eGrade Plus

for *Organizational Behaviour*, Canadian Edition

Check with your instructor to find out if you have access to eGrade Plus!

Study More Effectively with a Multimedia Text

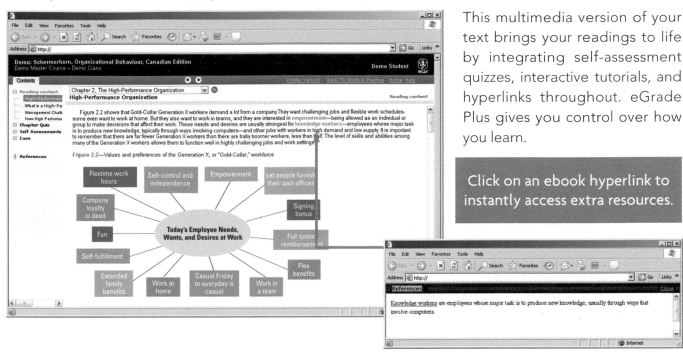

This multimedia version of your text brings your readings to life by integrating self-assessment quizzes, interactive tutorials, and hyperlinks throughout. eGrade Plus gives you control over how you learn.

Click on an ebook hyperlink to instantly access extra resources.

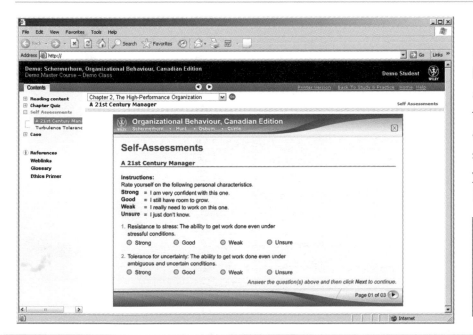

Preparing for a test has never been easier! eGrade Plus brings all of your course materials together and takes the stress out of organizing your study aids. A streamlined study routine saves you time and lets you focus on learning.

Grasp key concepts by exploring the various interactive tools in Study & Practice.

John Wiley & Sons Canada, Ltd.

Complete and Submit Assignments Online Efficiently

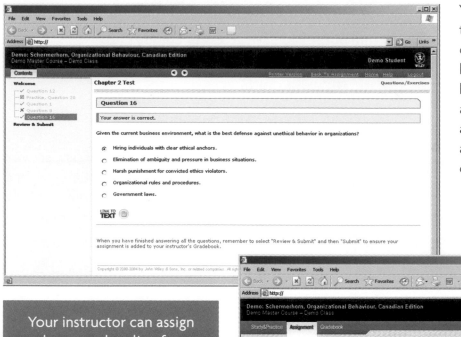

Your homework questions contain links to the relevant section of the multimedia text, so you know exactly where to go to get help solving each problem. In addition, use the Assignment area of eGrade Plus to monitor all of your assignments and their due dates.

> Your instructor can assign homework online for automatic grading and you can keep up-to-date on your assignments with your assignment list.

Keep Track of Your Progress

Your personal Gradebook lets you review your answers and results from past assignments as well as any feedback your instructor may have for you.

> Keep track of your progress and review your completed questions at any time.

ORGANIZATIONAL BEHAVIOUR

CANADIAN EDITION

SCHERMERHORN · HUNT · OSBORN · CURRIE

ORGANIZATIONAL BEHAVIOUR

CANADIAN EDITION

JOHN WILEY & SONS CANADA, LTD.

National Library of Canada Cataloguing in Publication Data
Organizational behaviour / John R. Schermerhorn, Jr. ... [et al.]. -- Canadian ed.

Includes index.
ISBN 0-470-83371-8

1. Organizational behavior--Textbooks. 2. Management--Textbooks. I. Schermerhorn, John R.

HD58.7.O683 2004   658   C2004-906394-4

Production Credits
Publisher: John Horne
Editorial Manager: Karen Staudinger
Publishing Services Director: Karen Bryan
Marketing Manager: Isabelle Moreau
Developmental Editor: Amanjeet Chauhan
Design: Interrobang Graphic Design Inc.
New Media Editor: Elsa Passera
Cover Image: Gray Mortimore / Allsport (Getty Images)
Printing & Binding: Tri-Graphic Printing Limited

Printed and bound in Canada
10 9 8 7 6 5 4 3 2 1

John Wiley & Sons Canada, Ltd.
6045 Freemont Blvd.
Mississauga, Ontario L5R 4J3
Visit our website at: www.wiley.com/canada

About the Authors

Dr. John R. Schermerhorn Jr. is the Charles G. O'Bleness Professor of Management in the College of Business Administration at Ohio University. He holds a PhD in organizational behaviour from Northwestern University, an MBA (with distinction) from New York University, and a BS from the State University of New York at Buffalo. He received an honorary doctorate from the University of Pecs (Hungary) in recognition of his international contributions to management research and education, and he presently serves as Adjunct Professor of Management at the National University of Ireland at Galway and is a member of the graduate faculty at Bangkok University in Thailand. He has also held appointments as the Kohei Miura Visiting Professor at Chubu University Japan, Visiting Professor of Management at the Chinese University of Hong Kong, and Visiting Scholar at Liaoning University in China and the Technical University of Wroclaw in Poland. At Ohio University he has been Director of the Center for Southeast Asia Studies and on-site Coordinator of EMBA and MBA programs in Malaysia. Dr. Schermerhorn has won awards for teaching excellence at Tulane University, the University of Vermont, and Ohio University, where he has been named a University Professor, the university's leading award for undergraduate teaching. He is the author or co-author of numerous journal articles, book chapters, and proceedings. His other Wiley books include *Management* (Eighth Edition, 2005), *Core Concepts of Management* (2004), and *Core Concepts of Organizational Behaviour* (Wiley, 2004).

Dr. James G. (Jerry) Hunt is the Paul Whitfield Horn Professor of Management, Trinity Company Professor in Leadership, Professor of Health Organization Management, Director, Institute for Leadership Research, and former department chair of Management, Texas Tech University. He received his PhD and master's degrees from the University of Illinois after completing a BS (with honours) at Michigan Technological University. Dr. Hunt has co-authored an organization theory text and *Basic Organizational Behaviour* (Wiley, 1998) and has authored or co-authored three leadership monographs. He founded the Leadership Symposia Series and co-edited the eight volumes based on the series. He has presented or published nearly 200 articles, papers, and book chapters, and among his most recent books are *Leadership: A New Synthesis*, published by Sage, and *Out-of-the-Box Leadership*, published by JAI. The former was a finalist for the Academy of Management's 1993 Terry Distinguished Book Award. Recently, Dr. Hunt received the Distinguished Service Award from the Academy of Management, the Sustained Outstanding Service Award from the Southern Management Association, and the Barnie E. Rushing. Jr. Distinguished Researcher Award from Texas Tech University for his long-term contributions to management research and scholarship. He has lived and taught in England and Finland and taught in China.

Dr. Richard N. Osborn is a Distinguished Professor at Wayne State University in the School of Business Administration and formerly a Board of Governors Faculty Fellow. He has received teaching awards at Southern Illinois University at Carbondale and Wayne State University, and he has also taught at Monash University (Australia), Tulane University, and the University of Washington. He received a DBA from Kent State University after earning an MBA at Washington State University and a BS from Indiana University. With over 175 presentations and publications, he is a charter member of the Academy of Management Journals Hall of Fame. Dr. Osborn is a leading authority on international alliances in technology-intensive industries and is co-author of an organization theory text and *Basic Organizational Behaviour* (John Wiley & Sons, 1995, 1998). He has served as a member of the editorial boards of the *Academy of Management Journal, Technology Studies, Journal of High Technology Management, The Academy of Management Review, The Journal of Management* and editor of international strategy for the Journal of World Business. He is very active in the Academy of Management, having served as divisional program chair and president, as well as the Academy representative for the International Federation of Scholarly Associations of Management. Dr. Osborn's research has been sponsored by the Department of Defense, Ford Motor Company, National Science Foundation, Nissan, and the Nuclear Regulatory Commission, among others. In addition to teaching, Dr. Osborn spent a number of years in private industry, including a position as a senior research scientist with the Battelle Memorial Institute in Seattle, where he worked on improving the safety of commercial nuclear power.

Elliott Currie, MBA, CMA, is an Assistant Professor in the Department of Agricultural Economics and Business at the University of Guelph. He has been teaching for 14 years at both Wilfrid Laurier and the University of Guelph. Prior to receiving his MBA from McMaster University, Mr. Currie held a wide variety of occupations, ranging from corporate pilot, general manager of a rock quarry, and management positions at both Gulf Canada and Petro-Canada. His industry experience also includes being a corporate lender for the Royal Bank, Director of Manufacturing for a plastics company, and Controller for an insurance broker. During his time at Guelph, Mr. Currie has been involved in consulting and training for First Nations Economic Developers in southern Ontario, consulting on marketing and communications for a number of high-growth firms in the areas of telecommunications, human resource management, and agriculture. He has become heavily involved in the development of the Agricultural Management Institute, primarily in the research, planning, and teaching areas. He has also been the recipient of numerous teaching awards.

Preface

People working individually and together are what should come to mind when looking at the cover of this book. It is not just an artistic expression; it symbolizes a basic fact of organizations and careers—individuals, acting together, do the work of our society and its organizations. The lesson for students of organizational behaviour is an important one: in the right environment, with the right blend of individuals, groups, and organizational structure, anything and everything is possible. The job of educators, too, is to bring together the great power of knowledge, understanding, and inquiry that characterizes the discipline and its commitment to understanding human behaviour in organizations.

Organizational Behaviour, Canadian Edition serves the needs of today's OB course in many important ways. Through nine best-selling U.S. editions and now in this Canadian edition, *Organizational Behaviour* is regarded as a text and teaching system that is easily integrated into the classroom. It presents OB in a manner that will help to inform and enthuse students with a rich variety of pedagogical and teaching aids. It simplifies the planning and delivery of courses in an increasingly complex teaching environment. And it offers the widest variety of topics, study tools, and lab resources that will benefit all students.

Organizational Behaviour, Canadian Edition is written for students who want to understand the discipline of OB in full awareness of its practical value and importance to their future careers. It provides the right amount of theoretical discussion blended with numerous real-world applications and unique opportunities to personally explore OB. All of this has been reviewed by an ESL expert and a business journalist to ensure that the material is accessible, interesting, and relevant to every student. The built-in Study Guide at the end of every chapter provides immediate opportunity to practice and understand. Students will grasp key OB concepts, understand how these OB concepts apply to the real world, and therefore be motivated to learn.

Organizational Behaviour, Canadian Edition was developed with a focus on educators who want to give their students a solid introduction to the discipline, a rich array of alternative learning activities, and a strong emphasis on and commitment to personal-skills development. It has briefer coverage of a wider variety of topic coverage, including three unique "macro" chapters on human resource management, globalization, and technology. It comes complete with *The OB Skills Workbook* that includes an outstanding set of professional self-assessments, experiential exercises, and cases. And it offers a DVD selection that shows OB at work in non-traditional environments. All of this allows instructors to design their course for any student audience.

Organizational Behaviour, Canadian Edition provides an unparalleled suite of teaching resources that provide complete flexibility in planning, delivering, and managing an OB course. The instructor's resources include an outstanding set of teaching tools developed and adapted by OB instructors. Teachers can choose from the widest variety of cases, experiential exercises, and self-assessments available on the market. And an innovative DVD-case collection helps demonstrate OB in action in unique and non-traditional ways, including Team Canada's successful bid for the Olympic gold medal in 2002.

Additionally, *Organizational Behaviour*, Canadian Edition is also available in Wiley's eGrade Plus on-line course information technology system, providing full electronic integration of all teaching resources. eGrade Plus comes complete with an "e-version" of the text, full on-line teaching tools, testing capability, lab resources, and a full course management program. With eGrade Plus, students can learn, practice, and follow their progress anywhere and at anytime.

We all live, work, and learn in a society that expects high performance and high quality of work life to go hand in hand, that considers ethics and social responsibility paramount measures of individual and organizational performance, that respects the talents of workforces increasingly rich in demographic and cultural diversity, and that knows the imprint of globalization. *Organizational Behaviour*, Canadian Edition was created with these realities in mind. It also applies the insights of OB across organizational and career settings—be they business, government, education, or public service. No matter what the reference point, we must all be prepared to perform in organizations challenged by uncertainty, bound for continuous change, and affected by the forces of technology. What students do with their talents will not only shape the contributions of the institutions of society but also fundamentally alter lives around the globe.

The goal of this book is to help students gain the understanding that can help them become leaders of tomorrow's organizations and to help educators become the most effective conduit in achieving that dream.

About the Book

Organizational Behaviour, Canadian Edition brings together a student-focused and accessible presentation of OB topics with outstanding in-text pedagogical aids, an innovative and pleasing design, and an innovative set of instructor and student resources.

Chapter Pedagogy

A primary goal in writing this book is to create a textbook that appeals to the student reader, while still offering solid coverage of the key aspects of organizational behaviour. Pedagogical aids were carefully selected and designed to enhance—rather than detract from—the learning experience of the reader. As is true for the entire book, the purpose of the pedagogy is to enliven the presentation of OB, to demonstrate to students how OB really works in actual organizations, and to highlight for students the managerial skills that will enable them to be successful in their careers.

In general order of when they appear, the chapter-by-chapter pedagogical system for *Organizational Behaviour*, Canadian Edition includes the following:

- **Chapter-Opening Essays**   Each chapter opens with a "real-world" vignette that showcases key OB concepts as they happen in actual Canadian and international organizations. These extended real-world examples show how people can make a difference in the way organizations operate or how they can maximize the potential of their employees. Special emphasis is given to organizations that students will find particularly interesting and relevant to their personal lives.

- **Study Questions**   Following the opening vignette, the chapter focuses the reader's attention on a set of key study questions that are tied to both the major headings of the chapter and the concluding summary. These are presented graphically and give students a visual image of how key topics relate to each other.

- **Embedded Boxes**   Throughout the chapter, embedded boxes enhance the richness of the material by highlighting best practices from Canadian and international organizations. These short and photo-enhanced boxes provide concise and relevant examples without disrupting the flow of the text. They focus on a variety of themes that includes ethics and social responsibility, technology, entrepreneurship, cultural diversity and globalization.

- **OB Across Functions**   This unique feature highlights real examples of how OB plays a role in all functions of an organization. These ensure that all students gain an understanding of how OB relates to them, no matter what their future plans.

- **Effective Manager Boxes**   These boxes organize key OB concepts and theories into useful practical tips and applications. They offer useful action guidelines on topics relevant to skills development and career readiness.
- **Chapter Study Guide**   Highly praised by instructors, a built-in Study Guide is included with each chapter to help students review and test their mastery of chapter content. Key components include: a Chapter Summary keyed to the chapter-opening Study Questions; a listing of Key Terms with page references; and a Self-Test that includes multiple-choice, true/false, short response, and applications essay questions. Students can access eGrade Plus or the website for interactive versions of self-tests, cases, and assessments, as well as to obtain self-test answers.

The OB Skills Workbook

The end-of-text *OB Skills Workbook* is a hallmark feature of *Organizational Behaviour*, Canadian Edition and includes a unique and unparalleled set of lab resources. It offers educators unprecedented flexibility in setting up and delivering their courses and provides students with numerous opportunities to apply OB theory in creative and interesting ways. Each resource is tied to relevant chapters, and an extensive set of teaching notes are available to instructors. *The OB Skills Workbook* includes:

- **Power Play Cases**   *The Gold Rush 2002* documentary is provided free-of-charge to instructors adopting *Organizational Behaviour*, Canadian Edition. It demonstrates how the gold-winning 2002 Canada Men's Olympic Hockey Team was planned, organized, managed, and lead through a variety of management challenges to reach its ultimate goal. Behind-the-scenes coverage, boardroom planning, and high-level politics highlight key OB concepts in a unique and student-motivating way. Five in-text cases are included and showcase how leadership, group dynamics, teamwork, goal-setting, and many other OB topics apply to Team Canada's successful Olympic bid.
- **Cases For Critical Thinking**   A selection of cases that are tied to various chapters and provide instructors with additional flexibility in setting up class discussions or creating assignments. Because they are at the end of the book, many can be used for a variety of chapters.
- **Experiential Exercises**   Over 40 experiential exercises are included to provide many unique opportunities to apply OB theory in the lab. These, too, are tied to a variety of chapters.

Instructional Support

Organizational Behaviour, Canadian Edition offers educators an exciting and innovative teaching system that allows you and your students to reach the ultimate goal—student success! *Organizational Behaviour*, Canadian Edition is supported by a comprehensive instructional package that assists instructors in creating a motivating and enthusiastic environment in which to learn and understand OB.

Instructor Resources   The Instructor's Resource CD (IRCD) offers a complete set of teaching tools, including an Instructor's Manual, PowerPoint slides, a fully automated computerized test bank, and Special Instructor Resources. All the resources on the IRCD are also available to instructors on the eGrade Plus system, providing a fully integrated system for planning, delivering, and managing their courses.

The Instructor's Manual is written and adapted by actual OB instructors to ensure that it focuses on the "in-class" experience and challenges of OB teachers. The Instructor's Manual provides the following for each chapter:

- A general philosophy and outline of the text
- Teaching ideas from learning theory and research
- Course development, sample assignments, and innovative instructional designs
- A description of the instructional support package
- Use of cases and the case method, which can be handed out to students
- Text highlights
- Teaching suggestions, including suggestions on how to use and integrate various media components
- An overview of chapter learning objectives
- Chapter overviews
- Lecture outlines and lecture notes to aid in pre-class preparation
- A summary of key definitions
- Answers to *The OB Skills Workbook* questions (including Experiential Exercises, Assessments, and Cases)
- Suggestions about how each aspect of *The OB Skills Workbook* should be used in class discussions and how each exercise is relevant to a particular chapter
- A Guide to both the *Gold Rush 2002* and CBC documentaries

The **Special Instructor Resources** include rich and substantive instructional aids, including the following:

- Using eGrade Plus provides instructors with a rich resource on how to maximize the full potential of Wiley's eGrade Plus system.
- The Creative Classroom by Robert E. (Lenie) Holbrook—a variety of ready-to-use enrichments to build creative learning opportunities ranging from social responsibility projects to special in-class exercises and activities.
- The Author's Classroom—additional PowerPoint selections from the authors' classrooms.
- The PowerPoint Slides provide a full set of slides to aid instructors in presenting key concepts of the text. These are fully adaptable by the instructor so as to modify course instruction to match their course outline.
- The Test Bank is fully automated and provides instructors with complete flexibility to choose, sort, edit, and add questions to tests, mid-terms, and final exams. It features approximately 130 questions per chapter, of which 75 are multiple-choice, 50 are true/false, and five are essay questions with suggested responses. The answers for the multiple-choice and true/false questions include the text page reference and the pedagogical element being tested. The Test Bank also tells the instructor whether a particular question is factual or applied in nature.
- Documentaries—Available exclusively with Organizational Behaviour, Canadian Edition, the Gold Rush 2002 documentary highlights Team Canada's 2002 Men's Olympic Hockey

Team and its successful quest for the gold medal. Behind the scenes and in the boardroom, the documentary shows the planning, organizing, goal-setting, and managing of this high-performance team. The documentary has numerous applications to OB that will motivate and involve students. Five cases are included in the book and can be used in class or in the lab to highlight OB concepts in a unique, student-motivating way. Also available are a collection of documentaries from the popular CBC television series Venture relating to topics in the text. A selection of cases is found in the Instructor's Manual, allowing instructors to integrate these into their lesson plans.

- eGrade Plus—*Organizational Behaviour,* Canadian Edition is available with Wiley's eGrade Plus course information technology system. It offers an on-line suite of teaching tools, assignments, interactive assessments, and a complete "e-version" of the book. It also includes an integrated set of on-line instructor's tools to help with class preparation, creation of assignments, automated assigning and grading of homework or quizzes, tracking of students' progress, and administration of courses. It provides instructors with the most comprehensive and flexible resources available on the market. Ask your Wiley sales representative for a demonstration of this powerful new tool, or visit www.wiley.com/canada/egradeplus for an on-line demonstration of the powerful teaching functionality now available.

Accessibility and Relevancy—Maximizing the OB Experience

As discussed, a primary goal of publishing *Organizational Behaviour,* Canadian Edition is to offer a presentation of the discipline that is accessible to all students while showing how concepts are applied in actual practice. All OB educators need to speak to a wide diversity of cultural backgrounds, work experiences, and career orientations. With that in mind, two experts were employed in the development of this text to ensure that the material is readable, understandable, and topical to all of its readers.

David Schwinghamer, an editor and translator, is the copy editor of *Organizational Behaviour*, Canadian Edition. He teaches English as a second language and is former coordinator for English courses at Collège Ahuntsic in Montreal, where his focus is on advanced courses that teach reading and writing skills. His contribution will ensure that *Organizational Behaviour*, Canadian Edition is readable and understandable to all readers of this book, whether English is their first language or not.

Alison Arnot researched numerous Canadian organizations, interviewed their key players, and wrote many of the chapter-opening essays, embedded boxes, and in-text examples for *Organizational Behaviour.* She has been a professional writer and editor since 1993, and she was the editor of CGA Magazine for more than six years. Alison holds a BA in English Literature, a diploma in Journalism, and a certificate in Teaching English as a Second Language. Her fun and informative examples of real companies enlivens *Organizational Behaviour*, Canadian Edition by making the material topical, interesting, and relevant to today's business environment.

Student Resources – An interactive website contains a rich variety of student and instructor resources. Students benefit from engaging in on-line activities based on Interactive Self-Testing, On-line Study Guide, and Interactive Self-Assessments. The website can be accessed at: www.wiley.com/canada/schermerhorn.

Acknowledgements

Organizational Behaviour, Canadian Edition benefits from insights provided by a dedicated group of organizational behaviour educators from across Canada who carefully read, critiqued, and provided suggestions on this project. Sincere appreciation is extended to the following OB teachers for their contributions to this edition:

Robert Bagg—Mount Saint Vincent University

Celeste Brotheridge—University of Regina

Marie-Hélène Budworth—University of Toronto

Louise Clarke—University of Saskatchewan

Susan Fitzrandolph—Ryerson University

Doug Fletcher—Kwantlen University College

Carolyn Gaunt—Cambrian College

Jean Helms Mills—Saint Mary's University

Fred Mandl—Kwantlen University College

Sudhir K. Saha—Memorial University

Carol Ann Samhaber—Algonquin College

Organizational Behaviour, Canadian Edition has benefited greatly from those educators whose materials are represented in *The OB Skills Workbook*. These individuals are identified in the workbook with their contributions, and are greatly appreciated for the range of innovative pedagogical options they help provide users of this book.

    Organizational Behaviour, Canadian Edition would not be complete without the efforts of the supplements authors, who worked to develop the comprehensive teacher's resource package described above. Thanks go to Rhona Berengut for preparing the Instructor's Resource Guide, Joan Condie for preparing the PowerPoint Presentations, Doug Fletcher for preparing the cases to accompany *Gold Rush 2002*, Carolyn Gaunt for preparing the Test Bank, Joan Rentsch for developing the Lecture Launch Video, and Hal Babson and John Bowen for case revisions. Robert E. (Lenie) Holbrook of Ohio University deserves a special acknowledgement for his contributions of The Creative OB Classroom.

Brief Contents

Contents

Organizational Behaviour

High Performance=People, People, People

Happy Employees Means Positive Bottom Line

A common philosophy that is shared by most high-performance companies is concern for employee job satisfaction and morale. More and more, today's employers are starting to realize that their employees are their most important asset and that by promoting a happy, healthy workforce, the return in profits is well worth the expense. In other words, the bottom line is only as good as the people building it. Stanford scholar Jeffrey Pfeffer believes that building an organization's performance capabilities has to start with the effective management of people. His research indicates that organizations that are getting the best from their people gain the competitive advantages of higher productivity and lower turnover. Pfeffer argues that the key is a leadership mindset that views and treats people in organizations as valuable assets, not as costs.[1]

Each year, *Report on Business* magazine publishes its list of the 50 Best Employers in Canada, with the assistance of Hewitt Associates, a global human resources outsourcing and consulting firm. The firms on this list come from a variety of industries, but Hewitt has identified five key traits that set "The Best" apart:

1. Leadership is aligned—among the leaders and with the employees.

2. Employees are intrinsically motivated.

3. The "basics" are done well.

4. People practices are effectively designed, communicated, and executed.

5. Employees are connected to the business.

Clearly, these five traits are in line with Pfeffer's view.

Husky Injection Molding Systems of Bolton, Ontario, is one company that made the 2004 list. The

five key traits are clearly present in Husky's employee practices. Husky also offers its employees such extrinsic benefits as an award-winning daycare centre, an on-site fitness centre, and the cafeteria pictured above that offers fresh, healthy food. All together, Husky spends about $4 million per year on employee benefits and programs, such as childcare, wellness, fitness, food, and landscaping. But the expense pays for itself in higher productivity and staff retention, leading to a savings of $6.2 million. Husky's turnover rate of 15 percent is about 5 percent below the industry average. Absenteeism averages four days per year for each employee, compared with an industry average of 9.1 days and injury claims are 1.5 for every 200,000 hours worked compared to an industry average of 7.2.

Nora Spinks, president of Toronto-based Work-Life Harmony Enterprises, believes that Husky has succeeded at keeping a happy, satisfied staff. "Husky has provided challenging work, career advancement opportunities, and the training, tools, and resources for people to take advantage of the opportunities." She further states that "Contented employees are good employees are good for business. Workers with higher job satisfaction create greater customer satisfaction. Happy customers mean more business, higher profits, and better shareholder values."

Chapter 1 introduces the field of organizational behaviour as a useful knowledge base for having a successful career in today's dynamic environment. As you read the chapter, keep in mind these key questions:

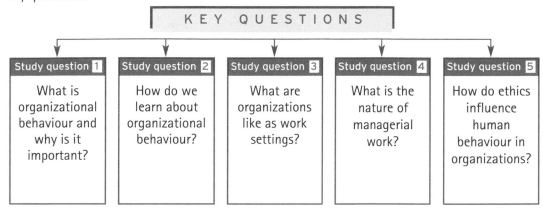

KEY QUESTIONS

Study question **1**	Study question **2**	Study question **3**	Study question **4**	Study question **5**
What is organizational behaviour and why is it important?	How do we learn about organizational behaviour?	What are organizations like as work settings?	What is the nature of managerial work?	How do ethics influence human behaviour in organizations?

Organizational Behaviour, Canadian Edition, is about people, everyday people like you and the authors of this book, who work and pursue careers in today's highly demanding settings. It is about people who look for fulfillment in their lives and jobs in a variety of ways and in changing times. It is about common themes that now characterize the modern workplace, including high performance, learning organizations, ethical behaviour, productivity improvement, use of technology, product and service quality, workforce diversity, work-life balance, and competitive advantage in a global economy. This book is also about how a complex environment challenges people and organizations to change, learn, and continuously develop themselves in their quest for promising futures.

Nothing is guaranteed. Whether your career develops in entrepreneurship, corporate enterprise, public service, or any other occupational setting, one thing remains sure: Success for people and organizations requires flexibility, creativity, learning, and a willingness to change. That is the message of today, and it will be the message for tomorrow.

Organizational Behaviour Today

People at work in organizations today are part of a new era. Society's institutions and the people who make them work are challenged in many and very special ways. The public in general expects high performance and high quality of life to go together; it thinks of ethics and social responsibility as core values; it respects the demographic and cultural diversity among people and understands the value of this diversity; and it sees the impact of globalization on everyday living and organizational competitiveness.

In this evolving era of work and organizations, the body of knowledge we call "organizational behaviour" offers many insights of great value. How does an organization and its workers learn new ways of work? How should they work together with their diverse backgrounds and perspectives? What roles and types of leadership are appropriate for the environments existing in the workplace? What opportunities are available and, to ensure the success of the organization and its members in achieving their respective goals, how should organizations and their members adapt to the evolving workplace and the demands of an ever-changing society?

For all members of the workforce, the demands are varied and constantly changing. This book helps its readers appreciate all these demands and challenges, and at the same time shows the many opportunities for effective functioning in today's organization for tomorrow's success.

WHAT IS ORGANIZATIONAL BEHAVIOUR?

Organizational behaviour is the study of individuals and groups in organizations.

Formally defined, **organizational behaviour**—OB for short—is the study of individuals and groups in organizations. Learning about OB will help you develop a better understanding of yourself and other people in the work environment. It can also increase your potential for a successful career in the dynamic, shifting, complex, and challenging new workplaces of today...and tomorrow.

Figure 1.1 Major topics in the study of OB: *Organizational Behaviour, Canadian Edition*

Environment
Ch 1 Organizational Behaviour
Ch 2 The High-Performance Organization
Ch 3 Globalization

Managing Organizations
Ch 11 Strategy and the Basic Attributions of Organizations
Ch 12 Strategic Competency and Organizational Design
Ch 13 High-Performance Organizational Cultures

Managing Groups
Ch 9 The Nature of Groups
Ch 10 Teamwork and High-Performance Teams

Managing Individuals
Ch 4 Diversity and Individual Differences
Ch 5 Perception and Attribution
Ch 6 Motivation and Reinforcement
Ch 7 Human Resource Management Systems
Ch 8 Job Designs

Managing Processes
Ch 14 High-Performance Leadership
Ch 15 Power and Politics
Ch 16 Information and Communication
Ch 17 Decision-Making
Ch 18 Conflict and Negotiations
Ch 19 Change and Innovation

Appendix
Dynamics of Stress

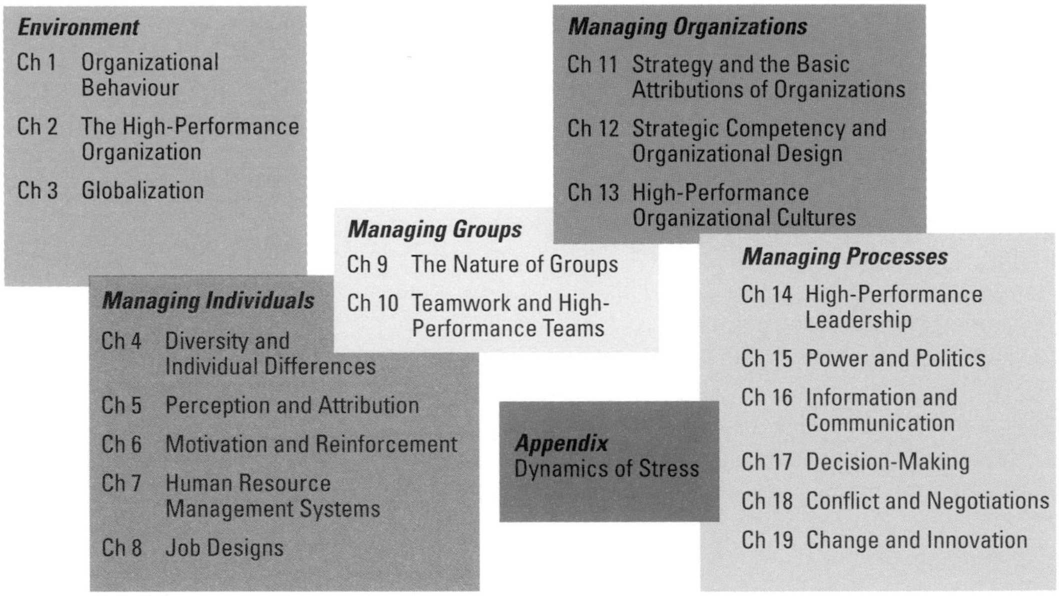

Figure 1.1 shows how *Organizational Behaviour, Canadian Edition* progresses logically from chapters on the current environment—including an emphasis on high performance and learning organizations, and the implications of globalization—to chapters on the dimensions of individual and group behaviour in organizations, and from there to chapters on the nature of organizations themselves and the core processes of OB—including leadership, power and politics, information and communication, decision-making, conflict and negotiation, and change, innovation, and stress.

SHIFTING PARADIGMS OF ORGANIZATIONAL BEHAVIOUR

Today's progressive workplaces look and act very differently from those of the past. They have different features, they approach work processes in new ways, and they serve different customer and client markets. The last decade of the twentieth century was especially dramatic in both the nature and speed of change. One observer called it a "revolution that feels something like this: scary, guilty, painful, liberating, disorienting, exhilarating, empowering, frustrating, fulfilling, confusing, challenging. In other words, it feels very much like chaos."[2]

What began as a revolution has become everyday reality. Intense global competition, highly interdependent national economies, constantly emerging information and biological technologies, changing forms of organizations, and shifting population demographics are now part of the norm. Today we are surrounded by change and uncertainty, with consequences for organizations (just look at current economic realities and the world of electronic commerce), as well as individuals (look also at the demand for the competencies and skills needed for evolving technologies and the commitment to continuous personal improvement).[3] What remains is the struggle for individuals and institutions to deal best with these changes and to keep up the pace as further challenges emerge in the new workplace.

Trends in the New Workplace

In an article entitled "The Company of the Future," Harvard professor and former U.S. Secretary of Labor Robert Reich says: "Everybody works for somebody or something—be it a board of directors, a pension fund, a venture capitalist, or a traditional boss. Sooner or later you're going to have to decide who you want to work for."[4] In making this decision, you will want to join a workplace that reflects values consistent with your own. This book can help you prepare for such choices while helping you be aware that work in this century includes these trends:[5]

- demise of "command-and-control"—Increasing competitiveness in organizational environments has made traditional hierarchical structures too unwieldy, slow, and costly to do well.

- emergence of new workforce expectations—The new generation of workers is less tolerant of hierarchy, is more informal, and is more concerned about performance merit than status.

- commitment to ethical behaviour—Investigations into the collapse of Enron, the actions of WorldCom and Parmalat, and questionable practices by many investment houses and some auditors, such as the now disbanded accounting firm Arthur Andersen, highlight concerns for ethical behaviour in the workplace. People are less and less tolerant of breaches of public faith by organizations and the executives or civil servants who run them.

- critical role of information technologies—Organizations now depend on computers, which have far-reaching implications for workflows and how information is used.

- belief in empowerment—A dynamic and complex environment places great importance on knowledge, experience, and commitment, all of which thrive in work settings that encourage high involvement and participation.

- emphasis on teamwork—Organizations today have a less vertical and more horizontal focus. Driven by complex environments and customer demands, work is increasingly team-based with a focus on peer and collaborative contributions.

- concern for work-life balance—As society and families become more complex, organizations are paying more attention to how their members balance conflicting demands and priorities at work and at home.

ORGANIZATIONAL BEHAVIOUR AND DIVERSITY

An important watchword in the twenty-first century is **workforce diversity**—the presence of differences based on gender, race and ethnicity, language, age, able-bodiedness, and sexual orientation.[6] Success in the new workplace requires a set of skills for working successfully

The Directors College

www.thedirectorscollege.com

In this era of corporate scandals and lack of accountability, a partnership of The Conference Board of Canada and the Michael G. DeGroote School of Business at McMaster University in Hamilton, Ontario has developed a program to help corporate directors become certified. The program is based on both the "hard" rules-based and the "soft" principle—and behaviour-based aspects of director-ships. This recently launched initiative is expected to build on the successes of the past involving boards of directors and to help future directors be better prepared for the increasing demands of our changing world.

Workforce diversity involves differences based on gender, race and ethnicity, age, able-bodiedness, and sexual orientation.

with a broad mix of people from different racial and ethnic backgrounds, of different ages and genders, and of different domestic and national cultures. Valuing diversity is a core OB theme.[7] It means managing and working with others in full respect for their individual differences (see The Effective Manager 1.1). Interpersonal and cultural sensitivity is essential to valuing diversity.

Even though valuing diversity is emphasized in our books and classrooms, much remains to be accomplished. A **glass ceiling effect** acts as a hidden barrier that limits the career advancement of minorities and women in some situations.[8]

According to the Statistics Canada report *The Changing Profile of Canada's Workforce*, from 1991 to 2001 the number of women managers increased by 40.5%, versus 7.4% for men, yet women account for only 35.4% of all managers in Canada. Women also accounted for two-thirds of the increase in the workforce but still earned on average only 70 cents as full-time employees for each dollar earned by a full-time male employee. In retrospect, women's earnings have increased steadily from 1980 through 2000, by 13.9% in the '80s and by another 12.9% in the '90s. In contrast, for men earnings decreased slightly during the '80s and only increased by 5.6% during the '90s.

The report also found that during the 1990s, 70% of the growth in the labour force was among immigrants to Canada, the majority of whom arrived in Ontario. New Canadians face tougher job prospects, with 8.9% fewer men and 21.8% fewer women working than their Canadian-born colleagues. Their wages have also not grown to equal those of their colleagues born in Canada, but immigrant Canadians who have been here longer tend to find jobs through greater acceptance and economic expansion.[9]

Progress is being made throughout Canada, the U.S.,[10] and elsewhere in the world, but much more needs to be done to achieve equality and fully realize the potential of all persons in our society and its organizations. After all, the diversity of an organization's workforce may open windows into new opportunities and new perspectives that may ultimately be the advantage an organization needs to achieve its goals.

The glass ceiling effect is a hidden barrier that limits the advancement of women and minorities in organizations.

The Effective Manager 1.1

How to Make Diversity Stick

- Focus on getting the best talent.
- Develop career plans for all employees.
- Provide career mentoring by diversity cohorts.
- Promote minorities to responsible positions.
- Maintain accountability for diversity goals.
- Make diversity part of organizational strategy.
- Build diversity into senior management.

Learning about Organizational Behaviour

We live and work in a knowledge-based economy that is always affected by the winds of change. This places a great premium on "learning" by organizations as well as individuals. Only the learners, so to speak, will be able to maintain the pace and succeed in a constantly changing environment.[11]

ORGANIZATIONAL BEHAVIOUR AND THE LEARNING IMPERATIVE

Organizational learning is the process of acquiring knowledge and using information to adapt successfully to changing circumstances.

Consultants and scholars emphasize **organizational learning** as the process of acquiring knowledge and using information to adapt successfully to changing circumstances.[12] Organizations must be able to change continuously and positively while searching for new ideas and opportunities. The same is true for each of us. We must strive for continuous improvement to maintain career readiness and keep pace with a dynamic and complex environment. Peter Senge, from the Center for Organizational Learning at MIT, helped make the concept of the Learning

Organization popular in the 1990s. The core concept is that the only way for an organization to succeed is to constantly change itself by learning new ways of conducting itself. This is also true for individuals—to succeed, you have to keep moving.

Lifelong learning is a popular concept these days, and the message is relevant. You can and must learn from day-to-day work experiences, conversations with colleagues and friends, counselling and advice from mentors, success models, formal training, seminars, and workshops, and the information available in the press and mass media. This textbook has a special section, The Organizational Behaviour Workbook, designed specifically to help you begin this process. Included in the workbook are many opportunities for you, individually and in study groups, to analyze readings and cases, participate in experiential exercises, and complete skills-assessment inventories to advance your learning.

HIGH-PERFORMANCE ORGANIZATION

Organizations that offer learning cultures are very attractive to today's graduates. Ernst & Young, the global accounting and consulting firm with over 106,000 employees and over $13 billion in annual revenues, is one of them. Visit the firm's Global Thought Center and you'll find insights from a professional staff and facility dedicated to learning. There is no "business as usual," states the Center's website. "Yesterday's strategies won't necessarily make you a success in tomorrow's world."[13]

ERNST & YOUNG
Quality In Everything We Do

SCIENTIFIC FOUNDATIONS OF ORGANIZATIONAL BEHAVIOUR

As far back as a century ago, consultants and scholars were paying more attention to the systematic study of management. Although at first the early focus was on physical working conditions, principles of administration, and industrial engineering principles, by the 1940s the interest had broadened to include the essential human factor. This led to research on individual attitudes, group dynamics, and the relationships between managers and workers. Eventually, the discipline of organizational behaviour emerged as a broader and all-inclusive approach. Today, it continues to evolve as a discipline devoted to the scientific understanding of individuals and groups in organizations, and of the impact of organizational structures, systems, and processes on performance.[14]

Interdisciplinary Body of Knowledge OB is an interdisciplinary body of knowledge with strong ties to the behavioural sciences—psychology, sociology, and anthropology, as well as to allied social sciences—such as economics and political science. Organizational behaviour is unique, however, in its commitment to applying and integrating these diverse insights. The ultimate goal is helping organizations achieve their objectives by improving how they function and their members' work experiences.

Use of Scientific Methods OB uses scientific methods to develop and empirically test generalizations about behaviour in organizations. Figure 1.2 describes the research methodologies that are commonly used. Scientific thinking is important to OB researchers and scholars for these reasons: (1) the process of data collection is controlled and systematic; (2) proposed explanations are carefully tested; and (3) only explanations that can be scientifically verified are accepted. The research concepts and designs used in OB are explained further in the end-of-book module "Research Methods in Organizational Behaviour."

Figure 1.2 Research methods in organizational behaviour

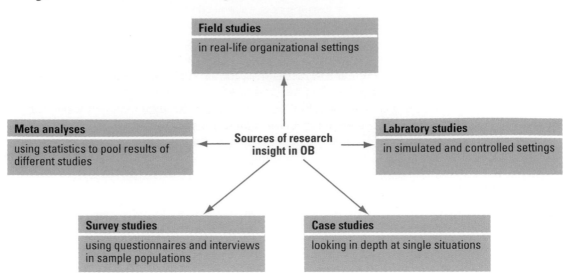

Focus on Application The field of organizational behaviour focuses on applications that can make a real difference in how organizations and the people in them perform. For example, the outcome or dependent variables studied by researchers include task performance, job satisfaction, job involvement, absenteeism, and turnover. Some of the practical questions the discipline of OB and this book address include these: How should rewards such as merit pay raises be allocated? How can jobs be designed for high performance? What are the ingredients of successful teamwork? How can organizational cultures be changed? Should decisions be made by individual, consultative, or group methods? In a negotiation, what is the best way to achieve "win-win" outcomes?

Contingency Thinking Rather than assume that there is one "best" or universal way to manage people and organizations, OB recognizes that management practices must be tailored to fit the exact nature of each situation. Using a **contingency approach**, researchers try to identify how different situations can best be understood and handled. In Chapter 3, for example, we recognize that culture can affect how OB theories and concepts apply in different countries.[15] What works well in one culture may not work as well in another. Other important contingency variables addressed in this book include the environment, technology, tasks, structures, and people.

> The contingency approach looks for ways to meet the needs of different management situations.

Organizations as Work Settings

The study of organizational behaviour depends on an understanding of organizations as work settings. An **organization** is formally defined as a collection of people working together in a division of labour to achieve a common purpose. This definition describes a wide variety of clubs, voluntary organizations, and religious bodies, as well as entities such as small and large businesses, labour unions, schools, hospitals, and government bodies. The insights and applications of OB can help all such organizations accomplish what is expected of them as social institutions and continue to meet the challenges of the future.

> An Organization is a collection of people working together to achieve a common purpose.

PURPOSE, MISSION, AND STRATEGIES

The *core purpose* of an organization may be stated as the creation of goods or services for customers or clients. Not-for-profit organizations produce services with public benefits, such as health care, education, elder care, judicial processing and correctional services, and highway maintenance. Large and small for-profit businesses produce goods and services, such as automobiles, banking, travel, food, housing, and entertainment.

Missions and *mission statements* focus the attention of an organization's members and its external constituents on the core purpose.[16] For example, WestJet of Calgary states that its mission is "To enrich the lives of everyone in WestJet's world by providing safe, friendly, affordable air travel." Retailer Wal-Mart states that it seeks "To give ordinary folk the chance to buy the same things as rich people."[17] Increasingly, mission statements are written to communicate a clear vision of long-term goals and future aspirations. The corporate vision at Hydro-Québec expresses the desire "To become a world leader in energy by developing its expertise for the benefit of its customers, employees and shareholder, by working with partners in business ventures."[18] Bold and challenging visions can attract attention and help draw members together in the quest for high performance. As Robert Reich states in his description of the company of the future: "Talented people want to be part of something that they can believe in, something that confers meaning on their work, on their lives—something that involves a mission."[19]

Once they have both a sense of purpose and a vision, organizations then develop and follow action *strategies* to accomplish their purpose and vision. The variety of mergers, acquisitions, restructurings, and divestitures found in business today are examples of corporate strategies to achieve and sustain an advantage in highly competitive environments. In this context, strategies must be both well formulated and well implemented for the organization to succeed.[20] A good plan is not enough by itself to achieve the broader strategic goal—to get and stay ahead of the competition. The plan has to be carried out.[21] It is here, at the level of action, that the field of organizational behaviour becomes especially important. For strategies to be implemented effectively, a knowledge of OB is essential. Things happen in organizations because of the efforts of people. How people work and perform together in organizations is what OB is all about.

> **Intellectual capital** is the sum total of knowledge, expertise, and energy available from an organization's members.

WORKPLACE DIVERSITY

At Murray Demolition of Toronto, management quickly realized that there was no advantage to be had in the equipment the company uses for demolitions. Only its employees and the style of management could give Murray an advantage over the competition and achieve the goal of becoming the number one company in the industry. Does your employer buy you lunch everyday? Murray does.[22] More and more, the leaders of today's organizations are realizing the importance of putting people first as they face new and sometimes very difficult times. The very best leaders understand the new significance of an old concept— people are an organization's most critical assets.

PEOPLE AND WORK SYSTEMS

One of the important directions in OB today is the emphasis on **intellectual capital**, which is the sum total of knowledge, expertise, and dedication of an organization's workforce.[23] It recognizes that even in the age of high technology, people are the indispensable **human resources** whose knowledge and performance advance the organization's purpose, mission, and strategies. Only through human efforts can great advantages be realized from an organization's other *material resources*, such as its technology, information, raw materials, and money. A

> **Human resources** are the people who do the work that helps organizations fulfill their missions.

Fortune survey of the U.S.'s most admired firms went as far as reporting that "the single best predictor of overall success was a company's ability to attract, motivate, and retain talented people." Interestingly, the service company selected by *Fortune* as a prime example was Clarica of Waterloo, now part of Sun Life.[24]

Today's strategic emphasis on customer-driven and market-driven organizations places great significance on understanding the relationship between an organization and its environment. As shown in Figure 1.3, organizations can be viewed as **open systems** that obtain resource inputs from the environment and transform them into outputs that are returned to the environment as goods or services. If everything works right, the environment values these outputs and creates a continuing demand for them. This sustains operations and allows the organization to survive and prosper over the long term. But things can and sometimes do go wrong in the organization-environment relationship. If the value chain breaks down and an organization's goods or services become unpopular, it will sooner or later have difficulty getting the resources it needs to operate. In the extreme case, it will be forced out of existence.

> **Open systems** transform human and material resource inputs into finished goods and services.

Figure 1.3 Organization and environment relationships

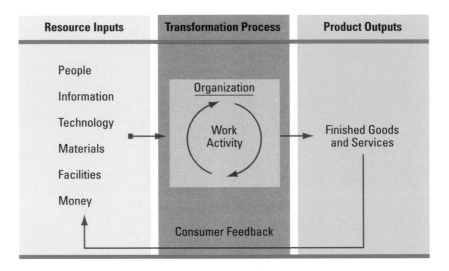

Organizational Behaviour and Management

Whatever your career direction and the level you start at, the field of organizational behaviour will someday become especially important to you as you try to master the special challenges of working as a **manager**. In all organizations, managers perform jobs that involve directly supporting the work efforts of others. Being a manager is a unique challenge that carries distinct performance responsibilities. Managers help other people get important things done in timely, high-quality, and personally satisfying ways. In the new workplace, this is accomplished more through "helping" and "supporting" than through traditional notions of "directing" and "controlling." Indeed, the word "manager" is increasingly being linked in the new workplace to roles described by such titles as "coordinator," "coach," or "team leader."[25]

> A **manager** is formally responsible for supporting the work efforts of other people.

THE NATURE OF MANAGERIAL WORK

Anyone who serves as a manager or team leader has a unique responsibility for work that is done mostly through the efforts of other people. The result is a very demanding and complicated job whose characteristics have been described by researchers as follows:[26] *Managers work long hours.* A work week of more than the standard 40 hours is typical. Heads of organizations often work the longest hours. *Managers are busy people.* The busy day of a manager includes a shifting mix of incidents that require attention, with the number of incidents being greatest for lower-level managers. *Managers are often interrupted.* Their work is fragmented and variable. Interruptions are frequent, and many tasks must be completed quickly. *Managers work mostly with other people.* In fact, they spend little time working alone. Time spent with others includes working inside the organization with bosses, peers, subordinates, and the subordinates of their subordinates. Externally, it includes working with customers, suppliers, and other such people. *Managers are communicators.* Managers spend a lot of time getting, giving, and processing information in both face-to-face and electronic communications. They participate in frequent formal and informal meetings, with higher-level managers typically spending more time in scheduled meetings.

THE MANAGEMENT PROCESS

An **effective manager** is a manager whose organizational unit, group, or team consistently achieves its goals while members remain capable, committed, and enthusiastic. Managers focus first on **task performance**—the quality and quantity of work produced or services provided by the work unit as a whole. They focus second on **job satisfaction**—how people feel about their work and the work setting. Just as a valuable machine should not be allowed to break down as a result of poor maintenance, the performance contributions of human resources should never be lost or compromised as a result of poor care for employees. Accordingly, OB directs a manager's attention to such matters as job satisfaction, job involvement, and organizational commitment, as well as measures of actual task performance.

An **effective manager's** team consistently achieves high performance goals.

Task performance is the quantity and quality of work produced.

Job satisfaction is a positive feeling about one's work and work setting.

Figure 1.4 The management process of planning, organizing, leading, and controlling

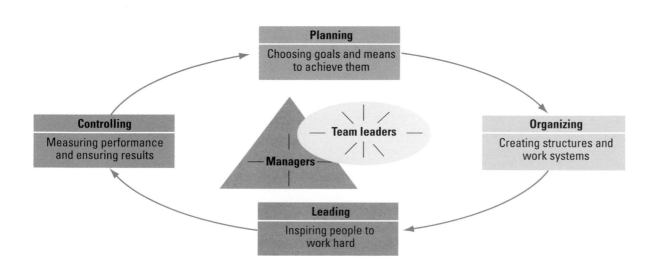

Four functions of management

- **Planning** sets objectives and identifies the actions needed to achieve them.
- **Organizing** divides up tasks and arranges resources to accomplish them.
- **Leading** instills enthusiasm to work hard to accomplish tasks successfully.
- **Controlling** monitors performance and takes any needed corrective action.

The job of any manager or team leader is largely one of adding value to the work setting by doing things that help others to accomplish their tasks. A traditional and still relevant way of describing this job is as a set of tasks or functions performed constantly and often at the same time. As shown in Figure 1.4, these four functions of management are planning, organizing, leading, and controlling. They form a framework for managerial action that can be described as follows:[27]

- **Planning**—defining goals, setting specific performance objectives, and identifying the actions needed to achieve them
- **Organizing**—creating work structures and systems, and arranging resources to accomplish goals and objectives
- **Leading**—instilling enthusiasm by communicating with others, motivating them to work hard, and maintaining good interpersonal relations
- **Controlling**—ensuring that things go well by monitoring performance and taking corrective action as necessary

MANAGERIAL ROLES AND NETWORKS

In what has become a classic study of managerial behaviour, Henry Mintzberg of McGill University moved beyond this functional approach in his description of what managers do. He identified 10 roles that managers must be prepared to perform on a daily basis, and classified the roles into the three categories shown in Figure 1.5.[28] The interpersonal roles involve working directly with other people. They include hosting and attending official ceremonies (figurehead), creating enthusiasm and serving people's needs (leader), and maintaining contacts with important people and groups (liaison). The informational roles involve exchanging information with other people. They include seeking out relevant information (monitor), sharing relevant information with insiders (disseminator), and sharing relevant information with outsiders (spokesperson). The decisional roles involve making decisions that affect other people. They include looking for problems to solve and opportunities to explore (entrepreneur), helping to resolve conflicts (disturbance handler), allocating resources to various uses (resource allocator), and negotiating with other parties (negotiator).

Figure 1.5 Ten roles of effective managers

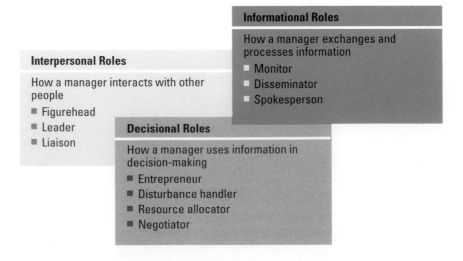

Good interpersonal relationships are essential to success in these roles and to all managerial work. Managers and team leaders should be able to develop and maintain relationships, and work well with a wide variety of people, both inside and outside the organization.[29] They must look for others and work with them in *task networks* composed of specific job-related contacts, *career networks* involving career guidance and opportunity resources, and *social networks*—made up of trustworthy friends and peers.[30]

MANAGERIAL SKILLS AND COMPETENCIES

A *skill* is an ability to turn knowledge into action that results in a desired performance. Robert Katz divides the essential managerial skills into three categories: technical, human, and conceptual.[31] He further suggests that how important each of these skills is varies across the different levels of management. Technical skills are considered more important at entry levels of management, where supervisors and team leaders must deal with specific problems in a particular job. Senior executives are concerned more with issues of organizational purpose, mission, and strategy. Broader, more ambiguous, and longer term decisions get the most attention at these higher levels, and conceptual skills are therefore more important. Human skills, which are a key element in the foundations of organizational behaviour, are equally important at all managerial levels.

Technical Skills A technical skill is the ability to perform specialized tasks. Such an ability comes from knowledge or expertise gained through education or experience. This skill involves being proficient at using selected methods, processes, and procedures to accomplish tasks. Perhaps the best current example is skill in using the latest communication and information technologies. Some technical skills require preparatory education, whereas others are acquired through specific training and on-the-job experience.

Technical skill is the ability to perform specialized tasks.

Human Skills Human skills, defined as the ability to work well with other people, are central to managerial work and team leadership. They show up as a spirit of trust, enthusiasm, and genuine involvement in interpersonal relationships. A person with good human skills will have a high degree of self-awareness and a capacity for understanding or empathizing with the feelings of others. People with this skill are able to interact well with others, engage in persuasive communications, deal successfully with disagreements and conflicts, and more.

Human skill is the ability to work well with other people.

Emotional Intellignce An important emphasis in this area of human skills is emotional intelligence (EI). Defined by Daniel Goleman as the ability to manage both oneself and one's relationships effectively, EI is now considered an important leadership competency.[32] Goleman's research suggests that a leader's emotional intelligence contributes significantly to his or her leadership effectiveness. Important dimensions of emotional intelligence that can and should be developed by any manager are shown in The Effective Manager 1.2. Human skills such as EI are indispensable in the new age of organizations, where traditional hierarchies and vertical structures are being replaced by lateral relations and peer structures.[33]

Emotional intelligence is the ability to manage oneself and one's relationships effectively.

Conceptual Skills All good managers are able to view the organization or situation as a whole and to solve problems in a way that benefits everyone concerned. This capacity to analyze and solve complex and interrelated problems is a **conceptual skill**. It involves the ability to see and understand how the whole organizational system works, and how the parts relate to each other. Conceptual skill is used to identify problems and opportunities, gather and interpret relevant information, and make good problem-solving decisions that serve the organization's purpose.

Conceptual skill is the ability to analyze and solve complex problems.

The Effective Manager 1.2
Developing Your Emotional Intelligence
• Self-awareness—ability to understand one's moods and emotions
• Self-regulation—ability to think before acting and to control disruptive impulses
• Motivation—ability to work hard and persevere
• Empathy—ability to understand the emotions of others
• Social skill—ability to gain rapport with others and to build good relationships

Ethics and Organizational Behaviour

Ethical behaviour is behaviour that is morally accepted as good and right.

The word "ethics" is important in OB. **Ethical behaviour** is behaviour that is accepted as morally good and right, as opposed to bad or wrong, in a particular setting. Is it ethical to hide information that might discourage a job candidate from joining your organization? Is it ethical to ask someone to take a job that you know will not be good for his or her career progress? Is it ethical to ask so much of someone that they continually have to choose between "having a career and having a life"? The list of questions can go on and on, but an important point remains: more and more, the public is demanding that people in organizations and the organizations themselves all act with high ethical and moral standards.

WAYS OF THINKING ABOUT ETHICAL BEHAVIOUR

Ways to rationalize unethical behaviour

- pretending the behaviour is not really unethical or illegal
- excusing the behaviour by saying it is really in the organization's or your best interest
- assuming the behaviour is okay because no one else is expected to find out about it
- presuming your superiors will support and protect you if anything should go wrong

Ethical behaviour respects not only a society's laws but also the broader moral code found in society as a whole. Exactly what the moral code is that governs a person's choices, however, is a subject of debate. There are at least four ways of thinking about whether the behaviour in and by organizations is ethical.[34]

Under the *utilitarian view*, behaviour is ethical if it delivers the greatest good to the greatest number of people. Those who follow the results-oriented utilitarian logic assess the moral aspects of their decisions according to the consequences that result from them. In utilitarianism, the needs of the many outweigh the needs of the few. From such a perspective, it may be ethical to close a factory in one town in order to keep the parent corporation profitable and operating in several other towns.

Under the *individualism view*, behaviour is ethical if it is the best behaviour for an individual's long-term self-interests. In principle, at least, someone who acts unethically in the short run—such as by denying a promotion to a qualified minority employee—should *not* succeed in the long run, because the short-run actions will not be tolerated. Thus, if someone acts with long-term self-interest in mind, his or her short-run actions will be ethical.

Under the *moral-rights view*, behaviour is ethical if it respects the fundamental rights shared by all human beings. This view is tied very closely to the principle of basic human rights, such as freedom of speech and movement, and fair treatment by law. In an organization, this principle is reflected in such issues as rights to privacy and due process. Ethical behaviour does not violate any of these fundamental human rights.

Procedural justice is the degree to which policies and procedures are properly followed.

Distributive justice is the degree to which all people are treated the same under a policy.

Interactional justice is the degree to which people are treated with dignity and respect.

Under the *justice view*, behaviour is ethical if it is fair and impartial in its treatment of people. This view is based on the concept of equitable treatment for all people concerned. In OB, three issues address this view of ethical behaviour:[35] **Procedural justice** is the degree to which the rules and procedures specified by policies are properly followed in all cases they apply to. In a sexual harassment case, for example, this may mean that required formal hearings are held for every case submitted for administrative review. **Distributive justice** is the degree to which all people are treated the same under a policy, regardless of their race, ethnicity, gender, age, or any other demographic characteristic. In a sexual harassment case, this might mean that a complaint filed by a man against a woman would receive the same consideration as one filed by a woman against a man. A third issue is **interactional justice**, the degree to which the people affected by a decision are treated with dignity and respect.[36] In a sexual harassment case again, this may mean making sure that both the accused and accusing parties feel they have received a complete explanation of any decision made.

ETHICAL DILEMMAS IN THE WORKPLACE

An **ethical dilemma** is a situation in which a person must decide whether or not to do something that, although it benefits the individual or the organization, or both, may be considered unethical. It is difficult to predict exactly what ethical dilemmas you will someday face. However, research suggests that people at work often encounter such dilemmas in their relationships with superiors, subordinates, customers, competitors, suppliers, and regulators. Common issues underlying the dilemmas involve honesty in communications and contracts, gifts and entertainment, kickbacks, pricing practices, and employee terminations.[37] More and more organizations are offering ethics training programs that offer advice (see The Effective Manager 1.3) for handling ethical dilemmas. In addition, the training helps participants learn how to identify and deal with common *rationalizations for ethical misconduct.*[38]

> An **ethical dilemma** requires a person to choose among actions that offer possible benefits but also violate ethical standards.

> ### The Effective Manager 1.3
>
> #### How to Deal with Ethical Dilemmas
> - Recognize and clarify the dilemma.
> - Get all the possible facts.
> - List all of your options.
> - Test each option by asking these questions: Is it legal? Is it right? Is it beneficial?
> - Make your decision.
> - Double-check your decision by asking these two questions: How will I feel if my family finds out? How will I feel if this is printed in the newspaper?
> - Then, and only then, take action.

ORGANIZATIONAL SOCIAL RESPONSIBILITY

Closely related to the ethics of workplace behaviour is **social responsibility**—the obligation of organizations to behave in ethical and moral ways as institutions of the broader society.[39] This means that an organization's members are responsible for making their ethical code extend to the whole organization. Managers and leaders should commit organizations to actions that support both the quest for high productivity and the objective of corporate social responsibility. Unfortunately, it does not always turn out this way.

> **Social responsibility** is the obligation of organizations to behave in ethical and moral ways.

Take, for example, the corporate scandal involving Canadian expatriate Conrad Black and his newspaper empire Hollinger Inc. Lord Black resigned as chairman and chief executive officer of Hollinger in November 2004 amid lawsuits alleging that he and other executives pilfered millions of dollars from the corporate coffers. A court-ordered forensic investigation, probing millions of dollars in loans, payments, transfers, and asset sales, was underway, and Hollinger's auditor KPMG had resigned almost a year earlier, saying the company had failed to take action "in respect of illegal acts" that materially affected its financial statements. Lord Black supposedly stepped down, not because of these allegations (he denies any wrongdoing), but to avoid any potential conflict of interest during the board's review his proposal to privatize Hollinger by buying back all the outstanding shares. (At the time he held 78% of the shares through his private holding company, Ravelston Corp.)

The Hollinger scandal followed not too long after the Enron case in the United States, where many employees lost their retirement savings after the company went bankrupt as a result of questionable accounting practices endorsed by Enron's executives. Enron's auditor Arthur Andersen was also ruined, and its investment houses and banks are still being investigated. Many of them, some Canadian, have been fined hundreds of millions of dollars.

Then, there is the federal sponsorship scandal resulting from the February 2004 Report from the Auditor General, which found that $100 million in fees and commissions had been paid to several communications agencies. The report said the sponsorship program was designed to generate commissions for the companies rather than benefit Canadians.

Cases like these often come to public awareness because of a **whistleblower**—someone in an organization who preserves high ethical standards by exposing the wrongdoings of others.[40] These issues are international in scope, and whistleblowers need to be protected from potential threats and retribution made by individuals who will be hurt by the truth. And there have been efforts to encourage such activity. Canada Post plans to set up a whistleblower service in the form of an independent toll-free hotline, web site, and e-mail service for employees to report any

> A **whistleblower** exposes the wrong doings of others.

TD Bank Financial Group

www.td.com

TD Bank Financial Group's web site states that the company believes employees' personal lives are as important as their professional lives.

"We understand that individuals who are able to balance the needs of work and home are more effective employees and more successful family and community members. That's why we strive to develop a supportive work environment. It's also why we provide our employees with a variety of options designed to help them achieve work/life balance. We offer temporary and personal leave of absence options that may enable employees to take between one and 12-month leaves. We also offer a number of flexible work arrangements that may help our employees better manage busy careers and busy lives."

potential improper activities going on at the corporation. This follows the federal government's proposed whistleblower legislation, the Public Servants Disclosure Act, which would make it easier for public servants and employees of Crown corporations to report improper activity.

Today, the spotlight is on. Corporate executives worldwide will never again be able to so easily hide from public scrutiny. Hopefully, the hard-learned management lessons of Hollinger and Enron will have long-term positive consequences for the ethical behaviour of organizations. It is hoped that the increasing level of power and responsibility given to the independent directors on organizations' boards will improve the ethical and transparent conduct of all organizations and their members.

WORK AND QUALITY OF LIFE

In many ways, the study of organizational behaviour is a search for practical ideas on how to help organizations achieve high performance outcomes while always acting in an ethical and socially responsible manner. A key concern in this quest is the well-being of an organization's entire workforce—this means everyone, not just the managers. The term **quality of work life**, or QWL, is a major indicator in OB of the overall quality of human experience in the workplace. It is a reminder that high performance in any work setting can and should be accomplished by high levels of job satisfaction.

A commitment to QWL is essentially a core value of OB. This commitment was set very early in the discipline's life by theorists with a strong human orientation, such as Douglas McGregor.[41] He contrasted what he called *Theory X assumptions*—that people basically disliked work, needed direction, and avoided responsibility—with *Theory Y assumptions*—that people liked work, were creative, and accepted responsibility. For McGregor, Theory Y assumptions were the most appropriate and tended to create positive *self-fulfilling prophecies*. That is, when people were treated well at work, the likelihood was that they would respond positively and as expected.

Today the many concepts and theories discussed in OB reflect QWL and Theory Y themes. The hallmarks of excellence in management and organizations now include empowerment: involving people from all levels of responsibility in decision-making; trust: redesigning jobs, systems, and structures to give people more personal discretion in their work; rewards: building reward systems that are fair, relevant, and consistent, and which also depend on work performance; responsiveness: making the work setting more pleasant and supportive of individual needs and family responsibilities; and **work-life balance**: making sure that the demands of the job are a reasonable fit with a person's personal life and non-work responsibilities.[42]

ENTREPRENEURSHIP

Most of the employees at Endpoint Research in Mississauga, Ontario are women who must stay in direct contact with medical researchers across the country. With all the travel required, there was incredible stress on these employees, who also often face the responsibilities of caring for young children or elderly parents. Traditionally, the industry faces a 20% turnover of staff due to burnout, the added stress of being away from home, and moves to competitors. The founder of Endpoint, Wendy Porter, faced the issue of keeping staff happy when she realized that money was not the major concern for these women. By introducing an employee assistance program that costs pennies per day for each employee, offering the staff opportunities to work from home, eliminating long-distance travel, permitting part-time work, and investing 5% of revenue in training, turnover has been reduced to 5% per year. In short, morale improved and the company saved the $25,000 it costs to hire a new research associate.

A commitment to QWL respects what was earlier called the intellectual capital of an organization. It involves putting people first in any list of organizational priorities. The next chapter will continue to explore how people help build high-performance organizations. For now, consider the leadership challenge posed in these comments made by Jeffrey Pfeffer in his book *The Human Equation: Building Profits by Putting People First*:[43]

> The key to managing people in ways that lead to profits, productivity, innovation, and real organizational learning ultimately lies in how you think about your organization and its people.... When you look at your people, do you see costs to be reduced?... Or, when you look at your people do you see intelligent, motivated, trustworthy individuals—the most critical and valuable strategic assets your organization can have?

Quality of work life is the overall quality of human experiences in the workplace.

Work–life balance is about the demands from a person's work and personal life.

CHAPTER 1 STUDY GUIDE

Summary

What is organizational behaviour and why is it important?

- Organizational behaviour is the study of individuals and groups in organizations.
- Dramatic changes signal the emergence of a new workplace with high technology, global competition, demanding customers, and high-performance systems.
- Valuing diversity and respecting differences is a key theme in OB; workforces are increasingly diverse in terms of gender, race and ethnicity, language, age, able-bodiedness, and sexual orientation.

How do we learn about organizational behaviour?

- Organizational learning is the process of acquiring knowledge and using information to adapt successfully to changing circumstances.
- Learning about organizational behaviour involves more than just reading a textbook; it also involves a commitment to continuous and lifelong learning from experience.
- OB is an applied discipline based on scientific methods and uses a contingency approach which recognizes that management practices must fit the situation.

What are organizations like as work settings?

- An organization is a collection of people working together in a division of labour for a common purpose—to produce goods or services for society.
- As open systems, organizations interact with their environments to obtain resources that are transformed into outputs returned to the environment for consumption.
- The resources of organizations are material, such as technology, capital, and information; and human, the people who do the required work.

What is the nature of managerial work?

- Managers in the new workplace are expected to act more like coaches and facilitators than like bosses and controllers.
- An effective manager is a manager whose work unit, team, or group accomplishes high levels of performance that can be sustained over the long term by enthusiastic workers.
- The four functions of management are (1) planning: to set directions; (2) organizing: to assemble resources and systems; (3) leading: to create workforce enthusiasm; and (4) controlling: to ensure desired results.

- Managers fulfill a variety of interpersonal, informational, and decisional roles while working with networks of people both inside and outside the organization.
- Managerial performance is based on a combination of essential technical, human, and conceptual skills.

How do ethics influence human behaviour in organizations?

- Ethical behaviour is that which is accepted as morally good and right instead of bad or wrong.
- Ways of thinking about ethical behaviour include the utilitarian, individualism, moral-rights, and justice views.
- The workplace is a source of possible ethical dilemmas in which people may be asked to do or are tempted to do things that violate ethical standards.
- Organizational social responsibility is the obligation of organizations as a whole to act in ethical ways.
- The insights of OB can help build and maintain high-performance organizations that offer their members a high quality of work life.

KEY TERMS

Conceptual skill (p. 13)

Contingency approach (p. 8)

Controlling (p. 12)

Distributive justice (p. 14)

Effective manager (p. 11)

Emotional intelligence (p. 13)

Ethical behaviour (p. 14)

Ethical dilemma (p. 15)

Glass ceiling effect (p. 6)

Human resources (p. 9)

Human skill (p. 13)

Intellectual capital (p. 9)

Interactional justice (p. 14)

Job satisfaction (p. 11)

Leading (p. 12)

Manager (p. 10)

Open systems (p. 10)

Organizations (p. 8)

Organizational behaviour (p. 4)

Organizational learning (p. 6)

Organization (p. 8)

Organizing (p. 12)

Planning (p. 12)

Procedural justice (p. 14)

Quality of work life (p. 17, 18)

Social responsibility (p. 15)

Task performance (p. 11)

Technical skill (p. 13)

Whistleblower (p. 15)

Workforce diversity (p. 5)

Work-life balance (p. 17, 18)

SELF-TEST 1

MULTIPLE CHOICE

1. The term "workforce diversity" refers to differences in race, age, gender, ethnicity, able-bodiedness, and _____ among people at work. (a) social status (b) personal wealth (c) sexual orientation (d) political preference

2. What is the best description of the setting facing organizational behaviour today? (a) Command-and-control is in. (b) The new generation expects much the same as the old. (c) Empowerment is out. (d) Work-life balance concerns are in.

3. The interest of OB researchers in outcome variables such as _____ is an indication that the discipline is concerned with practical issues and applications. (a) absenteeism and turnover (b) job satisfaction (c) job performance (d) all of these

4. The "glass ceiling effect" in organizations is _____. (a) a hidden barrier that limits the career advancement of minorities and women (b) an unpublicized limit on wages paid to top managers (c) an unpublicized limit on wages paid to operating workers (d) a restriction on the hiring of full-time permanent workers

5. Which statement about OB is most correct? (a) OB seeks "one-best-way" solutions to management problems. (b) OB is a unique science that has little relationship to other scientific disciplines. (c) OB is focused on using knowledge for practical applications. (d) OB is so modern that it has no historical roots.

6. Technology, information, and money are among the _____ in the open-systems view of organizations. (a) products (b) services (c) inputs (d) outputs

7. The management function of _____ is concerned with creating enthusiasm for hard work. (a) planning (b) organizing (c) controlling (d) leading

8. Justifying ethical behaviour based on the legality of the action is the _____ view. (a) utilitarian (b) individualism (c) moral-rights (d) justice

9. When employees excuse unethical behaviour by pointing out that it is really in the organization's best interest, they are _____. (a) doing the right thing for themselves (b) doing the right thing for society (c) rationalizing the unethical conduct (d) following the rule of procedural justice

10. When facing an ethical dilemma, final action should be taken only after _____. (a) recognizing the dilemma (b) checking whether or not the action will be legal (c) making sure no one will find out if the action is wrong (d) double-checking to make sure that you are personally comfortable with the decision

TRUE–FALSE

11. Organizational behaviour is defined as the study of how organizations behave in different environments.   T   F

12. The statement "OB seeks to meet the needs of different management situations" relates to contingency thinking.   T   F

13. Organizational learning is a process of acquiring knowledge and using information to adapt to changing circumstances.   T   F

14. The external environment is not as important to organizations as open systems.   T   F

15. When a president holds frequent meetings with a task force to stay informed about its progress, she is fulfilling the planning function of management.   T   F

16. Conceptual skills are probably the most important skills for top-level managers.   T   F

17. Managerial work involves major use of interpersonal networks.   T   F

18. A team leader who gives a friend special preference under a vacation-leave policy is violating distributive justice.   T   F

19. A whistleblower is someone who exposes unethical behaviour in organizations.   T   F

20. Research suggests that an organization's superiors are the causes of many ethical dilemmas faced by people at work.   T   F

SHORT ANSWER

21. What does "valuing diversity" mean in the workplace?

22. What is an effective manager?

23. How would Henry Mintzberg describe a typical executive's workday?

24. Why is QWL an issue of ethics and organizational social responsibility?

APPLICATIONS ESSAY

25. Indira Patel faces a dilemma in her role as the accounts manager for a local social service agency. One of the employees has reported to her that another employee is charging meals to his travel expense account even when he is attending a conference where meals are provided. What should Indira do in this situation so that (a) similar problems will not happen in the future, and that (b) the criteria of both procedural and distributive justice are satisfied?

The High-Performance Organization

Is There a Secret Code?

Headquartered in northern Europe, the Finnish-born company Nokia has the distinction of being the world's leading maker of mobile telephones. With a market share approaching 40 percent, approximately every third cellphone in use is from Nokia. This achievement has led many people to wonder: "What is Nokia's secret formula for success?" There seems to be no clear-cut answer, but what is clear is that Nokia reflects many aspects of a high-performance organization (HPO).

Nokia is team driven. During 2002, the company launched a diversity program to make sure the company culture considered individual needs and expectations, avoided exclusive practices, and increased the productivity and innovation of teams.

To encourage employees to accept this inclusive environment, a Diversity Advisory Team was created. This team was responsible for setting the overall direction for the program, and for enabling and supporting new diversity initiatives. Diversity awareness, skills development, and learning solutions were introduced, and diversity competence development was made part of Nokia Management and Leadership development programs. The program's success can be measured by current business results, but also by employee feedback, such as the employee satisfaction survey "Listening to You" that was used. The survey showed that 80 percent of employees felt personally responsible for creating inclusiveness.

Nokia also has a very definite business objective. It wants to strengthen its position as a leading producer of communication systems and products. The company targets sections of the communications market that it

believes will experience good growth, and it then works to expand into these sections during the early stages of development. Nokia looks at product development as an entire package. Every aspect of the Nokia brand is considered: design, production, and distribution are all carefully dissected and perfected. Advertising is only considered after all the other components are in place. These simple and effective rules have put Nokia at the top of the mobile phone industry.

Chapter 2 examines trends and directions in high-performance organizations, and their implications for the field of organizational behaviour. As you read the chapter, keep in mind these key questions:

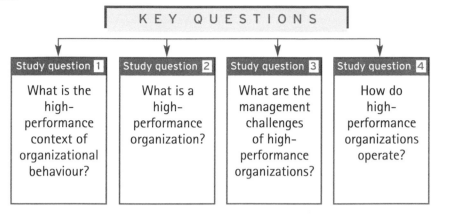

KEY QUESTIONS

Study question **1**	Study question **2**	Study question **3**	Study question **4**
What is the high-performance context of organizational behaviour?	What is a high-performance organization?	What are the management challenges of high-performance organizations?	How do high-performance organizations operate?

We live and work in an age of increasing global competition, new technologies, shifting demographics, and changing social values. In response to these forces, a new breed of organization has arrived—the high-performance organization (HPO). These organizations are designed to bring out the best in people and to create an extraordinary organizational capability which produces sustainable high-performance results.[1]

HPOs are fast, agile, and market driven. They emphasize respect for people, shown by the involvement of workers and managers at all levels and consistent use of teams like those at Nokia. Organizations with many HPO features now make up from one-fifth to one-third of the Fortune 1000 companies, and the growth trend will surely continue.[2] More and more careers will be lived in high-performance work settings.

High-Performance Context of Organizational Behaviour

Organizations today operate in a social context that is making high performance ever more essential for success. Some critical forces that are pushing organizations toward high performance include changing customer expectations, a changing workforce, and changing organizations.

OB AND CHANGING CUSTOMER EXPECTATIONS

Only those organizations that deliver what customers want in quality, service, and cost will prosper in today's highly competitive environments. Our current period is still a time of **total quality management** (TQM)—management dedicated to ensuring that an organization and all of its members are committed to high quality, continuous improvement, and customer satisfaction. Quality in this sense means that customers' needs are satisfied and all tasks are done right

Total quality management is a total commitment to high-quality results, continuous improvement, and meeting customer needs.

Continuous improvement is the belief that anything and everything done in the workplace should be continually improved.

the first time. An important hallmark of the total quality concept is continuous improvement—the belief that anything and everything done in the workplace should be constantly evaluated by asking these two questions: (1) Is this necessary? (2) If yes, can it be done better?[3]

Figure 2.1 The "upside-down pyramid" view of organizations and management

The creation of customer-driven organizations that are dedicated to quality and service is part of this approach. Figure 2.1 presents this notion as an *upside-down pyramid* view of organizations. The figure focuses attention on total quality service to customers and clients by placing them at the top of the organization. From this point of view, managing requires that workers act in ways that directly affect customers and clients; it requires that team leaders and middle managers do things that directly support the workers; and it requires that top managers clarify the organizational mission and objectives, set strategies, and make needed resources available.[4]

OB AND THE CHANGING WORKFORCE

Generation X workers are knowledge workers in short supply who were born between 1966 and 1977.

Canada's workforce is becoming more and more diverse, with a greater percentage of women, visible minorities, and older employees. Trends in North America and the European Union are similar.[5] Besides more diversity, two especially important and contradictory workforce characteristics are (1) the impact of **Generation X**, or "Gold-Collar," **workers** (those born between 1966 and 1977), and (2) the impact of less than ideal educational preparation of some high school graduates. In fact, U.S. test scores were the lowest in one comparison of 16 industrialized countries.[6] In another test by the Organization for Economic Cooperation and Development (OECD), Canada ranked second in literacy, sixth in mathematical literacy, and fifth in scientific literacy out of 28 industrialized countries, doing better than the U.S. in all measures.[7] These performance characteristics are now both a challenge and an opportunity for OB, but in very different ways, especially if your organization would like to establish a large facility somewhere in North America.

Figure 2.2 shows that Gold-Collar Generation X workers demand a lot from a company. They want challenging jobs and flexible work schedules—some even want to work at home. But they also want to work in teams, and they are interested in **empowerment**—being allowed as an individual or group to make decisions that affect their work. These needs and desires are usually strongest for **knowledge workers**—employees whose major task is to produce new knowledge, typically through ways involving computers—and other jobs with workers in high demand and low supply. It is important to remember that there are far fewer Generation X workers than there are baby boomer workers, less than half. The level of skills and abilities among many of the Generation X workers allows them to function well in highly challenging jobs and work settings.[8]

Empowerment allows individuals or groups to make decisions that affect them or their work.

Knowledge workers are employees whose major task is to produce new knowledge, usually through ways that involve computers.

Figure 2.2 Values and preferences of the Generation X, or "Gold-Collar," workforce

At the opposite end are those high school graduates who enter the workforce with skills deficiencies. An alarming number of them need a lot of basic skills training in math, writing, and reasoning so that they are able to function in many of today's organizations.[9] In a knowledge-driven economy, there are high costs for such remedial training. People without such basic skills can suffer long-term career and economic disadvantages. Some multinational firms, such as Toyota, prefer a college diploma or professional papers and will not hire people unless they have completed grade 12.

OB AND CHANGING ORGANIZATIONS

The last decade may eventually be seen as the one that fundamentally changed the way people work.[10] We experienced the stresses of downsizing and restructuring; we gained sensitivity to the peaks and valleys of changing economic times; and we witnessed the arrival of the Internet, with its impact on both people and organizations. Truly progressive organizations, however, are doing much more than simply cutting employees and adding technology to reduce the scale of operations and increase productivity. They are changing the very essence of the way things are done by learning new ways of operating, and they are adding new meaning to the traditional notions of employer–employee relationships.

Process re-engineering is the total rethinking and redesigning of organizational processes to improve performance and innovation. It involves analyzing, streamlining, and reconfiguring actions and tasks to achieve work goals.

Electronic commerce is business that is transacted through the Internet.

E-corporations use the Internet and information technologies to support the use of computers in all aspects of their operations.

Shamrock organizations are firms that have a core group of permanent workers to which they add outside contractors and part-time workers as needed.

One characteristic of this new and fast-paced world of organizations is constant change. And with this change there is an emphasis on reinventing ways of doing things and continuously improving all aspects of operations. Many organizations have pursued **process re-engineering**, which is to rethink and radically redesign business processes to encourage innovation and change and improve critical performance measures, such as cost, quality, service, and speed.[11] Organizations facing these new demands are being asked to "start over"—to forget how things were done in the past and to ask only how they should be done now to get the best results on these critical performance measures. The answers to how things should be done now lead to redesigning activities and workflows in order to give better value to both internal and external customers.

There has been an explosion of activity in new information technology in what may become a benchmark of twenty-first century organizations—**electronic commerce**, the name for business transacted through the Internet. Evergeek Media and e-corporations.ca are just two examples of Canadian **e-corporations** that use the Internet and information technology to support the use of computers in all aspects of their operations.[12] In a world that is more and more centred on the Internet, technology-driven *network organizations* act as virtual alliances of suppliers, customers, and even competitors, who link up with each other through the latest electronic information technologies and share such things as skills, costs, and access to global markets.[13] These alliances are formed, used, and disbanded with ease, all in quick response to business opportunities.

These and other related developments are creating what some observers call a *free-agent economy*—an economy in which individuals contract their services to a changing mix of employers over time.[14] British scholar and consultant Charles Handy has described the career implications of what he calls the **shamrock organization**.[15] A shamrock, the Irish national emblem, has three leaves per stem. Each leaf represents a different group of people. The first leaf is a core group of workers made up of permanent, full-time employees with critical skills. They follow standard career paths and form a relatively small group, perhaps made up of the employees who remain after major downsizing of a more traditional organization. The second leaf is a group of outside operators who are hired on contract by the core group to do a variety of jobs that are essential to the daily functioning of the organization. Many of these jobs would be performed by full-time staff (e.g., human resource personnel) in a more traditional organization. The third leaf is a group of part-timers who can be hired temporarily by the core group as the needs of the business grow and who can just as easily be let go when business falls. Today's college graduates must be prepared to succeed in the second and third leaves, not just the first.

What Is a High-Performance Organization?

The **high-performance organization** is designed to bring out the best in people and produce sustainable organizational results.

Intellectual capital is the sum total of knowledge, expertise, and energy available from an organization's members.

The free-agent economy and shamrock organizations are one aspect of the rapidly changing context of OB. Another is the **high-performance organization**, introduced earlier as an organization that is specifically designed to bring out the best in people in order to produce sustainable organizational results. Instead of treating people as disposable parts of constantly shifting temporary alliances, HPOs place people first.[16] They see people as the crucial resource that makes it possible to deliver sustainable high-performance results.

EMPHASIS ON INTELLECTUAL CAPITAL

The essential foundation for the high-performance organization is intellectual capital, defined in Chapter 1 as the sum total of knowledge, expertise, and energy of an organization's workforce.[17] This means that even in our days of high technology, people are the indispensable human resources whose contributions advance the organization's purpose, mission, and strategies. To make use of this intellectual capital, top organizations often organize their flow of work around the key business processes and often create work teams within these processes.[18] They follow human-resource policies that aim to increase employee flexibility, skills, knowledge, and motivation.[19] At the same time, these organizations have fewer levels of management and they change the way managers operate. Instead of being mostly directive order-givers, managers emphasize coaching, integrating the work of different work teams with each other, and facilitating the teams' work so that they can best complete their jobs and satisfy customers.[20]

COMPONENTS OF HIGH-PERFORMANCE ORGANIZATIONS

A high-performance organization's specific form depends on its setting. For example, an HPO bank would have a form different than an HPO auto manufacturer.[21] But, high-performance organizations often use the five components shown in Figure 2.3 when they adjust themselves to their environment. The key components are employee involvement, self-directing work teams, integrated production technologies, organizational learning, and total quality management.

Figure 2.3 Five components of high-performance organizations

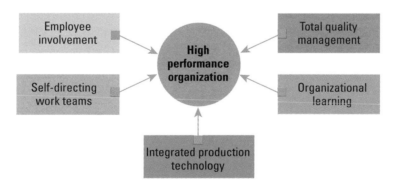

Employee Involvement   The amount of decision-making that workers at all levels are allowed to do is the amount of **employee involvement**. This can be thought of as a continuum.[22] At one end, there is no involvement (workers just do their jobs) or parallel involvement (workers have access to suggestion boxes, roundtable discussions about their jobs, and quality circles—members of a quality circle meet regularly to find ways to constantly improve quality operations). In the middle is moderate involvement or participative management (workers have increased responsibilities for day-to-day job decisions). At the opposite end from low involvement is high involvement, or what we earlier called empowerment, where workers make decisions affecting themselves and their work. Typically, these decisions are about almost all aspects of the job. Use of employee involvement increased when it was realized that

Crystal Decisions

www.businessobjects.com

Crystal Decisions of Vancouver, a developer of business reporting, analysis, and data management software, was one of Canada's Top 100 Employers. With over 14 million registered customers, this company is a strong contributor to business software provided by both itself and other companies, such as Microsoft, SAP, and People Soft. Its workplace is considered an exceptional facility thanks to its location near the water and public transit and its fitness and sleep rooms, foosball, free snacks, open-concept working arrangement, and natural light for employees. The company is so good at what it does that its largest competitor, Business Objects, acquired the company for $1.2 billion U.S. in December 2003. Crystal Decisions' ongoing commitment to its six values of leadership, customer focus, transnational identity, innovation, integrity, and passion will likely ensure future success and excellent staff.

Employee involvement is the amount of decision-making employees are allowed to do.

positive benefits could come from allowing employees to determine how their jobs should be done. Research shows that employee productivity and various aspects of satisfaction tend to be higher with more involvement.[23]

Self-directing work teams are teams that are empowered to make decisions about planning, doing, and evaluating their work.

Self-Directing Work Teams Teams or workgroups that are empowered to make decisions about planning, doing, and evaluating their work are **self-directing work teams**. They sometimes have other names, such as self-managing or self-leading work teams, or autonomous workgroups. We discuss them thoroughly in Chapter 10. There are at least two reasons for their role in high-performance organizations. First, the importance of using employee expertise and knowledge is now widely accepted. Second, there has been an increased need for employees to manage themselves as organizations have downsized and restructured for greater competitiveness.[24] Self-directing work teams strongly affect employee satisfaction and commitment, and these teams moderately affect performance.[25]

HIGH-PERFORMANCE ORGANIZATION

The junk removal company 1–800-GOT-JUNK? prides itself on the team-oriented environment of its Vancouver head office, nicknamed the Junktion. Each morning at exactly 10:55 a.m., all employees at the Junktion meet for a seven-minute huddle. The team shares good news, announcements, metrics, and any hurdles they are encountering. They also track the progress of their goals through company-wide games posted on the wall. At the end of the meeting, the team says a one-word cheer relating to good news. The company also has an open-book policy with its employees. They all meet once a month to go over the financial statements line-by-line. One person is accountable for each line item, and everyone is looking for innovative ways to cut costs, says Cameron Herold, VP, Operations. In return, the employees share a portion of the profits every year.

Integrated production technologies focus on making manufacturing and services flexible and making job design and information systems part of the technology.

Integrated Production Technologies All organizations use technology to combine the use of resources, knowledge, and techniques and create a product or service output. The concept of **integrated production technologies** focuses on making manufacturing and services flexible and making job-design and information systems part of the technology. Some aspects of integrated production technologies are key. These include using just-in-time production or service systems, and using computers extensively to help design products or services, control equipment in production processes, and integrate the various business functions.

When just-in-time systems are used, companies work closely with suppliers to make sure just the right amount of material is available to do the job.[26] Toronto-based electronics manufacturer Celestica Inc. implemented just-in-time principles to manage excess materials and capacity more efficiently. At P.E.I. mail-order company, Vesey's Seeds, this is done by buying seeds in large quantities but packaging them in increments, as orders come in.

Computers are used to integrate a variety of business functions. For example, order entry and accounting can be integrated with computer-aided design of the product or service and with computer-aided production. The integration may help control workflow and other aspects of the product or service. The Technology/Clothing Technology Corporation, for example, has developed a computer design process that allows clothing manufacturers to create "custom" clothing and then to use computers to turn the final design specifications into instructions for manufacturing the item.[27] K2 Corporation, a large manufacturer of skis, uses these approaches to produce custom-ordered skis.[28] These design and production functions are often integrated by computer into the just-in-time systems and business functions that are already integrated. The result is that placing the order, designing the product, making sure there are enough parts, and producing the product are all assisted by computer.

A particularly ambitious attempt at such integration has been made by Nygård International, which designs and manufactures five lines of women's clothing. Nygård has electronically connected the cash registers of its biggest customers to its Winnipeg manufacturing facility, called Arts2 (Automatic Re-order to Sales). Nygård's computer receives a download of the retailer's weekly point-of-sale data and generates re-orders automatically based on sales, allowing items to be manufactured and delivered to customers on a "just-in-time-basis." The system is also linked to major suppliers, who are notified as orders are placed, co-ordinating the flow of component parts like zippers and buttons. Currently, 85% of the company's customers and suppliers are linked, but Nygård plans to eventually restrict its supplier base to those who are similarly automated. This kind of integration may become an important part of many successful organizations in the future.[29]

Organizational Learning   Chapter 1 introduced *organizational learning* as a way for organizations to adapt to their settings and gather information to anticipate future changes.[30] High-performance organizations with the characteristics described next are designed for organizational learning. They put information into the organization's memory so that it can be used in new situations.[31] This type of learning became necessary because traditional, hierarchically structured organizations were not very good at anticipating changes in their environment or at sharing information across functions such as production, marketing, and engineering. For an organization to be evolving and learning, it must be able to function locally, share its successes with others if possible, and experiment with potential improvements.

Total Quality Management   As introduced earlier, total quality management involves a total commitment to high-quality results, continuous improvement, and meeting customer needs. In the mid-1980s, TQM was usually applied in separate, narrowly focused groups that emphasized various aspects of quality. The meetings of these groups were not considered part of the workers' regular jobs. Now total quality management has become a tightly integrated part of HPOs, where an emphasis on employee involvement and self-management encourages all workers to do their own quality planning and checking.

ETHICS AND SOCIAL RESPONSIBILITY

Intel is perhaps best known for its outstanding computer chip technology. However, it is also dedicated to being a responsible corporate citizen. Learning, education, and technology literacy programs are a major emphasis of Intel's outreach and giving programs. Intel especially supports mathematics, science, and engineering education in schools. Wherever Intel plants are located, a number of Intel employees volunteer at local schools and not-for-profits. The firm is known for its balanced and adaptive culture which emphasizes mutually beneficial outreach programs.

Management Challenges of High-Performance Organizations

There are many challenges on the journey to becoming an HPO. To respond to these challenges, a very strong leadership commitment is necessary. For those organizations that have made the HPO commitment, it has been well worth the effort. Studies of some 1,100 companies across a

30-year period show some interesting results. First, bottom-line financial performance tends to increase by 30 to 50 percent over a three- to five-year time period. Second, this bottom-line financial performance increased by at least 3 to 7 percent per year faster than it did in traditional organizations.[32] These results, however, depend on overcoming the challenges discussed next.

ENVIRONMENTAL LINKAGES

WestJet

www.westjet.ca

WestJet provided an innovative approach to the Canadian airline industry and customer expectations. Its mission, "To enrich the lives of everyone in WestJet's world by providing safe, friendly, affordable air travel," and its vision to "be the leading low-fare airline that: People want to work with... Customers want to fly with... and Shareholders want to invest with," guided the fledgling discount carrier to the top of the industry by addressing the desires of both its employees and customers.

Like other organizations, high-performance organizations are open systems that are influenced by the quickly moving *external environment*, with its global emphasis and rapidly changing customer expectations. Some of the most important *inputs* are the problems and opportunities that show up at the organizational worksite, and the organization's purpose, mission, strategy, and vision. HPOs typically develop a mission-and-vision package that ties these elements together and integrates them with the organization's core values.[33] In a true HPO, this vision-direction package must involve employees and managers at all organization levels. This complete involvement is crucial for making sure that everybody in the organization fully accepts the package. This high level of mutual acceptance is a key difference between HPOs and other more traditional organizations. Each of the previously mentioned *HPO components*—employee involvement, self-directed work teams, integrated manufacturing technologies, organizational learning, and total quality management—contributes in a special way to the transformation of inputs into outputs and to dealing with a changing environment.

The *outputs* are basically individual, group, and organizational effectiveness and contributions to society. Organizational effectiveness looks at how well the organization has done financially and what the quality of work life is for its members. Quality of work life refers to satisfaction, commitment to the organization, and many other measures of this kind, as indicated in Chapter 1. Contributions to society are what the organization contributes to society through the benefits of the products or services it provides, its charitable contributions, volunteer activities by its managers and workers, and many other similar activities.[34]

This open-systems perspective therefore means that the inputs, transformation processes, and outputs are all influenced by the external environment and by each other also. In other words, the outputs result in feedback for adjustments to the transformation components and inputs, and there is therefore continual adjustment to meet the environmental demands.

INTERNAL INTEGRATION

Integrating all five HPO components is a difficult challenge. For example, the self-directing teams must include the integrated production system in their plans and operations. For this reason, the teams are often heavily involved in the production system's design. Similarly, the teams must make total quality management part of their functioning. Finally, they must also create organizational learning and employee involvement functions and activities. In successful HPOs, there is a fit among all these activities and functions, just as there is with the open-system inputs and outputs.

Unlike traditional organizations, in which design comes from the top and moves downward, the design of an HPO involves a combination of top-down and bottom-up decision-making. Successful design requires a strong and sustained emphasis from the top which is supported by various design teams that have people from all levels of the organization. It is also essential to stay on course when the inevitable problems that come from changes need to be dealt with. If an organization can do all this, it has a chance to reap the kinds of benefits we will discuss in the concluding section of this chapter.

Sometimes there are **HPO "islands"** inside a larger, more traditional organization. These HPO islands are surrounded by organizations or units that do not function as HPOs and may even be opposed to them. Saturn Corporation within General Motors is one such example. Originally set up to help serve as an example for the rest of the corporation, Saturn has been in a constant struggle to remain a true HPO.[35] Indeed, some influential executives from GM and the United Auto Workers Union have not supported Saturn. Their opposition comes from concerns about losing the control they have elsewhere in GM's more traditional organization.[36]

Despite these internal pressures, Saturn had early success as a high-performance organization. Lately, however, external market forces have made it very difficult for Saturn to continue its success. For example, until a recent SUV addition, Saturn had not had any major changes or new additions to its traditional small-car line. A recent larger model, built at a different plant, did not sell well. In summary, despite Saturn's early success, its future remains uncertain. In general, however, well-run HPOs have been better at dealing with negative pressures than have traditional organizations.[37]

HPO "islands" are HPO units that are surrounded by organizations or units that do not function as HPOs and may even be opposed to them.

MIDDLE MANAGER ROLES

To build a true high-performance organization, middle managers must also handle many challenges. Managers are usually asked to help implement one or more of the components described earlier so that their organization can begin the journey toward becoming an HPO and learning organization. Implementing these components, however, can pose problems. One challenge that could result when self-directing work teams are implemented, for example, is resistance from employees and the managers themselves.[38] As self-directing work teams often decide what is to be done, and how and when it is to be done, middle managers in traditional organizations may be afraid that implementing such work teams will eliminate some or all of their own jobs.[39] With many traditional managerial functions now being done by the teams themselves, the middle managers must find new roles for themselves and adjust their traditional role of directing. They must become facilitators and coaches instead, something they may not enjoy or be prepared to do.

> **The Effective Manager   2.1**
>
> Managerial Challenges of High-Performance Organizations
>
> - Employee concern with effectiveness
> - Employee self-direction
> - Employee concern with organization design
> - Challenging jobs and/or work teams
> - Intense peer and customer feedback
> - Financial rewards and recognition

Although many Generation X employees may welcome new self-managing team environments, other workers may resist—particularly those without the appropriate educational skills. Some employees do not believe that working in teams is a fair way to work, and some do not like the additional challenge of teams. There is also a strong preference among many employees, especially in North America, to do individual work. A key challenge for middle managers in implementing any of these components (see The Effective Manager 2.1) is to help deal with possible employee resistance.[40]

Another challenge for middle managers is to resolve possible tensions between or among the various components. For example, the total quality management component often results in separate, narrowly focused groups which emphasize various aspects of quality. These groups typically have lots of management control. In contrast, an employee involvement component in the same organization could require a lot of worker empowerment in many issues, not just as regards quality. It would be difficult for managers and employees to reconcile the demands of these two different HPO components. The middle managers and the employees would need to be trained extensively to handle their new role in an HPO. In addition to getting additional training themselves, middle managers would also need to help design and implement training for other employees.[41] At least basic training in HPOs and possibly more would be needed for employees to be able to perform their new duties and to keep up with increasing competition. Conversely, the managers would have to learn to let go.

UPPER-LEVEL LEADERSHIP

The first challenge for upper-level management is to decide how far to go in becoming an HPO. Many organizations implement only one or two of the components above and are not true HPOs. They are traditional organizations with some HPO components. How far they attempt to go depends on the environment and input factors, as well as on how much top management values and is committed to a true HPO. For example, HPOs are particularly useful in constant, changing environments that demand innovation. Some firms, such as Procter and Gamble and Research in Motion, place a strong value on HPOs, and top management has a strong commitment to them.[42] Many managers of organizations, however, simply do not want to make this kind of commitment. Instead they are satisfied with trying to implement one or two components, or even just a small portion of a single component.

Another challenge for top-level managers is trying to extend North American business practices internationally. In countries where status, power, and prestige are a basic part of work-related values (e.g., Malaysia, Italy, Mexico), it can be very difficult to implement self-directing teams and employee involvement. In addition, workers with the appropriate abilities and education may not be available.[43] Finally, training and development of middle managers is a challenge. As we have stated, they no longer perform many of the managerial duties of traditional organizations.

GREENFIELD SITES VERSUS REDESIGNS

Greenfield sites are HPO sites that are started from zero at a new site.

A final challenge is the question of starting a high-performance organization from zero or redesigning a traditional organization to become one. HPOs started from zero at a new site are called **greenfield sites**. Saturn Corporation is an example of one. It took 10 years to develop Saturn from its original concept and open its plant. During that period, everything was designed from the ground up—typical for greenfield sites.[44] In contrast, redesigns start out as more traditional organizations, and management then tries to change the design so the organization can become an HPO.

Organizations that have implemented new designs have had an average financial increase of about 10 percent a year. In contrast, organizations that have redesigned themselves have realized average increases of 6.8 percent a year. Traditional organizations that have not been redesigned have seen improvements of 3.8 percent a year.[45] So, although all three design types have experienced financial increases due to external and internal pressures, the new HPOs—the greenfield sites—have done the best.

How High-Performance Organizations Operate—The Case of WestJet Airlines

On February 29, 1996, WestJet Airlines Limited began operations as a greenfield site out of Calgary and served five cities. By November 2004, it served 24 Canadian and eight U.S. cities, employing 4,500 people. When the team of Clive Beddoe, Don Bell, Mark Hill, and Tim Morgan started the firm, many observers thought they were "bonkers"—90 percent of all start-up airlines fail in very short time. With a plan based on the highly successful Southwest Airlines,[46] however, WestJet has built itself up on "WestJet Spirit," employee ownership, and teamwork—and has become part of the 10 percent that succeed. WestJet and Southwest have both been profitable, even after the downturn in travel since the September 11, 2001 terrorist attacks in New York City and Washington D.C. WestJet's third quarter of 2004 results showed net earnings of $21.1 million. The company has also received its share of attention. In 2001, WestJet was honoured in Monaco with an International Entrepreneurship award for Outstanding Teamwork; it was Canada's second most respected company in 2003; and in 2004 it was named one of the best 100 companies to work for in Canada. When a model that works is found, copying it makes sense.

Let's now briefly examine WestJet as an HPO by looking at it through the earlier five-component HPO model summarized in Figure 2.3. We start with *employee involvement*, which, as mentioned earlier, reflects the amount of decision-making that an organization's people at all levels of the organization are responsible for. From the beginning, WestJet's organizational hierarchy was flat and lean. It consisted of the CEO, department heads, managers, supervisors, and employees. There was a heavy team emphasis throughout, starting with the four founders, a senior management decision-making team, and now a board of directors reviewing all major policy areas. Even now, three of the four founders work closely together. (Mark Hill left WestJet in July 2004.) This lean-and-mean philosophy was everywhere in the organization. Paperwork was minimized, rapid decision-making was emphasized, and people were generally empowered to do "whatever it takes" to get the job done. These high-involvement notions were much easier to carry out when the organization started with only a few airplanes, but the WestJet culture has insisted that they be continued even with the rapid growth that the airline has experienced.

Often, as Chapters 10 and 14 will emphasize, HPOs have longer-term manufacturing or service teams that keep the same members for a long period of time. WestJet has teams like this wherever they are needed. HPOs also commonly have ad-hoc teams that are spontaneously created for specific projects or duties and then are disbanded until they are needed again. The HPO culture encourages these kinds of co-operative activities and many of WestJet's self-directing teams are of this nature—they are like task forces.

INTEGRATED PRODUCTION TECHNOLOGIES

The key word here is "integrated." WestJet's heaviest use of information technology has been in distribution, primarily sales through its website. Ticketless travel is the mainstay of WestJet as it eliminates the costs of printing, distributing, and tracking the tickets.

WestJet even offers discounts for booking a return flight through its website. At the time of writing this textbook, approximately 65% of WestJet's bookings were over the Internet. WestJet also uses information technology (IT) for many other functions. IT is used for dispatching flights and for revenue management through adjustments of prices and seats. "In-house" teams do both dispatch and revenue management through the use of highly technical computer programming. Ordering parts for maintenance is done over the Internet since most of the parts come from Seattle.

Of course, as IT is used more and more, there is more need to integrate its use. Management must pay attention to how IT affects the organization's culture as IT becomes more crucial to how the organization functions.

From its very beginning, like Southwest, WestJet has promoted *organizational learning*. Such learning is deeply rooted in each of these airlines' culture. In addition to many frequent letters to employees and newsletters that discuss details of the company's business, WestJet makes use of its special recovery/learning centre. The Business Recovery Centre/Training Centre has two roles. It has a complete system available at all times to take over the operation of the firm if the main computer at the Sales Super Centre fails. To make efficient use of it, however, the centre is also used as a training facility for most aspects of the business. To train flight crews, WestJet also has other learning systems nearby, including flight simulators that are rented out to other airlines when WestJet is not using them. Training is key to WestJet. As it grows, the number of skilled and committed employees it needs is critical to its success. Hiring pilots is ongoing at WestJet as it receives new aircraft and expands its fleet, and the training is rigorous, as you would expect.

The airline's culture and the kinds of learning tools mentioned above are used for both individual and organizational learning. As mentioned earlier, such learning is needed to deal with fast-changing environments and information sharing between functions.

Total quality management—a commitment to high-quality results, continuous improvement, and meeting customer needs—is another HPO component of the airline's culture. It is part of the "WestJet Spirit," defined as a strong work ethic, a strong desire for quality work, a desire to go beyond the call of duty, helping others, and "doing the right thing." These qualities are reinforced by empowerment and the previously mentioned learning and communication tools which inform employees about where the company stands and where it wants to go. There is always a vast supply of this information and a never-ending push to do better. WestJet pushes constantly to generate profits and this is reinforced by having 95 percent of the employees as company shareholders—many of the employees have shares worth over $500,000.

With all of its employees involved, the result is the collaborative effort and commitment that are needed for handling the issues that arise from growth and change. One of WestJet's biggest challenges is continuing to hire the right people—those who are not only qualified, but who can also embrace the WestJet spirit and values—while remaining the second most profitable airline in North America, second only to Southwest, its model of operation.

OTHER HPO CONSIDERATIONS

Other important considerations mentioned in this chapter that apply to WestJet are its vision-and-direction-setting package, its people, their compensation, dealing with the environment, and outcomes.

Vision-and-Direction-Setting Package The mission of WestJet Airlines is "To enrich the lives of everyone in WestJet's world by providing safe, friendly, affordable air travel."

Its vision reads, "WestJet will be the leading low-fare airline that: People want to work with…Customers want to fly with…and Shareholders want to invest with."[47]

The core values that are important to WestJet are growth, service, hard work, change and innovation, honesty and openness, the celebration of success, respect for everyone, training and tools for its people to do the job well, and taking their job seriously but not themselves. The airline's culture reflects these values.

The People Having an attitude that reflects the "WestJet Spirit" is a key hiring requirement, regardless of other qualifications. Previously mentioned core values, such as hard work and especially fun, are also important.

Compensation A straight proportion of the company's profits is shared twice a year with the employees. Employees may direct up to 20% of their salaries into WestJet shares and this investment can be directed into an RRSP. On top of that, the company matches any purchase of shares by an employee dollar for dollar.

Dealing with the Environment The airline industry has been deregulated and it has faced many challenges. While Canada's national carrier, Air Canada, has had difficulty dealing with this environment, WestJet has flourished in it. In this environment, competition from other airlines can be fierce, especially from the new entrants that are using similar tactics, and there is constant concern about fuel costs and decreases in pleasure and business flying. WestJet's culture, communication and learning, and employees are not only continuing to serve it well in dealing with this post 9/11 environment, but are also creating continued growth and profitability.

To summarize, according to the criteria discussed in this chapter, WestJet is an excellent example of a high-performance organization. It operates in a highly competitive industry that has suffered lots of economic turbulence and yet the company has been a consistent high performer on a wide range of measures. Southwest, the model, lost money in its first two years of operation—WestJet has yet to lose any. The model must be working.

CHAPTER 2 STUDY GUIDE

Summary

STUDY QUESTIONS

What is the high-performance context of organizational behaviour?

- Total quality management involves making sure customers are satisfied, making sure all tasks are done right the first time, and working toward continuous improvement.

- Customer-driven organizations can be seen as upside-down pyramids where workers work in ways that directly affect customers, and managers work in ways that directly support the workers.

- The diverse and changing workforce includes new pressures from "Generation X" workers who want their jobs to be challenging, flexible, and empowering.

- Organizations are embracing process re-engineering, electronic commerce, and free-agent employees who are added to a mix of permanent, part-time, and temporary workers.

What is a high-performance organization?

- A high-performance organization is designed to bring out the best in people and achieve sustained high performance.

- HPOs tend to organize workflow around key business processes and follow human-resource policies that are designed to increase employee flexibility, skills, knowledge, and motivation.

- The key components of HPOs include employee involvement, self-directing work teams, integrated production technologies, organizational learning, and total quality management.

What are the management challenges of high-performance organizations?

- Environmental linkages give rise to challenges for HPOs to be effective open systems whose inputs, transformation processes, and outputs support a clear and relevant vision.

- Internal integration creates a challenge for all HPO components to work successfully together in a changing and ever-improving fashion.

- Middle-manager challenges include implementing the HPO components, adapting to different managerial roles, and helping design and implement employee training.

- High-level leadership challenges include determining how far to go toward becoming an HPO, training and development of middle managers, and keeping an overall positive momentum during times of great change.

How do high-performance organizations operate?

- WestJet and Southwest airlines have essentially operated as evolving high-performance organizations since they were founded.

- WestJet's vision and mission focus on the kinds of mission, direction, and values that are characteristic of HPOs in relation to their customers and employees.

- Each of the key HPO components is emphasized by WestJet in its approach to the aviation environment and operations.

- For many years, WestJet's outcomes in terms of production activity measures, financial measures, employee quality of life measures, and general contributions have tended to be consistently superior.

KEY TERMS

Continuous improvement (p. 24)

Electronic commerce (p. 26)

Employee involvement (p. 27)

Empowerment (p. 25)

E-corporation (p. 26)

Generation X workers (p. 24)

Greenfield sites (p. 32)

High-performance organization (p. 26)

HPO islands (p. 31)

Integrated production technologies (p. 28)

Intellectual capital (p. 26)

Knowledge workers (p. 25)

Process re-engineering (p. 26)

Self-directing work teams (p. 28)

Shamrock organizations (p. 26)

Total quality management (p. 23)

SELF-TEST 2

MULTIPLE CHOICE

1. A high-performance organization _____. (a) is similar to a traditional organization (b) automatically occurs whenever self-managing work teams are used (c) produces the ability to deliver sustainable high-performance results (d) must have a very specific kind of organizational structure

2. The following is not listed as a characteristic of the changing workforce: _____. (a) a higher ranking in high school education scores (b) a lower ranking in high school education scores (c) more diversity (d) the arrival of Generation X workers

3. The following is not listed as an input of an HPO open-systems model: _____. (a) organizational worksite problems and opportunities (b) the external and global business environment (c) strategies (d) the vision-direction package

4. The five transformation components listed in the HPO open systems model _____. (a) are independent of one another (b) need to fit or match (c) assume there are very few employees (d) require little change after they are established

5. Compared to a traditional organization, a high-performance organization _____. (a) has a stronger functional orientation (b) is much simpler to design (c) is more productive (d) requires more employees

6. Because HPOs invest heavily in their employees' training, they apply the most important feature of _____ organizations. (a) learning (b) shamrock (c) vertical (d) e-commerce

7. HPOs _____. (a) are started mainly from the bottom (b) are started mainly from the middle (c) require little effort from top management (d) require much effort from all levels of an organization

8. An organization that is called an "island," such as Saturn Corporation, _____. (a) floats aimlessly (b) operates as an HPO inside a larger entity that is not an HPO (c) is early in its journey toward becoming an HPO (d) would operate worse if it were part of a larger HPO

9. The performance record of HPOs _____. (a) tends to be about the same as the record for traditional organizations (b) tends to be substantially higher than the record for traditional organizations (c) tends to be only slightly higher than the record for traditional organizations (d) shows benefits that are less than the costs

10. Once an HPO is established, it _____. (a) changes very little (b) changes constantly (c) reverts back to being a traditional organization (d) reduces the number of employees

TRUE–FALSE

11. True HPOs also have to be e-corporations.   T   F

12. HPOs emphasize employee involvement and self-management.   T   F

13. HPO results include organizational effectiveness; individual, team, and organizational learning; and benefits to society.   T   F

14. High-performance organizations tend to have fewer hierarchical levels than traditional organizations.   T   F

15. Any organization that uses employee work teams is an HPO.   T   F

16. Greenfield sites are traditional organizations that change into HPOs.   T   F

17. A traditional organization becomes an HPO from the bottom up.   T   F

18. Once the decision is made to go ahead, HPOs are easy to establish.   T   F

19. Strong, sustained, top-down leadership is required for an HPO.   T   F

20. HPOs appear to be a management fad.   T   F

SHORT ANSWER

21. Briefly discuss the role of the changing workforce in an HPO.

22. Briefly compare and contrast at least three components of traditional organizations and HPOs.

23. Briefly discuss the difficulties of HPO "islands" inside larger corporations.

24. Briefly discuss the major middle-management challenges in establishing an HPO.

APPLICATIONS ESSAY

25. Your manager recently heard about high-performance organizations. She has asked you to explain them to her so that she can decide whether her organization should become one. Answer her request.

Globalization

Culture and Competitive Advantage

Inco Walks a Fine Line

Inco Limited is one of the world's largest mining and metals companies and the world's second largest producer of nickel, with operations and an extensive marketing network in more than 40 countries. As a global company, Inco has had to adapt to the culture and environment of each of the countries in which it has a foothold.

In 1968, PT Inco officially began operations in Indonesia, signing a 30-year Contract of Work agreement with the Indonesian government, which granted mining rights in the provinces of South, Southeast, and Central Sulawesi. PT Inco opened Indonesia's first major nickel plant in Sorowako in 1977. And, in 1996, the company extended its contract for another 30-year period to 2025.

Establishing a foreign presence for upwards of 60 years no doubt requires consideration for the local environment, people, and culture. Inco endeavours to work in partnership with local community representatives and organizations, employees, governments, and various non-governmental organizations. It recognizes that the communities in which it operates play an important role in its operations and are vital to its long-term viability. Earning respect means pursuing relationships based on transparency, inclusion, and goodwill, and also acknowledging that there is always room for improvement.

PT Inco has provided support to improve the standard of living where it operates in Indonesia. Under the Contract of Work agreement, the company has paid royalties, water levy, land rent, and taxes. PT Inco and its subcontractors also use Indonesian services, raw materials produced from Indonesian sources, and Indonesian-manufactured products, if they are available on a competitive time, cost, and quality basis.

In 1990, PT Inco made a public offering in Indonesia of 20 percent of its shares to enable Indonesians to become PT Inco shareholders. Today, approximately four percent of its public shareholders are residents of Indonesia and about 11 percent of its employees own shares.

This chapter will broaden your understanding of people and organizations operating across cultures and in a complex global economy. As you read Chapter 3, keep in mind these key questions:

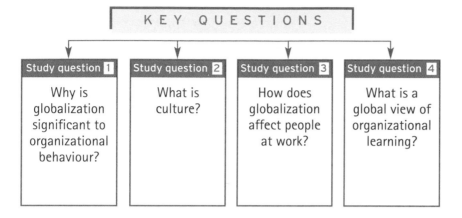

KEY QUESTIONS

Study question 1	Study question 2	Study question 3	Study question 4
Why is globalization significant to organizational behaviour?	What is culture?	How does globalization affect people at work?	What is a global view of organizational learning?

This is the age of globalization, a time when corporate success is increasingly linked to worldwide operations and a global staff.[1] All around the globe, people working in businesses large or small are facing the many challenges and opportunities that go with business competition in an increasingly complex and "borderless" world.[2] To successfully manage organizational behaviour across varied cultures, one of the keys is being able to respect differences and value diversity.

Today's organizations need managers with global awareness and cultural sensitivity. This does not mean that they all must work in foreign lands. But it does mean that they must be aware of how international events can affect the well-being of organizations. They must know how to deal with people from other countries and cultures. In other words, in an interconnected world, for those who cross cultural and national boundaries in their work, understanding these cultural differences is critical for success.

Today, managers must be curious and willing to learn quickly from management practices around the globe. Insights into effective management and high-performance organizations do not come from only one location or culture. Contributions to our understanding about people and organizations can be found from Africa to Asia and from Europe to North and South America. The variety of issues and topics in this chapter will help you understand the important global dimensions of organizational behaviour.

Organizational Behaviour and Globalization

Most organizations today must achieve high performance in the context of a competitive and complex global environment.[3] As we begin the twenty-first century, we are fully in the age of **globalization**, an age of complex economic networks of competition, resource supplies, and product markets that go beyond national boundaries and circle the globe.[4] No one can deny the impact of globalization on organizations, the people who work in them, and our everyday

Globalization involves growing worldwide interdependence of resource suppliers, product markets, and business competition.

lives. Consider globalization in terms of your own life and career: you already buy many products made by foreign firms; you may someday work overseas in the foreign operation of a domestic firm; you may someday work overseas as an expatriate employee of a foreign firm; and you may someday work as a domestic employee of a foreign firm operating in your home country. The field of organizational behaviour recognizes these realities and this book aims to help you understand how work in the global economy affects performance.

A GLOBAL ECONOMY

Google

www.google.ca

Google started as a research project at Stanford University, created by Ph.D. candidates Larry Page and Sergey Brin when they were 24 and 23 years old respectively. Google's index of more than four billion Web pages is the largest in the world; if printed, it would create a stack of paper more than 227 miles high. Google can search this huge collection of Web pages often in less than half a second. It receives search requests daily from all over the world, including Antarctica. Users can restrict their searches for content in 35 non-English languages, including Chinese, Greek, Icelandic, Hebrew, Hungarian, and Estonian. To date, no requests have been received from outer space, but the search engine has a Klingon interface just in case.

The rapid growth of information technology and electronic communications has increased the average person's awareness of the global economy. The international news brings the entire world into our homes and our thoughts daily. An explosion of opportunities on the Internet allows us to share and gather information from global sources at low cost and from the convenience of our desktops and laptops—at home, while travelling, or at work. And, always, the movement from country to country of products, trends, values, and innovations continues to change lifestyles at a rapid pace. At the same time that valuable skills and investments move among countries, cultural diversity among the world's populations is increasing. Immigration is having profound implications for many nations. More and more, tomorrow's employers will need to deal with *multicultural workforces*—made up of workers from non-traditional labour sources and from ethnic backgrounds representing every corner of our world.[5]

Being completely self-sufficient by relying only on what is available in their own country is no longer a realistic option for nations or businesses.[6] Commercial investments travel the trade routes of the world. Canadian businesses, for example, are highly interested in the U.S., having invested $30 billion there in 2000 alone. As of the end of 2003, Canadians had invested over $381 billion in fixed assets outside of Canada. These investments generate over $400 billion in annual sales and this amount is climbing. From the opposite side, there are foreign investments in Canada totalling $358 billion of fixed assets. All these investments have helped Canada's annual exports grow to $400 billion and they make a solid contribution to the $1.2-trillion Canadian economy.[7] Global investment networks are reinforced by events like the $15-billion merger of Manulife Insurance and John Hancock Insurance of Boston. With that merger, Manulife became the largest insurer in Canada, second largest in North America, and fifth largest in the world. Research in Motion (RIM), based in Waterloo, Ontario, is now the world's favourite producer of wireless technology for data and recently needed more production capacity as a result. With the $1 billion RIM netted in new money in January 2003, the company was able to fund its growth in Europe and 9 percent increase in workers in Canada. The U.S. automobile industry is highly integrated around the world. It imports Japanese, Canadian, Mexican, and Brazilian engines; uses German instruments and British electronics; and employs Italian designers. In 2003, over half of the automotive components in U.S. automobiles came from Mexico and Canada. Advances in technology even make it possible for software developers in places like Bangalore, India, to work for global employers without ever having to leave their homes.

REGIONAL ECONOMIC ALLIANCES

Economic alliances between countries of the same region are now an undeniable force in the global economy.[8] First and foremost, there is the European Union (EU), which is moving forward with its agenda of political, economic, and monetary union among its member countries. Remarkably, the EU has created a new world currency, the Euro, which has replaced the traditional currencies of many of its member nations. Within the EU, businesses from member countries have access to a market of almost 450 million customers. Some of the EU agreements include eliminating border controls and trade barriers, creating technical product standards that are the same for all member countries, making government procurement contracts more accessible, and standardizing financial regulations. These agreements are all designed to bring economic benefit and union to Europe, a region whose economy of some $8.5-trillion closely approaches the U.S.'s $9.1-trillion economy. With the inclusion of Poland, the Czech Republic, Hungary, and Cyprus in 2004, and potentially Turkey, Romania, and other countries in 2008 or later, the EU is becoming an economic powerhouse of the world.

The North American Free Trade Agreement (NAFTA) links the economies and customer markets of Canada, the United States, and Mexico in freer trade. NAFTA has been praised for uniting in trade a region with more potential customers than the European Union. The agreement may soon include other countries of the Americas as well. Some business and government leaders even speak of an all-encompassing Free Trade Agreement for the Americas (FTAA) early in the twenty-first century. At present, the Caribbean Community (CARICOM) is trying to negotiate free trade agreements with Latin American countries. In addition, the Andean Pact (linking Venezuela, Colombia, Ecuador, Peru, and Bolivia) and Mercosur (linking Brazil, Paraguay, Uruguay, and Argentina) are already active in South America. Canada and Chile have formalized their free trade agreement, the CCFTA.

Similar regional economic partnerships are appearing in other parts of the globe as well. In Asia, the Asia-Pacific Economic Co-operation Forum (APEC) is designed for joint economic development among member countries. Even with economic challenges worldwide, Asia remains an economic power and is the home of many world-class business competitors. Japan's economic influence is always visible, as is China's, whose size and power may well dominate the twenty-first century. Recent events have again confirmed the importance of other Asian countries, especially Taiwan, Singapore, South Korea, Malaysia, Thailand, and Indonesia. India, with its huge population, is an economy on the move and is recognized as a world-class supplier of software expertise.

Africa, led by developments in post-apartheid South Africa, has also become an important member of the global economy. Since apartheid was ended, for example, South Africa has steadily advanced to stand in 42nd place in the IMD (International Institute for Management Development)world competitiveness rankings.[9] Countries like Uganda, Ivory Coast, Botswana, South Africa, and Ghana are also recognized for their positive business potential. A report on sub-Saharan Africa concluded that the region's problems can be managed and that the region presents investment opportunities.[10]

GLOBAL QUALITY STANDARDS

The existence of international standards for quality is further proof of how important doing business across borders now is. The quality designation "ISO"—the Greek word for "same"— is for quality standards set by the International Organization for Standardization in Geneva, Switzerland. This mark of quality excellence has become a model for quality assurance worldwide. The European Union and more than 50 countries, including the United States, Canada, and Mexico, have endorsed the ISO's quality standard. ISO certification is fast becoming a goal for companies around the world that want to do business in Europe and want to win reputations as total quality, "world-class" manufacturers. In addition to having measures for product and service standards, ISO programs also have measures for environmental and human resource standards.

GLOBAL MANAGERS

A global manager has the international awareness and cultural sensitivity that are needed to work well across national borders.

Another consequence of globalization is the search for a new breed of manager—**the global manager**, someone who knows how to conduct business across borders.[11] Often multilingual, the global manager thinks with a world view; appreciates diverse beliefs, values, behaviours, and practices; and is able to map strategy accordingly. If you fit this description (see The Effective Manager 3.1), or soon will, get ready. Corporate recruiters are scrambling to find people with these skills and interests.

The global dimension that is now part of business and management poses many complications to be overcome. High performers with proven technical skills at home may find that their styles and attitudes just do not work well overseas. According to experienced international managers, having a "global mindset" of cultural adaptability, patience, flexibility, and tolerance is essential.[12] The failure rate for Western managers in overseas assignments has been measured as being as high as 25 percent, and a recent study criticized British and German companies for not preparing employees adequately before sending them abroad.[13]

Cultures and Cultural Diversity

The word "culture" is frequently used in organizational behaviour in discussions of corporate culture, the growing interest in workforce diversity, and the broad differences among people around the world. Specialists tend to agree that **culture** is the learned, shared way of doing things in a particular society. It is the way, for example, in which its members eat, dress, greet and treat one another, teach their children, solve everyday problems, and so on.[14] Geert Hofstede, a Dutch scholar and consultant, refers to culture as the "software of the mind," making the analogy that the mind's "hardware" is universal among human beings.[15] But the software of culture takes many different forms. Indeed, we are not born with a culture; we are born into a society that teaches us its culture. And because a culture is shared by people, it helps define the boundaries between different groups and affects how their members relate to one another.

Culture is the learned and shared way of thinking and acting among a group of people or a society.

The Effective Manager 3.1
ATTRIBUTES OF THE "GLOBAL MANAGER"
• adapts well to different business environments
• respects different beliefs, values, and practices
• solves problems quickly in new circumstances
• communicates well with people from different cultures
• speaks more than one language
• understands different government and political systems
• conveys respect and enthusiasm when dealing with others
• has high technical expertise for a job

POPULAR DIMENSIONS OF CULTURE

The popular dimensions of culture are those aspects that are most apparent to the individual travelling abroad—for example, language, time orientation, use of space, and religion.[16]

Language Perhaps the most conspicuous aspect of culture, and certainly the one the traveller notices first, is language. The languages of the world number into the thousands. Some, such as Maltese, are spoken by only a handful of people, whereas others, such as English, Spanish, and Mandarin, are spoken by hundreds of millions. Some countries, such as France and Malaysia, have one official language; others, such as Canada, Switzerland, and India, have more than one; and still others, like the United States, have none.

The idea that language is a central part of culture is expressed by the *Whorfian hypothesis*, which considers language to be a major determinant of our thinking.[17] The vocabulary and structure of a language reflect the history of a society and can also reveal how its members relate to the environment. Arabic, for example, has many different words for the camel, its parts, and equipment used with camels. As you might expect, English is very poor in its ability to describe camels. People who speak the same language do not necessarily share the same culture. The words of a language can have different meanings in different cultures or regions where the language is spoken, as is the case with English. A "truck" in Chicago is a "lorry" in London; "hydro" in Winnipeg is "electric power" in Boston; grocery shoppers in Canada put "pop" in their "bags," but U.S. shoppers put "soda" in their "sacks."

The anthropologist Edward T. Hall notes important differences in the ways different cultures use language.[18] Members of **low-context cultures** are very explicit in using the spoken and written word. In these cultures, such as those of Australia, Canada, and the U.S., the message is largely conveyed by the words someone uses, and not particularly by the "context" in which they are spoken. In contrast, members of **high-context cultures** use words to express only a limited part of the message. The rest of the message is found in the context, which includes body language, the physical setting, and past relationships—all of which add meaning to what is being said. Because this part of the message is not expressed directly, it must be inferred by the person receiving the message. According to Hall, many Asian and Middle Eastern cultures are high context, whereas most Western cultures are low context.

Time Orientation Hall also uses time orientation to classify cultures.[19] In **polychronic cultures**, people hold a traditional view of time that may be described as a "circle." This suggests repetition in the sense that time is "cyclical" and goes around and around. In this view, time does not create pressures for immediate action or performance. After all, one will have another chance to pass the same way again. If an opportunity is lost today, no problem, it may return again tomorrow. Members of polychronic cultures tend to emphasize the present and often do more than one thing at a time.[20] An important business or government official in a Mediterranean country, for example, may have a large reception area outside his or her office. Visitors wait in this area and may do business with the official and others who move in and about the room, conferring as they go.

> In low-context cultures, messages are expressed mainly by the spoken and written word.
>
> In high-context cultures, words express only part of a message, with the rest of the message expressed in body language and other contextual cues.
>
> In a polychronic culture, people tend to do more than one thing at a time.

OB ACROSS FUNCTIONS

Information Systems

Going Global by Staying High Tech

There is no shortage of help for those small and medium-sized businesses that want to "go global." Indeed, the information needed to get started as an exporter and become a participant in the marketplaces of the world is available at the touch of a keyboard—through the Internet. Those looking for a starting point can go to www.globalconnector.org, a useful global search engine. To look up travel guides and location information in a minute, www.go-global.com is a useful site. International business is well catalogued at www.fita.org, and information on free trade zones is available at www.escapeartist.com/ftz/ftz_index.html. The world of international business is a world of diverse peoples and cultures. The most talented individuals, the best of the best, know how to work across cultures with respect and delight. Visit www.ewinters.com/xculture.html for essays on a variety of cross-cultural business issues. This is only a small sample of the wealth of resources available that make international business ventures easier. But your company has to be linked and willing to explore the World Wide Web to take full advantage of these resources. With today's information technology, the potential for competitive advantage through expanded global commerce is there. It's yours for the asking, but you have to be quick.

In a monochronic culture, people tend to do one thing at a time.

Members of **monochronic cultures** view time more as a "straight line." In this "linear" view of time, the past is gone, the present is here briefly, and the future is almost upon us. In monochronic cultures, time is measured precisely and creates pressures for action and performance. People appreciate schedules and appointments and talk about "saving" and "wasting" time. Long-range goals become important, and planning is a way of managing the future. In contrast to the Mediterranean official in the earlier example, a British manager will typically schedule a certain amount of time in his or her daily calendar to deal with a business visitor. During this time, the visitor receives her complete attention. Only after one visitor leaves will another one be received, again based on the daily schedule.

Use of Space *Proxemics*, the study of how people use space to communicate, reveals important cultural differences.[21] Personal space can be thought of as the "bubble" that surrounds us, and how big this space should be depends on the culture. When others invade or close in on our personal space, we tend to feel uncomfortable. Then again, if people are too far away, communication becomes difficult. Arabs and South Americans seem more comfortable talking at closer distances than do North Americans; Asians seem to prefer even greater distances. When a Saudi moves closer to speak with a visiting Canadian executive, the visitor may back away to keep more distance between them. But the same Canadian may approach a Malaysian too closely when doing business in Kuala Lumpur, causing the host to back away. Cross-cultural misunderstandings due to differences in personal space are quite common.

In some cultures, often polychronic ones, space is organized in such a way that many activities can be carried out simultaneously. Spanish and Italian towns are organized around central squares (plazas or piazzas), whereas Canadian towns typically have a traditional "Main Street" laid out in a straight line. Similar cultural influences are seen in the layout of work space. Canadians, who seem to prefer individual offices or cubicles, may have difficulty adjusting to Japanese employers who prefer open floor plans.

Religion Religion is also a major element of culture and can be one of its more visible manifestations. Religions often specify rituals, holy days, and foods that can or cannot be eaten. Codes of ethics and moral behaviour often have their roots in religious beliefs. The influence of religion on economic matters can also be significant.[22] In the Middle East, there are interest-free "Islamic" banks that operate based on principles in the Koran. In Malaysia, business dinners are scheduled after 8 p.m. so that Muslim guests can first attend to their evening prayer.

VALUES AND NATIONAL CULTURES

Cultures vary in their underlying patterns of values and attitudes. The way people think about such matters as achievement, wealth and material gain, and risk and change may influence how they approach work and their relationships with organizations. A framework developed by Geert Hofstede offers one approach for understanding how value differences across national cultures can influence human behaviour at work. The five dimensions of national culture in his framework can be described as follows:[23]

Hofstede's dimensions of national cultures

1. **Power distance** is the willingness of a culture to accept status and power differences among its members. It reflects the degree to which people are likely to respect hierarchy and rank in organizations. Indonesia is considered a high-power distance culture, whereas Sweden is considered a relatively low-power distance culture.

2. **Uncertainty avoidance** is a cultural tendency to be uncomfortable with risk and ambiguity. It reflects the degree to which people are likely to prefer structured versus unstructured

organizational situations. France is considered a high-uncertainty avoidance culture, whereas Hong Kong is considered a low-uncertainty avoidance culture.

3. **Individualism–collectivism** is the tendency of a culture to emphasize either individual or group interests. It reflects the degree to which people are likely to prefer working as individuals or working together in groups. The U.S. is a highly individualistic culture, whereas Mexico is a more collectivist one.

4. **Masculinity–femininity** is the tendency of a culture to value stereotypical masculine or feminine traits. It reflects the degree to which organizations emphasize competition and assertiveness versus interpersonal sensitivity and concern for relationships. Japan is considered a very masculine culture, whereas Thailand is considered a more feminine culture.

5. **Long-term/short-term orientation** is the tendency of a culture to emphasize values associated with the future, such as thrift and persistence, or values that focus largely on the present. It reflects the degree to which people and organizations view performance from a long-term or short-term perspective. South Korea is high on long-term orientation, whereas Canada is a more short-term oriented country.

The first four dimensions in Hofstede's framework came from an extensive study of thousands of employees of a multinational corporation operating in more than 40 countries.[24] The fifth dimension of long-term/short-term orientation was added from research using the Chinese Values Survey conducted by cross-cultural psychologist Michael Bond and his colleagues.[25] Their research suggested the cultural importance of Confucian dynamism, which emphasizes persistence, the ordering of relationships, thrift, sense of shame, personal steadiness, reciprocity, protection of "face," and respect for tradition.[26]

Figure 3.1 Sample country clusters on Hofstede's dimensions of individualism–collectivism and power distance

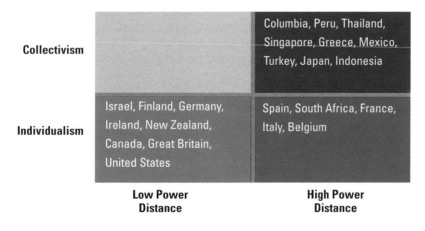

When using the Hofstede framework, it is important to remember that the five dimensions are interrelated and not independent.[27] National cultures may best be understood as collages that combine multiple dimensions. For example, Figure 3.1 shows a sample grouping of countries based on individualism–collectivism and power distance. Note that high power distance and collectivism are often found together, as are low power distance and individualism. Whereas high collectivism may lead us to expect a work team in Indonesia to operate by consensus, the high power distance may cause the consensus to be heavily influenced by the desires of a formal leader. A similar team operating in Canada, which is more individualistic and lower power distance, might make decisions with more open debate, and might allow disagreement with a leader's stated preferences.

UNDERSTANDING CULTURAL DIFFERENCES

To work well with people from different cultures, you must first understand your own culture. People are usually unaware of their own culture until they come into contact with a very different one. Knowing your own culture will help guard you against two problems that frequently arise in international dealings. One is the danger of parochialism—assuming that the ways of your culture are the only ways of doing things. The other is the danger of ethnocentrism—assuming that the ways of your culture are the best ways of doing things.[28] It would be parochial for a travelling Canadian businesswoman to insist that all of her business contacts speak English or French. It would be ethnocentric for her to think that anyone who dines with a spoon rather than a knife and fork lacks proper table manners.

A framework developed by Fons Trompenaars offers a useful way of looking at cultural differences that can help us better understand and, hopefully, deal with them.[29] Working from a databank of respondents from 47 national cultures, he suggests that cultures vary in the way their members solve problems of three major types: (1) relationships with people, (2) attitudes toward time, and (3) attitudes toward the environment.

Trompenaars identifies five major cultural differences in how people handle relationships with other people. The orientations, as illustrated in Figure 3.2, are:

How cultures deal with relationships among people

1. universalism versus particularism—relative emphasis on rules and consistency, or on relationships and flexibility

2. individualism versus collectivism—relative emphasis on individual freedom and responsibility, or on group interests and consensus

3. neutral versus affective—relative emphasis on objectivity and detachment, or on emotion and expressed feelings

4. specific versus diffuse—relative emphasis on focused and narrow involvement, or on involvement with the whole person

5. achievement versus prescription—relative emphasis on performance-based and earned status, or on ascribed status

For problems based on different attitudes toward time, Trompenaars distinguishes between cultures with sequential orientations versus those with synchronic orientations. Time in a sequential view is a passing series of events; in a synchronic view, it consists of an interrelated past, present, and future. For problems based on different attitudes toward the environment, he contrasts how different cultures may relate to nature in inner-directed versus outer-directed ways. Members of an inner-directed culture tend to view themselves as separate from nature and believe they can control it. Those in an outer-directed culture view themselves as part of nature and believe they must go along with it.

Figure 3.2 Sample country clusters on Trompenaars's framework for understanding cultural differences

Canada, USA, Ireland	**Universalism vs. Particularism**	**Indonesia, China, Venezuela**
USA, Hungary, Russia	Individualism vs. Collectivism	Thailand, Japan, Mexico
Indonesia, Germany, Japan	**Neutral vs. Affective**	**Italy, France, USA**
Spain, Poland, USA	Specific vs. Diffuse	India, Great Britain, Egypt
Australia, Canada, Norway	**Achievement vs. Ascription**	**Philippines, Pakistan, Brazil**
Great Britain, Belgium, USA	Sequential vs. Synchronic	Malaysia, Venezuela, France

Globalization and People at Work

OB scholars are increasingly aware of the need for a better understanding of how management and organizational practices vary among the world's cultures. According to them, we must therefore be familiar with the importance of multinational employers, the diversity of multicultural workforces, and the special demands of international work assignments.

MULTINATIONAL EMPLOYERS

A true **multinational corporation** (MNC) is a business firm that has extensive international operations in more than one foreign country. MNCs are more than just companies that "do business abroad;" they are global concerns—exemplified by Toyota, Royal-Dutch Shell, Sony, Bombardier, and many others. The missions and strategies of MNCs apply to the whole world. In the public sector, multinational organizations (MNOs) are organizations with not-for-profit missions whose operations also span the globe. Examples are Amnesty International, the International Red Cross, the United Nations, and the World Wildlife Fund.

The truly global organization operates with a total world view and does not have special ties to any one national "home." Futurist Alvin Toffler labels them **transnational organizations** that "may do research in one country, manufacture components in another, assemble them in a third, sell the manufactured goods in a fourth, deposit surplus funds in a fifth, and so on."[30] Although the pure transnational corporation may not yet exist, large firms like Nestle, Gillette, and Ford are striving hard to move in that direction. New information technologies are making it a lot easier to become a transnational corporation. These technologies allow organizations to operate through virtual links with components and suppliers located around the world.

The MNCs have enormous economic power and impact. Toffler, in particular, warns that "the size, importance, and political power of this new player in the global game has skyrocketed." Their activities can bring both benefits and controversies to the countries they operate in. One example is in Mexico, where many maquiladoras (foreign-owned plants) assemble imported parts and ship finished products to the U.S. and Canada. Inexpensive labour is an advantage for the foreign operators. For its part, Mexico benefits from industrial development, reduced unemployment, and increased foreign exchange earnings. But there are complaints about the downsides of maquiladoras—stress on housing and public services in Mexican border towns, inequities in the way Mexican workers are treated (wages, working conditions, and production quotas) compared to workers doing the same jobs in other countries, and the environmental impact of pollution from the industrial sites.

ETHICS AND SOCIAL RESPONSIBILITY

When it was learned that while toiling under inhumane conditions Guatemalan workers were earning five cents a kilogram to pick coffee beans that Starbucks was selling for $20 a kilogram, the successful chain had a controversy to deal with. Starbucks CEO Howard Schultz responded by setting a new standard for socially responsible business. His firm put in place guidelines requiring overseas suppliers to pay wages that "address the basic needs of workers and their families," to ensure that work does not "interfere with mandated education" for children, and to help workers get "access to safe housing, clean water and health facilities and services." Global human rights activists praised Starbucks' policy as a benchmark for importers of agricultural commodities.[31]

Team Canada

www.dfait.gc.ca

Team Canada is a partnership between business and government to promote Canada's trade and investment interests abroad and to raise Canada's profile as a source of high technology and goods and ervices.

Since 1994, the prime minister has led business delegations to several emerging markets, including China (1994); India, Pakistan, Indonesia, and Malaysia (1996); Korea, Philippines, and Thailand (1997); Mexico, Brazil, Argentina, and Chile (1998); Japan (1999); Beijing, Shanghai and Hong Kong (2001); Russia and Germany (2002); Brazil (2004); and returning to China in 2005. More than 2,800 Canadian businesses and other organizations have taken advantage of this opportunity to access foreign markets.

A multinational corporation is a business with extensive international operations in more than one foreign country.

A transnational organization operates with a total world view, having no national home.

MULTICULTURAL WORKFORCES

What is the best way to deal with a multicultural workforce? There are no easy answers. Styles of leadership, motivation, decision-making, planning, organizing, leading, and controlling vary from country to country.[32] Managing a construction project in Saudi Arabia with employees from Asia, the Middle East, Europe, and North America working side by side will clearly present challenges that are different from the ones that go with a domestic project. Similarly, establishing and successfully operating a joint venture in Kazakhstan, Nigeria, or Sri Lanka will require a great deal of learning and patience. In these and other international settings, political risks and bureaucratic difficulties further complicate the already difficult process of working across cultural boundaries.

Domestic multiculturalism is cultural diversity within a national population.

The challenges of managing across cultures, however, are not limited to international operations. In fact, a new term has been coined—**domestic multiculturalism**—which describes cultural diversity within a specific national population. This diversity in the national population will be reflected in the workforces of local organizations.[33] If we look to Canada, we see that our largest city is teeming with such diversity. In Toronto, 47% of high school students have English as their second language. At the elementary level, 47,000—more than 12%—of the students in Toronto were born outside of Canada in over 175 countries. There are over 80 languages represented in the Toronto school system, from Urdu to Serbian and Swahili to Cantonese.[34] Toronto is home to over 43% of all the persons who immigrated to Canada in the 1990s and is the most cosmopolitan city in the world according to the United Nations.[35] As a result, people and companies can expect their coworkers and employees to be just as cosmopolitan.

EXPATRIATE WORK ASSIGNMENTS

An expatriate works and lives in a foreign country for an extended time.

People who work and live outside their own country for extended periods of time are called **expatriates**. The cost of an expatriate worker can be very expensive for the employer. An executive earning $100,000 per year, for example, might cost her company more than $300,000 in the first year of an assignment in England. The added cost would be due to compensation, benefits, transfer, and other relocation expenses. It is estimated that, on average, a three-year expatriate assignment will cost the employer $1 million.[36] To get the most out of the investment, progressive employers increase their expatriates' chances of performing successfully by doing many things to support them.[37] They carefully recruit employees who have the right sensitivities and skills, provide them with good training and orientation to the foreign culture, actively support them while working abroad, give extra attention to the needs of the expatriate's family members, and pay careful attention to relocation when the expatriate and family return home.

Expatriates usually face their greatest problems when they enter and work in a foreign culture, and when they are repatriated and return home. Figure 3.3 shows the stages in the typical expatriate work assignment. It begins with the initial assignment shock, which is the shock the person first feels upon being informed of the foreign posting. The ways in which recruitment, selection, and orientation are handled during this stage can have an important influence on the assignment's eventual success. Ideally, the employee, along with his or her spouse and family, is allowed to choose whether or not to accept the opportunity. Also ideally, proper pre-departure support and counselling are given so that the employee and his or her family have "realistic expectations" of what is to come.

The expatriate undergoes three phases of adjustment to the new country.[38] First is the *tourist stage*, in which the expatriate enjoys discovering the new culture. Second is the *disillusionment stage*, in which his or her mood is dampened as difficulties become more evident. Typical problems include communicating well in the local language and obtaining preferred personal products and food supplies. Third, the expatriate's mood often hits bottom in the stage of *culture shock*. This is where confusion, disorientation, and frustration in the ways of the local culture and living in the foreign environment become evident. If culture shock is handled well, the expatriate begins to feel better, function more effectively, and lead a reasonably normal life. If it is not, the employee's work performance may suffer, and can even become so poor that he or she will need to be reassigned back home.

Figure 3.3 Stages in the expatriate international career cycle: potential adjustment problems in the home and foreign countries

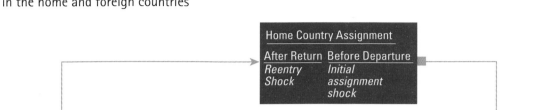

At the end of the expatriate assignment, perhaps after two to four years, there is the re-entry process. It, too, can be stressful. After an extended period away, the expatriate and his or her family have changed and the home country has changed as well. One does not simply "fall back in;" rather, it takes time to get used to living at home again. In too many instances, little thought is given to assigning the returned expatriate a job that matches his or her current skills and abilities. While abroad, the expatriate has often functioned with a great degree of independence—something that may or may not be possible at home. Problems caused by re-entry shock can be minimized with careful planning. This includes keeping enough contact with the home office during the expatriate assignment as well as having every possible support for the move back. Employers should also identify any new skills and abilities the expatriate has acquired, and assign returned expatriates to jobs that go well with their abilities. As organizations use more and more expatriate assignments, their systems for career planning and development must also take a global perspective.

GLOBALIZATION

When Laura Fennell graduated with a degree in psychology from the University of Guelph, she decided to further her career opportunities in human resource management by working for a year in India. She did this through AIESEC (www.ca.aiesec.org), the International Student Organization. This network of over 50,000 students in over 84 countries helps orient and train exchange students who then work in the host country in pre-arranged jobs. Laura found herself working at Next India (www.nextindia.net), a human resource company that primarily selects and trains personnel in Bangalore and Hyderabad, India, for such companies as Dell, Microsoft, and HSBC. These corporations require call centre operators for clients in Canada, the U.S., the UK, and Australia. Not only is training required in phonetics (the different sounds of a language) but also in areas of culture, attitude, political correctness, money matters, consumer rights, and more. Interestingly enough, Laura is making use of Hofstede's dimensions in the training manual and culture handbook she is helping develop.

Social Accountability International

www.sa–intl.org

Social Accountability International accredits auditors to evaluate whether or not an organization is respecting SA 8000. Auditors only give an organization SA 8000 certification after the auditors have consulted with human rights groups which visit and assess the businesses on a variety of issues. These include child labour, health and safety, freedom of association and the right to collective bargaining, discrimination, disciplinary practices, working hours, compensation, and management systems.

ETHICAL BEHAVIOUR ACROSS CULTURES

The importance of ethical issues in organizational behaviour and management was first introduced in Chapter 1. When companies do business internationally, there are special ethical challenges that they must deal with. These challenges result from our world's cultural diversity and varied governments and legal systems. Some of the important current issues include corruption and bribery in international business practices, poor working conditions and the employment of child and prison labour in some countries, and the role of international business in supporting repressive governments that fail to protect and respect the basic human rights of citizens.[39]

Canada does not have a specific law against firms acting in corrupt ways overseas, such as by giving bribes to government officials in order to get business contracts. However, our laws for business conduct in Canada could be used if a Canadian commits an illegal act abroad. In 1999, countries that belong to the Organization for Economic Development, including Canada, agreed to ban payoffs to foreign officials by their countries' businesses. In the U.S., the Foreign Corrupt Practices Act of 1977 makes it illegal for firms to engage in corrupt practives. The U.S. government is currently pushing for more countries to join the movement against bribe giving and taking. It has also been suggested that the World Bank consider corruption as a criterion when making loan decisions.[40]

The term *sweatshop* is increasingly in the news these days. It refers to organizations that force workers to labour under adverse conditions, which might include such things as long work days, unsafe conditions, and even the use of child labour. A variety of advocacy groups are now actively campaigning against sweatshops, and several well-recognized firms have been their targets—including multinationals Nike, Liz Claiborne, Gildan, Mattel, and Disney. Watchdog groups in Asia, for example, have criticized Disney for allowing some of its contract manufacturers in China to force workers to work seven days a week, up to 16 hours a day, and without overtime compensation. Mattel has been accused of engaging subcontractors who run "sweatshop Barbie" assembly lines that include extra-long work hours and heavy fines for workers' mistakes. In response to such criticisms, more multinational employers are now hiring independent consultants to conduct social audits of their international operations. They are also adopting formal codes of ethical practices that apply to subcontractors, and they are supporting external codes of conduct, such as *Social Accountability 8000*—a certificate awarded by Social Accountability International. Nike, Disney, and Mattel have each taken steps like these to ensure that products having their name are manufactured under conditions that meet acceptable standards.[41] Liz Claiborne and Gildan have joined the Fair Labor Organization of Washington, D.C. for their audit procedures. These two companies hope this will ensure that they and their subcontractors respect the fundamental rights of their workers, including the right to form unions and not be subjected to pregnancy tests. The following comment is pertinent, and was made by Jack Sheinkman, former president of the Amalgamated Clothing and Textile Workers Unions in the U.S., and member of the Council on Economic Priorities Advisory Board:

> As business becomes ever-more global in scope and its links in the chain of production extend further, the task of rating corporate social responsibility has become more complex. So, too, has the safeguarding of workers' rights…especially when responsibility is shared among manufacturers, contractors, subcontractors, buying agents…and other parties to business agreements which transcend time-zones, language barriers, and developing and industrialized country borders alike.[42]

One issue related to international business and management practices that is still debated is the influence of culture on ethical behaviour. Figure 3.4 presents a continuum that contrasts "cultural relativism" with "ethical absolutism."

Figure 3.4 The extremes of cultural relativism and ethical absolutism in international business ethics

Cultural relativism	Ethical absolutism
No culture's ethics are superior. The values and practices of the local setting determine what is right or wrong.	Certain absolute truths apply everywhere. Universal values transcend cultures in determining what is right or wrong.
"When in Rome, do as the Romans do."	*"Don't do anything you wouldn't do at home."*

Business ethicist Thomas Donaldson describes cultural relativism as the belief that there is no universal right way to behave and that ethical behaviour is determined by its cultural context.[43] In other words, international business behaviour is justified by the argument "When in Rome do as the Romans do." If a company accepts cultural relativism, a sweatshop operation would presumably be okay as long as it was consistent with the laws and practices of the local culture. At the opposite extreme on the continuum in Figure 3.4 is ethical absolutism, a universalistic assumption that there is a single moral standard that fits all situations, regardless of culture and national location. In other words, if a practice such as child labour is not acceptable in one's home environment, it should not be used elsewhere. Critics of the absolutist approach claim that it is a form of *ethical imperialism* because it attempts to impose external ethical standards unfairly or inappropriately on local cultures and fails to respect the local culture's needs and unique situations.

According to Donaldson, there is no simple answer to this debate. Indeed, he warns against the dangers of both cultural relativism and ethical absolutism. He argues that multinational businesses should adopt core or threshold values to guide behaviour in ways that respect and protect fundamental human rights in any situation by setting a minimum standard. However, he also argues that there is room beyond the threshold to adapt and tailor one's actions in ways that respect the traditions, foundations, and needs of different cultures.[44]

> **Cultural relativism** is the belief that ethical behaviour is determined by its cultural context.

> **Ethical absolutism** is the belief that a single moral standard applies to all cultures.

A Global View of Organizational Learning

Organizational learning was first defined in Chapter 1 as the process of acquiring the knowledge that an organization needs so that it can adapt to a changing environment. In the context and themes of this chapter, the concept can be extended to global organizational learning—the ability to gather from throughout the world the knowledge that is needed for long-term organizational adaptation. Simply stated, people from different cultures and parts of the world have a lot to learn from one another about organizational behaviour and management.

> **Global organizational learning** is the ability to gather from throughout the world the knowledge that is needed for long-term organizational adaptation.

ARE MANAGEMENT THEORIES UNIVERSAL?

One of the most important questions to be asked and answered in this age of globalization is whether or not management theories are universal. That is, can and should a theory developed in one culture be transferred and used in another? The answer, according to Geert Hofstede, is "no," at least not without careful consideration of cultural influences.[45] Culture can influence both the development of a theory or concept and how it is used. As an example, Hofstede cites the issue of motivation. He notes that Westerners have historically viewed motivation from the perspective of individual performance and rewards, which is consistent with their highly individualistic culture. However, concepts such as merit pay and job enrichment may not fit well in cultures where high collectivism places more emphasis on teamwork and groups. Hofstede's point—it is a point worth remembering—is that although we can and should learn from what is happening in other cultures, we should be informed consumers of that knowledge. We should always make adjustments for cultural factors when we transfer theories and practices from one setting to the next.

A good example of this point relates to the high interest there was several years ago in Japanese management approaches due to the success of Japanese industry at that time.[46] Although the Japanese economy and many of its firms have had problems of their own recently, management scholars and consultants recognize that many lessons can still be learned from Japanese practices. Japanese firms have traditionally been described as favouring *lifetime employment* with strong employee–employer loyalty, seniority pay, and company unions. Their operations have emphasized a *quality commitment*, the *use of teams* and *consensus decision-making*, and career development based on slow promotions and cross-functional job assignments.[47] In learning about these practices, however, management scholars have noted that cultural differences must be considered. Specifically, what works in Japan may not work as well in Canada, at least not without some modifications. Japan's highly collectivist society, for example, is very different from the individualistic cultures of Canada and other Western nations. It is only reasonable to expect differences in Japanese management and organizational practices.

BEST PRACTICES AROUND THE WORLD

An appropriate goal in global organizational learning is to find the "best practices" being used around the world. What is being done well in other settings may be of great value at home, whether that "home" is in Africa, Asia, Europe, North America, or anywhere else. Whereas organizations around the world once looked mainly to the North Americans and Europeans for management insights, today it is recognized that potential "benchmarks" of excellence for high-performance organizations can be discovered anywhere. There are, for example, the Japanese approaches discussed above, which have shown the value of global organizational learning and are evident in many of the workplace themes you will become familiar with in this book. They include growing attention to the value of teams and workgroups, consensus decision-making, employee involvement, flatter structures, and strong corporate cultures.

As the field of organizational behaviour continues to mature in its global research and understanding, we will all benefit from an expanding knowledge base that is made richer by cultural diversity. Organizational behaviour is a science of contingencies, and one of them is culture. No single culture has all of the "right" answers to today's complex management and organizational problems. As Canadian society evolves, the participants in our organizations will need ever more skills and awareness of the cultural diversity found abroad, but found also in our own communities. As the standards of human rights vary around the world, the ethical decisions facing managers and customers are complex, and at times overwhelming. But if we view our actions as being part of a learning environment and also use the tools of Trompenaars and Hofstede, we will find it easier to interact with others and to make such complex decisions. "When in Rome..." may apply to some countries, but for Canadians there seems to be a piece of Rome and every other city on every Canadian street. As a result, we need to be as international when away from home as when entering our workplaces here in Canada.

CHAPTER 3 STUDY GUIDE

Summary

Why is globalization significant to organizational behaviour?

- Globalization, with its complex, worldwide economic networks of business competition, resource supplies, and product markets, is having a major impact on businesses, employers, and workforces around the world.

- Nations in Europe, North America, and Asia are forming regional trade agreements, such as the EU, NAFTA, and APEC, to gain economic strength in the highly competitive global economy.

- More and more organizations, large and small, do an increasing amount of business in other countries; more and more local employers are partly or entirely foreign-owned; the local, domestic workforce is becoming multicultural and more diverse.

- All organizations need global managers who have the special interests and talents that are needed to excel in international work and cross-cultural relationships.

What is culture?

- Culture is the learned and shared way of doing things in a society; it has a profound effect on the way people from different societies think, behave, and solve problems.

- Some popular dimensions of culture include differences that can be observed in language, time orientation, use of space, and religion.

- Hofstede's five national culture dimensions are power distance, individualism–collectivism, uncertainty avoidance, masculinity–femininity, and long-term/short-term orientation.

- Trompenaars's framework for understanding cultural differences focuses on relationships among people, attitudes toward time, and attitudes toward the environment.

- Cross-cultural awareness requires a clear understanding of one's own culture and the ability to overcome the limits of parochialism and ethnocentrism.

How does globalization affect people at work?

- Multinational corporations (MNCs) are global businesses that operate with a worldwide scope; they are powerful forces in the global economy.

- Multiculturalism in the domestic workforce requires everyone to work well with people of different cultural backgrounds.

- Expatriate employees who work abroad for extended periods of time face special challenges, including possible adjustment problems abroad and re-entry problems when they return home.

- Ethical behaviour across cultures is examined from the perspectives of cultural relativism, universalism, and absolutism.

What is a global view of organizational learning?

- In a global view of learning about OB, the goal is to understand the best practices from around the world, while being sensitive to cultural differences.

- Management concepts and theories must always be considered in regard to the cultures in which they are developed and applied.

- Interest in Japanese management practices continues, with their traditional focus on long-term employment, quality commitment, use of teams, consensus decision-making, and careful career development.

- More and more, global learning will move beyond North America, Europe, and Japan to include best practices anywhere in the world.

KEY TERMS

Culture (p. 42)

Cultural relativism (p. 51)

Domestic multiculturalism
(p. 48)

Ethical absolutism (p. 51)

Expatriates (p. 48)

Globalization (p. 39)

Global manager (p. 42)

Global organizational

learning (p. 51)

High-context culture (p. 43)

Individualism–collectivism
(p. 42)

Long-term/short-term orientation (p. 43)

Low-context culture (p. 43)

Masculinity–femininity
(p. 43)

Monochronic culture (p. 44)

Multinational corporation
(p. 47)

Polychronic culture (p. 43)

Power distance (p. 42)

Transnational organization
(p. 47)

Uncertainty avoidance
(p. 42)

SELF-TEST 3

MULTIPLE CHOICE

1. NAFTA, APEC, and the EU are examples of _____. (a) multinational corporations (b) agencies of the United Nations (c) regional economic groupings (d) government agencies regulating international trade

2. In _____ cultures, people tend to complete one activity at a time. (a) parochial (b) monochronic (c) polychronic (d) ethnocentric

3. Cultural values that emphasize respect for tradition, ordering of relationships, and protecting one's "face" are associated with _____. (a) religious differences (b) uncertainty avoidance (c) masculinity–femininity (d) Confucian dynamism

4. One would expect to find respect for authority and acceptance of status differences in high _____ cultures. (a) power distance (b) individualism (c) uncertainty avoidance (d) aggressiveness

5. Asian countries like Japan and China are described on Hofstede's dimensions of national culture as generally high in _____. (a) uncertainty avoidance (b) short-term orientation (c) long-term orientation (d) individualism

6. _____ are foreign-owned plants that operate in Mexico, near the U.S. border, with special privileges. (a) estrellas (b) escuelas (c) maquiladoras (d) cabezas

7. In Trompenaars's framework for understanding cultural differences, _____ is used to describe different orientations toward nature. (a) inner-directed versus outer-directed (b) sequential versus polychronic (c) universal versus particular (d) neutral versus emotional

8. Management practices such as participative decision-making and an emphasis on teamwork are often characteristic of organizations in _____ cultures. (a) monochronic (b) collectivist (c) paternalistic (d) uncertain

9. The Mercosur is an example of how different countries may co-operate in a _____ for mutual gain. (a) franchise (b) strategic alliance (c) regional economic alliance (d) chaebol

10. Which of the following is most characteristic of Japanese management practices? (a) consensus decisions (b) fast promotion (c) highly specialized career paths (d) all of these

TRUE-FALSE

11. Globalization only affects persons who will work in foreign countries and/or for multinational corporations.   T   F

12. The notion of "ethical imperialism" fits the adage "When in Rome, do as the Romans do."   T   F

13. Language is important as a cultural variable only when one is dealing with a person who speaks a different language. T   F

14. A Canadian businessperson who expects foreign visitors to be able to conduct business negotiations in English is being very parochial about culture.   T   F

15. Respect that is earned based on an individual's performance is associated with an achievement-oriented culture.   T   F

16. A German doing business in Hong Kong should be sensitive to the "silent language" of culture, such as that reflected in the use of space.   T   F

17. The re-entry of expatriate employees returning from foreign assignments can be a source of problems for them and their employers.   T   F

18. Culture can be described as "software of the mind."   T   F

19. Promotion is typically faster in Japanese than in Western businesses.   T   F

20. A global manager thinks with a world view and is tolerant of differences.   T   F

SHORT ANSWER

21. Why is the individualism–collectivism dimension of national culture important in OB?

22. How do power-distance values affect management practices in different cultures?

23. What does the concept of ethnocentrism mean to you?

24. An organization trying to operate with Japanese management practices would do what?

APPLICATIONS ESSAY

25. Wayne C. Sales, the CEO of Canadian Tire, wants to keep his company "ahead of the pack" as foreign retailers try to enter the Canadian market. It used to be that American firms such as Wal-Mart and Home Depot were the major threats; now he has learned that the Asian giant Yaohan and the well-known Sainsbury's from Britain are thinking of having operations in Canada. The CEO has heard of your special consulting expertise in "global organizational learning." He is on the telephone now and wants you to explain how the concept may help him ensure Canadian Tire remains a world-class competitor. With a large consulting contract at stake, what do you tell him about this concept?

Diversity and Individual Differences

Building the Mosaic

Nowhere is our country's diversity more apparent than in the halls of Markham Gateway Public School in Markham, Ontario.

Almost all of the school's 792 students are the children of immigrants. Although many were born in Canada, some never speak English at home; instead, Tamil, Urdu, Cantonese, Punjabi, and Gujarati are the most common languages. In half the homes, more than one language is spoken.

Markham Gateway is not alone in its diversity. For example, at Milliken Mills High School in Unionville, 65 percent of the students speak English as a second language, and at Wilclay Public School in Markham, that figure is 70 percent.

This increased multiculturalism presents challenges. The Understanding the Early Years (UEY) research initiative, a federal study funded by Human Resources Development Canada, reveals that many students who know English as a second language are struggling in school.

A report from the UEY titled Early Childhood Development in the Dixie Bloor Community of Mississauga, Ontario, indicates that "the prevalence of children with low scores on the language test was particularly high: almost three times national norms. This observation reflects the high percentage of recent immigrants...as many such children would not be exposed to English at home."

These schools are microcosms of Canadian society. The 2001 census reports that the proportion of foreign-born Canadians is at its highest level in 70 years. With more than 200 ethnic origins represented, Canada is the second most diverse country in the world. Most immigrants come from China, the Philippines, and Hong Kong, and 13.4 percent of Canada's population is made up of visible minorities.

Markham Gateway's success lies in acclimatizing students, not in assimilating them. Despite the communication barriers, students are highly motivated to learn. In an interview with the *Toronto Star*, one kindergarten teacher says that she uses "signs to show them what to do.... Half of them don't speak even one word of English." She turns to "drumming and dance to teach children to count and learn the alphabet."

These unique teaching methods and the school's promise to recognize and respect all cultures are shaping a bright future for its students.

Understanding individual differences and similarities is crucial for today's diverse organizations. As you read Chapter 4, keep in mind these key questions:

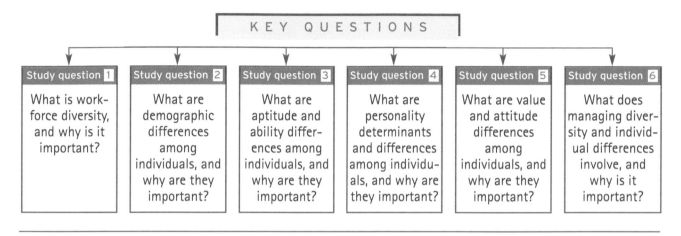

KEY QUESTIONS

Study question 1	Study question 2	Study question 3	Study question 4	Study question 5	Study question 6
What is workforce diversity, and why is it important?	What are demographic differences among individuals, and why are they important?	What are aptitude and ability differences among individuals, and why are they important?	What are personality determinants and differences among individuals, and why are they important?	What are value and attitude differences among individuals, and why are they important?	What does managing diversity and individual differences involve, and why is it important?

All of this suggests that diversity is, and should be, a major concern of organizations and that valuing diversity in all aspects of operations should be a top priority. With diversity come differences, and with differences comes the potential for problems in relationships. There is no denying this. But importantly, too, with diversity comes the great potential for new perspectives, as Markham Gateway Public School in our feature story has clearly shown. Creativity and expanded problem-solving can help meet the needs of our complex and dynamic work settings. In this chapter, we examine how diversity and differences affect our workplaces as factors in organizational behaviour.

Workforce Diversity

Most companies whose shares are traded on the Toronto Stock Exchange, including CN Rail, Suncor, and Royal Bank, are now providing incentives for their executives to deal successfully with workforce diversity.[1] **Workforce diversity** refers to the mix of individual human characteristics that make people different from one another.[2] More specifically, this diversity consists of the key demographic differences among members of a particular workforce—in other words, differences of gender, race and ethnicity, age, sexual orientation, and able-bodiedness. Sometimes these differences also include other factors, such as marital status, parental status, and religion.[3] The challenge is how to manage workforce diversity in a way that respects each individual's unique perspectives and contributions and also promotes a sense of organization vision and identity that is shared by the whole workforce.

Workforce diversity has increased in both Canada and the U.S., as it has in much of the rest of the world. Only Australia, with 22 percent of its population born out of country, has a higher proportion of new residents than Canada, where that figure is 18 percent. In the U.S., 11 percent of the population was born in a different country. From 1991 to 2001, over 46 percent of the 1.8

Workforce diversity is differences based on gender, race and ethnicity, age, sexual orientation, and able-bodiedness.

million immigrants to Canada, or 1.1 million people, were of working age (between 25 and 64). During the 1990s, almost 70 percent of the growth in Canada's labour force came from the 977,500 immigrants who entered the workforce in that decade. Immigrants were responsible for one-fifth of the workforce in Toronto and Vancouver. In the U.S., it is estimated that between 1990 and 2005 about 50 percent of the new entrants to the labour force will have been women and racial and ethnic groups, such as African Americans, Latinos, and Asians. It is projected that persons 55 and older will soon make up over 15 percent of the labour force.[4]

Stereotyping occurs when an individual is seen as belonging to a group or category (e.g., elderly persons) and is assumed to have the characteristics commonly associated with that group or category.

As the workforce becomes increasingly diverse, the possibility of stereotyping and discrimination increases and managing diversity becomes more important. **Stereotyping** occurs when an individual is thought of as belonging to a group or category—for instance, elderly persons—and the individual is assumed to have the characteristics commonly associated with that group or category—for instance, older people are not creative. Demographic characteristics can be the basis for stereotypes that prevent individual differences from being appreciated. In other words, stereotypes prevent people from getting to know each other as individuals and they prevent people from accurately assessing each other's performance potential. If you believe that older people are not creative, for example, you may mistakenly decide that a very inventive 60-year-old person should not be part of an important task force.

Discrimination against people in an organization is a violation of Canadian, U.S., and European Union (EU) laws. It is also counterproductive because it prevents organizations from fully using the contributions of people who are being discriminated against. Increasingly, firms are recognizing that having a diverse workforce that reflects society's differences helps bring the firms closer to their customers, both at home and abroad.

The Effective Manager | 4.1

TIPS IN DEALING WITH MALE AND FEMALE MANAGERS

- Do not assume that male and female managers have different personal qualities.
- Make sure that policies, practices, and programs provide equal management experiences regardless of gender differences.
- Do not assume that management success is more likely for either females or males.
- Recognize that there will be excellent, good, and poor managers of each gender.
- Understand that success requires the best use of human talent, regardless of gender.

Employment equity is a program designed to overcome employment disadvantages experieced by women, minorities, and Aboriginal peoples in Canada.

EQUAL EMPLOYMENT OPPORTUNITY

Equal employment opportunity refers to both workplace non-discrimination and employment equity. **Employment equity** is a comprehensive program designed to overcome employment disadvantages experienced by women, minorities, and Aboriginal peoples in Canada.

The Canadian Charter of Rights and Freedoms and the Employment Equity Act set out specific rules and standards to ensure that Canadians are not discriminated against and are treated equitably in the workplace. The Charter states, "Every individual is equal before and under the law and has the right to the equal protection and equal benefit of the law without discrimination and, in particular, without discrimination based on race, national or ethnic origin, colour, religion, sex, age or mental or physical disability." The purpose of the Employment Equity Act is to ensure this right in the workplace and "to correct the conditions of disadvantage in employment experienced by women, aboriginal peoples, persons with disabilities and members of visible minorities." It is also illegal in Canada to discriminate against someone because of his or her sexual orientation.[5]

Employment equity means more than treating people in the same way; it also requires special measures and the accommodation of differences. Under this legislation, the federal government and businesses regulated by federal law must have and follow employment equity programs to achieve equitable employment practices. Employment decisions are non-discriminatory if they are made without intending to exclude these legally protected groups or to disadvantage them.

While most provinces do not have individual employment equity acts, human rights legislation, which guarantees people equal treatment in relation to employment, falls under provincial jurisdiction. Each province has its own set of employment standards. Alberta has its Human Rights, Citizenship and Multiculturalism Act, and New Brunswick, Nova Scotia, and the Northwest Territories have their own Human Rights Acts, Newfoundland and Labrador its Human Rights Code, while British Columbia has the B.C. Human Rights Code. Ontario's Human Rights Code, created in 1962, was the first such code in Canada. It prohibits discrimination against an individual based on his or her "race, ancestry, place of origin, colour, ethnic origin, citizenship, creed, sex, sexual orientation, age, marital status, family status, or handicap." It also makes it possible to have special programs that can help overcome historic discrimination that was systematic. Quebec has its own Act Respecting Equal Employment in Public Bodies, as well as its own Charter of Rights and Freedoms, which set out the same standards and rights as found in the federal legislation.

In the United States, affirmative action is designed to remedy proven discrimination or to undo statistical imbalances in the labour force according to race or gender. The U.S. Civil Rights Act of 1964 makes it illegal for employers to discriminate against any individual—with respect to compensation, terms, or conditions of employment-based on the individual's race, colour, religion, sex, or national origin.

Canada's employment equity and the U.S.'s affirmative action are legally enforced by federal laws, provincial and state laws, and local laws, as well as by many court cases. These laws require organizations to write reports that give details about plans and statistical goals for specific groups of people. Specifically, the reports must give details about hiring, promotions, wages, layoffs, and other employment practices in regard to these groups.[6]

MANAGING DIVERSITY

Managing diversity in organizations is about appreciating differences by creating a setting where everyone feels valued and accepted. An organization's success or progress in managing diversity can be monitored with the help of organizational surveys of employees' attitudes and perceptions, among other means. An assumption in managing diversity is that groups will keep their own characteristics and will shape the firm, as well as be shaped by it, creating a common set of values that will strengthen ties with customers, improve recruitment, and so on. Sometimes, diversity management is resisted by individuals who are afraid of change or are uncomfortable with differences.

ENTREPRENEURSHIP

The Bank of Montreal is proud of its efforts to attract and build on a diverse team of individuals who come from and reflect the communities in which the bank operates. The bank sees this commitment as a competitive advantage and it works at it actively through hiring, training, and scholarships. Policies are in place to accommodate persons with disabilities through workplace adjustments and work balance. The bank's "Possibilities Program" is designed to help visible minorities, Aboriginal youth, and youth with disabilities by offering them educational assistance and work experience as interns. The intern positions are coordinated with local school boards and community groups and are for students in their last year of high school. The bank also offers bursaries for many of these students to attend post secondary institutions. Together, these efforts help BMO achieve its goal of being an "employer of choice." They also help it attract the talented and skilled future managers who will keep the Bank of Montreal competitive and successful.

Demographic Differences

Demographic characteristics are the background variables (e.g., age, gender) that help shape what a person becomes as time passes.

Demographic characteristics are the background characteristics that help shape what a person becomes as time passes. Such attributes may be thought of in current terms (for example, an employee's current medical status) and in historical terms (for instance, where and how long a person has worked at various jobs). Certain demographic characteristics are of special interest for matters of equal employment opportunity and workplace diversity. These include gender, age, race, ethnicity, sexual orientation, and able-bodiedness.

GENDER

According to research, very few differences between men and women affect job performance (see the Effective Manager 4.1). Men and women show no consistent differences in their problem-solving abilities, analytical skills, competitive drive, motivation, learning ability, or sociability. However, women are reported to be more conformist and to have lower expectations of success than men do. Women's absenteeism rates also tend to be higher than those of men. This latter finding may change, however, as we see men starting to play a more active role in raising children. Absenteeism is also likely to be less frequent as telecommuting, flexible working hours, and other similar measures become more common.[7]

Statistics Canada reports that women accounted for 47 percent of the employed work force in 2003, up from 37 percent in 1976. However, statistics from the 1999 Workplace and Employee Survey indicate that women were paid an average of 80 cents for every dollar earned by men. Specific workplace characteristics, such as the type of work, foreign ownership, and part-time rates, explained some of the wage difference, but not all. Wages increase with work experience, and in 1999, men averaged 18 years of full-time work experience compared with 14 for women. Men and women continued to hold different occupations, with women still clustered in low-wage industries. Women were also more likely to work part-time. Other factors, like teamwork, foreign ownership, and pay-for-performance, all of which were under-represented by women, but tended to include higher pay, played a role in the wage gap, as well.

Still a large chunk of the gender wage gap remains a mystery to Statistics Canada. After accounting for the differences in worker and workplace characteristics, women earned roughly 92 cents for every dollar earned by men. This means that worker and workplace characteristics account for 12 cents of the 20-cent gap. Considering the increased representation by women in recent decades and little difference in abilities and skills, what accounts for the remaining 8 cents?[8]

AGE

As Canada's workforce ages, research findings on age are particularly important. It is estimated that, by the end of 2005, people 50 years old and up will have accounted for 85 percent of the labour force growth since 1990.[9] Older workers are more likely to be stereotyped as inflexible and as undesirable in other ways. Workers as young as age 40 are considered by some as "old" and they complain that their experience and skills are no longer valued. Age-discrimination lawsuits are increasingly common in the U.S. Although there are fewer cases in Canada—the Canadian Human Rights Commission Tribunal has heard at least one case in recent years, that of a Quebec woman against Société Radio-Canada in 2001—we may soon see the same pattern here.[10] On the other hand, small businesses in particular tend to value older workers for their experience, stability, and low turnover—three qualities that research shows are typical of older workers. Research also shows that older workers have fewer avoidable absences.[11] Finally, to the extent that age is linked to experience or job tenure, there is a positive relationship between seniority and performance. More experienced workers tend to have low absence rates, relatively low turnover, and perform their jobs better.

As Canada's population ages, an important question arises. How will our school boards, colleges, universities, and hospitals replace senior staff who retire while these institutions are dealing with tight budgets imposed by the funding agencies, as well as the decreasing number of workers entering the workforce? With Canada's aging population, over half of education workers are eligible to retire in the next 12 years and the same proportion of health-care workers is likely to retire in less than 20 years.[12] These are the very individuals with the experience and better attendance who are required in high-performance organizations. The challenge of replacing our aging workforce may be a major reason that governments at all levels are discussing the possibility of eliminating mandatory retirement at age 65.

ABLE-BODIEDNESS

Even though recent studies report that disabled workers do their jobs as well as, or better than, non-disabled workers, nearly three-quarters of severely disabled persons are reported to be unemployed. Almost 80 percent of those with disabilities say they want to work.[13] Once again, it is predicted that the expected shortage of traditional workers will lead to a re-examination of hiring policies. More firms are expected to give serious consideration to hiring disabled workers, especially as it has been shown that the cost of accommodating these workers is low.[14]

RACIAL AND ETHNIC GROUPS

As is done in some current literature, here we use the term "racial and ethnic groups" to refer to the broad range of employees of different ethnicities or races who make up an always growing portion of the new workforce.[15] In the Canadian workplace, diversity is especially reflected in an increasing proportion of visible minorities. For Statistics Canada, the term "visible minorities" excludes Aboriginal peoples but includes people who are non-Caucasian in race or non-white in colour.[16] Statistics Canada estimates that visible minorities will amount to 20 percent of the population and workforce by the year 2016.[17] The potential for stereotypes and discrimination that can have a bad effect on career opportunities and progress for members of these and other groups must be recognized. Organizations that do not welcome this diversity may be missing the very employees they need to grow and, at the same time, may be passing up large numbers of potential customers.

Before leaving this section on demographic differences, it is important to repeat the following:

- Organizations must consider demographic variables so that they can respect and best deal with the needs and concerns of people of different genders, ethnic backgrounds, ages, and so on.

- These differences, however, are easily linked with stereotypes, which must be avoided.

- Demography is not a good indicator of how well an individual will fit a job. Rather, aptitude, ability, personality, values, and attitudes are what count.

Aptitude and Ability

Aptitude is a person's capability to learn something.

Ability is a person's existing capacity to perform the various tasks needed for a particular job.

Having discussed demographics, it is now time for us to consider aptitude and ability. **Aptitude** is a person's capability to learn something. **Ability** is a person's existing capacity to perform the various tasks needed for a specific job; it includes relevant knowledge and skills.[18] In other words, aptitudes are potential abilities, whereas abilities are the knowledge and skills that an individual already has.

Aptitudes and abilities are important considerations for a manager who is hiring or choosing candidates for a job. We all know about various tests used to measure mental aptitudes and abilities. Some of these give an overall intelligence-quotient (IQ) score (e.g., the Stanford-Binet IQ Test). Others give measures of more specific competencies that people entering various educational programs or career fields need to have. In many countries, there is a college or university entrance test. Such tests are designed to make it easier to screen and choose applicants for educational programs or jobs. In addition to mental aptitudes and abilities, some jobs, such as those of firefighters, police, and airline pilots, require tests of physical abilities. Muscular strength and cardiovascular endurance are two of the many dimensions of physical ability that may be tested.[19]

For legal reasons, evidence must be presented that shows that individuals who score better on these tests tend to be more successful in their educational program, career field, or job performance than those with lower scores. In other words, there must be a fit between specific aptitudes and abilities and the job requirements. If you want to be a surgeon, for instance, and cannot demonstrate good hand–eye coordination, there will not be a good ability–job fit. Good depth perception and a healthy constitution are important for airline pilots. The ability–job fit is so important that it is a core concept in Chapter 7 on managing human resources.

Personality

Personality is the overall profile or combination of characteristics that capture the unique nature of a person as that person interacts with others.

In addition to demographics and aptitude and ability, there is a third important individual attribute: **personality**. The term personality refers to the overall profile and combination of characteristics that capture the unique nature of a person as that person interacts with others. Consider the corporate banker who was asked in 1994 by two clients to join them in a mattress retail venture. Ten years later, Christine Magee is not only president of Sleep Country Canada, but also its main spokesperson, a face and voice familiar to most Canadians. As Sleep Country grew from an initial four to 87 stores, Magee became an icon of the executive woman: Retailer of the Year in 1996, one of the Globe and Mail's Top 40 Under 40 in 1997, and Entrepreneur of the Year in 1998. At 37, she also became a mother, and now juggles her high-profile, executive role at Canada's largest mattress retailer with the demands of her two young daughters.[20]

Personality combines a set of physical and mental characteristics that reflect how a person looks, thinks, acts, and feels. Sometimes attempts are made to measure personality with questionnaires or special tests. Other times, personality can be implied from behaviour alone, such as from the actions of Christine Magee. Either way, personality is an important individual characteristic for managers to understand. An understanding of personality contributes to an understanding of organizational behaviour because the interplay between an individual's personality and his or her tendency to behave in certain ways is somewhat predictable.

GLOBALIZATION

Many tech professionals are turning overseas assignments into opportunities for more challenging work and greater responsibility. These managers need knowledge about cultural differences, trade barriers, and other things that are likely to affect how they do business. They also need personality characteristics that will help them not only learn how to work effectively in another culture, but also keep up with developments in their homeland. People who are away for long periods can lose touch with their organization back home and, when returning, may be forced to take whatever job is available. However, if handled well, overseas assignments can provide important advantages for both the manager and the firm.

PERSONALITY DETERMINANTS AND DEVELOPMENT

What exactly determines personality? Is personality inherited—i.e., genetically determined—or is it formed by experience? You may have heard someone say something like, "She acts like her mother." Similarly, someone may argue that "Bobby is the way he is because of the way he was raised." These two arguments illustrate the nature/nurture controversy: Is personality determined by heredity, that is, by genetic makeup, or by one's environment? As Figure 4.1 shows, these two forces actually operate in combination. Heredity consists of those factors that are determined at conception, including physical characteristics, gender, and core personality factors. Environment consists of cultural, social, and situational factors.

The impact of heredity on personality continues to be debated greatly. Perhaps the most general conclusion we can draw is that heredity sets the limits on just how much personality characteristics can be developed; environment determines development within these limits. For instance, a person could be born with a tendency toward authoritarianism, and that tendency could be reinforced in an authoritarian work environment. These limits appear to vary from one characteristic to the next; and for all characteristics there is roughly an even split between the impact of heredity and that of the environment.[21]

Figure 4.1 The contribution of heredity and environment to personality

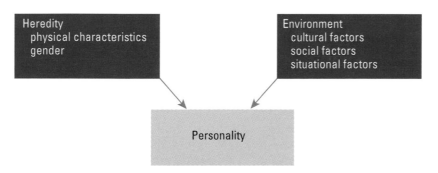

As we show throughout this book, cultural values and norms play a big role in the development of an individual's personality and behaviour. Contrast the individualism of U.S. culture with the collectivism of Chinese culture, for example.[22] Social factors that play a role include

such things as family life, religion, and the many kinds of formal and informal groups people join throughout their lives—friendship groups and athletic groups, for example, as well as formal workgroups. Finally, the demands of different situations bring out or constrain different aspects of an individual's personality. In class, for example, an individual would be likely to control his high spirits and related behaviours encouraged by his personality. However, at a sporting event, he might be seen jumping up, cheering, and loudly criticizing the referees.

Developmental approaches are systematic models of the ways in which personality develops over time.

The **developmental approaches** of Chris Argyris, Daniel Levinson, and Gail Sheehy systematically examine the ways in which personality develops over time. Argyris notes that people develop along a continuum of dimensions from immaturity to maturity, as shown in Figure 4.2. He believes that many organizations treat mature adults as if they were still immature and that this creates many problems for bringing out the best in employees. Levinson and Sheehy maintain that an individual's personality unfolds in a series of stages across time. Sheehy's model, for example, presents three stages: ages 18-30, 30-45, and 45-85+. Each of these has a crucial impact on the worker's employment and career, as we show in Chapter 7. The implications are that personalities develop over time and require different managerial responses accordingly. Thus, the personality aspects and needs of people when they first enter an organization will change sharply as they move through the different stages or toward increased maturity.[23]

Figure 4.2 Argyris's maturity–immaturity continuum

From Immaturity	To Maturity
Passivity	Activity
Dependence	Independence
Limited behaviour	Diverse behaviour
Shallow interests	Deep interests
Short time perspective	Long time perspective
Subordinate position	Superordinate position
Little self–awareness	Much self–awareness

Personality Traits and Classifications

Standardized personality tests determine how positively or negatively an individual scores on each of these dimensions. You can consider a person's individual personality profile across the five dimensions. For instance, a person scoring high on openness to experience tends to ask lots of questions and to think in new and unusual ways. In terms of job performance, research has shown that conscientiousness predicts job performance in five occupational groups of professions: engineers, police officers, managers, salespeople, and skilled and semi-skilled employees. What the other dimensions can predict about performance depends on the occupational group. For instance, not surprisingly, extraversion can predict performance in sales and managerial positions.

Many lists of personality traits—lasting characteristics that describe an individual's behaviour—have been developed, and many have been used in OB research. These lists can be looked at in different ways. First, recent research has used long lists of personality dimensions to examine people and, in the end, reduced these dimensions to the "Big Five":[24]

The "Big Five" personality dimensions

- *extraversion*—outgoing, sociable, assertive
- *agreeableness*—good-natured, trusting, co-operative
- *conscientiousness*—responsible, dependable, persistent
- *emotional stability*—unworried, secure, relaxed
- *openness to experience*—imaginative, curious, broad-minded

A second approach to looking at OB personality traits is to divide them into social traits, personal conception traits, and emotional adjustment traits, and then to consider how those categories come together dynamically; that is, what they produce as a whole.[25]

SOCIAL TRAITS

Social traits are surface-level traits that reflect the way a person appears to others when interacting in various social settings. Problem-solving style, based on the work of noted psychologist Carl Jung, is one measure of social traits.[26] It refers to the way a person gathers and evaluates information when solving problems and making decisions.

Information gathering is the first part of problem-solving. It involves getting and organizing data for use. Styles of information gathering vary from the sensation to intuitive styles. *Sensation-type individuals* prefer routine and order. They emphasize well-defined details in gathering information and would rather work with known facts than look for possibilities. In contrast, *intuitive-type individuals* prefer the "big picture." They like solving new problems, dislike routine, and would rather look for possibilities than work with facts.

The second part of problem-solving, *evaluation*, involves making judgements about how to deal with information once it has been collected. Styles of information evaluation vary from an emphasis on feeling to an emphasis on thinking. *Feeling-type individuals* are oriented toward conformity and try to accommodate themselves to other people. They try to avoid problems that may result in disagreements. *Thinking-type individuals* use reason and intellect to deal with problems and they downplay emotions.

When these two dimensions (information gathering and evaluation) are combined, four basic problem-solving styles result: sensation-feeling (SF), intuitive-feeling (IF), sensation-thinking (ST), and intuitive-thinking (IT). Figure 4.3 summarizes each of them.

> Social traits are surface-level traits that reflect the way a person appears to others when interacting in various social settings.

Figure 4.3 Four problem-solving styles

Sensation–*Feeling*	**Sensation–*Thinking***
Interpersonal	Technical detail-oriented
Specific human detail	Logical analysis of hard data
Friendly, sympathetic	Precise, orderly
Open communication	Careful about rules and procedures
Respond to people now	Dependable, responsible
Good at: Empathizing	*Good at:* Observing, ordering
Cooperating	Filing, recalling
Goal: To be helpful	*Goal:* Do it correctly
Illustrated by: Anita Rudick, CEO Body Shop International (International Cosmetics Organization)	*Illustrated by:* Enita Nordeck, President Unity Forest Products (a small and growing builder's supply firm)
Intuitive–*Feeling*	**Intuitive–*Thinking***
Insightful, mystical	Speculative
Idealistic, personal	Emphasize, understanding
Creative, original	Synthesize, interpret
Global ideas oriented to people	Logic-oriented ideas
Human potential	Objective, impersonal, idealistic
Good at: Imagining	*Good at:* Discovery, inquiry
New combinations	Problem-solving
Goal: To make things beautiful	*Goal:* To think things through
Illustrated by: Herb Kelleher, former CEO, Southwest Airlines (a fast-growing, large, regional airline)	*Illustrated by:* Paul Allaire, former CEO, Xerox Corporation (a huge multinational, recently innovatively reorganized)

(Figure axes: S at top, I at bottom, F at left, T at right)

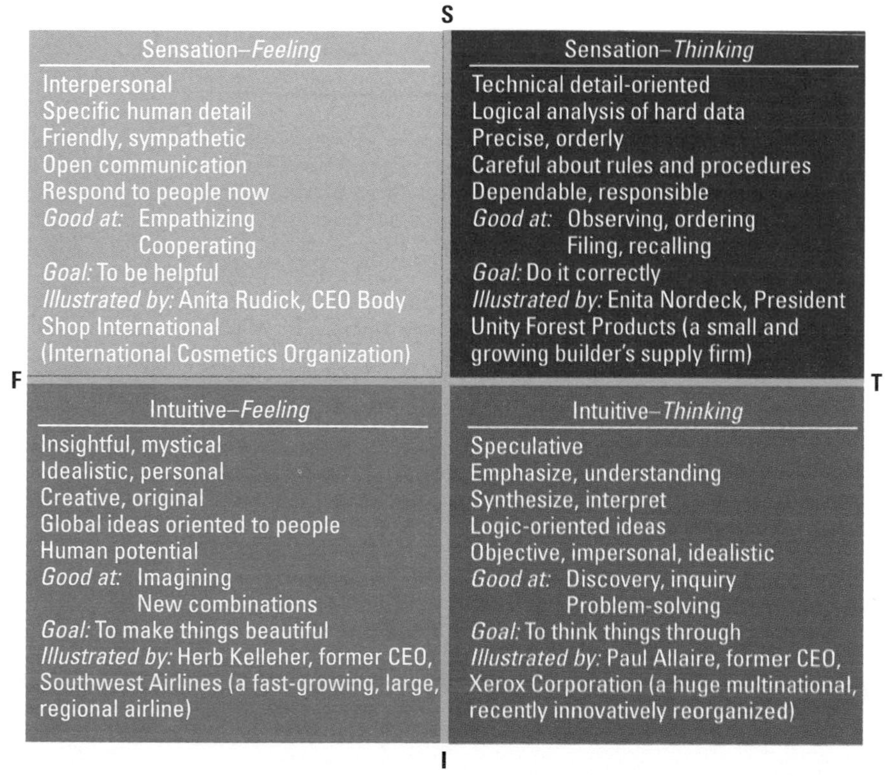

Research shows there is a fit between an individual's style and the kinds of decisions he or she prefers. For example, STs (sensation-thinkers) prefer analytical strategies-those that emphasize detail and method. IFs (intuitive-feelers) prefer intuitive strategies—those that emphasize an overall pattern and fit. Not surprisingly, mixed styles (sensation—feelers or intuitive-thinkers) select both analytical and intuitive strategies. Other findings also indicate that thinkers tend to be more motivated than feelers and that individuals who emphasize sensations tend to have higher job satisfaction than intuitives. These and other findings suggest a number of basic differences among different problem-solving styles, and they show how important it is to have a fit between these styles and a task's information processing and evaluation requirements.[27]

Problem-solving styles are most frequently measured by the *Myers-Briggs Type Indicator (MBTI)* questionnaire—usually the 100-item version—which asks individuals how they usually act or feel in specific situations. Firms such as RIM and Honda, as well as hospitals, educational institutions, and military organizations, have used the MBTI for various aspects of management development.[28]

ETHICS AND SOCIAL RESPONSIBILITY

Diversity pays off for such banks as the Royal Bank of Canada (RBC). It recognizes the business advantages of having employees who are as diverse as the markets it serves. However, such diversity is also becoming an increasingly important way of giving employees who are visible minorities and those with physical disabilities opportunities that they otherwise would not have. This is one way for astute firms to carry out their social responsibility concerns. As RBC says in its *Employment Equity Report*, "We value diversity, not only because it helps us meet our strategic business priorities in North America and globally, but because it is the right thing to do."[29]
www.rbc.com

PERSONAL CONCEPTION TRAITS

Personal conception traits are the way individuals tend to think about their social and physical setting, and also include their major beliefs and personal orientation on a range of issues.

Locus of Control How much a person feels able to control his or her own life has to do with the person's internal–external orientation, which can be measured by Rotter's locus of control instrument.[30] People have personal conceptions about whether events are controlled primarily by themselves, which indicates an internal orientation, or by outside forces—such as their social and physical environment—which indicates an external orientation. Internals, or persons with an internal locus of control, believe that they control their own fate or destiny. In contrast, externals, or persons with an external locus of control, believe that much of what happens to them is beyond their control and is determined by environmental forces.

In general, externals are more extraverted in their interpersonal relationships and are more oriented toward the world around them. Internals tend to be more introverted and are more oriented toward their own feelings and ideas. Figure 4.4 suggests that internals tend to do better on tasks requiring complex information processing and learning, as well as initiative. Many managerial and professional jobs have these kinds of requirements.

Figure 4.4 Some ways in which internals differ from externals

Information processing	Internals make more attempts to acquire information, are less satisfied with the amount of information they possess, and are better at utilizing information.
Job satisfaction	Internals are generally more satisfied, less alienated, less rootless, and there is a stronger job satisfaction/performance relationship for them.
Performance	Internals perform better on learning and problem-solving tasks, when performance leads to valued rewards
Self-control, risk, and anxiety	Internals exhibit greater self-control, are more cautious, engage in less risky behaviour, and are less anxious.
Motivation, expectancies, and results	Internals display greater work motivation, see a stronger relationship between what they do and what happens to them, expect that working hard leads to good performance, feel more control over their time.
Response to others	Internals are more independent, more reliant on their own judgement, and less susceptible to the influence of others; they are more likely to accept information on its merit.

Authoritarianism/Dogmatism   Both "authoritarianism" and "dogmatism" deal with the rigidity of a person's beliefs. A person high in authoritarianism tends to adhere rigidly to conventional values and to obey recognized authority. This person cares about toughness and power and is against using personal feelings. An individual high in dogmatism sees the world as a threatening place. This person regards legitimate authority as absolute and accepts or rejects others according to how much they agree with accepted authority. Superiors who possess these latter traits tend to be rigid and closed. At the same time, dogmatic subordinates tend to want certainty imposed on them.[31]

From an ethical standpoint, we can expect highly authoritarian individuals to present a special problem. Because they are so susceptible to authority, being eager to comply with instructions from someone who has more authority, they may behave unethically.[32] We might speculate, for example, that many of the Nazis who committed war crimes during World War II were high in authoritarianism or dogmatism; they believed so strongly in authority that they followed their unethical orders without question.

Machiavellianism   The third personal conception dimension is Machiavellianism, which owes its origins to Niccolo Machiavelli. The very name of this sixteenth-century author makes people think of a master of guile, deceit, and opportunism in interpersonal relations. Machiavelli earned his place in history by writing The Prince, a nobleman's guide to the acquisition and use of power.[33] The subject of Machiavelli's book is manipulation as the basic means of gaining and keeping control of others. Its pages describe the personality profile of a Machiavellian—someone who views and manipulates others for personal gain, someone who is focused on achieving a goal regardless of the means used.

Psychologists have developed a series of instruments called Mach scales to measure a person's Machiavellian orientation.[34] A high-Mach personality is someone who tends to behave in ways that are consistent with Machiavelli's basic principles. Such individuals approach situations logically and

Authoritarianism is a tendency to adhere rigidly to conventional values and to obey recognized authority.

Dogmatism leads a person to see the world as a threatening place and to regard authority as absolute.

thoughtfully and are even capable of lying to achieve personal goals. They are rarely swayed by loyalty, friendships, past promises, or the opinions of others, and they are skilled at influencing others.

Research using the Mach scales provides insight into the way high- and low-Machs may be expected to behave in various situations. A person with a "cool" and "detached" high-Mach personality can be expected to take control and try to exploit loosely structured environmental situations. He will perform in a perfunctory, even detached, manner in highly structured situations. Low-Machs tend to accept direction from others in loosely structured situations; they work hard to do well in highly structured ones. For example, we might expect that, where the situation permitted, a high-Mach would do or say whatever it took to get his or her way. In contrast, a low Mach would tend to be much more strongly guided by ethical considerations and would be less likely to lie or cheat or to get away with lying or cheating.

Self-Monitoring   A final personal conception trait of special importance to managers is **self-monitoring**. Self-monitoring is a person's ability to adjust his or her behaviour to external, situational (environmental) factors.[35]

Individuals with high self-monitoring are sensitive to external cues and tend to behave differently in different situations. Like high-Machs, high self-monitors can present a very different appearance from their true self. In contrast, low self-monitors, like their low-Mach counterparts, are not able to disguise their behaviour: "what you see is what you get." There is also evidence that high self-monitors are very attentive to the behaviour of others and conform more readily than do low self-monitors.[36] Thus, they appear flexible and may be especially good at responding to the kinds of situational contingencies emphasized throughout this book. For example, high self-monitors should be especially good at changing their leadership behaviour to fit subordinates with much or little experience, tasks with much or little structure, and so on.

> **Self-monitoring** is a person's ability to adjust his or her behaviour to external, situational (environmental) factors.

EMOTIONAL ADJUSTMENT TRAITS

Emotional adjustment traits measure how much emotional distress individuals experience or how often they act unacceptably. Their health is often affected. Many of these traits are mentioned in the literature, but one trait that is frequently encountered and is especially important for OB is the Type A/Type B orientation.

> **Emotional adjustment traits** measure how much emotional distress individuals experience or how often they act unacceptably.

Type A and Type B Orientation   To get a feel for this orientation, take the following quiz and then read on.[37] Circle the number that best characterizes you on each of the following pairs of characteristics:

Casual about appointments	1 2 3 4 5 6 7 8	Never late
Not competitive	1 2 3 4 5 6 7 8	Very competitive
Never feel rushed	1 2 3 4 5 6 7 8	Always feel rushed
Take one thing at a time	1 2 3 4 5 6 7 8	Try to do many things
Do things slowly	1 2 3 4 5 6 7 8	Do things fast
Express my feelings	1 2 3 4 5 6 7 8	Hold in my feelings
Many outside interests	1 2 3 4 5 6 7 8	Few outside interests

Total your points for the seven items in the quiz. Multiply this total by three to arrive at a final score. Use this total to locate your Type A/Type B orientation on the following list:

FINAL POINTS	A/B ORIENTATION
Below 90	B
90-99	B+
100-105	A-

106-119   A
120 or more   A+

Individuals with a **Type A orientation** are characterized by impatience, desire for achievement, and perfectionism. In contrast, those with **Type B orientations** are characterized as more easygoing and less competitive in relation to daily events.[38]

Type A people tend to work fast and to be abrupt, uncomfortable, irritable, and aggressive. Such tendencies indicate "obsessive" behaviour, a fairly common trait among managers, but not always a helpful one. Many managers are hard-driving, detail-oriented people who have high performance standards and thrive on routine. But when such work obsessions become extreme, they may lead to greater concerns for details than for results, resistance to change, overzealous control of subordinates, and various kinds of interpersonal difficulties, which may even include threats and physical violence. In contrast, Type B managers tend to be much more relaxed and patient in their dealings with co-workers and subordinates.

Type A orientations are characterized by impatience, desire for achievement, and perfectionism.

Type B orientations are characterized by an easygoing and less competitive nature than Type A.

PERSONALITY AND SELF-CONCEPT

All together, the ways in which an individual integrates and organizes the previously discussed categories and the traits they contain are referred to as **personality dynamics**. It is this category that makes personality more than just the sum of the separate traits. A key personality dynamic in your study of OB is the self-concept.

We can describe **self-concept** as the view individuals have of themselves as physical, social, and spiritual or moral beings.[39] It is a way of recognizing oneself as a distinct human being. A person's self-concept is greatly influenced by his or her culture. For example, Americans tend to reveal much more about themselves than do the English; that is, an American's self-concept is more assertive and talkative.[40]

Two related and crucial aspects of the self-concept are self-esteem and self-efficacy. *Self-esteem* is a belief about one's own worth based on an overall self-evaluation.[41] People with high self-esteem see themselves as capable, worthwhile, and acceptable, and they tend to have few doubts about themselves. The opposite is true of a person with low self-esteem. Some OB research suggests that, although high self-esteem generally can boost performance and lessen turnover, when they are under pressure, people with high self-esteem may become boastful and act egotistically. They can also be overconfident at times and therefore fail to get important information if they think they already know what needs to be known.[42]

Self-efficacy, sometimes called the "effectance motive," is a more specific version of self-esteem; it is an individual's belief about how likely he or she is to complete a specific task successfully. You could be high in self-esteem, yet have a feeling of low self-efficacy about performing a certain task, such as public speaking.

Personality dynamics are the ways in which individuals integrate and organize their social traits, values and motives, personal conceptions, and emotional adjustment.

Self-concept is the view individuals have of themselves as physical, social, and spiritual or moral beings.

Values and Attitudes

In addition to demographic and personality characteristics, which are important individual difference characteristics, there are also important differences in people's values and attitudes.

VALUES

Values can be defined as broad preferences about appropriate actions to take or outcomes. Values reflect a person's sense of right and wrong or what "ought to be."[43] The statements "Equal rights for all" and "People should be treated with respect and dignity" reflect values. Values tend to influence attitudes and behaviour. For example, if you value equal rights for all and you go to work for an organization that treats its managers much better than it treats its workers, you may form the attitude that the company is an unfair place to work. This attitude could then lead to you not producing well or you might even decide to leave the company. If the company had had a more egalitarian policy, your attitude and behaviour would likely have been more positive.

> Values can be defined as broad preferences about appropriate actions to take or outcomes.

Sources and Types of Values Parents, friends, teachers, and external reference groups can all influence individual values. Indeed, peoples' values develop from what they learn and experience in the cultural setting they live in. As learning and experiences differ from one person to another, value differences result. Such differences are likely to be deep-seated and difficult (though not impossible) to change; many have their roots in early childhood and the way a person has been raised.[44]

> Sources and types of values: Parents, friends, teachers, and external reference groups can all influence individual values.

Noted psychologist Milton Rokeach developed a well-known set of values that are classified into two broad categories.[45] **Terminal values** reflect a person's preferences about the "ends" to be achieved; they are the goals individuals would like to achieve during their lifetime. **Instrumental values** reflect the "means" for achieving desired ends. They represent how you might achieve your ends, depending on the relative value you place on the end results. Rokeach divides values into 18 terminal values and 18 instrumental values, as summarized in Figure 4.5.

> Terminal values reflect a person's preferences about the "ends" to be achieved.

> Instrumental values reflect a person's beliefs about the means for achieving desired ends.

Research shows, not surprisingly, that both terminal and instrumental values differ according to the type of group (for example, executives, activist workers, and union members).[46] These differences can encourage conflict or agreement when different groups have to deal with each other.

Another frequently used classification of human values was developed by psychologist Gordon Allport and his associates. These values fall into six major types:[47]

> **Allport's six value categories**

- *theoretical*—interest in the discovery of truth through reasoning and systematic thinking

- *economic*—interest in usefulness and practicality, including the accumulation of wealth

- *aesthetic*—interest in beauty, form, and artistic harmony

- *social*—interest in people and love in human relationships

- *political*—interest in gaining power and influencing other people

- *religious*—interest in unity and in understanding the cosmos as a whole

Once again, groups differ in the importance they give to each of these values, as follows:

- *ministers*—religious, social, aesthetic, political, theoretical, economic

- *purchasing executive*—economic, theoretical, political, religious, aesthetic, social

- *industrial scientists*—theoretical, political, economic, aesthetic, religious, social

The above value classifications have had a major impact on the values literature, but they were not specifically designed for people in a work setting. A more recent values schema, developed by Meglino and associates, is aimed at people in the workplace:[48]

> **Meglino and associates value categories**

- *achievement*—getting things done and working hard to accomplish difficult things in life

- *helping and concern for others*—helping other people and being concerned about them

- *honesty*—telling the truth and doing what one feels is right

- *fairness*—being impartial and doing what is fair for everyone concerned

Because these four values are especially important in the workplace, the framework developed by Meglino et al. should be particularly useful for studying values in OB.

In particular, values can be influential through **value congruence**, which occurs when individuals express positive feelings as they meet others who share similar values. When values differ, or are incongruent, conflicts over such things as goals and the means to achieve them may result. Researchers have used the Meglino et al. value schema to examine value congruence between leaders and followers. They found that followers were more satisfied with the leader when there was congruence in achievement, helping, honesty, and fairness values.[49]

Value congruence occurs when individuals express positive feelings as they meet others who share similar values.

Figure 4.5 Rokeach value survey

Terminal Values	Instrumental Values
A comfortable life (and prosperous)	Ambitious (hardworking)
An exciting life (stimulating)	Broad-minded (open-minded)
A sense of accomplishment (lasting contribution)	Capable (competent, effective)
A world of peace (free of war and conflict)	Cheerful (lighthearted, joyful)
A world of beauty (beauty of nature and the arts)	Clean (neat, tidy)
Equality (brotherhood, equal opportunity)	Courageous (standing up for beliefs)
Family security (taking care of loved ones)	Forgiving (willing to pardon)
Freedom (independence, free choice)	Helpful (working for others' welfare)
Happiness (contentedness)	Honest (sincere, ruthful)
Inner Harmony (Freedom from inner conflict)	Imaginative (creative, daring)
Mature love (sexual and spiritual intimacy)	Independent (self-sufficient, self-reliant)
National security (attack protection)	Intellectual (intelligent, reflective)
Pleasure (leisurely, enjoyable life)	Logical (rational, consistent)
Slavation (saved, eternal life)	Loving (affectionate, tender)
Self-respect (self-esteem)	Obedient (dutiful, respectful)
Social recognition (admiration, respect)	Polite (courteous, well-mannered)
True friendship (close companionship)	Responsible (reliable, dependable)
Wisdom (mature understanding of life)	Self-controlled (self-disciplined)

Patterns and Trends in Values   We should also be aware of applied research and insightful analyses of trends in values over time. Daniel Yankelovich, for example, is known for his informative public opinion polls of North American workers, and William Fox has written a carefully reasoned book that analyzes values trends.[50] Both Yankelovich and Fox note movements in our society away from earlier values. Fox emphasizes a decline in such shared values as duty, honesty, responsibility, and the like, while Yankelovich notes a movement away from valuing economic incentives, organizational loyalty, and work-related identity. The movement is toward valuing meaningful work, pursuit of leisure, and personal identity and self-fulfillment.

Yankelovich believes that the modern manager must be able to recognize value differences and trends among people at work. Yankelovich reports, for example, finding higher productivity among younger workers who are doing jobs that match their values and/or are supervised by managers who share their values—in other words, in jobs where there is value congruence.

In a large sample, managers and human-resource professionals were asked to identify the work-related values they believed to be most important to individuals in the workforce, both now and in the near future.[51] The nine most popular values named were recognition for competence and accomplishments; respect and dignity; personal choice and freedom; involvement at work; pride in one's work; lifestyle quality; financial security; self-development; and health and wellness.

These values are especially important for managers because they indicate some key concerns of the new workforce. Even though each individual worker places his or her own importance on these nine values, and even though Canada today very likely has the most diverse workforce in the world (Australia's, perhaps, is equally diverse), these values are a good starting place for managers in Canada. By considering them first, managers will be more likely to understand what motivates Canadian workers in the new workplace. Finally, it should be noted that although values are individual preferences many of them are usually shared within cultures and organizations.

ATTITUDES

Attitudes are influenced by values and come from the same sources as values: friends, teachers, parents, and role models. Attitudes focus on specific people or objects, whereas values have a more general focus and are more stable than attitudes. "Employees should be allowed to participate" is a value; your positive or negative feeling about your job because of the participation it allows is an attitude. Formally defined, an **attitude** is a predisposition to respond in a positive or negative way to someone or something in one's environment. For example, when you say that you like or dislike someone or something, you are expressing an attitude. It should be remembered that attitudes, like values, are hypothetical constructs; that is, one never sees, touches, or actually isolates an attitude. Rather, attitudes are *inferred* from the things people say, informally or in formal opinion polls, or from the things they do, their behaviour.

Figure 4.6 shows the three components of attitudes: the antecedents, the attitude itself, and the results.[52] The antecedents (the beliefs and values) are what come first. They form the **cognitive component** of an attitude: the person's beliefs, opinions, knowledge, or information. **Beliefs** are ideas about someone or something and the conclusions based on these ideas; they are an individual's sense of "what is." For example, in Figure 4.6, "My job lacks responsibility" is shown as a belief. Note that the beliefs may or may not be accurate. "Responsibility is important" is a related belief. It is another aspect of the cognitive component and reflects an underlying value.

The **affective component** of an attitude is a specific feeling about the personal impact of the antecedents or beliefs. This is the actual attitude itself, such as "I don't like my job." The **behavioural component** is an intention to behave in a certain way based on the specific feelings or attitudes. This intended behaviour results from an attitude and is a predisposition to act in a specific way, such as "I'm going to quit my job."

Attitudes and Behaviour   You should recognize that the link between attitudes and behaviour is tentative. An attitude results in *intended* behaviour, but this intention may or may not turn into actual behaviour, depending on the circumstances.

In general, the more specific the attitudes and behaviours are, the stronger the relationship between them is. Imagine, for example, that you are a French-Canadian webmaster and you are unhappy with your supervisor's treatment of you and other French-Canadian webmasters in the organization. As a result, you strongly intend to look for another webmaster job in a similar kind of organization within the next six months. Here, both the attitude and the behaviour are specifically stated (they refer to French-Canadian webmasters, and they identify a specific kind of organization and a specific time period). Thus, in this instance, we would expect to find a relatively strong relationship between your attitude and how aggressively you would actually start looking for another webmaster job.

There also has to be enough freedom to carry out the intent. In the example just given, the freedom to change jobs would be greatly limited if there were few jobs available for webmasters.

Finally, the relationship between the attitude and the behaviour tends to be stronger when the person has some prior experience related to the attitude. For example, if you are a busi-

Attitude is a predisposition to respond in a positive or negative way to someone or something in one's environment.

The **cognitive component** of an attitude refers to a person's beliefs, opinions, knowledge, or information.

Beliefs are ideas about someone or something and the conclusions based on these ideas.

The **affective component** of an attitude is a specific feeling about the personal impact of the antecedents (the beliefs and values).

The **behavioural component** is an intention to behave in a certain way based on specific feelings or attitudes.

Cognitive dissonance describes a state of inconsistency between an individual's attitude and his or her behaviour.

ness or commerce major, the relationship between, first, your attitude toward a course and/or your intention to drop the course and, second, your later behaviour of actually dropping the course will probably be stronger for a business course than it would be for a course in an unrelated field. In other words, the relationship would be stronger for this OB course than it would be for a course in pop culture that is in its first week.[53]

Figure 4.6 A work-related example of the three components of attitudes

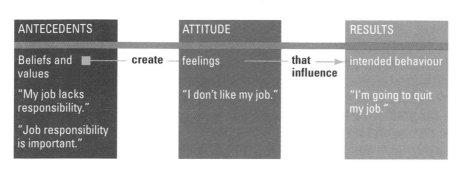

Encouraging Diversity in Business Relations

www.bchydro.com

BC Hydro has many power generation facilities located in First Nations territories. It also has more than 2,000 kilometres of transmission and distribution lines running through about 500 First Nations reserves in British Columbia.

BC Hydro is working to develop mutually beneficial relationships with First Nations and Aboriginal peoples. One initiative focuses on identifying and providing opportunities to Aboriginal-owned businesses. BC Hydro sponsors workshops explaining how it operates and the types of goods and services it requires, to provide Aboriginal-owned businesses with tools to put together successful bids.

Aboriginal suppliers currently provide BC Hydro with services including:
• line construction
• graphic design
• road construction
• maintenance
• archaeological and environmental assessment
• various consulting services

In addition, BC Hydro also publishes an online Aboriginal Business Directory, listing hundreds of companies that do business in B.C.

Even though attitudes do not always predict behaviour, the link between attitudes and potential or intended behaviour is important for managers to understand. Think about your work experiences or conversations with other people about their work. You have probably heard people express concerns about someone's "bad attitude." These concerns usually mean that the person is bothered by the behaviour that goes with the poor attitude. One of the manager's responsibilities is to recognize attitudes and to understand both their antecedents and what they may imply. As an unfavourable attitude, low job satisfaction, for example, can result in costly labour turnover, absenteeism, tardiness, and even impaired physical or mental health.

Attitudes and Cognitive Consistency Leon Festinger, a noted social psychologist, uses the term cognitive dissonance to describe a state of inconsistency between an individual's attitudes and his or her behaviour.[54] Let's assume that you have the attitude that recycling is good for the economy but you never recycle anything. Festinger predicts that an inconsistency like this will result in discomfort and a desire to reduce or eliminate the discomfort. This can be done by (1) changing the underlying attitude, (2) changing future behaviour, or (3) developing new ways of explaining or rationalizing the inconsistency.

There are two factors that influence which of the above choices will be made: (1) how much control a person thinks he or she has over the situation and (2) the size of the rewards involved. In terms of control, for example, if your boss does not let you recycle office garbage, you will be less likely to change your attitude than you will be if not recycling is entirely your own decision. You might therefore choose the rationalization option in this situation. In terms of rewards, if they are high enough, rewards tend to reduce feelings of inconsistency: "If I'm rewarded even though I don't recycle, the lack of recycling must not be so bad after all."

Managing Diversity and Individual Differences

Dealing with diversity and individual differences is one of the most important challenges for all managers in the quest for high performance and organizational competitiveness. This is true not only in Canada but also in the U.S., European Union countries, and several countries in Asia.[55] Only the details differ.

The Effective Manager 4.2

DIVERSITY CHECKUP REPORT

The *Employment Equity Survey* used by RBC asks four questions regarding Persons With Disabilities (PWD). The results are then separated to satisfy the Canadian Human Rights Commission and to ensure that the responses fully reflect the PWD population. Question (a) is separated in the analysis but it can be connected to one or more of the other questions to get a full picture of those who have disabilities and those who with or without assistance from the company have addressed their disability. The questions are as follows:

a. Do you consider yourself to be a person with a disability?

b. Do you consider yourself to be disadvantaged in employment by reason of this impairment (this includes persons whose limitations owing to their impairment have been accommodated in their current job or workplace)?

c. Do you believe RBC would be likely to consider you disadvantaged in employment by reason of this impairment?

d. Do you believe a potential employer would be likely to consider you disadvantaged in employment by reason of this impairment?

www.chrc.ccdp.ca

So how do managers deal with all this? To get a sense of what some of the more progressive employers have done in managing diversity, let's now consider the Royal Bank of Canada (RBC).[56] The CEO chairs the Diversity Leadership Council (DLC), which includes champions from all of the businesses in RBC as well as the various functions. There are three Executive Champions, one each for the employee groupings Visible Minorities and Aboriginals, Persons with Disabilities, and Women. From 1987 to 2002, the proportion of women employees declined from 75 percent to 68 percent while the proportion of Aboriginal people increased from 0.1 percent to 1.1 percent and the proportion of visible minorities increased from 7.8 percent to 19.0 percent, which is close to their participation in the Canadian workforce.

A lot is being done to ensure that diversity is more than just a passing fad at RBC. First, RBC conducts an Employment Equity Survey each year—it received a response rate of over 88 percent in 2002 and of 86 percent in 2001. RBC has also (1) included the Employment Equity Survey in its orientation package; (2) developed many educational tools, such as the Diversity-in-Action Video; (3) published its Corporate Responsibility Report at www.rbc.com/community/index.html; (4) increased the sensitivity training for managers and employees in regard to people with disabilities; (5) established a Code of Conduct with eight guiding principles governing behaviour standards; and (6) is partnering with Junior Achievement in Toronto to launch a "Diversity in the Workplace" program for high school students.

Each quarter, RBC also measures its progress through "Compliance Scorecards," which are focused on employment equity, and through "Business Diversity Scorecards," for monitoring hires, promotions, terminations, and other issues affecting the specific groups. New practices and policies of the human resources department are also reviewed to ensure that they do not have a negative impact on any of the groups.

The following factors, which include those of RBC but others as well, were obtained from in-depth interviews and focus groups and are important for keeping track of diversity programs: demographics, organizational culture, accountability, productivity, growth and profitability, benchmarking against the "best" programs, and measurement of the program.

Some firms, like Microsoft, have worked hard toward the measurement and computerization of key diversity measures. Three Microsoft employees—Stutz, Massengale, and Gordon—developed what is called the SMG Index, named after them. It gives a separate, bottom-line figure (the SMG index) that applies to Microsoft's women and minorities. This figure then allows managers to analyze Microsoft's affirmative action and diversity goals and accomplishments. When the SMG index is closer to zero (zero is best), fewer hires, promotions, and/or retentions are needed to correct group disparities. The index is compared from group to group and over time, which is similar to what RBC does.

Whether an organization is big or small, the characteristics of its employees will vary along many criteria, and this is regardless of how similar or different the employees' cultures are. Birth order, gender, age, and personality differ among all of us and when we include issues of ethnicity, language, and other factors, we realize that the challenges facing today's workers and managers are only getting more complex. Still these variables in our makeup, individually and collectively, also provide significant opportunities to advance our careers and the performance of the organizations we work for—provided, of course, that both we and the organizations are prepared to do the right thing and learn in the process.

CHAPTER 4 STUDY GUIDE

Summary

What is workforce diversity, and why is it important?

- Workforce diversity is the mix of gender, race and ethnicity, age, able-bodiedness, and sexual orientation in the workforce.
- Workforces in Canada, the U.S., and Europe are becoming more diverse, and valuing and managing this diversity is becoming increasingly important to improve organizational competitiveness and help individuals develop.

What are demographic differences among individuals, and why are they important?

- Demographic differences are background characteristics that help shape what a person becomes.
- Gender, age, race and ethnicity, sexual orientation, and able-bodiedness are particularly important demographic characteristics.
- The use of demographic differences in employment is covered by a series of federal, provincial/state, and local laws that make discrimination illegal.
- Demographic differences can be the basis for inappropriate stereotyping that can influence workplace decisions and behaviour.

What are aptitude and ability differences among individuals, and why are they important?

- Aptitude is a person's capability of learning something.
- Ability is a person's existing capacity to perform the various tasks needed for a given job.
- Aptitudes are potential abilities.
- Both mental and physical aptitudes and abilities are used in matching individuals to organizations and jobs.

What are personality determinants and differences among individuals, and why are they important?

- Personality is the overall profile or combination of characteristics that capture the unique nature of a person as that person reacts and interacts with others.
- Personality is determined by both heredity and the environment; for all personality characteristics, the impact of heredity and the environment is roughly equal.
- The Big Five personality framework reduces the dimensions of personality to extraversion, agreeableness, conscientiousness, emotional stability, and openness to experience.
- Another useful personality framework consists of social traits, personal conception traits, emotional adjustment traits—with each category representing one or more dimensions of personality—and personality dynamics.
- Personality characteristics are important because of their predictable interplay with an individual's behaviour. As with demographics and aptitude/ability differences, personality characteristics must be matched to organizations and jobs.

What are value and attitude differences among individuals, and why are they important?

- Values are broad preferences about appropriate actions to take or outcomes.
- Rokeach divides 18 values into terminal values (preferences about the ends to be achieved) and instrumental values (preferences about the means to achieve the ends).
- Allport and his associates identify six value categories, ranging from theoretical to religious.

- Meglino and his associates classify values into the categories of achievement, helping and concern for others, honesty, and fairness.

- There have been societal changes in value patterns: the move is away from economic and organizational loyalty and toward meaningful work and self-fulfillment.

- Attitudes are a predisposition to respond positively or negatively to someone or something in one's environment; they are influenced by values but are more specific.

- Individuals want consistency between their attitudes and their behaviour.

- Values and attitudes are important because they indicate predispositions toward certain behaviours.

- Values and attitudes—as is the case with demographics, aptitude/ability, and personality characteristics—need to be matched to organizations and jobs.

What does managing diversity and individual differences involve, and why is it important?

- Managing diversity and individual differences involves striving for a match between the firm, specific jobs, and the people recruited, hired, and developed. This must be done while also recognizing that the workforce is increasingly diverse.

- Employment equity in Canada; affirmative action in the U.S.; ethical considerations; local, national, and global competitive pressures; and a projected change in the nature of the workforce are contributing to increased workforce diversity.

- Once a match is found between organizational and job requirements and individual characteristics, it is still important to manage the increasing diversity in the workforce.

- Firms now use a wide variety of practices to manage workforce diversity. Some of these practices include interactive networks, recruitment, education, development, promotion, pay, and assessment.

KEY TERMS

Ability (p. 62)

Affective component (p. 72)

Aptitude (p. 62)

Attitude (p. 72)

Authoritarianism (p. 67)

Behavioural component (p. 72)

Beliefs (p. 72)

Cognitive component (p. 72)

Cognitive dissonance (p. 73)

Demographic characteristics (p. 60)

Developmental approaches (p. 64)

Dogmatism (p. 67)

Emotional adjustment traits (p. 68)

Employment Equity (p. 58)

Instrumental values (p. 70)

Personality (p. 62)

Personality dynamics (p. 69)

Self-concept (p. 69)

Self-monitoring (p. 68)

Social traits (p. 65)

Sources and types of values (p. 70)

Stereotyping (p. 58)

Terminal values (p. 70)

Type A orientations (p. 69)

Type B orientations (p. 69)

Value congruence (p. 71)

Values (p. 70)

Workforce diversity (p. 57)

MULTIPLE CHOICE

1. In Canada, the U.S., the EU, and much of the rest of the world, the workforce is _____. (a) becoming more homogeneous (b) more highly motivated than before (c) becoming more diverse (d) less motivated than before

2. Stereotyping occurs when one thinks of an individual _____. (a) as different from others in a given group (b) as having characteristics often associated with members of a particular group (c) as like some members of a particular group but different from other members of the group (d) as basically not very competent

3. Managing diversity and employment equity are _____. (a) similar terms for the same thing (b) both mandated by law (c) different but complementary (d) becoming less and less important

4. Demographic characteristics refers to _____. (a) aptitude and ability (b) personality traits (c) background characteristics that help shape what a person has become (d) values and attitudes

5. Aptitudes and abilities are divided into _____. (a) stereotypes (b) physical and mental characteristics (c) mental and personality characteristics (d) aggressive and passive traits

6. Personality characteristics tend to be determined by _____. (a) the environment (b) heredity (c) a mix of the environment and heredity (d) a person's aptitudes and abilities

7. The Big Five framework consists of _____. (a) five aptitudes and abilities (b) five demographic characteristics (c) extraversion, agreeableness, strength, emotional stability, and openness to experience (d) extraversion, agreeableness, conscientiousness, emotional stability, and openness to experience

8. Personality dynamics refers to a person's _____. (a) self-esteem, self-efficacy (b) Type A/Type B orientation (c) self-monitoring (d) Machiavellianism

9. Values and attitudes are _____. (a) similar to aptitudes and abilities (b) used interchangeably (c) related to each other (d) similar to demographic characteristics

10. Managing workforce diversity involves _____. (a) matching organizational and job requirements with increasingly diverse individuals (b) giving preference to traditional white males (c) giving preference to non-traditional, non-white male workers (d) making sure quotas of workers in various categories are emphasized

TRUE-FALSE

11. The EU workforce is becoming less diverse.   T   F

12. Workforce diversity is another name for employment equity.   T   F

13. Gender is a demographic characteristic.   T   F

14. Aptitude is another name for ability.   T   F

15. An individual's personality is determined by both the environment and heredity.   T   F

16. An individual's personality can develop over time.   T   F

17. The Big Five personality framework has been distilled from extensive lists of personality dimensions.   T   F

18. Attitudes often lead to values.   T   F

19. Both values and attitudes are predispositions to behave in certain ways.   T   F

20. An increasingly diverse workforce is only characteristic of the U.S.   T   F

SHORT ANSWER

21. What does managing diversity and individual differences mean in the workplace?

22. Why are diversity and individual differences important in the workplace?

23. In what ways are demographic characteristics important in the workplace?

24. Why are personality characteristics important in the workplace?

APPLICATIONS ESSAY

25. Your boss is trying to figure out how to get the kinds of people she needs for her organization to do well, while at the same time dealing appropriately with an increasing number of new Canadians. She has asked you to respond to this concern. Prepare a short report with specific suggestions for your boss.

More Connected than You Think

Thinking about Newfoundland and Labrador may conjure images of remote wilderness and of people disconnected from the mainstream. It doesn't summon visions of world-class strategies for using information and communication technologies. But it was exactly that attribute that won Labrador a place in Industry Canada's Smart Communities Program, beating out other communities in the province.

The SmartLabrador Initiative uses advanced communications technologies to give remote communities access to services in health care, education, community life, current issues, and culture—not an easy task, since the networks have to span all 300,000 square kilometres of Labrador. The network has 41 sites and was one of the first to integrate telephone and satellite IP network technology.

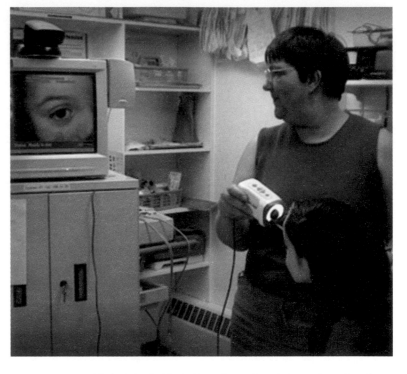

SmartLabrador's blending of satellite, land, and wireless technology into one of the largest wide-area networks in Canada has forever dispelled the illusion of Labrador as an isolated region. Instead Labrador is racing into the twenty-first century as a champion of the information superhighway.

Twelve regional staff, seven fieldworkers, and five technical support staff provide technical support, IT development support, and training in the community. Developing human resources is an important goal of the initiative. SmartLabrador will also create jobs and economic growth, and improve the quality of life in Labrador.

More than 60 partners contribute to SmartLabrador, including Collaborative Network Technologies, Inc.

(ColabNet). This Newfoundland-based technology company develops network services and software using wireless and satellite technologies. ColabNet played a key role in the design and implementation of SmartLabrador.

ColabNet now works with Telesat Canada, TETRA, and the Canadian Space Agency/European Space Agency on projects such as the Remote Community Services Telecentre (RCST) and Integrated Emergency Medicine Network (IEMN). These programs give remote communities access to services such as "telemedicine, distance education, high-speed Internet access, and government and community services." ColabNet and its partners are now selling these services nationally and internationally.

Perceptions and attributions influence an individual's interpretation of his or her environment. As you read Chapter 5, keep in mind these key questions:

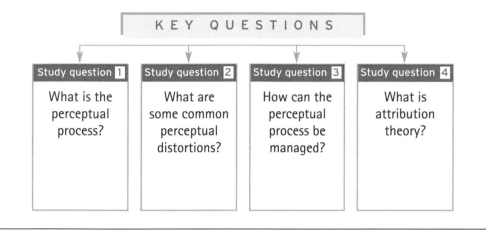

KEY QUESTIONS

Study question 1	Study question 2	Study question 3	Study question 4
What is the perceptual process?	What are some common perceptual distortions?	How can the perceptual process be managed?	What is attribution theory?

The Perceptual Process

A spectacular mid-air goal scored by Bobby Orr enshrined the Boston Bruin defenceman as a legendary hockey player, some say the greatest ever. Many would say that Paul Henderson scored an equally memorable winning goal in the 1972 Canada-Russia hockey series, but few of the readers of this textbook will recall either event. Whether or not a goal becomes memorable to those who saw it depends on many factors, including whether or not the team went on to win the game or championship. Wayne Gretzky is called "The Great One" but would he be as highly touted if he had never won the Stanley Cup or World Championship? Was Maurice "The Rocket" Richard the greatest ever or just in his era?

The questions of which goal is the most memorable and which hockey player is the greatest ever illustrate the notion of **perception**, the process through which people select, organize, interpret, retrieve, and respond to information from the world around them.[1] This information is gathered from the five senses of sight, hearing, touch, taste, and smell. As the differing views of Orr, Henderson, Gretzky, and Richard suggest, perception and reality are not necessarily the same thing. Even when they are describing the same event, any two people are likely to have perceptions or responses that are not identical.

Through perception, people process information inputs into responses that involve feelings and action. Perception is a way of forming impressions about oneself, other people, and daily life experiences. It also serves as a screen or filter which information passes through before it has an effect on people. The quality or accuracy of a person's perceptions, therefore, has a major impact on his or her responses to a specific situation. For example, Canadian and U.S. perceptions of the two countries' lumber policies vary when it comes to questions of true competitiveness and costing, and the result is recurring trade disputes between these neighbours. Likewise, beef farmers in Canada may have a more positive view of Canadian beef than U.S. farmers have, but the motives of Canadian and American farmers may also differ.

Perception is the process through which people receive, organize, and interpret information from their environment.

Figure 5.1 Contrasting perceptions of managers and their subordinates: the case of the performance appraisal interview

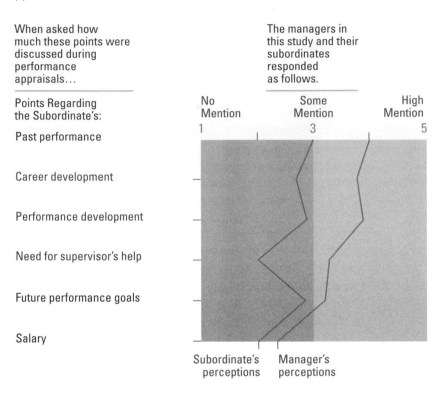

Perceptual responses are also likely to vary between managers and subordinates. Consider Figure 5.1, which shows the contrasting perceptions of managers and subordinates regarding a performance appraisal. There are important differences in the two sets of perceptions, and this can lead to responses that are quite different. In this case, managers who perceive that they already give enough attention to past performance, career development, and supervisory help are unlikely to emphasize these points more in future performance appraisal interviews. In contrast, their subordinates are likely to remain frustrated because they perceive that these subjects are not being given sufficient attention.

FACTORS INFLUENCING THE PERCEPTUAL PROCESS

The factors that contribute to perceptual differences and the perceptual process among people at work are summarized in Figure 5.2. They include the characteristics of the *perceiver*, the *setting*, and the *perceived*.

The Perceiver   A person's past experiences, needs or motives, personality, and values and attitudes may all influence the perceptual process. A person with a strong achievement need tends to perceive a situation in terms of that need. If you see doing well in class as a way to help meet your achievement need, for example, you will tend to emphasize how well you are doing in a class when you form an opinion of various classes. Similarly, a person with a negative attitude toward unions may look for antagonisms in the behaviour of local union officials even when the officials are only making routine visits to the organization. These and other perceiver factors influence the various aspects of the perceptual process.

Figure 5.2 Factors influencing the perceptual process

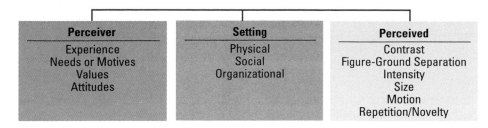

Perceiver	Setting	Perceived
Experience Needs or Motives Values Attitudes	Physical Social Organizational	Contrast Figure-Ground Separation Intensity Size Motion Repetition/Novelty

The Setting The physical, social, and organizational context of the perceptual setting can also influence the perceptual process. Kim Jeffrey, the former CEO of Nestlé Waters, was perceived by his subordinates as a frightening figure when he occasionally showed his temper and had confrontations with them. In the previous setting, before he was promoted, Jeffrey's flare-ups were tolerable; after his promotion to CEO, however, his outbursts caused intimidation, so his subordinates were afraid to express their opinions and recommendations. Fortunately, after he received feedback about this problem, he was able to change his subordinates' perceptions in the new setting.[2]

The Perceived The characteristics of the perceived person, object, or event—such as its contrast, intensity, figure-ground separation, size, motion, and repetition or novelty—are also important in the perceptual process. For example, one mainframe computer among six PCs will be perceived differently than one mainframe among six other mainframe computers as there is less contrast in the latter case. Likewise, one man among six women will be perceived differently than one man among six men. Intensity can vary in terms of brightness, colour, depth, sound, and so on. A bright red sports car stands out from a group of grey sedans; whispering or shouting stands out from ordinary conversation. This concept is known as figure-ground separation, and it involves which image is perceived as the background and which as the figure. For an example of this, look at Figure 5.3. What do you see? Faces or a vase?

Figure 5.3 Figure–ground separation

In the matter of size, very small or very large people tend to be perceived differently and more rapidly than average-sized people. Similarly, in terms of motion, moving objects are perceived differently from stationary objects. And, of course, advertisers hope that ad repetition or frequency will positively influence peoples' perception of a product. Television advertising blitzes for beverages or new models of cars or new personal computers are examples of this practice. Finally, the novelty or newness of a situation affects its perception. A purple-haired teenager is perceived differently than a blond or a brunette, for example.

STAGES OF THE PERCEPTUAL PROCESS

So far, we have discussed key factors that influence the perceptual process. Now we will look at the stages in processing the information that ultimately determines a person's perception and reaction, as shown in Figure 5.4. The information-processing stages are divided into information attention and selection; information organization; information interpretation; and information retrieval.

Attention and Selection Our senses are constantly bombarded with so much information that if we did not screen it, we would quickly become incapacitated with information overload. Selective screening lets in only a tiny proportion of all of the information available. Some of the selectivity comes from a person's controlled processing—consciously deciding what information to pay attention to and what to ignore. In this case, the perceivers are aware that they are processing information. Think about the last time you were at a noisy restaurant and screened out all the sounds except those of the person you were talking with.

In contrast to controlled processing, screening can also take place without the perceiver's conscious awareness. For example, you may drive a car without consciously thinking about the process of driving; you may be thinking about a problem you are having with your course work instead. In driving the car, you are affected by information from the world around you, such as traffic lights and other cars, but you do not pay conscious attention to that information. This selectivity of attention and automatic information processing works well most of the time when you drive, but if a nonroutine event occurs, such as an animal darting into the road, you may have an accident unless you quickly switch to controlled processing.

Figure 5.4 The perceptual process

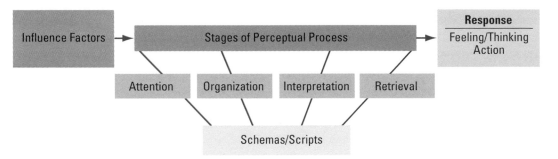

Organization   Even though selective screening takes place in the attention stage, it is still necessary to find ways to organize the information efficiently. **Schemas** help us do this. Schemas are cognitive frameworks that consist of organized knowledge, developed through experience, of a specific concept or stimulus.[3] A self schema contains information about a person's own appearance, behaviour, and personality. For instance, a person whose self schema includes decisiveness tends to perceive himself or herself in terms of this trait, especially in situations that require leadership.

Person schemas are the way individuals sort others into categories—such as types or groups—based on features that are perceived as being similar. The term "prototype," as well as the term "stereotype," is often used to represent these categories; it is an abstract set of features that are commonly associated with members of the category. Once the prototype is formed, it is stored in long-term memory. It is retrieved from memory when it is needed for a comparison that shows how well a person matches the prototype's features. For instance, if you have a "good worker" prototype in mind, which includes hard work, intelligence, punctuality, articulateness, and decisiveness, you may use that prototype to judge whether or not a specific individual is a good worker. Stereotypes, as discussed in Chapter 4, are prototypes that are based on such demographic characteristics as gender, age, able-bodiedness, and racial and ethnic groups.

A *script schema* is defined as a knowledge framework that describes the appropriate sequence of events in a particular situation.[4] For example, an experienced manager would use a script schema to think about the appropriate steps for running a meeting. Finally, person-in-situation schemas combine schemas built around persons (self and person schemas) and events (script schemas).[5] Thus, a manager might organize her perceived information in a meeting around a decisiveness schema for herself and key participants in the meeting. Here, a

Schemas are cognitive frameworks that consist of organized knowledge, developed through experience, of a specific concept or stimulus.

script schema would provide the steps and their sequence in the meeting; the manager would push through the steps decisively and would periodically call on selected participants to respond decisively. Note that, although this approach might make it easier to organize important information, the perceptions of the individuals at the meeting may not be completely accurate. This is because the decisiveness of the manager's person-in-situation schema does not allow enough time for open discussion.

As you can see in Figure 5.4, schemas are not important just in the organization stage; they also affect other stages in the perceptual process. Furthermore, schemas require a lot of automatic processing in order for people to be free to use controlled processing as necessary. Finally, as we will show, the perceptual factors described earlier, as well as the distortions we will discuss shortly, influence schemas in various ways.

Interpretation   Once your attention has been drawn to certain stimuli and you have grouped or organized this information, the next step is to uncover the reasons behind the actions. That is, even if you pay attention to the same information and you organize it in the same way as your friend does, you may interpret it differently or attribute different reasons for what you have perceived. For example, as a manager, you might attribute compliments from a friendly subordinate to his being an eager worker, whereas your friend might interpret the behaviour as insincere flattery.

Retrieval   So far, we have discussed the stages of the perceptual process as if they all occurred at the same time. However, this ignores an important component: memory. Each of the previous stages forms part of the memory and contributes to the stimuli or information that is already stored. To make use of it, the information stored in our memory must also be retrieved, which leads us to the retrieval stage of the perceptual process summarized in Figure 5.4.

All of us are at times unable to retrieve information stored in our memory. Our memory also decays, so that only some of the information is retrieved. Schemas play an important role in this area. They make it difficult for people to remember things that are not included in the schema. For example, based on your prototype about the traits comprising a "high-performing employee" (hard work, punctuality, intelligence, articulateness, and decisiveness), you may overestimate these traits as being present and underestimate others when you are evaluating the performance of a subordinate whom you generally consider good. Thus, you may overestimate the person's decisiveness since it is a key part of your high-performance prototype.

Indeed, people are as likely to recall non-existent traits as they are to recall those that are really there. Furthermore, once formed, prototypes may be difficult to change and they tend to last a long time.[6] Obviously, this distortion can cause major problems in performance appraisals and promotions, not to mention many other interactions on and off the job. At the same time, however, these prototypes make it possible to "chunk" information and reduce overload. In other words, prototypes are a double-edged sword.

RESPONSE TO THE PERCEPTUAL PROCESS

Throughout this chapter, we have shown how the perceptual process influences many OB responses. Figure 5.4 classifies these responses into thoughts, feelings, and actions. For example, in countries such as Mexico, bosses routinely greet their secretaries with a kiss as it is expected behaviour. In contrast, in Canada or the U.S., thoughts and feelings might be quite different about such behaviour. Indeed, you might perceive this as a form of sexual harassment. As you cover the other OB topics in the book, you should be alert to the importance of perceptual responses that involve thoughts, feelings, and actions.

Common Perceptual Distortions

Figure 5.5 shows some common kinds of distortions that can make the perceptual process inaccurate and affect the response. These are stereotypes and prototypes, halo effects, selective perception, projection, contrast effects, and self-fulfilling prophecy.

STEREOTYPES OR PROTOTYPES

Earlier, when discussing person schemas, we described prototypes and stereotypes as useful ways of combining information in order to deal

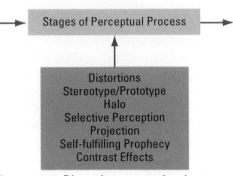

Figure 5.5 Distortions occurring in stages of the perceptual process

with information overload. At the same time, we pointed out how stereotypes can cause inaccuracies in retrieving information, as well as other problems. In particular, stereotypes hide individual differences; that is, they can prevent managers from getting to know people as individuals and from accurately assessing their needs, preferences, and abilities. We compared these stereotypes with research results and showed the errors that can occur when stereotypes are relied on for decision-making. Nevertheless, stereotypes continue to affect decisions at the board of directors level in organizations. A recent survey of 133 Fortune 500 firms showed that female directors were only favoured for membership on the relatively peripheral public affairs committee in these organizations. Males were favoured for membership on the more important compensation, executive, and finance committees, even when the females were equally or more experienced than their male counterparts.[7]

Here, we repeat our previous message: Both managers and employees need to be sensitive to stereotypes. They also have to try to overcome stereotypes and recognize that an increasingly diverse workforce can be a truly competitive advantage, as we showed in Chapter 4.

HALO EFFECTS

A halo effect occurs when one attribute of a person or situation is used to develop an overall impression of the person or situation.

A **halo effect** occurs when one attribute of a person or situation is used to develop an overall impression of the individual or situation. Like a stereotype, this distortion is more likely to occur in the organization stage of perception. Halo effects are common in our everyday lives. When we meet a new person, for example, a pleasant smile can lead us to a positive first impression of him or her as being overall a "warm" and "honest" person. Like stereotypes, halo effects also hide individual differences.

Halo effects are particularly important in the performance appraisal process because they can influence a manager's evaluations of how well subordinates do their work. For example, people with good attendance records tend to be viewed as intelligent and responsible; those with poor attendance records are considered poor performers. Such conclusions may or may not be valid. It is the manager's job to try to get true impressions rather than to allow halo effects to result in biased and inaccurate evaluations.

SELECTIVE PERCEPTION

Selective perception is the tendency to notice especially those aspects of a situation or person that emerge and are consistent with or reinforce existing beliefs, values, and needs.

Selective perception is the tendency to notice especially those aspects of a situation, person, or object that are consistent with one's needs, values, or attitudes. It affects the attention stage of the perceptual process the most. This perceptual distortion was shown clearly in a classic research study involving executives in a manufacturing company.[8] When asked to identify the key problem in a comprehensive business policy case, each executive selected a problem that was consistent with the functional area of his or her work assignments. For example, most marketing executives viewed the key problem area as sales, whereas production people tended to see the problem as one of production and organization. These differing viewpoints would affect how the executive would approach the problem; they might also create difficulties if the executives try to work together to improve things.

In a more recent study, 121 middle- and upper-lever managers attending an executive development program emphasized their own function but also expressed broader views. In addition to recognizing their own functions, for example, a chief financial officer indicated an awareness of the importance of manufacturing, and an assistant marketing manager recognized the importance of accounting and finance.[9] Thus, this more current research showed very little perceptual selectivity. The researchers were not, however, able to explain with certainty why the results were different.

These results suggest that selective perception is more important at some times than at others. Managers should be aware of this characteristic and test whether or not situations, events, or individuals are being selectively perceived. The easiest way to do this is to gather additional opinions from other people. When these opinions contradict those of the manager, an effort should be made to check the original impression.

PROJECTION

Projection is the assignment of one's personal attributes to other individuals; it is especially likely to occur in the interpretation stage of perception. One classic projection error is when managers assume that the needs of their subordinates and their own are the same. Suppose, for example, that you enjoy responsibility and achievement in your work. Suppose, too, that you are the newly appointed manager of a group of workers whose jobs seem dull and routine. You may move quickly to expand these jobs to help the workers achieve increased satisfaction from more challenging tasks because you want them to experience things that you, personally, value in work. But this may not be a good decision. If you project your needs onto the subordinates, individual differences are lost. Instead of designing the subordinates' jobs to fit their needs best, you have designed their jobs to fit your needs. The problem is that the subordinates may be quite satisfied and productive doing jobs that seem dull and routine to you. Projection can be controlled through a high degree of self-awareness and empathy—the ability to view a situation as others see it.

Projection is the assignment of one's personal attributes to other individuals.

ETHICS AND SOCIAL RESPONSIBILITY

Whether or not negotiation behaviours were perceived as ethical was investigated for 271 current and future North and South American business professionals in order to discover differences and similarities in their perceptions. The results showed that respondents had similar perceptions of behaviours which involved third parties to a negotiation (e.g., influencing an opponent's professional network and collecting information from third parties), but that the North and South American professionals had statistically significant differences in their perceptions of behaviours involving direct negotiating opponents (e.g., bluffing and misrepresenting information). The results suggest that the cultural setting influences perceptions of whether or not negotiating behaviour is ethical. It is through research in OB that we can more clearly recognize and possibly explain the various factors that affect our actions.

CONTRAST EFFECTS

Contrast effects occur when an individual's characteristics are contrasted with those of recently encountered and who rank higher or lower on the same characteristics.

Earlier, when discussing the perceived, we mentioned how a red sports car would stand out from other cars because of its contrast. Here, we show the perceptual distortion that can occur when, for example, a person gives a talk following a strong speaker or is interviewed for a job following a series of mediocre applicants. We can expect a contrast effect to occur when an individual's characteristics are contrasted with those of other persons who were recently encountered and who rank higher or lower on the same characteristics. Clearly, both managers and employees need to be aware of the possible perceptual distortion the contrast effect may create in many work settings.

SELF-FULFILLING PROPHECY

Self-fulfilling prophecy is the tendency to create or find in another situation or individual what one expects to find there.

A final perceptual distortion to be considered is the self-fulfilling prophecy—the tendency to create or find in another situation or individual what one expects to find there. Self-fulfilling prophecy is sometimes referred to as the "Pygmalion effect," named for a mythical Greek sculptor who created a statue of his ideal mate and then made her come to life.[10] Thus, his prophecy came true! Through self-fulfilling prophecy, you may also end up creating what you expect to find in the work situation.

Self-fulfilling prophecy can have both positive and negative results for you as a manager. Suppose you assume that your subordinates prefer to satisfy most of their needs outside the work setting and want only minimal involvement with their jobs. Consequently, you are likely to provide simple, highly structured jobs designed to require little involvement. Can you predict what response the subordinates would have to this situation? Their most likely response would be to show the lack of commitment you assumed they would have in the first place. Thus, your initial expectations are confirmed as a self-fulfilling prophecy.

Nonetheless, self-fulfilling prophecy can have a positive side (see The Effective Manager 5.1). Students introduced to their teachers as "intellectual bloomers" do better on achievement tests than other students who do not get such a positive introduction. A particularly interesting example of the self-fulfilling prophecy involves Israeli tank crews. One set of tank commanders was told that according to test data some members of their assigned crews had exceptional abilities but others were only average. In reality, the crew members were assigned randomly, so that the two test groups were equal in ability. Later, the commanders reported that the so-called exceptional crew members performed better than the "average" members. As the study revealed, however, the commanders had paid more attention to and praised the crew members they expected more from.[11] The self-fulfilling effects in these cases are a strong reason for managers to adopt positive and optimistic approaches to people at work.

> ### The Effective Manager   5.1
>
> Creating Positive Self-Fulfilling Prophecies for Employees
>
> - Create a warmer interpersonal climate between yourself and your subordinates.
> - Give more performance feedback to subordinates, and make it as positive as possible, given their actual performance.
> - Spend more time helping subordinates learn job skills.
> - Provide more opportunities for subordinates to ask questions.

Managing the Perceptual Process

To be successful, managers must understand the perceptual process, the stages involved, and the impact that the perceptual process can have on their own and others' responses. They must also be aware of what roles the perceiver, the setting, and the perceived have in the perceptual process. A particularly important concept that involves the perceived is impression management. This concept is important for managers, as well as others.

IMPRESSION MANAGEMENT

Impression management is a person's systematic attempt to behave in ways that will create and maintain impressions which the person wants others to have of him or her. First impressions are especially important and influence how people respond to one another. Impression management includes such activities as associating with the "right people," doing favours to gain approval, flattering others to make oneself look better, taking credit for a favourable event, apologizing for a negative event while seeking a pardon, agreeing with the opinions of others, and downplaying the severity of a negative event.[12] Successful managers learn how to use these activities to improve their own images. They are also more aware of when their subordinates and others in their organizations use these activities. In this context, job titles are particularly important.

DISTORTION MANAGEMENT

During the attention and selection stage, managers should try to balance automatic and controlled information processing. Most of their responsibilities, such as performance assessment and clear communication, involve controlled processing, which takes attention away from other job responsibilities. In addition to doing more controlled processing, managers need to focus on doing more observations and getting representative information. This is in contrast to simply responding to the most recent information about a subordinate or a production order, for instance. Some organizations, including 9-1-1 systems, have responded to the need for representative and more accurate information by using current technology. Managers should also not be afraid to look for disconfirming information that will help balance their typical perception of information.

Impression Management

www.babich.com

Often, job titles are designed for impression management, rather than to give accurate statements of duties. Basing himself on his experience, the owner of the recruitment and placement firm Babich and Associates states that "everybody wants to have a nice title." This impression management technique means that firms such as Babich often have to do extra research and dig beneath the surface to find a title's real significance.

TECHNOLOGY

Intrado Inc. is creating a technical solution to reduce the impact of perceptual distortions during emergencies. The company demonstrates how a 9-1-1 centre receives a signal from a car flipping over on the highway. Within seconds, emergency workers know how fast the car was moving, where it crashed, information about its driver and passengers, and whether they were wearing seatbelts. The system is patterned after the "black box" that records crucial data on airplane flights. The box uses a global positioning system to tell the 9-1-1 network how to relay the call and provide information to medical personnel who will treat the injured. The box also uses sensors to record a car's speed and the point of impact, and then radios the information into a central communication system. This stored information may even be used in court cases to ensure that the data for establishing driver fault is accurate.

The various kinds of schemas, and prototypes and stereotypes, are particularly important at the information organizing stage. Managers should try hard to broaden their schemas or should even replace them with more accurate or complete ones.

At the interpretation stage, managers need to be especially aware of how attribution affects information; we will discuss this concept more in the section later in this chapter on managing the attributional process. At the retrieval stage, managers should be aware of the weaknesses of memory. They should recognize the tendency to rely too much on schemas, especially prototypes or stereotypes that may bias which information is stored and retrieved.

Throughout the entire perception process, managers should be sensitive to the information distortions caused by halo effects, selective perception, projection, contrast effects, and self-fulfilling prophecy, in addition to the distortions of stereotypes and prototypes.

Attribution Theory

Attribution theory is the attempt to understand the cause of an event, assign responsibility for the outcomes of the event, and assess the personal qualities of the people involved.

Earlier in the chapter, we mentioned attribution theory in the context of perceptual interpretation. **Attribution theory** contributes to this interpretation by focusing on how people attempt to (1) understand the causes of a certain event, (2) assign responsibility for the outcomes of the event, and (3) assess the personal qualities of the people involved in the event.[13] In applying attribution theory, an important concern is whether behaviour has been internally or externally caused. Internal causes are believed to be under an individual's control—you believe Jake's performance, for example, is poor because he is lazy. External causes are seen as being outside a person—you believe Kellie's performance, for example, is poor because her machine is old.

According to attribution theory, three factors influence this internal or external determination: distinctiveness, consensus, and consistency. *Distinctiveness* considers how consistent a person's behaviour is in different situations. If Jake's performance is low regardless of the machine on which he is working, his poor performance will likely be given an internal attribution; if his poor performance is unusual, however, it is likely to be assigned an external cause to explain it.

OB ACROSS FUNCTIONS

PUBLIC RELATIONS

Enhancing Public Image Perception through Collaboration and Increasing Rigour

After the collapse of Enron—due in part, it is asserted, to the complicity of the company's auditors—accountants, auditors, and others involved in the reporting of financial statements came under great scrutiny. Members of the Canadian Institute of Chartered Accountants (CICA), which represents most auditors in Canada, quickly acted to assure its clients, investors, regulators, legislators, and the public in general that Canadian accountants and auditors were unlikely to be involved in similar illegal activities. The stock markets and their regulators, as well as the federal government, needed strong assurance that the accounting profession and the standards used in Canada could not fall prey to the same temptations as happened at Enron. Advertisements appeared in the national papers, committees reviewed standards, and submissions were made to regulators and the Senate. The profession's members were contacted and ultimately an independent body, the Canadian Public Accountability Board, was created to oversee the auditing standards. All this was done to assist CAs in "Keeping the Promise" as they act with objectivity and integrity—a perception endangered by Enron and its auditors—and keep their commitment to excellence and the public interest. Years of trust needed to be protected to ensure that the perceptions of financial markets as being safe and of reporting as being honest were in good hands.

Consensus involves whether all persons facing a similar situation respond in the same way. If all the people using machinery like Kellie's have poor performance, her performance will probably be given an external attribution. If other employees do not perform poorly, however, her performance will be attributed to internal causes.

Consistency involves whether an individual responds the same way as time passes. If Jake has a whole batch of low-performance figures, his poor performance will be given an internal attribution. In contrast, if Jake's low performance is an isolated incident, it will be attributed to an external cause.

ATTRIBUTION ERRORS

In addition to these three influences, two errors have an impact on internal versus external determination—the **fundamental attribution error** and the **self-serving bias**.[14] Figure 5.6 gives data from a group of health-care managers. When supervisors were asked to identify, or attribute, the causes of poor performance among their subordinates, the supervisors more often chose the individuals' internal deficiencies—lack of ability and effort—rather than external deficiencies in the situation—lack of support. This demonstrates a fundamental attribution error—the tendency to underestimate the influence of situational factors and to overestimate the influence of personal factors in evaluating someone's behaviour. When asked to identify the causes of their own poor performance, however, the supervisors overwhelmingly cited lack of support—an external, or situational, deficiency. This indicates a self-serving bias—the tendency to deny personal responsibility for performance problems but to accept personal responsibility for performance success.

Fundamental attribution error is the tendency to underestimate the influence of situational factors and to overestimate the influence of personal factors in evaluating someone's behaviour.

Self-serving bias is the tendency to deny personal responsibility for performance problems but to accept personal responsibility for performance success.

Figure 5.6 Health-care managers' attributions of causes for poor performance

Cause of Poor Performance by Their Subordinates	More Frequent Attribution	Cause of Poor Performance by Themselves
7	Lack of *ability*	1
12	Lack of *effort*	1
5	Lack of *support*	23

To summarize, we tend to overemphasize other people's internal personal factors in their behaviour and to underemphasize external factors in their behaviour. In contrast, we tend to attribute our own successes to internal factors and to attribute our failures to external factors.

Attribution theory is important for the management of subordinates because perceptions influence responses. For example, if a manager feels that subordinates are not performing well and perceives the reason to be an internal lack of effort, the manager will likely try to "motivate" the subordinates to work harder; the manager would probably ignore the possibility of changing external, situational factors that could remove job constraints and provide better organizational support. This oversight could mean losing major performance gains. Interestingly, because of the self-serving bias, when they evaluated their own behaviour, the supervisors in the study discussed earlier indicated that their performance would have benefited from having better support. Thus, the supervisors' own abilities or willingness to work hard were not questioned.

ATTRIBUTIONS ACROSS CULTURES

<table>
<tr><td>

The Effective Manager   5.2

Keys in Managing Perceptions and Attributions

• Be self-aware.

• Seek a wide range of differing information.

• Try to see a situation as others would see it.

• Be aware of different kinds of schemas.

• Be aware of perceptual distortions.

• Be aware of impression management used by yourself and others.

• Be aware of the implications of attribution theory.

</td></tr>
</table>

Research on the self-serving bias and fundamental attribution error has been done in cultures outside North America, with unexpected results.[15] In Korea, for example, the self-serving bias was found to be negative; that is, Korean managers attributed workgroup failure to themselves—"I was not a capable leader"—rather than to external causes. In India, the fundamental attribution error was to overemphasize external rather than internal causes for failure. There is some evidence that here in Canada, as well as in the U.S., women are less likely to emphasize the self-serving bias than males.[16]

Certain cultures, such as those of Canada and the U.S., tend to overemphasize internal causes and underemphasize external causes. This kind of overemphasis may result in negative attributions toward employees. These negative attributions, in turn, can lead to disciplinary actions, negative performance evaluations, transfers to other departments, and excessive reliance on training, when instead the focus should be on external causes, such as a lack of workplace support.[17] Employees, too, take their cues from managerial misattributions and, through negative self-fulfilling prophecies, they may reinforce their managers' original misattributions. Both employees and managers (see The Effective Manager 5.2) can be taught attributional realignment—in other words, to make corrections—to help them deal with such misattributions.[18]

CHAPTER 5 STUDY GUIDE

Summary

STUDY QUESTIONS

What is the perceptual process?

• Individuals use the perceptual process to pay attention to and to select, organize, interpret, and retrieve information from the world around them.

• The perceptual process involves the perceiver, the setting, and the perceived.

• Responses to the perceptual process involve thoughts, feelings, and actions.

What are some common perceptual distortions?

• Prototypes and stereotypes

• Halo effects

• Selective perception

• Projection

• Contrast effects

• Expectancy

How can the perceptual process be managed?

Managing the perceptual process involves the following:

• Impression management of the self and others

• Managing the information attention and selection stages

- Managing the information organization stage
- Managing the information interpretation stage
- Managing the information storage and retrieval stage
- Being sensitive to the effects of the common perceptual distortions

What is attribution theory?

- Attribution theory emphasizes the interpretation stage of the perceptual process and considers whether individuals' behaviours result mainly from external causes or from causes internal to the individuals.
- Three factors influence an external or internal causal attribution: distinctiveness, consensus, and consistency.
- Fundamental attribution error and self-serving bias are two errors that influence an external or internal causal attribution.
- Attributions can be managed by recognizing a typical overemphasis on internal causes of behaviour and an underemphasis on external causes.
- An overemphasis on internal causes tends to lead to assigning responsibility for failure to employees and results in disciplinary actions, negative performance evaluations, and so on.
- An underemphasis on external causes tends to lead to a lack of workplace support.

KEY TERMS

Attribution theory (p. 90)

Contrast effects (p. 88)

Fundamental attribution error (p. 91)

Halo effect (p. 86)

Perception (p. 81)

Projection (p. 87)

Schema (p. 84)

Selective perception (p. 86)

Self-fulfilling prophecy (p. 88)

Self-serving bias (p. 91)

SELF-TEST 5

MULTIPLE CHOICE

1. Perception is the process by which people _____ information. (a) generate (b) retrieve (c) transmute (d) transmogrify

2. Which of the following is not a perceptual process stage? (a) attention/selection (b) interpretation (c) follow through (d) retrieval

3. Which of the following is not a perceptual distortion? (a) prototypes/stereotypes (b) Barnum effect (c) halo effect (d) contrast effect

4. Perceptual distortions _____. (a) are quite rare (b) are quite common (c) affect only the interpretation stage (d) make the perceptual process more accurate

5. Impression management _____. (a) applies only to managers (b) applies only to subordinates (c) may involve agreeing with others' opinions and doing favours for others (d) may involve disobeying a superior to show how tough one is

6. Managing the perceptual process involves being concerned with _____. (a) information organization and interpretation (b) information processing (c) narrowing schemas (d) seeking confirming information

7. Which of the following does not influence internal or external attributions of causation? (a) distinctiveness (b) consensus (c) contrast (d) consistency

8. In the fundamental attribution error, the influence of _____. (a) situational factors is overestimated (b) personal factors is underestimated (c) self-factors is overestimated (d) situational factors is underestimated

9. Overemphasizing internal causes can lead to _____. (a) additional workplace support (b) training to correct deficiencies (c) the promotion of managers (d) positive self-fulfilling prophecies

10. Attribution _____. (a) is a trait managers are born or not born with (b) can be influenced by training (c) is almost impossible to manage (d) is strongly related to participative management

TRUE–FALSE

11. The perceptual process operates only in the perception of people.   T   F

12. The perceptual process involves four stages plus a response.   T   F

13. Stereotypes and prototypes are similar.   T   F

14. Expectancy is related to the self-fulfilling prophecy.   T   F

15. During the attention and selection stage, managers should concentrate mainly on automatic processing.   T   F

16. During the retrieval stage, there is a tendency to overemphasize schemas.   T   F

17. The fundamental attribution error seems to operate similarly throughout the world.   T   F

18. Distinctiveness influences internal or external causal determination.   T   F

19. There is a tendency in Canada to overemphasize external causes of employee behaviour.   T   F

20. Managerial misattributions can be influenced by training.   T   F

SHORT ANSWER

21. Draw and briefly discuss the model in this chapter of the perceptual process.

22. Select two perceptual distortions, briefly define them, and show how they influence the perceptual process.

23. What is the relation of attribution theory to the perceptual process?

24. Briefly discuss the perceptual response categories and relate them to one OB topic area.

APPLICATIONS ESSAY

25. Your boss has recently heard a little about attribution theory and has asked you to explain it to him in more detail. He would like you to focus on its potential for being useful in managing his department. Write a short response to his request.

Motivation and Reinforcement

Motivating an Entrepreneur

In 1980, Andrew Benedek left a secure professorship at McMaster University in order to start his own water purification company, ZENON ENVIRON-MENTAL INC. ZENON began selling membrane products and services for water purification, waste-water treatment, and water reuse. Twenty-four years later, ZENON now has 1,000 employees, offices in over 11 countries and had revenues of $184 million in 2003. However, it was not the lure of profit that pulled Benedek from McMaster but an urge to address potential global water problems. "I really wanted to make a difference in the world for water purification because I saw tremendous problems that the world would face with water shortages and I thought that these problems could best be solved by membranes."

The same philosophy of altruism has permeated the company. Employees receive an excellent benefits package, including access to on-site fitness and health services and an outdoor recreational area with forest hiking trails, natural ponds, and basketball and beach volleyball courts. But nothing is more motivating to the employees than the innovative and valuable work they are doing. ZENON'S employees have faith in the products they sell and have donated hundreds of volunteer hours to provide clean water to remote communities, such as Temagami First Nation Reserve on Bear Island, Ontario. ZENON donated a microfiltration-based water purification plant to the reserve, giving the community access to clean drinking water, which in turn has reduced the number of cases of intestinal illness caused by microscopic water-borne parasites.

Benedek also promotes a company culture that keeps his employees motivated and excited. Through an employee parliament, employees are involved in almost

every decision that affects them, and ZENON tries to attract employees who can share the company vision. Benedek explains, "From my visits to other companies, I saw that it was crucial to maintain a positive work environment. I resolved that ZENON would be different. At ZENON, we're committed to ensuring that our work environment is conducive to both professional and personal growth. We attract bright individuals who share our ambition to make a difference in the world."

And the company's mission statement clearly defines these ideals: *We are dedicated to solving urgent problems of humanity associated with water supply and wastewater management through advanced technology. As a team of dedicated employees, we benefit from professional growth, mutual respect, company ownership and the satisfaction that our success improves the environment we all share.*

Motivation and reinforcement are key issues in any firm. As you read Chapter 6, keep in mind these key questions:

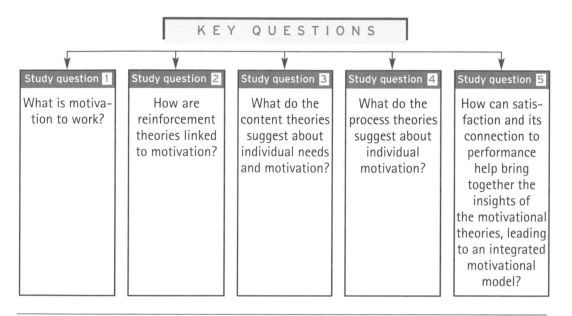

KEY QUESTIONS				
Study question 1	**Study question 2**	**Study question 3**	**Study question 4**	**Study question 5**
What is motivation to work?	How are reinforcement theories linked to motivation?	What do the content theories suggest about individual needs and motivation?	What do the process theories suggest about individual motivation?	How can satisfaction and its connection to performance help bring together the insights of the motivational theories, leading to an integrated motivational model?

What Is Motivation?

If asked to identify a major problem at work, a manager is very likely to cite a "motivational" concern and the need to do something that will encourage people to work harder to do "what I want." Formally defined, motivation refers to the forces inside an individual that lead to the direction, level, and persistence of the efforts he or she makes at work. *Direction* refers to an individual's choice when he or she has alternatives to choose from (e.g., whether to put effort into product quality or into product quantity). Level refers to the amount of effort a person makes (i.e., a lot or a little). *Persistence* refers to the length of time a person continues trying to do a specific action (e.g., trying to achieve product quality and giving up when it seems too difficult to attain).

The theories of motivation presented next seem both logical and realistic, and they can therefore help managers understand people and their motives.

Motivation refers to the forces inside an individual that lead to the level, direction, and persistence of the effort he or she makes at work.

REINFORCEMENT, CONTENT, AND PROCESS THEORIES

The theories of motivation can be divided into three broad categories: reinforcement theories, content theories, and process theories.[1] Reinforcement theories emphasize the means used in the process of controlling an individual's behaviour by manipulating its consequences. They

Reinforcement theories emphasize the means used in the process of controlling an individual's behaviour by manipulating its consequences.

Content theories identify different needs that may motivate individual behaviour.

Process theories seek to understand the thought processes that determine behaviour.

focus on what can be observed rather than on what is going on inside an employee's head. Thus, reinforcement theories focus on observing individuals to see which work-related outcomes are highly valued. By altering when, where, how, and why some types of rewards are given, the manager can change the apparent motivation of employees by providing a systematic set of consequences to shape behaviour. **Content theories** focus mainly on individual needs: the physiological or psychological deficiencies that we feel compelled to reduce or eliminate. These theories suggest that the manager's job is to create a work environment that responds positively to individual needs. They help to explain how poor performance, undesirable behaviours, low satisfaction, and so on can be caused by "blocked" needs or needs that are not satisfied on the job. **Process theories** focus on the thought or cognitive processes that take place in the minds of people and that influence their behaviour. Whereas a content approach may identify job security as an important need for an individual, a process approach goes further. It tries to identify why the person behaves in particular ways in the specific context of the available rewards and work opportunities. Although each type of theory adds to our understanding of motivation, none offers a complete explanation. At the end of this chapter, we use the insights of all three sets of theories to create an integrated view of motivational dynamics that should be useful in any work setting.[2]

MOTIVATION ACROSS CULTURES

Before we examine the motivation theories in detail, an important limitation must be noted. Motivation is a key concern in firms across the globe, but we must remember that North American theories (the only ones discussed in this chapter) have cultural limitations.[3] What determines motivation and the best ways to deal with it likely vary a lot across Asia, South America, Eastern Europe, and Africa. As we pointed out in Chapter 3, individual values and attitudes—which are both important aspects of motivation—have strong cultural foundations. What is motivating as a reward in one culture, for example, might not work in another. We should be sensitive to these issues and avoid being parochial or ethnocentric; in other words, we should not assume that people in all cultures are motivated by the same things in the same ways.[4]

Reinforcement

Reinforcement is the administration of a consequence as a result of behaviour.

In OB, reinforcement has a very specific meaning that has its origin in some classic studies in psychology.[5] **Reinforcement** is the administration of a consequence as a result of a behaviour. Managing reinforcement properly can change the direction, level, and persistence of an individual's behaviour. To understand this idea, we need to review some of the concepts on conditioning and reinforcement you may have learned in a basic psychology course. We will then move on to applications.

ETHICS AND SOCIAL RESPONSIBILITY

At Fairmont Hotels and Resorts, which owns Delta Hotels and historic resorts such as Banff Springs in Alberta, the employees are central to its strategy as are the communities in which Fairmont operates. The company encourages staff to participate in Fairmont's "Heart of the Community" charitable efforts, such as women's shelters and their second-stage housing, which the company supports by donating materials and goods to. Partnerships with colleges and universities in Canada and the U.S. help develop the future employees who will contribute to the company's growth while also contributing to Fairmont's "See the Forest AND the Trees" programs that help protect animals ranging from grizzly bears to belugas and bluebirds to sea turtles. The company's *Green Partnership Guide* is such a success in making hotels and resorts environmentally friendly that it is shared with colleges and universities throughout North America, and even with other hotel chains.

CLASSICAL AND OPERANT CONDITIONING

You may recall from other courses that Russian psychologist Ivan Pavlov studied classical conditioning. **Classical conditioning** is a form of learning through association that involves the manipulation of stimuli to influence behaviour. Pavlov "taught" dogs to salivate just by hearing the sound of a bell ringing. He did this by first ringing the bell whenever he fed the dogs. The sight of the food naturally caused the dogs to salivate. Eventually, the dogs "learned" to associate the bell ringing with the presentation of meat and to salivate at the ringing of the bell alone. Such "learning" through association is so common in organizations that it is often ignored until it causes considerable confusion. Take a look at Figure 6.1 for examples of this. The key to understanding classical conditioning is understanding a **stimulus** and a conditioned stimulus. A stimulus is something that already incites action and leads to a response (the meat for the dogs). The key in classical conditioning is associating one currently neutral but potential stimulus (the bell ringing) with another initial stimulus that already affects behaviour (the meat). The once-neutral stimulus is called a *conditioned stimulus* when it affects behaviour in the same way as the initial stimulus. In Figure 6.1, the boss's smiling becomes a conditioned stimulus because of its connection to his or her criticisms.

Operant conditioning, popularized by B. F. Skinner, is an extension of the classical case to much more practical affairs.[6] It includes more than just a stimulus-and-response behaviour. **Operant conditioning** is the process of controlling behaviour by manipulating its consequences. Classical and operant conditioning differ in two important ways. First, control in operant conditioning is achieved by manipulating consequences. Second, operant conditioning requires an examination of antecedents, behaviour, and consequences. The *antecedent* is the condition leading up to or "cueing" the behaviour. For example, in Figure 6.1, an agreement between the boss and the employee to work overtime as needed is an antecedent. If the employee works overtime, this would be the *behaviour*, and the *consequence* would be the boss's praise.

Classical conditioning is a form of learning through association that involves the manipulation of stimuli to influence behaviour.

A stimulus is something that incites action.

Operant conditioning is the process of controlling behaviour by manipulating, or "operating" on, its consequences.

Figure 6.1 Differences between classical and operant conditioning approaches for a boss and subordinate

Classical Conditioning	Stimulus		Behaviour
Learning occurs through conditioned stimuli	A person: sees the boss smile and hears boss's criticisms	→	feels nervous grits teeth
	and later: sees the smile	→	feels nervous grits teeth

Operant Conditioning	Behaviour		Behaviour
Learning occurs through consequences of behaviour	A person: works overtime	→	gets boss's praise
	and later: works overtime again		

The **law of effect** states that behaviour which results in a pleasing outcome is likely to be repeated and behaviour which results in an unpleasant outcome is not likely to be repeated.

If a boss wants a behaviour to be repeated, such as working overtime, she must manipulate the consequences. The basis for manipulating consequences is E. L. Thorndike's law of effect.[7] The **law of effect** is simple but powerful: behaviour that results in a pleasant outcome is likely to be repeated while behaviour that results in an unpleasant outcome is not likely to be repeated. The implications of this law are straightforward. If, as a supervisor, you want more of a specific behaviour, you must make the consequences for the individual positive.

Note that the emphasis is on consequences that can be manipulated rather than on consequences from just doing the behaviour itself. OB research often emphasizes specific types of rewards that are believed to influence individual behaviour from a reinforcement perspective. Extrinsic rewards are work outcomes that have a positive value and are given to the individual by some other person. They are important external reinforcers or environmental consequences that, through the law of effect, can substantially influence a person's work behaviours. Figure 6.2 presents a sample of extrinsic rewards that managers can give to their subordinates.[8] Some of these rewards are contrived (planned) rewards that have direct costs and affect budgets. Examples are pay increases and cash bonuses. Other rewards are natural and have no cost other than the manager's personal time and efforts. Examples are verbal praise and recognition in the workplace.

Figure 6.2 A sample of extrinsic rewards allocated by managers

Contrived Rewards: Some Direct Cost			Natural Rewards: No Direct Cost	
refreshments	profit-sharing	paid insurance	smiles	recognition
piped-in music	office parties	stock options	greetings	feedback
nice offices	promotion	gifts	compliments	asking advice
cash bonuses	trips	sport tickets	special jobs	
merit pay increases	company car			

REINFORCEMENT STRATEGIES

Organizational behaviour modification (OB Mod) is the systematic reinforcement of desirable work behaviour and the nonreinforcement or punishment of unwanted work behaviour.

We now bring the notions of classical conditioning, operant conditioning, reinforcement, and extrinsic rewards together to show how the direction, level, and persistence of individual behaviour can be changed. This combination is called "OB Mod," which is short for **organizational behaviour modification. OB Mod** is the systematic reinforcement of desirable work behaviour and the nonreinforcement or punishment of unwanted work behaviour. OB Mod includes four basic reinforcement strategies: positive reinforcement, negative reinforcement (or avoidance), punishment, and extinction.[9]

Positive Reinforcement   B. F. Skinner and his followers argue for **positive reinforcement**—the administration of positive consequences that tend to increase the likelihood of the desirable behaviour being repeated in similar settings. For example, a manager at Company A nods to her subordinate to express approval after he makes a useful comment during a sales meeting. Obviously, the boss wants more useful comments. Later, the subordinate makes another useful comment, just as the boss hoped he would.

To begin using a strategy of positive reinforcement, we first need to be aware that positive reinforcers and rewards are not necessarily the same. Recognition, for example, is both a reward and a potential positive reinforcer. Recognition only becomes a positive reinforcer, instead of a potential one, if a person's performance later improves. Sometimes, rewards turn out not to be positive reinforcers. For example, a supervisor at Company B might praise a subordinate in front of other group members for finding errors in a report. If the group members then give their co-worker the silent treatment, however, the worker may stop looking for errors in the future. In this case, the supervisor's "reward" does not serve as a positive reinforcer.

To have maximum reinforcement value, a reward must be delivered only if the desired behaviour is exhibited. That is, the reward must be contingent on the desired behaviour. This principle is known as the **law of contingent reinforcement**. Thus, in the earlier Company A example, the supervisor's praise depended on the subordinate first making constructive comments. Finally, the reward must be given as soon as possible after the desired behaviour. This is known as the **law of immediate reinforcement**.[10] If the boss waited for the annual performance review to praise the subordinate for providing constructive comments, the law of immediate reinforcement would be violated.

Now that we have presented the general concepts, it is time to look at two important issues related to implementing the concepts.[11] First, what should be done if the behaviour approximates what is wanted but is not exactly on target? Second, is it necessary to give reinforcement each and every time? These two issues are known as shaping and scheduling, respectively.

Shaping   If the desired behaviour is relatively specific and is difficult to achieve, a pattern of positive reinforcement, called shaping, can be used. **Shaping** is the creation of a new behaviour by the positive reinforcement of successive approximations leading to the desired behaviour. For example, new machine operators in the Ford Motor casting operation must learn a complex series of tasks in order to avoid gaps, overfills, and cracks when they pour molten metal into the casting.[12] The moulds are filled in a three-step process, with each step being more difficult than the one before it. Astute master craftspersons first show the new machine operators how to pour the first step and they give praise based on what the operators did right. As the apprentices gain experience, they are given praise only when all of the elements of the first step are completed successfully. Once the apprentices have mastered the first step, they progress to the second. Reinforcement is then given only when the entire first step and an aspect of the second step are completed successfully. Over time, apprentices learn all three steps and are immediately given contingent positive rewards for a complete casting that has no cracks or gaps. In this way, behaviour is shaped gradually rather than changed all at once.

Scheduling Positive Reinforcement   Positive reinforcement can be given according to either continuous or intermittent schedules. **Continuous reinforcement** rewards desired behaviour each time it occurs. **Intermittent reinforcement** rewards desired behaviour only periodically. These alternatives are important because the two schedules may have very different impacts on behaviour. In general, continuous reinforcement leads to a desired behaviour more quickly than does intermittent reinforcement. Thus, in the initial training of the apprentice casters, continuous reinforcement would be important. At the same time, however, continuous reinforcement is more costly because it uses up more rewards and the behaviour ends more easily when there is no longer any reinforcement of it. In contrast, behaviour acquired through intermittent

Positive reinforcement is the administration of positive consequences that tend to increase the likelihood of the behaviour being repeated in similar settings.

The law of contingent reinforcement states that, for a reward to have maximum reinforcing value, it must be delivered only if the desired behaviour is exhibited.

The law of immediate reinforcement states that the more immediate the delivery of a reward after a desired behaviour occurs, the greater the reinforcing effect on that behaviour.

Shaping is the creation of a new behaviour by the positive reinforcement of successive approximations leading to the desired behaviour.

Continuous reinforcement is a reinforcement schedule that rewards desired behaviour each time it occurs.

Intermittent reinforcement is a reinforcement schedule that rewards desired behaviour only periodically.

reinforcement lasts longer after reinforcement has stopped than does behaviour acquired through continuous reinforcement. In other words, it is more resistant to extinction. Thus, as the apprentices master an aspect of the pouring, the schedule is switched from continuous to intermittent reinforcement.

Figure 6.3 Four types of intermittent reinforcement schedules

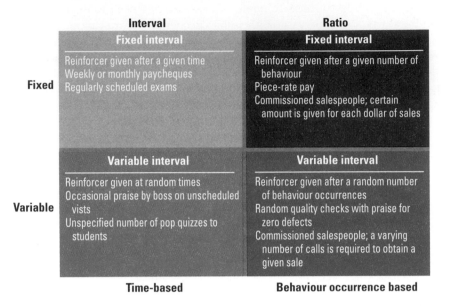

As shown in Figure 6.3, intermittent reinforcement can be given according to fixed or *variable schedules*. Variable schedules typically result in more consistent patterns of desired behaviour than do fixed reinforcement schedules. With *fixed interval schedules*, rewards are given at the first appearance of a behaviour after a specific time has elapsed. Fixed ratio schedules result in a reward each time a certain number of the behaviours have occurred. With a *variable interval schedule*, rewards are given for behaviour at random times, while a *variable ratio schedule* leads to rewards for behaviour after a random number of occurrences. In the Ford Motor example, as the apprentices perfect their technique for a stage of pouring castings, the astute masters switch to a variable ratio reinforcement.

Let's now look at an example from Metso Automation SCADA Solutions Ltd. of Calgary, Alberta. The Canadian division of Helsinki based Metso Corporation, Metso Automation SCADA Solutions, a maker of production automation systems, provides a relaxed work environment with personal offices and central common areas for teamwork. It also uses positive reinforcement to showcase employee accomplishments. The company not only brews its own beer for after-work get-togethers on Fridays, it also celebrates special awards nights. The company presents the "Get a Life" award for the most overtime worked and "Got a Life" award for the greatest decrease in overtime worked. Those working long hours receive spa packages, hockey tickets, and extra days off.[13]

The next element to consider is the kind of reinforcement scheduling that was used by Metso. The first schedule rewarded attendance behaviours occuring weekly and over extended periods of time. Thus, for each period that a person attended work on Fridays, the individual received a reward—a fixed ratio schedule reward. The reward, a free beer, is both social and mildly economic. At the same time, those working longer hours were given rewards and learned to expect to be rewarded for their dedication.

The second schedule, which remains in use, focuses on eligibility for the awards. It is a variable ratio because a random number of overtime hours must be worked before a specific employee receives an award. Employees can qualify for the rewards by either working long hours or improving their efficiency and thereby reducing overtime, but as they never know what number of overtime hours will "win" the next reward, it is similar to buying a lottery ticket. In this variable ratio system, people keep "buying tickets" because they have no idea when they will hit the jackpot.[14] Award systems similar to Metso's have been used by firms as different as new car dealerships and life insurance companies.[15]

Negative Reinforcement (Avoidance)   A second reinforcement strategy used in OB Mod is negative reinforcement or avoidance: it involves the withdrawal of negative consequences, which tends to increase the likelihood of desirable behaviour being repeated in a similar setting. An example of this would be if a manager regularly nags a worker about his poor performance and then one day stops nagging when the worker does not fall behind in his work. There are two aspects to focus on here: first, the negative consequences and, second, the withdrawal of these consequences when desirable behaviour occurs. The term negative reinforcement comes from this withdrawal of the negative consequences. This strategy is also sometimes called avoidance because the goal is for the person to avoid the negative consequence by performing the desired behaviour. Examples of this are when we stop at a red light to avoid a traffic ticket or when a worker who prefers the day shift is allowed to return to that shift if she performs well on the night shift.

> Negative reinforcement is the withdrawal of negative consequences, which tends to increase the likelihood of desirable behaviour being repeated in a similar setting; it is also known as avoidance.

Punishment   A third OB Mod strategy is punishment. Unlike positive reinforcement and negative reinforcement, punishment is not intended to encourage positive behaviour. Its goal is to discourage negative behaviour. Formally defined, punishment is the withdrawal of positive consequences or the administration of negative consequences that tend to reduce the likelihood of the behaviour being repeated in similar settings. An illustration of the first type of punishment would be if a manager assigns a worker who arrives late to an unpleasant job, such as cleaning the restrooms. An example of withdrawing positive consequences would be if the manager docks the employee's pay when she is late—in this example, the employee's pay is viewed as a positive consequence.

> Punishment is the administration of negative consequences that tend to reduce the likelihood of the behaviour being repeated in similar settings.

Research showing the importance of punishment has found that when punishment is administered for poor performance, performance improves without there being a significant effect on the workers' satisfaction. However, when workers see the punishment as being arbitrary and erratic, they end up being less satisfied and perform poorly.[16] In other words, punishment can be handled poorly and it can be handled well. Of course, the manager's challenge is to know when to use this strategy and how to use it correctly.

Finally, punishment may be weakened by positive reinforcement received from another source. It is possible for a worker to be reinforced by peers at the same time that the worker is receiving punishment from the manager. Sometimes the positive value of such peer support is so great that the individual chooses to put up with the punishment. Thus, the undesirable behaviour continues. Although, for example, a supervisor may have reprimanded an experienced worker many times for playing jokes on new employees, the worker may feel that the approving grins from co-workers make more jokes in the future worthwhile.

Does all of this mean that punishment should never be administered? Of course not. The important points to remember are to administer punishment selectively and then to do so correctly. The ultimate workplace punishment—firing someone—requires special attention to following the correct legal process and having documented support for the cause of the firing.

Figure 6.4 Applying reinforcement strategies

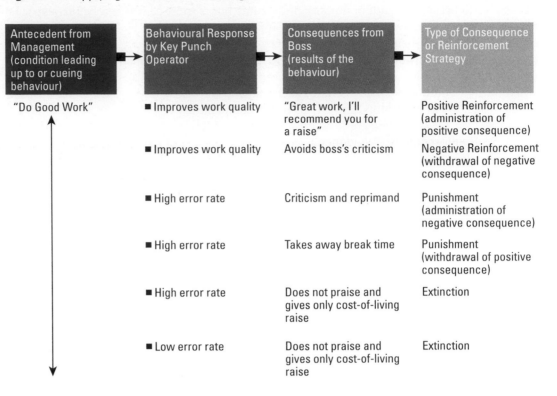

Extinction is the withdrawal of the reinforcing consequences for a particular behaviour.

Extinction   The final OB Mod reinforcement strategy is **extinction**—the withdrawal of the reinforcing consequences for a particular behaviour. Suppose an employee named Jack is often late for work and his co-workers cover for him (they provide positive reinforcement). To change Jack's behaviour, the manager tells the co-workers to stop covering for him, which takes away the reinforcing consequences for Jack. Thus, the manager has deliberately used extinction to get rid of an undesirable behaviour. This strategy decreases the frequency of or weakens the behaviour. The behaviour is not "unlearned;" it simply is not exhibited. Although the behaviour may no longer occur because it is no longer reinforced, it will reappear if it is reinforced again in the future. Whereas positive reinforcement seeks to establish and maintain desirable work behaviour, extinction aims to weaken and eliminate undesirable behaviour.

Summary of Reinforcement Strategies   Figure 6.4 summarizes and illustrates the use of each OB Mod strategy. They are all designed to direct work behaviour toward the practices that management wants. The boss uses both positive and negative reinforcement to strengthen the desirable behaviour of improving work quality when this behaviour occurs. Punishment is used to weaken the undesirable behaviour of having a high error rate, with the punishment being either the administration of negative consequences or the withdrawal of positive consequences. Similarly, extinction is used deliberately to weaken the undesirable behaviour of having a high error rate when this behaviour occurs. Note also, however, that the boss's unintended use of extinction weakens the desirable behaviour of having a low error rate. Finally, these strategies may be used together or separately.

REINFORCEMENT PERSPECTIVES: USAGE AND ETHICAL ISSUES

The effective use of reinforcement strategies can help manage human behaviour at work, which is no doubt why these strategies are used in many large firms, such as General Electric and B. F. Goodrich, and even in smaller firms, such as the Yanke Group of Companies. Yanke, a trucking firm from Saskatoon, pays $300 for referrals of new drivers. On top of that, it also recently introduced contests for employees who refer drivers, including a trip for two to Hawaii and $500 of spending money.

There has, however, been criticism of the use of these approaches by management in some instances. For example, some reports on the "success" of specific programs involve isolated cases that were analyzed without using scientific research designs. It is hard to conclude with certainty that the observed results were caused by reinforcement dynamics. In fact, one critic argues that the improved performance with these programs may only have occurred because of the goal setting involved; that is, because specific performance goals were clarified, and each worker was held accountable for his or her own accomplishments.[17]

Another major criticism involves the potential value dilemmas that are associated with using reinforcement to influence human behaviour at work. For example, some critics maintain that the systematic use of reinforcement strategies leads to a demeaning and dehumanizing view of people that limits human growth and development.[18] A related criticism is that, through reinforcement, managers abuse the power of their position and knowledge by exerting external control over individual behaviour. Advocates of the reinforcement approach attack the problem directly: they agree that behaviour modification involves the control of behaviour, but they also argue that behaviour control is an unavoidable part of every manager's job. The real question is how to ensure that any manipulation is done in an ethical, fair, and constructive fashion.[19]

Content Theories of Motivation
- -

Content theories, as noted earlier, suggest that motivation results from the individual's attempts to satisfy needs. Four of the better known content theories have been proposed by Abraham Maslow, Clayton Alderfer, David McClelland, and Frederick Herzberg. Each of these scholars offers a slightly different view of the needs individuals may bring with them to work.

HIERARCHY OF NEEDS THEORY

Abraham Maslow's **hierarchy of needs theory**, as shown in Figure 6.5, identifies five distinct levels of individual needs: from self-actualization and esteem, at the top, to social, safety, and physiological at the bottom.[20] Maslow assumes that some needs are more important than others and must be satisfied before the other needs can serve as motivators. For example, physiological needs must be satisfied before safety needs are activated, and safety needs must be satisfied before social needs are activated, and so on.

Maslow's view is quite popular in some organizations because it looks easy to implement. Unfortunately, however, research evidence does not show that there actually is a precise five-step hierarchy of needs. The needs more likely operate in a flexible hierarchy. Some research

Maslow's hierarchy of needs theory **is a pyramid of physiological, safety, social, esteem, and self-actualization needs.**

The higher order needs in Maslow's hierarchy are esteem and self-actualiza-tion needs.
The lower order needs in Maslow's hierarchy are physiological, safety, and social needs.

suggests that higher order needs (esteem and self-actualization needs) tend to become more important than lower order needs (physiological, safety, and social needs) as individuals move up the corporate ladder.[21] Other studies report that needs vary according to a person's career stage, the size of the organization, and even the geographic location.[22] There is also no consistent evidence that satisfying a need at one level makes this need less important and increases the importance of the next higher need.[23] Finally, when the hierarchy of needs is examined across cultures, values such as those discussed in Chapter 2 become important. For instance, social needs tend to dominate in more collectivist societies, such as Mexico and Pakistan.[24]

Figure 6.5 Higher order needs and lower order needs in Maslow's hierarchy of needs

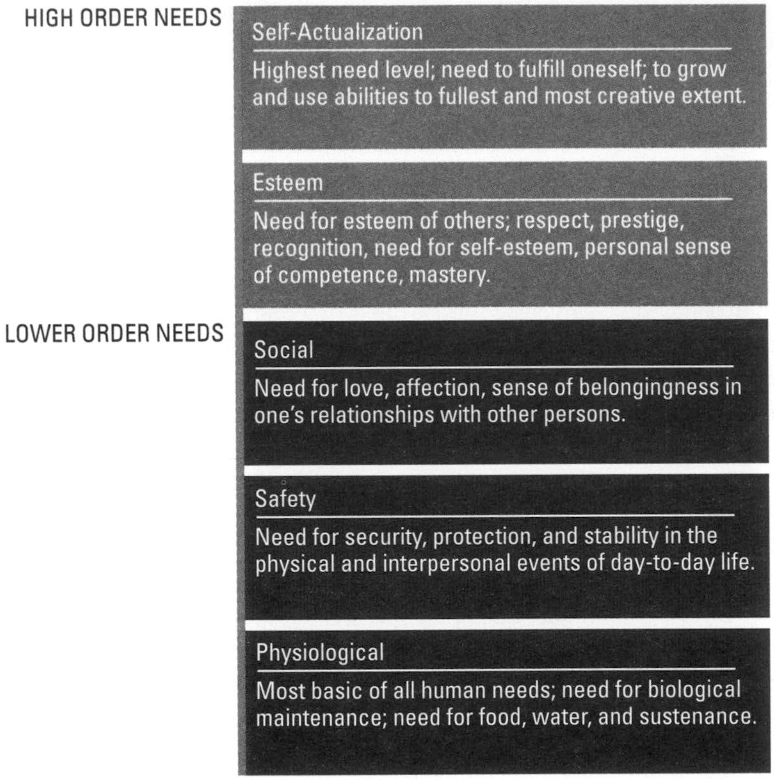

HIGH ORDER NEEDS

Self-Actualization
Highest need level; need to fulfill oneself; to grow and use abilities to fullest and most creative extent.

Esteem
Need for esteem of others; respect, prestige, recognition, need for self-esteem, personal sense of competence, mastery.

LOWER ORDER NEEDS

Social
Need for love, affection, sense of belongingness in one's relationships with other persons.

Safety
Need for security, protection, and stability in the physical and interpersonal events of day-to-day life.

Physiological
Most basic of all human needs; need for biological maintenance; need for food, water, and sustenance.

Alderfer's ERG theory identifies existence, relat-edness, and growth needs.

Existence needs are desires for physiological and mate-rial well-being.

Relatedness needs are desires for satisfying inter-personal relationships.

Growth needs are desires for continued personal growth and development.

ERG THEORY

Clayton Alderfer's ERG theory is also based on needs but differs from Maslow's theory in three basic ways.[25] First, the theory reduces Maslow's five need categories to three: existence needs—desires for physiological and material well-being; relatedness needs—desires for satisfying interpersonal relationships; and growth needs—desires for continued personal growth and development. Second, whereas Maslow's theory argues that individuals progress up the "needs" hierarchy, ERG theory emphasizes a unique *frustration–regression* component. An already satisfied lower level need can become reactivated when a higher level need cannot be satisfied. Thus, if a person is continually frustrated in his or her attempts to satisfy growth needs, relatedness needs can again surface as key motivators. Third, unlike Maslow's theory, ERG theory contends that more than one need may be activated at the same time.

Even though more research is needed to verify whether or not ERG theory is accurate, the supporting evidence is encouraging.[26] In particular, the theory's allowance for regression back to lower level needs is a valuable contribution to our thinking. It may help to explain why in some settings, for example, workers' complaints focus on wages, benefits, and working conditions—things relating to existence needs. Although these needs are important, they may become exaggerated precisely because the workers' jobs cannot satisfy relatedness and growth needs. ERG theory thus offers a more flexible approach to understanding human needs than does Maslow's strict hierarchy.

ACQUIRED NEEDS THEORY

In the late 1940s, psychologist David I. McClelland and his co-workers began experimenting with the Thematic Apperception Test (TAT) as a way of measuring human needs.[27] The TAT is a projective technique that asks people to view pictures and write stories about what they see. In one case, McClelland showed three executives a photograph of a man sitting down and looking at family photos arranged on his work desk. One executive wrote of an engineer who was daydreaming about a family outing scheduled for the next day. Another described a designer who had picked up an idea for a new gadget from remarks made by his family. The third described an engineer who was intently working on a bridge-stress problem that he seemed sure to solve because of his confident look.[28] McClelland identified three themes in these TAT stories, and related each one to an underlying need that he believes is important for understanding individual behaviour. These needs are (1) need for achievement (nAch), defined as the desire to do something better or more efficiently, to solve problems, or to master complex tasks; (2) need for affiliation (nAff), defined as the desire to establish and maintain friendly and warm relations with others; and (3) need for power (nPower), defined as the desire to control others, to influence their behaviour, or to be responsible for others.

McClelland argues that these three needs are acquired over time through life experiences. He encourages managers to learn how to identify the presence of nAch, nAff, and nPower in themselves and in others, and to be able to create work environments that go well with the different need profiles.

The theory is particularly useful because each need can be linked with a set of work preferences. An employee with a high need for achievement prefers individual responsibilities, challenging goals, and performance feedback. An employee with a high need for affiliation is drawn to interpersonal relationships and opportunities for communication. Finally, an employee with a high need for power seeks influence over others and likes attention and recognition. If individuals genuinely have these needs, it may be possible to match them with the need profiles that are required for success in various types of jobs. For instance, McClelland found that the combination of a moderate to high need for power and a lower need for affiliation is linked with senior executive success. High nPower creates the willingness to have influence or impact on others; lower nAff allows the manager to make difficult decisions without worrying too much about being disliked.[29]

Research has given a lot of insight into nAch in particular and includes some especially interesting applications in developing nations. For example, McClelland trained businesspeople in Kakinda, India, to think, talk, and act like high achievers by having them write stories about achievement and participate in a business game that encouraged achievement. The businesspeople also met with successful entrepreneurs and learned how to set challenging goals for their own businesses. Over a two-year period following these activities, the participants from the Kakinda study were involved in activities that created twice as many new jobs as those who had received no training.[30]

Need for achievement (nAch) is the desire to do better, solve problems, or master complex tasks.

Need for affiliation (nAff) is the desire for friendly and warm relations with others.

Need for power (nPower) is the desire to control others and influence their behaviour.

GLOBALIZATION

With the growing interest in more health-conscious fast food choices, the juice and smoothie industry has taken off. And Mississauga-based Juice Zone has taken advantage this trend by opening franchises across the country. Having entered the market in 2000, Juice Zone has already established a global presence, by selling master development rights to expand Juice Zone in India and surrounding countries. The company considers India a gateway to the Middle East and South and Southeast Asia. Juice Zone franchises are also present in several U.S. states, and there are plans to expand into more U.S. states and international markets in the near future.

Herzberg's two-factor theory identifies job context as the source of job dissatisfaction and job content as the source of job satisfaction.

TWO-FACTOR THEORY

Frederick Herzberg took a different approach to examining motivation. He simply asked workers to report the times they felt exceptionally good about their jobs and the times they felt exceptionally bad about them.[31] As shown in Figure 6.6, Herzberg and his associates noted that the respondents identified somewhat different things when they felt good or bad about their jobs. From this study, Herzberg and his fellow researchers developed the two-factor theory, also known as the motivator-hygiene theory, which presents different factors as the primary causes of job satisfaction and job dissatisfaction.

Figure 6.6 Sources of dissatisfaction and satisfaction in Herzberg's two-factor theory

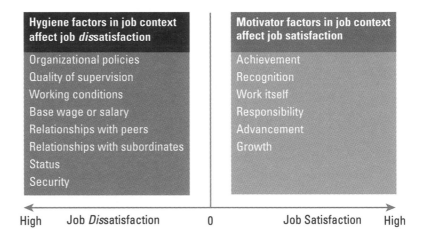

Hygiene factors in the job context (the work setting) are sources of job dissatisfaction.

According to this theory, the sources of job dissatisfaction are called hygiene factors. These factors are associated with the job context or work setting; that is, they relate more to the environment in which people work than to the type of work itself. Among the hygiene factors shown on the left in Figure 6.6, perhaps the most surprising is salary. Herzberg found that low salary makes people dissatisfied, but that paying them more does not necessarily satisfy or motivate them. In the two-factor theory, job satisfaction and job dissatisfaction are completely separate dimensions. This means that improving a hygiene factor, such as working conditions, will not make people satisfied with their work; it will only prevent them from being dissatisfied.

The way to improve job satisfaction, the theory states, is to pay attention to an entirely different set of factors—the **motivator factors** shown on the right in Figure 6.6. These factors are related to the job content—what people actually do in their work. Adding these satisfiers or motivators to people's jobs is Herzberg's link to performance. These factors include senses of achievement, recognition, and responsibility.

According to Herzberg, when these opportunities are not available, there is low job satisfaction, which causes a lack of motivation, and performance then suffers. He suggests the technique of job enrichment as a way of building satisfiers into job content. This topic is given special attention in Chapter 8. For now, the notion is well summarized in this statement by Herzberg: "If you want people to do a good job, give them a good job to do."[32]

OB scholars continue to debate the merits of the two-factor theory and its applications.[33] Many are unable to confirm the theory. Many criticize it as only repeatable under the same method. This is a serious criticism, because theories have to be verifiable under different research methods in the scientific approach. Furthermore, this theory, just like the other content theories, fails to explain individual differences, to link motivation and needs to both satisfaction and performance, or to consider cultural and professional differences.[34]

The content theories remain popular in management circles because of their simplicity and the apparently direct link between needs and behaviour. At the same time, however, none of the theories actually makes any direct links between specific needs and the behaviours that are desired by managers. As a result, managers can misinterpret the theories and inappropriately assume that they know the needs of their subordinates. For these reasons, we advise that these content theories not be used simplistically and instead be used very carefully. We will return to these theories when we add satisfaction to the discussion of motivation.

> **Motivator factors** in the job content (the tasks people actually do) are sources of job satisfaction.

Process Theories

The various content theories emphasize the "what" aspects of motivation. That is, they tend to look for ways to improve motivation by dealing with active or unsatisfied needs. They do not formally explore the thought processes through which people choose one action over another in the workplace. Process theories focus on thought processes. Although there are many process theories, we will concentrate on equity theory and expectancy theory.

EQUITY THEORY

Equity theory is based on social comparison and is best applied to the workplace by J. Stacy Adams.[35] Adams argues that when people judge the fairness of their work outcomes compared to those of other people, any perceived inequity (i.e., any unfairness they believe they have found) becomes a motivating state of mind. Perceived inequity occurs when individuals believe that the rewards which they are receiving for their work contributions are different than the rewards other people appear to be receiving for their work. Whenever there is a perceived inequity, the theory states that people will be motivated to act in ways that remove the discomfort and restore a sense of felt equity or fairness.

Felt negative inequity occurs when an individual feels that he or she has received less than others have received in proportion to their work inputs. *Felt positive inequity* occurs when an individual feels that he or she has received more than others have. When either feeling exists, the individual will likely behave in one or more of the following ways in order to restore a sense of equity:

> Adams' **equity theory** argues that people will act to eliminate any inequity (unfairness) that they feel there is in the rewards they receive for their work compared to what others receive.

How to restore perceived equity

- Change the work inputs (e.g., reduce the performance efforts).

- Change the outcomes (rewards) received (e.g., ask for a raise).

- Leave the situation (e.g., quit).

- Change the comparison points (e.g., compare oneself to a different co-worker).

- Psychologically distort the comparisons (e.g., rationalize that the inequity is only temporary and will be resolved in the future).

- Take actions to change the inputs or outputs of the comparison person (e.g., get a co-worker to accept more work).

The Effective Manager 6.1
STEPS FOR MANAGING THE EQUITY PROCESS
• Recognize that equity comparisons are inevitable in the workplace.
• Anticipate any felt negative inequities when rewards are given.
• Communicate clear evaluations of any rewards that are given.
• Communicate an appraisal of the performance on which the reward is based.
• Communicate comparison points that are appropriate in the situation.

Equity comparisons made by individuals determine how recipients will be affected by any rewards that they are given. What may seem fair and equitable to a group leader, for example, might be perceived as unfair and inequitable by a team member who has made comparisons to other teammates. Furthermore, such feelings of inequity are determined entirely by how the individual views the situation. It is not the reward giver's intentions that count; rather, it is how the recipient perceives the reward that will determine the actual motivational outcomes. The Effective Manager 6.1 offers some ideas on how to handle equity comparisons.

Research indicates that people who feel they are overpaid (a perceived positive inequity) increase the quantity or quality of their work, whereas those who feel they are underpaid (a perceived negative inequity) decrease the quantity or quality of their work.[36] The research is most conclusive with respect to felt negative inequity. It appears that people are less comfortable when they are rewarded too little than when they are rewarded too much. These results, however, are for individualistic cultures in which self-interests tend to govern social comparisons. In more collectivist cultures, such as those of many Asian countries, there is often more concern about equality than there is about equity. This encourages solidarity within the group and helps to maintain harmony in social relationships.[37]

EXPECTANCY THEORY

Vroom's **expectancy theory** argues that work motivation is determined by individual beliefs about effort-performance relationships and work outcomes.

Expectancy is the probability that work effort will be followed by goal or task achievement.

Instrumentality is the probability that performance will lead to particular work outcomes.

Valence is the value to the individual of various work outcomes.

Victor Vroom's **expectancy theory** argues that motivation results from a rational calculation.[38] A person is motivated to the degree that he or she believes that (1) effort will yield acceptable performance, (2) performance will be rewarded, and (3) the value of the rewards is highly positive. The interaction between all three elements influences motivation. (See Figure 6.7.) Thus, some key concepts are defined as probabilities, as follows:

- The individual's sense of the probability that work effort will be followed by an achieved goal or task performance is called **expectancy**. Expectancy would have a value of 0 if the person felt it were impossible to achieve the given performance level; it would have a value of 1 if a person were 100 percent certain that the performance could be achieved.

- The individual's sense of the probability that a particular level of achieved goals or tasks will lead to particular work outcomes is called **instrumentality**. Instrumentality also varies from 0 to 1.

- **Valence** is the value the individual gives to particular work outcomes, particularly a desired reward. Valences form a scale from -1 (a very undesirable outcome) to 1 (a very desirable outcome).

Figure 6.7 Key terms and managerial implications of Vroom's expectancy theory

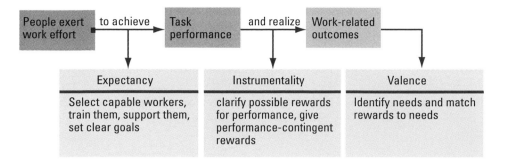

Vroom argues that motivation (M), expectancy (E), instrumentality (I), and valence (V) are related to one another accoridng to the following equation: M = E × I × V. This multiplier effect means that the motivational appeal of a particular work path goes down sharply whenever any one or more of these factors has a value close to zero. Conversely, for a reward to have a high and positive motivational impact as a work outcome, the expectancy, instrumentality, and valence associated with the reward must all be high and positive.

Suppose that a manager is wondering whether or not the chance to earn a merit raise will motivate an employee. Expectancy theory predicts that the motivation to work hard to earn the merit pay will be low if *expectancy* is low—i.e., if the employee feels that he or she cannot achieve the necessary performance level. Motivation will also be low if *instrumentality* is low—i.e., if the person is not confident that a high level of task performance will result in a high merit-pay raise. Motivation will also be low if *valence* is low—i.e., if the person places little value on a merit-pay increase or other reward offered. And motivation will remain low if any combination of these situations exists. Thus, the multiplier effect requires managers to act to create high expectancy, instrumentality, and valence when they want to have high levels of work motivation. A zero at any location on the right side of the expectancy equation will result in zero motivation.

Thus, with expectancy theory, the logical conclusion is that managers must intervene actively in work situations in order to create work expectancies, instrumentalities, and valences that support the organization's objectives.[39] To influence expectancies, managers should select people with the proper abilities, train them well, support them with needed resources, and identify clear performance goals. To influence instrumentality, managers should clarify performance–reward relationships and confirm these relationships when rewards are actually given for performance accomplishments. To influence valences, managers should identify the needs that are important to each individual and then try to adjust the available rewards to match these needs.

A large amount of research on expectancy theory has been done, and there are articles which review the research.[40] Although the theory has received substantial support, specific details, such as the operation of the multiplier effect, are still being questioned. One of the more popular modifications of Vroom's original version of the theory makes a distinction between two kinds of work outcomes for calculating the valence.[41] Researchers have separated **extrinsic rewards**—positively valued work outcomes (rewards) given to the individual by another person—from intrinsic rewards (see The Effective Manager 6.2). **Intrinsic rewards** are positively valued work outcomes that the individual receives directly from performing the

The Effective Manager | 6.2

WORK GUIDELINES FOR ALLOCATING EXTRINSIC REWARDS

- Clearly identify the desired behaviours.
- Keep an inventory of rewards that have the potential to serve as positive reinforcers.
- Recognize individual differences in which rewards will have a positive value for each person.
- Let each person know exactly what must be done to receive a desired reward. Set clear target goals beforehand and give performance feedback.
- Make the allocation of rewards contingent on the occurrence of the desired behaviours and then give the rewards immediately.
- Allocate rewards wisely when it comes to scheduling the delivery of positive reinforcement.

Extrinsic rewards are rewards that are given to the individual by another person in the work setting.

Intrinsic rewards are rewards that the individual receives directly from performing the task.

task. A feeling of achievement after accomplishing a particularly challenging task is an example of an intrinsic reward.

Expectancy theory does not specify exactly which rewards will motivate particular groups of workers. In this sense, the theory recognizes that rewards and their connection to performance are likely to be seen quite differently in different cultures. This helps to explain some apparently counterintuitive findings. For example, a pay raise motivated one group of Mexican workers to work fewer hours. They wanted a certain amount of money in order to enjoy things other than work rather than just more money. A Japanese sales representative's promotion to being the manager of a U.S. company decreased his performance. His superiors did not realize that the promotion embarrassed him and distanced him from his colleagues.[42]

Integrating the Motivation Theories

The reinforcement, content, and process approaches to motivation discussed in this chapter deal with one or more aspects of rewards, needs, cognitions, satisfaction, and performance. We have tended to treat each of these theories separately, and they may be used that way, but they can also be mixed and matched as the occasion demands, and in whichever way you are comfortable in using them. Next, we will examine the connection between satisfaction and performance, which will help integrate all the views we have discussed.

JOB SATISFACTION

Job satisfaction is how positively or negatively individuals feel about their jobs.

Formally defined, job satisfaction is how positively or negatively individuals feel about their jobs. It is the employee's attitude or emotional response to the tasks he or she has to do, as well as to the physical and social conditions of the workplace. At first glance, and from the perspective of Herzberg's two-factor theory, it may seem that some aspects of job satisfaction will involve motivation and lead to positive employment relationships and high levels of individual job performance. But as we will see, the issues are more complicated than this conclusion suggests.

HIGH-PERFORMANCE ORGANIZATION

Research In Motion (RIM), one of Canada's Top 100 Employers and based in Waterloo, Ontario, has been ranked by Deloitte and Touche for seven years in a row through 2004 as one of the 50 fastest growing technology companies. This growth is fostered by attracting talented, creative, and motivated persons. The company achieves this by offering desirable casual work environments, developing future employees through student co-op placements, encouraging learning and training, and offering valuable benefits such as subsidized fitness memberships and home and auto insurance, and free financial planning services. To help celebrate special achievements, the company has even put on private concerts for employees featuring such bands as The Barenaked Ladies, The Tragically Hip, and Aerosmith.

www.rim.com; www.blackberry.com

On a daily basis, managers must be able to infer the job satisfaction of others by observing subordinates carefully and interpreting what they say and do while going about their jobs. Sometimes, it is also useful to do more formal verifications of the levels of job satisfaction among groups of workers, especially through formal interviews or questionnaires. Increasingly, other methods are being used as well, such as focus groups and computer-based attitude surveys.[43]

Of the many available job satisfaction questionnaires that have been used over the years, two popular ones are the Minnesota Satisfaction Questionnaire (MSQ) and the Job Descriptive Index (JDI).[44] Both deal with aspects of employee satisfaction which good managers should be concerned about. For example, the MSQ measures satisfaction with working conditions, chances for advancement, freedom to use one's own judgment, praise for doing a good job, and feelings of accomplishment, among other items. The five facets of job satisfaction measured by the JDI are as follows:

- *the work itself*—responsibility, interest, and growth

- *quality of supervision*—technical help and social support

- *relationships with co-workers*—social harmony and respect

- *promotion opportunities*—chances for further advancement

- *pay*—adequacy of pay and perceived equity vis-à-vis others.

Five facets of job satisfaction

JOB SATISFACTION, RETENTION, AND PERFORMANCE

How important job satisfaction is can be better understood through two decisions people make about their work. The first is the decision to belong; that is, to join and remain a member of an organization. The second is the decision to perform; that is, to work hard in pursuit of high levels of task performance. Not everyone who belongs to an organization performs up to expectations.

The decision to belong concerns an individual's attendance and longevity at work. In this sense, job satisfaction influences *absenteeism*, or the failure of people to attend work. In general, workers who are satisfied with the job itself have more regular attendance and are less likely to be absent for unexplained reasons than are dissatisfied workers. Job satisfaction can also affect turnover, or decisions by people to terminate their employment. Simply put, dissatisfied workers are more likely than satisfied workers to quit their jobs.[45]

What is the relationship between job satisfaction and performance? There is considerable debate on this issue, with three points of view being evident: (1) satisfaction causes performance, (2) performance causes satisfaction, and (3) rewards cause both performance and satisfaction.[46]

Argument: Satisfaction Causes Performance   If job satisfaction causes high levels of performance, the message to managers is quite simple: to increase employees' work performance, make them happy. Research, however, indicates that no simple and direct link exists between individual job satisfaction at one point in time and work performance at a later point. This conclusion is widely recognized among OB scholars, although some evidence suggests that there is more of a relationship between satisfaction and performance for professionals or higher level employees than for nonprofessionals or those at lower job levels. Job satisfaction alone is not a consistent predictor of individual work performance.

Argument: Performance Causes Satisfaction   If high levels of performance cause job satisfaction, the message to managers is quite different. Rather than focusing first on peoples' job satisfaction, managers should instead be helping people achieve high performance; job satisfaction would then be expected to follow. Research indicates that there actually is a relationship between individual performance measured at a certain time period and later job satisfaction. A basic model of this relationship, based on the work of Edward E. Lawler and Lyman Porter, maintains that performance accomplishment leads to rewards that, in turn, lead to satisfaction.[47] In this model, rewards are intervening variables; that is, they are the middle link between performance and later satisfaction. In addition, a moderator variable—the perceived equity of rewards—further affects the relationship. The moderator indicates that performance will lead to satisfaction only if rewards are considered equitable or fair. If an individual feels that his or her performance is unfairly rewarded, the performance-causes-satisfaction connection breaks.

Argument: Rewards Cause Both Satisfaction and Performance   This final argument in the job satisfaction–performance controversy is the most compelling. It suggests that a proper allocation of rewards can positively influence both performance and satisfaction. The key word in the previous sentence is *proper*. Research indicates that people who receive high rewards report higher job satisfaction. But research also indicates that performance-contingent rewards influence a person's work performance. In this case, the size and value of the reward vary in proportion to the level of one's performance accomplishment. Large rewards are given for high performance; small or no rewards are given for low performance. And whereas giving a low performer only small rewards may at first lead to dissatisfaction, it is expected that the individual will try to improve performance in order to get greater rewards in the future.

The point here is that managers should consider satisfaction and performance as two separate but interrelated work results that are affected by the allocation of rewards. Whereas job satisfaction alone is not a good predictor of work performance, well-managed rewards can have a positive influence on both satisfaction and performance.

INTEGRATED MODEL OF MOTIVATION

Figure 6.8 outlines the integrated view. Note that the figure has much in common with the two process theories just discussed: Vroom's expectancy theory and the Porter-Lawler model.[48] In the figure, job performance and job satisfaction are separate results of work efforts, but they are also potentially interdependent. Performance is influenced most directly by the individual attributes presented in Chapter 4: these include, for example, ability and experience, organizational support such as resources and technology, and work effort, which is when an individual's level of motivation has a direct impact. Individual motivation directly determines work effort, and the key to motivation is the ability to create a work setting that positively responds to individual needs and goals. Whether or not a work setting ends up being motivating for a particular individual depends on the availability of rewards and their perceived value to the individual, not to the person granting the reward. Note also the importance of contingent rewards, reflecting the law of contingent reinforcement, and the importance of immediacy in rewarding.

The content theories contribute to the model by giving an understanding of individual attributes and by identifying the needs that make the possible rewards motivating. When the individual gets intrinsic rewards for work performance, the individual's motivation will be directly affected and increase. Motivation can also occur when job satisfactions result from either extrinsic or intrinsic rewards that are felt to be given out equitably. Again the extrinsic reward is from the employer but if one is always given undesirable jobs, this can reduce motivation. When there is felt negative inequity, satisfaction will be low and motivation will drop. Recall that equity comparison is a key aspect of process theory.

Having read this discussion of reinforcement, content, and process theories, you should now have a better understanding of motivation. Although it will always be difficult to motivate employees, the knowledge in this chapter should help you reach toward higher performance and satisfaction. One final point is that the integrating model makes cultural assumptions, which means that the meaning of the concepts may therefore only be culturally specific. In later chapters, we will explore the cultural aspects of motivation and their implications for managers. The importance of various intrinsic and extrinsic rewards may vary from culture to culture, as may the aspects of performance that are highly valued.

Figure 6.8 An integrated model of individual motivation to work

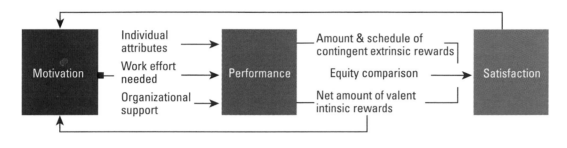

CHAPTER 6 STUDY GUIDE

Summary

What is motivation to work?

- Motivation refers to the forces inside an individual that lead to the level, direction, and persistence of the effort he or she makes at work.

- Reinforcement theories emphasize the means used in the process of controlling an individual's behaviour by manipulating its consequences. They focus on what can be observed rather than on what is going on inside an employee's head.

- Content theories, including the work of Maslow, Alderfer, McClelland, and Herzberg, focus on identifying individual needs that influence behaviour in the workplace.

- Process theories, such as equity theory and expectancy theory, examine the thought processes of people at work which affect their decisions about which actions to take.

What are reinforcement theories, and how are they linked to motivation?

- Reinforcement is based on the law of effect, which states that behaviour will be repeated or extinguished depending on whether the consequences are positive or negative.

- Positive reinforcement is the administration of positive consequences that tend to increase the likelihood that a person will repeat a specific behaviour in similar settings.

- Positive reinforcement should be contingent and immediate, and it can be scheduled continuously or intermittently, depending on the resources and desired outcomes.
- Negative reinforcement (avoidance) is used to encourage desirable behaviour by withdrawing negative consequences for previously undesirable behaviour.
- Punishment is the administration of negative consequences, or the withdrawal of positive consequences, which tends to reduce the likelihood of undesirable behaviour being repeated in similar settings.
- Extinction is the withdrawal of reinforcing consequences for a particular behaviour.

What do the content theories suggest about individual needs and motivation?

- Maslow's hierarchy of needs theory views human needs as being activated in a five-step hierarchy ranging from lowest to highest as follows: physiological needs, safety needs, social needs, esteem needs, and self-actualization needs.
- Alderfer's ERG theory reduces Maslow's five needs to three: needs for existence, relatedness, and growth; the theory maintains that more than one need can be activated at the same time.
- McClelland's acquired-needs theory focuses on the needs for achievement, affiliation, and power, and it views needs as developing over time through experience and training.
- Herzberg's two-factor theory links job dissatisfaction to hygiene factors associated with the job context, such as pay and working conditions.
- Herzberg's two-factor theory links job satisfaction to motivator factors associated with the job content, such as responsibility and challenge.

What do the process theories suggest about individual motivation?

- Equity theory points out that social comparisons take place when people receive rewards and that any felt inequity will motivate them to try to restore a sense of perceived equity or fairness.
- When felt inequity is negative, that is, when the individual feels unfairly treated, he or she may decide to work less hard in the future or to quit the job.
- Vroom's expectancy theory describes motivation as resulting from an individual's beliefs about effort—performance relationships (expectancy), work—outcome relationships (instrumentality), and the desirability of various work outcomes (valence).
- Expectancy theory states that Motivation = Expectancy $\times$ Instrumentality $\times$ Valence, and argues that managers should make each factor positive in order to ensure high levels of motivation.

How can satisfaction and its connection to performance help bring the insights of the motivational theories into an integrated motivational model?

- Job satisfaction is a work attitude that reflects how positively or negatively people feel about a job and its related aspects.
- Some common aspects of job satisfaction involve pay, working conditions, quality of supervision, co-workers, and the task itself.
- Research has shown that job satisfaction is related to employee turnover and absenteeism.
- The relationship between job satisfaction and performance is more controversial; currently, the focus is on how rewards influence both satisfaction and performance.
- Reinforcement views emphasize contingent rewards and how quickly these rewards are given.
- Content theories help identify important needs and determine what a person values as a reward.
- Equity theory argues that rewards must be perceived as equitable, or fair, in the social context of the workplace.
- Although motivation predicts work efforts, individual performance also depends on having abilities that are relevant to the job and organizational support.

Classical conditioning (p. 99)

Content theories (p. 98)

Continuous reinforcement (p. 101)

Equity theory (p. 109)

ERG theory (p. 106)

Existence needs (p. 106)

Expectancy (p. 110)

Expectancy theory (p. 110)

Extinction (p. 104)

Extrinsic rewards (p. 111)

Growth needs (p. 106)

Hierarchy of needs theory (p. 105)

Higher order needs (p. 106)

Hygiene factors (p. 108)

Instrumentality (p. 110)

Intermittent reinforcement (p. 101)

Intrinsic rewards (p. 111)

Job satisfaction (p. 112)

Law of contingent reinforcement (p. 101)

Law of effect (p. 100)

Law of immediate reinforcement (p. 101)

Lower order needs (p. 106)

Motivation (p. 97)

Motivator factors (p. 109)

Need for achievement (p. 107)

Need for affiliation (p. 107)

Need for power (p. 107)

Negative reinforcement (p. 103)

Operant conditioning (p. 99)

Organizational behaviour modification (OB Mod) (p. 100)

Positive reinforcement (p. 101)

Process theories (p. 98)

Punishment (p. 103)

Reinforcement (p. 98)

Reinforcement theories (p. 97)

Relatedness needs (p. 106)

Shaping (p. 101)

Stimulus (p. 99)

Two-factor theory (p. 108)

Valence (p. 110)

MULTIPLE CHOICE

1. Reinforcement emphasizes _____. (a) intrinsic rewards (b) extrinsic rewards (c) the law of diminishing returns (d) social learning

2. OB Mod reinforcement strategies _____. (a) have much carefully controlled research support (b) have been criticized because the observed results may confuse causality (c) are not used much in large firms (d) are useful mostly in large firms

3. Negative reinforcement _____. (a) is similar to punishment (b) seeks to discourage undesirable behaviour (c) seeks to encourage desirable behaviour (d) is also known as escapism

4. OB Mod emphasizes _____. (a) the systematic reinforcement of desirable work behaviour (b) noncontingent rewards (c) noncontingent punishment (d) extinction as being preferred over positive reinforcement

5. Reinforcement strategies _____. (a) violate ethical guidelines (b) involve the control of behaviour (c) work best when they restrict freedom of choice (d) have largely been replaced by computer technology

6. A content theory of motivation is most likely to focus on _____. (a) contingent reinforcement (b) instrumentalities (c) equities (d) individual needs

7. A person with a high need for affiliation is most likely to prefer _____ in his or her jobs. (a) group work (b) challenging goals (c) control over other people (d) little or no feedback

8. In equity theory, the _____ is a key issue. (a) social comparison of rewards and efforts (b) equality of rewards (c) equality of efforts (d) absolute value of rewards

9. In expectancy theory, _____ is the probability that a particular level of performance will lead to a particular work outcome. (a) expectancy (b) instrumentality (c) motivation (d) valence

10. Which statement about job satisfaction is most correct? (a) It causes performance. (b) It can affect turnover. (c) It cannot be measured. (d) It does not affect absenteeism.

TRUE–FALSE

11. Classical conditioning is another name for operant conditioning.   T   F

12. Because motivation is a universal concept, the theories apply equally well in all cultures.   T   F

13. The foundation for reinforcement is intrinsic rewards.   T   F

14. Reinforcement is the administration of a consequence as the result of behaviour.   T   F

15. OB Mod especially emphasizes the concepts of process and needs.   T   F

16. There is no equivalent to Maslow's social need in Aldefer's ERG theory.   T   F

17. In McClelland's acquired needs theory, a high need for socialized power results in the desire to control others in order to pursue group or organizational goals.   T   F

18. In equity theory, felt negative inequity is a motivating state, but felt positive inequity is not.   T   F

19. An extrinsic reward is a positively valued work outcome received directly by performing the task itself.   T   F

20. A reward is performance contingent when its size and value vary in proportion to the achieved performance level.   T   F

SHORT ANSWER

21. Briefly compare and contrast classical conditioning and operant conditioning.

22. Briefly discuss how reinforcement is linked to extrinsic rewards.

23. What is the frustration—regression component in Alderfer's ERG theory?

24. What is the multiplier effect in expectancy theory?

APPLICATIONS ESSAY

25. While attending a business luncheon, you overhear the following conversation at a nearby table. Person A: "I'll tell you this—if you make your workers happy they'll be productive." Person B: "I'm not so sure. If I make them happy, maybe they'll be real good about coming to work but not very good about working really hard while they're there." Which person do you agree with and why?

Human Resource Management Systems

Abilities, Certification, and Experience

The National Bank of Canada is the sixth largest bank in Canada, with more than 16,000 employees, assets of over $83 billion, 472 branches, and customers across the globe. In the last few years, the bank has increasingly used the Internet as a tool in its asset-based and commercial banking business, resulting in improved customer service levels and significant cost savings.

However, even as its customer service venues became more and more automated, the bank's recruiting methods were still almost 100 percent paper-based and relied on advertising in local newspapers, trade magazines, and referrals. As the National Bank of Canada was receiving more than 26,000 resumés per year from job seekers, a process was needed to efficiently identify potential employees, as well as to develop the employees already in the company. The basic in-house system stored only the name and contact information of some candidates, while at the same time other contacts were still stored as paper resumés in filing cabinets. The bank needed to develop an attractive front-end career website that would be well integrated with the back end in order to engineer the entire staffing process while also providing strategic benefits throughout the organization.

Enter Taleo. Founded in 1998 as Recruitsoft, the Quebec-based firm offers recruiting and talent-deployment software designed to help sizeable companies manage and optimize their hiring systems. Taleo's Internet management and WebTop suites handle job requisitions, resumés, and pre-screening of candidate communications, all of which results in more time for interactions with potential employees and less time on administrative tasks. The software enables hiring staff to translate job requirements into questions and required skills, then effectively pre-screen large volumes of candidates according to their Abilities, Certifications, and Experience (ACE). Taleo helps its clients implement the ACE system by doing a complete review of current

business practices, by finding a solution that fits the organization's structure and processes, and finally by developing a skills-based platform for complete staffing management, from entry to redeployment.

With the system overhaul:

- the staffing process has moved from being paper-based to skills-based, building a pool of over 25,000 candidates
- candidates are efficiently pre-screened and sourced, allowing recruiters to spend less time on administrative tasks and more time with candidates
- the average time-to-hire for first-level management positions declined by 50 percent
- the average cost-per-hire declined significantly, allowing financial resources to be strategically redeployed throughout the HR department as it grew its workforce by more than 30 percent
- the service level to candidates and hiring managers has improved significantly

Louise Desjardins, director of recruitment, states, "We were surprised how much Taleo had to offer and had no idea that we would find something so robust when we set out to re-engineer our staffing processes. From the very beginning, Taleo's company vision was in line with our business objectives."

Management of human resources and employee rewards are increasingly important in the new workplace. As you read Chapter 7, keep in mind these key questions:

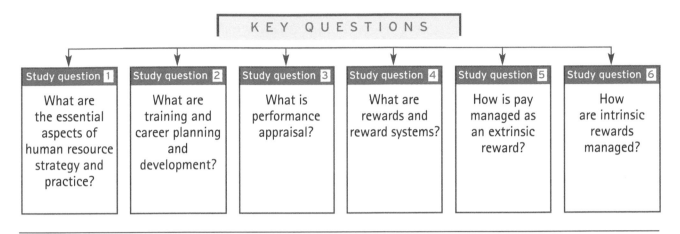

KEY QUESTIONS

Study question 1	Study question 2	Study question 3	Study question 4	Study question 5	Study question 6
What are the essential aspects of human resource strategy and practice?	What are training and career planning and development?	What is performance appraisal?	What are rewards and reward systems?	How is pay managed as an extrinsic reward?	How are intrinsic rewards managed?

Human Resource Strategy and Practice

Human resource (HR) strategic planning is the process of providing capable and motivated people who will carry out the organization's mission and strategy. A key part of this process is the staffing function. It involves (1) the recruitment of employees: getting people to apply for jobs in the organization; (2) selection: making hiring decisions for each applicant; and (3) socialization: orienting newly hired employees (hires) to the organization.[1] This function is a critical part of an organization's job requirements: the employee–characteristics match stressed in Chapter 4. Once an HR staffing strategy is established, managers must continue to assess current HR needs to make sure that the organization keeps the people it needs in order to meet its strategic objectives.[2] Matching the HR staffing strategy to the organization's strategy ensures that the correct employee is hired to do the correct job and so helps the organization follow its strategy and attain its goals. This notion will be discussed again in Chapter 12.

Human resource strategic planning is the process of providing capable and motivated people who will carry out the organization's mission and strategy.

JOB ANALYSIS

Staffing begins with an understanding of the positions (jobs) which the organization needs to have individuals doing. **Job analysis** provides this information; it is the process and procedures used to collect and classify information about tasks the organization needs to complete.[3] Job analysis makes it easier to understand the job activities a work process requires. Job analysis thus helps define jobs, how they relate to other jobs, and the demographic, aptitude and ability, and personality characteristics which people need to have to do these jobs. The results can be used in job descriptions, job evaluation and classification, training and career development, performance appraisal, and other HR aspects. Information about the job itself is specified in the job description. The job description typically contains such information as job duties and responsibilities, equipment and materials used, working conditions and hazards, type of supervision, work schedules, standards of performance, and relationships to other jobs.[4]

Job analysis is the procedure used to collect and classify information about tasks the organization needs to complete.

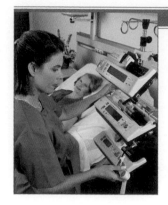

OB Across Functions

Medical Operations

The Alphabet Soup of Medical Care

In the old days, so they say, one warm and caring physician handled many problems and even made house calls. Those days are no more, if they ever were. Now, many people find the "alphabet soup" medical jargon of today overwhelming. The Canadian Nursing Association and the Canadian Physiotherapy Association, among other health-care providers, talk about NPs, PAs, PTs, OTs, and how they and others must work together for the patient's good. An NP is a Nurse Practitioner, someone who performs many traditional nurse and physician functions, along with physician assistants (PAs). Their tasks include, among others, taking medical histories and giving examinations. Both of these health-care providers work closely with registered nurses (RNs) in hospitals and in providing home health care. People in rehabilitation are likely to see physical therapists (PTs) and occupational therapists (OTs), who help restore daily living skills. These days, in addition to saying "aah," patients must be on top of lots of medical alphabet soup jargon to understand the team-oriented care they are getting.

After being determined in the job analysis, the worker characteristics that are needed to do the job and are specified in the job description are next stated in a job specification. For example, a safety supervisor must have knowledge of safety regulations. The job requirements and minimum qualifications are the job specification part of the job analysis.

In addition to making other important contributions, the job analysis helps organizations deal with legal requirements thanks to its description of the job content and how important some of the job duties and responsibilities are compared to others. This information is useful if legal challenges that allege discrimination or unfairness make it necessary to defend some of the company's actions. The standard defense against a charge of discrimination is that the decision being challenged (e.g., hiring someone, providing a pay raise, firing someone) was made for job-related reasons determined by the job analysis. For example, if job analysis finds that a firefighter may have to carry an 80 kg person from a burning building, this finding can help a city defend itself against sex discrimination if it chooses not to hire a woman who is unable to lift 80 kg.[5]

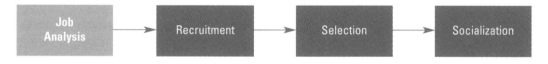

Job Analysis → Recruitment → Selection → Socialization

RECRUITMENT

Once job analysis has identified the necessary job requirements and employee characteristics, qualified people need to be attracted and encouraged to apply for various positions. **Recruitment** is the process of attracting and getting the best qualified individuals to apply for a particular job.[6]

It typically involves (1) advertisement of a position vacancy, (2) initial contact with potential job candidates, and (3) a first screening to obtain a pool of candidates. National Bank follows a variation of these steps in its hiring practices. These three steps are an example of external recruitment, which is the process of attracting individuals from outside the organization. External recruitment occurs through many different ways, including general advertisements, often in newspapers, trade journals, or via Internet; word-of-mouth suggestions from current employees; use of employment agencies; and applicant walk-ins. By contrast, internal recruitment is the process of attracting job applicants from those individuals already working for the firm. Posting vacant positions on bulletin boards, in internal memos, and over intranets are ways frequently used to recruit internally.

Recruitment is the process of attracting and getting the best qualified individuals to apply for a job.

Martin Ouellet and Louis Tetu founded Recruitsoft, now Taleo, in 1998 in Quebec City to assist visionary Fortune 500 companies such as Toyota, HP, and Proctor and Gamble develop on-line solutions to their recruiting problems. Many companies that hire over 1,000 people per year, some over 10,000 people, have recognized that the application of value-chain management techniques in manufacturing can be applied to recruiting and talent-management areas. Louis Tetu, who believes that the CEO of an organization should focus on deploying assets to maximize the return on assets, thought this principle could also be applied to people. And that is exactly what Taleo helps large firms accomplish. The company and its software is so much in demand that offices have been opened in Toronto, New York, Paris, Amsterdam, Singapore, and the UK since 1999. Revenue at Taleo grew by 11% per month throughout 2002—all by helping companies manage their hiring process.

www.taleo.com

Most firms tend to use a mix of external and internal recruitment. Some organizations, notably the armed forces, rely heavily on external recruitment for entry-level positions and then fill higher-level positions entirely from internal promotions. Both approaches have advantages. Internal recruitment is encouraging to current employees, and external recruitment tends to bring "new blood" and fresh ideas to an organization.

Traditionally, firms have attempted to "sell" their organization and jobs in order to strengthen the applicant pool. More recently, an increasingly popular approach called the **realistic job preview** is being used. In a realistic job preview, applicants are given an objective description of the prospective organization and job. These descriptions have been found to reduce turnover and to better prepare new hires to handle their jobs.[7]

> **Realistic job previews** give applicants an objective description of a job and organization.

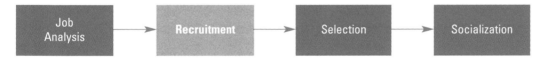

SELECTION

Once an applicant pool has been recruited, the selection aspect of staffing begins. **Selection** is the series of steps from initial applicant screening to final hiring of the new employee. The selection process involves reviewing completed application materials, conducting an interview, administering any necessary tests, doing a background investigation, and deciding to hire or not to hire.

> **Selection** is the series of steps from initial applicant screening to final hiring.

Application Materials These materials could include a traditional application form that asks for information about various aspects of a person's background and experience. These forms may be in traditional paper format or accessed through the Internet. Sometimes resumés (brief summaries of a person's background and qualifications) are used instead of, or in addition to, other materials. Tests may also be part of the application materials.

Employment Interviews You may have experienced employment interviews at one time or another. Interviews are almost always used in the selection process (see The Effective Manager 7.1), although they can be affected by the kinds of perceptual distortions discussed in Chapter 5, as well as other problems. Nevertheless, they are a standard part of the selection process, perhaps because they can serve as public relations tools for the organization. At their best, interviews provide rough ideas about how well an individual will fit the job and organization.[8]

The Effective Manager 7.1

STEPS TO EMPHASIZE IN HIRING INTERVIEWS

- Prepare yourself—check the applicant's resumé and prepare an agenda.
- First put the applicant at ease—use small talk.
- Guard against stereotypes—emphasize the applicant as an individual.
- Emphasize results-oriented questions—focus not only on what the applicant has done but on the results of these actions.
- Allow for pauses to gather thoughts.
- Bring the interview to a natural close.

Tests   Tests may be administered either before or after the interview. They include cognitive aptitude or ability tests, personality tests, and, increasingly, tests for drug use. Intelligence tests are the most common examples of cognitive tests. Other examples are clerical and mechanical tests. Personality tests evaluate the kinds of personality characteristics discussed in Chapter 4. For example, the California Personality Inventory measures such characteristics as dominance, sociability, and flexibility. Again, any test that is used must be validated by the job requirements; otherwise the organization may be found guilty of discrimination.

There are many types of performance tests, but in general they ask candidates to perform tasks that are identical to or at least closely related to what will be required on the job. As technology has become more important, performance tests involving computer skills have become more common. Also, a series of tests is often used to explore a range of job behaviours.

For managerial jobs in particular, but increasingly for other jobs as well, *assessment centres* are often used. Assessment centres give a firm a comprehensive view of a candidate by evaluating the candidate's performance in many situations. Such assessments typically involve one to four days of various tests, simulations, role-plays, and interviews. These are all based on dimensions the person occupying the job will need to demonstrate. The Public Service Commission of Canada provides a variety of assessment centres for positions ranging from directors, to senior executives, to middle management to management trainees.[9] Nortel, SunLife, and police forces are also among the organizations that use assessment centres for managerial selection and promotion.[10]

Background Investigation   Background investigation is another step that can be used in the selection process, either early on or later. Companies which do background audits say requests for their services have jumped sharply since the World Trade Center disaster. Hospitals, retailers, and firms that own private jets have been especially interested. Two-thirds of employers check on potential hires. Basic checks often include a verification of the candidate's employment history, educational records, criminal records, and driving records.

Typically, a background investigation also involves reference checks. Generally, reference letters tend to be positively biased and so are not highly related to job performance.[11] Moreover, unless the references, either written or provided over the phone, are very carefully worded, they can lead to lawsuits. References should only disclose information about the job duties the individual has been performing. Any personal descriptions should involve only information that can be objectively verified.

Decision to Hire   Based on the results of the previous steps, the organization may choose to make the hiring decision and present a formal job offer to the candidate. The offer may be made by the potential employee's future boss or by a group of people. At this point, the individual may be asked to undergo a physical examination if it is shown to be relevant to performing the job. For some jobs, negotiations concerning salary or other benefits may also now occur.

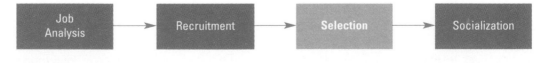

SOCIALIZATION

Socialization means orienting new employees to the firm and its work units.

Once hiring is completed, **socialization** is the final step in the staffing process. It involves orienting new employees to the firm and specifically to the work units in which they will be working. At this stage, the new employee is familiarized with the firm's policies and procedures and begins to understand the organization's culture. Orientation can be done formally or informally, or it may involve a combination of the two. In more complex jobs or positions, orientation can last an extended period of time. Socialization can help with the matching of job requirements and employee characteristics by filling in some gaps.

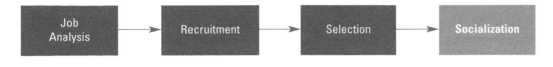

Training and Career Development

After an employee is hired, it is important that he or she undergo training and long-term career planning and development.

TRAINING

Training is a set of activities that provides the opportunity to acquire and improve job-related skills.[12] In addition to initial training, training to improve skills is important and might be for such areas as computer skills, awareness of diversity and sexual harassment issues, and the implementation of new systems or technology.

Training can be on the job, off the job, or both. *On-the-job training* (OJT) involves job instruction as the job is being done in the actual workplace. Internships, apprenticeships, and job rotation are common forms of OJT. *Internships* are an opportunity for students to gain real-world experience. They are often offered in the summer and may or may not be paid. *Apprenticeships* involve learning a trade from an experienced worker. They are quite common in Europe and relatively less common in Canada. Coaching or mentoring programs for managerial and professional jobs—which in some ways are like apprenticeships—are, however, quite common in Canada, the U.S., and other industrialized nations. *Job rotation* provides a broad range of experience in different kinds of jobs in a firm. It is often used as part of management training programs where future managers may spend from a few weeks to much longer in activities such as information processing, computer software usage, or computer sales. The total program could last up to one or two years, with varying amounts of mentoring.

Off-the-job training commonly involves lectures, videos, and simulations. E-training is becoming more popular. It includes classes or information modules delivered via computer or the Internet that may be completed at any time or place. It also includes group workshops offered through "virtual classroom" distance-learning technologies. Lectures give specific information and work well for problem-solving and technical skills. Videos are particularly good for demonstrating various skills. Simulations, such as experiential exercises, business games, and various computer-based exercises, are particularly useful for teaching interpersonal, leadership, and strategic management skills, as well as other complex skills, such as those required of police officers.

Rogers Communications Inc.'s "Customer Care Centres" located across the country provide complete on-the-job training to newly hired employees. The only requirements listed on its job advertisements are "individuals who are committed to providing outstanding customer service, have a keen interest in technology and troubleshooting, and who thrive in a fun, fast-paced, energetic, and team-based environment." New customer service consultants spend their first eight to ten weeks with the company in a comprehensive full-time, in-house training program that combines in-class and on-the-job training. In addition to this initial training program, employees also receive regular on-the-job mentoring and coaching.

Training provides the opportunity to acquire and improve job-related skills.

Job Rotation

www.waltecplastics.com

Baytech Plastics (of Midland, Ontario) engineers, manufactures, finishes, and assembles custom-molded plastic components. Its customers include manufacturers of household appliances, telecommunications equipment, electrical and electronic equipment, business machines, and automotive components, among others. Baytech uses self-directed job rotation to keep employees interested and challenged in their work. In its cellular manufacturing assembly operation, employees rotate jobs every two to four hours, as decided by the employee group. This employee-directed work practice, in which employees plan and execute tasks, eases the distribution and exchange of skills and knowledge throughout the plant. [13]

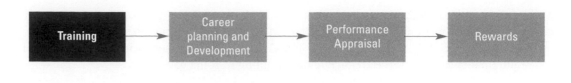

CAREER PLANNING AND DEVELOPMENT

In addition to being concerned about employee training for short-term jobs, both the employee and the organization need to be concerned about long-term career planning and development, in which individuals work with their managers and/or HR experts on career issues.[14]

Figure 7.1 Five steps in formal career planning

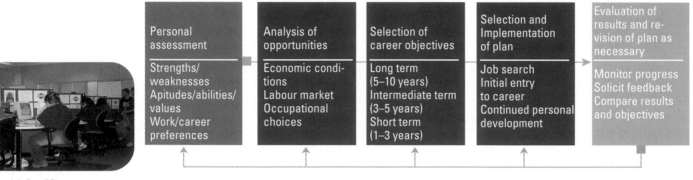

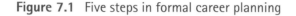

Rapid Staffing

www.onlinesupport.com

The changing nature of work is illustrated by On-Line Support (OLS), a P.E.I.-based call centre operator that provides customer relationship management services to a variety of clients, typically Internet or telephone service providers. Often OLS has to increase its staff complement very quickly. For example, OLS could get a call from an existing client asking for 20 or 30 more representatives within two to three months to aid with a specific marketing campaign. The company proudly claims it has launched new contact centres within in 60 days, and its Sprint Canada Customer Care centre was launched in 45 days.

Figure 7.1 shows a basic five-step framework for formal career planning. The process begins with personal assessment and then progresses through the analysis of opportunities, selection of career objectives, and implementation of strategies, to the final step, an evaluation of the results. The process is reused as necessary so that the career plan can be revised over time. Success in each of these steps requires a lot of self-awareness and honest assessment. Thus, a successful career begins with having enough insight to make good decisions about matching personal needs and capabilities with job opportunities over time. The manager's responsibility in career planning involves, first, planning and managing his or her own career and, second, helping subordinates become responsible for their own career planning and development.

Thoughts about careers are particularly relevant in the new workplace. We live and work in a time when the implications of constant change pressure us to continually review and reassess our career progress. Businesses are becoming smaller, are employing fewer people, and are moving beyond traditional organizational forms. Thus, there is more and more emphasis on horizontal and cross-functional relationships. Technical workers are becoming so important that they are being treated almost like high-level managers in terms of perquisites and rewards. The nature of "work" is changing and will be less bound by "nine-to-five" traditions. Continuous learning will be required, making training and electronic-education marketplaces more and more important.

In today's work setting, the old notion of having an entire career in a single organization that takes responsibility for a person's career development is becoming increasingly obsolete. In his book *The Age of Unreason*, British scholar and consultant Charles Handy argues forcefully that each of us must take charge of our own careers and prepare for inevitable uncertainties and changes by building a "portfolio" of skills.[15] This portfolio needs continuous development: each new job assignment must be well selected and rigorously pursued as a learning opportunity.

Initial Entry to a Career What a person needs to do in order to do well in the new workplace begins at the point of initial entry to a career. Choosing a job and a work organization are difficult decisions; our jobs inevitably exert a lot of influence over our lives. Whenever a job change is considered, the best advice is to know yourself and to learn as much as possible about the new job and the organization. This helps ensure the best possible match between you, the job, and the organization. By working hard to examine your personal needs, goals, and capabilities and to gather relevant information, share your views, and otherwise make the recruitment process as realistic as possible, you can help start a new job on the best possible note.

When considering a new job or a possible job change, a "balance sheet" analysis of possible "gains" and "losses" is important. Ask yourself at least two questions. First, what are my potential gains and losses? Things to consider in answering this question include salary and fringe benefits, work hours and schedules, travel requirements, use and development of skills and competencies, and opportunities for challenging new job assignments. Second, what are the potential gains and losses for significant others in my life? Here, you should consider the income available for family responsibilities, the time available to be with family and friends, the impact of a geographical move on your family and friends, and the implications of work stress for your nonwork life.

Adult Life Cycle and Career Stages Chapter 4 showed that as people mature they pass through an adult life cycle with many different problems and prospects. As a manager, it is especially important to recognize the effects of this cycle on the people you work with. Recall that the earlier-mentioned life cycle stages popularized by Gail Sheehy were as follows: provisional adulthood (ages 18 to 30), first adulthood (ages 30 to 45), and second adulthood (ages 45 to 85+).[16] These are only approximate ages, and there are transitional periods in moving from one stage to the next.

In our current era of constant change, the stages and transitions have become much less predictable than in earlier years. In the past, a person generally had one or two careers and a single spouse, but now it is common for individuals to have numerous careers and either no spouse or more than one spouse. In the provisional-adulthood period, people may move back with their parents, stretch out their education, and try many jobs, for example. And where people once retired at age 65, many are retiring at an earlier age to pursue other interests and activities.

It is useful to link the adult life cycle literature to the **career stages** literature. For those people who still follow a traditional career path, their career can be viewed as consisting of entry and establishment, which is roughly similar to the provisional-adulthood stage; advancement, similar to the first-adulthood stage; and maintenance, withdrawal, and retirement, similar to the second-adulthood stage.

Entry and establishment involve on-the-job development of relevant skills and abilities. Individuals also undergo the organizational and professional socialization mentioned earlier. At the same time, progressive organizations also actively mentor new employees.

In the advancement stage, the individual seeks growth and increased responsibility. There may be advancement through internal career paths within the organization or through external career paths outside the organization.

During the maintenance, withdrawal, and retirement stage of second adulthood, individuals may continue to add to their accomplishments or they may become more stable in their careers. Many people encounter a **career plateau**—they find themselves in a position from which they are unlikely to advance to a higher level of responsibility.

At some point during the maintenance career stage, individuals consider withdrawal and final retirement. Some of them prolong this stage well into the second-adulthood life cycle stage. Others start planning for an orderly retirement at about age 65.

Health-Care Pros

A key aspect of advancing through various career stages is continuing education. Nowhere is such education more important than in the health-care industry. For example, physicians who are members of the Royal College of Physicians and Surgeons of Canada must complete a minimum of 40 hours of continuing professional development annually, or a minimum of 400 credits during a 5-year cycle. All health-care professions recommend continuing education, and specialists require continuing education to maintain their specialization. Not surprisingly, there are more than 1,000 companies and colleges providing such training across North America.

Career stages are the different points of work responsibility and achievement which people pass through during their work lives.

A **career plateau** is a position from which someone is unlikely to advance to a higher level of responsibility.

Of course, as we have said, the traditional route just described is no longer typical. People may have many jobs and more than one career and they may choose to only retire when they can no longer work. All of these changes make it harder for managers to build and maintain a subordinate's commitment to the job and organization, thus creating many OB challenges.

Performance Appraisal

Performance appraisal is the process of systematically evaluating an employee's performance and providing feedback on which performance adjustments can be made.

Another key HR management function, the **performance appraisal**, helps both the manager and subordinate maintain the organization–job–employee characteristics match. Formally defined, performance appraisal is the process of systematically evaluating an employee's performance and providing feedback on which performance adjustments can be made.[17] If the desired level of performance is greater than the employee's actual level of performance, there is a performance variance and special attention becomes necessary. For example, if you have a sales quota of 20 CD-ROM drives per month (the desired performance) and you sell only two CD-ROM drives per month (your actual performance), your performance variance of 18 CD-ROMS will require the attention of the sales manager. The performance-appraisal process should be based on the job analysis mentioned earlier. The job description, which describes organizational job requirements, and the job specification, which describes individual worker characteristics, provide the basis for the evaluation.

PURPOSES OF PERFORMANCE APPRAISAL

Performance-appraisal systems are a central part of an organization's human-resource management activities. Performance appraisals are intended to:

Purposes of performance appraisal

- define the specific job criteria against which performance will be measured

- measure past job performance accurately

- justify the rewards given to individuals and/or groups, thereby discriminating between high and low performance

- define the development experiences the rated employee needs to undergo in order to improve performance in the current job and prepare for future responsibilities

These four functions describe two general purposes of good performance-appraisal systems: evaluation, and feedback and development. In terms of evaluation, performance appraisals let people know how well they are doing relative to objectives and standards. In this context, performance appraisals provide input for decisions about giving out rewards and running the organization's personnel functions. In terms of feedback and development, performance appraisals provide information that can support decisions involving planning for and remaining committed to the continued training and personal development of subordinates.

Evaluative Decisions   Evaluative decisions involve such issues as promotions, transfers, terminations, and salary increases. When these decisions are made on the basis of performance criteria, as opposed to some other basis (e.g., seniority), a performance-appraisal system is necessary.

Performance-appraisal information is also useful for making selection and placement decisions. In this case, performance results are matched against personal characteristics to determine which of these characteristics are most closely related to performance. For example, management checks characteristics such as education, mathematical ability, verbal ability, mechanical ability, and achievement motivation, to see how closely they are related to performance. Individuals who score well on the characteristics that have been found to be closely tied to performance for a specific job are then considered for that position. In addition, if specific aspects of an employee's performance are found to be inadequate, the performance-appraisal process may lead to remedial training so that the individual can perform better. Finally, appraisals are a basic part of any performance-contingent reward system (i.e., any system that ties rewards, such as pay, to an individual's or group's performance).

In Canada, if an organization decides to dismiss an employee, "just cause" must be substantiated. Not only must the employee first be permitted to review the negative performance evaluation, the employer and employee must also try to correct the shortcomings through better training and effort, respectively. In addition, the employee needs to be given a reasonable amount of time to respond to the poor evaluation. If the dismissal is due to misconduct, the employee must then be given a chance to correct the misconduct, unless the misconduct involves an illegal act. It is important to respect these requirements as no employer wants to see a former employee visiting the employment standards office or a labour lawyer.

Feedback and Development Decisions   Performance appraisals can also be used to let employees know how well they are doing relative to the organization's expectations and performance objectives. Performance-appraisal feedback should involve a detailed discussion of the employee's job-related strengths and weaknesses. This feedback can then be used for the individual's development. In terms of the expectancy motivation approach discussed in Chapter 6, feedback can help clarify the rated employee's sense of both instrumentality (it can help employees better understand what kinds of rewards they will receive if they perform well) and expectancy (it lets them know what actions they need to take to reach the desired level of performance and how likely they are to reach it). Performance-appraisal feedback can also be used by a manager as a basis for individual coaching or training to help a subordinate overcome performance deficiencies. Surveys typically indicate that around two-thirds of the sampled firms use performance appraisals to develop their employees.

WHO DOES THE PERFORMANCE APPRAISAL?

Performance appraisals have traditionally been done by an individual's immediate superior.[18] The assumption has been that since the immediate superior is responsible for the subordinate's performance, the superior should do the appraisal. In many cases, however, others may be better at doing at least some aspects of the appraisal. For example, peers are closest to the action, and their appraisals can be especially valuable when several peers are consulted. A rated employee's immediate subordinates can also provide insightful evaluations as long as the ratings remain anonymous.

To obtain as much appraisal information as possible, many organizations are now using not only the evaluations of bosses, peers, and subordinates, but also self-ratings, customer ratings, and ratings from other individuals whom the rated employee has contact with outside the immediate work unit. Such a comprehensive approach is called a **360-degree evaluation**. The number of appraisals typically ranges from five to ten for each person being evaluated. Firms such as Enbridge, Intuit, and Joseph Brant Hospital in Burlington, Ontario, now use 360-degree evaluations. They are ideal for the new, flatter, team-oriented organizations emphasizing total quality or high-performance management, for which input from many

The 360–degree evaluation is a comprehensive approach that uses self-ratings, customer ratings, and ratings from others who are outside the work unit.

sources is crucial. Moreover, computer technology can now make it easier to collect and analyze some or all of these 360-degree evaluations.[19]

One example of an innovative way in which computer technology is helpful involves the use of self-ratings and ratings by superiors. The subordinate rates how important a specific job function is to their own performance and how well the subordinate thinks he or she is performing the function. The supervisor does a similar evaluation of the employee. A computer program then compares the results and highlights those areas on which there is the most disagreement. Only the associate gets the printout of the results and may choose to discuss these areas with the supervisor. Both the timing and the specific content of such a meeting are decided by the subordinate.[20]

PERFORMANCE APPRAISAL DIMENSIONS AND STANDARDS

In addition to focusing on performance outcomes, performance appraisals also often make the behaviours or activities that result in these outcomes an important part of the evaluation.

Output Measures   The work output of many production and sales jobs is fairly easy to measure. For example, a final-stage assembler may have a goal of 15 completed computer monitors per hour. The number of monitors is easily measurable, and the organization can set standards for how many computer monitors should be completed per hour. Here, the performance dimension that is being focused on is a quantitative one: 15 completed computer monitors per hour. However, the organization also may introduce a quality dimension. The individual may be evaluated for not only of the number of monitors per hour but also the number of units that pass a *quality control inspection* per hour. Now, both quantity and quality are important, and the individual cannot trade one for the other. Assembling 20 monitors per hour will not be good if only 10 pass inspection, nor will having a higher percentage of monitors pass inspection if only 10 monitors are assembled each hour.

Management may also be interested in other performance dimensions, such as the downtime of the equipment used for assembling. In this case, the assembler would be evaluated in terms of the quantity and quality of assembly output and the equipment downtime. This would allow management to ensure not only that a desirable product is being assembled at a desirable rate but also that the employee is being careful with the equipment as well.

Activity Measures   In the preceding example, the output measures were straightforward, as was the measure of equipment downtime. Often, however, output measures may depend on group efforts, they may be extremely difficult to measure, or they may take so long to accomplish that they cannot be easily determined for a specific individual during a specific time period. For example, it may be very difficult to determine the output of a research scientist attempting to advance a company's knowledge. In such a case, activity or behavioural measures may be necessary, rather than output measures. The research scientist may be appraised in terms of his or her approach to problems, his or her interactions with other scientists, and so on.

Activity measures are typically obtained from the evaluator's observation and rating. In contrast, output measures are often obtained directly from written records or documents, such as production records. The difficulty of obtaining output measures may be one reason for using activity measures. Activity measures are also typically more useful for employee feedback and development than are output measures only. For example, a salesperson may sell 20 insurance policies a month when the quota is 25. However, activities such as the number of sales calls per day or number of community volunteer events attended per week (where some potential clients are likely to be found) can provide more specific information than simply the percentage of monthly quota output measures. For jobs which are easily put to a systematic analysis, the job analysis helps determine which activities are important.

PERFORMANCE-APPRAISAL METHODS

Performance-appraisal methods can be divided into two general categories: comparative methods and absolute methods.[21]

Comparative methods of performance appraisal try to identify how well an employee is doing compared to other employees who are being rated. In other words, for a particular performance dimension, comparative methods can establish that Bill is better than Mary, who is better than Leslie, who is better than Tom, and so on. Although comparative methods can indicate that one person is better than another on a specific dimension, they do not indicate how much better. These methods also fail to indicate if the person being rated is "good enough" in an absolute sense. It may be that Bill is merely the best of a group of underperforming employees. Three comparative performance-appraisal methods are (1) ranking, (2) paired comparison, and (3) forced distribution.

In contrast, absolute methods of performance appraisal specify precise measurement standards. For example, tardiness might be evaluated on a scale ranging from "never tardy" to "always tardy." Four of the more common absolute rating procedures are (1) graphic rating scales, (2) critical incident diaries, (3) behaviourally anchored rating scales, and (4) management by objectives. The comparative methods are less likely to be used than absolute measures in more collectivist-oriented cultures because of these cultures' emphasis on the collectivity.

Ranking   Ranking is the simplest of all the comparative techniques. It consists of merely rank ordering each individual from best to worst on each performance dimension being considered. For example, in evaluating work quality, I compare Smith, Jones, and Brown. I then rank Brown number one, Smith number two, and Jones number three. The ranking method, though relatively simple to use, can become burdensome when there are many people to consider.

Paired Comparison   In a paired-comparison method, each person is directly compared to every person being rated. The number of times a person gets a better rating across all pairs determines the person's final ranking. Every possible paired comparison within a group of individuals being rated is considered, as shown below (italics indicate the person rated better in each pair):

Bill vs. Mary   *Mary* vs. Leslie   *Leslie* vs. Tom

Bill vs. Leslie   *Mary* vs. Tom

Bill vs. Tom

Number of times Bill is better   =   3
Number of times Mary is better   =   2
Number of times Leslie is better   =   1
Number of times Tom is better   =   0

The best performer in this example is Bill, followed by Mary, then Leslie, and, last of all, Tom. When there are many people to compare, the paired comparison approach can be even more tedious than the ranking method.

Forced Distribution   Forced distribution uses a small number of performance categories, such as "very good," "good," "adequate," "poor," and "very poor." Each rater is instructed to rate a specific proportion of employees as belonging to each of these categories. For example, 10 percent of employees must be rated "very good", 20 percent must be rated "good", and so on. This method forces the rater to use all of the categories and to avoid rating everyone as very good or very poor, for example. It can be a problem if most of the people are truly superior performers or if most of the people perform about the same.

Ranking is a comparative technique of performance appraisal that involves rank ordering of each individual from best to worst on each performance dimension.

Paired comparison is a comparative method of performance appraisal in which each person is directly compared to every other person.

Forced distribution is a method of performance appraisal that uses a small number of performance categories, such as "very good," "good," "adequate," and "very poor" and forces a certain proportion of people into each.

A graphic rating scale is a scale that lists a variety of dimensions that are thought to be related to high performance outcomes in a specific job and that the individual is expected to exhibit.

Graphic Rating Scales **Graphic rating scales** list a variety of dimensions that are thought to be related to high performance outcomes in a specific job and that the individual is expected to exhibit, such as co-operation, initiative, attendance, and so on. The scales allow the manager to assign the individual scores on each dimension. An example is shown in Figure 7.2. These ratings are sometimes given point values and then combined to produce a numerical rating of an employee's performance.

The main appeal of graphic rating scales is how easy they are to use. They also use time and other resources efficiently, and they can be applied to a wide range of jobs. Unfortunately, because of generality, they may not be linked to job analysis or to other specific aspects of a particular job. This difficulty can be overcome by ensuring that only relevant dimensions of work that are based on sound job analysis procedures are rated. However, there is a trade-off: the more the scales are linked to job analyses, the less general they are for comparing people doing different jobs.

Figure 7.2 Sixth-month performance reviews for Burroughs and Watson

Employee: Jayne burroughs — Supervisor: Dr. cutter
Department: Pathology — Date: 11-28-02

Work Quantity		Work Quantity		Cooperation	
1. Far below average	___	1. Far below average	___	1. Far below average	___
2. Below average	✓	2. Below average	___	2. Below average	✓
3. Average	___	3. Average	✓	3. Average	___
4. Above average	___	4. Above average	___	4. Above average	___
5. Far above average	___	5. Far above average	___	5. Far above average	___

Employee: John Watson — Supervisor: Dr. cutter
Department: Pathology — Date: 12-24-02

Work Quantity		Work Quantity		Cooperation	
1. Far below average	___	1. Far below average	___	1. Far below average	___
2. Below average	___	2. Below average	___	2. Below average	___
3. Average	✓	3. Average	___	3. Average	___
4. Above average	___	4. Above average	✓	4. Above average	___
5. Far above average	___	5. Far above average	___	5. Far above average	✓

A critical incident diary is a method of performance appraisal that records incidents of unusual success or failure in a specific performance aspect.

Critical Incident Diary Supervisors may use **critical incident diaries** to record incidents of each subordinate's behaviour that led to either unusual success or failure in a specific performance aspect. These incidents are typically recorded in a diary-type log that is kept daily or weekly for pre-selected dimensions. In a sales job, for example, following up sales calls and communicating necessary customer information might be two of the dimensions recorded in a critical incident diary. Descriptive paragraphs can then be used to summarize each salesperson's performance for each dimension as the behaviour is observed.

This approach is excellent for employee development and feedback. Since the method consists of qualitative statements rather than quantitative information, however, it is difficult to use for evaluative decisions. To obtain quantitative information, the critical incident technique is sometimes combined with one of the other methods.

Behaviourally Anchored Rating Scales   The behaviourally anchored rating scale (BARS) is a performance appraisal approach that is becoming more popular. The procedure for developing this type of scale starts with the careful collection of descriptions of observable job behaviours. These descriptions are typically provided by managers and personnel specialists, and the descriptions are of both superior and inferior performance. Once a large sample of behavioural descriptions is collected, each behaviour is evaluated to determine how much it describes good versus bad performance. The final step is to develop a rating scale in which the anchors are specific critical behaviours, with each behaviour reflecting a different degree of performance effectiveness. An example of a BARS is shown in Figure 7.3 for a retail department manager. Note how specific the behaviours are and the scale values for each behaviour. Similar behaviourally anchored rating scales would be developed for other dimensions of the job.

A behaviourally anchored rating scale (BARS) is a performance appraisal approach that describes observable job behaviours, each of which is evaluated to determine good versus bad performance.

Figure 7.3   Example of a behaviourally anchored rating scale dimension

Supervising Sales Personnel
Gives sales personnel a clear idea of their job duties and responsibilities; exercises tact and consideration in working with subordinates; handles work scheduling efficiently and equitably; supplements formal training with his or her own "coaching;" keeps informed of what the salespeople are doing on the job; and follows company policy in agreements with subordinates.

Effective	9	Could be expected to conduct full day's sales clinic with two new sales personnel and thereby develop them into top salespeople in the department.
	8	Could be expected to give his or her sales personnel confidence and strong sense of responsibility by delegating many important tasks.
	7	Could be expected never to fail to conduct weekly training meetings with his or her people at a scheduled hour and to convey to them exactly what is expected.
	6	Could be expected to exhibit courtesy and respect toward his or her sales personnel.
	5	Could be expected to remind sales personnel to wait on customers instead of conversing with one another.
	4	Could be expected to be rather critical of store standards in front of his or her own people, thereby risking their development of poor attitudes.
	3	Could be expected to tell an individual to come in anyway even though he or she called in to say he or she was ill.
	2	Could be expected to go back on a promise to an individual who he or she had told could transfer back into a previous department if he or she did not like the new one.
Ineffective	1	Could be expected to make promises to an individual about his or her salary being based on department sales even when he or she knew such a practice was against company policy.

As you can see, the BARS approach is detailed and complex. It requires a lot of time and effort to develop. But the BARS also provides specific behaviours that are useful for counselling and feedback, and it can be combined with quantitative scales that are useful for comparing evaluations. When BARS were first used, the results suggested that they led to fewer common rating errors than more traditional scales did. More recent evidence, however, suggests that the scales may not be as superior as was originally thought, especially if an equivalent amount of developmental effort is put into other types of measures.[22] A somewhat simpler variation of behaviourally anchored rating scales is the *Behavioural Observation Scale* (BOS), which uses a five-point frequency scale (ranging from "almost always" to "almost never") for each separate statement of behaviour.

Management by objectives (MBO) is a process of joint goal-setting between a supervisor and a subordinate.

Management by Objectives   Of all the appraisal methods available, **management by objectives** (MBO) is the method that is most directly linked to means-ends chains and goal-setting, as will be discussed in Chapter 8.[23] When an MBO system is used, subordinates work with their supervisor to set specific task-related objectives for the subordinate's work which will help the supervisor accomplish his or her own higher-level objectives. Each set of objectives is worked out between a supervisor and a subordinate for a specific time period. The establishment of objectives is similar to a job analysis, except that it is done for a particular individual in his or her job rather than for any individual doing the job. As the MBO approach to goal-setting is more personalized, each individual is likely to have a custom-tailored set of work goals which still fits into the organization's overall means-ends chains.

Of all the appraisal systems, MBO is the most individualized. It tends to work well for counselling if the objectives do not just state desired outputs but also focus on important activities. In comparing one employee with another under the MBO approach, however, a key concern is the ease or difficulty of achieving the goals. If one person has an easier set of objectives to meet than another, comparisons are unfair. Since MBO tends to rely less on ratings than other appraisal systems do, rating errors are less likely to be a problem.

MEASUREMENT ERRORS IN PERFORMANCE APPRAISAL

To be meaningful, an appraisal system must be both *reliable* (it must provide consistent results each time it is used) and *valid* (it must measure people on relevant job content). There are several measurement errors that can threaten the reliability or validity of performance appraisals.[24] Note the strong tie between these errors and the discussion of perception and attribution in Chapter 5.

A halo error results when one person rates another person on several different dimensions and gives a similar rating for each dimension.

Halo Errors   A **halo error** results when one person rates another person on several different dimensions and gives a similar rating for each dimension. For example, a sales representative considered to be a "go-getter" and thus rated high on "dynamism" is also rated high on dependability, tact, and whatever other performance dimensions are used. The rater fails to discriminate between the person's strong and weak points; in other words, a "halo" carries over from one dimension to the next. This effect can create a problem when each performance dimension is considered an important and relatively independent aspect of the job. A variation is the single criterion error, in which only one of several important performance aspects is considered.

A leniency error is the tendency to give relatively high ratings to almost everyone.

A strictness error is the tendency to give almost everyone a low rating.

Leniency/Strictness Errors   Just as some professors are known as "easy A's," some managers tend to give relatively high ratings to almost everyone under their supervision. This is known as a **leniency error**. Sometimes the opposite occurs; some raters tend to give everyone a low rating. This is called a **strictness error**. The problem in both cases is the inadequate discrimination between good and poor performers. Leniency is likely to be a problem when peers assess one another, especially if they are asked to provide feedback to each other, because it is easier to discuss high ratings than low ones.

A central tendency error occurs when managers lump everyone together around the average, or middle, category.

A low differentiation error occurs when raters use only a small part of the rating scale.

Central Tendency Errors   A **central tendency error** occurs when managers lump everyone together around the "average," or middle, category. This tendency gives the impression that there are no very good or very poor performers on the dimensions being rated. No real differences are noted in the different performances. Both leniency and central tendency errors are types of **low differentiation errors**—the error of using only a small part of the rating scale.

A recency error is a biased rating that results from using the individual's most recent behaviour as the measure of his or her overall performance on a particular dimension.

Recency Errors   Another type of error is the **recency error**. It occurs when a rater allows recent events to influence a performance rating and ignores earlier events. Take, for example, the case of an employee who is usually on time but shows up one hour late for work the day before his or her performance rating. The employee is rated low on "promptness" because the one incident of tardiness overshadows his or her usual promptness.

Personal Bias Errors   Raters sometimes allow specific biases to affect performance evaluations. When this happens, **personal bias errors** occur. For example, a rater may intentionally give higher ratings to white employees than to nonwhite employees. In this case, the performance appraisal reflects a racial bias. Bias toward members of other demographic categories, such as age, gender, and disability, can also occur, depending on the stereotypes the rater may have. Such a bias appears to have existed at Monarch Paper Company when a former vice president was demoted to a warehouse-maintenance job for not accepting an early retirement offer. A federal jury found the firm guilty of age bias.[25] This example shows that raters must reflect carefully on their personal biases and ensure these biases do not affect performance-based ratings of subordinates.

A personal bias error occurs when a rater allows specific biases, such as race, age, or gender, to affect the performance appraisal.

Cultural Bias Errors   Managers must be aware of their cultural backgrounds when they do performance appraisals. They should be careful to avoid criticizing employees for the cultural differences described in Chapter 3, such as time orientation and ideas of appropriate power distance, unless these differences adversely affect performance on a regular basis.

IMPROVING PERFORMANCE APPRAISALS

As is true of most other issues in organizational behaviour, managers must be aware of certain trade-offs in setting up and using any performance-appraisal system. In addition to the pros and cons already mentioned for each method, some specific strategies to keep in mind in order to reduce errors and improve appraisals are include:[26]

- Train raters so that they understand the rationale of the evaluation process and can recognize the sources of measurement error.

- Make sure that raters observe employees being rated on an ongoing, regular basis and that they do not try to limit all their evaluations to the formally designated evaluation period, for instance, every six months or every year.

- Do not have the rater rate too many individuals. The ability to identify performance differences drops, and fatigue results, when evaluations are made of large numbers of people.

- Make sure that the performance dimensions and standards are stated clearly and that the standards are as specific and unique as possible.

- Avoid terms such as "average" because different evaluators tend to interpret these terms differently.

Steps to improve performance appraisals

   Remember that appraisal systems cannot be used to discriminate against employees on the basis of age, gender, race, ethnicity, and so on. To help create a legally defensible system under current legislation, the following recommendations are useful:[27]

- Appraisals must be based on an analysis of the job requirements and job description, with these reflected in performance standards.

- Appraisals are appropriate only if performance standards, goals, and expectations are clearly understood by employees.

- Clearly defined individual expectations, goals, and standards should be used rather than global measures.

- Standards should be based on behaviour and supported by observable evidence, with specific

Legal foundations of performance appraisals

consequences for failing to meet the goals or standards. The measurement process for achieving a goal must be clearly communicated. A failure to meet standards must be thoroughly documented to provide support for a final decision to dismiss the employee.

- If rating scales are used, abstract trait names, such as "friendly," should be avoided unless they can be defined as observable behaviours. What one person considers friendly, another person might consider overbearing.

- Rating scale anchors should be brief and logically consistent.

- The system must be validated and the measurement system psychologically sound, as must the ratings given by individual evaluators.

- Employees must be allowed to review the evaluation. An appeal mechanism must exist for cases where the evaluator and the rated individual disagree. If the decision is made to dismiss someone, "just cause" must be fully documented and attempts to improve the employee's performance must have taken place over a reasonable time period.

Technological advances have led to computer programs that are designed to make the rating process easier. Specifically, these programs offer easier and more comprehensive scale construction, faster feedback, and the additional flexibility needed in today's new workplace.[28]

The Effective Manager	7.2

SUGGESTIONS FOR A GROUP-PERFORMANCE EVALUATION SYSTEM

- Link the team's results to organizational goals.
- Start with the team's customers and the teamwork process needed to satisfy those needs:
  - customer requirements
  - delivery and quality
  - waste and cycle time
- Evaluate the team's and each individual member's performance.
- Train the team to develop its own measures.

GROUP EVALUATION

As indicated earlier, performance evaluations of groups or teams are becoming more common. This kind of evaluation is consistent with self-managed teams and high-performance organizations. Frequently, these evaluations are linked to group-based compensation systems, such as the ones discussed later in this chapter. For groups and teams, traditional, individually oriented appraisal systems are no longer appropriate and should be replaced by group systems which respect the suggestions made in The Effective Manager 7.2.

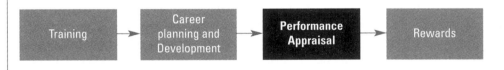

Rewards and Reward Systems

In addition to staffing, training, career planning and development, and performance appraisal, another key aspect of HR management is the design and use of reward systems. These reward systems emphasize a mix of extrinsic and intrinsic rewards. As we noted in Chapter 6, extrinsic rewards are positively valued work outcomes that are given to an individual, or group, by some other person or source in the work setting. In contrast, intrinsic rewards are positively valued work outcomes that the individual receives directly as a result of performing the task; intrinsic rewards do not involve another person or source. A feeling of achievement after accomplishing a particularly challenging task is an example of an intrinsic reward. With intrinsic work rewards, the challenge for managers is to design a work setting in which employees can, in effect, reward themselves for a job well done. Managers can also provide a variety of extrinsic rewards, as described in Chapter 6. Many of these—such as sincere praise for a job well done, or symbolic tokens of accomplishment, such as "employee-of-the-month" awards—are inexpensive for an organization. They are the main topic of Chapter 8. In the remainder of this chapter, we emphasize the management of pay as an extrinsic reward.

PAY AS AN EXTRINSIC REWARD

Pay is an especially complex extrinsic reward. It can help organizations attract and retain highly capable workers, and it can help satisfy and motivate these workers to work hard to achieve high performance. But if there is dissatisfaction with the salary, pay can also lead to strikes, grievances, absenteeism, turnover, and sometimes even poor physical and mental health.

Management expert Edward Lawler has contributed greatly to our understanding of pay as an extrinsic reward. His research generally concludes that, for pay to be a source of work motivation, high levels of job performance must be viewed as the path to achieving high pay.[29] **Merit pay** is defined as a compensation system that bases an individual's salary or wage increase on a measure of the person's performance accomplishments during a specified time period; that is, merit pay is an attempt to make pay depend on performance.

Although research supports the logic and theoretical benefits of merit pay, it also indicates that the use of merit-pay plans is not as universal or as easy as we might expect. In fact, surveys over the past 30 years have found that as many as 80 percent of respondents felt that they were not rewarded for a job well done.[30] An effective merit-pay system is one approach to dealing with this problem.

To work well, a merit-pay plan should be based on realistic and accurate measures of individual work performance and it should lead employees to believe that the way to achieve high pay is to perform at high levels. In addition, merit pay should clearly discriminate between high and low performers in the amount of pay received. Finally, managers should avoid confusing "merit" aspects of a pay increase with "cost-of-living" adjustments.

> **Merit pay** is a compensation system that bases an individual's salary or wage increase on a measure of the person's performance accomplishments during a specified time period.

CREATIVE PAY PRACTICES

Merit-pay plans are just one attempt to add to the positive value of pay as a work reward. But some critics argue that merit-pay plans are not consistent with the demands of today's organizations. They say these plans do not consider the fact that many tasks performed by employees depend on tasks performed by other employees (i.e., that there is a high degree of task interdependence among employees), which is particularly true of high-performance organizations. Also, as we argued earlier, HR management strategies should be consistent with overall organization strategies. For example, the pay system of a firm which depends on highly skilled individuals that are hard to find should emphasize employee retention rather than performance.[31]

With these points in mind, we can now examine a variety of creative pay practices. These practices are becoming more common in organizations with increasingly diverse workforces and increased emphasis on TQM or similar set-ups.[32] They include skill-based pay, gain-sharing plans, profit-sharing plans, employee stock ownership plans, lump-sum pay increases, and flexible benefit plans.

Skill-Based Pay   **Skill-based pay** rewards people for acquiring and developing job-relevant skills. This type of pay system pays people for the mix and depth of skills they possess, not for the particular job assignment they have. At Peace River Pulp Mill in Alberta, for example, skill-based bay is used for the mechanical maintenance, operations, and electrical services and instruction departments. Employees receive a standardized wage increase with each advance to another tier in the technical progression system.

> **Skill-based pay** is a system that rewards people for acquiring and developing job-relevant skills that fit the organization's needs.

Skill-based pay is one of the fastest growing pay innovations in progressive organizations.[33] Among the better known firms using this plan is the Hamilton-based steelmaker Dofasco. Besides flexibility, some advantages of skill-based pay are employee cross-training, through which workers learn to do each other's jobs; fewer supervisors, as workers can do some of their own supervision; and more individual control over compensation, with workers already knowing what is required to receive a pay raise. One disadvantage is that higher pay and training costs could result without there being greater productivity. Another disadvantage is the difficult task of deciding what is an appropriate monetary value for each skill.[34]

Gain-Sharing Plans   Cash bonuses, or extra pay for performance above standards or expectations, have been a common part of the compensation of managers and executives for a long time. Top managers in some industries earn annual bonuses of 50 percent or more of their base salaries. Attempts to give such opportunities to all employees are now becoming more frequent and important. One popular plan is called **gain sharing**, which links pay and performance by giving workers the opportunity to increase their earnings by sharing in productivity gains.

> Gain sharing is a system that links pay and performance by giving the workers the opportunity to increase their earnings by sharing in productivity gains.

Gain-sharing plans are similar in some ways to profit-sharing plans, but they are not the same. Typically, profit-sharing plans give individuals or workgroups a specified portion of any financial profits earned by the organization as a whole. In gain-sharing plans, a specific measurement of productivity is used to calculate a bonus for each worker that is intended as a mutual share of any increase in the organization's total productivity. The Scanlon Plan is probably the oldest and best known gain-sharing plan. Other examples include the Lincoln Electric Plan, the Rucker Plan™ and IMPROSHARE™

British Columbia Hydro and Power Authority has a gain-sharing plan that aligns the performance objectives of both union and non-union BC Hydro employees with the success of the organization. The program uses financial, customer satisfaction, and safety improvement measures. If targets are achieved, it provides a potential pensionable payment of up to four percent of annual earnings.

The intended benefits to the organization of gain-sharing plans are increased worker motivation because of the pay-for-performance incentives, and a greater sense of personal responsibility for making performance contributions to the organization. Because they can be highly participative, gain-sharing plans may also encourage co-operation and teamwork in the workplace. Although there is still much to be learned about gain sharing, organizations are paying more attention to these plans.[35]

Profit-Sharing Plans   Profit-sharing plans are like gain-sharing plans in some ways, but they are not identical. **Profit-sharing plans** reward employees based on the entire organization's performance. Unlike gain-sharing, profit-sharing does not try to reward employees for productivity gains, and profit-sharing is also affected by things over which employees have no control, such as economic conditions. In addition, gain-sharing plans generally use a "hard productivity" measure, while profit-sharing plans do not.

> Profit-sharing plans reward employees based on the entire organization's performance.

Profit-sharing also tends to use a formula for profit allocation which does not consider employee participation. Often, profit-sharing plans fund employee retirement plans and are therefore viewed as benefits rather than incentives.[36]

The Toronto Star Newspapers Ltd. has a profit-sharing provision, in which annual lump-sum payments are paid out if the gross profit of the company operations, before taxes, capital depreciation and interest payments, exceeds a certain percentage.

Employee Stock Purchase Plans (ESPPs)   Like profit-sharing plans, **ESPPs** are based on the entire organization's performance, but they are measured by the organization's stock price rather than its profit. The stock may be given to employees, or employees may be given an opportunity

> ESPPs, like profit-sharing plans, are based on the entire organization's performance, but they are measured by the organization's stock price rather than its profit.

to buy it at a price below market value. For example, WestJet employees can receive up to 20 percent of their salaries in WestJet shares. They can purchase the shares as common shares or direct them into their RRSPs, and WestJet will match their contributions dollar-for-dollar. Organizations often use ESPPs as a low-cost retirement benefit for employees because the organization may not be taxed for these stock purchase plans until the employees redeem the stock. Of course, like all investments in stock, ESPPs involve risk.[37]

Lump-Sum Pay Increases While most pay plans distribute increases as part of a regular paycheque, an interesting alternative is the **lump-sum increase** program. It allows employees to choose whether to receive an increase in one or more lump-sum payments. This makes it possible, for example, to take the full increase at the beginning of the year and use it for some valued purpose, such as a down payment on a car or a sizeable deposit in a savings account. Or a person may decide to take half of the raise early and get the rest at the start of the winter holiday season. In either case, the individual should be more motivated because of the larger sums or because these sums are associated with something he or she values highly.

Lump-sum increases are a pay system in which people choose to receive their wage or salary increase in one or more "lump-sum" payments.

A related, but more controversial, development in this area is the lump-sum payment, which differs from the lump-sum increase. The lump-sum payment is an attempt by employers to control labour costs while still giving workers more money—if corporate earnings allow. It involves giving workers a one-time lump-sum payment, often based on a gain-sharing formula, instead of a yearly increase in the worker's wage or salary. In this way, a person's base pay remains fixed, but how much money he or she ends up taking home varies according to the size of the annual lump-sum payment added to the base amount. Many unions are resistant to this approach because base pay does not increase and management determines the size of the bonus. However, surveys generally show that around two-thirds of the respondents have favourable reactions and think that the plans have a positive effect on performance.[38]

Flexible Benefit Plans An employee's total compensation package includes not only direct pay but also any fringe benefits that are paid by the organization. These fringe benefits often add an equivalent of 10 to 40 percent to a person's salary. It has been argued that organizations need to consider individual differences when developing such benefit programs. Otherwise, the motivational value of this indirect form of pay incentive can be lost. One approach is to let individuals choose their total pay package by deciding which benefits they will receive, up to a certain dollar amount, from a range of options offered by the organization. These **flexible benefit plans** allow workers to select benefits according to their individual needs. A worker who is single, for example, may prefer quite a different combination of insurance and retirement contributions than a married person would want.[39]

Flexible benefit plans are pay systems that allow workers to select their own benefits according to their individual needs.

As this chapter comes to a close, it is important to recall that, as mentioned by Charles Handy earlier, employees are responsible for their careers. Each person needs to be consistently maintaining and even upgrading his or her skills and proficiency. At the same time, the employer needs to manage the whole process from designing jobs through hiring the best available people for the positions, training them, and helping them with their performance and socialization in their new jobs. Effective evaluations that are appropriate to the tasks of the particular job and employee can be both disarming and complex, making it necessary to train those who do the appraisals and to first carefully choose the right method of appraisal. Ultimately, the appraisal should help managers focus their efforts on steadily strengthening their staff in order to follow the organization's strategy and achieve its goals.

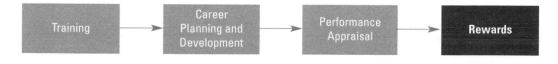

CHAPTER 7 STUDY GUIDE

Summary

STUDY QUESTIONS

What are the essential aspects of human resource strategy and practice?

- HR planning is the process of providing capable and motivated people who will carry out the organization's mission and strategy.
- HR staffing involves job analysis, attracting individuals through recruitment, selecting those best qualified through screening and hiring, and socializing employees through initial orientation and follow-up over time.

What are training and career planning and development?

- Training is a set of activities that provides the opportunity to acquire and improve job-related skills.
- On-the-job training involves job instruction in the workplace and commonly includes internships, apprenticeships, and job rotation.
- Off-the-job training takes place off the job and commonly involves lectures, videos, and simulations.
- Career planning and development for an employee involves working with managers and HR experts on careers and involves the following: a five-stage planning framework, personal responsibility for developing a portfolio of skills to keep oneself marketable at any time, a balance sheet approach to evaluating each career opportunity, and knowing the relationship between life stages and career stages and being aware of transition periods.

What is performance appraisal?

- Performance appraisal involves systematically evaluating performance and providing feedback on which performance adjustments can be made.

- Performance appraisals serve the two general purposes of evaluation, and feedback and development.
- Performance appraisals traditionally are done by an individual's immediate superior but are moving toward 360-degree evaluations involving the full circle of contacts a person may have in performing a job.
- Performance appraisals use either output measures or activity measures, or both.
- Performance appraisal methods include comparative methods and absolute methods.
- There are at least six important rater errors that can affect performance appraisal.
- There are six steps that can be used to reduce errors and improve performance appraisals.
- Group-performance evaluation systems are increasingly being used.

What are rewards and reward systems?

- Rewards are another key aspect of HR management and involve the design and use of positively valued work outcomes.
- Reward systems emphasize a mix of extrinsic and intrinsic rewards.

How is pay managed as an extrinsic reward?

- Pay as an extrinsic reward involves merit pay and creative pay practices.
- Creative pay practices include skill-based pay, gain-sharing plans, lump-sum pay increases, and flexible benefit plans.

How are intrinsic rewards managed?

- Managing intrinsic rewards involves the challenge of designing a work setting in which employees can, in effect, reward themselves for a job well done.

Behaviourally anchored rating scale (BARS) (p. 133)

Career planning and development (p. 126)

Career plateau (p. 127)

Career stages (p. 127)

Central tendency error (p. 134)

Critical incident diary (p. 132)

ESPPs (p. 138)

Flexible benefit plans (p. 139)

Forced distribution (p. 131)

Gain sharing (p. 138)

Graphic rating scales (p. 132)

Halo error (p. 134)

Human resource strategic planning (p. 121)

Job analysis (p. 121)

Leniency error (p. 134)

Low differentiation error (p. 134)

Lump-sum increases (p. 139)

Management by objectives (MBO) (p. 134)

Merit pay (p. 137)

Paired comparison (p. 131)

Performance appraisal (p. 128)

Personal bias error (p. 135)

Profit-sharing plans (p. 138)

Ranking (p. 131)

Realistic job preview (p. 123)

Recency error (p. 134)

Recruitment (p. 122)

Selection (p. 123)

Skill-based pay (p. 137)

Socialization (p. 124)

Strictness error (p. 134)

Training (p. 125)

360-degree evaluation (p. 129)

MULTIPLE CHOICE

1. HR staffing does not involve _____. (a) selection (b) socialization (c) recruitment (d) training

2. Job analysis is _____. (a) the same as job description (b) the same as job specification (c) involved with organizational tasks (d) the same as performance appraisal

3. Training _____. (a) is the same as socialization (b) is another name for career development (c) is a set of activities for improving job-related skills (d) precedes staffing

4. The notion of a career based entirely within a single organization _____. (a) is truer than ever (b) is increasingly obsolete (c) was never really true (d) applies to some industries but not others

5. A career plateau is when _____. (a) a person is demoted (b) promotions decrease (c) promotions increase (d) promotions end

6. Performance appraisal and job analysis are _____. (a) similar (b) unrelated (c) related because the job analysis should be based on the performance appraisal (d) related because the performance appraisal should be based on the job analysis

7. Performance appraisals have the two general purposes of _____. (a) rewards and punishments (b) evaluation and development decisions (c) rewards and evaluation decisions (d) feedback and job analysis decisions

8. The two kinds of rewards are _____. (a) extrinsic and intrinsic (b) internal and external (c) strong and weak (d) higher level and lower level

9. Merit pay _____. (a) rewards people for increased job-related skills (b) is a form of gain sharing (c) is similar to a lump-sum pay increase (d) adds to the positive value of pay as a work reward

10. In a flexible benefit plan, _____. (a) workers select benefits according to their needs (b) there are high benefits early in a job and lower ones later (c) there are low benefits early in a job and higher ones later (d) rewards can be split between salary and non-salary payouts.

TRUE–FALSE

11. Staffing is a smaller function than recruitment.   T   F

12. Selection follows socialization.   T   F

13. Training can be on the job or off the job.   T   F

14. The career-planning framework consists of five steps.   T   F

15. Adulthood transitions are linked to career stages.   T   F

16. Performance appraisals are best done by an immediate superior.   T   F

17. Performance appraisals can use output measures or activity measures.   T   F

18. Forced distribution is an absolute performance-appraisal method.   T   F

19. Pay is an intrinsic reward.   T   F

20. Gain-sharing plans and profit-sharing plans are the same.   T   F

SHORT ANSWER

21. Discuss the relationship between an organization's mission and HR strategic planning.

22. Discuss how training and career development relate to the match between the individual's characteristics, the job requirements, and the organization.

23. Discuss the link between adulthood stages, career stages, and transitions between the stages.

24. Compare and contrast the evaluative and the feedback and development aspects of a performance appraisal.

APPLICATIONS ESSAY

25. Assume you belong to a student organization on campus. Discuss, in some detail, how the human-resource management concepts in this chapter could be applied at the local and/or national level of your student organization. You can make up assumptions about the organization, as necessary.

Job Designs

8

One-Size Benefits Do Not Fit All

In today's competitive marketplace, corporations have learned-often the hard way-that in order to succeed and thrive, they have to value and respect their employees. Employees have more choices than ever before about where to work and the conditions of their employment. Gone are the days of lifetime employment with one company; employees are not afraid to go where the best opportunities are found. In order to retain people and bring out the best in them, organizations must offer incentives beyond salary and the basic benefits. The best organizations create a corporate culture where the focus is on continuous learning and ongoing change and development. And they know that a one-size-fits-all benefit package does not fit all employees.

The Royal Bank of Canada has committed itself to accommodating individual employees to the best of the bank's abilities. For some employees, pay raises are the most important, for others, better benefits, and some want more flexibility in working hours and job structure and a better work/life balance. RBC spent five months conducting thorough employee surveys to find out what its employees' priorities were and it discovered that you cannot treat all employees the same way. Employees are looking for different things in their employment at different stages in their lives, and RBC is now striving to find ways to support an employee at every stage of his or her career. Flexible work arrangements are one way to hold onto eligible retirees, who may be quite willing to stay on longer and prepare their younger colleagues to step into their jobs. At RBC, retirees can work part-time for 30 months without taking a penalty on their pension. Zabeen Hirji, senior vice-president of human resources at RBC, explains that this "encourages people to stay a little bit longer and to transfer some of their skills and knowledge. We are trying to build an organizational mindset where that kind of thing is encouraged and accepted."

Resources and tools are available to all employees, such as dependent care support, leave policies, and wellness resources. Other employees make use of the flexible work arrangements, such as job sharing, flextime, reduced hours, modified work weeks, and telecommuting. Employees are also encouraged to move within the company and across the various businesses to gain experience and expand their skills and abilities. To help them do this, RBC has made internal career-search software available. Employees also have access to experience-based learning, through projects and work assignments, and one-to-one coaching. Elearning gives employees the opportunity to access training and development sessions 24 hours a day, at their convenience.

RBC offers employees a variety of opportunities, benefits, and advantages. No wonder it was named the "Most Respected Corporation in Canada" and placed first in the category of "Human Resources Management" for the second year in a row in the annual KPMG/Ipsos Reid poll, published in *The Globe and Mail* in 2004.

This chapter introduces the essential aspects of job design, goal setting, and work scheduling as important strategies for developing high-performance work settings. As you read Chapter 8, keep in mind these key questions:

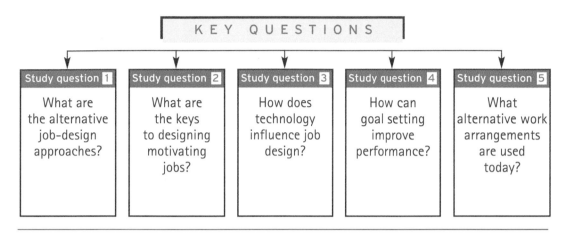

KEY QUESTIONS

Study question 1	Study question 2	Study question 3	Study question 4	Study question 5
What are the alternative job-design approaches?	What are the keys to designing motivating jobs?	How does technology influence job design?	How can goal setting improve performance?	What alternative work arrangements are used today?

Job Design Approaches

Through the process of **job design**, managers plan and specify job tasks and the work arrangements that are needed to accomplish them. Figure 8.1 shows how alternative job-design approaches differ in the way required tasks are defined and in the amount of intrinsic motivation provided for the worker. The "best" job design always does three things: it meets organizational requirements for high performance, offers a good fit with individual skills and needs, and provides opportunities for job satisfaction.

Job design is the process of defining job tasks and the work arrangements to accomplish them.

SCIENTIFIC MANAGEMENT

The history of scholarly interest in job design goes back in part to Frederick Taylor's work with *scientific management* in the early 1900s.[1] Taylor and his contemporaries wanted to increase people's efficiency at work. Their approach was to study a job carefully, break it down into its smallest components, establish exact time and motion requirements for each task to be done, and then train workers to do these tasks in the same way over and over again. These early efforts were forerunners of today's industrial-engineering approaches to job design that emphasize efficiency. These approaches try to determine the best processes, methods, work-flow layouts, output standards, and person–machine interfaces for various jobs.

Today the term **job simplification** is used to describe an approach to designing jobs that have standardized work procedures and employ people in clearly defined and highly specialized tasks. The machine-paced automobile assembly line is a classic example of this job-design strategy. Why is it used? Typically, the answer includes increasing operating efficiency by reducing the number of skills required to do a job, being able to hire low-cost labour, keeping the needs for job training to a minimum, and emphasizing the accomplishment of repetitive tasks. However, the very nature of such jobs creates potential disadvantages as well. These

Job simplification standardizes tasks and employs people in very routine jobs.

include loss of efficiency due to lower quality, high rates of absenteeism and turnover, and demands for higher wages to compensate for unappealing jobs.

Figure 8.1 A continuum of job-design strategies

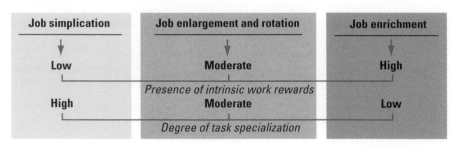

Job simplication	Job enlargement and rotation	Job enrichment
↓	↓	↓
Low	Moderate	High

Presence of intrinsic work rewards

High	Moderate	Low

Degree of task specialization

GLOBALIZATION

When Ford Motor Company purchased Volvo, it bought quality. At Volvo's Torslanda, Sweden, plant, the new S60 model is built with a unique combination of high technology and human contribution. The assembly line operates on a "platform" concept where large components come together in modules. It offers ergonomic advantages to the workers so that movements are easier to do and reaching and stretching are kept to a minimum. Instead of having monotonous individual jobs, workers are in teams that have broad responsibilities for planning and building large sections of the car. Workers also check their own quality and make corrections. Says a company spokesperson, "Responsibility, expertise, and collaboration are the key words when it comes to car production."[2]

JOB ENLARGEMENT AND JOB ROTATION

Job enlargement increases task variety by adding new tasks of similar difficulty to a job.

Job rotation increases task variety by shifting workers among jobs that have tasks of similar difficulty.

In job simplification, the number or variety of different tasks performed by the worker is limited. Although this makes the tasks easier to master, the repetitiveness can reduce motivation. Thus, a second set of job-design approaches has been created to add greater variety to the tasks performed. **Job enlargement** increases task variety by combining into one job two or more tasks that were previously done by different workers. Sometimes called *horizontal loading*, this approach increases job breadth by having the worker perform more and different tasks, but all at the same level of responsibility and challenge. **Job rotation**, another horizontal-loading approach, increases task variety by periodically rotating workers among jobs that have different tasks. Again, the responsibility level of the tasks stays the same. The rotation can be arranged according to almost any time schedule, whether hourly, daily, or weekly. An important benefit of job rotation is training. It allows workers to become more familiar with different tasks, which in turn gives management greater flexibility in moving workers from one job to another.

JOB ENRICHMENT

Frederick Herzberg's two-factor theory of motivation (described in Chapter 6) suggests that high levels of motivation should not be expected from jobs designed on the basis of simplification, enlargement, or rotation.[3] "Why," asks Herzberg, "should a worker become motivated when one or more 'meaningless' tasks are added to previously existing ones or when work assignments are rotated among equally 'meaningless' tasks?" Instead of pursuing one of these job-design strategies, therefore, Herzberg recommends an alternative approach that he calls "job enrichment."

In Herzberg's model, **job enrichment** is the practice of improving job content by building into it such motivating factors as responsibility, achievement, recognition, and personal growth. This job-design strategy differs significantly from the strategies previously discussed, as it adds to job content some planning and evaluating duties that would normally be done only by managers. These content changes (see The Effective Manager 8.1) involve what Herzberg calls vertical loading in order to increase the job depth. Enriched jobs, he states, help satisfy the higher-order needs that people bring with them to work, and the result is greater motivation to achieve high levels of job performance. Sales clerks in enriched jobs do not just sell; they are often empowered to order additional stock for customers and to follow up on the order so that a customer's needs are satisfied. Just getting to know a customer a little more can enrich a job and knowing that one has the power to help someone—and that the customer appreciates the effort—are just two higher-order needs that can be satisfied, which is better than simply saying, "Sorry, we don't have it in stock."

Despite the obvious appeal of Herzberg's ideas, two common questions suggest a need for caution. Is job enrichment expensive? Job enrichment can be very costly, particularly when it requires major changes in workflows, facilities, or technology. Will workers demand higher pay when they move into enriched jobs? Herzberg argues that if employees are being paid a truly competitive wage or salary, then the intrinsic rewards of performing enriched tasks will be adequate compensation. Other researchers are more skeptical, advising that pay must be considered carefully.[4]

Job enrichment increases job content by giving workers more responsibility for planning and evaluating duties.

The Effective Manager	8.1

JOB ENRICHMENT ADVICE FROM FREDERICK HERZBERG

- Allow workers to plan.
- Allow workers to control.
- Maximize job freedom.
- Increase task difficulty.
- Help workers become task experts.
- Provide performance feedback.
- Increase performance accountability.
- Provide complete units of work.

Designing Jobs to Increase Motivation

OB scholars have been reluctant to recommend job enrichment as a universal solution to all job-performance and job-satisfaction problems. The two questions just mentioned raise cost and pay concerns. Also, individual differences must be considered when answering the additional question, Is job enrichment for everyone? To design jobs that increase motivation, Richard Hackman and Greg Oldham developed a diagnostic approach that offers a broader framework for job design that is based on contingencies.[5] This model creates many opportunities for individualizing job designs.

JOB CHARACTERISTICS MODEL

Figure 8.2 presents the **job characteristics model**. It identifies five core job characteristics that are very important in job design. The higher a job scores on each characteristic, the more it is considered to be enriched. The core job characteristics are:

The **job characteristics model** identifies five core job characteristics that are very important in job design: skill variety, task identity, task significance, autonomy, and feedback.

Core job characteristics

- Skill variety—the degree to which a job includes a variety of different activities and involves the use of a number of different skills and talents.

- Task identity—the degree to which the job requires completion of a "whole" and identifiable piece of work, one that involves doing a job from beginning to end with a visible outcome.

- Task significance—the degree to which the job is important and involves a meaningful contribution to the organization or society in general.

- Autonomy—the degree to which the job gives the employee substantial freedom, independence, and discretion in scheduling the work and determining the procedures used in carrying it out.

• Job feedback—the degree to which carrying out the work activities provides direct and clear information to the employee regarding how well the job has been done.

For those who use this model in an actual work situation, Hackman and Oldham recommend determining the current status of each job on each core characteristic.[6] These characteristics can then be changed systematically to enrich the job and increase its motivational potential. Hackman and his colleagues have developed an instrument called the Job Diagnostic Survey (JDS) for such an assessment (see the end-of-book experiential exercise, "Job Design"). Scores on the JDS are then combined as follows to create a **motivating-potential score** (MPS), which indicates how capable the job is of motivating people:

The **motivating-potential score** describes how much the core characteristics of a job create motivating conditions.

$$\text{MPS} = \frac{\text{Skill variety} + \text{Task identity} + \text{Task significance}}{3} \times \text{Autonomy} \times \text{Feedback}$$

A job's MPS can be increased by combining tasks to create larger jobs, opening feedback channels so workers know how well they are doing, establishing client relationships so workers experience feedback directly from customers, and using vertical loading to create more planning and controlling responsibilities. When the core characteristics are enriched in these ways and the MPS for a job is raised as high as possible, it can be expected that three critical psychological states for the individual will improve: (1) experiencing meaningfulness in the work, (2) experiencing responsibility for the outcomes of the work, and (3) having knowledge of the actual results of the work activities. These favourable psychological states, in turn, can be expected to create more positive work outcomes in terms of individual motivation, performance, and satisfaction.

Individual Difference Moderators   The job characteristics model recognizes that the five core job characteristics do not affect all people in the same way. Rather than accept Herzberg's implication that enriched jobs should be good for everyone, this approach allows for individual differences. It accepts the idea that jobs should be designed to arrive at the best match between core characteristics and individual needs and talents. Specifically, the model suggests that enriched jobs will lead to positive outcomes only for those persons who are a good match for them. When the fit between the person and an enriched job is poor, positive outcomes are less likely and problems may result.

Figure 8.2   Job-design implications of job characteristics theory

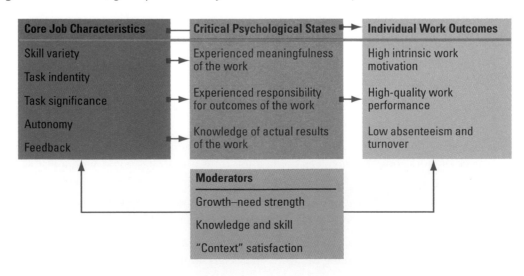

Figure 8.2 highlights three individual difference moderators that can influence how a person wants his or her job to be designed. The first moderator is *growth-need strength*—how much a person wants the opportunity for self-direction, learning, and personal accomplishment at work. It is similar to Abraham Maslow's esteem and self-actualization needs and Alderfer's growth needs, as discussed in Chapter 6. When applied here, the expectation is that people with high growth-need strengths at work will respond positively to enriched jobs, whereas people with low growth-need strengths will be anxious in enriched jobs. The second moderator is *knowledge and skill*. People with abilities that fit the demands of enriched jobs are predicted to feel good about these jobs and to perform well. Those who do not have the abilities, or who feel they do not have them even though they might, are likely to experience difficulties. The third moderator is *context satisfaction*, or how satisfied an employee is with such aspects of the work setting as salary levels, the quality of supervision, relationships with co-workers, and working conditions. In general, people who are more satisfied with their job context are more likely to support and do well with job enrichment than people who are dissatisfied.

Research Results   A lot of research has been done on the job characteristics model in a variety of work settings, including banks, dentist offices, corrections departments, telephone companies, and manufacturing firms, as well as in government agencies. Experts generally agree that the model and its diagnostic approach are useful guides to job design, but that they are not yet perfect.[7] On average, job characteristics do affect performance but not nearly as much as they affect satisfaction. The research also emphasizes the importance of growth-need strength as a moderator of the relationships between job design and job performance or job satisfaction. Positive job characteristics have more effect on the performance of individuals with high growth need than on those with low growth need. The relationship is about the same with job satisfaction. It is also clear that job enrichment can fail when job requirements are increased beyond an individual's capabilities or interests. Finally, the employee's perceptions of job characteristics often differ from the perceptions measured by managers and consultants. These perceptions are important and must be considered. After all, they will largely determine whether the workers view a job as high or low in the core characteristics, and work outcomes will be affected accordingly.

University of Alberta

www.ualberta.ca

The University of Alberta's human resources department has a compensation and job design team that plays a major role in helping university employees prepare position descriptions and job fact sheets. It assists departments in gathering information on the amount and types of duties performed, how duties are exchanged and inter-related, technology interventions, and opportunities to enrich or expand positions. The goal is to ensure timely, fair, and equitable compensation of employees throughout the university.

SOCIAL INFORMATION PROCESSING

Gerald Salancik and Jeffrey Pfeffer question whether or not jobs have stable and objective characteristics which individuals respond to predictably and consistently.[8] Instead, they view job design from the perspective of **social information processing** theory. This theory argues that individual needs, task perceptions, and reactions result from socially constructed realities. Social information in organizations is said to influence the way people perceive their jobs and respond to them. The same is true, for example, in the classroom. Suppose that several of your friends tell you that the instructor for a course is bad, the content is boring, and the requirements involve too much work. You may then think that the critical characteristics of the class are the instructor, the content, and the workload, and that they are all bad. All of this may substantially influence the way you perceive your instructor and the course and the way you deal with the class—regardless of its actual characteristics.

Research on social information processing indicates that both social information and core characteristics are important. Although social information processing influences how tasks are perceived and workers' attitudes, the job characteristics discussed earlier are also important. Indeed, how someone perceives job characteristics is likely to be influenced by both the objective characteristics themselves and the social information present in the workplace.

The social information processing approach argues that individual needs and task perceptions and reactions result from socially constructed realities.

MANAGERIAL AND GLOBAL IMPLICATIONS

Let's now use a question-and-answer approach to summarize some final points and implications about job enrichment that are worth remembering. *Should everyone's job be enriched?* The answer is clearly "No." The logic of individual differences suggests that not everyone will want an enriched job. Individuals most likely to have positive reactions to job enrichment are those who need achievement, who hold strong working values, or who are seeking higher-order growth–need satisfaction at work. Job enrichment also appears to be most advantageous when the job context is positive and when workers have the abilities needed to do the enriched job. Furthermore, costs, technological constraints, and workgroup or union opposition may make it difficult to enrich some jobs.[9] *Can job enrichment apply to groups?* The answer is "Yes." The application of job-design strategies at the group level is growing in many types of settings. In later chapters of this book, we discuss creative workgroup designs, including cross-functional work teams and self-managing teams.

A final question brings the issue of job enrichment to the global context. *What is the impact of culture on job enrichment?* The answer is that its impact is big. Research conducted in Belgium, Israel, Japan, the Netherlands, the United States, and Germany has found unique aspects of what work is considered in each country.[10] Work was seen as a social requirement most strongly in Belgium and Japan and least so in Germany. Work was regarded as something done for money in all countries but Belgium. In most cases, however, work was seen as having both an economic and a societal contribution component. These results, as well as differences in such national culture dimensions as power distance and individualism, suggest the need for a contingency approach to job enrichment, and further suggest that cultural differences should be considered in job design.

Technology and Job Design

Sociotechnical systems integrate people and technology into high-performance work settings.

The concept of **sociotechnical systems** is important in organizational behaviour: it refers to integrating people and technology to create high-performance work systems.[11] As computers and information technologies continue to dominate the modern workplace, this concept is an essential part of new developments in job design.

AUTOMATION AND ROBOTICS

Automation allows machines to do work that was previously done by people.

As mentioned earlier, highly simplified jobs often cause problems because they offer little intrinsic motivation for the worker. Such tasks have been defined so narrowly that they lack challenge and lead to boredom when someone has to repeat them over and over again. With today's high technology, one way to tackle this problem is to use complete **automation**. This means that a machine is used to do the work that was previously done by a human. Increasingly, this approach involves the use of robots, which are becoming ever more versatile and reliable. Robot prices are also now falling as the cost of human labour is rising. Japan presently leads the world in robot use; the U.S. and Canada are far behind, but our integrated industries are beginning to use more robots.[12] If you were to travel to Wolfsburg, Germany, you would find that Volkswagen's car plant, home of the Golf, is one of the world's largest and most highly automated plants. Robots do 80 percent of the welding work and can be programmed to perform different tasks. Computers control the assembly line, adjusting production so that it fits schedules for different models and options.[13]

FLEXIBLE MANUFACTURING SYSTEMS

In **flexible manufacturing systems**, adaptive computer-based technologies and integrated job designs are frequently used to shift work easily and quickly from one product to another. This approach is increasingly common, for example, in companies that supply the automobile industry with machined metal products, such as cylinder heads and gear boxes.[14] A cellular manufacturing system, for example, might contain a number of automated production machines that separately cut, shape, drill, and fasten together various metal components. The machines can be quickly changed from manufacturing one product to another.[15] Workers in flexible manufacturing cells do few routine assembly-line tasks. Rather, they ensure that the operations are handled correctly, and they deal with the changeover from one product setup to another. As a result, these workers develop expertise across a wide range of functions and their jobs have a high potential for enriched core-job characteristics.

Flexible manufacturing systems use adaptive technology and integrated job designs to easily shift production from one product to another.

ELECTRONIC OFFICES

Electronic office technology was the key when Consumer Impact Marketing (CIM), a private outsourcing company based in Toronto, was attempting to manage its sales force, data analysis, knowledge management, and payroll services. It offers all of its services in various packages to promote products and services ranging from Xbox to snack foods. With clients such as Microsoft and Quaker Tropicana Gatorade, CIM needed to manage a wide range of promotional events and mobile staff. The solution was a rapid integration of its functions and real-time communication. The more than 1,300 "road warriors" in its sales force use a software package called FieldMatrix on their PDAs to automate the analysis of the business by both the sales force and for the clients. The HR management system, including payroll, is done over the Internet using a software package called ISPHeRia (Interactive, Secure, Payroll and Human e-Resources). This program even ensures that all new labour rules are respected and that employees input their payroll information correctly. Essentially, the company tried to automate as many tasks as possible in order to make people available for more challenging work.

Continuing developments in electronic offices offer job enrichment possibilities for workers who are ready to handle the technology. But such jobs can be stressful and difficult for individuals who do not have the necessary education or skills. One survey showed that even in highly developed countries in Europe, 54 percent of workers had inadequate skills to operate a computer.[16] As technology continues to evolve, the proportion of older workers with difficulties will increase, yet, at the same time, they are the ones with valuable experiences they can share with newer employees. People who work continuously with computers are also beginning to have physical ailments caused by repetitious keyboarding and mouse movements. Clearly, the high technologies of the new workplace must be carefully integrated with the human factor.

WORKFLOW AND PROCESS RE-ENGINEERING

Another approach for improving job designs and performance is based on the concept of **process re-engineering**—the analysis, streamlining, and reconfiguration of actions and tasks required to reach a work goal.[17] The process-design approach systematically breaks processes down into their specific components and subtasks, analyzes each one for its relevance and simplicity, and then does everything possible to reconfigure the process to eliminate wasted time, effort, and resources. A classic example might be the various steps required to gain approval for a purchase order to buy a new computer. The process re-engineering approach looks at every step

Process re-engineering analyzes, streamlines, and reconfigures actions and tasks to achieve work goals.

in the process, from searching for items and vendors to obtaining bids, completing necessary forms, getting required signatures and approvals, actually placing the order, and so on to the point at which the new computer arrives, is checked in, is placed in an equipment inventory, and then is finally delivered to the workplace. In all this, one simple question drives the re-engineering approach: What is necessary and what steps can be eliminated?

TECHNOLOGY

Waterloo, Ontario-based Open Text Corporation recognizes that organizations face a number of common business process management challenges. It has developed Livelink for Business Process Management software, which provides tools to simplify business processes and help employees co-ordinate effectively with the organization and each other. It allows organizations to manage work-flow and integrate various forms—including engineering change orders, expense reports, and purchase requisitions—into automated processes to improve efficiency and productivity.[18]

Goal Setting and Job Design

Goals are important aspects of any job design. Without proper goals, employees may end up with a direction problem. Some years ago, for example, a professional football player gathered up an opponent's fumble. Then, with obvious effort and delight, he ran the ball almost the length of the field, into the wrong end zone. Clearly, the athlete did not lack motivation. Unfortunately, however, he failed to direct his energies toward the correct goal line. Similar problems are found in many work settings. They can be eliminated, or at least reduced, by properly setting and clarifying task goals. As baseball great Yogi Berra apparently said, "If you don't know where you're going, you'll probably end up somewhere else."

GOAL-SETTING THEORY

Goals play an important role in high-performance work environments. **Goal setting** is the process of developing, negotiating, and formally setting the motivational targets or objectives that a person is responsible for accomplishing.[19] Over many years, Edwin Locke and his associates have developed a comprehensive framework that links goals to performance as shown in Figure 8.3. The model uses elements of expectancy theory from Chapter 6 to help clarify the impact of goal setting on performance and at the same time considers other conditions that limit the impact of goals, such as ability and task complexity.

GOAL-SETTING GUIDELINES

Goal setting is the process of developing, negotiating, and setting motivational performance objectives.

There is now quite a lot of research on goal setting. Indeed, more research has been done on goal setting than on any other theory related to work motivation.[20] Nearly 400 studies have been conducted in several countries, including Australia, England, Germany, Japan, and the United States.[21] The basic precepts of goal-setting theory remain a very important source of advice for managing human behaviour in the work setting.

For managers, the implications of the Locke and Latham model and related goal-setting research can be summarized as follows.[22] First, *difficult goals are more likely to lead to higher performance than are less difficult ones.* However, if the goals are seen as too difficult or impossible, the relationship with performance ends. For example, you will likely perform better as a financial services agent if you have a goal of selling six RSPs a week than if you have a goal of three. However, if your goal is 15 RSPs a week, and you consider that impossible to achieve, your performance may be lower than what it would have been with a more realistic goal. Once again, we should recall expectancy theory and use it to help set realistic, achievable goals.

Second, *specific goals are more likely to lead to higher performance than are no goals or vague or very general ones.* All too often, people work with very general goals, such as the encouragement to "do your best." Research indicates that more specific goals, such as selling six computers a day, are much more motivating than a simple do-your-best goal.

Third, *task feedback, or knowledge of results, is likely to motivate people toward higher performance by encouraging the setting of higher performance goals.* Feedback lets people know how they are doing and whether their efforts are on course or off course. Just think about how eager you usually are to find out how well you did on an examination.

Fourth, *goals are most likely to lead to higher performance when people have the abilities and the feelings of self-efficacy that are needed to accomplish the goals.* The individual must be able to accomplish the goals and must feel confident about those abilities. Recall our earlier financial services example: You may be able to do what is required to sell six annuities a week and feel confident that you can. If your goal is 15, however, you may believe that your abilities are insufficient for the task and, as a result, you will lack the confidence that is needed to work hard enough to sell that many.

Fifth, *goals are most likely to motivate people toward higher performance when they are accepted and there is a commitment to them.* Making an employee part of the goal-setting process helps build the employee's acceptance and commitment to the goal. It helps create "ownership" of the goals. However, Locke and Latham report that goals assigned by someone else can in fact be equally effective. The persons who assign the goals, they explain, are likely to be authority figures, and that can have an impact. The assignment also implies that the subordinate can actually reach the goal. Moreover, assigned goals often are a challenge and help define the standards people use in deciding if they are satisfied with their performance. According to Locke and Latham, assigned goals most often lead to weak performance when they are stated sharply or they are poorly explained.

Figure 8.3 Essentials of the Locke and Latham goal-setting framework

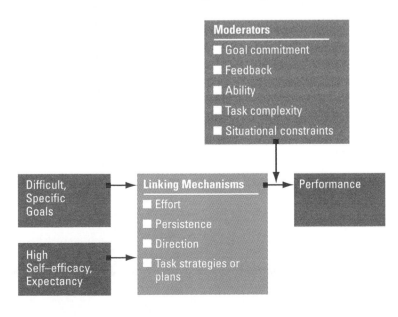

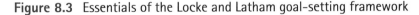

Domtar Inc.

www.domtar.com

When Raymond Royer left Bombardier for Domtar as CEO in 1996, he was greeted with skepticism. His goals for Domtar's return on equity and customer service were achieved despite his apparent lack of knowledge of his new company's industry. He set a goal for Domtar to be one of the top three companies in its industry by 2002. In the seven years since Royer joined the company, sales have grown from $1.9 billion to $5.5 billion and Royer was named Global CEO of the year by *Pulp and Paper Weekly* in 2003, a first for a Canadian. The goals Royer sets help motivate Domtar's staff—and the company and its CEO are now among the best.

ENTREPRENEURSHIP

Goals and motivation allowed Zero-Knowledge Systems (ZKS), an Internet security services technology company headquartered in Montreal, to ride the wave of the high-tech boom in the late 1990s and allowed it to survive the subsequent bust. ZKS describes the company culture as "casually intense." Although staff members are focused on developing cutting edge technology, they also know how to unwind and have a good time. For example, management once treated employees to a private sneak preview of *Star Wars: Episode I* as a reward for their hard work. [23]

GOAL SETTING AND MBO

When we speak of goal setting and its potential to influence individual performance at work, the concept of management by objectives (MBO) immediately comes to mind. Basically, MBO is a process of joint goal setting between a supervisor and a subordinate.[24] In MBO, managers work with their subordinates to set performance goals and plans that fit with the objectives of higher-level work units and the organization. When this process is followed throughout an organization, MBO helps clarify the different levels of objectives as a series of well-defined means-end chains.

Figure 8.4 shows a comprehensive view of MBO. The concept goes well with goal setting and the related principles discussed above. Notice how discussions between the supervisor and subordinate are designed to ensure there is joint participation from the point of setting the initial goals to the point of evaluating the results in terms of having attained the goals. In addition to having these goal-setting steps, a successful MBO system requires careful implementation. Not only must workers have the freedom to do the required tasks, managers should be prepared to actively support the workers' efforts to achieve the agreed-upon goals.

Figure 8.4 How management by objectives works

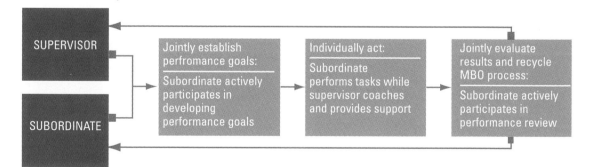

Although there is quite a lot of research based on case studies of MBO success, few of these studies were done with rigorous controls. The results of these reports are also mixed.[25] In general, and as a way of applying goal-setting theory, MBO has much to offer. But it is not at all easy to start MBO and keep it going. Many firms have started and then dropped the approach because of difficulties with it early on. Some of the specific problems it creates are too much paperwork documenting the goals and accomplishments and too much emphasis on goal-oriented rewards and punishments, on top-down goals, on goals that are easily stated in objective terms, and on individual instead of group goals. MBO also may need to be implemented throughout an organization for it to work well.

Alternative Work Arrangements

Alternative ways of scheduling time are becoming more common in the workplace. These arrangements are essentially reshaping the traditional 40-hour week with its nine-to-five day and work done on the company premises. Almost all alternative plans are designed to increase employee satisfaction and to help employees balance the demands of their work and nonwork lives.[26] These arrangements are becoming more and more important in fast-changing societies where demands are clearly growing for "work-life balance" and more "family-friendly" employers.[27] For example, dual-career families with children, single parents, part-time students, and older workers (retired or near retirement age) are all candidates for alternative work arrangements.

ETHICS AND SOCIAL RESPONSIBILITY

CANADIAN ONLINE SALES OF PRESCRIPTION PHARMACEUTICALS

Canadian online sales of prescription pharmaceuticals to U.S. customers have escalated in recent years. The Health Minister doesn't see any problems with pharmaceutical companies providing these medicines, since current sales levels don't pose a threat to domestic supply. However, he describes the practice of Canadian doctors signing prescriptions for U.S. customers without having seen the patients as unethical and unprofessional. In fact, the federal government is considering changing the Food and Drug Act to allow doctors to prescribe drugs only to Canadian residents and visitors to Canada. Provincial colleges of physicians also view the practice as unacceptable and have censured doctors for it. The Canadian International Pharmacy Association defends the practice, saying Canadian mail-order pharmacies fill only drug requests that are accompanied by an American doctor's prescription. The Canadian doctor simply checks an existing prescription from an American physician who has seen the patient. [28]

COMPRESSED WORKWEEKS

A **compressed workweek** is any scheduling of work that allows a full-time job to be completed in fewer than the standard five days. The most common form of compressed workweek is the "4/40" or 40 hours of work accomplished in four ten-hour days.

This approach has many possible benefits. For the worker, added time off is a major feature of this schedule. The individual often appreciates increased leisure time, three-day weekends, free weekdays to take care of personal matters, and lower commuting costs. The organization can benefit, too, in terms of lower employee absenteeism, and improved recruiting of new employees. But, there are also potential disadvantages. Individuals can experience increased fatigue from the extended workday and family-adjustment problems. For its part, the organization can experience work-scheduling problems and customer complaints because of breaks in work or service coverage. Some organizations may face occasional union opposition and laws requiring the payment of overtime for work exceeding eight hours of individual labour in any one day. Overall, reactions to compressed workweeks are likely to be most favourable when employees participate in the decision to adopt the new workweek, when their jobs are enriched as a result of the new schedule, and when the employees have strong higher-order needs in Maslow's hierarchy.[29] For some employees at the City of Edmonton, for example, a compressed workweek is available, at the discretion of the employer and employee.

A compressed workweek allows a full-time job to be completed in less than five full workdays.

FLEXIBLE WORKING HOURS

Flexible working hours give employees some daily choice in scheduling their arrival and departure times from work.

Another innovative work schedule, **flexible working hours** or flextime, gives individuals a daily choice in the timing of their work commitments. One such schedule requires employees to work four hours of "core" time but leaves them free to choose their remaining four hours of work from among flexible time blocks. One person, for example, may start early and leave early, whereas another may start later and leave later. This flexible work schedule is becoming increasingly popular and is a valuable alternative for structuring work in a way that accommodates individual interests and needs.

Flextime increases individual autonomy in work scheduling and offers many opportunities and benefits (see The Effective Manager 8.2). It is a way for dual-career couples to handle children's schedules as well as their own; it is also a way to meet the demands of caring for elderly parents or ill family members; and it is even a way to better attend to such personal affairs as medical and dental appointments, home emergencies, banking needs, and so on. Supporters of this scheduling strategy argue that the discretion it allows workers in scheduling their own hours of work encourages them to develop positive attitudes and to increase their commitment to the organization. An insurance manager, commenting on his firm's flexible working hours program, said, "We're not doing flexible work scheduling to be nice, but because it makes business sense."[30] A majority of Canadian workplaces already have flextime programs, and the number is growing.[31] The Royal Bank is one of these workplaces that has implemented flexible work arrangements and modified workweeks to allow employees to achieve a better work/life balance.

The Effective Manager 8.2
FLEXTIME BENEFITS
For organizations:
• less absenteeism, tardiness, turnover
• more commitment
• higher performance
For workers:
• shorter commuting time
• more leisure time
• more job satisfaction
• greater sense of responsibility

JOB SHARING

Job sharing allows one full-time job to be divided among two or more persons.

In **job sharing**, one full-time job is given to two or more persons who then divide the work according to agreed-upon hours. Often, each person works half a day, but job sharing can also be done on a weekly or monthly basis. Although it is used by only a small percentage of employers, human-resource experts believe that job sharing is a valuable alternative work arrangement.[32]

Organizations benefit from job sharing as it helps them attract talented people who would otherwise be unable to work. An example is the qualified teacher who also is a parent. This person may be able to work only half a day. Through job sharing, two such persons can be employed to teach one class. Some job sharers report less burnout and claim that they feel recharged each time they report for work. The tricky part of this arrangement is finding two people who will work well with each other. Karla Brown, a marketing services manager for Clearwater Fine Foods Inc. in Bedford, Nova Scotia, negotiated a job-sharing arrangement with her employer. The person who replaced her during maternity leave stayed on full-time, while Karla came back Monday, Tuesday, and Wednesday each week. This arrangement relieved Karla of the job's travel demands since her partner now did most out-of-town trips. The only drawback was that deadlines occasionally turned a day off into a telecommuting day.[33]

Job sharing should not be confused with a more controversial arrangement called work sharing. This occurs when workers agree to cut back on the number of hours they work in order to protect themselves from layoffs. Workers may agree to voluntarily reduce 20 percent of their hours worked and pay received, rather than have the employer cut 20 percent of the workforce during difficult economic times. Legal restrictions prohibit this practice in some settings.

WORK AT HOME AND THE VIRTUAL OFFICE

High technology is influencing yet another alternative work arrangement that is becoming increasingly visible in many employment sectors, ranging from higher education to government, and from manufacturing to services. **Telecommuting** is the term for working at home or in a remote location while using computers and advanced telecommunications links to stay in contact with a central office or other employment locations. At IBM Canada, an arrangement called *flexiplace* means some employees work most of the time from a home office and come into IBM corporate offices only for special meetings. In a practice known as *hotelling*, temporary offices are reserved for these workers during the times they visit the main office. Worldwide, some 20 percent of IBM's employees spend two or more days a week working at home or visiting customers.[34]

Telecommuting is the term for working at home or in remote locations while using computer and telecommunications links with the office.

The notion of telecommuting is associated more and more with the *virtual office*, where the individual works literally "from the road" and while travelling from place-to-place or customer-to-customer by car or airplane. In all cases, the worker remains linked electronically with the home office.[35] The number of workers who are telecommuting is growing daily, with organizations like Ernst and Young LLP and Mitra Imaging reporting that a significant proportion of their workers telecommute. At Cisco Systems, over 50 percent of the workers telecommute at least part of the time.[36] Bell Canada and Sun Life Insurance have had telecommute programs for ten years or longer. Most college and university instructors do some of their work either at home, at conferences, or en route.

Telecommuting offers the individual the potential advantages of flexibility, the comforts of home, and a choice of locations that fit one's lifestyle. In terms of advantages to the organization, this alternative often produces cost savings and efficiency as well as employee satisfaction.

OB ACROSS FUNCTIONS

Business Law

New Hiring Practices Have Legal Implications

Flexibility is the watchword in any consideration of work scheduling. The term applies not only to the needs of the workers who want more flexibility in their hours, but also to employers who want flexibility in expanding and shrinking their workforces. It is here that the role of the part-time or temporary worker becomes important. When companies employ temporary workers on a regular basis, for at least a year or more, these workers are sometimes called "permatemps." With new federal rules that permit part-time workers to collect Employment Insurance, important issues of labour law are being raised at the same time as part-time and contingency workers are becoming a key part of the human-resource strategies of many organizations. The question is mostly about the availability of benefits for permatemps, based on who is considered their true "employer." If the company is considered the employer, instead of the individual worker being considered an independent contractor, permatemps essentially become "common-law workers." As such, under employment laws, where the "master–servant" relationship exists, part-time employees may be eligible for the benefits available to other workers, unless they have been specifically excluded by policy. Labour lawyers and unions are watching current decisions carefully, since the rulings could open the door for future lawsuits.

On the negative side, telecommuters sometimes complain of isolation from co-workers, decreased identification with the work team, and technical difficulties with the computer links that are essential to their work arrangement. Yet overall, the practice continues to grow, with more organizations now offering special training in the *virtual management* of telecommuters.

PART-TIME WORK

Temporary part-time work is temporary work of fewer hours than the standard week.

Permanent part-time work is permanent work of fewer hours than the standard week.

Part-time work has become an increasingly prominent and controversial work arrangement. In **temporary part-time work**, an employee is classified as "temporary" and works less than the standard 40-hour workweek. In **permanent part-time work**, the person is considered a "permanent" member of the workforce but works less than the standard 40-hour workweek. An example of this is pre-retirement transition leave, allowing workers to reduce their hours up to two years before they retire. Federal government employees, as well as those working for the Province of New Brunswick have this option.[37]

Usually, temporary part-timers are easily released and hired according to the company's needs. Accordingly, many organizations use part-time work to lower labour costs and to help deal with ups and downs in the business cycle. Employers also may use part-time work to better manage what may be called "retention quality." In this context, the workers are highly skilled individuals who are committed to their careers and want to continue to develop professionally but can only work part-time. Part-time nurses and supply teachers, among others, fall into this category.[38]

The part-time work schedule can be a benefit to people who want to supplement other jobs or who want something less than a full workweek for a variety of personal reasons. For someone who is holding two jobs, including at least one part time, the added burdens can be stressful and his or her performance may be affected in either one or both work settings. Furthermore, part-timers often fail to qualify for fringe benefits, such as health care, life insurance, and pensions, and they may be paid less than their full-time counterparts. Nevertheless, part-time work schedules are becoming more of a factor because of the organizational advantages they offer.

Contract work is temporary work usually equal to the standard week but the employment ends after a set time.

Many organizations are turning to contract work to fill temporary needs as this allows them to get the full-time human resources that are needed without having more permanent employees. A person with **contract work** usually works a full set of standard hours in a week and is paid for a whole week's work. With this arrangement, the organization benefits by having an extra full-time employee only when it needs one, as it does not add another permanent member to its workforce. Such employees are usually excluded from benefit programs but they are usually well paid for their expertise. Here again, the employer enjoys the flexibility of growing and shrinking its workforce as needed and, for some contract workers, this arrangement provides exactly the freedom they desire.

Ultimately, the organization, through its managers, needs first to design jobs to achieve the goals of the organization and second to appropriately staff the jobs. By placing the right people in the jobs that they are best suited for and by keeping the employees motivated to complete their tasks, managers can achieve not only their own goals, but also those of the employees and the company. After all, if everyone is well directed and motivated, the jobs will be performed to everyone's satisfaction. Then, in addition to seeing the organization progress, employees will also feel that they, too, are advancing, whether they are full-time, part-time, or contract workers.

CHAPTER 8 STUDY GUIDE

Summary

What are the alternative job-design approaches?

- Job design is the creation of tasks and work settings for specific jobs.

- Job design by scientific management or job simplification standardizes work and employs people in clearly defined and specialized tasks.

- Job enlargement increases task variety by combining two or more tasks that were previously done by different workers.

- Job rotation increases task variety by periodically rotating workers among jobs involving different tasks.

- Job enrichment builds bigger and more responsible jobs by adding planning and evaluating duties.

What are the keys to designing motivating jobs?

- Job characteristics theory offers a diagnostic approach to job enrichment based on the analysis of five core job characteristics: skill variety, task identity, task significance, autonomy, and feedback.

- Job characteristics theory does not assume that everyone wants an enriched job; it indicates that job enrichment will be more successful for persons with high-growth needs, the needed job skills, and satisfaction with the context.

- The social information processing theory points out that information from co-workers and others in the workplace influences a worker's perceptions and responses to a job.

- Not everyone's job should be enriched; job enrichment can be done for groups as well as individuals; cultural factors may influence how successful job enrichment is.

How does technology influence job design?

- Well-planned sociotechnical systems integrate people and technology for high performance.

- Robotics and complete automation are increasingly used to replace people for jobs that are highly simplified and repetitive.

- Workers in flexible manufacturing cells use the latest technology to produce high-quality products with short setup times.

- The nature of office work is being changed by computer workstation technologies, networks, and various forms of electronic communication.

- Workflow and business process re-engineering analyzes all the steps in a work sequence in order to streamline activities and tasks, save costs, and improve performance.

How can goal setting improve job performance?

- Goal setting is the process of developing, negotiating, and formally stating performance targets or objectives.

- Research supports predictions that the most motivational goals are challenging and specific, allow for feedback on results, and create commitment and acceptance.

- The motivational impact of goals may be affected by individual difference moderators, such as ability and self-efficacy.

- Management by objectives is a process of joint goal setting by a supervisor and worker.

- The management by objectives process is a good way of putting goal-setting theory into practice throughout an organization.

What alternative work arrangements are used today?

- Today's complex society is giving rise to a number of alternative work arrangements that are designed to balance the workers' personal demands with their job responsibilities and opportunities.

- The compressed workweek allows a full-time workweek to be completed in less than five days, typically offering four ten-hour days of work and three days off.

- Flexible working hours allow employees some daily choice in timing their work and nonwork activities.

- Job sharing occurs when two or more people divide one full-time job according to agreements among themselves and the employer.

- Telecommuting involves work at home or at a remote location while communicating with the home office as needed via computer and related technologies.

- Part-time work requires less than a 40-hour workweek and, depending on the schedule, the worker is classified as temporary or permanent.

KEY TERMS

Automation (p. 150)

Compressed workweek (p. 155)

Contract Work (p. 158)

Flexible manufacturing systems (p. 151)

Flexible working hours (p. 156)

Goal setting (p. 142)

Job characteristics model (p. 147)

Job design (p. 145)

Job enlargement (p. 146)

Job enrichment (p. 147)

Job rotation (p. 146)

Job sharing (p. 156)

Job simplification (p. 145)

Motivating-potential score (p. 148)

Permanent part-time work (p. 158)

Process re-engineering (p. 151)

Social information processing (p. 149)

Sociotechnical systems (p. 150)

Telecommuting (p. 157)

Temporary part-time work (p. 158)

SELF-TEST 8

MULTIPLE CHOICE

1. Job simplification is closely associated with _____ as originally developed by Frederick Taylor. (a) vertical loading (b) horizontal loading (c) scientific management (d) self-efficacy

2. Job _____ increases job _____ by combining into one job several tasks of similar difficulty. (a) rotation; depth (b) enlargement; depth (c) rotation; breadth (d) enlargement; breadth

3. In job characteristics theory, _____ indicates how much an individual is able to make decisions that affect his or her work. (a) task variety (b) task identity (c) task significance (d) autonomy

4. The basic logic of sociotechnical systems is that _____ . (a) people must be integrated with technology (b) technology is more important than people (c) people are more important than technology (d) technology alienates people

5. _____ goals tend to be more motivating. (a) Challenging (b) Easy (c) General (d) No

6. The MBO process emphasizes _____ as a way of building a worker's commitment to accomplishing goals. (a) authority (b) joint goal setting (c) infrequent feedback (d) general goals

7. _____ is one of the concerns sometimes raised about MBO programs used throughout an organization. (a) Too much paperwork (b) Too little paperwork (c) Too little emphasis on top-down goals (d) Too much emphasis on group instead of individual goals

8. The "4/40" is a type of _____ work arrangement. (a) compressed workweek (b) flextime (c) job-sharing (d) permanent part-time

9. The flexible working hours schedule allows workers to choose _____. (a) which days to work (b) the total hours to work in a week (c) the location of work (d) the starting and ending times for workdays

10. Today's society is creating a demand for more jobs that by design _____. (a) are easy to perform (b) minimize the need for employee skills (c) are family-friendly (d) have low-performance goals

TRUE–FALSE

11. In some cases, job enrichment may be difficult to implement because of the expenses involved and/or union opposition.   T   F

12. The characteristic of task significance indicates how much a job is meaningful to the organization or society.   T   F

13. According to job characteristics theory, everyone's job should be enriched.   T   F

14. The social information processing approach stresses how important objective job characteristics are to motivation and performance.   T   F

15. Job enrichment is a management practice that does not apply in all cultural settings.   T   F

16. One sure way to motivate through goal-setting is to tell people simply to "do your best."   T   F

17. Goals are most likely to lead to higher performance for people who have high feelings of self-efficacy.   T   F

18. Flextime is unique because it offers advantages to the individual worker with no disadvantages for the employer.   T   F

19. Trends seem to indicate that telecommuting is becoming more attractive to organizations.   T   F

20. The presence of more part-time work is, from all perspectives and in all cases, a positive trend for society as a whole.   T   F

SHORT ANSWER

21. How can you create job enrichment by building job depth?

22. What role does growth-need strength play in job characteristics theory?

23. How can a manager increase an employee's commitment to stated task goals?

24. What is the difference between temporary part-time work and permanent part-time work?

APPLICATIONS ESSAY

25. When Jean-Paul Latrec opened his first Outfitter's Plus store, he wanted to create a motivational work environment for his sales associates. He therefore decided to implement MBO as a core management strategy. Over time, he became well known in Quebec City for his success. If you were to visit his store to study his MBO approach, what would you expect to find him doing to make the program work so well?

The Nature of Groups

Groups Can Bring Out the Best

Groups helped launch Apple Computer, Inc.'s early success, and they are still playing an important role in the company's future. The team that created Apple's original Macintosh computer was really "hot." The brainchild of Apple's co-founder Steve Jobs, it was composed of high-achieving members who were excited and turned on to their highly challenging task. They worked all hours and at an unrelenting pace. Housed in a separate building flying the "Jolly Roger," the Macintosh team combined youthful enthusiasm with great expertise and commitment to an exciting goal. The result was a benchmark computer produced in record time. Apple thrived.

Then came the computer wars. Intense competition in the ever-changing and fast-paced industry took its toll. Apple struggled against the likes of Compaq, Dell, Gateway, and the renewed IBM. Given the chance to return as CEO to the company he founded, Steve Jobs built another team charged with reinvigorating the company. This was the team "at the top." Building what he calls a "world-class" executive team, Jobs found an important key to corporate turnaround. On Apple's team were sales, hardware, software, services, inventory, and legal gurus. Together with Jobs, they brought major changes to such areas as human resources, manufacturing, and marketing. And what they created was first described as follows: "The iMac is the first desktop computer to get the whole industry excited since...well, since the original MacIntosh."

Jump forward to 2003 and Apple creates the iTunes Music Store, taking advantage of the controversy over music theft via the Internet. The iTunes Music Store allows consumers to access music with 99-cents-per-song pricing, free previews, one-click purchasing and downloading, and groundbreaking personal use rights. Recently celebrating its first anniversary, iTunes has become the number one on-line music service in

the world with more than 70 percent market share of legal downloads for singles and albums.

iTunes is the perfect companion for Apple's popular iPod digital music player, which has the battery life for 12 hours of music listening. iPods can store an entire music library—up to 10,000 songs—downloaded from either the Internet or CDs, and Apple has recently added photo storage and voice recording capabilities to the tiny devices, as well.

Product innovation continues to be a hallmark of Apple Computer, Inc. And that, so to speak, is what groups in organizations should be all about.

For organizations, groups can be important sources of performance, creativity, and enthusiasm. This chapter introduces you to the basic attributes of groups as they are found in today's progressive organizations. As you read Chapter 9, keep in mind these key questions:

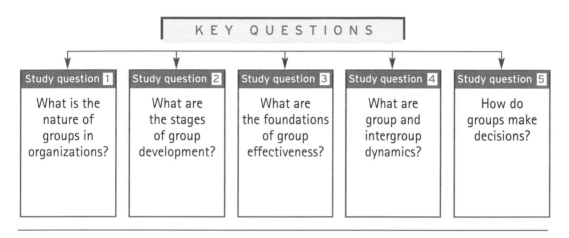

K E Y Q U E S T I O N S				
Study question 1	**Study question 2**	**Study question 3**	**Study question 4**	**Study question 5**
What is the nature of groups in organizations?	What are the stages of group development?	What are the foundations of group effectiveness?	What are group and intergroup dynamics?	How do groups make decisions?

Groups in Organizations

A **group** is two or more people who work together regularly to achieve common goals. In a true group, members (1) are dependent on each other to achieve common goals and (2) interact regularly to pursue those goals over a sustained period of time.[1] Groups are important resources that are good for both organizations and their members. They help organizations to accomplish important tasks. They also help maintain a high-quality workforce by satisfying employee needs. Consultant and management scholar Harold J. Leavitt is a well-known advocate for the power and usefulness of groups.[2] He describes "hot groups" as ones that thrive in crises and competition and whose creativity and innovation generate extraordinary benefits.[3]

A group is two or more people who work together regularly to achieve common goals.

WHAT IS AN EFFECTIVE GROUP?

An **effective group** is a group that achieves high levels of task performance, member satisfaction, and team viability. With regard to *task performance*, an effective group achieves its performance goals in the standard measures of quantity, quality, and timeliness of work results. For a formal workgroup, such as a manufacturing team, this may mean meeting daily production targets. For a temporary group, such as a new policy task force, this may involve meeting a deadline for submitting a new organizational policy to the company president. With regard to *member satisfaction*, an effective group is one whose members view their participation and experiences as positive and as meeting important personal needs. They are satisfied with their tasks, accomplishments, and interpersonal relationships. With regard to *team viability*, the members of an effective group are sufficiently satisfied with each other that they are willing to continue working together on an ongoing basis and/or they look forward to working together again at some future point in time. Such a group has all-important long-term performance potential.

An effective group is a group that achieves high levels of task performance, member satisfaction, and team viability.

UNIQUE CONTRIBUTIONS OF GROUPS

Synergy is the creation of a whole that is greater than the sum of its parts.

Effective groups help organizations accomplish important tasks. In particular, they offer the potential for **synergy**—the creation of a whole that is greater than the sum of its parts. When synergy occurs, groups accomplish more than the total of their members' individual capabilities. Group synergy is necessary for organizations to become competitive and achieve long-term high performance in today's rapidly changing times.

HIGH-PERFORMANCE ORGANIZATION

Whenever a company merges with or acquires a company like itself, there are extensive details to work out. There are legal factors involving labour contracts or such labour practices as working on holidays. There are the difficulties of integrating new people into current systems, which is especially challenging if the merger is international as language and culture can become even larger barriers. CGI Group, based in Montreal, and one of the top five IT companies in North America, has been expanding at a breakneck pace since its beginning in 1976. In 2003, it reported revenues of $2.7 billion and a profit of $177 million. CGI has also made more than 50 acquisitions. How does chief financial officer and co-founder André Imbeau do it so well? According to Louis Wermenlinger of Desjardins Securities, Imbeau "stresses teamwork."[4]

The Effective Manager 9.1

HOW GROUPS CAN HELP ORGANIZATIONS

- Groups are good for people.
- Groups can improve creativity.
- Groups can make better decisions.
- Groups can increase commitments to action.
- Groups help control their members.
- Groups help make large organizations feel smaller.

The Effective Manager 9.1 lists several benefits that groups can bring to organizations. In three specific situations, groups often perform better than an individual acting alone.[5] First, when there is no clear "expert" for a particular task or problem, groups seem to make better judgments than the average individual. Second, when problem-solving can be handled by dividing work and by sharing information, groups are usually more successful than individuals. Third, because they tend to make riskier decisions, groups can be more creative and innovative than individuals.

Groups are important settings where people learn from each other and share job skills and knowledge. The learning environment and combined experience of a group can help solve difficult and unique problems. This is especially helpful to newcomers who often need help in their jobs. When group members support and help each other in acquiring and improving job competencies, they may even overcome weaknesses in an organization's training systems.

Groups can satisfy their members' needs. They offer opportunities for social interaction and can give individuals a sense of security because they make help with work and technical advice available. They can also provide emotional support in times of special crisis or pressure, and allow for ego involvement in group goals and activities. The individual's ownership is the group's success.

Social loafing occurs when people work less hard in groups than they would by themselves.

Although they do have enormous performance potential, groups can still have problems. One concern is **social loafing**, also known as the Ringlemann effect. It is the tendency of people to work less hard in a group than they would if they were working alone.[6] Max Ringlemann, a German psychologist, pinpointed the phenomenon by asking people to pull on a rope as hard as they could, first alone and then in a group.[7] He found that average productivity dropped as more people joined the rope-pulling task. He suggested two reasons for why people may not work as hard in groups as they would individually: (1) their individual contribution is less noticeable in the context of the group, and (2) they prefer to see others carry the workload. Some ways for dealing with social loafing or trying to prevent it from occurring include the following:

- Define members' roles and tasks to maximize individual interests.

- Make the rewards an individual receives depend on the individual's performance contributions to the group.

- Make members feel more responsible for their personal performance by identifying what each individual has contributed to the group.

How to handle social loafing

Another issue in group work is social facilitation—the tendency for one's behaviour to be influenced by the presence of others in a group or social setting.[8] *Social facilitation theory* shows that, in general, working in the presence of others creates an emotional arousal or excitement that stimulates behaviour and therefore affects performance. Arousal tends to work positively when one is proficient with the task. Here, the excitement leads to extra effort at doing something that already comes quite naturally. An example is the play of a world-class athlete in front of an enthusiastic hometown crowd. On the other hand, the effect of social facilitation can be negative when the task is not well learned. You may know this best in the context of public speaking. When asked to speak in front of a class or larger audience about an unfamiliar topic, you may be more likely to stumble.

Social facilitation is the tendency for one's behaviour to be influenced by the presence of others in a group.

OB ACROSS FUNCTIONS

Human Resource Management

Stock Options Can Build the Companywide Team

The human resource function in any organization is dedicated to the attraction and maintenance of a high-quality and talented workforce. As executives struggle today with the complex challenges of social trends and shortages in specialized labour, they are rediscovering one of the foundations of teamwork in any setting: ownership. When workers own shares in their company, something happens. And the result is mostly good—good for them and good for the organization. Nearly one in every 10 private-sector employees, about 815,000, had a stock purchase plan in 1999, according to Statistics Canada. Employees with higher earnings or working in large workplaces, particularly those with 500 or more employees, were more likely to have these plans.

Janssen-Ortho Inc., a Toronto-based pharmaceutical research company, provides stock options beginning at the middle-management level. "We try to reach down to this level of managers as we feel those are the people who will impact on the long-term growth of the company, which is the kind of growth stock options are meant to support," says Greg Anderson, vice president, human resources. "We want people to see a clear link between managing for the long-term, which we ask them to do every day, and a long-term reward, which is what stock options can deliver."[9] This should mean more commitment to the job and a greater sense of teamwork around the company. After all, there is no greater bond between workers than a shared sense of ownership and shared responsibility for making their investments successful, whether the organization is large or small.

FORMAL GROUPS

Formal groups are groups that are officially designated for a specific organizational purpose.

There are many ways for groups to be used to great advantage in the new workplace. A **formal group** is a group that is officially designated for a specific organizational purpose. An example is the work unit headed by a manager and consisting of one or more people who report directly to the manager. The organization creates such a group to perform a specific task, which typically involves the use of resources to create a product such as a report, decision, service, or commodity. The head of a formal group is responsible for the group's performance accomplishments, but all members contribute required work. Also, the head of the group plays a key "linking-pin" role that ties the group horizontally and vertically to the rest of the organization.[10]

Formal groups may be permanent or temporary. *Permanent workgroups—*or *command groups* in an organization's vertical structure—often appear on organization charts as departments (e.g., market research department), divisions (e.g., consumer products division), or teams (e.g., product-assembly team). Such groups can vary in size from very small departments or teams of just a few people to large divisions employing a hundred or more people. As permanent workgroups, they are each officially created to perform a specific function on a regular basis. They continue to exist until a decision is made to change or reconfigure the organization for some reason.

In contrast, *temporary workgroups* are task groups that are specifically created to solve a problem or perform a defined task. They often disband after the assigned purpose or task has been accomplished.[11] Examples are the many temporary committees and task forces that are an important part of any organization. Indeed, today's organizations tend to make more use of *cross-functional teams* or *task forces* for special problem-solving efforts. The president of a company, for example, might create a task force to examine the possibility of implementing flexible work hours for non-managerial employees. Usually, such temporary groups appoint chairpersons or heads who are held accountable for results, much as the manager of a work unit is. Another common form is the project team that is formed, often cross-functionally, to complete a specific task with a well-defined end point. Examples include installing a new e-mail system and introducing a new product modification.

Members of virtual groups work together through computer networks.

Information technology is bringing a new type of group into the workplace. This is the **virtual group**, a group whose members meet and work together electronically through networked computers. In this electronic age, virtual groups are increasingly common in organizations. Helped by always better team-oriented software, or groupware, members of virtual groups can do the same things as members of face-to-face groups. They can share information, make decisions, and complete tasks. The important role of virtual groups or teams in the high-performance workplace is discussed in the next chapter.

WORKPLACE DIVERSITY

Virtual teams are a valuable development at Roche, one of the world's leading pharmaceutical companies. In 1996, Roche set up a subsidiary called Protodigm, which has as its mission to put new drugs through clinical trials for future approval and marketing. Because Protodigm operates with few managers, its overhead costs are lower and it has less bureaucracy, which means that it operates faster and is freer to negotiate hard bargains with its suppliers. With up to 20 companies involved in Roche's drug trials, coordination is important. There are also more opportunities because Roche operates not only in Canada and the U.S. but also in other countries and the result is faster approval of new drugs in many markets at the same time. Once the approval process is complete, responsibility for the new drugs returns to the parent company for marketing. Of course, Roche's involvement with so many other companies is not typical of the usual secrecy found in the pharmaceutical industry. According to Jon Court, managing director of Protodigm, however, "being able to ask the right questions is the key thing," and as a team, the nine employees of Protodigm in 1998 shared over 150 years of experience. Still, thanks to modern IT and communications systems, high-quality independent companies have access to more knowledge and larger companies can find the skills and culture of innovation that they sometimes lack.[12]

INFORMAL GROUPS

Informal groups are groups that form without being officially designated by the organization. They arise spontaneously from personal relationships or special interests, not because of any specific organizational decision. *Friendship groups,* for example, consist of persons with a natural liking for one another. They tend to work together, sit together, take breaks together, and even do things together outside of the workplace. *Interest groups* consist of persons who share common interests. These may be job-related interests, such as an intense desire to learn more about computers, or nonwork interests, such as community service, sports, or religion.

> **Informal groups** are groups that form without being officially designated by the organization.

    Informal groups can help people get their jobs done. These groups have the potential to speed up the workflow because people who are part of this network of interpersonal relationships often help each other in ways that formal lines of authority do not. They also help individuals satisfy needs that are blocked or unsatisfied in a formal group. In these and related ways, informal groups can provide their members with social satisfaction, security, and a sense of belonging.

Stages of Group Development

Whether it is a formal work unit, a temporary task force, or a virtual team, the group passes through a series of life cycle stages.[13] Depending on the stage the group has reached, the leader and members can face very different challenges. Figure 9.1 describes Bruce Tuckman's five stages of group development: (1) forming, (2) storming, (3) norming, (4) performing, and (5) adjourning.[14] In Allan Drexler and David Sibbet's model of group formation, the group passes through seven phases: (1) orientation, (2) trust building , (3) group/role clarification, (4) commitment, (5) implementation, (6) high performance, and (7) renewal. Both models of group formation are helpful and in both models the group must resolve the issues of the current stage before it can go to the next stage. The issues to be resolved include such things as goal clarification, role solidification, and performing, all of which lead to either the continuation or breakup of the group. We will focus on Tuckman's model as it is more widely recognized.

Figure 9.1 Five stages of group development

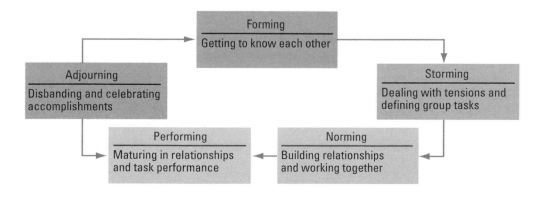

FORMING STAGE

In the *forming stage* of group development, one of the main concerns is the initial entry of members to the group. During this stage, individuals ask many questions as they begin to feel comfortable with other group members and with the group itself. Some of the questions they might ask themselves include these: What can the group offer me? What will I be asked to contribute? Can my needs be met at the same time as I contribute to the group? Members are interested in getting to know each other and discovering what is considered acceptable behaviour; in determining the real task of the group; and in defining group rules.

STORMING STAGE

The *storming stage* of group development is a period of high emotion and tension among the group's members. During this stage, hostility and infighting may occur, and the group typically experiences many changes. Coalitions or cliques may form as individuals compete to push their preferences on the group and to achieve a desired status position. Outside demands, including premature expectations for performance results, may create uncomfortable pressures. During this stage, members' expectations tend to be clarified, and the group's attention shifts toward obstacles standing in the way of group goals. Individuals begin to understand each other's interpersonal styles, and efforts are made to find ways to accomplish group goals while also satisfying individual needs. In Donald Trump's reality TV show, *The Apprentice*, this is the very core of the problems for the teams each week: they must work together and do it quickly to win. If a team loses the competition, however, only one person from the team is actually eliminated—a consequence that can work against team or group adhesion and collaboration.

NORMING STAGE

The *norming stage* of group development, sometimes called initial integration, is the point at which the group really begins to come together as a coordinated unit. Instead of the turmoil of the storming stage, there is now a precarious balancing of forces. With the pleasure that comes from a new sense of harmony, group members will strive to maintain a positive balance. Holding the group together may become more important to some members than successfully working on the group's tasks. Minority viewpoints, deviations from group directions, and criticisms may be discouraged as group members first experience a sense of closeness. Some members may mistakenly perceive this stage as one of ultimate maturity. In fact, a premature sense of accomplishment at this point needs to be carefully managed as a "stepping stone" to the next and higher level of group development.

PERFORMING STAGE

The *performing stage* of group development, sometimes called total integration, marks the emergence of a mature, organized, and well-functioning group. The group is now able to deal with complex tasks and handle internal disagreements in creative ways. The structure is stable, and members are motivated by group goals while being generally satisfied. The main challenges are continued efforts to improve relationships and performance. At this stage, the group members should also be able to adapt successfully as opportunities and demands change over time. A group that has achieved this level of total integration typically scores high on the criteria of group maturity shown in Figure 9.2.

Figure 9.2 Ten criteria for measuring the maturity of a group

	Immature group			Mature group
1. Feedback mechanisms	poor			excellent
2. Decision-making methods	dysfunctional			functional
3. Group loyalty/cohesion	low			high
4. Operating procedures	inflexible			flexible
5. Use of member resources	poor			excellent
6. Communications	unclear			clear
7. Goals	not accepted			accepted
8. Authority relations	independent			interdependent
9. Participation in leadership	low			high
10. Aceptance of minority views	low			high

ADJOURNING STAGE

A well-integrated group is able to disband, if required, when its work is accomplished. The *adjourning stage* of group development is especially important for the many temporary groups that are increasingly common in the new workplace, including task forces, committees, project teams, and so on. Members of these groups must be able to meet quickly, do their jobs on a tight schedule, and then adjourn—often to reform later if needed. Their willingness to break up when the job is done and to work well together in future group and non-group responsibilities is an important long-run test of group success.

Foundations of Group Effectiveness

To reach and then keep high levels of group effectiveness, any manager or leader must understand how groups work as organizational resources. The systems model in Figure 9.3 shows how groups, like organizations, try to be effective by interacting with their environments to transform resource inputs into product outputs.[15] The inputs are the initial givens or "ingredients" in any group situation. They are the foundations for all later action. In general, the stronger the foundations, the better the chances for long-term group effectiveness. The key group inputs are the task itself and the goals, rewards, resources, technology, membership diversity, and group size.

Figure 9.3 The workgroup as an open system transforming resource inputs into product outputs

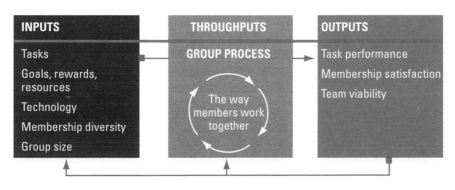

TASKS

The tasks that a group is asked to perform can make different demands on the group, and the group's effectiveness will be affected accordingly. The *technical demands* of a group's task are its routineness, difficulty, and information requirements. The *social demands* of a task involve relationships, ego involvement, controversies over ends and means, and so on. Tasks that are complex in technical demands require unique solutions and more information processing. Tasks that are complex in social demands involve difficulties in reaching agreement on goals or methods for accomplishing them. Naturally, group effectiveness is harder to achieve when the task is highly complex.[16] To master complexity, group members must apply and distribute their efforts broadly. They must also actively co-operate to achieve the desired results. When efforts to master complex tasks are successful, however, group members tend to experience high levels of satisfaction with the group and its accomplishments.

GOALS, REWARDS, AND RESOURCES

Appropriate goals, well-designed reward systems, and adequate resources are all essential as support for long-term performance accomplishments. Just as an individual's performance can suffer when goals are unclear, unchallenging, or arbitrarily imposed, so too can a group's performance. It can also suffer if goals and rewards are focused too much on individual achievements instead of group accomplishments. And it can suffer if adequate budgets, the right facilities, good work methods and procedures, and the best technologies are not available. In contrast, having the right goals, rewards, and resources can help create a strong foundation for group success. Once again we are back to expectance theory, as the group members must first want the reward, value the goal, and also believe they have what they need in order to succeed.

TECHNOLOGY

Technology provides the means to get work accomplished. It is always necessary to have the right technology available for the task to be done. The kind of workflow technology that is used can also influence the way group members interact with each other while performing their tasks. It is one thing to be part of a group that crafts products according to specific customer requests; it is quite another to be part of a group whose members staff one section of a machine-paced assembly line. The former technology permits greater interaction among group members. It will probably create a closer-knit group with a stronger sense of identity than the one formed around one small segment of an assembly line.

MEMBERSHIP CHARACTERISTICS

To achieve success, a group must have the right skills and competencies for performing the task and solving problems. Although abilities alone cannot guarantee desired results, they establish the potential for performance. When the competencies of the group's members are insufficient for the task, it is difficult to overcome the performance limits that result.

In homogeneous groups, where members are very similar to one another, members may find it very easy to work together. But they may still face performance limitations if their combined skills, experience, and perspectives are not a good match for complex tasks. In heterogeneous groups, whose members vary in age, gender, race, ethnicity, experience, culture and

EDS

www.eds.com

High-tech meeting facilities are to be expected at computer-services giant EDS which has locations across Canada. In the firm's Capture Labs, teams have full access to the Internet and the company's intranet in a fully integrated information network. Large-screen projections facilitate discussion.

so on, a wide pool of talent and viewpoints is available for problem-solving. But this diversity may create difficulties as members try to define problems, share information, and handle interpersonal conflicts. These difficulties may be especially significant in the early stages of group development. Once members learn how to work together, however, research confirms that diversity can lead to better performance potential.[17]

The Canadian Forces are currently facing such group issues as they prepare for missions, such as in Afghanistan, while bringing new recruits into the existing collective. Because our society encourages a more individualistic outlook, it is a challenge to increase the recruits' concerns for their comrades. On the other hand, the younger recruits are better at accepting other cultures, and their varied perspectives can be valuable to the changing military personnel and evolving roles expected of the modern armed forces.

Researchers identify what is called the **diversity–consensus dilemma**. This is the tendency for increasing diversity among group members to make it harder for group members to work together even though the diversity itself expands the skills and perspectives available for problem-solving.[18] The challenge to group effectiveness in a culturally mixed multinational team, for example, is to take advantage of the diversity without the group's processes being hurt by this same diversity.[19]

The mix of personalities is also important in a group or team. The **FIRO-B theory** (with "FIRO" standing for fundamental interpersonal orientation) identifies differences in how people in groups relate to each other based on their needs to express and receive feelings of inclusion, control, and affection.[20] Developed by William Schutz, the theory suggests that groups whose members have compatible needs are likely to be more effective than groups whose members have needs that do not go well together. Symptoms of incompatibilities in a group include withdrawn members, open hostilities, struggles over control, and domination of the group by a few members. Schutz states the management implications of the FIRO-B theory this way: "If at the outset we can choose a group of people who can work together harmoniously, we shall go far toward avoiding situations where a group's efforts are wasted in interpersonal conflicts."[21]

Another source of diversity in group membership is *status*—a person's relative rank, prestige, or standing in a group. Status in a group can be based on many different factors, including age, work seniority, occupation, education, performance, or position in other groups. **Status congruence** occurs when a person's position in the group is equivalent in status to the positions he or she has outside of the group. Problems can be expected when there is status incongruence. In high power distance cultures, such as Malaysia, for example, the chair of a committee is expected to be the highest-ranking member of the group. Such status congruence helps members feel comfortable in proceeding with their work. If the senior member is not appointed to head the committee, members are likely to feel uncomfortable and to have difficulty working as a group. Similar problems might occur, for example, when a young college graduate is appointed to chair a project group whose members include senior and more experienced workers.

GROUP SIZE

The size of a group can have an impact on group effectiveness. As a group becomes larger, more people are available to divide the work and accomplish needed tasks. This can boost performance and member satisfaction, but only up to a point. As a group continues to grow in size, communication and coordination problems often arise. Satisfaction may drop, and turnover, absenteeism, and social loafing may increase. Even logistical matters, such as finding times and locations for meetings, become more difficult for larger groups and can hurt performance.[22]

The diversity–consensus dilemma is the tendency for diversity in groups to create process difficulties even as it offers more potential for problem-solving.

FIRO–B theory examines differences in how people in groups relate to each other based on their needs to express and receive feelings of inclusion, control, and affection.

Status congruence refers to consistency between a person's status inside and outside the group.

A good size for problem-solving groups is between five and seven members. A group with fewer than five may be too small to adequately share responsibilities. With more than seven, individuals may find it harder to participate and offer ideas. Larger groups are also in more danger of being dominated by aggressive members and tend to split into coalitions or subgroups.[23] Groups with an odd number of members find it easier to use majority voting rules to resolve disagreements. When speed is required, using votes to manage conflict is useful, and odd-numbered groups may therefore be preferred. But when careful deliberations are required and the emphasis is more on consensus, such as in jury duty or very complex problem-solving, even-numbered groups may be more effective, unless, of course, an irreconcilable deadlock occurs.[24]

Group and Intergroup Dynamics

The effectiveness of any group as an open system (shown in Figure 9.3) always requires more than the correct inputs. It also depends on how well members work together at using these inputs to produce the desired outputs. When we speak about people working together in groups, we are dealing with issues of **group dynamics**—the forces operating in groups that affect the way members relate to and work with each other. In the open-systems model, group dynamics are the processes through which inputs are transformed into outputs.

> Group dynamics are the forces operating in groups that affect the way members relate to and work with each other.

WHAT GOES ON WITHIN GROUPS

George Homans described a classic model of group dynamics involving two sets of behaviours—required and emergent. In a workgroup, *required behaviours* are the behaviours that are formally defined and expected by the organization.[25] For example, they may include such behaviours as punctuality, customer respect, and assistance to co-workers. *Emergent behaviours* are the behaviours that group members display in addition to the required behaviours. They come from personal initiative rather than from outside expectations. Emergent behaviours often include things that people do beyond formal job requirements and that help get the job done in the best ways possible. It is rare for required behaviours to be specified so perfectly that they meet all the demands of a work situation. This makes emergent behaviours essential. An example might be someone taking the time to send an e-mail to two absent members to keep them informed about what happened during a group meeting. The concept of empowerment, often discussed in this book as being essential to the high-performance workplace, relies strongly on unlocking this positive aspect of emergent behaviours.

Homans' model of group dynamics also describes member relationships in terms of activities, interactions, and sentiments, all of which have their required and emergent forms. *Activities* are the things people do in groups while working on tasks. *Interactions* are interpersonal communications and contacts. *Sentiments* are the feelings, attitudes, beliefs, and values of group members.

ETHICS AND SOCIAL RESPONSIBILITY

Mount Sinai Hospital in Toronto has grown from a 30-bed maternity hospital to being one of the top six women's care centres in the world. Teams are at the core of all that goes on in the hospital. Starting on an employee's very first day, the approach is as a team of multidisciplinary professionals reaching out to the multicultural community. The goal is to provide focused care for patients and their families while building internal and external partnerships and being a top teaching hospital.

During the 2003 accreditation process, the surveyors commented that the "teams were enthusiastic, informative, and have a thirst for knowledge." This hospital was not only commended for its current outstanding performance but was also encouraged to "seize the future" in order to continue providing an excellent service to its population while also building on the leadership Mount Sinai brings to the international stage. [26]

WHAT GOES ON BETWEEN GROUPS

The term **intergroup dynamics** refers to the dynamics that take place between two or more groups. Ideally, organizations operate as co-operative systems in which the various parts support each other. In the real world, however, competition and intergroup problems often develop within an organization and lead to consequences, both good and bad. On the negative side— such as when manufacturing and sales units do not get along—intergroup dynamics may misdirect energies as members focus more on their dislike of the other group than on the performance of important tasks.[27] On the positive side, competition among groups can push their members to work harder, become more focused on key tasks, develop more internal loyalty and satisfaction, and achieve a higher level of creativity in problem-solving. Japanese companies, for example, often use competitive themes to motivate their workforces throughout the organization. At Sony, it has been said that the slogan "BMW" stands for "Beat Matsushita Whatsoever."[28]

Organizations and their managers make great efforts to avoid the negative and achieve the positive aspects of intergroup dynamics. Groups involved in destructive competition, for example, can be refocused on a common enemy or a common goal. Direct negotiations can be held among the groups, and members can be trained to work more co-operatively. It is important to avoid win-or-lose reward systems in which one group must lose something in order for the other to gain. Instead, rewards can be refocused on contributions to the total organization and on how much groups help each other. Co-operation also tends to increase as the interaction between groups increases.

> **Intergroup dynamics** are the relationships between groups that are co-operating and competing with each other.

Decision-Making in Groups

One of the most important activities in any group is decision-making—discussed in detail in Chapter 17 as the process of choosing among alternative courses of action. Clearly, the quality and timeliness of the decisions and the processes used to make them can have an important impact on group effectiveness.

HOW GROUPS MAKE DECISIONS

Edgar Schein, a respected scholar and consultant, has worked extensively with groups to analyze and improve their decision-making processes.[29] He observes that groups may make decisions through any of the following six methods: lack of response, authority rule, minority rule, majority rule, consensus, or unanimity.

In *decision by lack of response,* one idea after another is suggested without any discussion taking place. When the group finally accepts an idea, all the other ideas have been passed by and discarded by simple lack of response rather than by critical evaluation. In *decision by authority rule*, the chairperson, manager, or leader makes a decision for the group. This can be done with or without discussion and is very time efficient. Whether the decision is a good one or a bad one depends on whether the authority figure has the necessary information and on

The Effective Manager 9.2

GUIDELINES FOR GROUP
CONSENSUS

• Do not argue blindly; consider others'
  reactions to your points.

• Do not change your mind just to reach
  quick agreement.

• Avoid conflict reduction by voting,
  coin tossing, and bargaining.

• Try to involve everyone in the decision
  process.

• Allow disagreements to surface so
  that information and opinions can be
  discussed.

• Do not focus on winning versus losing;
  seek alternatives that are acceptable
  to all.

• Discuss assumptions, listen carefully,
  and encourage participation by everyone.

Consensus is a group decision that has the expressed
support of most members.

how well other group members accept this approach. In *decision by minority rule*, two or three people are able to dominate or "railroad" the group into making a decision the minority likes. This is often done by providing a suggestion and then forcing quick agreement by challenging the group with such statements as "Does anyone object?... No? Well, let's go ahead then."

One of the most common ways groups make decisions, especially when early signs of disagreement appear, is *decision by majority rule*. Formal voting may take place or members may be polled to find the majority viewpoint. This method parallels the democratic political system and is often used without awareness of its potential problems. The very process of voting can create coalitions; that is, some people will be "winners," and others will be "losers" when the final vote is tallied. Those in the minority—the "losers"—may feel left out or discarded without having had a fair chance to express themselves. As a result, they may be less enthusiastic about implementing the decision of the "winners." Lasting resentments may then damage the group's effectiveness in the future.

Another alternative is *decision by consensus*. Formally defined, consensus is what results when discussion leads to one alternative being favoured by most members and the other members agreeing to support it. When a consensus is reached, even those who may have opposed the chosen course of action know that they have been listened to and have had a fair chance to influence the outcome. Consensus, as suggested by the guidelines in The Effective Manager 9.2, does not require unanimity. What it does require is for any dissenting members to feel they have been able to speak and that their voices have been heard.[30]

A *decision by unanimity* may be the ideal state of affairs. Here, all group members agree totally on the course of action to be taken. This is a "logically perfect" group-decision method that is extremely difficult to achieve in actual practice. One reason that groups sometimes turn to authority decisions, majority voting, or even minority decisions is the difficulty of managing the group process to achieve consensus or unanimity.[31]

ASSETS AND LIABILITIES OF GROUP DECISION-MAKING

The best groups do not limit themselves to just one decision-making method, using it over and over again in all circumstances. Instead, they operate in contingency fashion by changing their decision methods to best fit the current problem and situation. Indeed, an important leadership skill is helping a group choose the "right" decision method—the one that can lead to a timely and quality decision that the group's members are highly committed to.

The choice among decision methods should be made with a full awareness of both the potential advantages and disadvantages of group decision-making. The *potential advantages of group decision-making* include the following:[32]

**Advantages of group
decision-making**

1. *information*—More knowledge and expertise is applied to solve the problem.

2. *alternatives*—A greater number of alternatives are examined, avoiding tunnel vision.

3. *understanding and acceptance*—The final decision is better understood and accepted by all group members.

4. *commitment*—There is more commitment among all group members to make the final decision work.

We also know that groups can experience problems when they are making decisions. *The potential disadvantages of group decision-making* include the following:[33]

1. *social pressure to conform*—Individuals may feel compelled to go along with the apparent wishes of the group.

2. *minority domination*—The group's decision may be forced or "railroaded" by one individual or a small coalition.

3. *time demands*—With more people involved in the dialogue and discussion, it usually takes longer for a group to make a decision than it takes an individual.

Disadvantages of group decision-making

GROUPTHINK

Identified by social psychologist Irving Janis, an important potential problem in group decision-making is **groupthink**—the tendency of members in highly cohesive groups to lose their ability to evaluate critically.[34] Janis believes that because highly cohesive groups demand conformity their members tend to become unwilling to criticize each other's ideas and suggestions. Desires to hold the group together and to avoid unpleasant disagreements lead to an overemphasis on agreement and an underemphasis on critical discussion. The possible result is a poor decision. Janis suggests that groupthink played a role in the lack of preparedness of U.S. forces at Pearl Harbor in World War II. It has also been linked to U.S. decision-making during the Vietnam War and to both space shuttle disasters. More recently, the Bush administration and the U.S. Congress's decision to invade Iraq based on a policy of "preemptive use of military force against terrorists and rogue nations" is seen as an example of groupthink. Repetition of phrases like "axis of evil" and "freedom-loving people" motivated this way of thinking.[35]

Group leaders and members should be alert to the symptoms of groupthink and quick to take any necessary action to prevent it.[36] The Effective Manager 9.3 identifies steps that can be taken to avoid groupthink.

Groupthink is the tendency of members of cohesive groups to lose their ability to evaluate critically.

The Effective Manager 9.3

HOW TO AVOID GROUPTHINK

- Assign the role of critical evaluator to each group member.
- Have the leader avoid seeming partial to one course of action.
- Create subgroups to work on the same problem.
- Have group members discuss issues with outsiders and report back.
- Invite outside experts to observe and react to group processes.
- Assign someone to be a "devil's advocate" at each meeting.
- Write alternative scenarios for competing groups to use.
- Hold "second-chance" meetings after consensus is apparently achieved.

HOW TO IMPROVE GROUP DECISION-MAKING

To take full advantage of the group as a decision-making resource, group dynamics must be managed so that individual contributions and group operations are balanced.[37] A particular concern is the process losses that often occur in free-flowing meetings, such as a committee deliberation or a staff meeting on a specific problem. In these settings, social pressures to conform, domination, time pressures, and even highly emotional debates can take away from the group's real purpose. They are also settings in which special group decision techniques may be used for better results.[38]

Brainstorming   In **brainstorming**, group members actively generate as many ideas and alternatives as possible, and they do this relatively quickly and without inhibitions. Four rules typically govern the brainstorming process. First, *all criticism is ruled out*. No one is allowed to judge or evaluate any ideas until the idea-generation process has been completed. Second, *"freewheeling" is welcomed*. The emphasis is on creativity and imagination; the wilder or more

Brainstorming generates ideas through "freewheeling" and without criticism.

radical the ideas, the better. Third, quantity is wanted. The emphasis is also on the number of ideas; the more ideas there are, the more likely a superior idea will appear. Fourth, *"piggybacking" is good.* Everyone is encouraged to suggest how others' ideas can be turned into new ideas or how two or more ideas can be joined into still another new idea. Typical results include enthusiasm, involvement, and a free flow of ideas that is useful in creative problem-solving.

Nominal Group Technique In any group, there will be times when the opinions of members differ so much that antagonistic arguments will develop during freewheeling discussions. At other times, the group will be so large that open discussion and brainstorming are awkward to manage. In such cases, a form of structured group decision-making called the **nominal group technique** may be helpful.[39] It puts people in small groups of six to seven members and asks everyone to respond individually and in writing to a "nominal question," such as "What should be done to improve the effectiveness of this work team?" Everyone is encouraged to list as many alternatives or ideas as they can. Next, one after the other, participants read aloud their responses to the question and the recorder writes each response on large newsprint. No criticism is allowed. The recorder then asks for any questions that may clarify items on the newsprint. This is again done with each person having a turn, and no evaluation is allowed. The goal is simply to make sure that everyone in the group fully understands each response. A structured voting procedure is then used to prioritize the responses to the nominal question. The nominal group procedure allows ideas to be evaluated without risking the inhibitions, hostilities, and distortions that may occur in an open meeting.

Delphi Technique A third group-decision approach, the **Delphi technique**, was developed by the Rand Corporation for when group members are unable to meet face to face. In this procedure, a series of questionnaires is distributed to a panel of decision makers, who then submit their first responses to a decision coordinator. The coordinator summarizes the responses and sends the summary back to the panel members, along with a follow-up questionnaire. Panel members again send in their responses, and the process is repeated until a consensus is reached and a clear decision emerges.

Computer-Mediated Decision-Making Today's information and computer technologies enable group decision-making across great distances with the help of group-decision support systems. The growing use of *electronic brainstorming* is one example of the trend toward virtual meetings. Assisted by special software, participants use personal computers to enter their ideas at will, either through simultaneous interaction or over a period of time. The software collects and sends out the results. The nominal group and Delphi techniques work well with computer mediation. Electronic approaches to group decision-making can offer several advantages, including the benefits of anonymity, a greater number of ideas being generated, the efficiency of recording and storing for later use, and the ability to handle large groups whose members are in different places.[40]

Ultimately, the success of our various organizations depends on the ability of their members to effectively and efficiently achieve the organizations' goals. With the complexity of the global workplace, the diversity of our workforces, and the quick-paced ever-changing marketplace, organizations and their managers must make the best use of the human resources available. By understanding the groups we deal with, the processes they evolve through, the pitfalls they need to avoid, and the successful procedures they can use, as managers we can make the teams of the future the best opportunity for our organizations to survive and prosper.

The nominal group technique uses structured rules for generating and prioritizing ideas.

The Delphi technique generates decision-making alternatives through a series of survey questionnaires.

CHAPTER 9 STUDY GUIDE

Summary

What is the nature of groups in organizations?

- A group is two or more people who work together regularly to achieve common goals.

- Groups can help organizations by helping their members improve their task performance and get more satisfaction from their work.

- One way to view organizations is as interlocking networks of groups whose managers serve as leaders in one group and subordinates in another.

- Synergy occurs when groups are able to accomplish more than their members could accomplish by acting individually.

- Formal groups are designated by the organization to serve an official purpose: examples are work units, task forces, and committees. Informal groups are unofficial and emerge spontaneously because of special interests.

What are the stages of group development?

- Groups pass through various stages in their life cycles, and each stage brings different management problems.

- In the forming stage, groups have problems managing the entry of individuals.

- In the storming stage, groups have problems managing their members' expectations and status.

- In the norming or initial integration stage, groups have problems managing their members' relations and task efforts.

- In the performing or total integration stage, groups have problems managing continuous improvement and self-renewal.

- In the adjourning stage, groups have problems managing task completion and the process of breaking up.

What are the foundations of group effectiveness?

- An effective group is one that achieves high levels of task accomplishment and member satisfaction, and achieves viability to perform successfully over the long term.

- As open systems, groups must interact successfully with their environments to obtain resources that are transformed into outputs.

- Group input factors establish the foundation for effectiveness. These inputs include goals, rewards, resources, technology, the task, membership characteristics, and group size, among other elements.

What are group and intergroup dynamics?

- Group dynamics are the way members work together to use inputs; these dynamics are another foundation of group effectiveness.

- Group dynamics are based on the interactions, activities, and sentiments of group members, and on the required and emergent ways in which members work together.

- Intergroup dynamics are the forces that operate between two or more groups.

- Although groups in organizations ideally co-operate with each other, they often become involved in dysfunctional conflicts and competition.

- The disadvantages of intergroup competition can be reduced through management strategies to direct, train, and reinforce groups to pursue co-operative instead of purely competitive actions.

How do groups make decisions?

- Groups can make decisions by lack of response, authority rule, minority rule, majority rule, consensus, and unanimity.

- The potential advantages of having more group decision-making include having more information available and generating more understanding and commitment.

- The potential disadvantages of having more group decision-making include social pressures to conform and the need for more time.

- Groupthink is the tendency of members of cohesive groups to lose their ability to evaluate critically.

- Techniques for improving creativity in group decision-making include brainstorming, the nominal group technique, and the Delphi method, with computer applications being a helpful resource.

KEY TERMS

Brainstorming (p. 177)

Consensus (p. 176)

Delphi technique (p. 178)

Diversity–consensus dilemma (p. 173)

Effective groups (p. 165)

FIRO-B theory (p. 173)

Formal groups (p. 168)

Groups (p. 165)

Group dynamics (p. 174)

Groupthink (p. 177)

Informal groups (p. 169)

Intergroup dynamics (p. 175)

Nominal group technique (p. 178)

Social loafing (p. 166)

Social facilitation (p. 167)

Status congruence (p. 173)

Synergy (p. 166)

Virtual groups (p. 168)

SELF-TEST 9

MULTIPLE CHOICE

1. The FIRO-B theory is about _____ in groups. (a) membership compatibilities (b) social loafing (c) dominating members (d) conformity

2. It is during the _____ stage of group development that members begin to really come together as a coordinated unit. (a) storming (b) norming (c) performing (d) total-integration

3. An effective group is defined as one that achieves high levels of task performance, member satisfaction, and _____. (a) coordination (b) harmony (c) creativity (d) team viability

4. Task characteristics, reward systems, and group size are all _____ that can make a difference in group effectiveness. (a) group processes (b) group dynamics (c) group inputs (d) human-resource maintenance factors

5. The best size for a problem-solving group is usually _____ members. (a) no more than 3 or 4 (b) 5 to 7 (c) 8 to 10 (d) around 12 to 13

6. When two groups are competing with each other, in each group _____ may be expected. (a) more group loyalty (b) less reliance on the leader (c) less task focus (d) more conflict

7. The tendency of members of highly cohesive groups to lose their ability to evaluate critically during decision-making is a phenomenon called _____. (a) groupthink (b) the Ringlemann effect (c) decision congruence (d) group consensus

8. When a decision requires a high degree of commitment for its implementation, a/an _____ decision is generally preferred. (a) authority (b) majority-vote (c) group-consensus (d) groupthink

9. What does the Ringlemann effect describe about group behaviour? (a) the tendency of groups to make risky decisions (b) social loafing (c) social facilitation (d) the satisfaction of members' social needs

10. Members of a multinational task force in a large international business should be aware that _____ might at first slow the progress of the group in meeting its task objectives. (a) synergy (b) groupthink (c) the diversity-consensus dilemma (d) intergroup dynamics

TRUE–FALSE

11. The creation of a whole that is greater than the sum of its parts defines synergy.   T   F

12. Informal groups tend to hurt organizations and should not be tolerated by managers.   T   F

13. Generally speaking, members of heterogeneous groups are expected to work easily and well with each other.   T   F

14. Poor attitudes toward work are examples of sentiments that may exist in group dynamics.   T   F

15. Decision by majority voting is the only group decision method that has no disadvantages.   T   F

16. The potential liabilities or disadvantages of group decision-making include social pressures to conform.   T   F

17. When group members are not getting along well together, the brainstorming technique is a good approach for improving creativity in decision-making.   T   F

18. Devil's advocate roles and second-chance meetings are good ways for members to avoid the dangers of groupthink.   T   F

19. Increasing interactions among members is one way of dealing with dysfunctional intergroup relationships.   T   F

20. Group decision-making is always better than individual decision-making.   T   F

SHORT ANSWER

21. How can groups be good for organizations?

22. What types of formal groups are found in organizations today?

23. What is the difference between required and emergent behaviours in group dynamics?

24. How can intergroup competition be bad for organizations?

APPLICATIONS ESSAY

25. Alex Cheung has encountered a dilemma in working with his quality-circle (QC) team. One of the team members claims that the QC must always be unanimous in its recommendations. "Otherwise," she says, "we will not have a true consensus." Alex, the current QC leader, disagrees. He believes that unanimity is desirable but not always necessary to achieve consensus. You are a management consultant specializing in the use of groups in organizations. Alex calls you for advice. What would you tell him and why?

Teamwork and High-Performance Teams

A Team With Heart

In February 2002 in Salt Lake City, Utah, years of hard work and team building came together to produce results—an Olympic gold medal for Canada and the 21 players who made up the women's hockey team. This kind of world-class success doesn't happen overnight, or without effort. Canada's team captain Cassie Campbell says it takes dedication, training, motivation to improve, and being prepared to win on the right day. "We were by far the fitter team come gold medal day at the Olympics," she says. "We had lost eight times in a row to the Americans prior to the Olympics. It was important to learn to work together as a team."

What Canada's hockey team had was a lot of **HEART**, an acronym Ms. Campbell uses in the motivational speeches she now gives on teamwork and leadership. Creating an effective team takes **H**ard work, **E**xperience and the ability to learn from experience, a good **A**ttitude and the willingness to push yourself, **R**espect for other team members and responsibility for your own actions, and **T**eam spirit.

The 2002 Olympic team—a gathering of the best women hockey players from across the country—began training together, both on and off the ice, in Calgary eight months before the games. Off-ice training included many team-building activities like obstacle courses, cross-country skiing, pond hockey, or simply visiting places together. By the end of the eight months, the women knew each other quite well. They were a mix of veteran players who were part of the team that won the silver medal four years earlier in Nagano, Japan, and eight new members with no Olympic experience.

"In 1998, we learned a lot of lessons that we were able to pass on to the younger players and help them keep their perspective," Ms. Campbell says. "And yet they helped us keep our perspective on how fun it is to play and be a part of this program. They brought some youth and energy to those of us who had been around a long time."

Each of the women on this high-performance team shared core values—a love and appreciation for the game of hockey; clear performance objectives—the Olympic gold; the right mix of skills—the best veteran and rookie players in the country; and creativity—the ability to analyze their opponents, find holes in their game, and adjust their performance in order to win.

Highly motivated and successful teams are a standard feature of successful organizations today. This chapter introduces the essentials of teams and teamwork for high-performance systems. As you read Chapter 10, keep in mind these key questions:

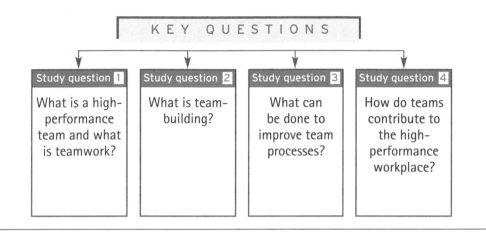

KEY QUESTIONS

Study question 1	Study question 2	Study question 3	Study question 4
What is a high-performance team and what is teamwork?	What is team-building?	What can be done to improve team processes?	How do teams contribute to the high-performance workplace?

High-Performance Teams

When we think of the word "team," a variety of popular sports teams usually comes to mind. Workgroups can also be considered teams to the extent that they match the following definition: a **team** is a small group of people with complementary skills who work together actively to achieve a common purpose that together they hold themselves accountable for.[1] Groups, on the other hand, involve two or more people interacting with each other either to achieve a common goal, as in a team, or, unlike teams, to satisfy more social or general purposes.

Teams are one of the major forces behind today's revolutionary changes in organizations. Management scholar Jay Conger calls the team-based organization the management system of the future and the business world's response to the need for speed in an always more competitive environment.[2] Employee productivity at Peace River Pulp, northwest of Edmonton, Alberta, is among the highest in the industry, largely due to its cross-functional team system, which has shifted decision-making autonomy to the shop floor. Mill production is much better than anticipated with 20 percent more output than had been originally planned when the plant started operations in 1990.[3] Clearly, we need to know more about such teams and the processes of teamwork in organizations.

Teams are groups of people who work together actively to achieve a purpose that together they hold themselves accountable for.

TYPES OF TEAMS

A major challenge in any organization is to turn formal groups, as discussed in Chapter 9, into true high-performance teams in any of the following settings.[4] First, there are *teams that recommend things*. Created to study specific problems and recommend solutions, these teams typically work with a target completion date and break up once they have achieved their purpose. They are temporary groups and include task forces, ad hoc committees, project teams, and so on. Members of these teams must be quick at learning how to work well together, accomplish the assigned task, and make good action recommendations for follow-up work by other people.

The federal government often relies on these types of teams, as seen in the various task forces it creates to study specific topics. For example, in January 2001, it established a National Broadband Task Force to advise it on how best to achieve its objective of ensuring that broadband networks and services are available in every Canadian community by 2005. The Task Force presented its report six months later, proposing a policy framework and action plan for extending broadband networks and services.

Second, there are *teams that run things*. Such management teams consist of people with the formal responsibility for leading other groups. These teams may exist at all levels of responsibility, from the individual work unit composed of a team leader and team members to the top-management team composed of a CEO and other senior executives. Teams can add value to work processes at any level and offer special opportunities for dealing with complex problems and uncertain situations. Key issues addressed by top-management teams, for example, include identifying overall organizational purposes, goals, and values; crafting strategies; and persuading others to support them.[5] Kevin Dee, CEO of Ottawa-based hi-tech staffing company Eagle Professional Resources Inc., explains that, in building a successful management team, you have to include good people and provide them with a meaningful way to contribute to the organization. "Sometimes people change your plan; great people can come along and do great things," he says.[6]

Third, there are *teams that make or do things*. These are functional groups and work units that perform ongoing tasks, such as marketing or manufacturing. Members of these teams must have good long-term working relationships with each other, solid operating systems, and the external support needed to achieve effectiveness over a sustained period of time. They also need energy to keep up the pace and meet the day-to-day challenges of sustained high performance. Woodstock, Ontario-based Sertapak Group, which manufactures custom packaging solutions for automotive, textile, plastics/resin, food processing, and other industries, says its manufacturing team members help to provide flexible manufacturing solutions. Employees provide input and ideas to improve production.

HIGH-PERFORMANCE ORGANIZATION

There was a lot of anxiety and uncertainty at B.C. Tel back in 1999 when it was getting ready to merge with Telus from Alberta. To help ease the anxiety, the firm hired Rock-Paper-Scissors Productions to set up a humorous event for the upcoming merger. A mock wedding, complete with church service and reception, was held for the B.C. Tel groom and the blushing bride Telus, as well as for 500 employees, at the Hyatt Regency and the Christ Church Cathedral across the road. The light-hearted effort gave the employees a chance to laugh at themselves, which is needed in periods of high stress, especially when there are expected cultural differences as in this merger that created Canada's second largest telecommunications company.[7]

www.telus.com
www.rpsinc.ca

THE NATURE OF TEAMWORK

Teamwork occurs when group members work together in ways that use their skills well to accomplish a purpose.

All teams need members who believe in team goals and are motivated to work actively with others to accomplish important tasks—whether those tasks involve recommending things, running things, or making or doing things. Indeed, an essential criterion of a true team is that the members feel "collectively accountable" (i.e., responsible as a group) for what they accomplish.[8]

This sense of collective accountability is the foundation for real teamwork, with team members actively working together in a way that enables each member's skills to be used well in achieving the team's common purpose.[9] A commitment to teamwork is found in the willingness of every member to "listen and to respond constructively to views expressed by others, give others the benefit of the doubt, provide support, and recognize the interests and achievements of others."[10] Teamwork of this type is the central foundation of any high-performance team. But developing teamwork is a challenging leadership task, regardless of the setting. It takes a lot more work to build a well-functioning team than to simply assign members to the same group and then expect them to do a great job.[11] See, for example, The Effective Manager 10.1.

High-performance teams have special characteristics that allow them to excel at teamwork and achieve special performance advantages. First, *high-performance teams have strong core values* that help guide their members toward attitudes and behaviours that fit the team's purpose. Such values act as an internal control system for a group or team and they can therefore replace direction and supervisory attention from outside the team. Second, *high-performance teams turn a general sense of purpose into specific performance objectives*. Although a shared sense of purpose gives general direction to a team, it is the commitment to specific performance results that makes this purpose truly meaningful. Specific objectives—such as reducing the time of getting the product to market by half—give a clear focus for solving problems and resolving conflicts. They also set standards for measuring results and obtaining performance feedback. Specific objectives also help group members understand the need for collective efforts, instead of purely individual ones. Third, members of *high-performance teams have the right mix of skills, including technical skills*, problem-solving and decision-making skills, and interpersonal skills. Finally, high-performance teams possess creativity. In the new workplace, teams must use their creativity to help organizations continuously improve their operations and develop new products, services, and markets.

The Effective Manager 10.1

HOW TO CREATE A HIGH-PERFORMANCE TEAM

- Communicate high performance standards.
- Set the tone in the first team meeting.
- Create a sense of urgency.
- Make sure members have the right skills.
- Establish clear rules for team behaviour.
- As a leader, model expected behaviours.
- Find ways to create early successes.
- Continually introduce new information.
- Have members spend time together.
- Give positive feedback.
- Reward high performance.

DIVERSITY AND TEAM PERFORMANCE

In order to create and maintain high-performance teams, all of the elements of group effectiveness discussed in Chapter 9 must be considered and successfully managed. As an important input to group and team dynamics, the diversity of a team's members has special significance in today's workplace.[12] When team members are homogeneous—that is, when members are alike in age, gender, race, experience, ethnicity, and culture—there are some potential benefits for group dynamics. It will probably be easy for members to quickly build social relationships and begin the interactions that are needed to work together harmoniously. On the other hand, a homogeneous membership may limit the group in terms of ideas, viewpoints, and creativity. Teams whose members have varied demographic characteristics, experiences, and cultures, by contrast, have a rich pool of information, talent, and varied perspectives that can help improve problem-solving and increase creativity. These assets are especially valuable to teams working on complex and very demanding tasks.

Research indicates that diversity among team members may create performance difficulties early in the team's life or development. This happens when interpersonal stresses and conflicts caused by diversity slow down group processes such as building relationships, defining the problem, and sharing information.[13] Even though teams with diversity may struggle in the beginning to resolve these issues, they are likely to develop better long-term performance potential once things are worked out.[14] Although it may take a bit more time and effort to create teamwork from foundations of diversity, long-term gains in creativity and performance can make it all worthwhile. Teamwork that is rich in diversity is one of the great advantages of high-performance organizations.

OB ACROSS FUNCTIONS

Research & Development

Working Together across Cultures

Air Liquide is a provider of industrial and medical gases and related services, based in France. It supplies oxygen, nitrogen, hydrogen, and other gases to most industries, including steel, oil refining, chemicals, glass, electronics, healthcare, food processing, metallurgy, paper, and aerospace. Founded in 1902, the company now operates in 60 countries, including Canada, and employs more than 30,000 people. Diversity among its employees—a mixture of gender, race, culture, nationality, education, and professional experience—is a driving force behind its success. Their combined competencies allow the company to capitalize on opportunities worldwide. In fact, 225 employees of 26 different nationalities are working specifically on international assignments in 45 countries. Air Liquide definitely provides an environment that honours, and even demands, the different perspectives of various cultures.

Team-Building

Teamwork does not always happen naturally in a group. It is something that team members and leaders must work hard to achieve. In the sports world, for example, coaches and managers focus on teamwork when they are building new teams at the start of each season. And, as you certainly know, even experienced teams often run into problems as a season progresses. Members slack off or become disgruntled; some have performance "slumps;" some are traded to other teams. Even world-champion teams have losing streaks, and the most talented players can lose motivation at times, quibble among themselves, and end up contributing little to their team's success. When these things happen, the owners, managers, and players have to examine their problems, take corrective action to rebuild the team, and restore the teamwork that is needed to achieve high-performance results.[15]

Workgroups and work teams have similar difficulties. When newly formed, they must master challenges in the early stages of group development. Even when they are mature, most work teams at times have problems of inadequate teamwork. When difficulties occur, or as a way of preventing them from occurring, a systematic process of **team-building** can help. This is a sequence of planned activities designed to first gather and analyze data on the functioning of a group and then make changes that will improve teamwork and increase group effectiveness.[16]

Team-building is a collaborative way to gather and analyze data to improve teamwork.

HOW TEAM-BUILDING WORKS

The action steps and continuous improvement theme of Figure 10.1 are typical of most team-building approaches. The process begins when someone notices that there is a problem with the team's effectiveness or that there may soon be one. Members then work together to gather data on the problem, analyze these data, plan for improvements, and implement the action plans. The entire team-building process is highly collaborative. Everyone is expected to participate actively as group operations are evaluated and decisions are made on what needs to be done to improve the team's functioning in the future. This process can and should become an ongoing part of any team's work agenda. It is an approach to continuous improvement that can be very beneficial to long-term effectiveness.

Team-building requires participation and is based on data. Whether the data are gathered by a questionnaire, interview, nominal group meeting, or other creative methods, the goal is to get good answers to questions like these: "How well are we doing in terms of task accomplishment? How satisfied are we as individual members with the group and the way it operates?" There are many ways for such questions to be asked and answered in a collaborative and motivating manner.

Figure 10.1 The team-building process

Cyberplex Inc.

www.cyberplex.com

The financial services industry, like all other industries today, requires Internet presence, and with its particular focus on providing integrated electronic systems for financial services companies, Toronto-based Cyberplex delivers. To begin the process, Cyberplex sets up a rigorous all-day meeting with its client. The meeting creates a joint team that must agree on all aspects of the electronic service system and on how it will be implemented. To create the joint team, one individual at the meeting plays the key role of bridge-builder between the initial client team and the Cyberplex team, covering a wall with notes of agreed upon actions, thus helping the two teams become one.

APPROACHES TO TEAM-BUILDING

In the *formal retreat approach*, team-building takes place during an off-site "retreat." During this retreat, which may last from one to several days, group members work intensively on a variety of assessment and planning tasks. These tasks begin with a review of the team's functioning based on data gathered through a survey, interviews, or other means. As part of the retreat, there is often a consultant—who is either hired from the outside or made available from in-house staff—to help take the group through the process. An example of such a consultant is Jim Clemmer of the Kitchener, Ontario-based Clemmer Group, which conducts intensive two-day offsite retreats with management teams, providing the opportunity to examine group accomplishments and operations.

Not all team-building is done in a formal retreat format or with the help of outside consultants. In a *continuous improvement approach*, the manager, team leader, or group members themselves take responsibility for regularly working on the team-building process. This method can be as simple as having periodic meetings that implement the team-building steps, and it can also include self-managed formal retreats. In all cases, the team members make a commitment to monitor the group's development and accomplishments continuously and to make the day-to-day changes that are needed to ensure team effectiveness. Such continuous improvement of teamwork is essential to the management themes of total quality and total service that are so important to organizations today.

The *outdoor experience approach* is an increasingly popular team-building activity that may be done on its own or in combination with other approaches. It places group members in a variety of physically challenging situations that must be mastered through teamwork, not individual work. By having to work together as they face difficult obstacles, team members are supposed to experience increased self-confidence, more respect for each other's capabilities, and a greater commitment to teamwork. Canadian Outback in Vancouver is one of many providers of outdoor team-building experiences. Its activities are designed to build morale and enhance productivity. They mentally challenge team members and also force them to interact and communicate, creating a more cohesive unit. For a group that has never done team-building before, the outdoor experience approach can be an exciting way to begin; for groups that are already familiar with team-building, it can be a way of further enriching the experience.

Improving Team Processes

Like many changes in the new workplace, the increased emphasis on teams and teamwork is a major challenge for people who are used to more traditional ways of working. As more and more jobs are turned over to teams and as more and more traditional supervisors are asked to function as team leaders, special problems with team processes may arise. As teams become more integral to organizations, having the number of members increase and seeing others come and go can cause complications. Team leaders and members alike must be prepared to deal positively with such issues as introducing new members, handling disagreements on goals and responsibilities, resolving delays and disputes when making decisions, and reducing friction and interpersonal conflicts. Due to the complex nature of group dynamics, the job of team-building is almost never finished. Something is always happening that creates the need for further leadership efforts to help improve a team's processes.

The members of most teams are expected to be creative and to function by interacting well among themselves. Team-building consulting group Getting in the Groove (GitG) and the comedy troupe Second City require active listening when they take part in corporate workshops. GitG uses team-building tools, and jazz in particular, to emphasize the need to be creative while remaining aware of and involved with the other members of a band so that the goal or core tune is always understood and followed. Second City includes participants in its improv sketches and each member needs to react at the right time to stay in tune with the other members, being ready to take the lead when called upon to do so. In both cases, creativity is improved by working with others while remaining fully aware of the other members' actions and reactions.

ENTREPRENEURSHIP

Succeeding in business requires a fair degree of improvisation. As it says on the Second City website, "You can plan all you want, but in the end, business is often about building relationships and adjusting to change as fast as it happens." With its corporate training and workshops, Canada's famous comedy troupe helps those in the business world become better communicators, build a stronger team, create a more positive work environment, and stimulate creativity. Using improvisation techniques, Second City helps people to think on their feet and create new ideas more quickly, communicate better and listen more effectively, and contribute and flourish in team environments, among other skills to help people and teams function better in the workplace.

NEW-MEMBER PROBLEMS

Special difficulties are likely to occur when members first get together in a new group or work team, or when new members join an existing one. Problems arise as new members try to understand what is expected of them and as they deal with the anxiety and discomfort of a new social setting. Some of the things that new members may worry about include these aspects:

- *participation*—"Will I be allowed to participate?"
- *goals*—"Do I share the same goals as others?"
- *control*—"Will I be able to influence what takes place?"
- *relationships*—"How close do people get to each other?"
- *processes*—"Are conflicts likely to be upsetting?"

Edgar Schein points out that people may try to cope with individual entry problems in ways that help the individual but hurt group operations.[17] He identifies three behaviour profiles that are common in such situations. The *tough battler* is frustrated by a lack of identity in the new group and may act aggressively or reject authority. This person wants answers to the question "Who am I in this group?" The *friendly helper* is insecure, suffering uncertainties of intimacy and control. This person may show extraordinary support for others, behave in a dependent way, and seek alliances in subgroups or cliques. The friendly helper needs to know whether she or he will be liked. The *objective thinker* is anxious about how personal needs will be met in the group. This person may act in a passive, reflective, and even single-minded, self-focused manner while struggling with the fit between individual goals and group directions.

TASK AND MAINTENANCE LEADERSHIP

Research in social psychology suggests that the achievement of sustained high performance by groups requires that both "task needs" and "maintenance needs" be satisfied.[18] Although the person who is formally appointed to be the group leader should help satisfy these needs, the other members should also be contributing. This responsibility for **distributed leadership** is an important part of the group dynamics in any high-performance team.[19]

Distributed leadership is the sharing of responsibility for satisfying group task and maintenance needs.

Figure 10.2 Task and maintenance leadership in group team dynamics

Leading by Task Contributions	How to lead groups and teams	Leading by Maintenance Contributions
• Offering ideas • Clarifying suggestions • Giving information • Seeking information • Summarizing discussion		• Encouraging others • Reconciling differences • Expressing standards • Offering agreement • Inviting participation

Figure 10.2 describes group **task activities** as the various things members do that make a direct contribution to the performance of important group tasks. They include starting discussions, sharing information, asking others for information, clarifying something that has been said, and summarizing the current state of a deliberation.[20] If these task activities are not done well, the group will have difficulty accomplishing its objectives. In an effective group, members

Task activities contribute directly to the performance of important tasks.

do important task activities as needed and these activities become building blocks for performance success.

Maintenance activities support the group's social and interpersonal relationships, thus helping the group stay intact and healthy as an ongoing social system. A member contributes maintenance leadership, for example, by encouraging the participation of others, trying to harmonize differences of opinion, praising the contributions of others, and agreeing to go along with a popular course of action. When maintenance leadership is poor, members become dissatisfied with each other and their group membership. This often leads to conflicts that can drain energies that are actually needed for task performance. In an effective group, maintenance activities help sustain the relationships that are needed for group members to work well together over time.

> Maintenance activities support the emotional life of the team as an ongoing social system.

In addition to helping meet a group's task and maintenance needs, group members share the additional responsibility of avoiding disruptive behaviours—behaviours that harm the group process. Full participation in distributed leadership means taking individual responsibility for avoiding the following types of behaviours, and helping others avoid them also:

> **Disruptive behaviours that harm teams**

- being overly aggressive toward other members
- withdrawing and refusing to co-operate with others
- fooling around when there is work to be done
- using the group as a forum for self-confession
- talking too much about irrelevant matters
- trying to compete for attention and recognition

ROLES AND ROLE DYNAMICS

In groups and teams, both new and old members need to know what others expect of them and what they can expect from others. A role is a set of expectations associated with a job or with a position on a team. When roles are unclear or they conflict with each other, performance problems can occur. Groups and work teams sometimes have problems that are caused by difficulties in defining and managing their members' roles.

> A role is a set of expectations for a team member or person in a job.

Role ambiguity occurs when a person is uncertain about his or her role. To do any job well, people need to know what is expected of them. In new group or team situations, role ambiguities may create problems if members feel that their work efforts are wasted or unappreciated by others. Even in mature groups and teams, the failure of members to share expectations and listen to each other may at times create a lack of understanding. Being asked to do too much or too little can also create problems. **Role overload** occurs when too much is expected and the individual feels overwhelmed with work. **Role underload** occurs when too little is expected and the individual feels underused. All groups benefit from clear and realistic expectations regarding the contributions of each member.

> Role ambiguity occurs when an individual is uncertain about what is expected of him or her.

> Role overload occurs when too much work is expected of an individual.

> Role underload occurs when too little work is expected of an individual.

Role conflict occurs when a person is unable to satisfy expectations that conflict with each other. The individual understands what needs to be done but has a reason for not doing it. The resulting tension can reduce the individual's job satisfaction and affect his or her work performance and relationships with other group members. There are four common forms of role conflict: (1) *Intrasender role conflict* occurs when the same person sends the individual conflicting expectations. (2) *Intersender role conflict* occurs when different people send the individual conflicting expectations that are contradictory. (3) *Person-role conflict* occurs when the individual's personal values and needs conflict with role expectations. (4) *Interrole conflict*

> Role conflict occurs when an individual is unable to satisfy role expectations that conflict with each other.

occurs when the expectations of two or more roles held by the same individual become incompatible, such as the conflict between work and family demands.

Figure 10.3 A sample role negotiations agreement

> **ROLE NEGOTIATIONS**
>
> Issue Diagnosis Form
>
> Messages from   Jim
>   to   Diane
>
> If you were to do the following, it would help me to increase my performance:
> - Be more receptive to my suggestins for improvement
> - Provide help when new software is installed
> - Work harder to support my staffing request
> - Stop asking for so many detailed progress reports
> - Keep providing full information in our weekly meetings
> - Keep being available when I need to talk with you

One way of managing role dynamics in any group or work setting is by *role negotiation*. In this process, individuals negotiate to clarify the role expectations they have of each other. Sample results from an actual role negotiation are shown in Figure 10.3. Note the "give and take" between negotiators.

POSITIVE NORMS

The **norms** of a group or team are ideas or beliefs about how members are expected to behave. They can be considered as rules or standards of conduct.[21] Norms help clarify the expectations associated with a person's membership in a group. They allow members to adjust their own behaviour and to predict what others will do. They help members gain a common sense of direction, and they reinforce a desired culture for the group or team. When someone violates a group norm, other members typically respond in ways that are intended to enforce the norm. These responses may include direct criticisms, reprimands, expulsion, and social ostracism.

Norms are rules or standards for the behaviour of group members.

Managers, task-force heads, committee chairs, and team leaders should help their groups adopt positive norms that support the organization's goals (see The Effective Manager 10.2). A key norm in any setting is the *performance norm*, which expresses how hard group members should work. Other norms are important, too. In order for a task force or a committee to operate effectively, for example, norms for attendance at meetings, punctuality, preparedness, criticism, and social behaviours are needed. Groups also commonly have norms on how to deal with supervisors, colleagues, and customers, as well as norms that set guidelines for honesty and ethical behaviours. Norms are often evident in the everyday conversations of people at work. The following examples show the types of norms that operate with positive and negative implications for groups and organizations:[22]

- *organizational and personal pride norms*—"It's a tradition around here for people to stand up for the company when others criticize it unfairly" (positive); "In our company, they're always trying to take advantage of us" (negative).

> **The Effective Manager | 10.2**
>
> **SEVEN STEPS TO POSITIVE NORMS**
>
> 1. Act as a positive role model.
> 2. Hold meetings to agree on goals.
> 3. Select members who can and will perform.
> 4. Provide support and training for members.
> 5. Reinforce and reward desired behaviours.
> 6. Hold meetings for performance feedback.
> 7. Hold meetings to plan for improvements.

Types of group norms

- *high-achievement norms*—"On our team, people always try to work hard" (positive); "There's no point in trying harder on our team—nobody else does" (negative).

- *support and helpfulness norms*—"People on this committee are good listeners and actively seek out the ideas and opinions of others" (positive); "On this committee, it's dog-eat-dog and save your own skin" (negative).

- *improvement and change norms*—"In our department, people are always looking for better ways of doing things" (positive); "Around here, people hang on to the old ways even after they've outlived their usefulness" (negative).

TEAM COHESIVENESS

Cohesiveness is how much the members are attracted to a group and motivated to remain part of it.

The **cohesiveness** of a group or team is how much the members are attracted to and motivated to remain part of the group or team.[23] Persons in a highly cohesive group value their membership and try hard to maintain positive relationships with other group members. In this sense, cohesive groups and teams are good for their members. In contrast to less cohesive groups, members of highly cohesive ones tend to be more energetic when working on group activities, are less likely to be absent, and are more likely to be happy about performance success and sad about failures. Cohesive groups generally have low turnover and satisfy a broad range of individual needs, often providing a source of loyalty, security, and esteem for their members.

Cohesiveness tends to be high when group members are similar in age, attitudes, needs, and backgrounds. It also tends to be high in groups of small size, where members respect each other's competencies, agree on common goals, and work on interdependent tasks. Cohesiveness tends to increase when groups are physically isolated from people who are not in the group and when they experience performance success or crisis.

Conformity to Norms   Even though cohesive groups are good for their members, they may or may not be good for the organization. This will depend on the match of cohesiveness with performance norms. Figure 10.4 shows how performance can be affected by the following basic *rule of conformity in group dynamics*: the more cohesive the group, the greater the conformity of its members to group norms.

Figure 10.4 How cohesiveness and conformity to norms affect group performance

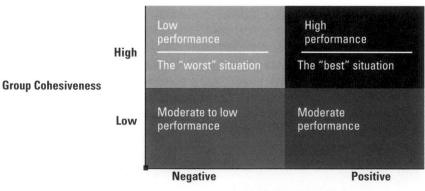

When the performance norms are positive in a highly cohesive workgroup or team, the resulting conformity to the norm should have a positive effect on task performance and member satisfaction. This is a best-case situation for everyone. When the performance norms are negative in a highly cohesive group, however, the same power of conformity creates a worst-case situation for the organization. Although team members in this worst-case situation are highly motivated to support group norms, the organization ends up with poor performance results because the norms are negative. In between these two extremes are mixed-case situations in which a lack of cohesion lessens conformity to the norm. With its strength reduced, the outcome of the norm is somewhat unpredictable and performance will most likely be moderate or low.

Figure 10.5 Ways to increase and decrease group cohesiveness

How to Decrease Cohesion	TARGETS	How to Increase Cohesion
Create disagreement	Goals	Achieve agreement
Increase heterogeneity	Membership	Increase homogeneity
Restrict within team	Interactions	Enhance within team
Make team bigger	Size	Make team smaller
Focus within team	Competition	Focus on other teams
Reward individual results	Rewards	Reward team results
Open up to other teams	Location	Isolate from other teams
Disband the team	Duration	Keep team together

Influencing Cohesiveness Team leaders and managers must be aware of the steps they can take to create more cohesiveness when a group has positive norms but also has low cohesiveness. They must also be ready to deal with situations when cohesiveness adds to the problems of negative performance norms that are hard to change. Figure 10.5 shows how group cohesiveness can be increased or decreased by making changes in group goals, membership composition, interactions, size, rewards, competition, location, and duration.

Teams and the High-Performance Workplace

As mentioned in Chapter 2, the staff at 1-800-GOT-JUNK? approach the company's finances as a team. With each person accountable for a portion of the budget, everyone looks for ways to cut costs. The company's frugal approach to day-to-day costs has been integral to its budgeting success. Employees have established a strategic relationship with the local coffee shop, which now provides free coffee for meetings. Others will continuously assess their options for courier services or other suppliers to ensure they're getting the best deal. Staff will buy office furniture in bulk from liquidators, or even help themselves to some of the good quality "junk" removed from other businesses. Central to the company's budgeting process is educating and involving employees, creating a sense of personal ownership, and sharing the wealth—or savings. Like 1-800-Got-Junk?, organizations everywhere in the new workplace are finding creative ways of using teams to solve problems and make changes to improve performance. The catchwords of these new approaches to teamwork are empowerment, participation, and involvement. And the setting these approaches are used in is increasingly described as an organization that looks much more "lateral" or "horizontal" than vertical and that acts that way as well.[24]

PROBLEM-SOLVING TEAMS

One way for organizations to use teams is in creative problem-solving. The term **employee involvement team** applies to a wide variety of teams whose members meet regularly to examine important workplace issues. They discuss ways to improve quality, better satisfy customers, raise productivity, and improve the quality of work life. In this way, employee involvement teams use all of the workers' know-how and they gain the commitment that is needed to fully implement solutions.

Members of employee involvement teams meet regularly to examine work-related problems and opportunities.

A special type of employee involvement group is the **quality circle**, or QC for short. It is a small group of persons who meet periodically (e.g., for an hour or so once a week) to discuss and find solutions for problems related to quality, productivity, or cost.[25] QCs are popular in organizations around the world, but they cannot be seen as the answer for all of an organization's ills. To be successful, members of QCs should receive special training in group dynamics, information gathering, and problem-analysis techniques. Leaders of quality circles should also be trained in participation and team-building. When solutions for problems are found, both the QC members and the organization's management should follow up on the solutions. QCs work best in organizations that place a clear emphasis on quality in their mission and goals, promote a culture that supports participation and empowerment, encourage trust and willingness to share important information, and develop a "team spirit."

Members of a quality circle meet regularly to find ways for continuous improvement of quality operations.

CROSS-FUNCTIONAL TEAMS

In today's organizations, teams are an essential part of efforts to achieve more horizontal integration and better lateral relations. The **cross-functional team**, consisting of members from different functional departments or work units, plays an important role in this regard. Traditionally, many organizations have suffered from what is often called the **functional silos problem**. This problem occurs when members of functional units stay focused on matters that involve their own function and they have as few interactions as possible with members of other functions. Thus, the functional departments or work units are essentially creating artificial boundaries or "silos" that make integrative thinking and active coordination with other parts of the organization less likely, rather than more likely.

Cross-functional teams bring together persons from different functions to work on a common task.

The functional silos problem occurs when individuals in one function do not communicate with individuals in other functions.

The new emphasis on team-based organizations, discussed in Chapter 11, is designed to help break down these barriers and improve lateral communication.[26] Members of cross-functional teams can solve problems with a positive combination of each member's expertise in his or her function and the team's integrative or total-systems thinking. They are also better at solving problems thanks to the great advantages of having better information and being able to act faster. The Bombardier Aerospace's Amphibious Aircraft support team in Montreal, for example, comprises more than 60 support specialists in service engineering, technical support, customer training, technical publications, and spares support. The support process begins before aircraft are delivered to clients, with training, maintenance, and operational support programs. Within each group, a technically qualified person is the single-point-of-contact responsible for managing customers' needs.[27]

VIRTUAL TEAMS

A virtual team meets and operates with members who are linked together electronically through networked computers.

Until recently, teamwork was limited as a concept and limited also in practice by the need for members to meet face-to-face. This has now changed, however, thanks to new technologies and sophisticated computer programs known as groupware. **Virtual teams**—introduced in the last chapter as teams whose members meet at least part of the time electronically with the help of computers—are more and more a fact of life now.[28] The real world of work in today's businesses and other organizations involves a variety of electronic communications that allow people to work together through computers, and often with the group's members geographically far away from each other. *Groupware*, which comes in many popular forms, easily allows for virtual meetings and group decision-making in many different situations.[29] There have also been advancements in conferencing and collaboration technologies, resulting in more audio, data, and videoconferencing options.[30] In sum, groupware makes it possible for people in different locations and with different opinions, training, culture, and so on to meet electronically at a common location to exchange their views and information and, as a result, more easily collaborate as team members.

Virtual teams have several potential advantages. They bring cost-effectiveness and speed to teamwork when members are unable to meet easily face-to-face. They also allow the power of the computer to help out with typical team needs for information processing and decision-making.[31] When the computer is the "go-between" among virtual team members, however, group dynamics can be different from the dynamics of face-to-face settings.[32] Although technology makes communication possible among people separated by great distances, the team members may have very little, if any, direct "personal" contact. Virtual teams may suffer from less social rapport and less direct interaction among members. Although computer mediation may have the advantage of focusing interaction and decision-making on facts and objective information, rather than on emotional considerations, it may also increase risks as group decisions are made in a limited social context.

Just as with any form of teamwork, to achieve effectiveness, virtual teams rely on the efforts and contributions of their members as well as on support from the organization. Teamwork in any form always takes work. The same stages of development, the same input considerations, and the same process requirements are as relevant for a virtual team as they are for any team. Where possible, the advantages of face-to-face and virtual teamwork should be combined for maximum benefit. The computer technology should also be appropriate and team members should be well trained in using it.[33] Above all, the technology should simply help the team achieve its goal; it should not become the focus itself.

PeopleSoft
www.peoplesoft.com

At PeopleSoft, the firm's director of global telecommunications gives Sony Videoconferencing technology credit for helping PeopleSoft manage its explosive growth: "It's simply better when you meet someone over video than the phone. It's much more like a live meeting."

SELF-MANAGING TEAMS

The **self-managing team** is a high-involvement workgroup design that is becoming increasingly common today. These are small groups that are empowered to make decisions about how to manage themselves on a day-to-day basis.[34] Although there are different variations on this theme, Figure 10.6 shows that members of a true self-managing work team make decisions on scheduling work, allocating tasks, training for job skills, evaluating performance, selecting new team members, and controlling the quality of work. Members are collectively held accountable for the team's overall performance results.

Self-managing teams are empowered to make decisions about planning, doing, and evaluating their daily work.

How Self-Managing Teams Work   Self-managing teams, also called self-directed teams or empowered teams, are permanent and formal elements in the organizational structure. They replace the traditional workgroup headed by a supervisor. What makes self-managing teams different from the more traditional workgroup is that the members of self-managing teams have duties that would traditionally belong to a manager or first-line supervisor. The team members, not a supervisor, perform and are collectively accountable for such activities as planning and work scheduling, performance evaluation, gatekeeping (focusing and limiting access to the team), and quality control.

Multiskilling occurs when team members are trained in skills to perform different jobs.

A self-managing team should probably include between five and 15 members. The teams must be large enough to provide a good mix of skills and resources, but small enough to function efficiently. Members must have a lot of control over determining the work pace and the distribution of tasks. This is made possible, in part, by **multiskilling**, which is the training of team members to perform more than one job on the team. In self-managing teams, each person is expected to perform many different jobs—even all of the team's jobs—as needed. The more skills someone masters, the higher the base pay he or she receives. Team members themselves do the job training and certify each other as having mastered the required skills.

At Alberta-Pacific Forest Industries Inc., north of Edmonton, each employee is a member of a self-directed work team, who manage their day-to-day activities, as well as budgeting, hiring, and discipline. They take responsibility for their work results and are encouraged to show initiative and innovation in achieving those results. The company provides all team members with training in effective meeting administration, conflict resolution, and coaching. In addition, employees are encouraged to expand their education levels in both the technical and personal aspects of their work. Team members are also expected to coach and mentor others in order to transfer their knowledge wherever possible.

Operational Implications of Self-Managing Teams The expected benefits of self-managing teams include productivity and quality improvements, production flexibility and faster response to technological change, reduced absenteeism and turnover, and improved work attitudes and quality of work life. But these results are not guaranteed. Like all organizational changes, the shift to self-managing teams can create difficulties. Structural changes in job classifications and management levels will affect supervisors and others who are used to more traditional ways. Simply put, with a self-managing team you no longer need the formal first-line supervisor. The full impact of this change is shown in Figure 10.6, where the first level of supervisory management in the traditional organization has been eliminated and replaced by self-managing teams. Note also that the supervisor's tasks are transferred to the team.

For individuals who are used to more traditional work, the new team-based work arrangements can be challenging. Managers must learn to deal with teams rather than with individual workers. For any supervisors who become displaced by self-managing teams, the implications are even more personal and threatening. Given this situation, a question must be asked: *Should all organizations operate with self-managing teams?* The best answer is "No." Self-managing teams are probably not right for all organizations, work situations, and people. They have great potential, but they also require a proper setting and support. At a minimum, the basic features of any self-managing team—high involvement, participation, and empowerment—must be consistent with the values and culture of the organization.

GLOBALIZATION

If you visit the Texas Instruments plant in Malaysia, you will find many workers and no traditional supervisors. The plant uses self-managing teams that make decisions on quality and production issues, schedule work and work breaks, and keep track of work hours on the honour system. When teams were first introduced, people were anxious. Management styles had to be changed, and rigid job descriptions were eliminated. But the changes increased productivity, improved product quality, and reduced staff absenteeism. Says a TI senior executive, "Teams bring about better sharing of ideas and learning. Better decisions are made and the implementation of ideas takes less time."[35]

Figure 10.6 Organizational and management implications of self-managing teams

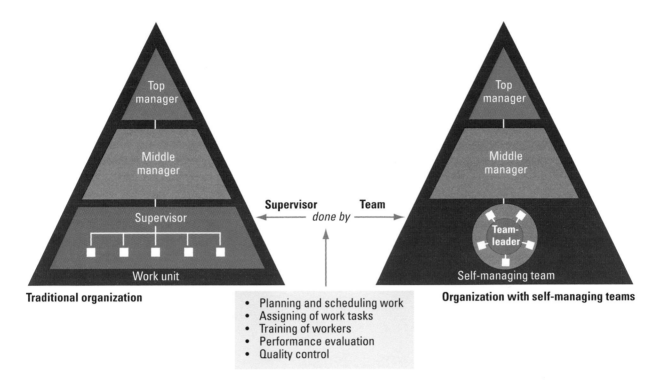

Throughout the chapter, we have emphasized the need to work in teams, whether the team's purpose is to recommend things, run things, or make or do things. Central to a team's success is how well its members agree about and understand the team's goal and how willing they are to address differences so that they can achieve the performance standards expected of them. Teams can be built in many ways, with the formal retreat being a popular method and the outdoor experiential method, as offered by companies like Outward Bound, becoming well known. In these situations, the members must learn to rely on each other and to work together despite personal differences. Team processes need constant maintenance, especially those which involve bringing in new members, keeping the team on track, and ensuring that every member knows his or her role. Hopefully, the team will be cohesive and will build on norms that reinforce positive behaviour and success. Different kinds of teams were discussed in the chapter, but many of us can now expect to join virtual teams whose members are spread around the world and who only meet electronically. Probably the most complex and responsible teams are the self-managing teams that are empowered to make decisions about their goals, schedule their training, and even do their own performance evaluations, among other functions. No organization today can function without teams. As members of an organization, therefore, we should be prepared to commit ourselves to both the team and the organization by remaining flexible and adaptable to new teams and challenges.

CHAPTER 10 STUDY GUIDE

Summary

STUDY QUESTIONS

What is a high-performance team and what is teamwork?

- A team is a small group of people who work together to achieve a common purpose that they hold themselves collectively accountable for.

- High-performance teams have core values, clear performance objectives, the right mix of skills, and creativity.

- Teamwork occurs when members of a team work together so that their skills are well used to accomplish common goals.

What is team-building?

- Team-building is an approach that uses data to analyze group performance and take steps to improve it in the future.

- Team-building is participative and involves all of the group's members in collaborative problem-solving and action.

What can be done to improve team processes?

- Individual entry problems are common when new teams are formed and when new members join already existing teams.

- Task leadership involves starting and summarizing discussions, and making direct contributions to the performance of the group's tasks; maintenance leadership involves gatekeeping, encouraging, and helping support the social fabric of the group over time.

- Role difficulties occur when expectations for group members are unclear, too high, too low, or conflicting.

- Norms, as rules or standards for what is considered appropriate behaviour by group members, can have a significant impact on group processes and outcomes.

- Members of highly cohesive groups value their membership and are very loyal to the group; they also tend to conform to group norms.

How do teams contribute to the high-performance workplace?

- An employee involvement team is a team whose members meet regularly to examine important work-related problems and opportunities.

- Members of a quality circle—a popular type of employee involvement group—meet regularly to deal with issues of quality improvement in work processes.

- Self-managing teams are small workgroups that operate with empowerment and basically manage themselves on a day-to-day basis.

- Members of self-managing teams typically plan, complete, and evaluate their own work; train and evaluate each other in job tasks; and share tasks and responsibilities.

- Self-managing teams have structural and management implications for organizations because they largely eliminate the first-line supervisors.

KEY TERMS

Cohesiveness (p. 192)

Cross-functional teams (p. 194)

Distributed leadership (p. 189)

Employee involvement team (p. 194)

Functional silos problem (p. 194)

Maintenance activities (p. 190)

Multiskilling (p. 196)

Norms (p. 191)

Quality circle (p. 194)

Role (p. 190)

Role ambiguity (p. 190)

Role conflict (p. 190)

Role overload (p. 190)

Role underload (p. 190)

Self-managing team (p. 195)

Task activities (p. 189)

Teams (p. 183)

Teamwork (p. 184)

Team-building (p. 186)

Virtual team (p. 194)

SELF-TEST 10

MULTIPLE CHOICE

1. A group could have difficulty becoming a high-performance team if it has _____.
   (a) specific performance objectives (b) high creativity (c) a poor mix of membership skills
   (d) strong core values

2. The team-building process can best be described as being _____. (a) participative (b) based on data (c) oriented toward action (d) all of these

3. When a new team member has questions such as "Will I be able to influence what takes place?" the team member is actually worried about _____. (a) relationships (b) goals (c) processes (d) control

4. A person who is facing an ethical dilemma that involves differences between personal values and team expectations is experiencing _____ conflict. (a) person-role (b) intrasender role (c) intersender role (d) interrole

5. The statement "On our team, people always try to do their best" is an example of a(n) _____ norm. (a) support and helpfulness (b) high-achievement (c) organizational pride (d) organizational improvement

6. Highly cohesive teams tend to _____. (a) be bad for organizations (b) be good for their members (c) have more social loafing among members (d) have greater membership turnover

7. One way of increasing team cohesiveness is to _____. (a) make the group bigger (b) increase membership diversity (c) isolate the group from others (d) relax performance pressures

8. Self-managing teams _____. (a) reduce the number of different job tasks that members need to master (b) largely eliminate the need for a traditional supervisor (c) rely heavily on outside training to maintain job skills (d) add another management layer to overhead costs

9. Which statement about self-managing teams is correct? (a) They can improve performance but not satisfaction. (b) They should have limited decision-making authority. (c) They should operate without any team leaders. (d) They should let members plan work schedules.

10. A team member who does a good job at summarizing discussion, offering new ideas, and clarifying points made by others is contributing _____ activities to the group process. (a) required (b) disruptive (c) task (d) maintenance

TRUE-FALSE

11. Collective accountability for results is essential for a true team.   T   F

12. Team-building should only be done in a formal retreat with the help of an outside consultant.   T   F

13. Team members work best with role ambiguity and unclear expectations.   T   F

14. Role overload is bad; role underload is good.   T   F

15. The only norm that is really important to team success is the performance norm.   T   F

16. A quality circle is an example of an employee involvement team.   T   F

17. What makes virtual teams unique is that they work well for all tasks and in all situations.   T   F

18. Through multiskilling, members of self-managing teams become capable of switching job tasks.   T   F

19. Diversity in team membership can be a valuable performance asset.   T   F

20. In any team, only the formal leader should have task leadership behaviours.   T   F

SHORT ANSWER

21. What is the team-building process?

22. How can a team leader help build positive group norms?

23. How do cohesiveness and conformity to norms influence group performance?

24. What are members of self-managing teams typically expected to do?

APPLICATIONS ESSAY

25. While surfing the Internet, you encounter this message posted in your favourite discussion group: *Help, I have just been assigned to head a new product-design team at my company. The division manager has high expectations for the team and me, but I have been a technical design engineer for four years since graduating from university. I have never "managed" anyone, let alone led a team. The manager keeps talking about her confidence that I will create a "high-performance team." Does anyone out there have any tips to help me master this challenge? Help. /s/Galahad.* As a good citizen of the Internet you decide to answer. What will your message say?

Strategy and the Basic Attributes of Organizations

11

Executive Boot Camp Teaches Teamwork

Every day for over 30 years, Michael Tatham has stood and watched top executives fail miserably with his business. Luckily for Tatham, his business is Boot Camp for Executives and he expects them to fail as they proceed through his business simulator. Tatham is CEO of the Toronto-based Tatham Group, a management consulting firm, and his business simulator—Push Corp.—is a production system designed to trip up visiting executives and illuminate what they are doing wrong.

In working with Push Corp., teams of 20 are presented with the task of producing a dozen terminal boards (metal sheets soldered with pieces of wire) within 40 minutes. Invariably the teams fail, but not because of the complexity of the exercise; these teams usually fail due to a lack of co-operation or too much bureaucracy. By the end of the two-day seminar, executives begin to recognize that they already have the knowledge to complete the task, but they need to work together as a team in order to accomplish the task. Each person usually jumps into the experience, naturally drawing upon the skills that they have used successfully in their daily business context. And usually they fail when trying to solve the presented problem.

They are then presented with the technique of using a systematic approach to create an integrated business and management system that is focused on the problem at hand. Once they start using this simple, systematic approach and management process, the teams usually do finally manage to complete the terminal boards and ship them on time to their imaginary

customers. Participants also learn that it is much more effective to focus on the underlying process that is causing the trouble, than to blame others for mistakes.

Tatham explains: "The reason the team fails is the same in business: the functions and the department are not connected. Unless the people recognize that and look at the business from an end-to-end perspective, then connect the functions and departments, there's no way the customer will get what they want. Every business is a simple production company. It has specific tasks that contribute to an end product. If you can't get this terminal board together, then you can't get your product together."

The basic attributes of organizations create the setting for individual and group action in the workplace. This setting may both liberate and limit individuals as they pursue their careers. As you read Chapter 11, keep in mind these key questions:

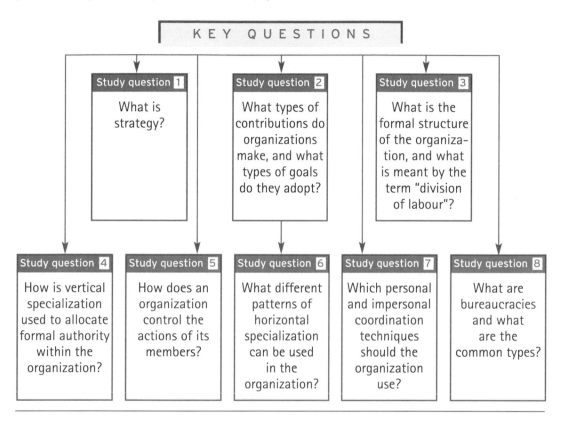

KEY QUESTIONS

Study question 1
What is strategy?

Study question 2
What types of contributions do organizations make, and what types of goals do they adopt?

Study question 3
What is the formal structure of the organiza-tion, and what is meant by the term "division of labour"?

Study question 4
How is vertical specialization used to allocate formal authority within the organization?

Study question 5
How does an organization control the actions of its members?

Study question 6
What different patterns of horizontal specialization can be used in the organization?

Study question 7
Which personal and impersonal coordination techniques should the organization use?

Study question 8
What are bureaucracies and what are the common types?

Strategy and the Basic Attributes of Organizations

Strategy is the process of positioning the organization in its competitive environment and implementing actions so it can compete successfully. It is seen through the pattern in a series of decisions.[1]

This strategizing is evident in Canadian National (CN) Railway's move to become North America's largest railroad. In the 1990s, major U.S. railroads were merging, as the North American Free Trade Agreement increased trade among Canada, the United States, and Mexico. Feeling the increased competition from the new rail giants, CN decided it would have to expand. It bought the common stock of Illinois Central (IC) Railway in 1999 to merge the two companies and create a Y-shaped network spanning across North America, from Vancouver to Halifax, and south into the United States through Chicago to New Orleans. CN and IC also created an alliance with the Kansas City Southern Railway, extending their reach southwest to Kansas City and Dallas, and into Mexico. CN became the only network to link the three coasts of North America.

Strategy is the process of positioning the organiza-tion in its competitive environment and imple-menting actions so it can compete successfully.

**Mission Statement
St. John Ambulance**

www.sja.ca

Founded over 900 years ago, the Most Venerable Order of the Hospital of St. John of Jerusalem came to Canada in 1882 as a non-denominational charitable organization. It stated its mission in this way: To enable Canadians to improve their health, safety and quality of life by providing training and community service. Today, St. John Ambulance is the nation's leader in first aid, setting standards for first aid training, CPR, and other life-saving skills.

Societal goals are goals that reflect what an organization intends to contribute to the broader society.

Mission statements are written statements of an organization's purpose.

Choosing the types of contributions the firm wants to make to its larger society, precisely who it will serve, and exactly what it will provide to others are the usual way in which a firm begins the pattern of decisions and related actions that define its strategy. At this stage of defining a strategy, the reason for the organization is made clear—although this is an ongoing process. Strategy should involve individuals at all levels of the firm so that there is a recognizable, consistent pattern up and down the firm and across all of its activities. Doing this leads to better capability compared to rivals. This continuous process may start with a top-down perspective, but over time and through inputs from the front-line staff, the intended strategy truly evolves into the pattern or strategy of the organization. The strategy can be unique to a firm and it always involves many facets. In the following sections, we will show how choices about the goals of the firm and the way it organizes itself to accomplish these goals are an important part of the overall positioning of the organization.

STRATEGY, CONTRIBUTIONS, AND GOALS

No choices are more important than the ones which decide the firm's goals. No firm can be all things to all people. By selecting goals, firms also define who they are and what they will try to become. From these basic choices, executives can work with subordinates to develop ways of accomplishing the chosen targets. They can also make decisions about allocating available resources, especially the current employees and those to be hired.

The notion that organizations have goals is very familiar to us simply because our world has many organizations. Most of us are born, go to school, work, and retire in organizations. Without organizations and their limited, goal-directed behaviour, modern societies would simply not function. We would need to go back to older forms of social organization based on loyalties, clans, and tribes. Organizational goals are everywhere, however, so much so that we rarely pay real attention to them. One organization that does pay attention to them is the Vancouver-based non-profit, Envirnmental Youth Alliance, which outlines its organizational goals on its website (www.eya.ca).

SOCIETAL CONTRIBUTIONS OF ORGANIZATIONS

Organizations that are better at turning the positive character of their societal contribution into a favourable image have an advantage over firms that neglect this sense of purpose. Moreover, smart executives who link their firm to a desirable mission can increase employee motivation by creating a shared sense of noble purpose.

Organizations do not operate separately from society. Rather, they reflect the needs and desires of the societies they operate in. Societal goals are goals that reflect what an organization intends to contribute to the broader society.[2] Organizations normally serve a specific function or enduring need of the society. Astute top-level managers build on what the organization states as its contribution to society by relating the organization's specific tasks and activities to higher purposes. Mission statements—written statements of an organization's purpose—may include these corporate ideas of service to the society. Putting together a mission statement that includes an emphasis on implementation and therefore provides direction and motivation is a highly important executive responsibility. A good mission statement says who the firm will serve and how it will accomplish its societal purpose.[3] A mission statement is often the first visible outcome in developing a strategy. It may be several paragraphs long or as simple as that of St. John Ambulance.

A political party may see its mission as being to generate and allocate power to improve the well-being of its citizens. Universities profess to both develop and disseminate knowledge.

Churches wish to instill values and protect the spiritual well-being of all. Courts are expected to integrate the interests and activities of citizens. Finally, business firms are expected to provide economic sustenance and material well-being to society, in other words, to keep the economy healthy and generate wealth for a society's citizens.

By claiming to provide specific types of societal contributions, an organization can make legitimate claims over a society's resources, individuals, markets, and products. When its contributions are questionable, it will have far less working in its favour. For instance, which business would have to pay you more in order for you to want to work for it: a tobacco firm or a health-food store? Tobacco firms are heavily taxed and under increasing pressure for regulation because their societal contribution is highly questionable.

Primary Beneficiaries

Organizations need to define their societal contributions so that their efforts benefit a particular group.[4] In Canada, for example, the main beneficiary of business success is generally expected to be the shareholder. Interestingly, in Japan employees are much more important, with shareholders only being as important as banks and other financial institutions.

Although each organization may have a primary beneficiary (i.e., people who benefit the most from what the organization does), its mission statement may also recognize the interests of many other parties. Thus, business mission statements often include service to customers, the organization's obligations to employees, and its intention to support the community.

STRATEGY AND OUTPUT GOALS

Firms need to consider how they will accomplish their missions. This refinement can begin with a very clear statement of which business they are in.[5] This statement can then become the basis for long-term planning and may help prevent huge organizations from diverting too many resources to areas that are less related to the main business. For some corporations, answering the question of which business they are in may result in a more detailed statement about their products and services. Product and service goals, in turn, can provide an important basis for judging the firm. **Output goals** are a way of defining the type of business an organization is in and making the more general aspects of mission statements more specific.

> Output goals are the goals that define the type of business an organization is in.

SYSTEMS GOALS AND ORGANIZATIONAL SURVIVAL

Fewer than 10 percent of the businesses founded in a typical year can be expected to survive to their twentieth birthday.[6] The survival rate for public companies is not much better. Even in organizations that do not have their own survival as an immediate problem, managers work toward having specific types of conditions that minimize the risk of failure and increase the likelihood of survival. These conditions are positively stated as systems goals.

Systems goals are goals about conditions in the organization that are expected to increase the organization's survival potential. The list of systems goals is almost endless, since each manager and researcher links today's conditions to tomorrow's existence in a different way. For many organizations, however, the list includes growth, productivity, stability, harmony, flexibility, prestige, and human-resource maintenance. In some businesses, analysts consider market share and current profitability to be important systems goals. Other recent studies suggest that innovation and quality are also considered important.[7] In a very practical sense, systems goals

> Systems goals are goals about conditions in the organization that are expected to increase the organization's survival potential.

reflect the short-term organizational characteristics that higher-level managers want to encourage. Systems goals must often be balanced against each other. For instance, a push for ever-higher productivity and efficiency, if taken too far, may reduce the flexibility of an organization.

Different parts of the organization are often asked to pursue different types of systems goals. For example, higher-level managers may expect to see efficiency from their production operations, innovation from their R&D lab, and stability in the firm's financial affairs.

How important different systems goals are, relative to each other, can vary substantially across different types of organizations. Although we may expect the University of British Columbia or the University of New South Wales to emphasize prestige and innovation, few observers would expect such businesses as Nike or Telus to favour prestige over growth and profitability.

Systems goals are important to firms because they provide a road map that helps a firm link together various units of its organization, which will help it survive. Well-defined systems goals are practical and easy to understand; they focus the attention of managers on what needs to be done. Accurately stated systems goals also offer managers flexibility in figuring out ways to meet important targets. They can be used to balance the demands, constraints, and opportunities facing the firm. In addition, they can form a basis for dividing the work of the firm—in other words, a basis for developing a formal structure.

Strategy, Formal Structures, and the Division of Labour

Since the work of Alfred Chandler in the 1960s, OB scholars have known that successful organizations develop a structure that fits the pattern of goals chosen by senior management.[8] That is, decisions about what to accomplish must be matched with decisions on an appropriate way of organizing to reach these goals. The formal structure shows the planned configuration (i.e., the arrangement) of positions, job duties, and the lines of authority among different parts of the enterprise. The configuration that is selected gives the organization specific strengths that will help it reach toward some goals more than others.

Figure 11.1 A partial organization chart for a university

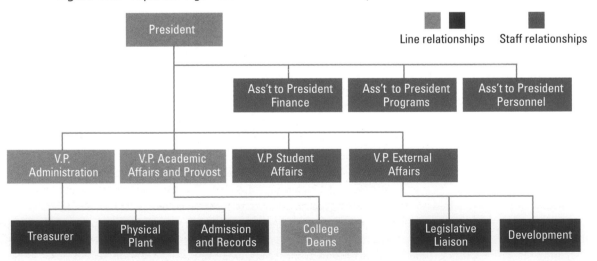

Traditionally, the formal structure of the firm has also been called the *division of labour*. This terminology is still sometimes used to make a clear distinction between decisions about the formal structure and decisions about the division of markets and/or technology. We will

deal with environmental and technology issues in the next chapter after discussing the structure as a foundation for managerial action. Here we emphasize that the formal structure outlines the jobs to be done, the persons (in terms of positions) who are to perform specific activities, and the ways the total tasks of the organization are to be accomplished. In other words, the formal structure is the skeleton of the firm.

Organization charts are diagrams that depict the formal structures of organizations. A typical chart shows the various positions, the position holders, and the lines of authority that link them to each other. Figure 11.1 presents a partial organization chart for a university. The total chart allows university employees to locate their positions in the structure and to identify the lines of authority linking them with others in the organization. For instance, in this figure, the treasurer reports to the vice president of administration, who, in turn, reports to the president of the university. (In Figure 11.2, the Royal Bank of Canada and IVACO, the steel manufacturer, are structured by product or region and then each subsidiary or division is structured according to the strategy and goals it must accomplish, thus reflecting more of the company's market rather than the skeleton of the company.)

> Organization charts are diagrams that depict the formal structures of organizations.

Figure 11.2 RBC and Ivaco structures

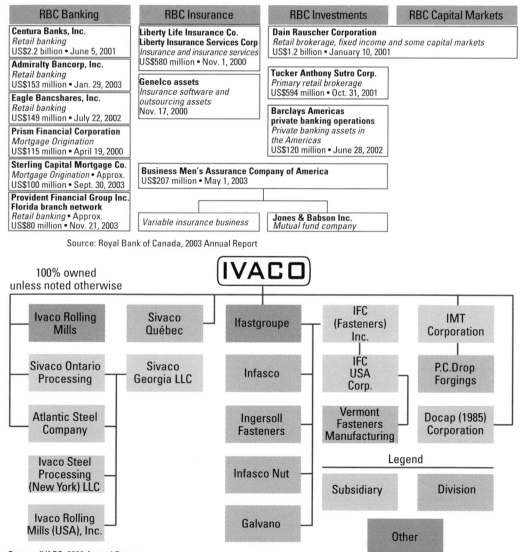

Source: Royal Bank of Canada, 2003 Annual Report

Source: IVACO, 2002 Annual Report

Vertical Specialization

Vertical specialization is a hierarchical division of labour that distributes formal authority.

In larger organizations, there is a clear separation of authority and duties by hierarchical rank. This separation is known as **vertical specialization**, a hierarchical division of labour that distributes formal authority and establishes where and how critical decisions are to be made. The division creates a hierarchy of authority—that is, an arrangement of work positions in order of increasing authority.

In Canada, the distribution of formal authority can be seen in the responsibilities that managers typically have. Top managers or senior executives plan the overall strategy of the organization and plot its long-term future.[9] They also act as the final judges for internal disputes and they certify promotions, reorganizations, and so on.

Middle managers guide the daily operations of the organization, help formulate policy, and translate top-management decisions into more specific guidelines for action. Lower-level managers supervise the actions of subordinates to ensure that the strategies authorized by top management are implemented and that the related policies established by middle management are complied with.

Managers in Japan often have different responsibilities than their counterparts in the typical North American firm. Japanese top managers do not develop and decide the firm's overall strategy. Instead, they manage a process involving middle managers. The process involves a lot of dialogue about actions the firm needs to take. Lower-level managers are also expected to act as advocates for the ideas and suggestions of their subordinates. The strategy of the firm is developed from dialogue and discussion, and implementation occurs according to the ideas and suggestions of lower-level managers and non-managers.

In many European firms, the senior managers are highly trained in the core of their business. For example, it is not unusual for the head of a manufacturing firm to have a Ph.D. in engineering. Thus, many European executives become more centrally involved in plotting the technical future of their firm. In contrast, few Canadian or Japanese executives have the necessary technical background to tackle this responsibility. Despite the differences in managerial responsibilities across Japan, Europe, and North America, all organizations have some vertical specialization.

Broad Span of Control

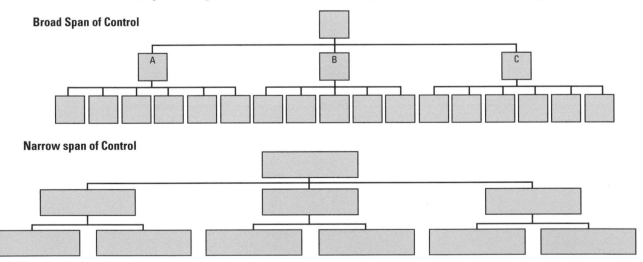

Narrow span of Control

CHAIN OF COMMAND AND THE SPAN OF CONTROL

Executives, managers, and supervisors are hierarchically connected through the *chain of command*—a listing of who reports to whom up and down the firm. Individuals are expected to follow their supervisor's decisions in the areas of responsibility outlined in the organization chart. Traditional management theory suggests that each individual should have one boss and each unit one leader. Under these circumstances, there is a "unity of command." Unity of command is considered necessary to avoid confusion, to make specific individuals responsible for something, and to provide clear channels of communication up and down the organization. Under traditional management with unity of command, the number of individuals a manager can supervise directly is obviously limited.

The number of individuals reporting to a supervisor is called the **span of control**. Narrower spans of control are expected when tasks are complex, when subordinates are inexperienced or poorly trained, or when tasks require team effort. Unfortunately, narrow spans of control create an organization with many levels. The excessive number of levels is not only expensive, but it also makes the organization unresponsive to necessary change. Communications in such firms often become less effective because messages are screened and modified as they move from one level to the next. The result is that subtle but important changes get ignored. Furthermore, with many levels, managers are removed from the action and become isolated.

New information technologies, discussed in the next chapter, now allow organizations to broaden the span of control, flatten their formal structures (i.e., have fewer levels), and still stay in control of complex operations.[10] At Nucor, for instance, senior managers pioneered the development of "minimills" for making steel and developed what they call "lean" management. At the same time, management there has expanded the span of control through extensive employee education and training that is backed by sophisticated information systems. The result: Nucor has only four levels of management from the bottom to the top.

> Span of control refers to the number of individuals reporting to a supervisor.

LINE AND STAFF UNITS

A very useful way to examine the vertical division of labour is to separate line and staff units. **Line units** and personnel do the major business of the organization. The production and marketing functions are two examples. In contrast, **staff units** and personnel assist the line units by providing specialized expertise and services, such as accounting and public relations. For example, the vice president of administration in a university (Figure 11.1) heads a staff unit, as does the vice president of student affairs. All academic departments are line units since they constitute the basic production function of the university.

> Line units are workgroups that conduct the major business of the organization.

Two other useful distinctions are often made in firms. One distinction is the type of relationship a unit in the chain of command has to the units above it. A staff department, such as the office of the V.P. for External Affairs in Figure 11.1, may be divided into subordinate units, such as Legislative Liaison and Development (again see Figure 11.1). In Figure 11.1, Legislative Liaison and Development are two staff units with a line relationship to the unit immediately above them in the chain of command—the V.P. for External Affairs. Why the apparent confusion of having line relationships between what are all staff units? The reason is historical: the notion of line and staff originally comes from the military where there is great emphasis on command. In a military sense, the V.P. for External Affairs is the commander of this staff effort—the individual responsible for this activity and the one held accountable—and the subordinate staff units are providing a line function for the staff unit they belong to.

> Staff units are groups that assist the line units by performing specialized services in the organization.

A second useful distinction for both line and staff units concerns the amount and types of contacts each unit has with outsiders to the organization. Some units are mainly internal in orientation; others have a more external focus. In general, internal line units (e.g., production) focus on transforming raw materials and information into products and services, whereas external line units (e.g., marketing) focus on maintaining links to suppliers, distributors, and customers. Internal staff units (e.g., accounting) assist the line units in performing their function. Normally, they specialize in specific technical or financial areas. External staff units (e.g., public relations) also assist the line units, but the focus of their actions is on linking the firm to its environment and buffering internal operations. Returning to Figure 11.1, then, the Legislative Liaison unit would be described as an external staff unit with a line relationship to the office of the V.P. for External Affairs.

CONFIGURING STAFF AND INFORMATION SYSTEMS FOR IMPLEMENTATION

Staff, particularly internal staff, contribute indirectly was corporate goals by using their specialized knowledge and talents. Traditionally, someone was needed to keep the books, hire and train the personnel, and do the research and development. Figure 11.3 shows how the placement of staff changes the look of a firm.

Staff units can be assigned mostly to senior, middle, or lower-level managers. When staff are assigned mostly to senior management, the capability of senior management to develop alternatives and make decisions is expanded. It allows senior executives to directly develop information and alternatives and check on the implementation of their decisions. Here, the amount of vertical specialization in the firm is smaller because senior managers plan, decide, and control through their centralized staff. With new information technologies, fewer and fewer firms are placing most staff at the top. They are replacing internal staff with information systems and placing talented individuals further down the hierarchy. When staff are moved to the middle of the organization, middle managers now have the specialized help that is needed to expand their role.

Many firms are also beginning to ask whether certain staff should be a permanent part of the organization at all. Some firms are outsourcing many of their staff functions.

Figure 11.3 How the placement of staff changes the look of an organization

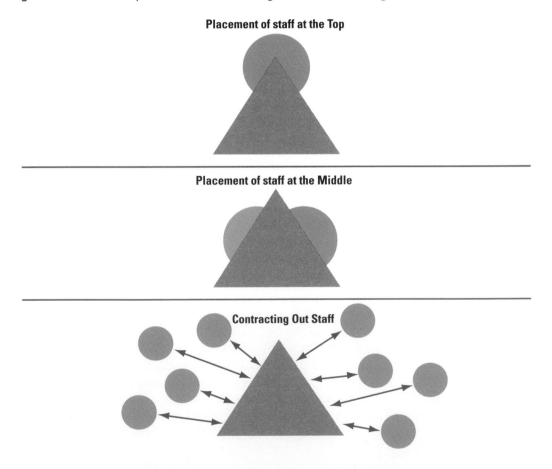

Manufacturing firms are contracting much of their accounting, personnel, and public relations activities to small, specialized firms.[11] Outsourcing by large firms has been a boon for smaller support corporations. Figure 11.3 illustrates the use of staff through "contracting out."

Finance

High Finance at the Click of a Button

Today's highly volatile global stock market, combined with the immediacy of the Internet, has created a wealth of online information for investors and their advisers. The difficulty is choosing where to point the mouse. Canada's Stockwatch is a subscription-only source of real-time quotes, trades, and market information on companies listed on the major North American stock markets, including NYSE, AMEX, NASDAQ, OTCBB, Pink Sheets, Toronto, Montreal, and CNQ. It provides unlimited real-time market data, company news bulletins, charts, analytical tools for casual, serious, and professional investors, as well as many other advanced features for active traders. It has essentially all the information a person would need to make a buy or sell decision.

One of the biggest trends in management today is to use information technology to streamline operations and reduce staff, with the ultimate goal being to lower costs and raise productivity.[12] One way of accomplishing this is to provide line managers and employees with information and managerial techniques that will expand their analytical and decision-making capabilities—and so make certain internal staff unnecessary. For instance, students of financial management know the importance of financial planning models (in detecting problems); financial decision aids, such as capital budgeting models and discounted cash-flow analyses (for selecting among alternatives); and budgets (to monitor progress and ensure that managers stay within financial limits). With computer programs, each of these is now accessible to all levels of management instead of only being available to financial staff.[13]

Although a great variety of managerial techniques have been available to managers for decades, only with the widespread use of computers have the costs of these techniques been reduced. Most organizations use a combination of line and staff units, alliances with specialized providers, and managerial techniques to specialize their division of labour vertically (e.g., to distribute formal authority).

The most appropriate pattern of vertical specialization depends on the environment of the organization, its size, its technology, and its goals. For instance, as organizations grow, vertical specialization typically increases just to keep up with the amount of work. We will return to this theme in the next chapter and pay special attention to information technology and its role in changing organizations. For now, however, we should turn our attention to issues involving control of the organization, because control is closely related to the division of labour.

Control

Control is the set of mechanisms an organization uses to ensure that actions and outputs respect predetermined limits. Control involves setting standards, measuring results versus standards, and taking corrective actions. Although all organizations need controls, having just a few controls may be all that is needed. Astute managers need to be aware of the danger of too much control in the organization.

> **Control** is the set of mechanisms an organization uses to ensure that actions and outputs respect predetermined limits.

OUTPUT CONTROLS

Output controls are controls that focus on desired targets and allow managers to use their own methods for reaching these targets.

Earlier in this chapter, we suggested that systems goals could be used as a road map to bring together the various units of the organization by directing them all towards achieving a common practical objective. Developing targets or standards, measuring results against these targets, and taking corrective action are all steps in developing output controls.[14] **Output controls** focus on desired targets and allow managers to use their own methods to reach these targets. Most modern organizations use output controls as part of an overall method of managing by exception (for example, a process should only be dealt with if it is not working well).

Output controls are popular because they promote flexibility and creativity, and also make it easier to discuss possible corrective actions. Having output controls separates what is to be accomplished from how it is to be accomplished. Thus, the discussion of goals is separated from the dialogue about methods. This separation can help power move down through the organization, as senior managers can be sure that individuals at all levels will be working toward the goals that senior management believes are important. Significantly, this still allows lower-level managers to innovate and introduce new ways to accomplish these goals.

PROCESS CONTROLS

Process controls are controls that try to specify how tasks are to be accomplished.

Few organizations only use output controls. Once a solution to a problem is found and successfully implemented, managers do not want the problem to happen again, so they create process controls. **Process controls** try to specify how tasks are to be accomplished. There are many types of process controls, but three groups of them have received considerable attention: (1) policies, procedures, and rules; (2) formalization and standardization; and (3) total quality management controls.

Policies, Procedures, and Rules Most organizations use a variety of policies, procedures, and rules to help specify how goals are to be accomplished. In general, a *policy* is a guideline for action that outlines important objectives and broadly indicates how an activity is to be performed. A policy allows for individual discretion and minor adjustments without the need for direct approval by a higher-level manager. *Procedures* indicate the best method for performing a task, show which aspects of a task are the most important, or outline how an individual is to be rewarded.

Many firms link *rules and procedures*. Rules are more specific, rigid, and impersonal than policies. They typically describe in detail how a task or a series of tasks is to be performed, or they indicate what cannot be done. They are designed for all individuals, under specified conditions. For example, most car dealers have detailed instruction manuals for repairing a new car under warranty, and they must follow very strict procedures to obtain a reimbursement from the manufacturer for warranty work.

Rules, procedures, and policies are often used as substitutes for direct managerial supervision. With the help of written rules and procedures, the organization can specifically direct the activities of many individuals. It can ensure virtually identical treatment across even distant work locations. For example, a hamburger and fries at McDonald's taste much the same whether they are purchased in Hong Kong, Indianapolis, London, or Toronto, simply because the ingredients and the cooking methods follow the same written rules and procedures.

Formalization is the written documentation of work rules, policies, and procedures.

Formalization and Standardization **Formalization** refers to the written documentation of rules, procedures, and policies that guide behaviour and decision-making. In addition to being a substitute for direct management supervision, formalization can also often simplify jobs. Written instructions allow individuals with less training to perform comparatively sophisticated tasks. Written procedures may also be used to ensure that a series of tasks is done in the proper sequence, even if this sequence is performed only occasionally.

Most organizations have developed additional methods for dealing with recurring problems or situations. **Standardization** is the degree to which the range of actions in a job or series of jobs is limited. It involves the creation of guidelines so that similar work activities are repeatedly performed in a similar manner. Such standardized methods may come from years of experience in dealing with typical situations, or they may come from outside training. For instance, a typical method your bank may use if you are late in paying your credit card is to automatically send you a notification and start an internal process of monitoring your account.

Standardization is the degree to which the range of actions in a job or series of jobs is limited.

Total Quality Management   The process controls discussed so far—policies, procedures, rules, formalization, and standardization—represent the lessons an organization learns from experience. That is, managers institute these process controls based on past experience, and usually one at a time. Often there is no overall philosophy for using control to improve the overall operations of the company. Another way to institute process controls is to establish a total quality management process for the firm.

The late W. Edwards Deming is the modern-day founder of the total quality management movement.[15] When Deming's ideas were not generally accepted in the U.S., he found an audience in Japan. Thus, for some managers, Deming's ideas have become known through the best Japanese business practices.

Deming's basic idea is to use a process approach for continual improvement that is based on statistical analyses of the firm's operations. Around this core idea, Deming built a series of 14 points for managers to use. As you look at the following points, note the emphasis on having both managers and employees working together and using statistical controls to continually improve:

- Create a consistency of purpose in the company to:
    - (a) innovate
    - (b) put resources into research and education
    - (c) put resources into maintaining equipment and new production aids

Deming's 14 Points

- Learn a new philosophy of quality to improve every system.

- Require statistical evidence of process control and eliminate financial controls on production.

- Require statistical evidence of control in purchasing parts; this will mean dealing with fewer suppliers.

- Use statistical methods to isolate the sources of trouble.

- Institute modern on-the-job training.

- Improve supervision to develop inspired leaders.

- Drive out fear and instill learning.

- Break down barriers between departments.

- Eliminate numerical goals and slogans.

- Constantly revamp work methods.

- Institute massive training programs for employees in statistical methods.

- Retrain people in new skills.

- Create a structure that will push, every day, on the above 13 points.

All levels of management are to be involved in the quality program. The specific role of managers is to improve supervision, train employees, retrain employees in new skills, and create a structure that pushes the quality program. Where the properties of the firm's outcomes are well defined, as in most manufacturing operations, Deming's system and emphasis on quality appears to work well when it is implemented along with empowerment and participative management. Quality Solutions® Inc., based in London, Ontario, is a professional training and consulting group that provides Total Quality Management Training, based on the philosophy of Edward Deming. It includes a set of guiding principles for continuous improvement within an organization. Small teams focus on continually improving what they do by tracking their quality and reviewing it, then problem solving and making changes in how they do their job.

HIGH-PERFORMANCE ORGANIZATION

ALCAN, ISO CERTIFIED

ISO (International Organization for Standardization)—a worldwide federation of national standards bodies from some 100 countries—has a mission to promote quality. It has established rigorous quality process standards that are in part based on Deming's work. Firms that want to have ISO certification must be assessed by a third party and go through periodic audits to ensure that they meet the standards defined in the ISO 9000 series. Few small firms based in Canada have an ISO 9000 certification unless it is required by their customers. As expected, a multinational corporation like Alcan is certified. In fact, in 2003 Alcan was certified or completing certification in all 42 countries in which it operated. This includes ISO 14000, the environmental system. President and CEO Travis Engen says the benefits of the process of obtaining the ISO 9001 designation include "fewer rejects, less lost time accidents, better productivity, greater employee pride in their facility, improved housekeeping —the list goes on."

www.alcan.com

ALLOCATING FORMAL AUTHORITY: CENTRALIZATION AND DECENTRALIZATION

Centralization is when the authority to make decisions is restricted to higher levels of management.

Decentralization is when the authority to make decisions is given to lower levels in an organization's hierarchy.

Different firms use very different mixes of vertical specialization, output controls, process controls, and managerial techniques to allocate the authority or freedom to act.[16] The higher the level of authority that is needed for making decisions that involve spending money, hiring people, and so on, the greater the degree of **centralization**. The more such decisions are delegated, or moved down the hierarchy of authority, the greater the degree of **decentralization**. Greater centralization is often preferred when the firm faces a single major threat to its survival. Thus, it is no surprise that armies tend to be centralized and that firms facing bankruptcy increase centralization.

Generally speaking, greater decentralization leads to higher satisfaction in subordinates and a quicker response to a series of unrelated and varied problems. Decentralization also makes it easier to do on-the-job training of subordinates for higher-level positions. Decentralization is now a popular approach in many industries. For instance, Alcan is pushing responsibility down the chain of command, by creating six business groups which are responsible for the value creation of their own business units. They provide leadership and operating oversight to meet customer, shareholder, and employee expectations. With this decentralization, senior managers hope to improve both performance quality and organizational responsiveness. Closely related to decentralization is the notion of participation. Many people want to be involved in making decisions that affect their work. There is participation when a manager delegates some authority for such decision-making to subordinates in order to include them in the choosing process. Employees may want to have some influence on both what the unit objectives should be and on how they can be achieved.[17]

Firms such as AMJ Campbell Movers and Dofasco have also experimented by moving decisions down the chain of command and increasing participation. These firms found that just cutting the number of organizational levels was not enough. They also needed to change their controls over quality, to stress constant improvement, and to change other basic features of the organization. As these firms have increased participation, they have emphasized the importance of ethical decision-making and adherence to national and international human rights laws. In the case of TI, discussed below, this emphasis takes a very visible form. As these firms changed their degree of vertical specialization, they also changed the division of work among units—in other words, they changed the firm's horizontal specialization.

In the case of VanCity, discussed below, this emphasis takes a very visible form.

ETHICS & SOCIAL RESPONSIBILITY

ETHICS AT VANCITY

Vancouver City Savings Credit Union (VanCity) takes its role as an advocate for socially and environmentally responsible business behaviour seriously. An example of this commitment is its sponsorship and support of the Ethics in Action Awards, which recognize organizations and individuals who exemplify good corporate citizenship by making corporate social responsibility a key aspect of their daily operations.

www.vancity.com

Horizontal Specialization

Vertical specialization and control are only half the picture. Managers must also divide the total task into separate duties and group similar people and resources together.[18] **Horizontal specialization** is a division of labour that establishes specific work units or work groups within an organization; it is often referred to as the process of departmentation. There are several pure forms of departmentation.

Horizontal specialization is the division of labour by forming work units or work groups within an organization.

DEPARTMENTATION BY FUNCTION

Grouping individuals by skill, knowledge, and action results in a pattern of **functional departmentation**. Recall Figure 11.1, which shows the partial organization chart for a large university in which each department has a technical specialty. Marketing, finance, production, and personnel are important functions in business. In many small firms, this functional pattern dominates. Even large firms use this pattern in technically demanding areas or when low cost is a major competitive focus.

Functional departmentation is grouping individuals by skill, knowledge, and action yields.

Figure 11.4 summarizes the advantages of the functional pattern. With all these advantages, it is not surprising that the functional form is extremely popular. It is used in most organizations, particularly toward the bottom of the hierarchy. Functional specialization also has some disadvantages, summarized in Figure 11.4. Organizations that rely heavily on functional specialization should expect the following tendencies to develop over time: an emphasis on quality from a technical standpoint, rigidity to change, and difficulty in coordinating the actions of different functional areas.

Figure 11.4 Major advantages and disadvantages of functional specialization

Major Advantage and Disadvantages of Functional Specialization	
Advantages	Disadvantages
1. Yields very clear task assignments, consistent with an individual's training.	1. May reinforce the narrow training of individuals.
2. Individuals within a department can easily build on one another's knowledge, training, and experience.	2. May yield narrow, boring, and routine jobs.
3. Provides an excellent training ground for new managers.	3. Communication across technical areas is complex and difficult.
4. It is easy to explain.	4. "Top management overload" with too much attention to cross-functional problems.
5. Takes advantage of employee technical quality.	5. Individuals may look up the organizational hierarchy for direction and reinforcement rather than focus attention on products, services, or clients.

DEPARTMENTATION BY DIVISION

Divisional departmentation groups individuals and resources by products, territories, services, clients, or legal entities.[19] Figure 11.5 shows a divisional pattern of organization grouped around products, regions, and customers for three divisions of a conglomerate. This pattern is often used to respond to diverse external threats and opportunities.

Divisional departmentation groups individuals and resources by products, territories, services, clients, or legal entities.

As shown in Figure 11.5, the major advantages of the divisional pattern are its flexibility in responding to external demands, spotting external changes, integrating specialized individuals deep within the organization, and focusing on the delivery of specific products to specific customers. Among its disadvantages are a duplication of effort by function, the tendency for divisional goals to be placed above corporate interests, and conflict among divisions. It is also not the best structure for training individuals in technical areas, and firms relying on this pattern may fall behind competitors who use a functional pattern.

Many larger, geographically dispersed organizations that sell to national and international markets may rely on departmentation by geography. The savings in time, effort, and travel can be substantial, and each territory can adjust to regional differences. Organizations that rely on a few major customers may organize their people and resources by client. Here, the idea is to focus attention on the needs of the individual customer.[20] To the extent that customer needs are unique, departmentation by customer can also reduce confusion and increase synergy.

Organizations that are expanding internationally may also form divisions to respond to the demands of complex host-country ownership requirements. For example, Sony, Nissan, Mazda, Panasonic, and many other Japanese corporations have developed Canadian, U.S., or North American divisional subsidiaries to serve their customers in these markets. Some huge European-based corporations such as Philips and Nestlé have also adopted a divisional structure in their expansion to North America. Similarly, most of the internationalized Canadian and U.S.-based firms, such as Nortel, Alcan, CanWest Global, Bombardier, Alliance-Atlantis, IBM, and GE have incorporated the divisional structure as part of their internalization programs.

Figure 11.5 A divisional pattern of departmentation

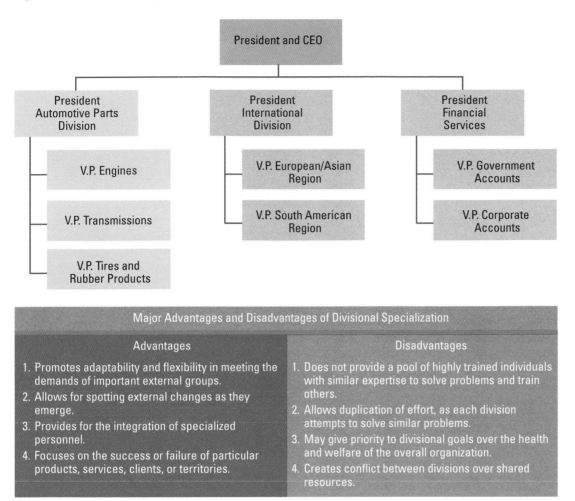

DEPARTMENTATION BY MATRIX

Originally developed in the aerospace industry, a third unique form of departmentation is now becoming more popular—**matrix departmentation**.[21] In aerospace efforts, projects are technically very complex, involving hundreds of subcontractors located throughout the world. Precise integration and control are needed across many sophisticated functional specialties and corporations. This is often more than a functional or divisional structure can provide, because many firms do not want to trade the responsiveness of the divisional form for the technical emphasis of the functional form. The solution, matrix departmentation, uses both the functional and divisional forms at the same time. Figure 11.6 shows the basic matrix arrangement for an aerospace program. Note the functional departments on one side and the project efforts on the other. Workers and supervisors in the middle of the matrix have two bosses—one functional and one project.

Matrix departmentation is a combination of functional and divisional patterns which assigns an individual to more than one type of unit.

Figure 11.6 A matrix pattern of departmentation in an aerospace division

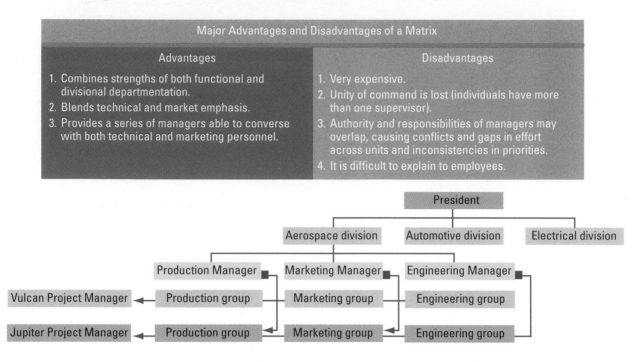

Major Advantages and Disadvantages of a Matrix	
Advantages	Disadvantages
1. Combines strengths of both functional and divisional departmentation. 2. Blends technical and market emphasis. 3. Provides a series of managers able to converse with both technical and marketing personnel.	1. Very expensive. 2. Unity of command is lost (individuals have more than one supervisor). 3. Authority and responsibilities of managers may overlap, causing conflicts and gaps in effort across units and inconsistencies in priorities. 4. It is difficult to explain to employees.

The major advantages and disadvantages of the matrix form of departmentation are also summarized in Figure 11.6. The key disadvantage of the matrix method is the loss of unity of command. Individuals can be unsure about what their jobs are, who they report to for specific activities, and how various managers will oversee the effort. It can also be a very expensive method because it relies on individual managers to coordinate efforts deep within the firm. In Figure 11.6, note that the number of managers in a matrix structure is almost double the number needed in either a functional or a divisional structure. Despite these limitations, the matrix structure provides a balance between functional and divisional concerns. Many problems can be solved at the working level, where the balance among technical, financial, customer, and organizational concerns can be dealt with.

GLOBALIZATION

SNC-LAVALIN FROM MONTREAL TO THE WORLD

SNC-Lavalin Group Inc. began as a small engineering consulting office that opened in 1911 and evolved into a partnership. In 1991, what had by then become SNC Inc., merged with another large Canadian engineering firm, Lavalin Inc., to form one of the world's leading groups of engineering and construction companies. Today, SNC-Lavalin offers engineering and construction services, owns and manages infrastructure in terms of large, completed projects and provides facilities and operations management in sectors as varied as agrifood, aluminum, pharmaceuticals, chemicals and petroleum, the environment, infrastructure, mass transit, mining and metallurgy, and power. It also offers project financing services. SNC-Lavalin's vast network of offices and subsidiaries stretches worldwide and is present on every continent. In Canada, the firm's engineers and other professionals are located in cities from coast to coast. In SNC-Lavalin's multicultural workforce (in which 50 languages are spoken, representing 80 nationalities), the matrix concept is used in structuring major projects, allowing the firm to coordinate, for the purposes of a specific project in a specific country, the use of its own specialists from around the world. The process works this way: senior staff members in a local office first identify the specific needs of a client's project, then "matrix" across the firm's global locations to find those individuals whose unique skills are needed for the project to supplement the qualifications of local staff.

www.snc-lavalin.com

Many organizations also use elements of the matrix structure without officially using the term "matrix." For example, special project teams, coordinating committees, and task forces can be the beginnings of a matrix. These temporary structures can be used in a mostly functional or divisional form and without upsetting the unity of command or hiring additional managers.

MIXED FORMS OF DEPARTMENTATION

Which form of departmentation should be used? As the matrix concept suggests, it is possible to departmentalize by two different methods at the same time. In reality, organizations commonly use a mixture of departmentation forms. It is often desirable to divide the effort (i.e., to group people and resources) by two methods at the same time in order to balance the advantages and disadvantages of each method. In the next chapter, we will discuss several mixed forms. These mixed forms help firms use their division of labour to take advantage of opportunities, reap the benefits of larger size, and realize the potential of new technologies as they pursue their strategies.

Coordination

Whatever is divided up horizontally must also be integrated.[22] **Coordination** is the set of mechanisms an organization uses to link the actions of its units into a consistent pattern. Much of the coordination within a unit is done by its manager. Smaller organizations may rely on their management hierarchy to provide the necessary consistency and integration. As the organization grows, however, managers become overloaded. The organization then needs to develop more efficient and effective ways of linking work units to each other.

Coordination is the set of mechanisms an organization uses to link the actions of its units into a consistent pattern.

PERSONAL METHODS OF COORDINATION

Personal methods of coordination produce synergy by promoting dialogue, discussion, innovation, creativity, and learning, both within and across organizational units. Personal methods allow the organization to respond to the particular needs of distinct units and individuals simultaneously. There is a wide variety of personal methods of coordination.[23] Perhaps the most popular is direct contact between and among organizational members. As new information technologies have been adopted, the potential for developing and maintaining effective contact networks has expanded. For example, many executives use e-mail, Corporate Time, Lotus Notes, and other computer-based links in addition to direct personal communication (face-to-face or by phone). Direct personal contact is also associated with the ever-present "grapevine." Although information that travels unofficially from person to person is notoriously inaccurate when it comes to rumours, it is often both accurate enough and quick enough that managers cannot ignore it. Instead, managers need to work with and supplement this rumour mill with accurate information.

The Effective Manager	11.1

ADJUSTING COORDINATION EFFORTS

The astute manager should recognize that some individuals and/or units:

- have their own views of how best to move toward organizational goals
- emphasize immediate problems and quick solutions; or stress underlying problems and longer-term solutions
- have their own unique vocabulary and standard way of communicating
- have strong preferences for formality or informality

Managers are also often assigned to committees to improve coordination across departments. Even though committees are generally expensive and have a very poor reputation, they can become an effective personal mechanism for unit heads to make adjustments so that their styles and actions are better coordinated. Committees can be effective in communicating complex qualitative information. They can also help managers whose units must work together to adjust schedules, workloads, and work assignments to increase productivity.

As more organizations develop flatter structures with a greater delegation of responsibility, they are finding that task forces can be quite useful. Whereas committees tend to be long-lasting, task forces are typically formed with a more limited agenda. Individuals from different parts of the organization are brought together into a task force to identify and solve problems that involve several different departments.

There is no magic in selecting the appropriate mix of personal coordination methods and tailoring them to the individual skills, abilities, and experience of subordinates. Managers simply need to know the individuals involved, their preferences, and the accepted approaches in different organizational units. Different personal methods can be made to match different individuals (see The Effective Manager 11.1). Personal methods are only one important part of coordination. The manager may also establish a series of impersonal mechanisms.

IMPERSONAL METHODS OF COORDINATION

Impersonal methods of coordination produce synergy by stressing consistency and standardization so that individual pieces fit together well. Impersonal coordination methods are often refinements and extensions of process controls, but with extra emphasis on formalization and standardization. Most larger organizations have written policies and procedures, such as schedules, budgets, and plans, that are designed to bring the operations of several units into a whole. The policies and procedures do this by providing predictability and consistency.

The most highly developed form of impersonal coordination is the matrix form of departmentation. As noted earlier, this form of departmentation is specifically designed to coordinate the efforts of diverse functional units. Natural Resources Canada's CANMET—Materials Technology Laboratory—uses a matrix system since organizational design, development and performance, and organizational structure cannot be considered in isolation. In fact, its structure must be conceived, implemented, and operated in the context of other key organizational variables. Although a few organizations rely exclusively on a matrix structure, many firms are simply using cross-functional task forces to replace specialized staff units that had coordination as their main role.

The final example of an impersonal coordination mechanism is now changing radically in many modern organizations. Originally, management information systems were developed and designed so that senior managers could coordinate and control the operations of diverse subordinate units. These systems were supposed to be computerized substitutes for schedules, budgets, and so on. In some firms, the management information system still operates as a combined process control and impersonal coordination mechanism. In the hands of astute managers, however, the management information system has become an electronic network, linking individuals throughout the organization. Using decentralized communication systems, supplemented by the telephone, fax machine, and e-mail, a once centrally controlled system becomes another aid to personal coordination.

The fundamental change that is now happening in most larger organizations is the transformation of the potential of information technologies into real benefits. This fundamental change is so important and so pervasive that it is altering the way firms put together their specialization of labour, control, and coordination. This will be shown in the next chapter. For now it is important to understand the basic combinations of specialization, control, and coordination.

Bureaucracy

In the developed world, most firms are bureaucracies. In OB, this term has a very special meaning, beyond its negative connotation (see The Effective Manager 11.2). The famous German sociologist Max Weber suggested that organizations would thrive if they became **bureaucracies** by emphasizing legal authority, logic, and order.[24] Bureaucracies rely on a division of labour, hierarchical control, promotion by merit, career opportunities for employees, and administration by rule.

Weber argued that the rational and logical idea of bureaucracy was superior to building a firm based on charisma or cultural tradition. The "charismatic" ideal-type organization, he argued, relies too much on the talents of one individual and would likely fail when the leader left. Too much reliance on cultural traditions blocked innovation, stifled efficiency, and was often unfair. Since the bureaucracy values efficiency, order, and logic, Weber hoped that it could also be fair to employees and provide more freedom for individual expression than is allowed when tradition dominates. Although he knew it was far from perfect, Weber predicted that the bureaucracy, or some variation of this ideal form, would dominate modern society. He was right. While charismatic leadership and cultural traditions are still important today, it is the rational, legal, and efficiency aspects of the firm that characterize modern corporations.

> **The Effective Manager   11.2**
> THE NATURAL DYSFUNCTIONAL TENDENCIES OF A BUREAUCRACY
> - overspecialization and a failure to lessen the resulting conflicts of interest
> - overuse of the formal hierarchy and an emphasis on adherence to official channels rather than on problem-solving
> - treatment of senior managers as superior performers on all tasks and as rulers of a political system rather than as individuals who should help others reach goals
> - overemphasis on insignificant conformity that limits individual growth
> - treatment of rules as being what matters rather than as poor mechanisms for control and coordination

TYPES OF BUREAUCRACIES

The notion of a bureaucracy has evolved over time. Figure 11.7 illustrates three popular, basic types of bureaucracies: the mechanistic, the organic, and the divisionalized approaches. And it shows how some huge corporations called conglomerates are collections of very different firms. Each type of bureaucracy is a different mix of the basic attributes discussed in this chapter, and each mix results in firms with a slightly different blend of capabilities and natural tendencies.

The Mechanistic Type   The **mechanistic type** emphasizes vertical specialization and control.[25] Organizations of this type stress rules, policies, and procedures; specify techniques for decision-making; and emphasize developing well-documented control systems that are backed by a strong middle management and supported by a centralized staff. The functional pattern of departmentation is often used throughout the firm. Henry Mintzberg uses the term *machine bureaucracy* to describe an organization that is entirely structured in this way.[26]

To achieve efficiency in the mechanistic design, management emphasizes routine. Until the arrival of new information systems, most very large firms in basic industries were machine bureaucracies. Included in this long list were all the automobile manufacturers, banks, insurance companies, steel mills, large retail establishments, and government offices. Efficiency was achieved through extensive vertical and horizontal specialization that was held together by elaborate controls and informal coordination mechanisms.

There are, however, limits to the benefits of specialization that relies on rigid controls. Employees do not like rigid designs, so motivation becomes a problem. Unions make narrow job descriptions stay narrow by demanding very specific work rules and regulations to protect employees from the many vertical controls. Key employees may leave because of these limitations. In short, using a machine bureaucracy can limit an organization's ability to adjust to subtle external changes or new technologies.

Bureaucracy is an ideal form of organization, with its characteristics defined by the German sociologist Max Weber.

Mechanistic type or machine bureaucracy emphasizes vertical specialization and control, with impersonal coordination and a heavy reliance on standardization, formalization, rules, policies, and procedures.

Figure 11.7   Different basic bureaucratic patterns

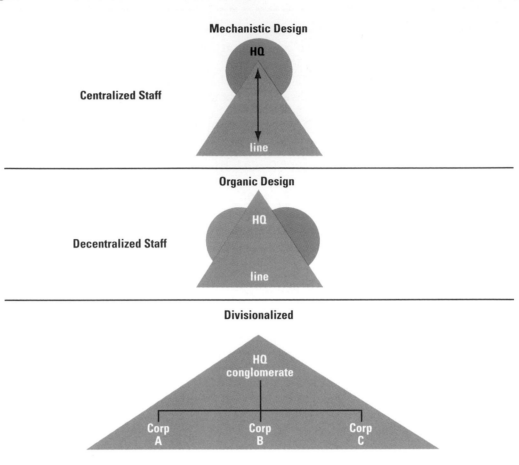

The Organic Type   The **organic type** of bureaucracy is much less vertically oriented than the mechanistic type; it emphasizes horizontal specialization. There are few procedures, and they are not as formalized. The organization relies on the judgements of experts and personal coordination. When controls are used, they generally back up professional socialization, training, and individual reinforcement. Staff units are generally placed toward the middle of the organization. Because this is a popular design in professional firms, Mintzberg calls it a professional bureaucracy.[27]

Your university or college is probably a professional bureaucracy that looks like a broad, flat pyramid with a large bulge in the centre for the professional staff. Power in this ideal type goes with knowledge. Historically, the staff helped the line managers and often had very little formal power, other than to block action. Control is achieved by the standardization of professional skills and the use of professional routines, standards, and procedures. Other examples of organic types include most hospitals, libraries, and social service agencies.

Although it is not as efficient as the machine bureaucracy, the professional bureaucracy is better for problem-solving and for satisfying individual customer needs. Since lateral relations and coordination are emphasized, there is less centralized direction by senior management. Thus, this type of bureaucracy is good for detecting external changes and adjusting to new technologies, but it is not as efficient at responding to direction from central management.[28]

Hybrid Types   Many very large firms find that neither the mechanistic nor the organic approach is suitable for all their operations. Adopting a machine bureaucracy would overload

> Organic type or professional bureaucracy emphasizes horizontal specialization, extensive use of personal coordination, and loose rules, policies, and procedures.

senior management and result in too many levels of management. On the other hand, adopting an organic type would mean losing control and becoming too inefficient. Senior managers may then choose one of several hybrid types.

We have already introduced two hybrid types. One is an extension of the divisional pattern of departmentation and allows different divisions to be more or less organic or mechanistic. Here the divisions may be treated as separate businesses, even though they share a similar mission and output and systems goals.[29]

A second hybrid is the true conglomerate. A **conglomerate** is a single corporation that contains a number of unrelated businesses. On the surface, these firms look like divisionalized firms, but when the various businesses of the divisions are unrelated, the term "conglomerate" is used.[30] For instance, Bell Canada Enterprises (BCE) is a telecommunications and media conglomerate, though, with the growth of convergence, the lines between the various business divisions are beginning to blur. Bell Canada provides phone and long distance services, Bell Mobility provides wireless services, Bell Sympatico provides Internet services, and Bell ExpressVu provides satellite television services. In addition BellGlobemedia owns and operates *The Globe and Mail*, CTV Inc., TSN, RDS, and Report on Business Television. Nestlé was created through a series of financial manoeuvres that brought together several food companies from around the world and is now based in Switzerland. Many provincial and federal entities are also, by necessity, conglomerates. For instance, a premier is the chief executive officer of those units concerned with higher education, health, prisons and courts, highway construction and maintenance, police, and so on.

The conglomerate type also illustrates two important points that will be the highlight of the next chapter: (1) All structures are combinations of the basic attributes. (2) There is no one best structure—it all depends on factors such as the size of the firm, its environment, its technology, and, of course, its strategy.

> **Conglomerates** are firms that own several different unrelated businesses.

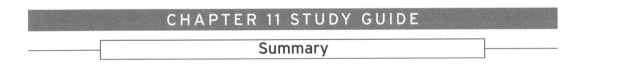

CHAPTER 11 STUDY GUIDE

Summary

What is strategy?

- Strategy is a process.
- Strategy is positioning the organization in its competitive environment.
- Strategy is implementing actions.
- Strategy is seen through the pattern in a series of decisions.

What types of contributions do organizations make, and what types of goals do they adopt?

- Organizations make specific contributions to society.
- Firms often concentrate on primary beneficiaries and specify output goals (specific products and services).

- In their mission statement, firms may mention a societal contribution focused on a primary beneficiary.
- Corporations have systems goals that state the conditions which managers believe will lead to survival and success.

What is the formal structure of the organization, and what is meant by the term "division of labour"?

- The formal structure defines the planned configuration of positions, job duties, and lines of authority among different parts of the firm.
- The formal structure is also known as the firm's division of labour.

How is vertical specialization used to allocate formal authority within the organization?

- Vertical specialization is a hierarchical division of labour that specifies where formal authority is located.
- Typically, there is a chain of command that links lower-level workers with senior managers.
- The distinction between line and staff units also indicates how authority is distributed, with line units doing the major business of the firm and staff providing support.
- Managerial techniques, including the use of information technology, are used to expand the analytical and decision-making capability of managers and to minimize staff.

How does an organization control the actions of its members?

- Control is the set of mechanisms an organization uses to ensure that actions and outputs respect predetermined levels.
- Output controls focus on desired targets and allow managers to use their own methods for reaching these targets.
- Process controls specify how tasks are to be accomplished through (1) policies, rules, and procedures; (2) formalization and standardization; and (3) total quality management controls.
- Firms are learning that decentralization often provides substantial benefits.

What different patterns of horizontal specialization can be used in the organization?

- Horizontal specialization is the division of labour that creates various work units and departments in the organization.
- There are three main types or patterns of departmentation: functional, divisional, and matrix. Each pattern has advantages and disadvantages.
- Organizations may successfully use any type of departmentation, or a mixture, as long as the strengths of what is chosen match the needs of the organization.

Which personal and impersonal coordination techniques should the organization use?

- Coordination is the set of mechanisms an organization uses to link the actions of separate units into a consistent pattern.
- Personal methods of coordination produce synergy by promoting dialogue, discussion, innovation, creativity, and learning.
- Impersonal methods of control produce synergy by stressing consistency and standardization so that individual pieces fit together well.

What are bureaucracies and what are the common types?

- The bureaucracy is an ideal form of organization that is based on legal authority, logic, and order and that provides superior efficiency and effectiveness.
- Mechanistic, organic, and hybrids are common types of bureaucracies.
- Hybrid types include the divisionalized firm and the conglomerate. No one type is always superior to the others.

Bureaucracy (p. 221)

Centralization (p. 214)

Conglomerate (p. 223)

Control (p. 211)

Coordination (p. 219)

Decentralization (p. 214)

Divisional departmentation (p. 216)

Formalization (p. 212)

Functional departmentation (p. 215)

Horizontal specialization (p. 215)

Line units (p. 209)

Matrix departmentation (p. 217)

Mechanistic type (p. 221)

Mission statements (p. 204)

Organic type (p. 222)

Organization charts (p. 207)

Output controls (p. 212)

Output goals (p. 205)

Process controls (p. 212)

Societal goals (p. 204)

Span of control (p. 209)

Staff units (p. 209)

Standardization (p. 213)

Strategy (p. 203)

Systems goals (p. 205)

Vertical specialization (p. 208)

MULTIPLE CHOICE

1. The strategy of an organization is _____. (a) a process (b) positioning the organization in the competitive environment (c) consistent implementation actions (d) seen through the pattern in a series of actions (e) all of these

2. The formal structures of organizations may be shown in a(n) _____. (a) environmental diagram (b) organization chart (c) horizontal diagram (d) matrix depiction (e) labour assignment chart

3. A major distinction between line and staff units is _____. (a) the amount of resources each is allowed to use (b) how their jobs link to the goals of the firm (c) the amount of education or training they possess (d) their use of computer information systems (e) their link to the outside world

4. The division of labour by grouping people and material resources deals with _____. (a) horizontal specialization (b) coordination (c) divisionalization (d) vertical specialization (e) goal setting

5. Control involves all but _____. (a) measuring results (b) establishing goals (c) taking corrective action (d) comparing results with goals (e) selecting manpower

6. Grouping individuals and resources in the organization around products, services, clients, territories, or legal entities is an example of _____ specialization. (a) divisional (b) functional (c) matrix (d) mixed form (e) outsourced

7. Grouping resources into departments by skill, knowledge, and action is the _____ pattern. (a) functional (b) divisional (c) vertical (d) means-end chains (e) matrix

8. A matrix structure _____. (a) reinforces unity of command (b) is inexpensive (c) is easy to explain to employees (d) gives some employees two bosses (e) results in very little organizational politics

9. _____ is the concern for proper communication so that units can understand each other's activities. (a) Control (b) Coordination (c) Specialization (d) Departmentation (e) Division of labour

10. Compared to the machine bureaucracy (mechanistic type), the professional bureaucracy (organic type) _____. (a) is more efficient for routine operations (b) has more vertical specialization and control (c) is larger (d) has more horizontal specialization and coordination mechanisms (e) is smaller

TRUE–FALSE

11. Mission statements are written statements of organizational purpose.   T   F

12. A specific group, such as a political campaign, is an example of a primary beneficiary.   T   F

13. The configuration of positions, job duties, and lines of authority among the component parts of an organization is called its structure.   T   F

14. The hierarchy of authority is the process of breaking work into small components that serve the organization's purpose.   T   F

15. Specialization and coordination are two core issues in the concept of organizational structure.   T   F

16. The span of control distributes formal authority and establishes where and how critical decisions are to be made.   T   F

17. Grouping people together by skill, knowledge, and action results in a divisional pattern of departmentation.   T   F

18. Line units and personnel in an organization provide specialized expertise and services to staff units and personnel.   T   F

19. One of the advantages of the matrix structure is that it provides a mix of technical and market emphases that is helpful to organizations which operate in highly complex environments.   T   F

20. As opposed to committees, task forces are typically formed with a limited agenda to identify and solve problems that involve several different departments.   T   F

SHORT ANSWER

21. Compare and contrast output goals to systems goals.

22. Describe the types of controls that are typically used in organizations.

23. What are the major advantages and disadvantages of functional departmentation?

24. What are the major advantages and disadvantages of matrix departmentation?

APPLICATIONS ESSAY

25. Describe some of the side effects of organizational controls in a large mechanistically-structured organization such as Canada Post.

Strategic Competency and Organizational Design

WestJet Balances Design and Culture

In 1996, a small upstart Canadian airline took to the skies with a plan to offer short flights on selected routes, and the attraction of low-cost fares and excellent customer service. Several years later, WestJet now ranks among the most profitable airlines in North America, in an industry where 90 percent of startups collapse. Clive Beddoe, one of the founding partners, insists that it is the company's organizational design that drives the airline's success: "The entire environment is conducive to bringing out the best in people; it's the culture that creates the passion to succeed."

The basis of the organizational design is a company managed from the bottom. Employees are able to perform their jobs without a great deal of supervisory attention. Standards and expectations are set, but the rest is left up to the worker as long as customers are served in a caring, positive, and attentive manner. By structuring the organization in this way, WestJet avoids the cost of a huge layer of supervisory personnel and has a much higher level of productivity per person. While a typical full-service airline operates with more than 140 staff per aircraft, WestJet uses just 59.

However, it takes more than having fewer supervisors to ensure that employees have ownership in their jobs. The structure of the company also supports a generous profit-sharing program that is designed to motivate employees in providing that little bit extra in customer service. If the profit margin comes in at 5 percent, then that 5 percent of net income is spread among the employees, prorated to salary; if net profit is 10 percent, then the staff receives 10 percent, up to a maximum of 20 percent. Cheques are distributed twice a year and average about $9,000. Beddoe insists that it is not just the money that motivates the employees: "When they receive this cheque they have a tremendous pride and sense of major accomplishment. They know their contributions have gone above and beyond anything we've asked of them, and that's what generated the profits." The employees are also offered shares in the company. For every $1 an employee spends, the company matches it, in effect allowing employees to buy shares at a 50 percent discount. This has resulted in 83 percent of employees being shareholders, some with portfolios near $1 million.

The company receives about 3,000 to 4,000 resumés per week and it is not the applicant with the most experience who gets the job. WestJet looks for enthusiasm and a sense of humour in its employees. The company culture supports a philosophy of having fun, even down to the passengers. It is not uncommon to find a flight attendant playing games with passengers and holding contests. It seems passengers enjoy this in-flight entertainment. Most people do not seem to mind and it is this element of fun that helps to support the organizational design and competency at WestJet.

Strategy and organizational design are important for a firm to reach its goals. As you read Chapter 12, keep in mind these key questions:

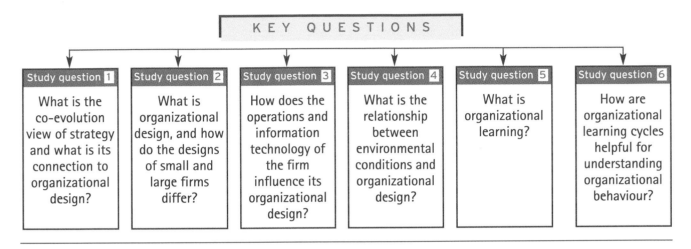

KEY QUESTIONS

Study question **1**	Study question **2**	Study question **3**	Study question **4**	Study question **5**	Study question **6**
What is the co-evolution view of strategy and what is its connection to organizational design?	What is organizational design, and how do the designs of small and large firms differ?	How does the operations and information technology of the firm influence its organizational design?	What is the relationship between environmental conditions and organizational design?	What is organizational learning?	How are organizational learning cycles helpful for understanding organizational behaviour?

Strategy and Organizational Design

ASPECTS OF STRATEGY

The notions of strategy discussed in the previous chapter are critical for an organization's success, so they are worth repeating now and discussing further.[1] Strategy is the positioning of the organization in its competitive environment so that it can succeed, and strategy is seen through the pattern in a series of decisions. In Chapter 11, we emphasized that goals and the basic aspects of structure are important elements in this positioning. The structure, staffing, and systems of the organization must be appropriate so that they effectively and efficiently focus human resources toward achieving the organization's goals and implementing its strategy. It must be emphasized that for an organization to be able to do what it intends to do it must have the capabilities, usually human ones, to successfully implement its strategy. The setting of the organization should also be designed to make it easier to achieve the goals and implement the strategy.

At one time, executives were told that firms had a limited number of economically determined standard strategies that they could choose from—such as strategies involving growth, niches, cost leadership, etc.—and that these strategies were based on such factors as efficiency and innovation. If the firm wanted efficiency, it should simply adopt the machine bureaucracy (i.e., have many levels of management backed with extensive controls and many written procedures). If it wanted innovation, it should simply adopt a more organic form (i.e., have fewer levels of management and emphasize coordination). Today, however, the world of corporations is much more complex and executives have found much more sophisticated ways of competing.

Today many senior executives are emphasizing the skills and abilities that their firms need, not only to compete, but also to remain agile and dynamic in a rapidly changing world. The structural configuration or organizational design of the firm should do two things: in addition to making it easier to accomplish what senior management wants, the design should also allow individuals to experiment, grow, be entrepreneurial, and develop competencies so that the strategy of the firm can evolve. Over time, the firm may develop specialized administrative and technical skills as middle and lower-level managers make minor adjustments to solve specific problems. As a firm's employees learn, so can the firm: this will happen if the individual learning of employees can be transferred across and up the organization's hierarchy. As the skills of employees and managers develop, these skills may be noticed by senior management and become a foundation for revisions in the firm's overall strategy.

Just as employees and managers are always changing, the world in which we operate is also constantly changing. There are new technologies, such as new administrative systems created by the information revolution. Competitors continue to innovate and present new challenges. And, of course, customers want new products and services and lower prices. Thus, the position of the firm in its environment must change. The firm must develop new capabilities to respond to all these changes even as it, too, tries to be the source of changes and innovations.

STRATEGY AND CO-EVOLUTION

With astute senior management, a firm can co-evolve. That is, the firm can adjust to external changes even as it shapes some of the challenges facing it. Co-evolution is a process. One aspect of this process is repositioning the firm in its setting as the setting itself changes, the firm's operations expand, and its technology shifts. Senior management can guide the process of positioning and repositioning the firm in its environment. However, senior management can also help shape some of these influences, particularly the capabilities of organizational members and the ability of the firm's administrative and technical systems. Shaping these influences is the other aspect of co-evolution.

Successful firms must adjust to the ever-changing competitive world and at the same time develop internal capabilities to match their intentions and shape their competitive landscape. All the while, successful firms also need to build upon and refine their unique experience and specific competencies. These competencies include the technology used to produce goods and services, the individuals in the firm, and the administrative support systems, particularly the firm's information technology.

Bombardier's CRJ regional jets have changed the way people travel. It's the most successful regional aircraft program in history, having sold 1,000 jets by 2003. Bombardier began making these smaller jets in the mid-1980s, when there was no apparent market for them. It has since sparked a revolution in airline transportation. Regional jets allow airlines to replace and complement larger aircraft on weaker routes. As a result, regional airline traffic growth in the United States averaged 12.3 percent per year between 1978 and 2000. From 2000 and 2003, U.S. regional jet seat capacity grew by 97 percent.

ORGANIZATIONAL DESIGN AS PART OF A RECOGNIZABLE PATTERN IN DECISIONS AND IMPLEMENTATION

Obviously, co-evolution is complex and challenging. Fortunately, firms have developed successful patterns for handling co-evolution. That is, there are successful and recognizable decisions and implementations that consistently bring clarity out of the complexity. One aspect that consistently contributes to effective co-evolution is organizational design.

Organizational design is the process of choosing and implementing a structural configuration.[2] Choosing an appropriate organizational design depends on several factors, including the size of the firm, its operations and information technology, its environment, and the strategy

Organizational design is the process of choosing and implementing a structural configuration for an organization.

it selects for growth and survival. Raymond Miles and Charles Snow have identified three patterns of design: prospector, defender, and analyzer. Prospector companies like Hewlett-Packard look for change and opportunities. Compared to a leading innovator such as Intel, National Semiconductor would be considered a defender that specializes in a narrow field of products. Analyzers, on the other hand, tend to be fast followers, such as Matsushita—the maker of Panasonic—rather than leaders, such as Sony.

Above all, the design of the organization encourages the development of individual skills and abilities. To understand how firms develop a successful pattern, in this chapter we show how firms can use their organizational design to both respond to their various operations, technology, and environment, and to shape their competitive landscape.

Organizational Design and Size

For many reasons, large organizations cannot be just bigger versions of their smaller counterparts. As the number of individuals in a firm increases, the number of possible connections among the individuals increases even more. To be successful, large organizations need to manage this direct interpersonal contact among their members. When the tasks and interaction are more complex, there will be greater motivation for the organization to choose a matrix structure, as outlined in the previous chapter. Highly repetitive and cost-focused functions require strong specialization and are more likely to move an organization toward a hierarchical form of structure. Of course, in this situation the cost of having too many layers of management can cancel out efforts to reduce costs and make it necessary to again adjust the structure so that the organization can achieve its needs and goals. If an organization needs to be proactive or reactive, it will likely try to imitate the design of smaller firms that have greater flexibility because they have fewer layers and people, and therefore need less coordination. A large organization can imitate these smaller firms by using a divisional structure.

Whereas the design of a small firm is directly influenced by its core operations technology, larger firms have many core operations technologies in a wide variety of much more specialized units. In short, larger organizations are often more complex than smaller firms, but require the attributes of smaller organizations. For example, Belleville, Ontario-based Bioniche Life Sciences is a biopharmaceutical research company with more than 300 employees. The company has three business divisions: Human Health (consisting of two business units—Bioniche Therapeutics and Bioniche Pharma Group), Animal Health, and Food Safety.

THE SIMPLE DESIGN FOR SMALLER UNITS AND FIRMS

The **simple design** is a configuration that uses only one or two ways of specializing individuals and units. This means that vertical specialization and control are usually achieved by having different levels of supervision, but without elaborate formal mechanisms (e.g., rule books and policy manuals), and the manager is responsible for most of the control. Thus, the simple design tends to minimize bureaucratic aspects and depends mostly on the leadership of the manager.

The simple design is appropriate for many small firms, such as family businesses, retail stores, and small manufacturing firms.[3] The strengths of the simple design are simplicity, flexibility, and responsiveness to the desires of a central manager—in many cases, the owner. Because a simple design relies heavily on the manager's personal leadership, however, this configuration is only as effective as the senior manager is.

Simple design is a configuration that uses only one or two ways of specializing individuals and units.

Student Express Ltd. of Richmond Hill, Ontario, has grown a lot since its founding in 1989. In 2000 alone, growth exceeded 45%. Unfortunately, complaints also started increasing that year. Operating a student transportation service has certain standards. "If a bus is a half hour late, that's not good enough." To solve the problems of increasing work, greater stress on employees, and too many over-time hours being worked, Marnie Walker first surveyed her customers to identify their concerns. Then she created an employee task force responsible for fixing problems. After nine months, the team that included drivers, administrators, dispatchers, and order takers—all of whom were assured that no one was to blame—had learned to treat each other as customers and had successfully addressed many issues. Changes in orders were now being sent to dispatch instead of having order takers try to deal with them. Everyone also agreed that new order-taking software was necessary and Walker decided to hire a consultant to deal with that need. The follow-up survey carried out by Student Express showed that its customers were delighted with the improved service made possible by changes to the company's process and technology.

www.studentexpress.org

Operations Technology and Organizational Design

Although the design for an organization should reflect its size, it must also be adjusted to fit technological opportunities and requirements.[4] That is, successful organizations usually arrange their internal structures so that the structures fit well with the organization's dominant "technologies" or workflows and, more recently, take advantage of information technology opportunities.[5] **Operations technology** is the combination of resources, knowledge, and techniques that creates a product or service output for an organization.[6] **Information technology** (CIT) it is the combination of machines, artifacts, procedures, and systems that are used to gather, store, analyze, and disseminate information so that it can be transformed into knowledge.[7]

For over 30 years, researchers in OB have charted the links between operations technology and organizational design. For operations technology, three common classifications have received most of the attention: those of Perrow, of Thompson, and of Woodward.

Operations technology is the combination of resources, knowledge, and techniques that creates a product or service output for an organization.

Information technology is the combination of machines, artifacts, procedures, and systems that are used to gather, store, analyze, and disseminate information so that it can be transformed into knowledge.

VIEWS OF TECHNOLOGY

Charles Perrow developed a continuum that goes from routine technologies at one end to nonroutine technologies at the other. He claims that all organizations can be classified in this continuum, and that how complex the technology is will determine how complex the organization needs to be. The more routine the technology is, the simpler the organization's structure can be. Conversely, the more nonroutine the technology is, the better complex organizations are at managing it.

Using categories that he named intensive, mediating, and long-linked, James D. Thompson classified technologies based on how specifically the technology could be described and how much interdependence there was among the work activities.[8] Under *intensive technology*, there is uncertainty about how to produce desired outcomes. A group of specialists must be brought together to interact in a variety of ways that will help them find solutions for problems. An example of intensive technology is found in a research and development laboratory at a pharmaceutical company like GlaxoSmithKline (GSK) Inc. GSK invests more than $100 million in research and development each year. In 2002, it conducted more than 60 academic research proposals with physicians across Canada. GSK develops vaccines, such as for hepatitis A and hepatitis B, and its medicines treat a variety of illnesses from allergies, infections, and migraines, to depression and gastrointestinal disorders, to HIV/AIDS, cancer, and Parkinson's Disease. Coordination and the exchange of knowledge are of critical importance with this kind of technology.

Mediating technology links parties that want to become interdependent. For example, banks link creditors and depositors and store money and information to facilitate such exchanges. Whereas all depositors and creditors are indirectly interdependent, their reliance on each other is handled or pooled by the bank. With pooled technology, much less coordination is needed among the tasks, and information management becomes more important than applying coordinated knowledge.

Under *long-linked technology*, also called mass-production or industrial technology, the way to produce the desired outcomes is known. The task is broken down into a number of sequential steps. A classic example is the automobile assembly line. Control is critical, and coordination is only needed for making the links in the sequence work in harmony.

Joan Woodward also divides technology into three categories: small-batch production, mass production, and continuous-process manufacturing.[9] In units of *small-batch production*, a variety of custom products are tailor-made to fit customer specifications, such as tailor-made suits. The machinery and equipment used are generally not very elaborate, but considerable craftsmanship is often needed. In *mass production*, the organization produces one or a few products through an assembly-line system. The work of one group is highly dependent on that of another, the equipment is typically sophisticated, and the workers are given very detailed instructions. Automobiles and refrigerators are produced in this way. Organizations using *continuous-process technology* produce a few products using a lot of automation. Classic examples are automated chemical plants and oil refineries.

ETHICS AND SOCIAL RESPONSIBILITY

ETHICS AT SUNCOR INC.
Suncor is the world leader when it comes to producing oil from tar sands, but it takes more than that to please this company as it has also invested over $100 million in alternative energy sources. Not the typical oil company, especially as Suncor has had its share of technical problems extracting the oil from the tar sands in northern Alberta. Now the goal is to turn Alberta's oil sands into North America's primary oil source, while at the same time preaching for the importance of the Kyoto Accord and the need to reduce greenhouse gases. Even Greenpeace members have attended two annual general meetings quite respectfully. Suncor's president himself was the one to personally and reluctantly lay off staff during the downsizing of the early 1990s. Since that time, the company has reduced its harmful discharges by over 77 percent, committed itself to having Aboriginals make up 12 percent of its workforce, and thanks to its social record, Suncor has even earned a spot on the Dow Jones Sustainability Index three years in a row. When he was asked about the investment in alternative energy sources, company president Rick George replied, "It's the right thing to do, we'll find a way." Suncor's culture reflects this attitude, and with 50 years of reserves, this oil producer plans on supplying one quarter of North America's oil for some time to come, but always responsibly.

www.suncor.ca

Based on her studies, Woodward concluded that the combination of structure and technology was critical to the success of organizations. When technology and organizational design were properly matched, a firm was more successful. Specifically, successful small-batch and continuous-process plants had flexible structures with small workgroups at the bottom; more rigidly structured plants were less successful. In contrast, successful mass-production operations were rigidly structured and had large workgroups at the bottom. Since Woodward's studies, this technological necessity has been supported by various other investigations. Still, today we also know that operations technology is just one factor that contributes to the success of an organization.[10]

WHERE OPERATIONS TECHNOLOGY DOMINATES: THE ADHOCRACY

The influence of operations technology is most clearly seen in small organizations and in specific departments within large organizations. In some instances, managers and employees simply do not know the appropriate way to service a client or to produce a particular product. This situation is the extreme example of Thompson's intensive type of technology, and it can happen in some small-batch processes when a team of individuals must develop a unique product for a particular client.

Mintzberg suggests that at these technological extremes, the "adhocracy" may be an appropriate design.[11] An **adhocracy** is an organizational structure that is characterized by substantial decentralization; shared decision-making among members; extreme horizontal specialization (as each member of the unit may be a distinct specialist); few levels of management; almost no formal controls; and few rules, policies, and procedures.

The adhocracy is particularly useful when an aspect of the organization's operations technology presents two sticky problems: (1) the tasks facing the organization vary considerably and provide many exceptions, as in a hospital, or (2) problems are difficult to define and resolve.[12] The adhocracy places a high value on professionalism and coordination in problem-solving.[13] Large firms may use temporary task forces, form special committees, and even contract consulting firms to provide the creative problem identification and problem-solving that the adhocracy encourages. For instance, Microsoft creates new autonomous departments to encourage talented employees to develop new software programs. Kraft and 3M also set up quasi-autonomous groups to explore new ideas.

> Adhocracy is an organizational structure that emphasizes shared, decentralized decision-making; extreme horizontal specialization; few levels of management; an almost complete absence of formal controls; and few rules, policies, and procedures.

Information Technology and Organizational Design

Today, information technology, the World Wide Web, and computers may seem to be inseparable.[14] Some commentators even suggest that IT only refers to computer-based systems used in the management of an enterprise.[15] Certainly, the computer and extensions of the personal computer are a major force in most corporations. However, substantial advances have also been made in telecommunication options. Furthermore, advances in the computer as a machine are much less profound than is the impact of information technology on how firms manage.

It is important to understand just what IT does from an organizational perspective—not from the view of the PC user.[16] For organizations, IT can be used, among other things, (1) as a partial substitute for some operations as well as some process controls and impersonal methods of coordination, (2) as a capability for transforming information into knowledge for learning, and (3) as a strategic capability.

INFORMATION TECHNOLOGY AS A SUBSTITUTE

Old bureaucracies prospered and dominated other forms, in part, because they provided more efficient production through specialization and their approach to dealing with information.

Where the organization used mediating technology or long-linked technology, the machine bureaucracy was the norm. In these firms, the rules, policies, and procedures, as well as many other process controls, could be rigidly enforced based on very little information.[17] Such was the case for the post office: postal clerks even had rules telling them how to hold their hands when sorting mail.

OB Across Functions

Marketing

OB Skills Needed in Marketing

The position advertised on Workopolis.com by Waterloo-based Research In Motion (RIM) was for a product marketing manager, someone who would be responsible for launching RIM products in new markets. Besides marketing experience, the required skills listed for the position included these: a broad understanding of the marketplace and industry trends; proven project management, team leadership, and organizational skills; excellent written and verbal communication skills; experience creating a business case; and experience in business planning and execution, including experience predicting and tracking ROI (Return on Investment). RIM also wanted candidates who were creative and "driven to take wireless technologies to the next level."

www.rim.com

In many organizations, the initial use of IT eliminated the most routine, highly specific, and repetitious jobs.[18] The clerical tasks in bookkeeping, writing cheques for payroll, and keeping track of sales were some of the first targets of computerization. In these instances, IT often first appeared as a large, centralized mainframe computer. In fact, mainframe computers were still the major business for IBM well into the 1990s. This early type of implementation did not change the fundamental character or design of the organization. It simply substituted IT for more routine tasks. To continue the example of the post office, initial computerization focused mainly on replacing the tracking of mail by hand. This was achieved by implementing IT through automated reading machines that helped sort mail. This also made postal codes necessary.

A second wave of substitution replaced process controls and informal coordination mechanisms. Rules, policies, and procedures could be replaced with a decision support system (DSS). In the case of a DSS, repetitive, routine choices could be programmed into a computer-based system. For instance, if you applied for a credit card, a computer program would check your credit history and other financial information. If your application passed several pre-set tests, you would be issued a credit card. If your application failed any of the tests, it would either be rejected or sent to an individual for further analysis.

The second wave of implementation resulted in some small changes in organizational design. Specifically, the firm often needed fewer levels of management and less internal staff. A small number of firms also recognized that they could outsource some internal staff operations. For instance, for many firms, outside organizations actually do the entire employee payroll.

The emphasis on direct substitution was still the norm in many organizations well into the 1990s, and in smaller firms it continues today. This is to be expected when a new-to-the-world technology is first implemented. It takes decades to move from the lab to full implementation, and the first applications are often substitutes for existing solutions. For instance, cars were once just substitutes for the horse and buggy. Both computer technology and the automobile took about 20 years to enter the mass market. However, IT, just like the automobile, has transformed our society because it added new capability.

INFORMATION TECHNOLOGY AS A CAPABILITY FOR LEARNING

IT has also long been recognized for its potential to add capability.[19] For over 20 years, OB scholars have talked of using IT to improve the efficiency, speed of responsiveness, and effectiveness of operations. Used with machines, IT became advanced manufacturing technology when computer-aided design (CAD) was combined with computer-aided manufacturing (CAM) to create the automated manufacturing cell. More complex decision support systems have provided middle and lower-level managers with programs that help them analyze complex problems rather than just approve routine choices for them. Computer-generated reports now give even senior executives the opportunity to track the individual sales performance of the lowliest salesperson.

More recently, instead of substituting for existing operations or process controls, IT has given individuals deep within the organization the information they need to plan, make choices, coordinate with others, and control their own operations.

Although simple substitution could continue occurring one application at a time, the real impact of adding IT capability could not come until it was broadly available to nearly everyone.[20] To use the automobile analogy again, the real impact of the automobile was felt only after Henry Ford sold hundreds of thousands of his Model T and new roads were constructed. For IT to have a similar impact on organizational design, the seamless use of computerized information across the organization was needed. The extremely powerful mainframe of the 1970s and 1980s was not up to the task simply because the information individuals needed to have in order to do their jobs more quickly and better was often unique information that only they needed. This therefore meant that they needed a common technology with the capability for uniqueness. And nearly everyone would have to have it and use it in co-operation with others.

Enter WINTEL—that is, Microsoft Windows in combination with an Intel microprocessing chip. This combination provided a relatively cheap, easy-to-use personal computer with an almost standardized technology that could be individually tailored at a modest cost. WINTEL was the PC equivalent of the Tin Lizzie—Henry Ford's Model T designed for the masses.

With the adoption of WINTEL, three important changes occurred. First, IT applications for tasks being done in a wide range of organizations were quickly developed and received broad acceptance. Thus, the era of the spreadsheet and word processing programs began and the old mainframes were displaced. Individuals could develop and transfer information to others and be pretty sure that the other party could read their output and duplicate their processes. Second, WINTEL expanded by incorporating existing telecommunications systems such as the Internet.[21] Thus, the era of connectivity also arrived. Tied to parallel developments in telecommunications, a whole world of electronic commerce, teleconferencing—with combinations of data, pictures, and sound—and cellphones emerged. Third, IT was transformed from being a substitute to being a mechanism for learning.[22] For example, in this book we ask you to learn by using Internet connections and offer the option of learning with eGrade Plus, an electronic version of this book.

As a whole, the impact of IT on organizational design was and remains profound. The changes can often occur from the bottom up. New IT systems empower individuals, expanding jobs and making them both interesting and challenging. Jobs that used to be narrowly defined and limited by process controls imposed by middle management can be transformed into broadly envisioned, interesting jobs based on IT-embedded processes with output controls. A new series of coordination devices based on IT can replace both the memo and the coordinating department as firms are now able to put together temporary teams and task forces using "virtual meetings"—meetings via e-mail to solve cross-departmental problems.[23] The whole world of staff units has changed as bureaucratic professionals have adjusted to the new world of IT. And many middle managers and all their staff assistants are no longer needed.

For the production segments of firms that use long-linked technology, such as in auto assembly plants and canneries, IT can be linked to total quality management (TQM) programs and be made part of the machinery. Data on operations can be transformed into knowledge of operations and used to systematically improve quality and efficiency. This has also meant that firms have had to rethink their view of employees as brainless robots. To make TQM work with IT, all employees must plan, do, and control. As was stated in the discussion of job enrichment and job design in Chapter 8, combining IT and TQM with empowerment and participation is a basic requirement for success. In the mid-1990s, for example, two computer equipment manufacturers started improvement programs by combining IT and TQM. One manufacturer imposed the program on all employees. There was some success at first, but in the end this program failed. The second manufacturer combined the IT-TQM program with extensive empowerment and participation. Although implementation was slower, today the combination has produced a constantly improving learning environment.[24]

Information Technology as a Strategic Capability

Just as the automobile gave birth to the mobile society and led to the development of a multitude of auto-related businesses, IT has spawned a whole new series of corporations called e-businesses. It is also transforming aging bricks-and-mortar firms as they incorporate a new type of capability.

IT AND E-BUSINESS

E-business is here to stay.[25] Whether it is business to business (B2B) or business to consumers (B2C), there is a whole new set of dot-com firms that have information technology at the core of their operations. One of the more exciting entrants to the B2C world is the now-familiar Amazon.com. Opened in 1995 to sell books directly to customers through the Internet, it rapidly expanded to toys and games, health and beauty products, computers and video games, and even cameras and photography. It is now a virtual general store. After over six years of losses, Amazon.com posted a modest profit in 2002, which increased further in 2003 and continued to increase through 2004. The U.S.-based Amazon has also expanded with international sites serving France, Germany, Japan, the United Kingdom, and Canada (www.amazon.ca).

It is very interesting to examine the transformation of Amazon.com's organizational design as it illustrates the notion of co-evolution presented in the introduction. Initially, the firm was organized as a simple structure. As it grew, it became more complex by adding divisions for each of its separate product areas. To remain flexible and promote growth in both the volume of operations and the capabilities of employees, it did not develop an extensive bureaucracy. There are still very few levels of management. It built separate organizational components based on product categories (divisional structure, as described in Chapter 11), with minimal rules, policies, and procedures. In other words, the organizational design it adopted appeared relatively conventional. What was not conventional was the use of IT for learning about customers and the use of IT for coordinating and tracking operations. Although its website was not the most technically advanced site, you could easily order the book you wanted, track the delivery, and feel confident that it would arrive as promised. This use of IT was also adopted by others, such as Indigo Books and Music Inc. Indigo's website sells not only books online, but also music, DVDs, videos, iPods, and gifts. Amazon.com changed the competitive landscape.

Unlike Amazon.com, many other new dot-com firms adopted a variation of the adhocracy as their organizational design. The thinking was that e-business was fundamentally different from the old bricks-and-mortar operations. Thus, an entirely new structural configuration was needed to fit the development of new e-products and services. However, the managers of these firms forgot two important limitations of the adhocracy as their firms grew. First, there are limits on the size of an effective adhocracy. Second, the actual delivery of their products and services did not require continual innovation. It depended more on responsiveness to clients and maintaining efficiency. Thus, the adhocracy design did not deliver what was needed. In sum, they had great websites, but they were highly inefficient. One such business was Pets.com Inc., which ventured to sell pet supplies purely online. It went out of business in January 2001.

IT AS A STRATEGIC CAPABILITY FOR THE BRICKS-AND-MORTAR FIRMS

IT as a strategic capability is now changing many traditional bricks-and-mortar firms. Perhaps IT's most profound effect can be seen in firms that rely on a mediating technology, such as banks, finance companies, dating services, and employment agencies. The job of the firm, as we know, is to make exchanges easier by matching types of individuals. In the case of banks, individuals who want to borrow are matched with those who want to lend by placing individual interests into categories. For example, those who have a savings account are put in a category of precisely that type of savings account and are pooled with others. IT can revolutionize the categorization process that results in the matching by helping to create much more sophisticated categories and linking these categories in new ways.

For example, IT has made auctioneering and trade in second-hand goods extremely profitable with websites like eBay.ca. Millions of dollars trade hands every day through eBay. The online marketplace brings together buyers and sellers of a variety of items, each divided into categories, such as antiques, art, books, clothing, musical instruments, sporting goods, and toys, to name a few. The "eBay community" has more than 100 million registered members worldwide. The website claims: "People spend more time on eBay than any other online site, making it the most popular shopping destination on the Internet." Information technology has provided people with a bigger market and wider geographical reach to sell or seek prized possessions and superfluous stuff, at very competitive prices since, on eBay, many people can bid on the same thing.

TECHNOLOGY

More firms are recognizing the strategic value of information technology and using IT as a basis for global operations. The RBC Financial Group has set the priority of establishing strategic alliances to better serve its customers by giving them access to support and many financial tools and solutions in the digital world of e-commerce. To achieve this goal, RBC has partnered with AOL Canada Inc. Institutional customers can manage their portfolios on-line, and allied car dealerships can access a number of financing sources for the car-buying consumer. Soon-to-be brides and grooms can even access services at idoido.com and weddingbells.ca, a branch of the leading Canadian wedding magazine, and organize their wedding from reception to invitations to obtaining advice, all through the RBC Financial Group set of alliances.

www.rbc.com

Other industries could not exist today without IT, for example, the travel industry in which online research and bookings have become the norm. Expedia Canada Corp. provides travelers with flight, car, and hotel reservations, as well as package deals. The website essentially helps customers plan and book their business trip or vacation with a few clicks of the mouse. Expedia is a subsidiary of U.S.-based InterActiveCorp, which operates a variety of online interactive businesses, including Ticketmaster, Citysearch, and Evite. Revenues for 2003 were US$6.3 billion.

Of course, IT has not developed in isolation, and for it to be effective it often requires that others adopt common IT standards and operations. Just because IT presents a potential capability does not automatically mean that a firm should adopt it or change its organizational design to make IT easier to use. The appropriate design also depends on external factors and the firm's strategy. We turn to these issues now.

Environment and Organizational Design

An effective organizational design also considers powerful external forces in addition to size and technological factors. As open systems, organizations need to both receive inputs from and sell outputs to their environment. Clearly, understanding the environment is therefore important.[26]

The *general environment* is the set of cultural, economic, legal-political, and educational conditions found in the areas in which the organization operates. Much of Chapter 3 on international concerns was about the influences of the general environment, and throughout this book we have shown examples of globalization. The owners, suppliers, distributors, government agencies, and competitors that an organization must interact with in order to grow and survive are its *specific environment*. A firm typically has much more choice about what its specific environment is like than its general environment.

Although it is often convenient to separate the general and specific environmental influences on the firm, managers need to recognize the combined impact of both. Choosing some lines of businesses, for instance, means entering global competition with advanced technologies. In exhibit 12.1, the forces are described as the environment, industry, and the current organization, all of which affect the design of the organization and the resulting selection of staff and the systems to be implemented. It is this challenge of designing the organization so that it responds well to the external forces and its internal needs and demands that makes management vital to the success of the organization. This also means that having an understanding of the environment is where management's task begins.

ENVIRONMENTAL COMPLEXITY

A basic concern that must be considered in analyzing the environment of the organization is its complexity. A more complex environment gives an organization more opportunities and more problems. **Environmental complexity** is how large the problems and opportunities in the organization's environment are, which is shown by how much richness, interdependence, and uncertainty there is in the general and specific environments.

Environmental complexity is how large the problems and opportunities in the organization's environment are, which is shown by how much richness, interdependence, and uncertainty there is.

Environmental Richness   Overall, the environment is richer when the economy is growing, when individuals are improving their education, and when the people and other organizations the firm relies on are prospering. For businesses, a richer environment means that economic conditions are improving, customers are spending more money, and suppliers (especially banks) are willing to invest in the organization's future. In a rich environment, more organizations survive, even if they have poorly functioning organizational designs. A richer environment is also filled with more opportunities and dynamism—the potential for change. The organizational design must allow the company to recognize these opportunities and take advantage of them.

The indications were that the mid-2000s were going to be more prosperous in Canada than the preceding years. Statistics Canada reported that, in 2004, businesses, governments and institutions planned to allocate more than $223 billion for total capital spending, a 3.1 percent increase from 2003. In addition, private sector investment was to grow for the first time since 2001. This is in contrast to the decline in investment activity that took place at the end of the 1990s. Investment intentions for 1999 were expected to slip to $122.3 billion, down 0.6 percent from 1998. Statistics Canada reported that this was the first slowdown in a trend of increased investment spending that had averaged 5.6 percent per year since 1994.

The opposite of richness is decline. For business firms, a general recession is a good example of a leaner environment. Although corporate reactions vary, it is instructive to examine typical responses to decline. In Canada and the U.S., firms have traditionally reacted to decline by first laying off nonsupervisory workers and then moving up the organizational ladder as the environment becomes leaner. As global competition has increased and new IT options have become more widely available, firms have also started to change their organizational designs by cutting staff units and the number of organizational levels. Although it is traumatic, the downsizing of a firm can be managed to reduce its impact.

Nortel Networks was hard-hit by the slowdown in the economy at the close of the century. Its stock fell from heights in the $120 range to less than $2. And the job losses soon followed. In 2000, the company employed 15,000 people in Ottawa alone, but by 2002, the staff complement was more in the neighbourhood of 5,000. Recognizing that former employees are valuable resources, Nortel has implemented an alumni program that provides former employees the opportunity to learn about and apply for any new job openings that may arise. Still, Nortel's Ottawa office, its biggest Canadian operation, employed only about 6,000 people in September 2004, and continued to face threats of more downsizing.

Many European firms find it very difficult to cut full-time employees legally when the economy worsens. In extended periods of decline, many firms have therefore turned to national governments for help. Much like Canadian- and U.S.-based firms, European-based firms view changes in organizational design as a last but increasingly necessary resort because they must now compete globally.

GLOBALIZATION

MONSTER WORLDWIDE REORGANIZES
Monster Worldwide recognizes that its technology is key to the success of its websites Monster.com in the U.S. and Monster.ca in Canada, two of the best e-links to finding a new job. It has one of the largest Dell server installations in the world and the second largest Windows installation (second only to Microsoft). It also recently reorganized its worldwide operations into regions to focus on Europe, Asia, and North America in an attempt to build its capabilities in advertising and communications as well as executive searches. Its plan is to improve its capabilities in these areas by having more direct contact with local firms and clients.

www.monster.ca

Environmental Interdependence The link between external interdependence and organizational design is often subtle and indirect. The organization may co-opt powerful outsiders by including them. For instance, many large corporations have financial representatives from banks and insurance companies on their boards of directors. The organization may also adjust its overall design strategy to absorb or soften the demands of a more powerful external element. Perhaps the most common adjustment is the development of a centralized staff department to handle an important external group. For instance, most large corporations have some form of governmental relations group near the top of their hierarchy (Air Canada and BCE both have VPs of Government Relations). Where service to a few large customers is considered critical, the organization's departmentation is likely to switch from a functional form to a divisionalized form.[27]

Uncertainty and Volatility Environmental uncertainty and volatility can be particularly damaging to large bureaucracies. In times of change, investments quickly become outmoded, and internal operations no longer work as expected. The obvious organizational-design response to uncertainty and volatility is to switch to a more organic form. In extreme cases, moving toward an adhocracy may be necessary. However, these pressures may be in opposition to pressures created by large size and operations technology. In these cases, it may be too hard or too time consuming for some organizations to make the design adjustments. Thus, the organization may continue to struggle while adjusting its design just a little bit at a time.

USING ALLIANCES WHERE ENVIRONMENTAL FACTORS DOMINATE

In high-tech areas and businesses dominated by IT—such as robotics, semiconductors, advanced materials (ceramics and carbon fibres), and advanced information systems—a single company often does not have all the knowledge that it needs in order to bring new products to market. Often, the firms with the necessary knowledge are not even in the same country. The organizational design must therefore go beyond the boundaries of the organization into **interfirm alliances**—official co-operative agreements or joint ventures between two independent firms. These agreements often involve corporations that are headquartered in different nations.[28]

> Interfirm alliances are official co-operative agreements or joint ventures between two independent firms.

Alliances are quite common in such high-technology industries. In these international alliances, high-tech firms want not only to develop technology but also to ensure that their solutions become standardized across regions of the world. The Canadian Advanced Technology Alliance is an alliance of high-technology businesses across the country, 80 percent of which are active exporters. Its goal is to promote its members' resources and stimulate "Global Business Growth" with Canadian innovation and strategic partnerships.

Firms may also develop alliances to explore potential future collaboration. One of the largest and potentially most influential strategic alliances is the co-operation between Germany's DaimlerChrysler and Japan's Mitsubishi. The two companies agreed to share technology and to develop joint ventures, market-based co-operations, or high-tech consortia, as the need arises. As part of Sony's restructuring, it announced an alliance with Samsung of Korea. Some alliances to share technology even go as far back as the turn of the twentieth century.

In more developed industries, interfirm alliances are also quite popular, but they are often known by other names. In Europe, for example, they are called *informal combines* or *cartels*. Competitors work co-operatively to share the market in order to decrease uncertainty and improve conditions for all. Except in rare cases, these arrangements are often illegal in the U.S. but not as often in Canada. For example, De Beers, the South African diamond company, may legally operate in Canada, and usually does as a partner, but until recently, it was illegal for the firm to operate in the U.S., let alone sell diamonds there. Charges of price fixing dating back to the 1940s had forced the diamond company to sell in the United States only through intermediaries. De Beers recently plead guilty in a 10-year-old price-fixing case, paying a US$10-million fine, which opened the U.S. market to the company once more.

In Japan, the network of relationships among well-established firms in many industries is called a keiretsu. There are two common forms. The first is a bank-centred keiretsu, in which firms are linked to one another directly through cross-ownership and historical ties to one bank. The Mitsubishi group is a good example. In the second type, a vertical keiretsu, a key manufacturer is at the hub of a network of supplier firms or distributor firms. The manufacturer typically has both long-term supply contracts with members and cross-ownership ties. These arrangements help isolate Japanese firms from shareholders and they provide a mechanism for sharing and developing technology. Toyota is an example of a firm at the centre of a vertical keiretsu.

The network organization is beginning to evolve in the North America as well. Here, the central firm specializes in a core activity, such as design and assembly, and works with a fairly small number of participating suppliers on a long-term basis for both component development and manufacturing efficiency. Bombardier Aerospace, for example, has a worldwide network of "Authorized Service Facilities" for its Global Express corporate jet operators, including Harrods Aviation in Standsted and Luton, England, ExecuJet South Africa near Johannesburg, and Jet Aviation Geneva, in Switzerland. Bombardier Aerospace now has these facilities in Australia, England, Japan, Singapore, South Africa, the United States, the United Arab Emirates, as well as Canada.

More extreme variations of this network design are also emerging as a way of responding all at once to apparently conflicting environmental, size, and technological demands. Firms are spinning off staff functions to reduce their overall size and take advantage of new IT options. With these new environmental challenges and technological opportunities, firms must choose and not just react blindly.

GLOBALIZATION

The town of Markham, Ontario, implemented an Economic Alliance Program in 1990 to "create a global network of business relationships with communities and business groups in strategic market locations and to create an international awareness of Markham's business assets and locational benefits." It has since negotiated more than a dozen economic alliance agreements, including those with the Hong Kong Trade Development Council, the Haidian District of Beijing, China (Zhongguancun Science Park) and the town of Cary, North Carolina. The program has provided Markham and its business community with a larger presence in the global marketplace and a network of contacts.

www.markham.ca

Strategic Competency through Learning

Organizational learning is the process of knowledge acquisition, information distribution, information interpretation, and organizational retention.

Throughout this chapter we have emphasized co-evolution. The firm must not only adapt to its size, technology, and environment, but must also shape these forces. In the introduction, we stressed the development of individuals and their skills. In the OB literature, the development of individual skills and capabilities throughout an organization is discussed under the topic of *organizational learning*. Organizational learning is the key to successful co-evolution. **Organizational learning** is defined as the process of knowledge acquisition, information distribution, information interpretation, and organizational retention in adapting successfully to changing circumstances.[29] In simpler terms, organizational learning involves the adjustment of the organization's actions and those of the individuals working for it based on their experiences and the experiences of others. The challenge, then, is doing to learn and learning to do. Peter Senge, a strong proponent of organizational learning, believes that in the long run, the only sustainable source of competitive advantage is the organization's ability to learn faster than its competition.

KNOWLEDGE ACQUISITION

Firms get information in a variety of ways and at different rates during their histories. Perhaps the most important information is obtained from sources outside the firm at the time of its founding. During a firm's early years, many managers attempt to simplify, copy, or mimic, what they believe are the successful practices of others.[30] As they mature, however, firms can also acquire knowledge through experience and systematic search.

Mimicry   Mimicry is important to the new firm because (1) it provides workable, if not ideal, solutions to many problems; (2) it reduces the number of decisions that need to be analyzed separately, allowing managers to concentrate on more critical issues; and (3) it establishes legitimacy or acceptance by employees, suppliers, and customers and narrows the choices calling for detailed explanation.

> Mimicry is the action of copying the successful practices of others.

One of the key factors to look at when examining mimicry is how much managers try to isolate cause-effect relationships. Simply copying others without trying to understand the issues often leads to failure. The literature is filled with examples of firms that have tried to implement quality circles, empowerment, and decentralization simply because other firms have used them successfully. Many such firms have ended up abandoning these techniques because their managers failed to understand why and under what conditions the techniques worked for other firms. When mimicking others, managers need to make adjustments that fit the unique circumstances of their corporation.

Experience   One of the main ways of acquiring knowledge is through experience. All organizations and managers can learn in this manner. Besides learning by doing, managers can also systematically follow structured programs to capture the lessons to be learned from failure and success. For instance, a well-designed research and development program allows managers to learn as much through failure as through success.

Learning by doing in an intelligent way is at the heart of many successful corporations, which emphasize modern management techniques such as statistical quality control, quality circles, and other such practices. Many firms have discovered that making many small improvements can lead to a major improvement in both quality and efficiency. The major problem with learning by doing is not being able to forecast precisely what will change and how it will change. Managers need to believe that improvements can be made, listen to suggestions, and actually implement the changes. This is key to why many successful organizations focus on ways to increase employee retention.

Vicarious Learning   Vicarious learning is learning through the lessons taught by others' experiences. At the individual level, managers can build on individualized "social learning" and use it to help transform their organization's potential for improvement into actual results.

Individual Social Learning   *Social learning* is learning that happens through the interactions among people, their behaviours, and the environment. Figure 12.1 illustrates and explains more about this individualized view of learning from the work of Albert Bandura.[31] According to the figure, the individual uses modelling or vicarious learning to acquire behaviour by first observing and imitating others. The person then attempts to make these behaviours his or her own by modelling them through practice. In a work situation, the model may be a manager or co-worker who demonstrates desired behaviours. Mentors or senior workers who become friends with younger and more inexperienced protegés can also be important models.[32]

The symbolic processes presented in Figure 12.1 are also important in social learning. The words and symbols used by managers and others in the workplace can help communicate values, beliefs, and goals, and they can therefore serve as guides for the individual's behaviour. For example, a "thumbs up" or a symbol from the boss lets you know that your behaviour is appropriate. Another important influence on behaviour is the person's self-control. Self-efficacy—the person's belief that he or she can perform adequately in a situation—is an important part of such self-control. People with self-efficacy believe that they have the ability that is needed for doing a particular job; that they are capable of the effort required; and that no outside events will stop them from reaching their desired performance level.[33] In contrast, people with low self-efficacy believe that, no matter how hard they try, they cannot manage their environment well enough to be successful. For example, if you feel self-efficacious as a student, a low grade on one test is likely to encourage you to study harder, talk to the instructor, or do other things that will help you do well the next time. In contrast, a person who feels low self-efficacy as a student would probably drop the course or give up studying. Of course, even people who are high in self-efficacy do not control their environment entirely.

Figure 12.1 Social learning model

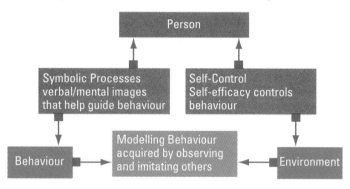

Much of the learning in corporations is less systematic than what is shown in Figure 12.1. Some firms have learned that the process of searching for new information does not have to always be structured or planned in relation to a specific problem or opportunity. Managers may instead learn in less systematic ways through scanning, grafting, and contracting out.

Scanning involves looking outside the firm and bringing back useful solutions. At times, these solutions may be used for known problems. More often, these solutions simply float around in the minds of management until they are needed to solve a problem that arises later.[34] Astute managers can contribute to organizational learning by scanning external sources, such as competitors, suppliers, industry consultants, customers, and leading firms. For instance, by reverse engineering the competitor's products (developing the engineering drawings and specifications by examining an already finished product), an organization can quickly match all standard product features. By systematically exploring the proposed developments from suppliers, a firm may become a lead user and be among the first to take advantage of a supplier's latest development.

Grafting is the process of bringing in useful knowledge by acquiring individuals, units, or firms. Almost all firms try to hire experienced individuals from other firms simply because

Scanning is looking outside the firm and bringing back useful solutions to problems.

Grafting is the process of acquiring individuals, units, and/or firms to bring in useful knowledge to the organization.

experienced individuals may bring a whole new series of solutions with them. For instance, after Fred Jaekel was fired by Magna for the second time, he started up a competitor to his former employer called Martinrea. A former executive from Magna then joined Jaekel as chief financial officer, another became the chairman of the board, and by November 2003, over 30 former Magna managers and executives had joined the growing firm.

The challenge in grafting is much the same as that in scanning: obtaining the knowledge is not enough; it must be translated into action. A key problem with grafting one unit onto an existing organization is discussed in Chapter 13, which is about organizational culture. The basic problem is that a clash of cultures could result. When this happens, instead of getting new solutions, both units may experience a lot of conflict.

Contracting out or outsourcing is the reverse of grafting and involves asking outsiders to perform a particular function. Whereas almost all organizations contract out or outsource, the key question for managers is often what functions to keep in the firm. As we have already noted, firms often outsource peripheral or staff functions to specialized firms.

INFORMATION DISTRIBUTION

Once information is obtained, managers must create mechanisms to distribute relevant information to the individuals who may need it. A primary challenge in larger firms is to locate quickly who has the appropriate information and who needs it. A partial solution is the development of disbursed IT networks that connect related organizational units through IT. The development of intranets (internal networks that use Internet technology) has made this information distribution easier. Statistics Canada reports that intranets have become much easier and less expensive to set up than traditional networks and are now accessible to small firms as well as large. In 2003, 16 percent of all Canadian firms used an intranet, a proportion that is most likely to increase greatly with the increase in broadband access, allowing employees to always be connected. Although collecting information or data is helpful, it is not enough, however. What is collected must also be correctly interpreted.

INFORMATION INTERPRETATION

Information within organizations is a shared understanding of the firm's goals and of how the organization's data relate to one of the firm's stated or unstated objectives in the current setting. Unfortunately, the process of developing multiple interpretations is often made more difficult by some common problems.[35]

Self-Serving Interpretations Almost all managers have the tendency to interpret events, conditions, and history to their own advantage. Managers, just like employees, often see what they have seen in the past or see what they want to see. Rarely do they see what actually is or can be.

Managerial Scripts A managerial script is a series of well-known routines that is commonly used by managers in a firm for identifying problems and generating and analyzing alternative solutions.[36] Different organizations have different scripts, often based on what has worked in the past. In a way, the script is a ritual that shows what is in the organization's "memory banks." Scripts can be harmful, however, because managers can become bound by what they have seen. When this happens, the danger is that they may not be open to what is actually occurring. In other words, they may not be able to unlearn.

Larger, older firms are rarely structured for learning; rather, they are structured for efficiency. That is, the organizational design emphasizes repetition, volume processing, and routine. In order to learn, therefore, the organization needs to be able to unlearn, to break out of routines which simply obtain information quickly, and to provide various interpretations of events rather than just go to external archives.[37]

Few managers question a successful script. Scripts can be elaborate enough that they provide an apparently well-tested series of solutions that are based on the firm's experience. Consequently, managers start solving today's problems with yesterday's solutions. Indeed, this is not surprising as managers have been trained, both in the classroom and on the job, to take corrective actions that are based on a historically shared view of the world. Unfortunately, however, this means that managers often make small, incremental improvements that are based on existing solutions when instead they should be creating new approaches to identify the underlying problems.

Common Myths An **organizational myth** is the common belief in an organization that a cause-effect relationship exists or an assertion is true even if it cannot be proven by fact.[38] Even though myths cannot be proven true, both managers and workers may base their interpretations of problems and opportunities on potentially faulty views. Three common myths often make it harder to develop multiple interpretations of a situation.

The first common myth is the presumption that *there is a single organizational truth*. This myth is often expressed as, "Although others may be biased, I am able to define problems and develop solutions objectively." We are all biased in varying degrees and in varying ways. The more complex the issue, the more likely it is that there are many different supportable interpretations.

A second common myth is the *presumption of competence*. It is common for managers at all levels to believe that their part of the firm is okay and just needs minor improvements in implementation. As we have documented throughout this book, this is rarely true. We are in the middle of a managerial revolution in which all managers need to reassess their general approach to managing organizational behaviour.

A third common myth is the *denial of trade-offs*. Most managers believe that their group, unit, or firm can avoid making undesirable trade-offs and can at the same time please nearly everyone. Whereas the denial of trade-offs is common, it can be a dangerous myth in some firms. For instance, when complex, dangerous technologies are being used, in order for operations to be safe, efficiency sometimes has to be sacrificed. Some firms, however, simply believe that "an efficient operation is a safe one" and aggressively move to improve efficiency. As a result, while their managers are stressing efficiency, they may be failing to work on improving safety. The final result may be a serious accident.[39]

An organizational myth is the common belief that a cause-effect relationship exists or an assertion is true even if it cannot be proven by fact.

INFORMATION RETENTION

Organizations have a variety of mechanisms that can be used to retain useful information.[40] Seven important mechanisms are individuals, culture, transformation procedures, formal structures, ecology, external archives, and internal information technologies.

Individuals are the most important storehouses of information for organizations. Organizations that keep a large and fairly stable group of experienced individuals are expected to have a higher capacity to acquire, retain, and retrieve information. Viewed as a whole, the organizational *culture* is an important repository of the shared experiences of the organization's members, past and present. The culture often maintains the organizational memory through rich, vivid, and meaningful stories that outlive those who experienced the event.

Documents, rule books, written procedures, and even standard but unwritten methods of operation are all *transformation mechanisms* that are used to store accumulated information. In cases where operations are extremely complex but rarely needed, written sources of information are often invaluable. The Treasury Board of Canada, for example, has a guide on the *Management of Government Information Holdings*. It states that the corporate memory of the government includes all information holdings that are created, collected, or received by government institutions to meet their operational needs and legislation and policy requirements. To preserve this corporate memory, information is stored on a variety of media (paper, books, microfilm, computer diskettes, magnetic computer tape, etc.) depending on its use and length of time departments need to keep it, as long as it is useful for decision making, program operations, and service delivery. The information also helps record the evolution of policy and program decisions. Once the departments no longer need it, the information is disposed of, either by destruction or transfer to the National Archives or National Library of Canada.

An organization's *formal structure* and the positions in the organization are less obvious but equally important mechanisms for storing information. When an aircraft lands on the deck of a U.S. Navy aircraft carrier, for example, there are typically dozens of individuals on the deck who look like they are just watching the aircraft land. Each person on the deck is actually there for a specific purpose. Each of them can often trace his or her position to a specific accident that would not have occurred had some individual originally been assigned that position.

Physical structures (or *ecology*, in the language of learning theorists) are potentially important but often neglected mechanisms that can be used to store information. For example, a traditional way of ordering parts and subcomponents in a factory is known as the "two-bin" system. One bin is always kept in reserve. Once an individual opens the reserve bin, he or she automatically orders replacements. In this way, the plant never runs out of components. This is considered a way of storing information because having two bins instead of one reminds the individual of the need to order parts.

External archives can be used as sources of valuable information about most larger organizations. Former employees, stock market analysts, suppliers, distributors, and the media are all examples of such sources. These external archives are important because they may provide a view of events that is quite different from the organization's view.

Finally, the IT system of the organization—its *internal information technology*—can provide a powerful and individually tailored mechanism for storing information. Many firms are using new IT programs that database, organize, and catalogue historical data in ways that better allow them to make decisions for the future.

TECHNOLOGY

The loss of key personnel can blindside a firm as it loses not only years of expertise but also the learning accumulated by the lost personnel. This is where Toronto-based ProCarta, Inc. steps in. With its ProCarta software installed on the organization's intranet, the firm can store network documents such as reports, schedules, manuals, memos, letters, and e-mail, and the software even organizes the information by task. Thanks to ProCarta, staff at such organizations as Hudson's Bay Co., the Bank of Montreal, and the U.S. Marine Corps can search their databases for information about the standard steps to follow and pitfalls to avoid concerning a task that used to be done by the lost personnel. Comments can then be added, changes suggested, and contacts reached for help, but only experts in the area can modify the actual process. According to Craig Stevens, the director of e-commerce at HBC, the system allows firms like his to "re-engineer our processes based on performance and best practices." Many companies feel that having the ability to search for processes in databases amounts to a far superior knowledge base than shelffuls of manuals and directives.

www.procarta.com

The Effective Manager   12.1

AVOIDING MORE PROBLEMS WITH DOWNSIZING

When downsizing, firms should keep in mind that they must:

- accurately identify the causes of the decline
- avoid grandiose attempts to reverse past history
- avoid the tendency to increase centralization and rigidity and to reduce participation
- target cuts and retrain employees wherever possible
- keep employees informed to lessen fear
- systematically work to rebuild morale and emphasize more participation

Organizational Learning Cycles

In the very first years of our current century, a common headline in the business press read "Major Corporation Downsizes." Whether the corporation was Nortel, General Motors, or Air Canada, the message appeared to be the same: major North American-based corporations were in trouble. They were finally adjusting to a new competitive reality—but on the backs of their workers and managers. As we have noted in this chapter, today the message from these firms is quite different. All are emphasizing competency through individual development and empowerment to learn and they are making the incremental changes and decisions that are needed along the way, rather than all at once. Essentially, they are trying to avoid their past mistake of making massive attempts to redirect themselves only once it was apparent to everyone that change was long overdue (see The Effective Manager 12.1). Some recent work on learning cycles helps explain why many organizations apparently fail to learn, while others appear to improve rapidly.[41]

DEFICIT CYCLES

A **deficit cycle** is a pattern of deteriorating performance that is followed by even further deterioration.

A **deficit cycle** is a pattern of deteriorating performance that is followed by even further deterioration. Firms that are continually downsizing, such as Nortel Networks, are examples of firms in a deficit cycle. The same problems keep reoccurring, and the firm fails to develop adequate mechanisms for learning. The firm often has problems in one or more phases of the learning process. The inability to adjust in the past leads to more problems and fewer resources being available to solve the next wave of problems, and the firm continues to deteriorate.

Major factors that are associated with deficit cycles are still being discovered, but current research has found three that stand out especially.[42] One is *organizational inertia*. It is very difficult to change organizations, and the larger the organization, the more inertia it often has. A second is *hubris*. Because they see a history of success, few senior executives are willing to challenge their own actions or those of their firms. They fail to recognize that yesterday's successful innovations are today's outmoded practices. A third major factor is *detachment*. Executives often believe they can manage widely distributed and diverse operations simply by analyzing reports and financial records. They lose touch and fail to make the unique and special adaptations that all firms need. One consultant has made millions by advising executives to focus on improvement and have managers walk around the office to avoid becoming detached.

BENEFIT CYCLES

A **benefit cycle** is a pattern of successful adjustment followed by further improvements.

Inertia, hubris, and detachment are common maladies, but they are not the automatic fate of all corporations. Firms can successfully co-evolve. As we have repeatedly demonstrated, managers are trying to reinvent their firms each and every day. They hope to initiate a **benefit cycle**—a pattern of successful adjustment followed by further improvements. Microsoft is an example of a firm experiencing a benefit cycle. In this cycle, the same problems do not keep reoccurring as the firm develops adequate mechanisms for learning. The firm has few major difficulties with the learning process, and managers continually attempt to improve knowledge acquisition, information distribution, information interpretation, and organizational memory.

Organizations that successfully co-evolve can ride the benefit cycle. Inertia can be a good thing for managers if they have the habit of not becoming overconfident, of staying directly involved with the firm's key operations, and of accurately forecasting changes in the environment and technology.

CHAPTER 12 STUDY GUIDE

Summary

What is the co-evolution view of strategy and what is its connection to organizational design?

- Firms need to adjust to their environments and contexts and to influence them.

- The capabilities of organizational members are critical in both reacting to and changing the firm's environment, size, and technology.

- Strategy and organizational design are interrelated. For the firm to be successful, the organization's design must support the strategy.

What is organizational design, and how do the designs of small and large firms differ?

- Organizational design is the process of choosing and implementing a structural configuration for an organization.

- Smaller firms often choose a simple structure, whereas larger firms often choose a bureaucratic form.

How does the operations and information technology of the firm influence its organizational design?

- Operations technology and organizational design are interrelated.

- In highly intensive and small-batch technologies, organizational designs may tend toward the adhocracy, a very decentralized form of operation.

- Information technology and organizational design can be interrelated.

- IT provides an opportunity to change the design by substitution, through capability for learning, and through the ability to capture strategic advantages.

What is the relationship between environmental conditions and organizational design?

- Environmental conditions and organizational design are interrelated.

- In analyzing environments, both the general environment (background conditions) and specific environment (key actors and organizations) are important.

- The more complex the environment, the greater the demands on the organization; firms should respond with more complex designs, such as the use of interfirm alliances.

What is organizational learning?

- Organizational learning is the process of knowledge acquisition, information distribution, information interpretation, and organizational memory that is used to adapt successfully to changing circumstances.

How are organizational learning cycles helpful for understanding organizational behaviour?

- Organizational learning cycles help us understand how some organizations continually decline while others appear to be rising stars.

KEY TERMS

Adhocracy (p. 234)

Benefit cycle (p. 248)

Deficit cycle (p. 248)

Environmental complexity
  (p. 239)

Grafting (p. 244)

Information technology

(p. 232)

Interfirm alliances (p. 241)

Mimicry (p. 243)

Operations technology
  (p. 232)

Organizational design
  (p. 230)

Organizational learning
  (p. 242)

Organizational myth (p. 246)

Scanning (p. 244)

Simple design (p. 231)

SELF-TEST 12

MULTIPLE CHOICE

1. The design of the organization needs to be adjusted to all of the following except _____. (a) the environment of the firm (b) the strategy of the firm (c) the size of the firm (d) the operations and information technology of the firm (e) the personnel to be hired by the firm

2. _____ is the combination of resources, knowledge, and techniques that creates a product or service output for an organization. (a) Information technology (b) Strategy (c) Organizational learning (d) Operations technology (e) The general environment (f) The benefit cycle

3. _____ is the combination of machines, artifacts, procedures, and systems that is used to gather, store, analyze, and disseminate information for translating it into knowledge. (a) The specific environment (b) Strategy (c) Operations technology (d) Information technology (e) Organizational decline

4. Which of the following is an accurate statement about an adhocracy? (a) The design makes it easier to exchange information and learn. (b) There are many rules and policies. (c) Use of IT is always minimal. (d) It handles routine problems efficiently. (e) It is quite common in older industries.

5. The set of cultural, economic, legal-political, and educational conditions in the areas in which a firm operates is called the _____. (a) task environment (b) specific environment (c) industry of the firm (d) environmental complexity (e) general environment

6. The segment of the environment that refers to the other organizations that an organization must interact with in order to obtain inputs and sell outputs is called _____. (a) the general environment (b) the strategic environment (c) the learning environment (d) the technological setting (e) the specific environment

7. _____ are official co-operative agreements or joint ventures between two independent firms. (a) Mergers (b) Acquisitions (c) Interfirm alliances (d) Adhocracies (e) Strategic configurations

8. The process of acquiring knowledge, retaining information in the organization, and distributing and interpreting information is called _____. (a) vicarious learning (b) experience (c) organizational learning (d) an organizational myth (e) a self-serving interpretation

9. Three methods of vicarious learning are _____. (a) scanning, grafting, and contracting out (b) grafting, contracting out, and mimicry (c) maladaptive specialization, scanning, and grafting (d) scanning, grafting, and mimicry (e) experience, mimicry, and scanning

10. Three important factors that block information interpretation are _____. (a) detachment, scanning, and common myths (b) self-serving interpretations, detachment, and common myths (c) managerial scripts, maladaptive specialization, and common myths (d) contracting out, common myths, and detachment (e) common myths, managerial scripts, and self-serving interpretations

TRUE–FALSE

11. The organizational design for a small firm and a large firm are almost the same.   T   F

12. Organizations that have well-defined and stable operations technologies have more opportunity to substitute informational techniques for managerial judgement than do firms that rely on more variable operations technologies.   T   F

13. Adhocracies tend to favour vertical specialization and control.   T   F

14. When IT is used extensively, more staff are typically added.   T   F

15. The general environment of an organization includes other organizations that the organization must interact with in order to get inputs and sell outputs.   T   F

16. The specific environment of an organization includes other organizations that the organization must interact with in order to get inputs and sell outputs.   T   F

17. An organizational alliance is an extreme example of an adhocracy.   T   F

18. Mimicry is the action of copying the successful practices of others.   T   F

19. The key to effective organizational learning is manipulation.   T   F

20. A deficit cycle is a pattern of deteriorating performance that is followed by further deterioration.   T   F

SHORT ANSWER

21. Explain why a large firm could not use a simple structure.

22. Explain the deployment of IT and its uses in organizations.

23. Describe the effect that operations technology has on an organization from both Thompson's and Woodward's points of view.

24. What are the three main determinants of environmental complexity?

APPLICATIONS ESSAY

25. Why might Ford Motors want to shift to a matrix organization structure for the design and development of cars and trucks but not use this structure for its manufacturing and assembly operations?

Organizational Cultures

The Company that Cares

www.vancity.com

Vancouver City Savings Credit Union is the largest credit union in Canada with $9 billion in assets and 305,000 members. It is also an innovative industry leader, but it is Vancity's reputation as an exceptional and progressive employer that makes the company proudest.

Vancity employees are encouraged to be both intellectually and emotionally involved in their work and to focus on delivering the best service to the credit-union members. The company tries to meet this commitment by:

- creating a healthy, diverse, stimulating, and rewarding workplace

- providing the necessary leadership, tools, resources, and opportunities for employees to do their best work and achieve their full potential

- especting and honouring employees' responsibilities to their families, friends, and communities

Vancity has indeed put its money where its mouth is, as it has a number of programs to ensure that Vancity employees are happy and satisfied.

Tonya Frizzell is just one employee who was able to take advantage of Vancity's commitment to its employees. A communications specialist, Frizzell was given a year's leave to work as a volunteer in Albania. She arrived in Albania with five other people, but she was the only one who had a job waiting for her upon her arrival home; the others had to quit their jobs to make this trip. "Companies should be more open to this," Frizzell confirms. "I brought back skills and, after a good long break, a fresh perspective. It's important to shake things up and not get too comfortable." Other

flexible work arrangements help employees cope with the demands of family and work. Part-time, on-call, job-sharing, and reduced and compressed workweeks all allow employees to find the right balance. The company also offers a living-well program by providing services and programs that contribute to an excellent quality of work-life experience. This includes health clinics, awareness campaigns and information, and online tools. Vancity has partnered with local organizations to offer employees free, confidential support and counselling for personal or work-related problems, such as locating child- or elder-care services.

Corporate social responsibility is also part of the package. The credit union tries to support not only employees and their families, but also the environment and the communities that its members and employees live in. Vancity takes its role as an advocate for socially and environmentally responsible business behaviour seriously. An example of this commitment is its sponsorship and support of the Ethics in Action Awards, which recognize organizations and individuals who exemplify good corporate citizenship by making corporate social responsibility a key aspect of their daily operations.

The not-so-hidden advantage of many leading high-performance organizations is their corporate culture. As you read Chapter 13, keep in mind these key questions:

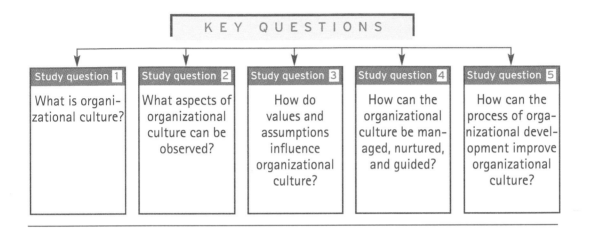

KEY QUESTIONS

Study question **1**	Study question **2**	Study question **3**	Study question **4**	Study question **5**
What is organizational culture?	What aspects of organizational culture can be observed?	How do values and assumptions influence organizational culture?	How can the organizational culture be managed, nurtured, and guided?	How can the process of organizational development improve organizational culture?

The Concept of Organizational Culture

Organizational or corporate culture is the system of shared actions, values, and beliefs that develops within an organization and guides the behaviour of its members.[1] In the business setting, this system is often called the *corporate culture*. Calgary-based WestJet prides itself on its distinct corporate culture, emphasizing a "can-do" attitude and team spirit. Just as no two individual personalities are the same, no two organizational cultures are identical. Very significantly, management scholars and consultants increasingly believe that differences in organizational cultures can have a major impact on the performance of organizations and the quality of work life experienced by their members. Some cultures encourage flexibility and seeking opportunities, while others encourage leaving things as they are. For an organization to not only realize its strategy but also evolve and adapt to the ever-changing environment in which it operates, it must have the appropriate culture for the strategy it has chosen.

The "culture iceberg" in Figure 13.1 presents the organizational culture as having three basic components. There are the artifacts or concrete and recognized portions of the culture; the espoused values as expressed in the strategies, goals, and so on; and the basic underlying assumptions or beliefs regarding the environment and other intangible aspects of the organization's culture.

> **Organizational or corporate culture** is the system of shared actions, values, and beliefs that develops within an organization and guides the behaviour of its members.

FUNCTIONS AND COMPONENTS OF ORGANIZATIONAL CULTURE

Through their collective experience, members of an organization solve two extremely important survival issues.[2] The first is the question of external adaptation: what precisely needs to be accomplished, and how can it be done? The second is the question of internal integration: how do members resolve the daily problems that come with living and working together?

External Adaptation **External adaptation** involves reaching goals and dealing with outsiders. Concerns include the tasks to be accomplished, methods used to achieve the goals, and methods of coping with success and failure.

> **External adaptation** involves reaching goals and dealing with outsiders; concerns include the tasks to be accomplished, methods used to achieve the goals, and methods of coping with success and failure.

Figure 13.1 The culture iceberg

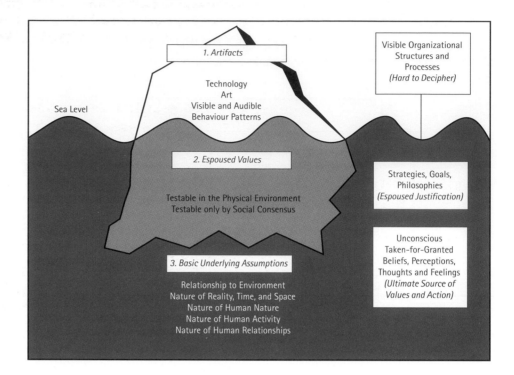

IMS Health Canada

www.imshealthcanada.com

IMS Health Canada is a health industry information management company with offices in Montreal and Toronto. Its employees observe, measure, and report what is actually happening in health care delivery to help stakeholders (including physicians, pharmacists, medical researchers, pharmaceutical manufacturers, public health authorities, and patient advocacy groups) understand, shape, and advance health care. Employees believe that it is their responsibility to be creators, innovators, and risk takers. They see these responsibilities as being important to achieving the goal of providing superior quality business solutions to advance health care in Canada and contribute to the well being of society.

Through their shared experiences, members may develop common views that help guide their day-to-day activities. Organizational members need to know the real mission of the organization, not just what is officially said to key constituencies (i.e., shareholders or other interested parties). Through their interactions with others, members will naturally develop an understanding of how they contribute to the mission. Perceptions in the organization may emphasize: the importance of employees as vital to the organization; the view that employees are merely cogs in a machine; or the idea that employees are simply a cost to be reduced.

Closely related to the organization's mission and view of its contribution are the questions of responsibility, goals, and methods. For instance, at IMS Health Canada, an information management company in the health industry, employees believe that it is their responsibility to be creators, innovators, and risk takers. They see these responsibilities as being important to achieving the goal of providing superior quality business solutions to advance the state of health care and contribute to the well-being of society.

Each grouping of individuals in an organization also tends to (1) separate more important external forces from less important ones; (2) develop ways to measure their accomplishments; and (3) create explanations for why goals are not always met. At Dell, for example, managers have moved away from judging their progress based on specific targets and instead now estimate how much they have moved a development process forward. And instead of blaming a poor economy or upper-level managers for the firm's failure to reach a goal, Dell managers have set hard goals that are difficult to reach and have doubled their efforts to improve participation and commitment.[3]

The final issues in external adaptation are two important but often neglected aspects of dealing with external reality. First, individuals need to develop acceptable ways of telling outsiders just how good they really are. At 3M, for example, employees talk about the quality of their products and the many new, useful products they have brought to market. Second, individuals must know together when to admit defeat. At 3M, admitting defeat for new projects is straightforward: at the beginning of the development process, members establish "drop" points—specific points in the development process at which to decide whether or not to quit the development effort and redirect it.[4]

In sum, external adaptation involves answering important instrumental or goal-related questions that deal with reality: What is the real mission? How do we contribute? What are our goals? How do we reach our goals? What external forces are important? How do we measure results? What do we do if specific targets are not met? How do we tell others how good we are? When do we quit?

Internal Integration   The corporate culture also provides answers to the problems of internal integration. **Internal integration** involves the creation of a collective identity and finding ways of working and living together.

The process of internal integration often begins with the establishment of a unique identity; that is, each collection of individuals and each subculture within the organization develops some type of unique definition of itself. Through dialogue and interaction, members begin to develop beliefs about their world. They may see it as changeable or fixed, filled with opportunity or threatening. Real progress toward innovation can begin when group members collectively believe that they can change important parts of the world around them and that what appears to be a threat is actually an opportunity for change.[5]

Three important aspects of working together are (1) deciding who is a member and who is not; (2) developing an informal understanding of acceptable and unacceptable behaviour; and (3) separating friends from enemies. For there to be effective total quality management, subgroups in the organization need to view their immediate supervisors as members of the group who will represent them in front of friendly higher managers.

To work together effectively, individuals need to decide collectively how to allocate power, status, and authority. They need to establish a shared understanding of who will get rewards and sanctions for specific types of actions. Too often, managers fail to recognize these important aspects of internal integration. For example, a manager may fail to explain the reason for a promotion and to show why this reward, the status that goes with it, and the power given to the newly promoted individual are consistent with the beliefs shared by members of the organization.

Internal integration is particularly challenging during a corporate merger. In April 2002, Calgary-based oil and gas company EnCana was created out of the merger of Alberta Energy Company Ltd. and PanCanadian Energy Corporation, and the company did not miss a beat. "In the seven months since creating EnCana, our teams have come together in an efficient integration as we build a best-in-class independent," said Gwyn Morgan, EnCana's President and Chief Executive Officer in a November 2002 news release.

When individuals are part of a collectivity, they need to decide on acceptable ways of communicating and to develop guidelines for friendships. Although these aspects of internal integration may appear unimportant, they are vital. To function effectively as a team, individuals must accept that some members will be closer to each other than others; friendships are inevitable.

In sum, internal integration is about answers to important questions associated with living together. What is our unique identity? How do we view the world? Who is a member? How do we allocate power, status, and authority? How do we communicate? What is the basis for friendship? Answering these questions is important to organizational members because the organization is more than a place to work; it is a place where individuals spend much of their adult life.[6]

Internal integration involves the creation of a collective identity and finding ways of working and living together.

Ethics Quality, Inc.
Ethics and Culture
Management Services

DOMINANT CULTURE, SUBCULTURES, AND COUNTERCULTURES

Smaller firms often have a single, dominant culture with a unified set of shared actions, values, and beliefs. Most larger organizations contain several subcultures as well as one or more countercultures.[7] **Subcultures** are unique patterns of values and philosophies within a group that fit with the organization's dominant values and philosophy.[8] Interestingly, strong subcultures are often found in high-performance task forces, teams, and special project groups in organizations. The culture helps create cohesion between individuals who are working together intensely to accomplish a specific task. For example, the accountants at WestJet call their department "Beanland" and have created a subculture counter to the traditional accountant image by trying to keep the atmosphere informal and not taking themselves too seriously.

In contrast, **countercultures** are patterns of values and philosophies that reject the surrounding culture.[9] When Steve Jobs returned to Apple computer as its interim CEO in 1997, he quickly formed a counterculture within Apple. Over the next 18 months, numerous clashes occurred as the followers of the old CEO (Gil Amelio) fought to maintain their place. Jobs won and Apple won. His counterculture became dominant.

Within an organization, mergers and acquisitions may produce countercultures. Employers and managers of an acquired firm may hold values and assumptions that go against those of the acquiring firm. This is known as a "clash of corporate cultures."[10]

Importing Subcultures Every large organization imports potentially important subcultures when it hires employees from the larger society. In North America, for instance, subcultures and countercultures may naturally form based on ethnic, racial, gender, generational, or locational similarities. In Japanese organizations, subcultures often form based on gender, geographic location, or the date of graduation from a university. In European firms, ethnicity and language play an important part in developing subcultures, as does gender. In many less

Subcultures are unique patterns of values and philosophies within a group that fit with the dominant culture of the larger organization or social system.

Countercultures are the patterns of values and philosophies that reject those of the larger organization or social system.

developed nations, language, education, religion, or family social status are often grounds for forming popular subcultures and countercultures in society. As more firms globalize and use mergers and acquisitions to expand, they often have to deal with both importing subcultures and clashes of corporate cultures. For instance, when Daimler-Benz said it was merging with Chrysler Corporation, it was presented as a merger of equals that would give the new combined firm a global reach. The corporate culture clash came quickly, however, when Chrysler managers and employees realized that Daimler executives would control the new firm and shape it around the Daimler-Benz culture.

OB ACROSS FUNCTIONS

Marketing

Marketing at a High-Performance Organization: Hewlett-Packard

A corporation with 145,000 employees worldwide and 2004 revenues of more than $79 billion U.S., Hewlett-Packard (HP) is a leader in many information technology fields. In all of its product-line advertising, one HP core value is repeated again and again—the spirit of innovation. For instance, in 2002, HP launched its Invent America campaign, "celebrating the Nation's spirit of inventiveness." The event was the largest consumer product rollout in HP's history, unveiling almost 50 new imaging and printing products. Dick Clark was on-hand to unveil the world's largest digital image, a football field-sized Photomosaic™, featuring more than 113,000 images of favourite inventions, sent in from people across the United States. "Invent" now applies to everything the company does, from the home and office, to large, medium, and small business services, to public sector, health and education. It also has an Invent Center to help customers come up with innovative business solutions. Business and technology specialists from HP's worldwide network provide consulting services to help executives on their choice technology products, solutions, and services.

When people who share a subculture in the larger society are brought into an organization, the challenge for the firm involves how well these groups will fit with the organization as a whole. At one extreme, senior managers may simply accept these internal divisions and work with the organization's larger, dominant culture. There are three main problems with this approach, however. First, subordinated groups, such as members of a specific religion or ethnic group, are likely to form into a counterculture and to work harder to change their status than to improve the firm. Second, the firm may find it extremely difficult to handle broader cultural changes. For instance, in Canada and the U.S., ideas about how women, ethnic minorities, and the disabled should be treated have changed dramatically over the last 30 to 40 years. Firms that merely accept old customs and prejudices have experienced a greater loss of key personnel and increased communication difficulties, as well as greater interpersonal conflict, than have more progressive firms. Third, firms that accept and build on natural divisions in society may find it extremely difficult to develop solid international operations. For example, many Asian firms have had major difficulties in adjusting to the equal treatment of women in their North American operations.[11]

Valuing Cultural Diversity Managers can work to eliminate all naturally occurring subcultures and countercultures in their organization. Firms are indeed struggling to develop what Taylor Cox calls the multicultural organization. The multicultural organization is a firm that values diversity but systematically works to block the transfer of subcultures from society into the fabric of the organization.[12] Because Cox focuses on some problems that are unique to the United States, his solutions may not apply to organizations located in countries that have much more homogeneous populations, but they may still apply in Canada's diverse society.

Cox suggests a five-step program for developing the multicultural organization. First, the organization should develop pluralism in order to reach the objective of multibased socialization. To accomplish this objective, members of different naturally occurring groups need to educate each other about their groups to increase knowledge and information and to eliminate stereotyping. Second, the firm should fully integrate its structure so that there is no direct relationship between a naturally occurring group and any particular job—for instance, there should be no distinctly male or female jobs. Third, the firm must integrate informal networks by eliminating barriers and increasing participation. That is, it must break down existing informal groups that are based on divisions in society. Fourth, the organization should break the link between naturally occurring group identity and the identity of the firm. In other words, the firm should not be just for the young, old, men, or women, and so on. Fifth, the organization must actively work to eliminate conflict between individuals that is based on either group identity or the natural backlash of the largest group in society against smaller groups.

Key problems with trying to fully implement Cox's program involve separating the firm from the larger culture in which it must operate and eliminating some groupings from society that would help the firm achieve its goals. For instance, the U.S. military cannot fully implement Cox's recommendations simply because it is not currently legal to put women into all combat roles. The issue of generational groupings provides another example. Implementing Cox's recommendations would call for 20-year-olds to be represented proportionally in the senior management ranks; most corporations, however, want and need the quality of judgement that comes from many years of experience. Still, astute senior managers are recognizing that they may be out of touch with younger employees. For example, John Chambers, president of Cisco Systems, has breakfast each month with all head office employees who have their birthday that month, and he meets them without their supervisors present.[13]

LEVELS OF CULTURAL ANALYSIS

Three important levels of cultural analysis in organizations are observable culture, shared values, and common assumptions.[14] These levels may be imagined as layers. The deeper the layer is, the more difficult it is to discover the culture associated with it.

The first level is *observable culture*, or "the way we do things around here." These are the methods that the group has developed and teaches to new members. The observable culture includes the unique stories, ceremonies, and corporate rituals that make up the history of a successful workgroup.

The second level of analysis recognizes that shared values can play a critical part in linking people together and can provide a lot of motivation for members of the culture. Many consultants suggest that organizations should develop a "dominant and coherent set of shared values."[15] The term "shared" in cultural analysis implies that the group is a whole. Every member may not agree with the shared values, but they have all been exposed to them and have often been told these values are important. At Hewlett-Packard Canada, for example, "innovation" is part of everyone's vocabulary. The spirit of innovation is an integral part of HP Canada and its employees are valued for their ideas and input.

At the deepest level of cultural analysis are common assumptions, or the taken-for-granted truths that groups of corporate members share as a result of their joint experience. It is often extremely difficult to isolate these patterns, but discovering them can help explain why culture invades every aspect of organizational life.

Observable Aspects of Organizational Culture

Important parts of an organization's culture develop from the collective experience of its members. These aspects of the culture help make it unique and may even create a competitive advantage for the organization. Some of these aspects may be directly observed in day-to-day practices. Others may have to be discovered—for example, by asking members to tell stories of important incidents in the history of the organization. We often learn about the unique aspects of the organizational culture through descriptions of specific events.[16] By observing employee actions, listening to stories, and asking members to interpret what is going on, one can begin to understand the organization's culture.

STORIES, RITES, RITUALS, AND SYMBOLS

Organizations are rich with stories of winners and losers, successes and failures. Perhaps one of the most important stories is the one that tells the founding of the organization. The founding story often contains the lessons learned from the heroic efforts of an embattled entrepreneur whose vision may still guide the firm. The story of the founding may be so embellished that it becomes a saga—a heroic account of accomplishments.[17] Sagas are important because they are used to tell new members the real mission of the organization, how the organization operates, and how individuals can fit into the company. Rarely is the founding story totally accurate, and it often skips over some of the distractive events along the way.

> **Sagas** are embellished heroic accounts of the story of the founding of an organization.

ENTREPRENEURSHIP AND ETHICS

BAKING GREAT BREADS

In 1982, Martin Connell set out to bake a great baguette in his family's kitchen. In 1993, he and his wife, Linda Haynes, opened the ACE Bakery in Toronto as an artisan bakery creating hand-made, European-style rustic breads. Outgrowing its operation on King Street in 1997, ACE moved to North York. In 1998, ACE opened The ACE Fresh Bread Store and Cafè on Yonge Street. While the cafè was closed in 2000 in order to focus on the wholesale business, ACE maintains a fresh bread store and cafè at the bakery in North York. Community involvement is an essential part of ACE's philosophy. The company donates a percentage of its net profits to charitable organizations in the principal centres where ACE breads are sold. ACE's focus is on food and nutrition programs that assist low-income members of the community, financing culinary scholarships and supporting organic farming initiatives. Now one of North America's leading artisan bakeries (with the Toronto Star calling it the 'Best Bakery' in 2003) ACE Bakery's famous baguettes and artisan breads are sold to hundreds of restaurants, hotels, caterers, grocery and gourmet food shops throughout Ontario, Quebec, New York and the Midwest U.S.A.

www.ace-bakery.com

If you have job experience, you may well have heard stories based on the following questions: How will the boss react to a mistake? Can someone move from the bottom to the top of the company? What will get me fired? These are common story topics in many organizations.[18] Often, the stories provide valuable hidden information about who is "more equal" than others, whether jobs are secure, and how things are really controlled. In essence, the stories give some notion of how an organization's members view their world and live together.

Rites are standardized and recurring activities that are used at special times to influence the behaviours and understanding of organizational members.

Rituals are systems of rites.

Some of the most obvious aspects of organizational culture are rites and rituals. **Rites** are standardized and recurring activities that are used at special times to influence the behaviours and understanding of organizational members. **Rituals** are systems of rites. It is common, for example, for Japanese workers and managers to start their workdays together with group exercises and singing of the company song. Separately, the exercises and song are rites. Together, they form part of a ritual. In other settings, such as the Mary Kay Cosmetics company, scheduled ceremonies that resemble the Miss America pageant (a ritual) are used regularly to spotlight positive work achievements and reinforce high-performance expectations with awards, including gold and diamond pins and fur stoles.

Subcultures often develop based on the type of technology used by the unit, the specific function being performed, and the specific collection of specialists in the unit. The boundaries of the subculture may even be maintained by a unique language that becomes a form of jargon that only the subculture's members understand. In some cases, the special language starts to move outside the firm and begins to enter the larger society. For instance, Hewlett-Packard advertises its new iPAQ pocket PC as having an Intel® XScale™ processor (400MHz), Windows Mobile 2003 Premium for Pocket PC, 64MB SDRAM, 32MB Flash ROM, Bluetooth® wireless technology, a 3.5-inch transflective TFT screen with LED backlight, SD and CF slots, and a 900 mAh battery. Not everyone considered this a user-friendly ad, but it did appeal to knowledgeable individuals.[19]

A cultural symbol is any object, act, or event that serves to transmit cultural meaning.

Another observable aspect of corporate culture is the symbols found in organizations. A **cultural symbol** is any object, act, or event that serves to transmit cultural meaning. Good examples are the corporate uniforms worn by UPS and Federal Express delivery personnel. Although many such symbols are quite visible, their importance and meaning may not be. The HP logo includes the word "invent." This encouragement to invent may encourage the employees by reinforcing the culture of creating new products and renewing the organization and may encourage the customers to use HP products in their endeavours to invent on their own.

CULTURAL RULES AND ROLES

Organizational culture often specifies when various types of actions are appropriate and what each individual member's role is in the social system. These cultural rules and roles are part of the normative controls of the organization and come from its daily routines.[20] For instance, the timing, presentation, and methods of communicating authoritative directives are often quite specific to each organization. In one firm, meetings may be forums for dialogue and discussion, where managers set agendas and then let others offer new ideas, critically examine alternatives, and fully participate. In another firm, the "rules" may be quite different, with the manager going into meetings with fixed expectations. Any new ideas, critical examinations, and so on are expected to be worked out in private before the meeting takes place. The meeting is a forum for letting others know what is being done and for passing out orders on what to do in the future.

THE EVOLUTION OF SHARED MEANINGS FROM OBSERVABLE CULTURE

What you may recall or see as an outside observer may not be what an organization's members see. We see film of Canadian peacekeepers driving in military vehicles, but they may not see themselves as stopping a war or being police; rather, they see themselves as helping rebuild Afghanistan. Through their interactions with each other, and with the reinforcement they receive from the rest of their organization and the larger society, these peacekeepers' work has deeper meaning. In this deeper sense, organizational culture is a "shared" set of meanings and perceptions. In most corporations, these shared meanings and perceptions may not be as dramatic as those shared in Afghanistan, but in most firms employees do still create and learn a deeper aspect of their culture.[21]

Values and Organizational Culture

To describe more fully the culture of an organization, it is necessary to go deeper than the observable aspects. For many researchers and managers, shared common values are the very heart of organizational culture. Shared values help turn routine activities into valuable, important actions; tie the corporation to the important values of society; and may provide a very distinctive source of competitive advantage. In organizations, what works for one person as a solution for a problem is often taught to new members as being the correct way to think and feel. Important values are then attributed to these solutions to everyday problems. By linking values and actions, the organization gains access to some of the strongest and deepest realms of the individual. The tasks a person performs are given not only meaning but value: what one does is not only workable but correct, right, and important.

Successful organizations sometimes share some common cultural characteristics.[22] Organizations with "strong cultures" have a value system that is broadly and deeply shared by their members. Unique, shared values can give a strong corporate identity, increase the commitment of employees as a group, provide a stable social system, and reduce the need for formal and bureaucratic controls. A strong culture can be a double-edged sword, however, as it can also bring problems. A strong culture and value system can reinforce a one-dimensional view of the organization and its environment. Stelco Inc. may have a "strong" culture, for example, but the firm met with enormous resistance from the Steelworkers Union in negotiating its restructuring and financing deal.

In many corporate cultures, there is a series of common assumptions that are shared by almost everyone in the corporation: "We are different;" "We are better at...;" or "We have unrecognized talents." Cisco Systems provides an excellent example. Senior managers often share common assumptions, such as, "We are good stewards;" "We are competent managers;" and "We are practical innovators." Like values, these assumptions influence and show up in the organizational culture. These values can result in a strong and successful company such as Wal-Mart, the world's largest retailer, or in marginal companies like the former Woolco department stores that were eventually bought by Wal-Mart, renamed, and outfitted with a McDonald's in each store.

The Effective Manager 13.1 presents some assumptions and other elements of a strong organizational culture.

> **The Effective Manager 13.1**
>
> ELEMENTS OF STRONG CORPORATE CULTURES
>
> - a widely shared real understanding of what the firm stands for, often expressed in slogans
> - a greater concern for individuals than for rules, policies, procedures, and adherence to job duties
> - a recognition of heroes whose actions illustrate the company's shared philosophy and concerns
> - a belief in ritual and ceremony as important to members and to building a common identity
> - a well-understood sense of the informal rules and expectations so that employees and managers understand what is expected of them
> - a belief that what employees and managers do is important and that it is important to share information and ideas

ORGANIZATIONAL MYTHS

In many firms, the management philosophy is supported by a series of organizational myths. Organizational myths are unproven and often unstated beliefs that are accepted uncritically. In a study of safety in nuclear power plants, senior managers were asked whether they felt there was a trade-off between safety and efficiency. Their response was clear: a safe plant is an efficient plant. Most of these executives, however, had seen data which proved that measures of safety and efficiency were quite independent. To admit there was a trade-off would have meant having to choose between efficiency and safety, but they all wanted to believe that to do one was to promote the other.[23]

Although some individuals may look down on these organizational myths and want to see rational, hard-nosed analysis instead of mythology, each firm needs a series of managerial myths.[24] Myths allow executives to redefine impossible problems into more manageable components. Myths can encourage experimentation and creativity, and they allow managers to govern. For

An organizational myth is an unproven and often unstated belief that is accepted uncritically.

instance, senior executives are not just decision-makers or rational allocators of resources. All organization members hope these individuals will also be fair, just, and compassionate.

NATIONAL CULTURE INFLUENCES

Common assumptions that are widely shared in an organization may often be traced to the larger culture of the society the firm is in.[25] The difference between Sony's corporate emphasis on group achievements and Zenith's emphasis on individual engineering excellence, for example, can be traced to the Japanese emphasis on collective action versus the U.S. emphasis on individualism.

National cultural values may also show up in the expectations of important organizational constituencies and in generally accepted solutions to problems. When moving from one national culture to another, managers need to be sensitive to national cultural differences so that their actions do not violate common assumptions in the underlying national culture. In Japan and Western Europe, for example, executives are expected to work co-operatively with government officials on an informal basis. Informal business-government relations that are perfectly acceptable in these countries are considered influence peddling in the U.S. and, depending on the situation, may or may not be acceptable in Canada.

Inappropriate actions that violate common assumptions that come from a national culture can affect performance greatly and may alienate organizational members, even if managers have the best intentions. To improve morale at General Electric's new French subsidiary, American managers invited all the European managers to a "get acquainted" meeting near Paris. The Americans gave out colourful T-shirts with the GE slogan, "Go for One," a typical manoeuvre in many American training programs. The French resented the T-shirts. One outspoken individual said, "It was like Hitler was back, forcing us to wear uniforms. It was humiliating."

Managing Organizational Culture

The culture is as critical as structure and strategy when the organizational foundations of high performance are being established. Good managers are able to reinforce and support an existing strong culture; good managers are also able to help build effective cultures in situations where such cultures are absent. For instance, when Rick George assumed the helm at Suncor, the company was said to be a source of toxic fires, large fish kills in the Athabasca River caused by spills from a tailing pond, and the death of workers on the job. George assured everyone that there was a way out of the financial losses and the accidents, and a way to have fun in the process. With a five-year environmental plan and a 50-year business plan, "George has really set the bar for the oil sands business," according to Neil Camarta, senior vice-president of tar sands at Shell Oil. Under George, morale has improved and Suncor has quadrupled production. Today, the tar sands oil producer is more than just profitable and environmentally sound; it is growing beyond Canada into Australia and the U.S.

MANAGEMENT PHILOSOPHY AND STRATEGY

Management philosophy is a philosophy that links key goal-related issues with key collaboration issues to come up with general ways for the firm to manage its affairs.

Perhaps the first step in managing an organizational culture is for management to recognize its own subculture. In OB, this is often referred to by the term "management philosophy." A **management philosophy** links key goal-related issues with key collaboration issues to come up with a series of general ways for the firm to manage its affairs.[26] A well-developed management philosophy is important because it links strategy to a more basic understanding of how the firm is to operate. Specifically, it (1) establishes generally understood boundaries for all members of the firm; (2) provides a consistent way of approaching new situations; and (3) helps keep individuals together by assuring them that the path toward success is known.

Cisco Systems, which has several offices across the country and a Canadian head office based in Toronto, has a clearly identified management philosophy that links the strategic concerns of growth, profitability, and customer service to observable aspects of its culture and selected underlying values. For instance, Sue Bostrom heads Cisco's Internet Business Solutions Group. She emphasizes the link between strategy and culture in three important elements of Cisco's management philosophy. These three aspects emphasize (1) empowering employees to generate the best ideas quickly and to implement them successfully, (2) hiring the best people because it is the ideas and intellectual assets of these colleagues that drive success, and (3) developing and disseminating information to compete in the world of ideas. While elements of a management philosophy may be formally written in a corporate plan or statement of business philosophy, it is the well-understood fundamentals which these documents try to express that form the heart of a well-developed management philosophy. In the case of Sue Bostrom, her unit in Cisco is not waiting on the competition, building bricks-and-mortar monuments, or developing elaborate bureaucratic procedures. Her unit's philosophy is clear, and it forms a basis for managing the shared actions and values that emerge in her group.

Two broad strategies for managing an organization's corporate culture have received considerable attention in the OB literature. One strategy encourages managers to help modify observable culture, shared values, and common assumptions directly. The other strategy involves the use of organizational development techniques to modify specific elements of the culture.

GLOBALIZATION

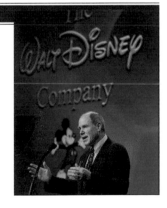

All new Disney employees are told the story of Walt Disney. He is said to have emphasized that everyone is a child at heart and that every individual in the Disney theme parks is a performer. This emphasis is commonly linked to his founding philosophy. Actually, Walt Disney was a perfectionist. A harder boss would be difficult to find, and, several times, Disney bet the entire firm on the success of one picture. The emphasis on "Everyone is a performer" did not come from a philosophy but from hard-won experience. In fact, the initial opening of Disneyland Park in California was not a success until the firm eliminated much of the staff who only had experience in county fairs. They were replaced by an inexperienced crew of young employees trained by Disney. In France, Disneyland Paris Resort took almost five years to answer the question of how to match European culture and Disney's created culture. The Disney challenge now is what to do with CapCities/ABC. Instead of just Disney, the corporation now includes well-known entities such as ABC and ESPN, as well as a host of lesser-known daily newspapers, 50 trade publications, several feature film companies, and even a hockey and a baseball team. The big challenge, then, is managing a corporate culture within the framework of a conglomerate.

www.disney.com

BUILDING, REINFORCING, AND CHANGING CULTURE

Managers can modify the visible aspects of culture, such as the language, stories, rites, rituals, and sagas. They can change the lessons to be drawn from common stories and even encourage individuals to see the reality they see. Because of their positions, senior managers can interpret situations in new ways and can adjust the meanings attached to important corporate events.

WestJet

www.westjet.ca

WestJet is known for no-frills, low cost airfares. But the company is also an example of participatory democracy in a way. Ninety-five percent of WestJet employees participate in the Employee Stock Ownership Program.

They can even create new rites and rituals. This takes time and enormous energy, but the long-term benefits can also be great.

Top managers, in particular, can set the tone for a culture and for cultural change. Even in the highly cost-competitive pulp and paper industry, CEO Raymond Royer of Domtar built on basic human values of respect in Canadian society to improve service and Domtar is now the third largest producer of freesheet in North America. And at Procter & Gamble, Richard Nicolosi evoked the shared values for greater participation in decision-making and dramatically improved creativity and innovation.

Each of these examples shows how managers can help create a culture that gives answers to important questions about external adaptation and internal integration. Recent work on the links among corporate culture and financial performance reaffirm the importance of helping employees adjust to the environment. It also suggests that just emphasizing this is not enough. Paying attention only to shareholders or customers is not associated with long-term economic performance either. Instead, managers must work to pay attention to all three groups simultaneously. This emphasis on customers, shareholders, and employees does come at a price—less emphasis on management. Large offices, multimillion-dollar salaries, golden parachutes (protections for executives if the firm is bought by others), as well as the executive plane, dining room, and country club are out.

Early research on culture and culture change often emphasized direct attempts to change the values and assumptions of individuals by resocializing them—that is, trying to change their hearts so that their minds and actions would follow.[27] The goal was to establish a clear, consistent consensus throughout the organization. More recent work suggests that this one-dimensional approach of working through values may not be either possible or desirable.

Trying to change people's values from the top down without also changing how the organization operates and recognizing the importance of individuals does not work very well. Take another look at the example of Cisco Systems. Here managers realize that keeping a dynamic, change-oriented culture is a mix of managerial actions, decisions about technology, and initiatives from all employees. The values are not set and forced on employees by someone high up. Instead, the shared values emerge from the firm itself, and they are not identical in all of Cisco's operating sites. For instance, there are subtle but important differences across their operations in Silicon Valley, the North Carolina operation, and the Australian setting. The differences may be even greater at their offices in Halifax, Nova Scotia; Caracas, Venezuela; Hamburg, Germany; and the Malaysian office in Selangor Darul Ehsan.

It is also a mistake for managers to try to revitalize an organization by forcing major changes and ignoring shared values. Although things may change a bit on the surface when changes are dictated, a deeper look often shows whole departments resisting change and many key people who are unwilling to learn new ways. Such reactions may indicate that the managers are not sensitive to the effects of their proposed changes on shared values. They fail to ask whether the changes go against the important values of participants within the firm, are a challenge to historically important assumptions shared throughout the corporation, or violate important common assumptions that come from the national culture outside the firm. Remember the example of Steve Jobs who returned to Apple when the company appeared to be failing. He did not make all the changes himself. Rather, he worked with others to make changes in strategy, structure, products, and marketing and to build on deep-seated common assumptions that long-term employees shared. The Effective Manager 13.2 provides some key characteristics that managers should encourage in Internet companies.

The Effective Manager 13.2

ENCOURAGING AN EFFECTIVE INTERNET CULTURE

To respond to the constant, rapid changes in e-business, some experts recommend developing an Internet culture. Key distinguishing characteristics of such a culture include:

- embracing open communication in all forms and in all possible media
- emphasizing constant learning and individual development
- stressing leadership that reinforces courage and risk-taking

CONTINUOUS CULTURAL DEVELOPMENT

To keep an organization's culture fresh and competitive, the challenge today is to be part of a process of continuous self-assessment and planned change in order to stay on top of problems and opportunities in a complex and demanding environment. **Organizational development (OD)** is a comprehensive approach to planned change that is designed to improve the overall effectiveness of organizations. Formally defined, OD is the use of behavioural-science knowledge in a long-term effort to improve an organization's ability to respond to change in its external environment and increase its internal problem-solving capabilities.[28]

Organizational development is used to improve performance in organizations of many types, sizes, and settings. It includes a set of tools that any manager whose goal is to achieve and maintain high levels of productivity will want to be familiar with. In its early years, because of its comprehensive nature and scientific foundations, OD was frequently implemented with the aid of an external consultant. Today, as OD techniques have been combined with a better understanding of organizational culture, OD's basic concepts can and should be used routinely by all managers.

Organizational development (OD) is the use of behavioural-science knowledge in a long-term effort to improve an organization's ability to respond to change in its external environment and increase its problem-solving capabilities.

Organizational Development Processes and Applications

Organizational development provides a set of well-proven methods for developing and changing what cultural analysts call external adaptation and internal integration. Importantly, the goal of OD is to create change in a way that results in the organization's members being more active and confident in taking similar steps to maintain the culture and long-term effectiveness of the organization. Whether or not an OD program will succeed in achieving this goal depends largely on the program's assumptions, values, and action-research foundations.

UNDERLYING ASSUMPTIONS OF OD

In organizational development, efforts to achieve change are based on underlying assumptions about individuals, groups, and organizations. At the *individual level*, OD is guided by an underlying respect for people and their capabilities. It assumes that individual needs for growth and development are most likely to be satisfied in a supportive and challenging work environment. It also assumes that most people are capable of taking responsibility for their own actions and of making positive contributions to organizational performance.

At the *group level*, OD is guided by the belief that groups can be good for both people and organizations. It assumes that groups help their members satisfy important individual needs and can also be helpful in supporting the organization's objectives. And it assumes that effective groups can be created by people working together to meet individual and organizational needs.

At the *organizational level*, OD is guided by respect for the complexity of an organization as a system of interdependent parts. It assumes that changes in one part of the organization will affect other parts as well. And it assumes that organizational structures and jobs can be designed to meet the needs of individuals and groups, as well as those of the organization.

SHARED VALUES AND PRINCIPLES UNDERLYING OD

Organizational development offers a systematic approach to planned change in organizations by addressing two main goals: outcome goals, which are mainly issues of external adaptation, and process goals, which are mainly issues of internal integration. Outcome goals include achieving improvements in task performance by improving the organization's capability for external adaptation. In OD, these goals focus on what is actually accomplished through individual and group efforts. Process goals include achieving improvements in such things as communication, interaction, and decision-making among an organization's members. These goals focus on how well people work together, and they stress improving internal integration.

OD helps organizations and their members reach these goals by (1) creating an open problem-solving climate throughout an organization, (2) supplementing formal authority with authority based on knowledge and competence, (3) moving decision-making to points where relevant information is available, (4) building trust and maximizing collaboration among individuals and groups, (5) increasing the sense of organizational "ownership" among members, and (6) allowing people to use self-direction and self-control at work.[29] Thus, using OD means supporting these values. That is, organizational development is designed to improve the contributions of individual members in achieving the organization's goals, and it tries to do this in ways that respect the organization's members as mature adults who need and deserve high-quality experiences in their working lives.

ACTION-RESEARCH FOUNDATIONS OF OD

Action research is the process of systematically collecting data on an organization, feeding it back for action planning, and evaluating results by collecting and reflecting on more data.

Organizational development practitioners refer to a process they call **action research**. This is the process of systematically collecting data on an organization, feeding it back to the members for action planning, and evaluating results by collecting and reflecting on more data after the planned actions have been taken. This is a data-based and collaborative approach to problem-solving and the evaluation of an organization.

When used in OD, action research helps identify action directions that may improve an organization's effectiveness. In the typical action-research sequence shown in Figure 13.2, the sequence begins when someone senses a performance gap and decides to analyze the situation systematically for problems and opportunities. The next steps are data gathering, data feedback, data analysis, and action planning. The process then continues with action being taken and results being evaluated. The evaluation or reassessment stage may or may not reveal another performance gap. If it does, the action-research cycle begins again.

Figure 13.3 identifies one set of frameworks that can help OD practitioners do the required diagnoses. These foundations use the open-systems framework and OB concepts which you are already familiar with from earlier chapters. At the organizational level, the figure indicates that effectiveness is judged according to forces in the external environment and major organizational aspects, such as strategy, technology, structure, culture, and management systems. At the group level, effectiveness is judged according to forces in the internal environment of the organization and major group aspects, such as tasks, membership, norms, cohesiveness, and group processes. At the individual level, effectiveness is judged according to the internal environment of the workgroup and individual aspects, such as tasks, goals, needs, and interpersonal relationships.

Figure 13.2 An action-research model for organizational development

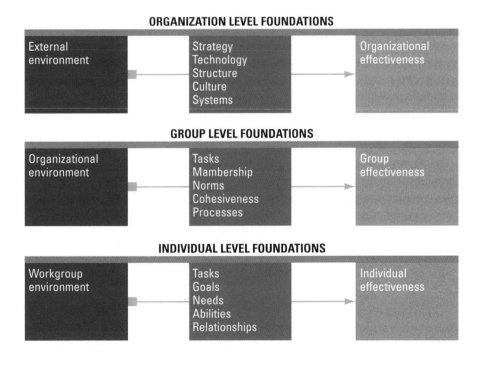

Figure 13.3 Diagnostic foundations of organizational development and OD techniques: concerns for individual, group, and organizational effectiveness

ORGANIZATION LEVEL FOUNDATIONS

| External environment | Strategy Technology Structure Culture Systems | Organizational effectiveness |

GROUP LEVEL FOUNDATIONS

| Organizational environment | Tasks Mambership Norms Cohesiveness Processes | Group effectiveness |

INDIVIDUAL LEVEL FOUNDATIONS

| Workgroup environment | Tasks Goals Needs Abilities Relationships | Individual effectiveness |

ORGANIZATIONAL DEVELOPMENT INTERVENTIONS

The action-research process should involve members of an organization in activities that are designed to accomplish the required diagnoses and to develop and implement plans for positive change. Action research, data collection, and the diagnostic foundations should come together in the choice and use of OD "interventions." **Organizational development interventions** are activities begun by the consultant to help planned change occur and to help the client organization develop its own problem-solving capabilities. With less formality, many of these techniques are also now being used by managers to help understand and improve their own operations. Major OD interventions can be categorized according to their major impact at the organizational, group, and individual levels of action.[30]

Organizationwide Interventions   An organization is effective if it achieves its major performance objectives while maintaining a high quality of work life for its members. OD interventions that are designed for the organization's entire system include the following:

   Survey feedback begins with the collection of data from questionnaires answered by organization members. The data can include the answers of all members or a representative sample of their answers. The data are then presented, or fed back, to the members. They then work together to interpret the data and develop action plans in response.

   Confrontation meetings are designed to help determine quickly how an organization may be improved and what initial actions to take to improve the situation.[31] The intervention involves a one-day meeting conducted by an OD facilitator for a representative sample of organizational members, including top management. In a structured format, the consultant asks participants to make individual lists of what they feel can be done to improve things. Then, through a series of small-group work sessions and the sharing of results, these ideas are refined into a tentative set of actions that top management then approves for immediate implementation. The major trick here is to get senior managers to propose changing their part of the firm. Confrontation meetings fail if all the proposed changes call for adjustments by subordinates without any alterations by the top managers.

   Structural redesign involves realigning the structure of the organization or major subsystems in order to improve performance. It includes examining the best fit between structure, technology, and environment. In today's highly changeable environments, with the increasing involvement of organizations in international operations and with rapid changes in information technology, a structure can easily grow out of date. Thus, structural redesign is an important OD intervention that can be used to help maintain the best fit between organizational structures and the demands of different situations.

   Collateral organization is designed to make creative problem-solving possible by putting a representative set of members from the formal organization structure into periodic, small-group, problem-solving sessions.[32] These collateral, or "parallel," structures are temporary and are only used to supplement the activities of the formal structure.

Group and Intergroup Interventions   OD interventions at the group level are designed to improve group effectiveness. The major interventions at this level are team-building, process consultation, and intergroup team-building.

   In **team-building**, a manager or consultant involves the members of a group in a series of activities that are designed to help them examine how the group functions and how it may function better. Like survey feedback at the organizational level, team-building uses some form of data collection and feedback. The key elements, however, are a collaborative assessment of the data by all members of the group and the achievement of consensus about what can be done to improve the group's effectiveness. Team-building is often done at "retreats" or

---

Organizational development interventions are activities for supporting planned change and improving work effectiveness.

Survey feedback begins with the collection of data from questionnaires answered by organization members.

A confrontation meeting helps determine how an organization may be improved and start action toward improvement.

Structural redesign involves realigning the structure of the organization or major subsystem in order to improve performance.

Collateral organization is having a representative set of members in periodic, small-group, problem-solving sessions.

Team-building gathers and analyzes data about how a group functions, and makes changes to increase the group's operating effectiveness.

off-site meetings, where group members spend two to three days working intensely together on this process of reflection, analysis, and planning.

Process consultation involves structured activities that are guided by an OD practitioner and that are designed to improve how the group functions. Process consultation has a more specific focus than does team-building, however: its attention is directed toward the key "processes" through which members of a group work with each other. The process consultant is concerned about helping a group function better on such things as norms, cohesiveness, decision-making methods, communication, conflict management, and task and maintenance activities.

Intergroup team-building is a special form of team-building. It is designed to help two or more groups improve their working relationships with each other and, it is hoped, to experience improved group effectiveness as a result. Here, the OD practitioner involves the groups or their representatives in activities that increase members' awareness of how each group sees the other. Given this increased awareness, collaborative problem-solving can improve the coordination between the groups and encourage them to support each other more, with each group recognizing the other as an important part in the total organization.

Individual Interventions
Task performance and job satisfaction are important considerations for improving an individual's effectiveness in the workplace. OD interventions at this level range from those that involve personal issues to those that deal more with specific job and career considerations. OD interventions at the individual level include the following:

Role negotiation is a way of clarifying what individuals expect to give to and receive from each other in their work relationship. Because roles and personnel change over time, role negotiation can be an important way to maintain understanding among individuals about the tasks in an organization. This kind of understanding is quite easily accomplished by helping people who work together clarify what they need from each other to do their jobs well.

Job redesign is the process of creating a long-term fit between individual goals and career opportunities in an organization. A good example is the Hackman and Oldham diagnostic approach to job enrichment discussed in Chapter 8.[33] Recall that this approach involves (1) analyzing the core characteristics of a job or group of jobs, (2) analyzing the needs and capabilities of workers in those jobs, and (3) taking action to adjust the core job characteristics either to enrich or to simplify the jobs to best match individual preferences.

Career planning consists of structured opportunities for individuals to work on career issues with their managers or staff experts from the personnel or human resources department. These opportunities can be used to map career goals, assess personal development needs, and actively plan short-term and long-term career moves. Increasingly, career planning is becoming a major part of the support that highly progressive organizations provide for their members.

OD and the Continuous Evolution
Today, even if they do not use the term OD, there is a new wave of successful high-tech firms that are fine examples of using organizational development assumptions, values, and techniques to improve performance. Firms such as Domtar, Suncor, and Starbucks are not trying to force change on their employees. Rather, the managers in these systems take a very practical approach to managing culture. They realize that both external adaptation and internal integration are important for a variety of subcultures within their firms. They use OD intervention techniques to improve both. They do not dictate values or set common assumptions on their own; instead, they involve their fellow employees in this process. They are working with others to help nurture and guide the continual evolution of organizational culture from day to day.

Process consultation helps a group improve such things as norms, cohesiveness, decision-making methods, communication, conflict management, and task and maintenance activities.

Intergroup team-building helps different groups improve their working relationships with each other and experience improved group effectiveness.

Role negotiation is a process which helps individuals clarify their expectations about what each should be giving and receiving as group members.

Job redesign creates a long-term fit between individual goals and career opportunities in an organization.

Career planning is structured opportunities for individuals to work with their managers on career issues.

Summary

What is organizational culture?

- Organizational or corporate culture is the system of shared actions, values, and beliefs that develops within an organization and guides the behaviour of its members.

- Corporate culture can help an organization respond to both external adaptation and internal integration issues.

- Most organizations contain a variety of subcultures, and some organizations have countercultures that can cause potentially harmful conflicts.

- Organizational cultures may be analyzed in terms of observable actions, shared values, and common assumptions (truths that are taken for granted).

What aspects of organizational culture can be observed?

- Observable aspects of culture include the stories, rites, rituals, and symbols that are shared by organization members.

- Cultural rules and roles specify when various types of actions are appropriate and where individual members stand in the social system of the organization.

- Shared meanings and understandings help everyone know how to act and what to expect others to act like in various circumstances.

How do values and assumptions influence organizational culture?

- Common assumptions are the taken-for-granted truths that are shared by groups of corporate members.

- Some organizations express these truths in a management philosophy that links key goal-related issues to key collaboration issues to come up with general ways for the firm to manage its affairs.

How can the organizational culture be managed, nurtured, and guided?

- The management philosophy is supported by a series of corporate myths.

- Executives may manage many aspects of the observable culture directly. New goals or structures and systems can be instituted. Personnel may be moved around or new teams may be created to encourage different attitudes and capabilities. Processes can be used to change an organization's culture, but, as with any adaptation of a culture, management's decisions are limited because the changes need to be more evolutionary than revolutionary. Otherwise, employees may resist the changes. Details are discussed more in later chapters.

- Nurturing values that are shared by the members of the organization is a major challenge for executives.

- When actions are adjusted, they must respect common understandings, which limits what even the CEO can try to change.

How can the process of organizational development improve organizational culture?

- All managers may use organizational development (OD) techniques in their attempts to manage, nurture, and guide a change in culture.

- OD is a special application of knowledge that comes from behavioural science and its purpose is to create a comprehensive effort to improve organizational effectiveness.

- OD has outcome goals, which involve improved task accomplishments, and process goals, which involve improvements in the way organization members work together.

- With a strong commitment to collaborative efforts and human values, OD uses basic behavioural-science principles regarding individuals, groups, and organizations.
- Organizationwide interventions include survey feedback, confrontation meetings, structural redesign, and collateral organization.

- Group and intergroup interventions include team-building, process consultation, and intergroup team-building.
- Individual interventions include sensitivity training, role negotiation, job redesign, and career planning.

KEY TERMS

Action research (p. 266)

Career planning (p. 269)

Collateral organization (p. 268)

Confrontation meeting (p. 268)

Countercultures (p. 256)

Cultural symbol (p. 260)

External adaptation (p. 253)

Intergroup team-building (p. 269)

Internal integration (p. 255)

Job redesign (p. 269)

Management philosophy (p. 262)

Organizational development (OD) (p. 265)

Organizational development interventions (p. 268)

Organizational myth (p. 261)

Organizational or corporate culture (p. 253)

Process consultation (p. 269)

Rites (p. 260)

Rituals (p. 260)

Role negotiation (p. 269)

Sagas (p. 259)

Structural redesign (p. 268)

Subcultures (p. 256)

Survey feedback (p. 268)

Team-building (p. 268)

SELF-TEST 13

MULTIPLE CHOICE

1. Culture concerns all of the following except _____. (a) the concepts shared by all members of a firm (b) acquired capabilities (c) the personality of the leader (d) the beliefs of members (e) members' view of their collective personality

2. The three levels of cultural analysis that are highlighted in the text are _____. (a) observable culture, shared values, and common assumptions (b) stories, rites, and rituals (c) symbols, myths, and stories (d) manifest culture, latent culture, and observable artifacts (e) cultural symbols, myths, and sagas

3. External adaptation concerns _____. (a) the unproven beliefs of senior executives (b) the process of responding to outside forces (c) the vision of the founder (d) the processes working together (e) standard, recurring activities that are used at special times

4. Internal integration concerns _____. (a) the process of deciding the collective identity and how members will live together (b) the total daily life of members as they see and describe it (c) expressed, unproven beliefs that are accepted uncritically and used to justify current actions (d) groups of individuals with a pattern of values that rejects those of the larger society (e) the process of responding to outside forces

5. When Japanese workers start each day with the company song, this is an example of a(n) _____. (a) symbol (b) myth (c) underlying assumption (d) ritual (e) saga

6. _____ is a sense of broader purpose that workers put into their tasks as a result of interactions with each other. (a) A rite (b) A cultural symbol (c) A foundation myth (d) A shared meaning (e) An internal integration

7. The story of a corporate turnaround thanks to the efforts of a visionary manager is an example of a(n) _____. (a) saga (b) foundation myth (c) internal integration (d) latent cultural artifact (e) common assumption

8. OD is designed primarily to improve _____. (a) the overall effectiveness of an organization (b) intergroup relations (c) synergy (d) the planned-change process (e) group dynamics

9. The three stages in the OD process are _____. (a) data collection, intervention, and evaluation (b) diagnosis, intervention, and reinforcement (c) intervention, application, and innovation (d) diagnosis, intervention, and evaluation (e) planning, implementing, and evaluating

10. OD is planned change plus _____. (a) evaluation (b) intervention (c) the ability for self-renewal (d) any future changes that may occur (e) reinforcement

TRUE–FALSE

11. The system of shared beliefs and values that develops within an organization is called the organizational culture.   T   F

12. The belief that senior managers can manage all levels of the corporate culture is a myth.   T   F

13. External adaptation concerns such issues as the real mission of the firm, its goals, and how goals are reached.   T   F

14. Who gets rewards and sanctions is part of external adaptation.   T   F

15. Rites and rituals often develop from a subculture.   T   F

16. A ritual is a standardized activity used to manage anxiety.   T   F

17. Any object, art, or event that serves to transmit cultural meaning is called a rite.   T   F

18. The organizationwide OD interventions are survey feedback, confrontation meeting, structural redesign, management by objectives, and collateral organization.   T   F

19. The confrontation meeting is an OD intervention used to handle conflicts.   T   F

20. MBO is an organizationwide OD intervention.   T   F

SHORT ANSWER

21. Describe Taylor Cox's five steps for helping generate a multicultural organization or pluralistic company culture.

22. List the three aspects that help individuals and groups work together effectively and illustrate them with examples.

23. Give an example of how cultural rules and roles affect the atmosphere in a university or college classroom. Provide specific examples from your own perspective.

24. What are the major elements of a strong corporate culture?

APPLICATIONS ESSAY

25. Discuss the process of OD and write an overview of its diagnostic foundations in a small business such as ACE Bakery.

Leadership

Suncor and the Seven Principles of Leadership

In 1991 when Rick George joined Calgary-based Suncor Inc. as president and CEO, it was known to be a struggling company. Although it was best known for developing the extraction of tar-like crude from petroleum reserves in 1967, the company was not doing well in 1991 with employee morale at a similar level. But George rose to the challenge and today Suncor is one of Canada's leading companies. Part of Suncor's turnaround was due to George's policy of hiring some of the best and brightest—including those able to replace him. "It just makes more sense than having one brain at the top telling 3,000 people what to do," he says.

George decided to begin by attacking the low morale. He tried to restore confidence by assuring everyone that there was a directional path to follow, but not a detailed map. He encouraged senior managers to try to have some fun. He believed that it was impossible to "overcommunicate" with employees and that open leadership squelched the rumour mill fostered by office politics. He demanded a five-year environmental plan, as well as a clear vision for the future. And he consistently applied seven principles of leadership, encouraging his management team to also do so. The results spoke for themselves as the company began to revive and prosper. Today Suncor has nearly quadrupled its oil production and is leading a $50-billion project to turn the oil sands into North America's number one oil source. George's seven principles have a universal appeal and could be used in any business situation:

1. Earn the trust and the commitment of the people you lead. Listening to them will only enhance your own leadership abilities.

2. Set clear goals and communicate them well.

3. Keep your focus on the outside world—on your customers, on your markets, on your investors. It is one way to avoid bureaucracy.

4. Do the right things. Take no shortcuts, accept no simple compromises and easy answers—especially when it comes to your relationships with each other and the communities you operate in.

5. Communicate openly and honestly with your employees, your customers, your shareholders, and your communities.

6. Back up communication with responsible actions. Actions speak louder than words.

7. Look to the future.

George claims that putting these principles into practice can be the biggest challenge one can face in business and as a society. But if Suncor is an example, then the challenge is definitely worth the effort.

Leadership requires vision and the ability to make a difference. As you read Chapter 14, keep in mind these key questions:

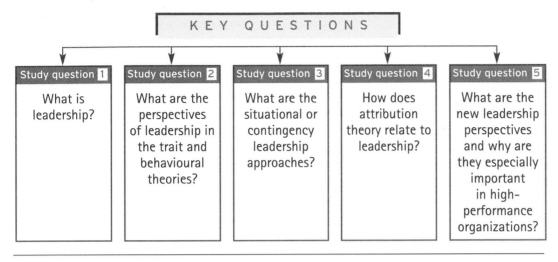

KEY QUESTIONS

Study question 1	Study question 2	Study question 3	Study question 4	Study question 5
What is leadership?	What are the perspectives of leadership in the trait and behavioural theories?	What are the situational or contingency leadership approaches?	How does attribution theory relate to leadership?	What are the new leadership perspectives and why are they especially important in high-performance organizations?

Leadership and Management

In the chapters in Part 1, we discussed managers and the functions, roles, activities, and skills of management. The question to ask now is how leaders and leadership are linked to all this.

The role of leadership is to promote adaptive and useful changes. We elect new prime ministers and premiers to be the leaders of our nation or provinces. Legal panels and task forces require effective leaders to achieve their goals. In every organization, whether religious, governmental, business, or volunteer, there are always leaders. We appear to need these leaders in every part of life and work and some of us are good at leading and others are not. Whatever our abilities, however, we must all consider the roles we are asked to perform. Most of us will, at some point in our careers, be asked to take on the role of manager. A manager's role, however, is to promote stability or to enable the organization to run smoothly, which is a slightly different but more supportive role than that of a leader.[1] Persons in managerial positions can be involved with both management and leadership activities, or they could emphasize one activity over the other. Both management and leadership are needed in organizations, however, and if managers choose not to be responsible for both, then they should ensure that someone else handles the other role.

For our purpose, we treat **leadership** as a special case of interpersonal influence that gets an individual or group to do what the leader or manager wants done. Broader ideas about influence are dealt with in Chapter 15. Leadership appears in two forms: (1) formal leadership, which is leadership by persons appointed or elected to positions of formal authority in organizations; and (2) informal leadership, which is leadership by persons who become influential because they have special skills that are needed by others. Although both types are important in organizations, this chapter will emphasize formal leadership.

Leadership is a special case of interpersonal influence that gets an individual or group to do what the leader wants done.

The leadership literature is vast—10,000 or so studies at least—and consists of many approaches.[2] We have grouped these into the following categories: trait and behavioural theory perspectives; situational or contingency perspectives; attributional leadership perspectives; and "new leadership" perspectives, which include charismatic approaches, transformational approaches, and the leadership of self-directing work teams. The new leadership theories are especially important for high-performance organizations. In each of these perspectives, there are several models. While each of these models may be useful to you in a particular work setting, we recommend that you mix and match them as necessary in your particular setting, just as we did earlier with the motivational models in Chapter 6. This is a trial-and-error process, but it is a good way to bring together the contributions from each model in a combination that responds to your needs as a manager.

Trait and Behavioural Theories Perspectives

TRAIT THEORIES

Trait perspectives assume that personality traits play a central role in differentiating leaders
from non-leaders (i.e., leaders must have the "right stuff")[3] or in predicting leader or organizational outcomes. The *great person-trait approach* assumes there is a difference in personality traits between leaders and non-leaders. It is the earliest approach used to study leadership, having been first used more than a century ago. What traits differentiated "great persons" from the masses? For example, how did Catherine the Great differ from her subjects?[4] Later studies that used this approach examined differences between leaders and non-leaders as well as trait predictions of outcomes. For various reasons, including inadequate theorizing and trait measurement, the studies were not successful enough to provide consistent findings.

More recent work has produced more promising results. Several traits that help identify important leadership strengths have been identified (see Figure 14.1). Most of these traits also tend to predict leadership outcomes.[5]

Figure 14.1 Traits with positive implications for successful leadership

> **Energy and adjustment or stress tolerance:** Physical vitality and emotional resilience.
>
> **Prosocial power motivation:** A high need for power exercised primarily for the benefit of others.
>
> **Achievement orientation:** Need for achievement, desire to excel, drive to success, willingness to assume responsibility, concern for task objectives.
>
> **Emotional maturity:** Well adjusted, does not suffer from severe psychological disorders.
>
> **Self-confidence:** General confidence in self and in the ability to perform the job of a leader.
>
> **Integrity:** Behaviour consistent with espoused values; honest, ethical, trustworthy.
>
> **Perseverance or tenacity:** Ability to overcome obstacles; strength of will.
>
> **Cognitive ability, intelligence, social intelligence:** Ability to gather, integrate, and interpret information; intelligence; understanding of social setting.
>
> **Task-relevant knowledge:** Knowlege about the company, industry, and technical aspects.
>
> **Flexibility:** Ability to respond appropriately to changes in the setting.

Trait perspectives assume that personality traits play a central role in differentiating leaders from non-leaders or in predicting leader or organizational outcomes.

Leaders tend to be energetic and to operate from a balanced perspective. They crave power not as an end in itself but as a way of achieving a vision or desired goals. Leaders are also very ambitious and have a high need for achievement. At the same time, they have to be emotionally mature enough to recognize their own strengths and weaknesses, and they are oriented toward self-improvement. Furthermore, to be trusted they must have integrity; without trust, they cannot hope to keep the loyalty of their followers. Leaders must also not be easily discouraged. They need to stick to a chosen course of action and to push toward goal accomplishment. At the same time, they must be cognitively sharp enough to deal well with the large amount of information they receive. However, they do not need to be brilliant; they just need to show above-average intelligence. In addition, leaders must have a good understanding of their social setting. Finally, they must possess lots of specific knowledge about their industry, firm, and job.

BEHAVIOURAL THEORIES

Like the trait perspectives covered above, the behavioural perspective assumes that leadership has a big impact on performance and other outcomes. In this case, however, instead of examining personality traits, behaviours are considered. Two classic research programs—one at the University of Michigan and the other at Ohio State University—provide useful insights into leadership behaviours.

The behavioural perspective assumes that leadership is central to performance and other outcomes.

Michigan Studies In the late 1940s, researchers at the University of Michigan started a research program on leadership behaviour. They wanted to identify the leadership pattern that results in effective performance. From interviews of high- and low-performing groups in different organizations, the researchers concluded that there were two basic forms of leader behaviours: employee centred and production centred. Employee-centred supervisors place strong emphasis on their subordinates' welfare. In contrast, production-centred supervisors are more concerned about getting the work done. In general, employee-centred supervisors were found to have more productive workgroups than did the production-centred supervisors.[6]

These behaviours may be viewed on a continuum, with employee-centred supervisors at one end and production-centred supervisors at the other. Sometimes, the more general terms "human-relations oriented" and "task-oriented" are used to describe these two leader behaviours.

Ohio State Studies At about the same time as the Michigan studies, an important leadership research program was started at Ohio State University. A questionnaire was used in both industrial and military settings to measure subordinates' perceptions of their superiors' leadership behaviour. The researchers identified two dimensions that are similar to the ones found in the Michigan studies: consideration and initiating structure.[7] A highly considerate leader is sensitive to people's feelings and, much like the employee-centred leader, tries to make things pleasant for his or her followers. In contrast, a leader who is high in initiating structure is more concerned about defining task requirements and other aspects of the work agenda; he or she might be seen as similar to a production-centred supervisor. These dimensions are related to what people sometimes call socio-emotional and task leadership tendencies, respectively.

At first, the Ohio State researchers believed that a leader who is high in consideration, or socio-emotional warmth, would have more highly satisfied or better performing subordinates. Later results indicated that leaders should be high in both consideration and initiating structure behaviours, however. This dual emphasis appears in the leadership grid approach.

Consideration is the dimension of leadership which focuses on being sensitive to people's feelings and trying to make things pleasant for the followers.

Initiating structure is the dimension of leadership which focuses on defining the task requirements and clarifying other aspects of the work agenda.

The Leadership Grid Robert Blake and Jane Mouton developed the leadership grid approach based on the Ohio State dimensions. Results are plotted on a nine-position grid that places concern for production on the horizontal axis and concern for people on the vertical axis, where 1 is minimum concern and 9 is maximum concern. As an example, those with a 1/9 concern for production/concern for people are termed "country club management." They do not emphasize task accomplishment but do stress the attitudes, feelings, and social needs of people. Similarly, leaders with a 1/1, style, low concern for both production and people, are termed "impoverished," while a 5/5 style is labelled "middle of the road." A 9/1 leader, high on task and low on people, has a "task management" style. Finally, a 9/9 leader, high on both dimensions, is considered to have a "team management" style, ideal in Blake and Mouton's framework.

Cross-Cultural Implications   It is important to consider how the kinds of behavioural dimensions discussed above work in other countries. Studies done in the United States, Britain, Hong Kong, and Japan show that the behaviours must be expressed in different ways in different cultures. For instance, British leaders are seen as considerate if they show subordinates how to use equipment, whereas in Japan the highly considerate leader helps subordinates with personal problems.[8]

Situational Contingency Theories

The trait and behavioural perspectives assume that leadership, by itself, has a strong impact on outcomes. Another development in leadership thinking recognized, however, that outcomes are more accurately predicted when leader traits and behaviours are considered in relation to *situational contingencies*—other important aspects of the leadership situation.

House and Aditya argue that the effects of traits are greater if they are relevant to the leader's situational contingencies.[9] For example, achievement motivation should be more effective in situations where there are challenging tasks that require initiative and taking personal responsibility for success. Leader flexibility should have more impact on the outcome when the environment is unstable or when leaders lead different people over time. Prosocial power motivation is likely to have more impact in complex organizations where getting people to implement a decision requires lots of persuasion and social influence. "Strong" or "weak" situations also make a difference. An example of a strong situation is a highly formal organization with lots of rules, procedures, and so on. Here, traits will have less impact than in a weaker, more unstructured situation (e.g., "I can't show my dynamism as much when the organization restricts me"). Traits sometimes have a direct relationship to outcomes or to leaders versus non-leaders. They may also make themselves felt by influencing leader behaviours (e.g., when a leader who is high in energy shows directive, take-charge behaviours).[10]

FIEDLER'S LEADERSHIP CONTINGENCY THEORY

Fred Fiedler's work began the situational contingency era in the mid-1960s.[11] His theory is that for a group to be effective there has to be a match between the leader's style (essentially a trait measure) and the demands of the situation. Specifically, Fiedler considers **situational control**—how much a leader can determine what his or her group is going to do and what the outcomes of the group's actions and decisions are going to be.

**Energy Savings
Income Fund**

www.energysavingsincome-fund.ca

In 2001, Rebecca MacDonald took the firm she founded in 1997 public. Only two years later, she had quadrupled her customer base and was generating revenue of over $500 million a year, compared to $2 million in 1998. These achievements are based on training and encouraging her door-to-door salespeople to help and educate their potential customers about the value of long-term energy contract purchases. Integrity and the daily training of her first "customer," the salespeople working for her, are critical for this CEO.

Situational control is how much a leader can determine what his or her group is going to do and what the outcomes of the group's actions and decisions are going to be.

Fiedler uses an instrument called the **least preferred co-worker (LPC) scale** to measure a person's leadership style. Respondents are asked to describe the person whom they have the most trouble working with—their least preferred co-worker, or LPC—using a series of adjectives such as the following two:

Unfriendly $\frac{\quad}{1}$ $\frac{\quad}{2}$ $\frac{\quad}{3}$ $\frac{\quad}{4}$ $\frac{\quad}{5}$ $\frac{\quad}{6}$ $\frac{\quad}{7}$ $\frac{\quad}{8}$ Friendly

Pleasant $\frac{\quad}{1}$ $\frac{\quad}{2}$ $\frac{\quad}{3}$ $\frac{\quad}{4}$ $\frac{\quad}{5}$ $\frac{\quad}{6}$ $\frac{\quad}{7}$ $\frac{\quad}{8}$ Unpleasant

Fiedler argues that high-LPC leaders (leaders who describe their LPC very positively) have a relationship-motivated style, whereas low-LPC leaders have a task-motivated style. He considers this relationship or task motivation to be a trait that leads to either directive or nondirective behaviour, depending on the amount of situational control that the leader has. A task-motivated leader tends to be non-directive in high- and low-control situations and directive in situations that are in between. A relationship-motivated leader tends to be the opposite.

Figure 14.2 shows the task-motivated leader as having a more effective group in situations of high or low control. The relationship-motivated leader is shown as having a more effective group in in-between situations. The figure also shows that to measure how much control there is in the situation, Fiedler arranges the following three variables in the different combinations used in the figure:

- *leader–member relations* (good/poor)—membership support for the leader
- *task structure* (high/low)—clearly stating the leader's task goals, procedures, and guidelines in the group
- *position power* (strong/weak)—the leader's task expertise and reward or punishment authority

Consider an experienced and well-trained supervisor of a group that manufactures a part for personal computers. The leader is highly supported by his group members and can give raises and make hiring and firing decisions. This supervisor has very high situational control and is operating in situation I in Figure 14.2. Leaders operating in situations II and III would have high situational control, but less than our production supervisor has. For these latter two high-control situations, a task-motivated leader who gives directives would have the most effective group.

The least preferred co-worker (LPC) scale measures a person's leadership style based on a description of the person whom respondents have the most trouble working with.

Fiedler's three situational control variables

Figure 14.2 Summary of Fiedler's situational variables and preferred leadership styles

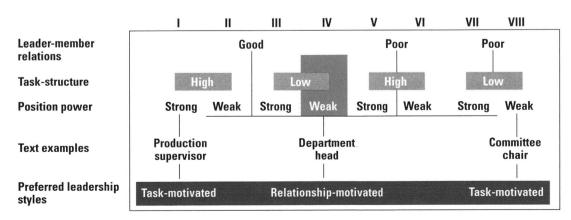

Now consider the chair of a student council committee of volunteers (the chair's position power is weak) who are unhappy about this person being the chair and who have the low-structured task of organizing a Parents' Day program to improve relations between the university and parents. This is low-control situation VIII. For this situation, it is essential to have a task-motivated leader who gives directives that keep the group together and focused on the ambiguous task. Finally, consider a well-liked academic department chair with tenured faculty. This is a cell IV moderate-control situation with good leader-member relations, low task structure, and weak position power. This is the right context for a relationship-motivated leader. The leader should emphasize non-directive and considerate relationships with the faculty.

Fiedler's Cognitive Resource Theory   Fiedler recently moved beyond his contingency theory by developing the cognitive resource theory.[12] Cognitive resources are abilities or competencies. According to this approach, whether or not a leader should give directives depends on the following situational contingencies: (1) the ability or competency of the leader or subordinate group members, (2) the amount of stress, (3) the amount of experience, and (4) group support of the leader. Basically, cognitive resource theory is useful because it directs us to the ability of the leader or subordinate group members, an aspect that is not usually considered in other leadership approaches.

The theory views directiveness (i.e., giving many specific instructions) as most helpful for performance when the leader is competent, relaxed, and supported. In this case, the group is ready, and directiveness is the clearest means of communication. When the leader feels stressed, he or she is diverted. In this case, experience is more important than ability. If support is low, then the group is less receptive, and the leader has less impact. The ability of group members becomes most important when the leader is non-directive and has strong support from the group. If support is weak, then the difficulty of the task or other factors will have more impact than the leader or subordinates will.

Evaluation and Application   Fiedler's contingency approach began in the 1960s and reactions to it have been positive and negative. The biggest controversy concerns exactly what Fiedler's LPC instrument measures. Some critics question Fiedler's behavioural interpretation, in which the specific behaviours of high- and low-LPC leaders change depending on the amount of situational control. Furthermore, the approach makes the most accurate predictions in situations I and VIII, and IV and V; results are less consistent in the other situations.[13] Tests of cognitive resource theory have shown mixed results.[14]

In leader match training, leaders are trained to diagnose the situation to match their high and low LPC scores with situational control.

To help organizations use the theory, Fiedler has developed **leader match training**, which Sears and other organizations have used. In this program, leaders are trained to diagnose the situation to match their high and low LPC scores with situational control—measured by leader–member relations, task structure, and leader position power—following the general ideas shown in Figure 14.2. If there is no match, the training teaches how each of these situational control variables can be changed to obtain a match. Another way of getting a match is through leader selection or placement based on LPC scores.[15] For example, a high-LPC leader would be selected for a position with high situational control, as in our earlier example of the manufacturing supervisor. Studies have been designed to test leader match, just as Fiedler's contingency theory has been studied. Although the results are not always supportive, more than a dozen of these studies have found increases in group effectiveness after the training.[16]

We conclude that although there are still unanswered questions about Fiedler's contingency theory, especially concerning the meaning of LPC, the theory and the leader match program have fairly strong support.[17] The approach and training program are also especially useful in encouraging managers to think about the contingencies of a situation.

HOUSE'S PATH-GOAL THEORY OF LEADERSHIP

Another well-known approach to situational contingencies is the one developed by Robert House based on earlier work of others.[18] This theory is based in part on the expectancy model of motivation discussed in Chapter 6. The term **path–goal** is used because of its emphasis on how a leader influences subordinates' perceptions of, first, work goals and personal goals and, second, the links or paths found between these two sets of goals.

The theory assumes that a leader's key function is to adjust his or her behaviours by providing what is missing in situational contingencies, such as those in the work setting. House argues that when the leader is able to compensate for things that are missing in the setting, subordinates are likely to be satisfied with the leader. For example, the leader could help remove job ambiguity or show how good performance could lead to more pay. Performance should improve as the paths by which (1) effort leads to performance—expectancy—and (2) performance leads to valued rewards—instrumentality—become clarified.

House's path–goal theory of leadership assumes that a leader's key function is to adjust his or her behaviours by providing what is missing in situational contingencies.

Figure 14.3 Summary of major path–goal relationships in House's leadership approach

LEADERSHIP FACTORS	CONTINGENCY FACTORS	CONTINGENCY FACTORS
Leadership Behaviours: Directive Supportive Achievement oriented Participative	Subordinate Attributes: Authoritarianism Internal–external orientation Ability Work-Setting Attributes: Task Formal authority system Primary workshop	Job Satisfaction: Job leads to valued rewards Acceptance of leader: Leader leads to valued rewards Motivational Behaviour: Expectancy that effort leads to performance Instrumentality that such performance is the path to valued rewards

House's approach is summarized in Figure 14.3. The figure shows four types of leader behaviours—directive, supportive, achievement oriented, and participative—and two categories of situational contingency variables—subordinate attributes and work-setting attributes. The leader behaviours are adjusted to complement the situational contingency variables in order to influence subordinate satisfaction, acceptance of the leader, and motivation for task performance.

Directive leadership involves clearly stating what subordinates' tasks are and how the tasks should be done; it is a lot like the initiating structure dimension mentioned earlier. **Supportive leadership** focuses on subordinates' needs and well-being and on developing a friendly work climate; it is similar to consideration. **Achievement-oriented leadership** emphasizes creating challenging goals, stressing excellence in performance, and showing confidence in people's ability to achieve high standards of performance. **Participative leadership** focuses on consulting subordinates and getting and considering their suggestions before making decisions.

Directive leadership clearly states what subordinates' tasks are and how the tasks should be done.

Supportive leadership focuses on subordinates' needs and well-being, and on developing a friendly work climate.

Achievement-oriented leadership emphasizes creating challenging goals, stressing excellence in performance, and showing confidence in people's ability to achieve high standards of performance.

Participative leadership focuses on consulting subordinates and getting and considering their suggestions before making decisions.

Important subordinate characteristics are *authoritarianism* (closed-mindedness, rigidity), *internal-external orientation* (i.e., locus of control), and ability. The key work-setting factors are the nature of the subordinates' tasks (task structure), the *formal authority system*, and the *primary workgroup*.

Predictions from Path–Goal Theory   Directive leadership is predicted to have a positive impact on subordinates when the task is ambiguous; it is predicted to have just the opposite effect for clear tasks. In addition, the theory predicts that when ambiguous tasks are being performed by highly authoritarian and closed-minded subordinates, even more directive leadership is needed.

Supportive leadership is predicted to increase the satisfaction of subordinates who work on highly repetitive tasks or on tasks considered to be unpleasant, stressful, or frustrating; the leader's supportive behaviour helps compensate for these adverse conditions. For example, many people would consider traditional assembly-line auto worker jobs to be highly repetitive, perhaps even unpleasant and frustrating. A supportive supervisor could help make these jobs more pleasant.

Achievement-oriented leadership is predicted to encourage subordinates to try to have higher performance standards and to have more confidence in their ability to meet challenging goals. For subordinates in ambiguous, non-repetitive jobs, achievement-oriented leadership should increase their expectation that effort leads to desired performance.

Participative leadership is predicted to promote satisfaction on non-repetitive tasks that allow for the ego involvement of subordinates (i.e., that allow workers to get involved in how things are done). For example, on a challenging research project, participation allows employees to feel good about dealing with the challenge of the project on their own. On repetitive tasks, open-minded or non-authoritarian subordinates will also be satisfied with a participative leader. On a task where employees screw nuts on bolts hour after hour, for example, employees who are non-authoritarian will appreciate having a leader who allows them to get involved in ways that may help break the monotony.

Evaluation and Application   House's path–goal approach has now been around for 30 years or so. Early work provided some support for the theory in general and for the particular predictions discussed earlier.[19] However, current assessments by well-known scholars have pointed out that many aspects have not been tested adequately, and there is very little recent research on the theory.[20] House himself recently revised and extended path–goal theory into the Theory of Work Unit Leadership. It is beyond this text to discuss the details of this new theory, but the new theory basically expands the list of leader behaviours used in path–goal theory by including aspects of both traditional and new leadership.[21] It remains to be seen how much research it will generate.

Regarding how to use the theory in organizations, there is enough support for original path–goal theory to suggest two possibilities. First, training could be used to change leadership behaviour to fit the situational contingencies. Second, the leader could be taught to diagnose the situation and to learn how to try to change the contingencies, as in leader match.

Hersey and Blanchard's Situational Leadership Model   Like other situational contingency approaches, the situational leadership model developed by Paul Hersey and Kenneth Blanchard claims that there is no single best way to lead.[22] Hersey and Blanchard focus in particular on the situational contingency of followers' maturity or "readiness." Readiness is how able and willing people are to accomplish a specific task. Hersey and Blanchard argue that "situational" leadership require leaders to adjust their emphasis on task behaviours (for example, by giving guidance and direction) and relationship behaviours (for example, by providing socio-emotional

Figure 14.4 Hersey and Blanchard model of situational leadership

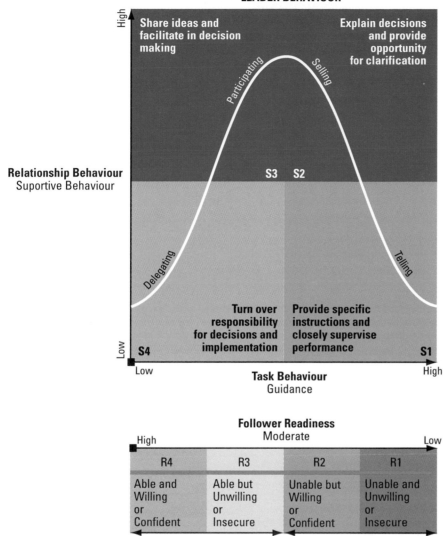

support) according to the readiness of followers to perform their tasks. Figure 14.4 identifies four leadership styles: delegating, participating, selling, and telling. (Note that the four types of leaders in House's path–goal theory are quite similar to the Hersey-Blanchard model's leadership styles.) Each leadership style emphasizes a different combination of task and relationship behaviours by the leader. The figure also suggests the following situational matches as the best choice of leadership style for followers who are at four different readiness levels:

- A *"telling" style (S1) is best for low follower readiness* (R1). The direction provided by this style defines roles for people who are unable and unwilling to take responsibility themselves; it eliminates any insecurity about the task that must be done.

- A *"selling" style (S2) is best for low to moderate follower readiness* (R2). This style offers both task direction and support for people who are unable but willing to take task responsibility; it involves combining a directive approach with explanation and reinforcement in order to maintain enthusiasm.

- A *"participating" style (S3) is best for moderate to high follower readiness* (R3). Able but unwilling followers require supportive behaviour in order to increase their motivation; by allowing followers to share in decision-making, this style helps increase the desire to perform a task.

- A *"delegating" style (S4) is best for high readiness* (R4). This style offers little direction and support for the task at hand; it allows able and willing followers to take responsibility for what needs to be done.

This situational leadership approach requires the leader to develop the ability to diagnose the demands of situations and then to choose and use the appropriate leadership response. The model gives specific attention to followers and their feelings about the task at hand and suggests that an effective leader focus especially on signs that the level of readiness of the people involved in the work may be changing.

Although it has an important history and has been used in training programs by many firms, the situational leadership approach has only recently begun to receive systematic research attention.[23]

SUBSTITUTES FOR LEADERSHIP

In contrast to the traditional leadership approaches discussed above, in the substitutes for leadership theory, it is argued that hierarchical leadership sometimes makes no real difference. John Jermier and others believe that certain individual, job, and organizational variables can either be substitutes for leadership or neutralize or cancel a leader's impact on subordinates.[24] Some examples of these variables are shown in Figure 14.5.

Figure 14.5 Examples of leadership substitutes and neutralizers

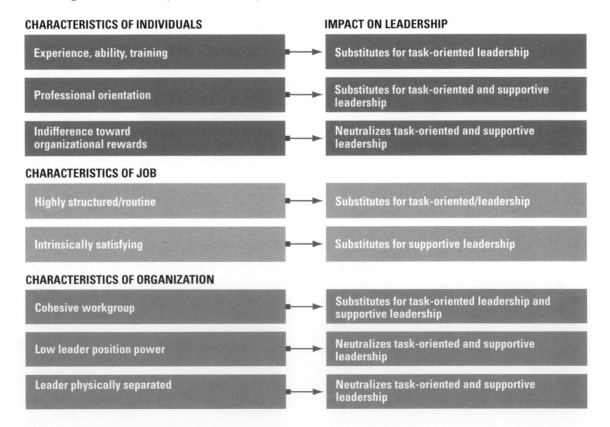

CHARACTERISTICS OF INDIVIDUALS — **IMPACT ON LEADERSHIP**

Characteristics of Individuals	Impact on Leadership
Experience, ability, training	Substitutes for task-oriented leadership
Professional orientation	Substitutes for task-oriented and supportive leadership
Indifference toward organizational rewards	Neutralizes task-oriented and supportive leadership

CHARACTERISTICS OF JOB

Characteristics of Job	Impact on Leadership
Highly structured/routine	Substitutes for task-oriented/leadership
Intrinsically satisfying	Substitutes for supportive leadership

CHARACTERISTICS OF ORGANIZATION

Characteristics of Organization	Impact on Leadership
Cohesive workgroup	Substitutes for task-oriented leadership and supportive leadership
Low leader position power	Neutralizes task-oriented and supportive leadership
Leader physically separated	Neutralizes task-oriented and supportive leadership

Substitutes for leadership make a leader's influence either unnecessary or redundant since they replace a leader's influence. For example, in Figure 14.5, it will be unnecessary and perhaps not even possible for a leader to provide the kind of task-oriented direction already available from an experienced, talented, and well-trained subordinate. In contrast, neutralizers prevent a leader from behaving in a certain way or cancel the effects of a leader's actions. If a leader has little formal authority or is physically separated from subordinates, for example, his or her leadership may have no impact even though support for the task may still be needed.

Some of the research comparing Mexican and U.S. workers, as well as workers in Japan, suggests there are similarities and differences between the various leadership substitutes in these countries. More generally, a review of 17 studies in the U.S. and other countries found mixed results for the substitutes theory. Among other things, the authors argued that the kinds of characteristics and leader behaviours should be broadened and that the approach appeared to be especially important for high-performance work teams.[25] For these teams, for example, instead of having a hierarchical leader who specifies the standards and ways of achieving goals (task-oriented behaviours), the team might set its own standards and substitute those for the leader's.

Substitutes for leadership make a leader's influence either unnecessary or redundant since they replace a leader's influence.

Attribution Theory and Leadership

The traditional leadership theories discussed so far have all assumed that leadership and the real effects it has can be identified and measured objectively. This is not always the case, however. Attribution theory addresses this very point—that is, it looks at the issue of trying to understand causes, to assess responsibilities, and to evaluate personal qualities, and sees each of these as having an impact on certain events. Attribution theory is particularly important in understanding leadership.

To begin, think about a workgroup or student group that you see as performing really well. Now assume that you are asked to describe the leader on one of the leadership scales discussed earlier in the chapter. If you are like many others, the group's high performance will probably encourage you to describe the leader favourably; in other words, you will attribute good things to the leader based on the group's performance. Similarly, leaders themselves make attributions about the performance of their subordinates and react differently depending on those attributions. For example, if leaders attribute an employee's poor performance to lack of effort, they may issue a reprimand, whereas if they attribute the poor performance to an external factor, such as work overload, they will probably try to fix the problem. A great deal of evidence supports these attributional views of subordinates and leaders.[26]

LEADERSHIP PROTOTYPES

There is also evidence that people have a mental picture of what makes a "good leader" or ways in which "real leaders" would act in a given situation. The image that people have in their minds of what a model leader should look like is sometimes called a **leadership prototype**.[27] These theories in people's minds about leaders or prototypes of them are usually a mix of specific and more general characteristics. For example, a prototype of a bank president would differ in many ways from that of a high-ranking military officer. However, there would probably also be some core characteristics that reflect leaders in our society in general—for example, integrity and self-efficacy.

We also would expect differences in prototypes by country and by national culture.[28] To examine differences between countries, a study asked people from eight different nations to describe

A **leadership prototype** is an image that people have in their minds about what a model leader should look like.

how well several leadership attributes previously identified described their image of a business leader. In each country, five attributes were identified as most prototypical of such a leader. Note the differences in the prototype of the typical business leader between the U.S. and Japan:

U.S.: determined, goal-oriented, verbally skilled, industrious, persistent

Japan: responsible, educated, trustworthy, intelligent, disciplined

Similar differences exist in other countries, although there are also similarities.

The closer the behaviour of a leader is to the implicit theories of his or her followers, the better the leader's relations with them tend to be. Outcomes also improve accordingly.[29] Both of the attributional prototypes above emphasize leadership as something that is largely symbolic or dependent on what someone sees. Another study determined that the management styles of the U.S. and Germany are very similar but that in the former USSR the power distance measure, the level of perceived masculinity, and a longer time horizon were seen as more typical qualities of managers than in the West. This general notion has also appeared in related directions of research. Ironically, the first of these directions argues that leadership makes little or no real difference in organizational effectiveness. The second tends to attribute greatly exaggerated importance to leadership and ultimately leads us into charisma and other aspects of the new leadership.

EXAGGERATION OF THE LEADERSHIP DIFFERENCE

Jeffrey Pfeffer has looked at what happens when leaders at the top of an organization are changed. Pfeffer is among those who claim that even CEOs of large corporations have little impact as leaders on their firms' profits and effectiveness compared to environmental and industry forces, such as cutbacks in government budgets. Furthermore, these leaders are typically accountable to so many groups of people for the resources they use that their leadership impact is greatly limited. Pfeffer argues that, because of these forces and limits, much of the impact that a top leader does have is symbolic; in other words, Pfeffer believes that leaders and others develop explanations based on leadership to justify the actions they take.[30]

The symbolic treatment of leadership occurs particularly when performance is either extremely high or extremely low or when the situation is such that many people could have been responsible for the performance. James Meindl and his colleagues call this phenomenon the **romance of leadership**. This refers to when people attribute romantic, almost magical qualities to leadership.[31] Consider the firing of a baseball manager or hockey coach whose team is not performing well. Neither the owner nor anyone else is really sure why performance is poor. But the owner cannot fire all the players, so a new coach is brought in to symbolize "a change in leadership" that is "sure to turn the team around."

> The romance of leadership view attributes romantic, almost magical qualities to leadership.

From Traditional to New Leadership Perspectives

The focus on leadership attributions and symbolic aspects moves us away from traditional leadership and into new leadership. **New leadership** emphasizes charismatic and transformational leadership approaches and various related aspects. We also extend the term to include the leadership of self-directing work teams. New leadership is considered especially important for changing and transforming individuals and organizations that have a commitment to high performance.[32]

> New leadership emphasizes charismatic and transformational leadership approaches and various related aspects of vision; it also includes self-directing work teams.

CHARISMATIC APPROACHES

Robert House and his associates have done a lot of work recently that is based on an earlier theory of charisma that House developed. (Do not confuse this with House's path–goal theory or its extension, discussed earlier in the chapter.)[33] Of special interest is the fact that House's theory uses both trait and behaviour combinations.

House's **charismatic leaders** are leaders who, because of their personal abilities, can have a profound and extraordinary effect on followers. These leaders are high in need for power and have high feelings of self-efficacy and conviction in the moral rightness of their beliefs. That is, the need for power motivates these people to want to be leaders. This need is then reinforced by their conviction of the moral rightness of their beliefs. The feeling of self-efficacy, in turn, makes these people feel that they are capable of being leaders. These traits then influence such charismatic behaviours as role modelling, image building, articulating goals (focusing on simple and dramatic goals), emphasizing high expectations, showing confidence, and arousing motivation in followers.

Charismatic leaders are leaders who, because of their personal abilities, can have a profound and extraordinary effect on followers.

ENTREPRENEURSHIP

Recently, Bryan Payne, managing partner for Spacial Audio Solutions LLC, and his South African partner, Louis Louw, signed a Webcasting performance licence with the Recording Industry Association of America. They have developed a piece of software that helps the recording industry monitor Webcasters who use music. There is concern in the recording industry that MP3, a technology that allows people to download music from their computers, will cause the industry to eventually lose control of the music it produces. The software monitors such actions and helps assure accountability to the recording industry. It documents everything from audience listening habits to play lists. The two partners are highly entrepreneurial and are now implementing their entrepreneurial vision. Next up is implementation of a plan to establish the firm's own music store, supported by the recording industry. Moving the firm ahead will require a broad range of leadership behaviours.

Some of the more interesting and important work that is based on aspects of House's theory of charisma involves a study of U.S. presidents.[34] The research showed that behavioural charisma was substantially related to presidential performance and that the kind of personality traits in House's theory, along with responses to a crisis, among other things, predicted the behavioural charisma for each president in the sample. Related studies of presidents also show that voters who saw Bill Clinton as charismatic followed through by voting for him.[35] This characteristic is not as true for Canada, as we do not directly elect our prime ministers or premiers. While presidents and kings and queens are heads of state, prime ministers and premiers are heads of governments. Still, the role of the leader of a political party can be pivotal in a parliamentary system like Canada's and that of the UK.

House and his colleagues summarize other work that partially supports their theory of charisma. Some of the more interesting related work has shown that negative, or "dark-side," charismatic leaders emphasize personalized power-focus on themselves—whereas positive, or "bright-side," charismatic leaders emphasize socialized power that tends to empower their followers. This helps explain differences between such dark-side leaders as Adolf Hitler and David Koresh, and bright-side leaders Martin Luther King, Jr., Nelson Mandela, and Mahatma Gandhi.[36]

Jay Conger and Rabindra Kanungo have developed a three-stage charismatic leadership model.[37] In the initial stage, the leader critically evaluates the status quo (the current situation). Deficiencies in the status quo lead to decisions about future goals. Before developing these goals, the leader assesses available resources and limits that stand in the way of the goals. The leader also assesses follower abilities, needs, and satisfaction levels. In the second stage, the leader decides and states the goals along with an idealized future vision. Here the leader emphasizes communication and impression management skills. Then in the third stage, the leader shows how these goals and the vision can be achieved. The leader emphasizes innovative and unusual ways of achieving the vision. Mahatma Gandhi illustrated these three stages in his non-violent independence movement and human rights approach, an approach that changed the methods that people resisting more powerful forces can use. Martin Luther King Jr. successfully transferred Gandhi's methods and applied the three stages to the civil rights movement in the U.S., with the result that he advanced human rights movements around the world. Nelson Mandela continued their efforts by turning away from destructive postures to expressing a vision of a South Africa that included all people and offered opportunity for all South Africans, regardless of their race.

Conger and Kanungo have argued that if leaders use behaviours such as vision articulation (stating one's vision), environmental sensitivity, and unconventional behaviour, rather than maintaining the status quo, followers will attribute charismatic leadership to them. Such leaders are also seen as behaving quite differently than leaders who are labelled "non-charismatic."[38]

Figure 14.6 Descriptions of the characteristics of distant and close-up charismatics

Distant Charismatics Should Demonstrate

- Persistence
- Rhetorical skills
- Courage
- Emphasizing social courage (expressing opinion, not conforming to pressure)
- Ideological orientation

Close-up Charismatics Should Demonstrate

- Sociability
- Expertise
- Humour
- Dynamism, activity
- Physical appearance
- Intelligence
- Setting high standards
- Originality

Both Distant and Close-up Charismatics Should Demonstrate

- Self-confidence
- Honesty
- Authoritativeness
- Sacrifice

Finally, an especially important question about charismatic leadership is whether it is described in the same way for close-up and at-a-distance leaders. Close-up leaders are those who followers have close contact with; at-a-distance leaders are those who followers have little contact with. Boas Shamir recently examined this issue in Israel.[39] He found that descriptions of distant charismatics, for instance, former Israeli prime minister Golda Meir, and close-up charismatics, for instance, a specific teacher, were generally more different than they were similar. Figure 14.6 shows the high points of his findings. Clearly, leaders who followers have close contact with and those they seldom, if ever, have direct contact with are both described as charismatic but possess quite different traits and behaviours.

TRANSFORMATIONAL VERSUS TRANSACTIONAL APPROACHES

Building on notions originally expressed by James MacGregor Burns, as well as ideas from House's work, Bernard Bass has developed an approach that focuses on both transformational and transactional leadership.[40]

Transactional leadership involves leader–follower exchanges that are necessary for achieving routine performance that leaders and followers agree about. These exchanges involve four dimensions, as shown in The Effective Manager 14.1.

Transformational leadership goes beyond this routine accomplishment, however. For Bass, transformational leadership occurs when leaders broaden and elevate their followers' interests, when they generate awareness and acceptance of the group's purposes and mission, and when they get their followers to look beyond their own self-interests for the good of others.

Dimensions of Transformational Leadership Transformational leadership has four dimensions: charisma, inspiration, intellectual stimulation, and individualized consideration. *Charisma* provides vision and a sense of mission, and it instils pride, along with respect and trust from followers. For example, Steve Jobs, the founder of Apple Computer, showed charisma by emphasizing the importance of creating the Macintosh as a radical new computer. Inspiration communicates high expectations, uses symbols to focus efforts, and expresses important purposes in simple ways. In the movie *Apollo 13*, Tom Hank's portrayal of the astronaut James Lovell's calmness under pressure, while leading pilot John Swigert and module driver Fred Haise through the tense Apollo 13 lunar mission crisis, is another example. *Intellectual stimulation* promotes intelligence, rationality, and careful problem-solving. An example of this would be if your boss encourages you to look at a very difficult problem in a new way. Individualized consideration *involves personal attention, treating each employee* individually, and coaching and advising. An example of individualized consideration would be when your boss drops by and makes remarks that strengthen your feeling of worth as a person.

Bass concludes that transformational leadership is likely to be strongest at the top-management level, where there is the greatest opportunity for proposing and communicating a vision. However, it is not *restricted* to the top level; it is found throughout the organization. Furthermore, transformational leadership operates *in combination with* transactional leadership. Transactional leadership is similar to most of the traditional leadership approaches mentioned earlier. Leaders need both transformational and transactional leadership skills in order to be successful, just as they need both leadership and management.[41]

> Transactional leadership involves leader–follower exchanges that are necessary for achieving routine performance that leaders and followers agree about.

> Transformational leadership occurs when leaders broaden and elevate followers' interests and get followers to look beyond their own interests for the good of others.

The Effective Manager 14.1

FOUR DIMENSIONS OF TRANSACTIONAL LEADERSHIP

- contingent rewards: giving various kinds of rewards in exchange for accomplishing goals the leader and subordinates agree upon
- active management by exception: watching for deviations from rules and standards and taking corrective action
- passive management by exception: intervening only if standards are not respected
- laissez-faire: neglecting responsibilities and avoiding decisions

---

TECHNOLOGY

Helen McDonald is the Government of Canada's Acting Chief Information Officer (CIO). McDonald guides the use of information and communications technology in the federal government, promoting a whole-of-government approach. She is responsible for policies and strategic directions in the areas of privacy, security, access and information management as well as articulating a Government of Canada service delivery vision and identifying changes that can improve service quality and cost-effectiveness. McDonald is well aware that the decisions made by managers affect the employees and their performance every day. On a daily basis, she uses her managerial skills, takes risks, motivates, communicates, and establishes guidelines to keep projects on track and to promote quality performance.

Evaluation and Application   Reviews have summarized a large number of studies of Bass's approach. These reviews report significant, favourable relationships between Bass's leadership dimensions and various aspects of performance and satisfaction. The reviews also find a favourable relationship with regard to extra effort, burnout and stress, and predispositions for followers to act as champions of innovation. The strongest relationships tend to be associated with charisma or inspirational leadership, although, in most cases, the other dimensions are also important. These findings are consistent with those reported elsewhere.[42] They broaden the possible outcomes of leadership compared to traditional leadership studies.

LEADERSHIP IN HIGH-PERFORMANCE WORK TEAMS

An extension of the new leadership approaches discussed above is the leadership in self-directing work teams. As mentioned previously, such teams are particularly important in high-performance organizations, and the workers in these teams are the teams' leaders.[43] The question, then, is whether or not they have a leader from outside the team. The answer is "yes," but what the leader does is quite different from what a traditional supervisor does. Indeed, even the title is different—two widely used titles are "coordinator" and "facilitator."

Figure 14.7 Sample leader behaviours for high-performance work teams

COORDINATOR BEHAVIOUR	ACTIVITIES INVOLVED IN COORDINATOR TEAM ENCOURAGEMENTS*
Encourage rehearsal Work team goes over an activity and "thinks it through" before actually performing the activity	• Go over activity • Practise new task • Go over new task • Think about how to do a job
Encourages self-goal setting Work team sets performance goals	• Define team goals • Define own goals • Establish task goals • Set team performance goals
Encourages self-criticism Work team self-critical of low team performance	• Be critical of ourselves • Be tough on ourselves • Be self-critical • Be critical when we do poorly
Encourages self-reinforcement Work team self-reinforcing of high team performance	• Praise each other • Feel positive about ourselves • Praise each other for a good job • Feel good about ourselves
Encourages self-expectation Work team has high expectations for team performance	• Think we can do very well • Expect high performance • Expect a lot from ourselves
Encourages self-observation/evaluation Work team monitors, is aware of, and evaluates levels of performance	• Be aware of performance level • Know how our performance stands • Judge how well we are performing

*These activities were specifically described in a questionnaire, and some of the questions were designed to be very similar to increae the reliability of the questionnaire.

Figure 14.7 shows some of the key leadership behaviours of coordinators. These behaviours focus on coordinator encouragements, and the team activities show the specific actions that help the members satisfy the coordinator's expectations. A reasonable question that can be asked is whether there really is a difference when team members perform the team activities encouraged by the coordinator. The answer is that these leader behaviours do seem to be important. One study showed that when team members perceived that there was coordinator encouragement of the team's self-leadership activities, coordinator effectiveness was higher. Another study showed that coordinator leader behaviour was related to positive team performance and various aspects of satisfaction.[44] An example is the Tillsonburg, Ontario facility of TRW Canada Ltd., a world-leading supplier of automotive suspension components to the Big Three automakers and Nissan. It uses self-led work teams and has team coordinators responsible for one of six tasks that each team is responsible for completing. Each coordinator also represents the team in best practices meetings with other team coordinators to spread successful processes across the plant.

OB ACROSS FUNCTIONS

Production

Production Module Leaders Handle Shop Floor Complexity

Deere & Company is the world's leading manufacturer of farm machinery, with Canadian sales in 2003 of approximately $930 million (US). It produces more than 80 different seed planter frames, with several million options. Dealing with this complexity involves using a process flow, moving machines closer together, and reorganizing the work into nine modules, with each module responsible for building particular subassemblies and attaching them to planter frames. To help leaders and workers handle the immensely complex tasks involved, Deere provides them with information on everything from assembly schedules to quality control. As much as possible, Deere distributes authority to where the information and incentives are. Module leaders thus have the information that they need to have in order to control their budgets for staffing, overtime, maintenance, and other functions. In addition, each employee is charged with continuous improvement, and work groups have goals for safety, quality, delivery, and efficiency. This in turn makes it possible for module leaders and team members to plan ahead and deal with the many issues in their own module and elsewhere on the line. For example, if there is a quality problem as a planter rolls past an assembler's module, the assembler fixes it or finds the person responsible, regardless of the person's job, and gets it fixed.

www.Deere.com

Take another look at Figure 14.7. Notice that while these behaviours are important, they only focus on self-leadership activities. They do not examine other leadership functions such as managing resources and boundary spanning with other units. In other words, they emphasize the social system and not the technical system. Indeed, Manz and Sims[45] suggest that the coordinator, who is outside the group, has the fundamental responsibility to get the team to lead itself and therefore needs to emphasize various team self-leadership behaviours. In contrast to the coordinator, these authors argue, the team leader within the team becomes a member who helps the team organize itself by coordinating job assignments and making sure resources are available. Another team of authors points out that even though coordinator self-leadership encouragement has been related to team effectiveness and satisfaction in studies, the relationship probably would have been much stronger if these other kinds of leadership dimensions had been included, in addition to the self-leadership ones.[46]

To conclude, note two other considerations. First, these self-leadership activities from the team members themselves can be considered a partial substitute for hierarchical leadership, even though the coordinator encourages them. For example, members can praise each other rather than look to the coordinator for praise. As we have shown previously, such behaviours are becoming increasingly important in high-performance organizations.

Second, although these behaviours encourage a lot of participation from team members, they do not appear to be particularly charismatic. They should work best when they are combined with the kinds of resource and coordination behaviours that were mentioned above and when they are reinforced by new leadership from bright-side leaders higher up in the organization.

SOME NEW LEADERSHIP ISSUES

We now examine some issues related to charismatic and transformational leadership, and new leadership that focuses on a vision. The first issue is whether or not people can be *trained in new leadership*. According to research in this area, the answer is "yes." Bass and his colleagues have put a lot of work into such training efforts. For example, they have created a workshop where leaders are given initial feedback on their scores on Bass's measures. The leaders then plan improvement programs that will help them overcome their weaknesses and they work with the trainers to develop their leadership skills. Bass, and Bass and Avolio report findings that demonstrate the beneficial effects of this training. They also report improvements from team training and programs tailored to individual firms' needs.[47] Similarly, Conger and Kanungo propose using training to develop the kinds of behaviours that are summarized in their model, as suggested in The Effective Manager 14.2.[48]

Approaches that have a special emphasis on vision often emphasize training. Kouzas and Posner have reported on the results of a week-long training program at AT&T. The program involved training leaders on five dimensions that are oriented around developing, communicating, and reinforcing a shared vision. According to Kouzas and Posner, leaders showed an average 15 percent increase in these visionary behaviours 10 months after partici-pating in the program.[49] Similarly, Sashkin has developed a leadership approach that emphasizes various aspects of vision and changing an organization's culture. Sashkin discusses several ways to train leaders to be more visionary and to improve the change of culture.[50] All of the new leadership training programs emphasize hands-on workshop so that leaders do more than just read about vision.

A program begun by Henry Mintzberg of McGill University has been cus-tomized to create a training program for leadership at the Royal Bank, which was concerned that its culture was too risk-averse. Problems were approached in vari-ous ways and the first 50 participants recognized the need for a balance between analysis and instinct in their leadership behaviours. The vice-president of leader-ship effectiveness at the Royal Bank, Frank McAuley, says, "you can't go complete-ly on instinct, but if you do too much analysis you'll be paralysed." Meanwhile, at the Banff Centre for Management, the inclusion of rock climbing encourages risk-taking and teamwork, while improvisation teaches leaders to loosen up.

A second issue is whether or not new leadership is always good. As we point-ed out earlier, dark-side charismatics, such as Adolf Hitler, can have negative effects on their population of followers. Similarly, new leadership is not always needed. Sometimes, emphasis on a vision takes energy away from more important day-to-day activities. It is also important to note that new leadership by itself is not enough. New leadership needs to be used in combination with traditional leadership. Finally, new leadership is not only important at the top of an organiza-tion. Several experts argue that it applies at all levels of organizational leadership.

It appears critical for organizations to choose the correct leaders and managers for their long-term survival and growth. At the same time, the individuals who are chosen have to be aware of the diverse cultures they operate in, the different situations they will encounter, and the different roles they should expect to have as leaders and managers. Because they must achieve a variety of goals, leaders and managers must adapt themselves to the kinds of leader-ship that are required. This means that they must choose an appropriate style of leadership for the organizational culture and the business situation they find themselves immersed in.

The Effective Manager 14.2

FIVE CHARISMATIC SKILLS

- sensitivity to the most appropriate con-texts for charisma: emphasis on critical evaluation and problem detection

- visioning: emphasis on creative think-ing to learn and think about profound change

- communication: working with oral and written language

- impression management: emphasis on modelling, appearance, body lan-guage, and verbal skills

- empowering: emphasis on communi-cating high-performance expecta-tions, improving participation in decision-making, loosening up bureaucratic constraints, setting meaningful goals, and establishing appropriate reward systems

What is leadership?

- Leadership is a special case of interpersonal influence that gets an individual or group to do what the leader wants done.

- Leadership and management differ in that management is designed to promote stability or to make the organization run smoothly, whereas the role of leadership is to promote adaptive change.

What are the perspectives of leadership in the trait and behavioural theories?

- Trait, or great person, approaches argue that leader traits have a major impact on differentiating between leaders and non-leaders and predicting leadership outcomes.

- Traits are considered relatively innate and hard to change.

- Similar to trait approaches, behavioural theories argue that leader behaviours have a major impact on outcomes.

- The Michigan and Ohio State approaches are particularly important leader behaviour theories.

- Leader behaviour theories are especially suitable for leadership training.

What are the situational or contingency leadership approaches?

- Situational contingency approaches to leadership argue that leadership, in combination with various situational contingency variables, can have a major impact on outcomes.

- The effects of traits are greater when they relate to the situational contingencies faced by the leader.

- Strong or weak situational contingencies influence the impact of leadership traits.

- Fiedler's contingency theory, House's path–goal theory, Hersey and Blanchard's situational leadership theory, and Kerr and Jermier's substitutes for leadership theory are particularly important, specific situational contingency approaches.

- Sometimes, as in the case of the substitutes for leadership approach, the role of the situational contingencies replaces the role of leadership, and leadership then has little or no impact.

How does attribution theory relate to leadership?

- Attribution theory extends traditional leadership approaches by recognizing that real effects cannot always be objectively identified and measured.

- Leaders form attributions about why their employees perform well or poorly and leaders respond accordingly.

- Leaders and followers often infer that there is good leadership when their group performs well.

- Leaders and followers often have in mind a good leader prototype, compare the leader to this prototype, and conclude that the closer the fit, the better the leadership.

- Some observers claim that leadership makes no real difference and is largely symbolic; others, following the "romance of leadership" notion, embrace this symbolic emphasis and attribute almost magical qualities to leadership.

What are the new leadership perspectives and why are they especially important in high-performance organizations?

- New leadership consists of charismatic, transformation, and visionary leadership, and leadership of self-directing work teams.

- Charismatic, transformational, and visionary attributions encourage followers to achieve goals that go beyond their own self-interests and help transform the organization.

- Particularly important new leadership approaches are Bass's transformational theory, and the charismatic theories of House and of Conger and Kanungo.

- Transformational approaches are broader than charismatic approaches and often include charisma as one of their dimensions.

- Leadership in self-directing teams, particularly such teams in high-performance organizations, changes the external leadership role by making the focus that of encouraging team members to lead themselves.

- Behaviours of team coordinators are assumed to work best when they are reinforced by leaders who provide empowerment and stress various aspects of the new leadership.

- The new leadership, in general, is important because it goes beyond traditional leadership by helping changes occur in the increasingly fast-moving and high-performance workplace.

KEY TERMS

Achievement-oriented leadership (p. 281)

Behavioural perspective (p. 277)

Charismatic leaders (p. 287)

Consideration (p. 277)

Directive leadership (p. 281)

House's path–goal theory of leadership (p. 287)

Initiating structure (p. 277)

Leader match training (p. 280)

Leadership (p. 275)

Leadership prototype (p. 285)

Least preferred co-worker (LPC) scale (p. 279)

New leadership (p. 286)

Participative leadership (p. 281)

Romance of leadership (p. 286)

Situational control (p. 278)

Substitutes for leadership (p. 285)

Supportive leadership (p. 281)

Trait perspectives (p. 276)

Transactional leadership (p. 289)

Transformational leadership (p. 289)

SELF-TEST 14

MULTIPLE CHOICE

1. "Leadership is central, and other variables are less important" best describes _____ theories. (a) trait and behavioural (b) attribution (c) situational contingency (d) substitutes for leadership

2. Trait and behavioural approaches assume that traits and behaviours are _____. (a) as important as other variables (b) more important than other variables (c) caused by other variables (d) symbolic of leadership

3. A comparison of leadership and management would find that _____. (a) leadership promotes stability, and management promotes change (b) leadership promotes change, and management promotes stability (c) leaders are born, but managers are developed (d) the two are pretty much the same

4. The earliest theory of leadership stated that individuals become leaders by _____. (a) the behaviour of those they lead (b) the traits they possess (c) the particular situation in which they find themselves (d) being very tall

5. In Fiedler's contingency theory, the three situational control variables are leader–member relations, task structure, and _____. (a) command power (b) position power (c) discretionary power (d) complexity

6. Which leadership theory argues that a leader's key function is to act in ways that provide what is missing in the work setting? (a) trait (b) behavioural (c) path–goal (d) multiple influence

7. A leadership prototype _____. (a) is useful primarily for selection and training (b) uses LPC as an important component (c) is the image of a model leader (d) emphasizes leadership skills

8. Conger and Kanungo's model emphasizes all of the following except _____. (a) active management by exception (b) vision articulation (c) environmental sensitivity (d) unconventional behaviour

9. Leadership of self-directing teams _____. (a) emphasizes charisma (b) emphasizes team-member empowerment (c) emphasizes leader traits (d) has been replaced by technology

10. Leadership of high-performance organizations _____. (a) uses traditional, new, and self-directing perspectives (b) uses only a self-directing perspective (c) has largely been replaced (d) is very autocratic

TRUE–FALSE

11. The earliest studies of leadership tended to focus on leader behaviours.   T   F

12. Leadership and management are usually considered the same.   T   F

13. The University of Michigan studies concluded that employee-centred leaders tended to have more productive workgroups.   T   F

14. Hersey and Blanchard's situational leadership theory focuses on the maturity or readiness of followers.   T   F

15. Neutralizers prevent a leader from behaving in a certain way or nullify the effects of a leader's actions.   T   F

16. In romance of leadership, it is argued that leaders are unimportant.   T   F

17. Transformational leadership acts in combination with transactional leadership.   T   F

18. Charismatic and transformational leadership are part of the "new leadership."   T   F

19. Team coordinators and team leaders each perform the same functions.   T   F

20. Leadership of self-directing teams emphasizes charisma in the team.   T   F

SHORT ANSWER

21. Define leadership and contrast it with management.

22. Discuss the application of the trait and behaviour approaches in leadership.

23. Discuss the application of situational contingency approaches in leadership.

24. Compare and contrast traditional leadership and the new leadership.

APPLICATION ESSAY

25. You have just been called in as a consultant to analyze the role of leadership at Suncor Inc. in the chapter's feature story and to suggest ways to develop it further. Making any necessary assumptions, discuss how you would handle this assignment.

Power and Politics

15

Microsoft Flexes its Corporate Power

November 2001 was a banner month for Bill Gates and Microsoft. Microsoft announced two new products—the Xbox and Windows XP. Just as important to the long-term strategic success of the firm was the announced settlement of both a federal lawsuit and several nagging private lawsuits related to Microsoft's power.

In 1998, the U.S. government had sued the company, claiming that the software giant was a monopolist. With 95 percent of new computers using Windows, the suit claimed Microsoft used its power to unfairly eliminate existing and potential competitors. Microsoft bundled a browser into its Windows operating system and required computer makers to incorporate the new system into virtually all of their machines. A federal judge ordered massive payments by the firm, cession of coercive practices, and a breakup of the firm.

Microsoft, however, negotiated a settlement. Without pleading guilty, Microsoft agreed to stop coercive practices; it made some elements of Windows more open to rival developers; and it agreed to spend over a billion dollars on computers and software to be sent to deserving public schools. But this is only one side of power, politics, and Microsoft. On the other side are Windows XP and the Xbox. They signal the virtually unstoppable innovation at Microsoft. An initial key to this innovation was Bill Gates's willingness to empower his researchers and project managers by arranging them in small groups. Microsoft's CEO, Steven A. Ballmer, now follows Gates's philosophy. He realizes that by minimizing bureaucracy new products can make it from conception to production much more quickly.

Understanding power and politics is crucial to understanding the roles of individuals in organizations. As you read Chapter 15, keep in mind these key questions:

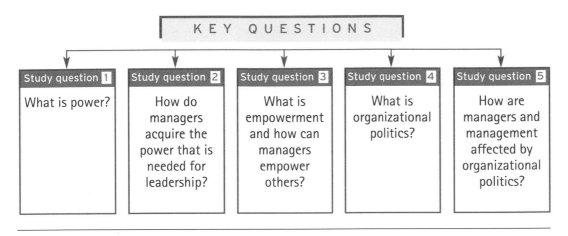

KEY QUESTIONS

Study question 1	Study question 2	Study question 3	Study question 4	Study question 5
What is power?	How do managers acquire the power that is needed for leadership?	What is empowerment and how can managers empower others?	What is organizational politics?	How are managers and management affected by organizational politics?

Individuals rarely join a corporation simply to work for the organization's stated goals. They join for their own reasons to achieve their own goals. Because individuals in a hierarchical setting will compete for their own interests, understanding power and politics is a key to understanding the behaviour of individuals in organizations. An important part of power and politics is that managers find there are never enough resources—i.e., money, people, time, or authority—to get things done. They see a power gap.[1] As discussed throughout this chapter, power and politics have two sides. On the one hand, power and politics represent the unpleasant side of management, since organizations are not democracies composed of individuals with equal influence. On the other hand, power and politics are important organizational tools that managers must use to get the job done. In effective organizations, power is delicately developed, nurtured, and managed by astute individuals. There are politics in every organization and there are actually many specific instances where the interests of individuals and organizations fit together well. The astute manager knows how to find these opportunities.[2]

Power

In OB, **power** is defined as the ability to get someone to do something you want done, or the ability to make things happen in the way you want them to. In Chapter 14, we examined leadership as a key power mechanism to make things happen. Now is the time to discuss other ways. The essence of power is control over the behaviour of others.[3] While power is the force you use to make things happen in an intended way, **influence** is what you have when you use power, and it is seen in how others respond to your use of power. Managers get power from both organizational and individual sources. These sources are called position power and personal power, respectively.[4]

Power is the ability to get someone else to do something one wants done, or the ability to make things happen or get things done the way one wants.

Influence is a behavioural response to the exercise of power.

POSITION POWER

There are six popular bases of power in today's organizations that a manager can use just because of his or her position in the organization: legitimate, reward, coercive, process, information, and representative power.

The first base of "position" power is **legitimate power**, or formal hierarchical authority. It comes from how much a manager can use subordinates' internalized values or beliefs that the "boss" has a "right of command" to control their behaviour. For example, the boss may have the formal authority to approve or deny such employee requests as job transfers, equipment purchases, personal time off, or overtime work. Legitimate power is the special kind of power that a manager has because his or her subordinates believe it is legitimate for a person in the managerial position of being their boss to have the right to command them. If this legitimacy is lost, subordinates will not accept the manager's authority.

Reward power is how much a manager can use extrinsic and intrinsic rewards to control other people. Examples of such rewards include money, promotions, compliments, and enriched jobs. Although all managers have some access to rewards, how successful a manager is at accessing and using these rewards to achieve influence depends on the manager's skills.

Power can also be based on punishment instead of reward. For example, a manager may threaten to not give a pay raise, or to transfer, demote, or even recommend the firing of a subordinate who does not act as the manager wants. Such **coercive power** is how much a manager can deny desired rewards or administer punishments to control other people. How much coercive power is available varies from one organization to another and from one manager to another. The presence of unions and organizational policies on employee treatment can make this basis of power much weaker.

Process power is the control over the methods of production and analysis. This power comes from placing an individual in a position where he or she can influence how inputs are transformed into outputs for either the firm, a department in the firm, or even a small group in the firm. Firms often have process specialists who work with managers to ensure that production is efficient and effective. There can also be control over the analytical processes that are used to make choices. For example, many organizations have individuals with specialties in financial analysis. They may review investment proposals from other parts of the firm. Their power does not come from doing the actual calculations, but from being responsible for deciding which analytical procedures will be used to judge the proposals. Process power may be separated from legitimate hierarchical power if a firm's operations are complex. A manager may have the formal hierarchical authority to decide, but he or she may need to use the analytical schemes of others and/or to consult with process specialists on the most effective way to implement a process. As you may have suspected, the issue of position power can get quite complex very quickly in sophisticated operations. This leads us to another related aspect of position power—access to and control of information.

Information power is the access to and/or control of information. It is one of the most important aspects of legitimacy. The "right to know" and use information can be given to a position holder. Thus, information power may complement legitimate hierarchical power. Information power may also be given to specialists and managers who are in the middle of a firm's information systems. For example, the chief information officer of the firm may not only control all the computers, but may also have access to almost any information desired. Managers jealously guard the formal "right to know," because it means they are in a position to influence events, not just react to them. For example, most chief executive officers believe they have the right to know about everything in "their" firm. Deeper in the organization, managers often protect information from others because they believe that outsiders would not understand it. For instance, engineering drawings are not typically allowed outside of engineering.

Legitimate power or formal authority is how much a manager can use the "right of command" to control other people.

Reward power is how much a manager can use extrinsic and intrinsic rewards to control other people.

Coercive power is how much a manager can deny desired rewards or administer punishment to control other people.

Process power is the control over the methods of production and analysis.

Information power is the access to and/or control of information.

In other instances, information needs to be protected from outsiders. Marketing plans may be labelled "top secret." In most instances, the standard reason for controlling information is to protect the firm. The real reason is often to allow information holders to increase their power.

Representative power is the formal right given by the firm for someone to speak for and to a potentially important group of individuals from the firm's different departments or a group of individuals from outside the firm. In most complex organizations, there are a wide variety of different constituencies (individuals with a common interest) that may have an important impact on a firm's operations and/or its success. Many of the constituencies are outside the firm. They include such groups as investors, customers, alliance partners, and, of course, unions. Astute executives often hire individuals to act as representatives of and to these constituencies to ensure that these constituencies have some influence over the firm, but do not dominate it. So, for instance, investor relations managers are expected to deal with the everyday inquiries of small investors, anticipate the questions of financial analysts, and inform senior management about investors' concerns. The investor relations manager may also be asked to anticipate the questions of investors, and to guide the type of responses senior management may make. The influence of the investor relations manager comes in part from being assigned to represent the interests of this important group.

Finally, it is important to stress the unstated basis for legitimacy in most organizations. This is an implicit moral and technical order. As we will note later in this chapter, from the crib to school to work to retirement, individuals in our society are taught to obey "higher authority." In Western firms, "higher authority" means those individuals who are close to the top of the corporate pyramid. In other societies, "higher authority" does not have a bureaucratic or organizational reference. Instead it belongs to individuals who have moral authority, such as tribal chiefs, religious leaders, and so on. In firms, the legitimacy of those at the top comes more and more from their positions as representatives for various constituencies. This is a technical or instrumental role. Many senior executives also refer to ethics and social causes in their role as authority figures.

> **Representative power** is the formal right given by the firm for someone to speak for and to a potentially important group.

ETHICS AND SOCIAL RESPONSIBILITY

LEADERSHIP LEADS TO RESPONSIBILITY

For five years in a row, G.A.P. Adventures has been one of the top 100 growth firms in the Profit 100 awards. This is not surprising as global marketing of the firm has resulted in its name being known around the world for ecotourism. In fact, the company now generates 70 percent of its business from overseas clients, and has experienced growth of 3,500 percent over five years. With the company also having been chosen as one of the "Top 40 Under 40," company founder and president Bruce Poon Tip is dedicated to keeping his company's high standards. G.A.P. Adventures has maintained its integrity by using small scale accommodations and local transportation, and by supporting locally owned and operated low impact businesses. This effort has resulted in G.A.P. Adventures receiving the Ethics in Action Millennium Award (www.ethicsinaction.com) for its continuing effort to be a responsible tour operator while providing its customers with face-to-face travel experiences. www.gap.ca

PERSONAL POWER

Personal power is in the individual and is unrelated to that individual's position. Personal power is important in many well-managed firms. Three bases of personal power are expertise, rational persuasion, and reference.

Expert power is the ability to control another person's behaviour by having knowledge, experience, or judgement that the other person needs but does not have.

Rational persuasion is the ability to control another person's behaviour through efforts that convince the person that a goal is desirable and the way to achieve it is reasonable.

Referent power is the ability to control another's behaviour because the other person wants to identify with the power source.

Expert power is the ability to control another person's behaviour by having knowledge, experience, or judgement that the other person needs but does not have. A subordinate obeys a supervisor who has expert power because the boss ordinarily knows more about what is to be done or how it is to be done than does the subordinate. Expert power is relative, not absolute. In other words, it depends on one person having more expertise than the other person.

Rational persuasion is the ability to control another's behaviour through efforts that convince the person that a goal is desirable and the way to achieve it is reasonable. Rational persuasion involves both explaining the desirability of expected outcomes and showing how specific actions will achieve these outcomes. Much of what a supervisor does each day involves rational persuasion up, down, and across the organization.

Referent power is the ability to control another's behaviour because the other person wants to identify with or be like the power source. In this case, a subordinate obeys the boss because he or she wants to behave, perceive, or believe as the boss does. This obedience may occur, for example, because the subordinate likes the boss personally and therefore tries to do things the way the boss wants them done. In a sense, the subordinate tries to avoid doing anything that would hurt the enjoyable boss-subordinate relationship. A person's referent power can be increased when the individual makes use of morality or shows a clearer long-term path to a morally desirable end. In common language, individuals who are able to use these more esoteric aspects of corporate life have "charisma" and "the vision thing." Followership is not based on what the subordinate will get for specific actions or specific levels of performance; instead it is based on what the higher-placed individual represents—a path toward a loftier future.

ACQUIRING AND USING POWER AND INFLUENCE

A large part of any manager's time is spent on what is called *power-oriented behaviour*. Power-oriented behaviour is action that is done mainly to develop or use relationships in which the other person is willing to follow one's wishes, at least to some extent.[5] Figure 15.1 shows three basic dimensions of power and influence which a manager is involved with in this regard: downward, upward, and lateral. The figure also shows some basic ideas for achieving success in each of these dimensions.

Figure 15.1 Three dimensions of managerial power and influence

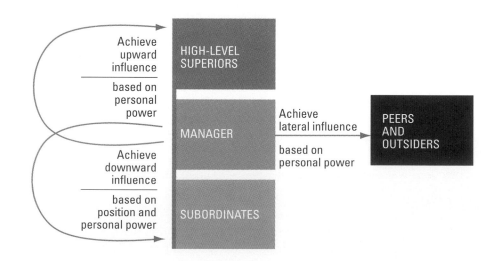

An effective manager succeeds in building and maintaining high levels of both position and personal power over time. When there is enough power of the right types, the manager can use his or her influence on downward, lateral, and upward dimensions whenever this is needed.

Building Position Power   Position power increases when managers can show others that the manager's work units are highly relevant to organizational goals and can respond to urgent organizational needs. To become more central and critical to an organization, managers may try to have a more central role in the workflow. They can do this either by having information filtered through them, by making at least part of their job responsibilities unique, by expanding their network of communication contacts, or by occupying an office that is close to the company's main traffic flows of personnel.

Managers may also try to make their tasks and those of their unit more relevant to the organization. There are many ways to do this. Executives may try to become internal coordinators within the firm or external representatives. They may suggest that their subordinates take on these roles, particularly when the firm is downsizing. When the firm is in a dynamic setting of changing technology, the executive may also try to provide unique services and information to other units. This is particularly effective if the executive moves his unit so that it becomes involved with decisions that are central to the organization's top-priority goals. To expand their position, managers may also delegate routine activities, expand the task variety and novelty for subordinates, initiate new ideas, and get involved in new projects. We will have more to say about this when we discuss empowerment.

Some of the ways that some managers try to build influence can actually hurt the organization, however. Managers may try to define tasks so that they are hard to evaluate—for example, by creating an ambiguous job description or developing a unique language for their work.

Building Personal Power   Personal power comes from the personal characteristics of the manager rather than from the location and other characteristics of his or her position in the organization's hierarchy of authority.

Three personal characteristics—expertise, political savvy, and likeability—have special potential for increasing personal power in an organization. The most obvious is *building expertise*. A person can get additional expertise through advanced training and education, participation in professional associations, and involvement in the early stages of projects.

A less obvious way to increase personal power is to learn *political savvy*: this means learning better ways to negotiate, persuade individuals, and understand the goals and means that others are most willing to accept. The novice believes that most individuals are very much the same, see the same goals, and will accept much the same paths toward these goals. The more astute individual is aware that there are important individual differences.

A manager's referent power is increased by characteristics that contribute to his or her *likeability* and create personal attraction in relationships with other people. These include pleasant personality characteristics, agreeable behaviour patterns, and an attractive personal appearance. Sincere hard work by an individual on behalf of task performance can also increase personal power by increasing both expertise and reference. A person who is perceived as trying hard may be seen as being someone who knows more about the job and should therefore be spoken to when advice is needed. A person who tries hard is also likely to be respected for his or her effort and others may even depend on that person to maintain that effort.

Combined Building of Position and Personal Power   In a true analysis, most sources of power can be traced to position power or personal power. However, many influential actions and behaviours are combinations of position and personal power.

Most managers try to increase the visibility of their job performance by (1) expanding the number of contacts they have with senior people, (2) making oral presentations of written work, (3) participating in problem-solving task forces, (4) sending out notices of accomplishment, and (5) generally seeking additional opportunities that will make their name better known in the organization. Most managers also recognize that, between superiors and subordinates, access to or control over information is an important element. A boss may appear to increase his or her expert power over a subordinate by not giving the individual access to critical information. Although the denial might add to the boss's expert power, it could also make the subordinate less effective. In a similar manner, a supervisor may also decide to control access to key organizational decision-makers. However, an individual's ability to contact key persons informally can partly overcome this disadvantage. Indeed, astute senior executives routinely develop "back channels" to lower-level individuals deep within the firm as a way of dealing with the tendency of bosses to control information and access.

Expert power is often relational and embedded within the organizational context, formally and informally. Many important decisions are made outside formal decision channels and are influenced greatly by key individuals who have the knowledge that is needed. By developing and using coalitions and networks, an individual can build on his or her expert power. Through coalitions and networks, an individual may change the flow of information and the context for analysis. By developing coalitions and networks, executives can also increase their access to information and their opportunities for participation.

Executives also try to control, or at least influence, decision premises. A decision premise is a basis for defining the problem and for choosing among alternatives. If a problem is defined in a way that fits the executive's expertise, it will be natural for that executive to be in charge of solving it. In this way, the executive can subtly shift his or her position power.

Executives who want to increase their power often make their goals and needs clear and bargain effectively to show that their preferred goals and needs are best. They do not show their power base directly but instead provide clear "rational persuasion" for their preferences. In other words, the astute executive does not make threats or use sanctions to build power. Instead, he or she combines personal power with the position of the unit to increase total power. As illustrated in The Effective Manager 15.1, it is important for the aspiring manager to build trust. As the organizational context changes, different personal sources of power may become more important alone and in combination with the individual's position power. There is an art to building power.

| The Effective Manager | 15.1 |

DEVELOPING TRUST

One key to ethically developing power is to build trust. To build trust a manager should, at a minimum:

- always honour implied and explicit social contracts
- try to prevent, avoid, and correct harm to others
- respect the unique needs of others

TURNING POWER INTO RELATIONAL INFLUENCE

For most managers, using position and personal power well to achieve the desired influence over others is a challenge. Practically speaking, there are many useful ways of exercising relational influence. The most common strategies involve the following:[6]

Strategies for Exercising Influence

Reason	Using facts and data to support a logical argument
Friendliness	Using flattery, goodwill, and favourable impressions
Coalition	Using relationships with other people for support
Bargaining	Using the exchange of benefits as a basis for negotiation
Assertiveness	Using a direct and forceful personal approach
Higher authority	Gaining higher-level support for one's requests
Sanctions	Using the organization's rewards and punishments

Research on these strategies suggests that reason is the most popular strategy overall.[7] In addition, friendliness, assertiveness, bargaining, and higher authority are used more frequently to influence subordinates than to influence supervisors. This pattern of influence usage is consistent with Figure 15.1, which showed earlier that downward influence generally includes using both position and personal power sources, whereas upward influence is more likely to rely on personal power.

There is very little research about upward influence in organizations. This is unfortunate, since truly effective managers are able to influence their bosses as well as their subordinates. One study reports that both supervisors and subordinates view reason, or the logical presentation of ideas, as the most frequently used strategy of upward influence.[8] When the two groups were asked about the reasons for success and failure, however, their viewpoints showed both similarities and differences. The perceived causes of success in upward influence were similar for both supervisors and subordinates: these involve the favourable content of the influence attempt, the favourable way it was presented, and the competence of the subordinate.[9] The two groups disagreed about the causes of failure, however. Subordinates attributed failure in upward influence to the close-mindedness of the supervisor, unfavourable content of the influence attempt, and unfavourable interpersonal relationships with the supervisor. In contrast, supervisors attributed failure to the unfavourable content of the attempt, the unfavourable way in which it was presented, and the subordinate's lack of competence.

POWER, FORMAL AUTHORITY, AND OBEDIENCE

As we have shown, power is the potential to control the behaviour of others, and formal authority is the potential to use such control through the legitimacy of a managerial position. Yet, we also know that people who seem to have power do not always get what they want. Why do some people obey directives and others do not? More specifically, why should subordinates respond to a manager's authority, or "right to command," in the first place? Furthermore, since subordinates are willing to obey, what determines the limits of obedience—that is, what sometimes stops them from obeying?

The Milgram Experiments   The mythology of Western personal independence and unrestrained individualism is so strong that we need to spend some time showing that most people, including those in the West, are really quite obedient. So we turn to the seminal studies of Stanley Milgram on obedience.[10] Milgram designed experiments to determine to what extent people would obey the commands of an authority figure, even if they believed they were endangering the life of another person. Subjects, ranging in age from 20 to 50 and representing a diverse set of occupations (engineers, salespeople, schoolteachers, labourers, and others), were paid a small fee for their participation in the project.

The subjects were falsely told that the purpose of the study was to determine the effects of punishment on learning. The subjects were to be the "teachers." The "learner" was a confederate (a secret associate) of Milgram's, who was strapped to a chair in an adjoining room with an electrode attached to his wrist. The "experimenter," another confederate of Milgram's, was dressed in a grey laboratory coat. Appearing impassive and somewhat stern, the experimenter instructed the teacher to read a series of word pairs to the learner and then to reread the first word along with four other terms. The learner was supposed to indicate which of the four terms was in the original pair by pressing a switch that caused a light to flash on a response panel in front of the teacher.

The teacher was instructed to administer a shock to the learner each time a wrong answer was given. This shock was to be increased by one level of intensity each time the learner made a mistake. The teacher controlled switches that were indicated as giving shocks ranging from

Building Consortiums Helps Smaller Firms

www.aerosystems-international.com

By working with other organizations, such as Bombardier on aeronautical testing systems and the federal government on radio monitoring, Aerosystems International Inc. has been able to expand its market well beyond our borders. As marketing director Mark Connolly put it, "Cooperation with successful Canadian exporters by way of coat-tailing or consortium can be a fast and less expensive route for small entry-level exporters."

15 to 450 volts. In reality, there was no electric current in the apparatus, but the teacher did not know this. The learners then purposely made mistakes often and responded to each level of "shock" in more distressing ways. If a teacher (the subject) was unwilling to administer a shock, the experimenter used the following sequential prods to get him or her to perform as requested. (1) "Please continue" or "Please go on"; (2) "The experiment requires that you continue"; (3) "It is absolutely essential that you continue"; and (4) "You have no choice, you must go on." Only when the teacher refused to go on after the fourth prod would the experiment be stopped. When would you expect the "teachers" to refuse to go on?

Milgram asked some of his students and colleagues the same question. Most felt that few, if any, of the subjects would go beyond the "very strong shock" level. Actually, 26 subjects (65 percent) continued to the end of the experiment and shocked the "learners" to the maximum. None stopped before 300 volts, the point at which the learner pounded on the wall. The remaining 14 subjects refused to obey the experimenter at different intermediate points.

Most people are surprised by these results, as was Milgram. The question is why people would have a tendency to accept or comply with authoritative commands under such extreme conditions. Milgram did further experiments to try to answer this question. The subjects' tendencies toward compliance were somewhat reduced (1) when experimentation took place in a rundown office (rather than a university lab), (2) when the victim was closer, (3) when the experimenter was farther away, and (4) when the subject could observe other subjects. However, the level of compliance was still much higher than most of us would expect. In short, there is a tendency for individuals to comply and be obedient—to switch off and merely do exactly what they are told to do.

Obedience and the Acceptance of Authority   Direct defiance in organizations is quite rare, as is the individual who develops new and different ways to get the job done. If the tendency to follow instructions is high and defiance is rare, then why do so many organizations appear to drift into what looks like chaos?

The answer to this question can be found in work done by the famous management writer Chester Barnard.[11] Barnard's argument focused on the "consent of the governed" rather than on the rights that come from ownership. He argued that subordinates accepted or followed a directive from the boss only under special circumstances.

All four of these circumstances must be met: (1) the subordinate can and must understand the directive; (2) the subordinate must feel mentally and physically capable of following the directive; (3) the subordinate must believe that the directive is consistent with the purpose of the organization; and (4) the subordinate must believe that the directive is consistent with his or her personal interests.

These four conditions are very carefully stated. For instance, to accept and follow an order, the subordinate does not need to understand how the proposed action will help the organization. He or she only needs to believe that the requested action is consistent with the purpose of the firm. The astute manager will not take these guidelines for granted. In giving directives, the astute manager recognizes that the acceptance of the request is not assured.

Obedience and the Zone of Indifference   Most people look for a balance between what they put into an organization (contributions) and what they get from an organization in return (inducements). Within the boundaries of the psychological contract (boss–subordinate), therefore, employees will agree to do many things in and for the organization because they think they should. In exchange for certain inducements, subordinates accept the authority of the organization and its managers to direct their behaviour in certain ways. Based on his acceptance view of authority, Chester Barnard calls this area in which directions are obeyed the "zone of indifference."[12]

A **zone of indifference** is the range of authoritative requests that a subordinate is willing to follow without first critically evaluating or judging the directives. Directives that are within the zone are obeyed. Requests or orders that are outside the zone of indifference are not considered legitimate under the terms of the psychological contract. Such "extraordinary" directives may or may not be obeyed. This link between the zone of indifference and the psychological contract is shown in Figure 15.2.

A zone of indifference is the range of authoritative requests that a subordinate is willing to follow without first critically evaluating or judging the directives.

Figure 15.2 Hypothetical psychological contract for an administrative assistant

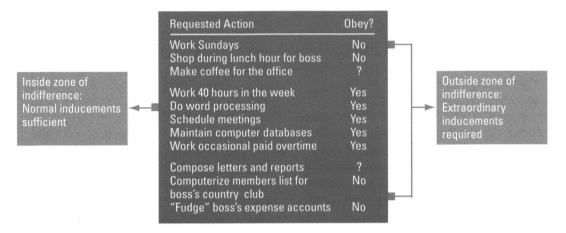

The zone of indifference can change. There may be times when a boss would like a subordinate to do things that are outside the zone. In this case, the manager must enlarge the zone to include the additional behaviours. In these attempts, a manager most likely will have to use more incentives than pure position power. In some instances, no power base may be capable of accomplishing the desired result. Consider your own zone of indifference and tendency to obey. When will you say "No" to your boss? When should you be willing to say "No"? At times, the situation may involve ethical dilemmas, where you may be asked to do things that are illegal, unethical, or both.

Research on ethical managerial behaviour shows that supervisors can become sources of pressure for subordinates to do such things as support incorrect viewpoints, sign false documents, overlook the supervisor's wrongdoing, and do business with the supervisor's friends.[13] Most of us will face such ethical dilemmas during our careers. For now, we must simply remember that saying "No" or "refusing to keep quiet" can be difficult and potentially costly.

Empowerment

Empowerment is the process a manager uses to help others get and use the power they need to have to make decisions that affect themselves and their work. More than ever before, managers in progressive organizations are expected to be good at (and highly comfortable with) empowering the people they work with. Rather than seeing power as something to be held only at higher levels in the traditional "pyramid" of organizations, this view considers power to be something that can be shared by everyone working in flatter and friendlier structures.

The concept of empowerment is part of the sweeping change happening in today's corporations. Corporate staff is being cut back; layers of management are being eliminated; and the number of employees is being reduced as the volume of work increases. What is left is a leaner

Empowerment is the process a manager uses to help others get and use the power they need to have to make decisions that affect themselves and their work.

and trimmer organization staffed by fewer managers, who must share more power as they accomplish their daily tasks. Indeed, empowerment is a key foundation of the increasingly popular self-managing work teams and other creative worker involvement groups.

THE POWER KEYS TO EMPOWERMENT

One of the bases for empowerment is a radically different view of power itself. So far, our discussion has focused on power over other individuals. In this traditional view, power is relational as it depends on the relationships between individuals. In contrast, the concept of empowerment emphasizes the ability to make things happen. Power is still relational, but in terms of problems and opportunities, not individuals. Cutting through everything that corporations say about their empowerment efforts is quite difficult, because this word has become quite fashionable in management circles and management therefore likes to use it. As the term is sometimes misused, however, each empowerment attempt needs to be examined for how it will actually change power in the organization.

Changing Position Power   When an organization tries to move power down the hierarchy, it must also change the existing pattern of position power. Changing this pattern raises some important questions. Can "empowered" individuals give rewards and sanctions based on task accomplishment? Has their new right to act been made legitimate by giving them formal authority? All too often, attempts at empowerment disrupt well-established patterns of position power and threaten middle- and lower-level managers. As one supervisor said, "All this empowerment stuff sounds great for top management. They don't have to run around trying to get the necessary clearances to implement the suggestions from my group. They never gave me the authority to make the changes, only the new job of asking for permission."

Expanding the Zone of Indifference   When it begins a new empowerment program, management needs to be aware of the current zone of indifference and work systematically to expand it. All too often, management assumes that its directive for empowerment will be followed; management may fail to show precisely how empowerment will benefit the individuals involved, however.

POWER AS AN EXPANDING PIE

Along with empowerment, employees need to be trained to expand their power and their new influence potential. This is the most difficult task for managers and a difficult challenge for employees because it often changes the dynamic between supervisors and subordinates. The key is to change the concept of power in the organization from a view that stresses power over others to one that emphasizes using power to get things done. Under the new definition of power, all employees can be more powerful.

A clearer definition of roles and responsibilities may help managers empower others. For instance, senior managers may choose to concentrate on long-term, large-scale adjustments to a variety of challenging and strategic forces in the external environment. If top management tends to concentrate on the long term and pay less attention to quarterly results, other individuals throughout the organization must be ready and willing to make critical operating decisions to maintain the organization's current profitability. By providing opportunities for creative problem-solving as well as the discretion to act, real empowerment increases the total power available in an organization. In other words, the top levels do not have to give up power in order for the lower levels to gain it. Note that senior managers must only give up the illusion of control—the false belief that they can direct the actions of employees five or six levels of management below them.

TECHNOLOGY

Lynn Tyson is vice president, Investor Relations and Corporate Communications for Dell, the "world's most preferred computer systems company." She is responsible for Dell's relationships with investors and financial analysts, and strategic direction and global oversight of Corporate Communications. If you think "high-tech" is all about engineering and software, think again. Ms. Tyson received a bachelor's degree in psychology from The City College of New York and a master's degree in finance/international business from The Stern School of Business, New York University. She is a member of the Executive Leadership Council, on the Board of Directors for the National Investor Relations Institute (NIRI) and she frequently contributes to NIRI's monthly publications on topics such as investor relations best practices. Her experience and expertise contribute to the company's ability to better inform customers, investors, and others about Dell's unique product and service capabilities.

www.dell.ca

Getting the most out of any manager–subordinate relationship involves the same basic arguments. Empowerment means that all managers need to emphasize different ways of exercising influence. In other words, appeals to higher authority and sanctions need to be replaced by appeals to reason. Friendliness must replace coercion. And bargaining must replace orders for compliance.

As the emphasis on coercion and compliance within firms has a long history, individuals may need special support to become comfortable with developing their own power over events and activities. What executives fear, and all too often find, is that employees will passively resist empowerment by looking for directives they can obey or reject. In these instances, the problem starts with executives and middle managers who need to rethink what they mean by power and rethink their use of traditional position and personal power sources. The key is to lead, not push; reward, not sanction; build, not destroy; and expand, not shrink. To expand the zone of indifference, inducements must be expanded for thinking and acting, not just for obeying.

Organizational Politics

Any study of power and influence inevitably leads to the subject of "politics." For many people, this word makes them think of illegal deals, favours, and special personal relationships. Perhaps this image of shrewd, often dishonest, practices used to get what one wants is reinforced by Machiavelli's classic fifteenth-century work The Prince, which outlines how to obtain and hold power through political action. It is important, however, to adopt a perspective that allows politics in organizations to function in a much broader way.[14]

THE TWO TRADITIONS OF ORGANIZATIONAL POLITICS

There are two quite different traditions in the analysis of **organizational politics**. One tradition builds on Machiavelli's philosophy *and defines politics in terms of self-interest and the use of non-sanctioned means* (unapproved ways). In this tradition, organizational politics may be formally

Organizational politics is defined as managing influence to obtain ends that are not approved by the organization or to obtain approved ends in ways that are not approved, and it is the art of creative compromise between individuals with different self-interests.

defined as managing influence to obtain ends that are not approved by the organization or to obtain approved ends in ways that are not approved.[15] Managers are often considered political when they seek their own goals or use ways that are not currently authorized by the organization or that push legal limits. Where there is uncertainty or ambiguity, it is often extremely difficult to tell whether a manager is being political in this self-serving sense.[16] For instance, was John Meriwether a great innovator when he established Long Term Capital Management (LTCM) as a hedge fund to bet on interest rate spreads?[17] At one time, the firm included two Nobel laureates, one of whom was Canadian, and some 25 Ph.D.s. Or was he a real insider when he got the U.S. Federal Reserve to bail him out when it looked like he would either go broke or lose control to a rich investor? Or as often happens in the world of corporate politics, could both of these statements be partially true?

The second tradition *treats politics as a necessary function that results from individuals' different self-interests*. Here, organizational politics is viewed as the art of creative compromise among competing interests. When Air Canada was going through the bankruptcy process, the manoeuvres of management, the unions, and potential investors were always being examined very carefully. Unions were trying to protect their pensions (that were severely underfunded for all employees) and the government was trying to correctly apply the laws on the funding of pensions. Management wanted not only wage concessions, which they got, but also a waiver of the pension debts that the company owed. One investor, who later pulled out, used the pension issue as a key matter—when the pension obligations were not waived by either the unions or the government, he cancelled his offer to invest. Air Canada went back to the drawing board but still progressing toward getting out of its difficult financial situation and resuming normal business practices. In a heterogeneous society, individuals will disagree about whose self-interests are most valuable and whose concerns should therefore be limited by collective interests. Politics arise because individuals need to develop compromises, avoid confrontation, and live together. The same is true for organizations, where individuals join, work, and stay together because their self-interests are satisfied. Furthermore, it is important to remember that the goals of the organization and the acceptable ways to achieve them are decided by organizationally powerful individuals in negotiation with others. Thus, organizational politics is also the use of power to develop socially acceptable ends and means that balance individual and collective interests.

The Effective Manager 15.2

POLITICAL SKILL AS AN ANTIDOTE FOR STRESS

Ever wonder why executives under tremendous daily stress don't burn out? Some argue it is their political skill that saves them. Which specific political skills? Think of these:

- the ability to use practical intelligence (as opposed to analytical or creative intelligence)
- the ability to be calculating and shrewd about social connections
- the ability to inspire trust and confidence
- the ability to deal with individuals who have a wide variety of backgrounds, styles, and personalities

THE DOUBLE-EDGED SWORD OF ORGANIZATIONAL POLITICS

The two different traditions of organizational politics can be seen in how executives describe the effects of politics on managers and their organizations. In one survey, 53 percent of those interviewed indicated that organizational politics increased the achievement of organizational goals and survival.[18] At the same time, 44 percent suggested that politics distracted individuals from organizational goals. In this same survey, 60 percent of respondents suggested that organizational politics were good for career advancement, and 39 percent reported that they led to a loss of power, position, and credibility. As shown in The Effective Manager 15.2, political skill has been linked to lower executive stress.

Organizational politics are not automatically good or bad. They can serve a number of important functions as they can help organizations overcome personnel inadequacies and deal with change, and they can also be a substitute for formal authority.

Even in the best managed firms, mismatches arise among managers who are learning, burned out, without needed training and skills, overqualified, or lacking the resources they need for accomplishing the duties they have been given. Organizational politics provide a mechanism for getting around these inadequacies and getting the job done. Organizational politics can make it easier to adapt to changes in an organization's environment and technology.

Organizational politics can help identify where there are problems like the ones above and help move ambitious, problem-solving managers into the problem area. This is quicker than restructuring. It allows the firm to respond to unanticipated problems quickly with the right people and resources, before small headaches become major problems. Finally, when a person's formal authority is lost or does not apply to a particular situation, political actions can be used to prevent a loss of influence. Managers may also use political behaviour to maintain operations and to achieve task continuity in circumstances where the failure of formal authority may otherwise cause problems.

ORGANIZATIONAL POLITICS AND SELF-PROTECTION

Although organizational politics may be helpful to the organization as a whole, it is probably more commonly known and better understood in terms of self-protection.[19] Whether or not management likes it, all employees understand that in any organization they must watch out for themselves first. In too many organizations, if the employee does not protect himself or herself, no one else will.

Individuals can use three common strategies to protect themselves. They can (1) avoid action and risk-taking, (2) redirect accountability and responsibility, or (3) defend their turf.

Avoidance   *Avoidance* is quite common in controversial areas where the employee must risk being wrong or where actions may result in a sanction. Perhaps the most common reaction is to "work to the rules." That is, employees are protected when they follow all the rules, policies, and procedures strictly and do not allow deviations or exceptions. Perhaps one of the most frustrating but effective techniques is to "play dumb." We all do this at some time or another. When was the last time you said something like "Officer, I didn't know the speed limit was 60. I wouldn't have been going 80 if I had"?

Although working to the rules and playing dumb are common techniques, experienced employees often practise somewhat more subtle techniques of self-protection. These include depersonalization and stalling. Depersonalization involves treating individuals, such as customers, clients, or subordinates, as numbers, things, or objects. Senior managers do not fire long-term employees; the organization is merely "downsized" or "delayered." Routine stalling involves slowing down the pace of work to expand the task so that the individuals look as if they are working hard. With creative stalling, the employees may spend their time supporting the organization's ideology, position, or program and, as a result, delaying implementation.

Redirecting Responsibility   Individuals who are concerned about politics will always protect themselves from accepting blame for the negative consequences of their actions. Again, a variety of well-worn techniques may be used for *redirecting responsibility*. "Passing the buck" is a common method employees and managers use. The trick here is to define the task in a way that makes it someone else's formal responsibility. The ingenious ways individuals can redefine an issue to avoid action and transfer responsibility are often amazing.

Both employees and managers may avoid responsibility through *buffing or rigorous documentation*. Here, individuals take action only when all the paperwork is in place and it is clear that they are merely following procedure. Closely related to rigorous documentation is the "blind memo," which explains an objection to an action implemented by the individual. Here, the required action is taken, but the blind memo is prepared in case the action is questioned. Politicians are particularly good at this technique. They will meet with a lobbyist and then send a memo to the files confirming the meeting. Any relationship between what was discussed in the meeting and the memo is accidental.

As the last example suggests, a convenient method that some managers use to avoid responsibility is to simply *rewrite history*. If a program is successful, the manager claims to have been an early supporter. If a program fails, the manager was the one who expressed serious reservations in the first place. Although a memo in the files is often nice to have to show one's early support or objections, some executives do not bother with such niceties. They simply start a meeting by summarizing what has happened so far—but in a way that makes them look good.

For the really devious, there are three other techniques for redirecting responsibility. One technique is to blame the problem on someone or some group that has difficulty defending themselves. Fired employees, outsiders, and opponents are often targets of such scapegoating. Closely related to scapegoating is blaming the problem on uncontrollable events. The really astute manager goes far beyond the old "the-dog-ate-my-homework" routine. A perennial favourite is, "Given the unexpected severe decline in the overall economy, firm profitability was only somewhat below reasonable expectations." Meaning, the firm lost a bundle.

If these techniques fail, there is always another possibility: facing apparent defeat, the manager can increase commitment to a losing cause of action. That is, when all appears lost, assert your confidence in the original action, blame the problems on not spending enough money to implement the plan fully, and begin actions that call for increased effort. The hope is that you will be promoted or retired by the time the negative consequences are recognized.

Defending Turf   Defending turf—that is, protecting one's territory—is a time-honoured tradition in most large organizations. As noted earlier in the chapter, managers who want to improve their power try to expand the jobs their groups perform. Defending turf also results from the coalitional nature of organizations. That is, an organization can be seen as a collection of various departments and groups that have competing interests. As each group tries to expand its influence, it starts to move in on the activities of other groups. Turf protection can be seen more easily in the following analysis of political action and the manager.

Political Action and the Manager

Managers can get a better understanding of political behaviour by imagining themselves in the positions of the other individuals who are involved in a critical decision or event that the manager is involved in. Each action and decision can be seen as having benefits for and costs to all parties that the decision will affect. Where the manager's costs exceed the manager's benefits, the manager may act to protect his or her position.

Figure 15.3 shows a sample payoff table for two managers, Lee and Leslie, in a problem situation involving a decision on whether or not to allocate resources to a special project. If both managers authorize the resources, the project gets completed on time, and their company keeps a valuable client. Unfortunately, if they do this, both Lee and Leslie will overspend their budgets. Taken on its own, a budget overrun would be bad for the managers' performance records. Assume that the overruns are acceptable only if the client is kept. Thus, if both managers act, both they and the company win, as shown in the upper left block of the figure. Obviously, this is the most desirable outcome for all parties.

Figure 15.3 Political payoffs for the allocation of resources on a sample project

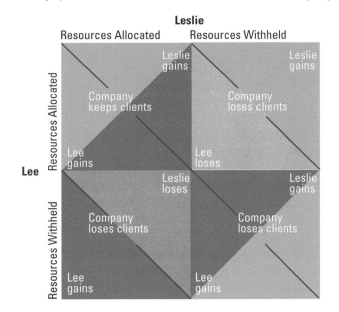

Assume that Leslie acts, but Lee does not. In this case, the company loses the client, and Leslie overspends the budget in a wasted effort, but Lee ends up within budget. While the company and Leslie lose, Lee wins. This scenario is shown in the lower left block of the figure. The upper right block shows the reverse situation, where Lee acts but Leslie does not. In this case, Leslie wins, while the company and Lee lose. Finally, if both Lee and Leslie fail to act, each stays within the budget and therefore gains, but the company loses the client.

The company clearly wants both Lee and Leslie to act. But will they? Would you take the risk of overspending the budget, knowing that your colleague may refuse? The question of trust is critical here, but building trust among co-managers and other workers takes time and can be difficult. The involvement of higher-level managers may be needed to better prepare the decisions of both Lee and Leslie. Yet, in many organizations both Lee and Leslie would fail to act because the "climate" or "culture" too often encourages people to maximize their self-interest at minimal risks.

POLITICAL ACTION AND SUBUNIT POWER

Political action links managers more formally to one another as representatives of their work units. Five of the more typical lateral, intergroup relations in which you may be involved as a manager are workflow, service, advisory, auditing, and approval relations.[20] Workflow linkages are contacts with units that come before or after in a sequential production chain. Service ties are contacts with units that have been created to help with problems. For instance, an assembly-line manager may develop a service link by asking the maintenance manager to fix an important piece of equipment on a priority basis. In contrast, advisory connections are contacts with formal staff units that have special expertise, such as a manager seeking the advice of the personnel department on evaluating subordinates. Auditing linkages are contacts with units that have the right to evaluate the actions of others after action has been taken, whereas approval linkages are contacts with units whose approval must be obtained before action may be taken.

To be effective in political action, managers should understand the politics of subunit relations. Line units are typically more powerful than are staff groups, and units toward the top of the hierarchy are often more powerful than are those toward the bottom. In general, units gain power as more of their relations with others are approval and auditing relations. Workflow relations are more powerful than advisory relations, and both are more powerful than service relations.

POLITICAL ACTION IN THE CHIEF EXECUTIVE SUITE

Whether it is a description of such 1890s robber barons as Andrew Carnegie and John D. Rockefeller, or a story about the actions of Microsoft's Bill Gates, Gerry Schwartz of Onex, or the Desmarais family of Power Corp., people have long been fascinated with the politics of the chief executive suite. The analysis that we will now do of the executive suite should take away some of the mystery about what goes on behind the political veil at the top levels in organizations.

Resource Dependencies Executive behaviour can sometimes be explained in terms of resource dependencies—the firm's need for resources that are controlled by others.[21] Essentially, the resource dependence of an organization increases as (1) needed resources become harder to get, (2) outsiders have more control over needed resources, and (3) there are fewer substitutes for a particular type of resource that is controlled by a limited number of outsiders. Thus, one political role of the chief executive is to develop workable compromises among the competing resource dependencies facing the organization—compromises that increase the executive's power. To create such compromises, executives need to first evaluate how powerful each outsider is compared to other outsiders and then develop strategies that respond differently to various suppliers of external resources.

For larger organizations, many strategies focus on changing the firm's amount of resource dependence. Through mergers and acquisitions, a firm may bring key resources within its control. By changing the "rules of the game," a firm may also find protection from particularly powerful outsiders. Markets may be protected by trade barriers, or labour unions may be put in check by laws such as Nova Scotia's so-called "Michelin Bill." Yet, there are limits on the ability of even our largest and most powerful organizations to control all the external resources they depend on.

International competition has given chief executives fewer choices; they can no longer ignore the rest of the world. As a result, some companies may need to fundamentally redefine how they expect to do business. For instance, in the past, U.S. firms could do business on their own without the assistance of foreign corporations. Canadian firms were always internationally aware due to our proximity to the U.S. and ties to England. Now, chief executives in the U.S. are increasingly leading their companies in the direction of more joint ventures and strategic alliances with foreign partners from around the globe. Such "combinations" give partners access to scarce resources and technologies, as well as new markets and shared production costs.

On the more unpleasant side, there is a new wrinkle in the discussion of resource dependencies—executive pay. Traditionally, U.S. CEOs made about 30 times the pay of the average worker. This was similar to CEO pay scales in Europe and Japan.[22] Today, many U.S. CEOs are making 3,000 times the average pay of workers. How did they get so rich? CEOs may tie themselves to the short-term interests of powerful stockholders. They can do this by directly linking their pay to short-term stock price increases. The problem with this is that CEOs are most often expected to focus on the long-term health of the firm. When a CEO downsizes, begins a series of mergers, or cuts such benefits as worker health care, short-term profits may jump dramatically and lift the stock price. Although the long-term health of the firm may be put at risk, few U.S. CEOs seem able to resist the temptation. It is little wonder that there is renewed interest in how U.S. firms are governed.

Politics and Corporate Strategy While much of the strategy literature is about the economic and organizational aspects of strategy, there is growing awareness of the importance of political strategy. Three aspects have received much attention recently. First is the absence of a political strategy in some corporations, mainly Silicon Valley and software firms. It can be argued, for example, that Microsoft's antitrust problems were partly the result of Gates and Ballmer not wanting to consider the political consequences of their attempts to block competitors by coercing computer manufacturers into incorporating Windows software in their new computers. In contrast, consider the approach of John Chambers, CEO of Cisco Systems. Cisco has over 80 percent of the high-speed server market, clearly almost a monopolistic position. He met with U.S. Justice Department officials to pre-empt government action. He assured regulators his firm was not acting like Microsoft. It just had the patents and a superior technology.[23] In general, it is better for firms to reject passive reaction to government policy or even passive anticipation. Rather, they should participate in the public political process.[24]

A second aspect of a corporate political strategy is trying to transform the government from being a regulator against the industry to being one of its protectors. Immediately after the events of September 11, 2001, a wounded U.S. airline industry collectively sought government help and received an immediate financial bailout in the billions of dollars.[25] Here in Canada, Air Canada did not directly look for government assistance and wound up in bankruptcy court. On a more routine basis, U.S. steel companies and lumber companies have tried to get protection from foreign competition for over 40 years. In this instance, the industry's largest firms dominated the politics surrounding trade protection. They sought and generally received protection when U.S. demand was weakest. They used a variety of tactics, ranging from political contributions to information campaigns, to create a government agenda that favoured their view.[26] Despite all the efforts made by these two industries, global efforts to reduce their influence eventually forced the U.S. government to reach agreements with the Europeans on steel and Canada on softwood lumber.

Of course, a third and highly critical aspect of any corporate political strategy is deciding when and how to get involved in the public policy process. There are no easy answers. Smaller firms with less government regulation of their industry may be willing to take what is called a transactional approach. On a specific issue, they become involved with specific public policy officials who deal with that issue. Larger firms that operate in areas that have a lot of government regulation should not wait for the agenda to be formed by the government. Instead they should be more relationally oriented. That is, they should monitor the environment, help shape emerging issues, and build solid relationships with a broad range of policy-makers. While firms may try to do this alone, most of them look for allies and build coalitions of firms that can help shape and guide how an issue develops.

As our economy continues to globalize and firms move across national boundaries, the development and implementation of an effective political strategy has become both more important and more difficult. For example, CN Rail's attempt to acquire Burlington Northern Railway was blocked by U.S. regulators despite the strenuous lobbying efforts of CN regulators. In the U.S., regulators were willing to allow General Electric to buy a firm called Honeywell. Unfortunately for General Electric, European Union representatives were not, and the proposed merger fell through. While Microsoft has apparently resolved its U.S. antitrust problems, the European Union had only late in 2004 reached its decision on this matter.

Organizational governance is the pattern of authority, influence, and acceptable managerial behaviour that is decided at the top of the organization.

Organizational Governance   Organizational governance is to the pattern of authority, influence, and acceptable managerial behaviour that is decided at the top of the organization. This system establishes what is important, how issues will be defined, who should and should not be involved in key choices, and the boundaries for acceptable implementation.

Those who study organizational governance suggest that a "dominant coalition" of powerful individuals in the organization or involved with the organization in some way is the key to understanding a firm's governance.[27] Although one expects many top officers within the organization to be members of this coalition, the dominant coalition sometimes includes outsiders who have access to key resources. Thus, the analysis of organizational governance involves the notion of resource dependencies as the people who control such key resources may be members of the dominant coalition.

ETHICS AND SOCIAL RESPONSIBILITY

Montreal-based Alcan is a multinational, market-driven aluminum company that employs more than 88,000 people and has operating facilities in more than 60 countries. With all the different cultures, ethical standards, and business practices involved, it would be easy for Alcan employees to violate corporate ethical standards if they adopted some foreign practices. Recognizing how critical this potential problem is, Alcan has developed a Worldwide Code of Employee and Business Conduct, which is available in eight languages and applies to contractors, consultants, and suppliers, as well as employees. "[I]n our working lives we often experience situations where the 'right thing to do' is not immediately apparent. The interests of Alcan and those of fellow employees, customers, suppliers, families, communities, and ourselves may seem to conflict at times. When we're faced with such complex situations, it can be difficult to decide just where the ethical path lies," says Alcan's President and CEO Travis Engen in the introduction to the Code. Alcan has attempted to provide guidance on the "right" choice on a variety of issues, including confidential information and intellectual property, conflicts of interest, government relations, human rights and the workplace, improper payments to officials, international business, and political activity. Violation of the code could result in legal liability. A set of standards may not ensure ethical behaviour, but it does create rules that can be enforced when necessary.
www.alcan.ca

Our view of the executive suite recognizes that the daily practice of organizational governance is the development and resolution of issues. Through the governance system, the dominant coalition tries to define reality. By accepting or rejecting proposals from subordinates, by directing questions toward the interests of powerful outsiders, and by choosing individuals who appear to have particular values and qualities, the coalition slowly creates a pattern of governance in the organization. Furthermore, this pattern is built, at least in part, on very political foundations.

While organizational governance was an internal and a rather private matter in the past, it is now becoming more public and openly controversial. Some critics argue that senior managers do not represent shareholder interests well enough. Others are concerned that they give too little attention to broader constituencies throughout community groups, government, and industry partners.

It has been estimated that the Fortune 500 companies cut some eight million positions over 15 years of downsizing.[28] As the new millennium dawned, managers and employees who were once confident their firm's management philosophy included their interests no longer felt this way. However, with the recent upswing in the economy, perhaps this confidence will return. The eighth annual Watson Wyatt *Canadian Strategic Rewards*™ Survey found organizations are moving away from many of the cost-cutting measures they had put in place. More than one-third of the 163 companies surveyed (34 percent) planned to increase their hiring of critical-skill employees in 2004, while only three percent planned to make reductions.

However, nearly 30 percent expected to hire only a limited number of non-critical-skill employees and 17 percent planned to freeze hiring altogether. Companies like the multinational Alcan face tough decisions in changing economic and market conditions. Alcan recently announced a restructuring of its European operations, which included the downsizing of four sites in Italy, the Czech Republic, France, and Switzerland, the potential sale of two business sites in France, and three plant closures in Belgium, France, and Italy. The measures would result in the loss of 520 jobs, offset by the creation of only 40 new jobs in France, Switzerland, and Italy. Even when a company attempts to operate as a high-performance organization, difficult choices have to be made.

Organizational Governance and Ethics Public concern about all corporations, especially those organizations with high-risk technologies such as chemical processing, medical technology, and integrated oil refineries, seems to be increasing. For instance, Dow Corning's survival is questionable because it has been accused of selling breast implants that cause immune-system problems. Dow Corning claims there is not enough scientific evidence to link their product with such problems, but jury after jury is awarding damages to women who have had Dow Corning implants and immune-system problems. Without a doubt, juries are holding Dow Corning management accountable.

Imbalanced organizational governance by some corporations may limit their ability to manage global operations effectively. Although some senior managers may blame such external factors as unfavourable trade laws for their inability to compete in Japan, China, or other Asian competitors, their critics suggest that a lack of global operating savvy is the only thing that limits the corporations these managers are supposed to be leading. Organizational governance, it is argued, is too closely tied to shareholders' short-term interests and the CEO's pay.

On a more positive note, there are bright spots which suggest that the governance of some firms is going well beyond the limited interests of their owners and now includes the well-being of employees and communities.

Cavanagh, Moberg, and Velasquez argue that organizational governance should have an ethical base.[29] They suggest that from the CEO to the lowest employee, a person's behaviour must satisfy the following criteria to be considered ethical. First, the behaviour must create as much satisfaction as possible for people both inside and outside the organization, resulting in the greatest good for the greatest number of people. Second, the behaviour must respect the rights of all affected parties, including the human rights of free consent, free speech, and freedom of conscience, privacy, and due process. Third, the behaviour must respect the rules of justice by treating people equitably and fairly, as opposed to arbitrarily.

ETHICS AND SOCIAL RESPONSIBILITY

CEOS SOMETIMES NEED TO TAKE A STAND
Wayne Sales took a stand that others chose not to and by 2004 his employer, Canadian Tire, had been the 12-year corporate partner of Project: Warmth, collecting and distributing over 135,000 sleeping bags and blankets to the homeless across Canada. This effort eventually grew to delivering truckloads of relief for the ice storm in Quebec and Ontario, the floods in Manitoba, and other locations as well, with the result that lives have been saved and hope given to those hurting the most. This initiative now extends even beyond our borders to international disaster areas.
www.canadiantire.ca

There may be times when an action does not match these criteria but it can still be considered ethical in the specific situation. This special case must satisfy the criterion of there being overwhelming factors. This means that the special nature of the situation must either result in (1) conflicts among criteria (e.g., an action results in some good and some bad being done), (2) conflicts within criteria (e.g., an action uses questionable ways to achieve a positive result), or (3) the inability to use the criteria (e.g., a person's behaviour is based on inaccurate or incomplete information).

Choosing to be ethical often involves considerable personal sacrifice, and, at all corporate levels, it involves avoiding common rationalizations or excuses. Both CEOs and employees may justify unethical actions by suggesting that (1) the behaviour is not really illegal and so could be moral; (2) the action appears to be in the firm's best interests; (3) the action is unlikely ever to be detected; or (4) it appears that the action demonstrates loyalty to the boss, the firm, or short-term shareholder interests. Although these rationalizations may appear attractive at the moment of action, each action must be carefully examined. Otherwise, the firm's organizational governance system could end up being dominated by the more unsavoury side of organizational politics.

CHAPTER 15 STUDY GUIDE

Summary

STUDY QUESTIONS

What is power?

- Power is the ability to get someone else to do what one wants him or her to do or the ability to make things happen or get things done the way one wants.

- Power in managerial positions comes from three sources: rewards, punishments, and legitimacy (formal authority).

How do managers acquire the power that is needed for leadership?

- Formal authority is based on the manager's position in the hierarchy of authority, whereas personal power is based on one's expertise and referent capabilities.

- Managers can pursue various ways of acquiring both position and personal power.

- Managers can also become skilled at using various tactics, such as reason, friendliness, agreeability, and bargaining, to influence superiors, peers, and subordinates.

- People may have a tendency to obey directives coming from others who appear powerful and authoritative.

- The zone of indifference for people in an organization defines which of their behaviours they will let others influence.

- Ultimately, power and authority work only if the individual "accepts" them.

What is empowerment and how can managers empower others?

- Empowerment is the process through which managers help others get and use the power others need to have to make decisions that affect themselves and their work.

- Empowerment emphasizes power as the ability to get things done rather than as the ability to get others to do what one wants.

- Clear delegation of authority, integrated planning, and the involvement of senior management are all important to implementing empowerment.

What is organizational politics?

- Organizational politics are inevitable.

- Organizational politics involves the use of power to obtain ends that are not officially approved and the use of power to find ways of balancing individual and collective interests in otherwise difficult circumstances.

How are managers and management affected by organizational politics?

- For the manager, there are often politics in decision situations where the interests of another manager or individual must be reconciled with the manager's.

- For managers, politics also involves subunits that try to increase their power and get advantageous positions compared to other subunits.

- For chief executives, politics involves strategically managing the resource dependencies from the external environment.

- Politics can also be used strategically.

- Organizational governance is the pattern of authority, influence, and acceptable managerial behaviour that is decided at the top of the organization.

- CEOs and managers can develop an ethical organizational governance system that is free from rationalizations.

KEY TERMS

Coercive power (p. 300)

Empowerment (p. 307)

Expert power (p. 302)

Influence (p. 299)

Information power (p. 300)

Legitimate power (p. 300)

Organizational governance (p. 316)

Organizational politics (p. 309)

Power (p.299)

Process power (p. 300)

Rational persuasion (p. 302)

Referent power (p. 302)

Representative power (p. 301)

Reward power (p. 300)

Zone of indifference (p. 307)

SELF-TEST 15

MULTIPLE CHOICE

1. Three bases of position power are _____. (a) reward, expertise, and coercive power (b) legitimate, experience, and judgement power (c) knowledge, experience, and judgment power (d) reward, coercive, and knowledge power (e) reward, coercive, and legitimate power

2. _____ is the ability to control another's behaviour because, through the individual's efforts, the person accepts the desirability of an offered goal and a reasonable way of achieving it. (a) Rational persuasion (b) Legitimate power (c) Reward power (d) Coercive power (e) Charismatic power

3. A worker who behaves in a certain way to ensure an effective boss–subordinate relationship shows that the boss has _____ power. (a) expert (b) reward (c) coercive (d) approval (e) referent

4. When implementing a successful empowerment strategy _____. (a) the delegation of authority should be left ambiguous and open to individual interpretation (b) managers should stop communicating effectively to subordinates (c) planning should be separated according to the level of empowerment (d) it can be assumed that any empowering directives from management will be automatically followed (e) the authority delegated to lower levels should be clear and precise

5. The major lesson of the Milgram experiments is that _____. (a) Westerners are very independent and unwilling to obey (b) individuals are willing to obey as long as it does not hurt another person (c) individuals will obey an authority figure even if it does appear to hurt someone else (d) individuals will always obey an authority figure (e) individuals will hardly ever obey unless an authority figure repeatedly tells them to

6. The range of authoritative requests that a subordinate is willing to respond to without first evaluating or judging the directives critically is called the _____. (a) psychological contract (b) zone of indifference (c) Milgram experiment (d) functional level of organizational politics (e) power vector

7. The three basic power dimensions to ensure success are _____. (a) upward, downward, and lateral (b) upward, downward, and oblique (c) downward, lateral, and oblique (d) downward, lateral, and external (e) internal, external, and oblique

8. In which dimension of power and influence would a manager find the use of both position power and personal power most advantageous? (a) upward (b) lateral (c) downward (d) workflow (e) advisory

9. Reason, coalition, bargaining, and assertiveness are strategies for _____. (a) increasing personal power (b) increasing position power (c) using referent power (d) using influence (e) increasing coercive power

10. Negotiating the interpretation of a union contract is an example of _____. (a) organizational politics (b) lateral relations (c) an approval relationship (d) an auditing relation (e) unethical behaviour

TRUE–FALSE

11. Coercion is a behavioural response to the use of power.   T   F

12. Reference power is an example of power that comes from personal, as opposed to organizational, sources.   T   F

13. Position power includes the ability to control another's behaviour through an appeal to reason.   T   F

14. Legitimate power and formal authority are the same.   T   F

15. Reward power is how much a manager can use extrinsic and intrinsic rewards to control other people.   T   F

16. The acceptance theory of authority indicates that subordinates will always accept the orders of their superiors in organizations.   T   F

17. The Milgram experiments demonstrate that individuals are generally unwilling to obey the commands of authoritative persons.   T   F

18. The process a manager uses to help others get and use the power they need to have to make decisions that affect them is called organizational politics.   T   F

19. A resource-dependence perspective suggests that one of the key roles played by top management is to develop and allocate power.   T   F

20. Increasing one's knowledge and attractiveness are ways to increase one's position power.   T   F

SHORT ANSWER

21. Explain how the various bases of position and personal power do or do not apply to the classroom relationship between an instructor and student. What sources of power do students have over their instructors?

22. Identify and explain at least three guidelines for the acquisition by managers of (a) position power and (b) personal power.

23. Identify and explain at least four strategies of managerial influence. Give examples of how each strategy may or may not work when one is using influence in organizations (a) downward and (b) upward.

24. Define "organizational politics" and give an example of how they operate in both functional and dysfunctional ways.

APPLICATIONS ESSAY

25. If mergers and acquisitions were found to rarely produce financial gains for shareholders, what explanations would you give shareholders for why mergers and acquisitions happen?

Information and Communication

16

Using Technology to Enhance Communication and Employee Satisfaction

As a large retailer with 453 stores across Canada, in the late 1990s Canadian Tire found itself being challenged to effectively communicate with its 45,000 employees. The company had been steadily losing staff and market share due to training and communication difficulties in large part, and with its retail outlets independently owned, the challenge was even greater.

Enter "eLearning." This Internet-based training program, introduced in spring 2001, has allowed employees to access and participate in interactive lessons concerning, among other things, new employee orientation, customer service, job descriptions, and product knowledge on thousands of products and brands. Employees also have the option of logging on to the system at any time using computers at work or home, a cell phone, or even a PDA. All lessons are available in both English and French and take different provincial laws into consideration.

Although Canadian Tire had developed the eLearning program, before using it, the company first had to convince the corporate dealers to climb on board. Soon 85 percent of the dealers had signed up for the program, but the challenge lay in enticing employees to participate and to complete the lessons. Canadian Tire then developed a "Gold Status" program that required employees to complete a specific number of lessons in order to get the reward of a gold, silver, or bronze pin. Then, once all of a store's departments had attained the gold status, the store, too, was awarded gold status.

At the same time, the company developed a televised program in conjunction with the Canadian Automotive Repair and Service Council for its auto technicians and auto service counter employees. Called Interactive Distant Learning (IDL), the training is avail-

able in two-hour modules taught by professional trainers and requires only a television, a dedicated phone line, and a satellite hookup. Students also have access to follow-up exams to test their knowledge. Besides automotive skills, the IDL system is used to offer training in leadership, management, and computer software use. Employees also have unlimited access to a technical help desk.

With so much going into it, has the program been a success? Janice Wismer, vice-president of human resources, confirms that it has, from an employee satisfaction perspective: "People say the lessons have increased their confidence, that they're happier working here because the company is committing to their growth and development."

Chapter 16 examines the process of communication, with special attention to its interpersonal and organizational challenges, as well as the opportunities from new developments in information technology. As you read this chapter, keep in mind these key questions:

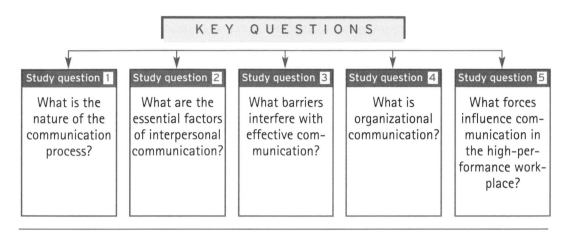

KEY QUESTIONS

Study question 1	Study question 2	Study question 3	Study question 4	Study question 5
What is the nature of the communication process?	What are the essential factors of interpersonal communication?	What barriers interfere with effective communication?	What is organizational communication?	What forces influence communication in the high-performance workplace?

Communication is vital to an organization. But it takes hard work and true commitment to create the information-rich environment that exists at Canadian Tire. This is especially true in an age where speed is critical for organizations and in an age where Microsoft's chairman Bill Gates can say, "Only managers who master the digital universe will gain competitive advantage."[1]

Using information and technology to get a high-performance advantage requires a commitment to opening up the communication linkages and opportunities among people in organizations, and between them and their customers. It also requires a culture of trust throughout the organization, a culture that encourages a free flow of ideas and suggestions up and down the hierarchy, as well as among peers and colleagues. In a recent survey by the American Management Association, however, respondents gave their managers only a 63 percent success rating in respect to "communicating information and direction." Respondents in another sample rated their managers' skills in "listening and asking questions" at only an average 3.36 on a five-point scale.[2] Clearly, communication is an area where organizations can focus their efforts in their goal to become a high-performance organization.

The Nature of Communication

Have you ever stopped to think about how information technology is critical to the way we communicate? It is safe to estimate that there will be more than a billion voice-mail messages exchanged today; 450 trillion e-mails will be sent this year; over 100 million Internet users will come on-line this year; and Internet traffic will double as fast as every 100 days.[3] The figures are amazing, and the implications are clear. The need for information is enormous, and the future of organizations is increasingly linked to their abilities to use information and information technology to realize and maintain a competitive advantage. At the centre of all this are the great demands and opportunities of the process we call "communication."

THE COMMUNICATION PROCESS

Communication is the process of sending and receiving symbols with attached meanings.

Noise is anything that interferes with the effectiveness of communication.

It is useful to think of **communication** as the process of sending and receiving symbols that have attached meanings. The key elements in the communication process are illustrated in Figure 16.1. They include a source, who encodes an intended meaning into a message, and a receiver, who decodes the message into a perceived meaning. The receiver may or may not give feedback to the source. Although this process may appear to be very elementary, it is not quite as simple as it looks. **Noise** is the term used to describe any disturbance that disrupts this process and interferes with the transfer of messages in the communication process.

Figure 16.1 The communication process and possible sources of "noise"

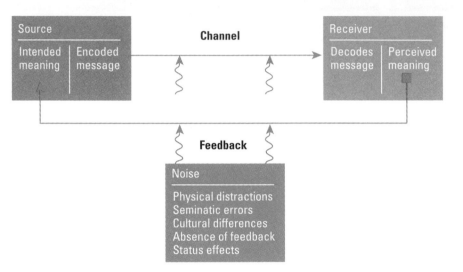

The information source is a person or group trying to communicate with someone else. The source seeks to communicate, at least in part, to change the attitudes, knowledge, or behaviour of the receiver. A team leader, for example, may want to communicate with a division manager in order to explain why the team needs more time or resources to finish an assigned project. This involves *encoding*—the process of translating an idea or thought into a message consisting of verbal, written, or non-verbal symbols (such as gestures), or some combination of them. Messages are transmitted through various **communication channels**, such as face-to-face meetings, electronic mail, written letters or memorandums, and telephone communications or voice-mail, among others. The choice of channel can have an important impact on the communication process. Some people are better at using certain channels than others, and some messages fit better with specific channels. In the case of the team leader who needs to communicate with the division manager, for example, it can make quite a difference if the message is delivered face to face, in a written memo, by voice-mail, or by e-mail.

Communication channels are the pathways through which messages are communicated.

The communication process is not completed just because a message is sent. The receiver is the individual or group of individuals that a message is directed to. In order for meaning to be assigned to any received message—that is, for the message to be given a meaning—its contents must be interpreted through decoding. This process of translation is complicated by many factors, including the knowledge and experience of the receiver and his or her relationship with the sender. The points of view of other individuals—such as friends, co-workers, or superiors in the organization—can also influence the way the receiver interprets the message. Ultimately, the decoding may result in the receiver interpreting a message in a way that is different from what the source originally intended.

Stratford Internet Technologies was a hot technology firm attracting many talented employees even though such employees were the hardest to find at that time. Sales grew to over $10 million in four years and there was always a profit for this company that designed websites. Investors from across North America lauded the firm for its excellent communication methods. A free lunch actually happened. If you and another employee wanted to go to lunch, the company would pay up to $20 per person on one condition: you had to eat with someone from the company whom you didn't know. At monthly dinners, employees were treated to expensive meals and beverages, but the CEO, Robert Craig, always filled his table with people he didn't know. With the technological crash of 2001, clients such as The Keg, Ballard Power, and The David Suzuki Foundation continued on, but, unfortunately, Stratford failed. Many of its clients could now create and manage their own websites in house. The model for Stratford was well received but the technology changed, exceeding the firm's ability to survive.

Feedback communicates how one feels about something another person has done or said.

360-degree feedback provides performance feedback from peers, co-workers, and direct reports, as well as from the supervisor.

FEEDBACK AND COMMUNICATION

Most receivers are very aware of the potential gap there can be between the intended message of the source and the meaning the receiver has given to the message. One way in which these gaps are identified is through feedback. This is the process in which the receiver communicates with the sender by returning another message. The exchange of information through feedback can be very helpful in improving the communication process, and the popular advice to always "keep the feedback channels open" is good to remember.

In practice, giving "feedback" is often thought of as involving one or more persons who are communicating an evaluation of what another person has said or done. The practice of 360-degree feedback—in which not just a supervisor, but also one's peers, co-workers, and direct reports provide feedback on performance—was introduced in Chapter 7. As said earlier, firms such as Enbridge, Intuit, and Joseph Brant Hospital in Burlington, Ontario, now use 360-degree evaluations. This is an increasingly popular approach to performance reviews that makes feedback processes even more challenging. Like any feedback situation, all parties must engage in the 360-degree feedback situation carefully and with interpersonal skill.[4]

There is an art to giving feedback so that the receiver accepts the feedback and uses it constructively (see The Effective Manager 16.1). Words that are intended to be polite and helpful can easily end up being perceived as unpleasant and even hostile. This risk is particularly high in the performance appraisal process. A manager or team leader must be able to do more than just complete a written appraisal that documents another person's performance for the record. To help the person develop, feedback on the results of the appraisal—both the praise and the criticism—must be well communicated.

The Effective Manager 16.1
HOW TO GIVE CONSTRUCTIVE FEEDBACK
• Give directly and in a spirit of mutual trust.
• Be specific, not general; use clear examples.
• Give when the receiver is most ready to accept.
• Be accurate; check validity with others.
• Focus on things the receiver can control.
• Limit how much the receiver gets at one time.

Essential Factors of Interpersonal Communication

Organizations today are information-rich and integrate technology from basic, entry-level positions to top executive positions. They are also increasingly "high-tech." But we always need to remember that people still drive the system. And for people to work together well and put their mutual talents and energies into creating high-performance organizations, they must excel at interpersonal communication.

EFFECTIVE AND EFFICIENT COMMUNICATION

When people communicate with each other, at least two important things are at issue. One is the accuracy of the communication—an issue of effectiveness. The other is the cost of the communication—an issue of efficiency.

Effective communication occurs when the intended meaning of the source and the perceived meaning of the receiver are virtually the same.[5] Although this should be the goal in any communication, it is not always achieved. Even now, as you read this, we worry about whether or not you are interpreting these written words exactly as we intend. Our confidence would be higher if we were face to face in class together and you could ask clarifying questions. Opportunities to offer feedback and ask questions are important ways of increasing the effectiveness of communication.

Efficient communication costs as little as possible in the resources it uses. Time, for example, is an important resource. Picture your instructor taking the time to communicate individually with each student about the course content. It would be virtually impossible to do so. Even if it were possible, it would be very costly in terms of time. It is much more efficient to communicate the course content to a larger class at one time. People at work often choose not to visit each other personally to communicate messages. Instead, they rely on the efficiency of written memos, posted bulletins, group meetings, e-mail, or voice-mail, as does your instructor.

As efficient as these forms of communication may be, they are not always effective. A change in policy posted by efficient e-mail may save time for the sender, but it may not achieve the desired interpretations and responses. Similarly, an effective communication may not be efficient. For a business manager to visit each employee and explain a new change in procedures may guarantee that everyone understands the change, but it may also be far too expensive in terms of the required time expenditure.

NON-VERBAL COMMUNICATION

People communicate in ways other than the spoken or written word. **Non-verbal communication** takes place through facial expressions, body position, eye contact, and other physical gestures and is important both to understand and master. It is basically the act of speaking without using words. Kinesics, the study of gestures and body postures, has achieved a rightful place in communication theory and research.[6] The non-verbal side to communication can often hold the key to what someone is really thinking or meaning. It can also affect the impressions we make on others. Interviewers, for example, tend to respond more favourably to job candidates whose non-verbal cues, such as eye contact and erect posture, are positive than to those displaying negative non-verbal cues, such as looking down or slouching. The art of impression management during interviews and in other situations requires careful attention to both the verbal and non-verbal aspects of communication, including one's dress, timeliness, and demeanour.

Just how important non-verbal communication is to humans is made clear even by our emails, which become more expressive with the inclusion of "smileys" that allow us to frown :-(, shout :-<, smile :), and so on. Humans are able to enrich many means of communication in order to increase understanding, no matter what the technology.

Non-verbal communication can also take place through the physical arrangement of space, such as that found in various office layouts. Proxemics, the study of the way space is used, is important to communication.[7] Figure 16.2 shows three different office arrangements and the messages they may communicate to visitors. Compare the diagrams to the furniture arrangement in your office or that of your instructor or a person you know. What are you or they saying to visitors through the way the furniture is placed?[8]

Effective communication is when the intended meaning equals the perceived meaning.

Efficient communication is low cost in its use of resources.

Non-verbal communication occurs by facial expressions, body motions, eye contact, and other physical gestures.

Figure 16.2 Furniture placement and non-verbal communication in the office

"I am the boss!" "I am the boss, but let's talk." "Forget I'm the boss, let's talk."

ACTIVE LISTENING

The ability to listen well is a distinct asset for anyone whose job involves a large amount of time "communicating" with other people. After all, there are always two sides to the communication process: (1) sending a message, or "telling," and (2) receiving a message, or "listening." Unfortunately, too many people emphasize the telling and neglect the listening.[9]

Everyone in the workplace should develop good skills in **active listening**—the ability to help the source of a message say what he or she really means. This concept comes from the work of counsellors and therapists, who are trained to help people express themselves and talk about things that are important to them.[10] Take some extra time to carefully think about the guidelines for active listening that are given in The Effective Manager 16.2. Then read the conversations below. One involves active listening by the branch manager; the other does not. How would you feel as the group leader in each case?[11]

Active listening encourages people to say what they really mean.

Example 1

Group leader: Hey, Sal, I don't get this work order. We can't handle this today. What do they think we are?

Branch manager: But that's the order. So get it out as soon as you can. We're under terrific pressure this week.

Group leader: Don't they know we're behind schedule already because of that software problem?

Branch manager: Look, I don't decide what goes on upstairs. I just have to see that the work gets out, and that's what I'm going to do.

Group leader: The team won't like this.

Branch manager: That's something you'll have to work out with them, not me.

Example 2

Group leader: Hey, Kelly, I don't get this work order. We can't handle this today. What do they think we are?

Branch manager: Sounds like you're pretty sore about it, John.

Group leader: I sure am. We're just about getting back to schedule while fighting that software breakdown. Now this comes along.

Branch manager: As if you didn't have enough work to do?

The Effective Manager 16.2

GUIDELINES FOR ACTIVE LISTENING

1. Listen for content—try to hear exactly what is being said.

2. Listen for feelings—try to identify how the source feels about things.

3. Respond to feelings—let the source know that his or her feelings are recognized.

4. Note all cues—be sensitive to both verbal and non-verbal expressions.

5. Reflect back—repeat in your own words what you think you are hearing.

Group leader: Right, I don't know how to tell the team about this. They're under a real strain today. Seems like everything we do around here is rush, rush, rush.

Branch manager: I guess you feel like it's unfair to load anything more on them.

Group leader: Well, yes. But I know there must be plenty of pressure on everybody up the line. If that's the way it is, I'll get the word to them.

Branch manager: Thanks. If you'll give it a try, I'll do my best to hold with the schedule in the future.

The branch manager in the second example has active listening skills. She responded to the group leader's communication in a way that increased the flow of information. The manager learned more about the situation. The group leader felt better after having been able to really say what she thought, and after being heard!

Communication Barriers

It is important to understand six sources of noise that are common in most interpersonal exchanges: physical distractions, semantic problems, mixed messages, cultural differences, absence of feedback, and status effects. They were shown earlier in Figure 16.1 as potential threats to the communication process.

PHYSICAL DISTRACTIONS

There are many physical distractions that can interfere with the effectiveness of a communication attempt. Some of these distractions are evident in the following excerpt of a conversation between an employee, George, and his manager:[12]

> Okay, George, let's hear your problem (phone rings, boss picks it up, promises to deliver the report, "just as soon as I can get it done"). Uh, now, where were we—oh, you're having a problem with marketing. They (the manager's secretary brings in some papers that need immediate signatures; he scribbles his name and the secretary leaves)...you say they're not co-operative? I tell you what, George, why don't you (phone rings again, lunch partner drops by)...uh, take a stab at handling it yourself. I've got to go now.

In addition to what may have been the manager's poor intentions in the first place, George's manager also allowed physical distractions to create an information overload. As a result, the communication with George suffered. This mistake can be eliminated by setting priorities and planning. If George has something to say, his manager should set aside enough time for the meeting. In addition, interruptions such as telephone calls, drop-in visitors, and so on should be prevented from happening. At a minimum, George's manager could start by closing the door to the office and instructing his secretary not to disturb them.

SEMANTIC PROBLEMS

Semantic barriers to communication include a poor choice or use of words, and mixed messages. The following examples of the "bafflegab" that was once presented as actual "executive communication" are a case in point:[13]

A. "We solicit any recommendations that you wish to make, and you may be assured that any such recommendations will be given our careful consideration."

B. "Consumer elements are continuing to stress the fundamental necessity of a stabilization of the price structure at a lower level than exists at the present time."

One has to wonder why these messages were not stated more simply: (A) "Send us your recommendations. They will be carefully considered"; and (B) "Consumers want lower prices." When you have doubts about how clear your written or spoken messages are, the popular **KISS principle** of communication is always worth remembering: "Keep it short and simple."

The KISS principle stands for "Keep it short and simple."

MIXED MESSAGES

Mixed messages occur when a person's words communicate one thing while his or her actions or "body language" communicate something else. They are important to notice since non-verbal elements can help one understand what is really being said in face-to-face communication.[14] For instance, someone may voice a cautious "Yes" during a business meeting at the same time that her facial expression shows stress and she begins to lean back in her chair. The body language in this case may suggest the person has important reservations, even though her words indicate agreement.

Mixed messages occur when words say one thing while non-verbal cues say something else.

CULTURAL DIFFERENCES

People must always be careful when they are involved in cross-cultural communication—whether the communication is between persons of different geographical or ethnic groupings within the same country, or between persons of different national cultures. A common problem is *ethnocentrism*, first defined in Chapter 3 as the tendency to believe one's culture and its values are superior to those of others. This often leads to an unwillingness to try to understand alternative points of view and to take the values expressed by these views seriously. This way of thinking can easily create communication problems among people with diverse backgrounds.

The difficulties with cross-cultural communication are perhaps most obvious in respect to language differences. Advertising messages, for example, may work well in one country but not work so well when they are translated into the language of another country. There were problems like this when Ford introduced its European model, the "Ka," in Japan—in Japanese, Ka means mosquito. Gestures may also be used quite differently in the various cultures of the world. For example, crossed legs are quite acceptable in the United Kingdom but they are rude in Saudi Arabia if the sole of the foot is directed toward someone. Similarly, pointing at someone to get his or her attention may be acceptable in Canada, but in Asia it is considered inappropriate.[15]

International business experts advise that one of the best ways to gain understanding of cultural differences is to learn at least some of the language of the country that one is dealing with. Although the prospect of learning another language may sound daunting, The Effective Manager 16.3 shows that it can be well worth the effort.[16]

> **The Effective Manager 16.3**
>
> **WHY BUILD FOREIGN LANGUAGE SKILLS?**
> - Increase your self-confidence as a traveller.
> - Show respect to local hosts.
> - Build relationships with locals.
> - Earn the trust and respect of locals.
> - Gain insights into local culture.
> - Prepare for emergencies.
> - Find greater pleasure in day-to-day interactions.
> - Experience less frustration with local ways.

ABSENCE OF FEEDBACK

One-way communication flows only from the sender to the receiver, as in the case of a written memo or a voice-mail message. There is no direct and immediate feedback from the receiver. Two-way communication, by contrast, goes from sender to receiver and back again. This is typical of the normal interactive conversations in our daily experiences. Research indicates that two-way communication is more accurate and effective than one-way communication, even though it is also more costly and time consuming. Because of their efficiency, however, one-way forms of communication—memos, letters, e-mails, voice-mail, and so on—are frequently used in work settings. One-way messages are easy for the sender but often frustrating for the receiver, who may be left unsure about just what the sender means or wants done.

STATUS EFFECTS

Status differences in organizations create potential communication barriers between persons of higher and lower ranks. On the one hand, because of the authority of their positions, managers may have a tendency to do a lot of "telling" but not much "listening." On the other hand, we know that communication is frequently biased when it flows upward in organizational hierarchies.[17] Subordinates may filter information and tell their superiors only what they think the boss wants to hear. Whether the reason is a fear of punishment for bringing bad news, an unwillingness to identify personal mistakes, or just a general desire to please, the result is the same: the higher-level decision-maker may end up taking the wrong actions because of biased and inaccurate information from below. This is sometimes called the **mum effect**, named after the expression "to keep mum" or "stay mum" about something, which means to say nothing—usually out of a desire to be polite, a reluctance to give bad news, or simply the wish to keep something secret.[18]

The **mum effect** occurs when people are reluctant to communicate bad news.

To avoid such problems, managers and group leaders must develop trust in their working relationships with subordinates and team members, and they have to take advantage of all opportunities for face-to-face communications. *Management by wandering around*, or **MBWA** for short, is now popularly acclaimed as one way to achieve this trust.[19] It simply means getting out of the office and talking to people regularly as they do their jobs. Managers who spend time walking around can greatly reduce the perceived "distance" between themselves and their subordinates. It helps to create an atmosphere of open and free-flowing communication between the ranks. As a result, more and better information is available for decision-making and decisions become more relevant to the needs of workers.

MBWA involves getting out of the office to directly communicate with others.

Organizational Communication

Communication among members of an organization, as well as between them and external customers, suppliers, distributors, alliance partners, and many other outsiders, provides vital information for the enterprise. **Organizational communication** is the specific process through which information moves and is exchanged throughout an organization.[20] Information flows through both formal and informal structures, and it flows downward, upward, and laterally. Encana, for example, states in its corporate constitution that it expects employees to "communicate freely and openly, exchanging views, ideas, and lessons learned." For its part, Royal Bank of Canada says it has removed restrictive barriers to enable the sharing of ideas and information and increase productivity.

Organizational communication is the process through which information is exchanged in organizations.

Technology plays a major role in how information is shared and used in organizations. Research in the area of channel richness—that is, the capacity of a channel to carry information effectively—offers insight into how various channel alternatives may be used depending on the type of message to be carried. In general, the richest channel is face to face. Next are the telephone, electronic methods (such as videoconferencing), e-mail, written memos, and letters. The leanest channels are posted notices and bulletins. When messages get more complex and open-ended, richer channels are necessary to achieve effective communication; leaner channels work well for more routine and straightforward messages, such as announcing the location of a previously scheduled meeting.

FORMAL AND INFORMAL CHANNELS

Information flows in organizations through both formal and informal channels of communication. **Formal channels** follow the chain of command that has been established by an organization's hierarchy of authority. For example, an organization chart indicates the proper routing for official messages that pass from one level or part of the hierarchy to another. Because formal channels are recognized as authoritative, it is typical for communications about policies, procedures, and other official announcements to use only these channels. On the other hand, much "networking" takes place through the use of **informal channels** that do not follow the organization's hierarchy of authority.[21] They exist beside the formal channels and often split away from them by skipping levels in the hierarchy or cutting across vertical chains of command. Informal channels help to create open communications in organizations and ensure that the right people are in contact with each other.[22]

Formal channels follow the official chain of command.

Informal channels do not follow the chain of command.

HIGH-PERFORMANCE ORGANIZATION

Intuit Canada encourages communication and the best in amenities for its employees. When it designed its new offices, management chose a site that offered nearby shopping, highway access, public transit, and free parking. The employee lounge and rest area includes a fireplace and rest rooms for a quick nap. Fitness classes are available onsite and the fitness facility is open 24 hours a day. There is a monthly newsletter, and an Intranet site keeps all employees up to date on developments. There is even a satisfaction survey of the employees called "Great Place to Work" conducted every 12 months by an outside consultant.[23] How people work and what they think and feel are important enough to warrant effective listening by management.

One familiar informal channel is the **grapevine** or network of friends and acquaintances that rumours and other unofficial information passes through from person to person. Grapevines have the advantage of being able to transmit information quickly and efficiently. Grapevines also help satisfy the needs of people involved in them. Being part of a grapevine can provide a sense of security by "being in the know" when important things are going on. It also provides social satisfaction as information is exchanged interpersonally. The primary disadvantage of grapevines occurs when they transmit incorrect or untimely information. Rumours can be very dysfunctional, to both people and organizations. One of the best ways to avoid them is to make sure that key persons in a grapevine get the right information to begin with.

A **grapevine** transfers information through networks of friends and acquaintances.

COMMUNICATION FLOWS AND DIRECTIONS

As shown in Figure 16.3, *downward communication* follows the chain of command from top to bottom. One of its major functions is to have an influence through information. Lower-level personnel need to know what the higher levels are doing and they need to be regularly reminded of key policies, strategies, objectives, and technical developments. Of special importance are feedback and information on performance results. Sharing such information limits the spread of rumours and inaccuracies about the intentions of people at the higher levels. It also helps create a sense of security and involvement among the receivers, because they feel they know the whole story. Unfortunately, not having enough downward communication is often mentioned as a management failure. On the issue of corporate downsizing, for example, one sample in a study showed that 64 percent of employees did not believe what management said, 61 percent felt uninformed about company plans, and 54 percent complained that decisions were not well explained.[24]

Figure 16.3 Directions for information flows in organizations

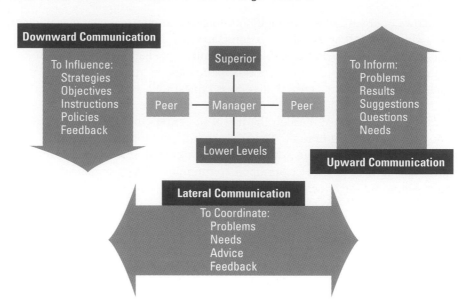

The flow of messages from lower to higher levels is upward communication. As shown in Figure 16.3, it serves several purposes. Upward communication keeps the higher levels informed about what lower-level workers are doing, what their problems are, what suggestions they have for improvements, and how they feel about the organization and their jobs. But, as you should recall, status effects can potentially interfere with the effectiveness of upward communication.

The importance of *lateral communication* in the high-performance organization has been a recurrent theme in this book. Today's customer-sensitive organizations need timely and accurate feedback and product information. To satisfy customer needs, they must get the right information into the hands of workers—and get it there fast enough. Furthermore, inside the organization, people must be willing and able to communicate across departmental or functional boundaries and to listen to each other's needs as "internal customers." High-performance organization designs are emphasizing lateral communication in the form of cross-departmental committees, teams, or task forces, and the matrix organization. One recent development is the growing attention being given to *organizational ecology*—the study of how building design may influence communication and productivity by improving lateral communications, something Intuit is big on.

COMMUNICATION NETWORKS

Figure 16.4 shows three interaction patterns and communication networks that are common in organizations.[25] Having the right interaction pattern and communication network can make a big difference in the way groups function and in the performance results they achieve.

Some work arrangements involve interacting groups. The members of such groups work closely together on tasks, and activities are closely coordinated. Information flows to everyone. This interaction pattern results in a **decentralized communication network** in which all group members communicate directly and share information with each other. Sometimes these are also called all-channel or star communication networks.[26] They work best for complex and non-routine tasks. They also tend to create high levels of member satisfaction.

Decentralized communication networks link all group members directly with each other.

Figure 16.4 Interaction patterns and communication networks found in groups

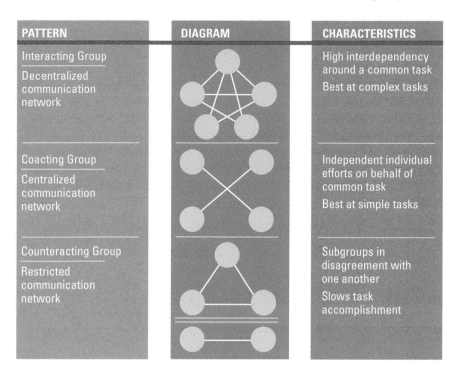

PATTERN	DIAGRAM	CHARACTERISTICS
Interacting Group Decentralized communication network		High interdependency around a common task Best at complex tasks
Coacting Group Centralized communication network		Independent individual efforts on behalf of common task Best at simple tasks
Counteracting Group Restricted communication network		Subgroups in disagreement with one another Slows task accomplishment

Another work arrangement is *coacting groups*. The members of these kinds of groups work on tasks independently, but they are linked through some form of central coordination. The required work is divided up and then largely completed by individuals working alone. Each individual's activities are coordinated and the results are brought together by a central control point. Information flows to a central person and is redistributed. This creates a **centralized communication network**, with the central person serving as the hub. Sometimes this arrangement is also called a wheel or chain communication network. It works best when tasks are easily routinized or subdivided. In these groups, it is usually the central or hub person who experiences satisfaction. After all, he or she is the only person involved in all aspects of the group's information processing.

Counteracting groups exist when subgroups disagree about some aspect of the workplace operations. The subgroups may have issue-specific disagreements—such as a temporary debate over the best way to achieve a goal—or the disagreements may be longer-term—such as labour–management disputes. In either case, the resulting interaction pattern is a **restricted communication network**, a situation in which polarized subgroups argue against each other's positions and sometimes have antagonistic relations with each other. As would be expected, communication between the groups is often limited and biased. There are also likely to be problems of destructive competition between the groups under such circumstances.

Centralized communication networks link group members through a central control point.

Restricted communication networks link subgroups that disagree with each other's positions.

Communication and the High-Performance Workplace

One of the greatest changes in organizations and in everyday life in the last five years has been the complete integration of new communication technologies. We have moved from the world of just the telephone, mail, photocopying, and face-to-face meetings into one which includes voice-mail, e-mail, tele-conferencing, and use of the Internet and intranets. Being able to participate effectively in all forms of the electronic office and communications environment has become an essential career skill. E-commerce is also transforming the very nature of business in modern society.[27] Given the pace and extensiveness of these changes, everyone must continuously keep themselves up to date with the full range of information technologies and emerging issues in organizational communication.

CHANGING TECHNOLOGIES

Technology is discussed throughout this book for how it has affected job design and the growth of telecommuting; organizational design and the growth of network organizations; and teamwork and software for electronic meetings and decision-making, among many other applications. Advances in information technology are allowing organizations to (1) distribute information much faster than before; (2) make more information available than ever before; (3) allow broader and more immediate access to this information; (4) encourage participation in the sharing and use of information; and (5) integrate systems and functions, and use information to link with environments in unprecedented ways.

The potential disadvantages of e-communications must also be recognized. To begin, the technologies are largely impersonal; people interact with machines, not with each other. Electronics also remove non-verbal communications from the situation, which, as we saw earlier, can add important, and perhaps unintentional, context to an interaction. The electronic medium can also influence the emotional aspects of communication. Some observers argue, for example, that it is far easier to be blunt, overly critical, and insensitive when messages are sent electronically rather than given face-to-face. Indeed, the term "flaming" is sometimes used to describe rudeness in electronic communication. This suggests that the use of computers as a means of communication may make people less inhibited and more impatient in what they say.

Another risk of e-communication technologies is information overload. In some cases, too much information may find its way into the communication networks and e-mail systems, and the systems basically get overloaded—both organizational and individual. Individual users may have difficulty sorting the useful from the trivial and may become impatient while doing so. Even the IT giant Intel experiences e-mail problems. Employees at the firm reportedly handle over 3 million e-mail messages a day; some individuals handle as many as 300 in a day. Says one employee, "We're so wrapped up in sending e-mail to each other, we don't have time to be dealing with the outside." Intel offers training in e-mail processing as a way of helping employees gain the advantages and avoid the disadvantages of electronic messaging. The Effective Manager 16.4 lists several suggested guidelines.[28]

In all this, one point remains undeniable: e-communication technologies will continue to change the nature of work and of office work in particular. The non-conventional office incorporates telecommuting, electronic networks, and wireless technology. Workers in the future will continue to benefit as new technologies allow them to spend more time out of the traditional office and working with customers—and according to the hours and other conditions that best fit their individual needs.

The Effective Manager 16.4

HOW TO STREAMLINE YOUR E-MAIL

- Read items once.
- Take action immediately to answer, move to folders, or delete.
- Regularly purge folders of outdated messages.
- Send group mail and use "reply to all" only when really necessary.
- Get off distribution lists that do not offer value to your work.
- Send short messages in the subject line, avoiding a full-text message.
- Place large files on company intranets or FTP sites, instead of sending them as attachments.
- Subscribe to a SPAM filter service, such as Symantec.
- Do not use all capitals to communicate.

COMPLEX SOCIAL CONTEXT

There are many issues that affect communication in the complex social context of organizations today. Of continuing interest, for example, is the study of male and female communication styles. In her book *Talking 9 to 5*, Deborah Tannen argues that men and women learn or are socialized into different styles and, as a result, often end up having difficulties communicating with each other.[29] She sees women as being more oriented toward relationship building in communication, for example, while men are more likely to seek status through communications.[30] Because people tend to surround themselves with other people whose communication styles fit with their own, this could mean that women or men may dominate communications in situations where they are in the majority.[31]

OB ACROSS FUNCTIONS

Management Information Systems

Enterprise Resource Planning Builds the E-Corporation

Total enterprise integration is one of the big pushes these days. Consider the example of VF Corporation, the world's largest apparel manufacturer. It manufactures over $2 billion of jeans each year for major brands including Lee, Wrangler, Britannia, and Rustler, and also manufactures many other products under names such as North Face, JanSport, Nautica, and Vanity Fair, among others. When Mackey McDonald took over as the firm's CEO, his vision was to create a computer-savvy company that would use the latest in technologies to continually identify customer demographics and point-of-sale and other relevant information to drive its production and distribution systems. In short, information and technology were to be used for a competitive advantage. VF's integrated information systems begin with SAP software, which is used for resource planning at the corporate level and for the entire organization. SAP acts as the information systems hub and communicates with special software programs that individually deal with such needs as product development, micromarketing, forecasting, capacity and raw materials planning, manufacturing control, and warehouse control. It's all sophisticated and integrated, and with a purpose. The investment cost over $100 million, but it also brought the goals of speed to market and cost efficiency within reach. McDonald is confident that the returns will be high. After all, he began the process by involving employees from all levels of the firm in planning and identifying systems needs. He sums it up this way: "Our people designed the products and the processes. That's why I think we can have success."

An interesting debate exists about today's organizations: "Are women better communicators than men?" A study by the consulting firm Lawrence A. Pfaff and Associates suggests that they may well be.[32] The survey shows that supervisors rank women managers higher than men managers on communication, approachability, evaluations, and empowering others; the subordinates also rank women higher on these same items. A possible explanation is that early socialization and training better prepare women for the skills involved in communication and may make them more sensitive in interpersonal relationships. In contrast, men may be more socialized in ways that cause communication problems—such as aggression, competitiveness, and individualism.[33] In considering such possibilities, however, it is important to avoid gender stereotyping and to focus instead on what really matters—finding out how communication in organizations can be made most effective.[34]

One of the controversies in organizational communication today is the issue of *privacy*. An example that involves questions of privacy is when employers eavesdrop on their employees' use of electronic messaging in corporate facilities. A study by the American Management Association found that electronic monitoring of employee performance increased by over 45 percent in a year's time. Almost one-third of the U.S. employers monitored their employees' communications. You may be surprised to learn that the most frequently reported things bosses watch for are the number of telephone calls and time spent on telephone calls (39%), e-mail messages (27%), computer files (21%), telephone conversations (11%), and voice-mail messages (6%).[35]

Progressive organizations are developing internal policies regarding the privacy of employee communications, and the issue is gaining attention from legislators. Canada's Personal Information Protection and Electronic Documents Act (PIPEDA), which was finalized in January 2004, applies to personal information about employees of an organization that collects, uses, or discloses the information in connection with federal work or business. And, wherever similar provincial legislation doesn't apply, PIPEDA also applies to all organizations in Canada that collect, use, or disclose personal information in the course of commercial activities. While PIPEDA doesn't specifically apply to all employers and employees in Canada, it does provide best practices guidelines.

An employer's need for information should be balanced with an employee's right to privacy. Recognizing that employers may consider electronic monitoring and other surveillance necessary to ensure productivity, stop confidential information leaks, and prevent workplace harassment, the Privacy Commissioner provides the following basic rules for handling personal information:

- The employer should say what personal information it collects from employees, why it collects it, and what it does with it.

- Collection, use, or disclosure of personal information should normally be done only with an employee's knowledge and consent.

- The employer should only collect personal information that's necessary for its stated purpose, and collect it by fair and lawful means.

- The employer should normally use or disclose personal information only for the purposes that it collected it for, and keep it only as long as it's needed for those purposes, unless it has the employee's consent to do something else with it, or is legally required to use or disclose it for other purposes.

- Employees' personal information needs to be accurate, complete, and up-to-date.

- Employees should be able to access their personal information, and be able to challenge the accuracy and completeness of it.[36]

Employers need to inform employees of their policies on web, e-mail, and telephone use, and if employees are subject to random or continuous surveillance, they need to be told so.

Still such eavesdropping is common in some service areas, such as airline reservations, where union concerns are sometimes expressed by the phrase: "Big brother is watching you!" The privacy issue is likely to remain controversial as communication technologies continue to make it easier for employers to electronically monitor the performance and communications of their workers. The obligation of the employee to work for the benefit of the employer overlaps with the right and expectation of privacy. This issue will take a long time to resolve.

CHAPTER 16 STUDY GUIDE

Summary

What is the nature of the communication process?

- Communication is the process of sending and receiving messages with attached meanings.

- The communication process involves encoding an intended meaning into a message, sending the message through a channel, and receiving and decoding the message into perceived meaning.

- Noise is anything that interferes with the communication process.

- Feedback is a return message from the original receiver back to the sender.

- To be constructive, feedback must be direct, specific, and given at an appropriate time.

What are the essential factors in interpersonal communication?

- Communication is effective when both the sender and the receiver interpret a message in the same way.

- Communication is efficient when messages are transferred at a low cost.

- Non-verbal communication occurs through facial expressions, body position, eye contact, and other physical gestures.

- Active listening encourages a free and complete flow of communication from the sender to the receiver; it is non-judgemental and encouraging.

- Communication in organizations uses a variety of formal and informal channels; the richness of the channel, or its capacity to carry information, must be adequate for the message.

What barriers interfere with effective communication?

- The possible barriers to communication include physical distractions, semantic problems, and cultural differences.

- Mixed messages that give confused or conflicting verbal and non-verbal cues may interfere with communication.

- The absence of feedback can make it difficult to know whether or not an intended message has been accurately received.

- Status effects in organizations may result in restricted and filtered information exchanges between subordinates and their superiors.

What is organizational communication?

- Organizational communication is the specific process through which information moves and is exchanged in an organization.

- Organizations depend on complex flows of information, upward, downward, and laterally, to operate effectively.

- Groups in organizations work with different interaction patterns and use different communication networks.

- Interacting groups with decentralized networks tend to perform well on complex tasks; coacting groups with centralized networks may do well at simple tasks.

- Restricted communication networks are common in counteracting groups experiencing subgroup disagreements.

What forces influence communication in the high-performance workplace?

- As new electronic communication technologies change the workplace, they bring many advantages of rapid and greater information-processing capability.

- These same technologies have the potential to bring disadvantages, including a loss of emotion and personal feeling in the communication process.

- Researchers are interested in possible differences in communication styles among men and women and in how effective these styles are in the new workplace.

- Current controversies in organizational communication include the issues of privacy and political correctness in workplace communications.

KEY TERMS

Active listening (p. 327)

Centralized communication networks (p. 333)

Communication (p. 324)

Communication channels (p. 324)

Decentralized communication networks (p. 332)

Effective communication (p. 326)

Efficient communication (p. 326)

Feedback (p. 325)

Formal channels (p. 331)

Grapevine (p. 331)

Informal channels (p. 331)

KISS principle (p. 329)

MBWA (p. 330)

Mixed messages (p. 329)

Mum effect (p. 330)

Noise (p. 324)

Non-verbal communication (p. 326)

Organizational communication (p. 330)

Restricted communication networks (p. 333)

360-degree feedback (p. 325)

SELF-TEST 16

MULTIPLE CHOICE

1. When criticism is given to someone, it should be _____. (a) general and non-specific (b) given when the sender feels the need to give it (c) related to things the recipient can do something about (d) given all at once to get everything over with

2. In _____ communication the cost is low, whereas in _____ communication the intended message is fully received. (a) effective, electronic (b) efficient, electronic (c) electronic, face-to-face (d) efficient, effective

3. Which channel is more appropriate for sending a complex and open-ended message? (a) a face-to-face meeting (b) a written memorandum (c) an e-mail (d) a telephone call

4. When someone's words express one meaning and their body posture expresses something else, a(n) _____ is occurring. (a) ethnocentric message (b) mixed message (c) semantic problem (d) status effect

5. Management by wandering around is a technique that can help to overcome the limitations of _____ in the communication process. (a) status effects (b) semantics (c) physical distractions (d) proxemics

6. A coacting group is most likely to use a(n) _____ communication network. (a) interacting (b) decentralized (c) centralized (d) restricted

7. A complex problem is best dealt with by a group using a(n) _____ communication network. (a) all-channel (b) wheel (c) chain (d) linear

8. Although new communication technologies have the advantage of handling large amounts of information, they may also make organizational communication _____. (a) less accessible (b) less immediate (c) more impersonal (d) more personal

9. The physical arrangement of office furniture and its impact on communication is an issue of _____. (a) kinesics (b) proxemics (c) semantics (d) status

10. In _____ communication the sender is likely to be most comfortable, whereas in _____ communication the receiver is likely to feel more informed. (a) one-way, two-way (b) top-down, bottom-up (c) bottom-up, top-down (d) two-way, one-way

TRUE-FALSE

11. Encoding in the communication process translates an intended message into perceived meaning. T   F

12. Proxemics is the study of mixed messages in organizations.   T   F

13. A rule of active listening is to avoid reflecting back or paraphrasing what the other person has said. T   F

14. Grapevines can have a positive impact on communication in organizations.   T   F

15. Poor downward communication is a common management failure.   T   F

16. New trends in organizational design emphasize more lateral communications.   T   F

17. Developments in organizational ecology recognize the importance of informal communication. T   F

18. Members in a coacting group tend to interact frequently and share information directly with each other.   T   F

19. A tendency toward "flaming" to express intense anger is a possible drawback of electronic communication.   T   F

20. There is little concern for the political correctness of communications in organizations today. T   F

SHORT ANSWER

21. Why is channel richness a useful concept for managers?

22. What place do informal communication channels have in organizations today?

23. Why are communications between lower and higher organizational levels sometimes filtered?

24. Is there a gender difference in communication styles?

APPLICATIONS ESSAY

25. "People in this organization don't talk to each other anymore. Everything is e-mail, e-mail, e-mail. If you are mad at someone, you can just say it and then hide behind your computer." With these words, Wesley expressed his frustrations with Delta General's operations. Xiaomei echoed his concerns, responding, "I agree, but surely the managing director should be able to improve organizational communication without losing the advantages of e-mail." As a consultant overhearing this conversation, how would you suggest the managing director respond to Xiaomei's challenge?

Decision-Making

Deciding When and How to Pass the Wealth

Passing a family business from one generation to the next involves making a number of decisions, many of which can cause a lot of conflict. The SuccessCare® Program is a consulting service provided by Guelph, Ontario, accounting firm Robinson & Company to help business owners avoid the problems that may arise during succession planning.

"Most people know how to build businesses; they don't know how to transition them," says Grant Robinson, director of the SuccessCare® Program, adding that three out of four businesses in North America will change leadership over the next decade. "It ties in with the great wealth transfer that's going on," he says. SuccessCare® guides large companies through the important decision-making process surrounding the transfer of not only this wealth, but also the business values that created it.

"You have two choices," Mr. Robinson says, "you can build your business or you can shut it down someday." Once business owners have decided their operations will continue upon their retirement, their remaining decisions will significantly affect members of their family. The SuccessCare® Program looks at three areas—the relationships among family members, the business ownership, and the management of the business —separating them out in order to deal with them effectively. SuccessCare® Consultants coach owners through the succession-planning process, identifying the best solutions in each area, and helping to create plans and prepare the required documentation. They work with other advisers, such as the businesses' own accountants or lawyers, to ensure that the appropriate structures and processes are in place to support the execution of the owners' plans.

There is a lot of emotional capital involved in a family business, so strong communication is essential to deal with areas of conflict. The SuccessCare® process sets out rules for participation and defines the context for fair and equal treatment of all family members. In addition to deciding who will get what and what roles various family members will play, owners must include contingency and continuity plans, including tax, estate, and personal financial planning. Management choices must consider building and continuing a competitive and profitable business using strategies that incorporate leadership development, good governance, organizational planning, research and development, and assurance services.

Succession planning involves much more than simply handing the cash to the next generation, Mr. Robinson points out. It involves passing on values as well. "We help the kids to realize that the family has built a wealth-base called a family business, and their obligation is to take that family business and the surrounding wealth, use it during their generation, do good things with it, and pass it on to the next generation healthier and stronger than when they got it."

Chapter 17 examines the many aspects of decision-making in organizations. As you read this chapter, keep in mind these key questions:

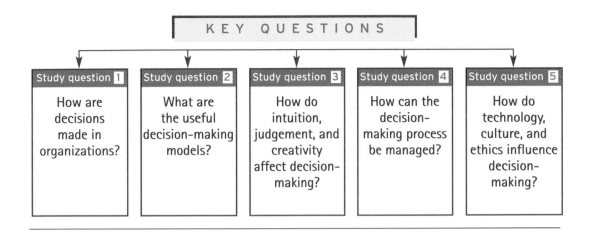

KEY QUESTIONS				
Study question 1	**Study question 2**	**Study question 3**	**Study question 4**	**Study question 5**
How are decisions made in organizations?	What are the useful decision-making models?	How do intuition, judgement, and creativity affect decision-making?	How can the decision-making process be managed?	How do technology, culture, and ethics influence decision-making?

Organizations depend for their success on day-to-day decisions made by their members. The quality of these decisions influences both the long-term performance of an organization and its day-to-day "character"—as seen by employees, customers, and society in general. Today's challenging environments also demand ever more rigour and creativity in the decision-making process. New products and new manufacturing and service processes all come from ideas. Organizations must provide opportunities for decision-making that encourages the free flow of new ideas and supports the efforts of people who want to make their ideas work. And just as organizations depend on quality decisions, the success of our individual careers depends on the quality of the decisions we make about our jobs and employment situations.

Decision-Making Process

Formally defined, **decision-making** is the process of choosing a course of action (i.e., which actions to take) to deal with a problem or opportunity.[1] The five basic steps in systematic decision-making are as follows:

1. Recognize and define the problem or opportunity.

2. Identify and analyze alternative courses of action, and estimate their effects on the problem or opportunity.

3. Choose a preferred course of action.

4. Implement the preferred course of action.

5. Evaluate the results and follow up as necessary.

Decision-making is the process of choosing a course of action to deal with a problem.

Five Steps in Decision-Making

We must also be aware that in organizations where there has been a lot of change and there are many new technologies, this step-by-step approach may not be followed. Occasionally, a non-traditional sequence works and actually results in superior performance compared to the traditional approach. It is also important to consider the ethical consequences of decision-making. Finally, to understand when and where to use either the traditional or the novel decision techniques, it is necessary to first understand decision environments and the types of decisions to be made.

TECHNOLOGY

Analog Devices, Inc. is the world leader in signal processing solutions, including the development of digital signal processing (DSP) chips. Converters such as an analog-to-digital converter take real-world signals, like voice, audio, and video, and turn them into the digital code. The DSP then takes over, capturing the digitized information, processing it, and feeding it back for use in the real world. This is all done at amazing speed. But DSP chips' speed wouldn't be quite so amazing without the help of Ottawa-based MOSAID Technologies, which in 2000 designed and developed a fast-access embedded DRAM macrocell, allowing more than 10 times more memory to be integrated with DSP chips. This benefited wireless and broadband communications by reducing the number of chips in the system, which in turn reduced system power consumption and size. Perhaps that explains the multitude of cellular phones, digital television stations, and MP3 players available today.

DECISION ENVIRONMENTS

Certain environments are environments that give definite information about the expected results of decision-making alternatives.

Risk environments give probabilities about the expected results of decision-making alternatives.

Uncertain environments give no information that can help predict the expected results of decision-making alternatives.

Problem-solving decisions in organizations are typically made under three different conditions or environments: certainty, risk, and uncertainty.[2] **Certain environments** exist when there is enough information to predict the results of each alternative before anything is implemented. When a person invests money in a savings account, for example, there is absolute certainty about the interest that will be earned on that money over a specific period of time. Certainty is an ideal condition for managerial problem-solving and decision-making. The challenge is simply to find the alternative that is the best solution. Unfortunately, certainty is the exception instead of the rule in decision environments—in other words, it does not happen very often.

Risk environments exist when decision-makers do not have complete certainty about the outcomes of various courses of action, but they are aware of the probabilities associated with each course of action. A *probability* is how likely it is that an event will occur. Probabilities can be calculated using objective statistical procedures or through personal intuition. For instance, managers can make statistical estimates of quality rejects in production runs, or a senior production manager can make similar estimates based on past experience. Risk is a common decision environment in today's organizations.

Uncertain environments exist when managers have so little information that they cannot even assign probabilities to various alternatives and their possible outcomes—in other words, any prediction is no better than a wild guess. This is the most difficult of the three decision environments. Uncertainty forces decision-makers to rely heavily on individual and group creativity to succeed in problem-solving. It requires unique, novel, and often totally innovative alternatives instead of the existing patterns of behaviour. Responses to uncertainty are often heavily influenced by intuition, educated guesses, and hunches. Furthermore, an uncertain decision environment can also be an organizational setting that is changing rapidly because of changes in (a) external conditions, (b) the information technology requirements that are needed to analyze and make decisions, and (c) the personnel who are influencing the definitions of the problem and choices. Together, these changes describe what has been called an **organized anarchy**: a firm or division in a firm that is in transition and is characterized by very rapid change and having no legitimate hierarchy or collegiality. Although this was once a very unique setting, many high-tech firms and those with expanding global operations have many of the characteristics of an organized anarchy.

Organized anarchy is a firm or division in a firm that is in transition and is characterized by very rapid change and having no legitimate hierarchy.

As the following example shows, by using a systematic process, firms can more clearly identify which aspects of their environment and operations are risky and which ones are truly uncertain. KPMG LLP, a member of KPMG International, one of the world's largest and most prestigious consulting firms, provides governance and enterprise risk management, which not only helps firms identify and manage risks, it also helps them report these risks to key stakeholders—an aspect of risk management that has become increasingly necessary. KPMG helps managers identify, assess, and proactively manage the risks that threaten their business goals. By using established methodologies for risk assessment, measurement, and reporting, the firm provides clients with full awareness of what could go wrong in all aspects of their business, from strategic goals to business risks, earnings, financing, and stakeholder value. It aids in the development of a contingency plan for all material risks and helps develop strategies for knowledge transfer. It also provides managers with a way to report to stakeholders on the spectrum of risks facing the organization and how they are being managed. And, it provides a more strategic view of risk, helping managers decide when to take specific risks that represent business opportunities.[3]

TYPES OF DECISIONS

The many routine and non-routine problems in the modern workplace call for different types of decisions. Routine problems are problems that happen regularly and can be handled through standard responses, called **programmed decisions**. These decisions simply use solutions that have already been determined by past experience that is appropriate for the current problem. Examples of programmed decisions are reordering inventory automatically when stock falls below a predetermined level and issuing a written reprimand to someone who violates a certain personnel procedure.

Programmed decisions are standard responses to a current problem that are based on past experience as appropriate.

Routine operations are at the heart of many corporations, and such corporations are finding that when they or their customers face programmed decisions, they can use Web-based technologies to get speedier and better decisions. For example, REI (Recreational Equipment, Inc.) linked its website to inventory-monitoring systems to quickly offer its customers discounts on overstocked items.

TECHNOLOGY

HBC AND DECISION-MAKING
When you think of The Bay, Canada's largest department store, you probably see shopping malls and Christmas shopping crushes, not the technology that is behind it all. In July 2000, HBC formed an alliance with IBM Canada, Microsoft, and Oracle Corporation to solve technology issues and implement HBC's strategic technology needs. The goal was to ensure that HBC would be competitive through streamlining, planning, evaluation, and acquisition and implementation activities that would make use of its technology solutions. This, in turn, would help HBC compete in the emerging e-enabled world and, of course, be a leader in electronic retail in North America.

Non-programmed decisions create unique solutions for a problem that is occurring for the first time.

Non-routine problems are unique and new, as they have never occurred before. Because standard responses are not available, these circumstances need creative problsolving. These **non-programmed decisions** are specifically crafted or tailored to fit the current situation. Higher-level managers generally spend a greater proportion of their decision-making time on non-routine problems. An example is a senior marketing manager who has to respond to the introduction of a new product by a foreign competitor. Although past experience may help deal with this competitive threat, the immediate decision requires a creative solution based on the unique characteristics of the current market situation.

Associative choices are decisions that can be loosely linked to nagging, chronic problems but that were not specifically developed to solve the problem.

For firms in a state of "organized anarchy," there are also a third class of decisions, called associative choices. **Associative choices** are decisions that can be loosely linked to nagging, chronic problems but that were not specifically developed to solve the current problem. When the setting is chaotic, when action needs to be taken instead of just waiting, and when the employees can make nearly any "decision" work, it can still be worthwhile to use a series of associative choices that may improve the setting, even if they will not solve the problem.

Decision-Making Models

The field of organizational behaviour has historically emphasized two alternative approaches to decision-making—the classical and behavioural models (see Figure 17.1).[4] Models based on **classical decision theory** view the manager as acting in a world of complete certainty. Models based on **behavioural decision theory** accept the notion of bounded rationality (explained below) and suggest that people act only according to what they perceive about a specific situation.

Classical decision theory views decision-makers as acting in a world of complete certainty.

Behavioural decision theory views decision-makers as acting only according to what they perceive about a specific situation.

Figure 17.1 Decision-making viewed from the classical and behavioural perspectives

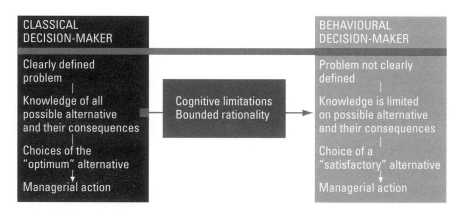

CLASSICAL AND BEHAVIOURAL DECISION THEORY

Ideally, the manager faces a clearly defined problem, knows all the possible alternatives for action and their consequences, and then chooses the alternative that offers the best, or "optimum," solution to the problem. This optimizing style is an ideal way to make decisions. This classical approach is normative and prescriptive, and is often used as a model for how managers should make decisions. Managers follow a normal process and it prescribes an optimum solution.

Behavioural scientists are cautious about applying classical decision theory to decision situations. They recognize that the human mind is a wonderful creation, capable of infinite achievements. But they also recognize that human beings have *cognitive limitations* that limit their information-processing capabilities. Information deficiencies and overloads reduce the ability of decision-makers to be completely certain, which makes it harder to make decisions according to the classical model of decision-making. As decision-makers, humans also operate with bounded *rationality*.[5] Bounded rationality is a short way of saying that, while humans are reasoned and logical, they have their limits. Individuals interpret and make sense of things within the context of their personal situation. Their decision-making occurs "within the box"—in other words, with a simplified view of a more complex reality. This makes it difficult to achieve the ideal decision-making situation assumed by the classical model. As a result, the classical model does not give a full and accurate description of how most decisions are made in organizations.[6]

Classical decision theory does not appear to fit today's chaotic world of globalizing high-tech organizations, yet it would be a mistake to dismiss it and the types of progress that can be made with classical models. Classical models can be used toward the bottom of many firms. For instance, even the most high-tech firm faces many clearly defined problems with known alternatives where firms have already selected an optimal solution. When a firm's managers do not know the answer to a standard problem, the situation may appear to be non-classical when, in fact, it should not be.

As noted above, models based on *behavioural decision theory* accept the notion of bounded rationality. They suggest that people act only according to what they perceive about a specific situation. Because these perceptions are frequently imperfect, most decision-making in organizations does not occur in a world of complete certainty. Rather, the behavioural decision-maker is viewed as acting most of the time in uncertain conditions and with limited information. In organizations, decision-makers face problems that are often ambiguous, and they have only partial knowledge of the available alternatives for action and their consequences. This leads to a phenomenon which Herbert Simon has described as **satisficing**—this is when decision-makers choose the first alternative that appears to give an acceptable or a satisfactory resolution of the problem. As Simon states: "Most human decision-making, whether individual or organizational, is concerned with the discovery and selection of satisfactory alternatives; only in exceptional cases is it concerned with the discovery and selection of optimal decisions."[7]

> **Satisficing** is choosing the first alternative that appears to give an acceptable or satisfactory resolution of the problem.

GLOBALIZATION

Nokia, initially a Finnish corporation, is the world's second largest mobile phone manufacturer and a leading supplier of digital and fixed networks. Its ability to maintain its leadership position in the fastest growing telecommunications segments is based squarely on its employees and the way they make decisions. It is not just a Finnish way—it is a Nokia way. The decision-making process is characterized by an emphasis on technology development and goal attainment, not bureaucracy, so that Nokia can quickly apply and refine the newest technologies. The decision-making process is supported by four Nokia values—customer satisfaction, respect for the individual, achievement, and renewal. Moreover, Nokia managers recognize that the application and emphasis on these values, as well as their incorporation into the decision-making process, will vary substantially across different cultures.

THE GARBAGE CAN MODEL

The garbage can model views the main components of the choice process—problems, solutions, participants, and choice situations—as all mixed up together in the garbage can of the organization.

A third view of decision-making stems from the so-called **garbage can model**.[8] In this view, the main components of the choice process—problems, solutions, participants, and choice situations—are all mixed up together in the "garbage can" of the organization. In many organizations where the setting is stable and the technology is well known and unchanging, tradition, strategy, and the administrative structure help organize the contents of the garbage can. Specific problems can be matched to specific solutions, an orderly process can be maintained, and the behavioural view of decision-making may be appropriate.

But when the setting is dynamic, the technology is changing, and demands are conflicting or the goals are unclear, the garbage can's contents can get mixed up. There can be more action than thinking going on. Solutions appear as "potential capabilities"—that is, as capabilities that have nothing to do with the problems or opportunities. Solutions often emerge not to solve specific problems but as lessons learned from the experience of other organizations. These new solutions/capabilities may be in the form of new employees, new technical experts, consultants, or reports on best practices. Many solutions might be used even if they cannot be linked to a specific problem. Solutions may also be implemented when no other solution has solved a chronic problem. Although solutions that are implemented change the organization, they are unlikely to solve specific problems.

The garbage can model highlights an important feature of decision-making in many large organizations. Making choices and actually implementing them may be done by quite different individuals. Often, the job of subordinates is to make the decisions of senior managers work. They must interpret the intentions of their bosses and solve local problems. The actual implementation becomes an opportunity to make many changes that are related to the choice of more senior executives. So it is not always only the choice from higher up that is implemented—many other changes may also be implemented. The link between a choice and its implementation can become even weaker when senior managers are vague or do not vigorously follow up on the implementation. The net result for those who implement the choice can be the impression that what was chosen does not exactly match what was implemented.

There is a final aspect of the garbage can view. Many problems go unsolved. That is, all organizations have chronic deficiencies that never seem to get much better. In the garbage can view, this is because decision-makers cannot agree to match these problems with solutions, make a choice, and implement it on a timely and consistent basis; nor do they know how to resolve chronic problems. It is only when a problem and a solution "bump into each other," under a decision-maker who is willing to implement a choice, that problems, solutions, and choice come together as they are expected to under other views. Thus, one key job challenge for the astute manager is to make the appropriate links between problems and solutions.

DECISION-MAKING REALITIES

All three of these models highlight specific features of the complex choice processes managers must engage in as professionals. A key difference between a manager's ability to make an optimum decision in the classical style and the manager's tendency to make a satisfying decision in the behavioural style is the availability of information. The organizational realities of bounded rationality and cognitive limitations affect the way people define problems, identify alternatives for action, and choose preferred courses of action. By necessity, most decision-making in organizations involves more than the linear, step-by-step rational choice that models often suggest. While the process may not be as chaotic as the garbage can model suggests, it is often not as rational as even a behavioural view suggests either. In real organizations, decisions must be made under risk and uncertainty. Decisions must be made to solve non-routine problems.

And decisions must be made under the pressures of time and information limitations. And last, but not least, hopefully decisions will be made on an ethical foundation.

ETHICS AND SOCIAL RESPONSIBILITY

ETHICS AT IKEA
IKEA is one of the world's leading manufacturers and retailers of home furnishings. Working with manufacturers around the world with the customer in mind, the company focuses on providing a wide range of effective and economical products for all households. It also pays a lot of attention to the environment. First, all the wood it uses must come from a certified, managed, and intact forest or woodlot. Then, to ensure that it wastes as little wood as possible, the wood left over from the manufacture of one product is often used in the manufacture of another product. But wood is not the only concern. When you visit an IKEA store, you can even have your light bulbs that contain mercury recycled.

www.ikea.ca

Intuition, Judgement, and Creativity

Choices always carry the unique imprint of the individuals who make them, of the organization's politics, and of the challenges facing the organization's decision-makers. As a result, the intuition, judgement, and creativity of an organization's personnel are as critical to decision-making as is their understanding of how decisions can be made.

A key element in decision-making under risk and uncertainty is intuition. **Intuition** is the ability to quickly know or recognize the possibilities of a specific situation.[9] Intuition adds elements of personality and spontaneity to decision-making. As a result, it offers potential for creativity and innovation.

> **Intuition** is the ability to quickly know or recognize the possibilities of a situation.

In an earlier time, scholars debated about how managers should plan and make decisions.[10] On one side of the issue were those who believed that planning could be accomplished in a systematic, step-by-step fashion. On the other side were those who believed that the very nature of managerial work made a systematic approach hard to achieve in actual practice. Indeed, we now know of several factors that make the systematic approach hard to follow. We know that managers prefer verbal communication. Thus, they are more likely to gather data and make decisions in a relational or interactive way than in a systematic, step-by-step fashion.[11] Managers often deal with impressions. Thus, they are more likely to synthesize data than to analyze it as they search for the "big picture" that helps them redefine problems and link them with a variety of solutions. Managers also work fast, do a variety of things, and are frequently interrupted. Thus, they do not have a lot of quiet time alone to think, plan, or make decisions systematically (see The Effective Manager 17.1).

Are managers correct when they favour the more intuitive and less systematic approach? The more chaotic environments and technologies of many of today's organizations seem to demand this emphasis on intuition. Unfortunately, many firms are better at implementing the solutions that are commonly used by others than at uniquely solving their own particular problems. Since managers do work in chaotic settings, this reality should be accepted and decision-makers should be

> **The Effective Manager** **17.1**
>
> WAYS TO IMPROVE INTUITION
>
> Relaxation Techniques
> - Drop the problem for a while.
> - Spend some quiet time by yourself.
> - Try to clear your mind.
>
> Mental Exercises
> - Use images to guide your thinking.
> - Let ideas run freely without a specific goal.

confident in using their intuitive skills. Ideally, they should combine the analytical and intuitive approaches to create new and novel solutions to complex problems.

JUDGEMENTAL HEURISTICS

Judgement, or the use of one's intellect, is important in all aspects of decision-making. When we question the ethics of a decision, for example, we are questioning the "judgement" of the person making it. Research shows that people tend to make mistakes because of biases that often interfere with the quality of the decision-making.[12] These mistakes can be traced to the use of **heuristics**—simplifying strategies or "rules of thumb" that are used to make decisions. Heuristics serve a useful purpose as they make it easier to deal with uncertainty and limited information in problem situations. But they can also lead to systematic errors that affect the quality, and perhaps the ethical implications, of any decisions that are made. There are three common judgemental heuristics that it is helpful to understand: availability, representativeness, and anchoring and adjustment.[13]

The **availability heuristic** is when a current event is assessed based on past occurrences that are easily available in the person's memory. An example is the product development specialist who bases a decision not to launch a new product on her recent failure with another product offering. In this case, the existence of a past product failure has negatively, and perhaps inappropriately, biased the decision-maker's judgement of how to best handle the new product.

The **representativeness heuristic** is when the assessment of how likely it is that an event will occur is based on similarities between the event and the person's stereotypes of similar occurrences. An example is the team leader who selects a new member, not because of any special qualities the person has, but because the individual comes from a department that has produced high performers in the past. In this case, it is the individual's current place of employment—and not his or her job qualifications—that is the basis for the selection decision.

The **anchoring and adjustment heuristic** is when an event is assessed by taking an initial value from a historical precedent or an outside source, and then incrementally adjusting this value to make a current assessment. An example is the executive who makes salary increase recommendations for key personnel by simply adjusting their current base salaries by a percentage amount. In this case, the existing base salary becomes an "anchor" that affects later salary increases. In some situations, this anchor may be inappropriate, such as in the case of an individual whose market value has become a lot higher than what the base salary plus increment amounts to.

In addition to using the common judgemental heuristics, decision-makers also tend to have more general biases in their decision-making. One bias is the **confirmation trap**, where the decision-maker seeks confirmation for what is already thought to be true and ignores opportunities to find or admit disconfirming information. This bias is a type of selective perception, as it involves only looking for the cues in a situation that support a pre-existing opinion. A second bias is the **hindsight trap**, where the decision-maker overestimates how much he or she could have predicted an event that has already taken place. One risk of hindsight is that it can lead to feelings of inadequacy or insecurity in dealing with future decisions.

CREATIVITY FACTORS

Creativity in decision-making involves the development of unique and novel responses to problems and opportunities. In a changing environment that is full of non-routine problems, creativity in finding solutions often determines how well people and organizations respond to complex challenges.[14]

Heuristics are simplifying strategies or "rules of thumb" that are used to make decisions.

The *availability heuristic* bases a decision on recent events that are related to the current situation.

The *representativeness heuristic* bases a decision on similarities between the current situation and stereotypes of similar occurrences.

The *anchoring and adjustment heuristic* bases a decision on incremental adjustments to an initial value that is determined by historical precedent or some reference point.

The *confirmation trap* is the tendency to seek confirmation for what is already thought to be true and to not search for disconfirming information.

The *hindsight trap* is a tendency to overestimate how much an event that has already taken place could have been predicted.

Creativity generates unique and novel responses to problems.

In Part 3 of this book, we examined the group as an important resource for improving creativity in decision-making. Indeed, making good use of such traditional techniques as brainstorming, nominal groups, and the Delphi method can greatly expand the creative potential of people and organizations. The addition of technology-based group meeting and decision-making techniques takes this great potential even further.

Creative thinking may unfold in a series of five stages. First is *preparation*.[15] Here people do the active learning and day-to-day sensing that is needed for dealing successfully with complex environments. The second stage is *concentration*, where actual problems are defined and framed so that alternatives can be considered for dealing with them. In the third stage, *incubation*, people look at the problems in diverse ways that make it possible to consider unusual alternatives, and they avoid the tendency to use only linear, systematic problsolving. The fourth stage is *illumination*, in which people respond to flashes of insight and recognize when all the pieces of the puzzle suddenly fit into place. The fifth and final stage is certification, which involves using logical analysis to confirm that good problem-solving decisions have really been made.[16]

All of these stages of creativity need support and encouragement in the organizational environment. However, creative thinking in decision-making can be limited by a number of factors. Judgemental heuristics like those just mentioned can limit the search for alternatives. When attractive options are left unconsidered, creativity can be limited. Cultural and environmental blocks can also limit creativity. This occurs when people are discouraged from considering alternatives that would be viewed as inappropriate by cultural standards or as inconsistent with prevailing norms.

Managing the Decision-Making Process

As our discussion of creativity suggested, people working at all levels, in all areas, and in all types and sizes of organizations are not supposed to simply make decisions. They must make good decisions—the right decisions in the right way at the right time.[17] Managing the decision-making process also involves choices. Some of the critical choices include which "problems" to work on, who to involve and how to involve them, and when to quit.

CHOOSING PROBLEMS TO ADDRESS

Most people are too busy and have too many valuable things to do with their time to personally make the decisions on every problem or opportunity that comes their way. The effective manager and team leader knows when to delegate decisions to others, how to set priorities, and when to do nothing at all. When a manager is faced with the dilemma of whether or not to deal with a specific problem, asking and answering the following questions can sometimes help.[18]

Is the problem easy to deal with? Small and less significant problems should not get the same time and attention as bigger ones. Even if a mistake is made, the cost of a decision error on a small problem is also small. *Might the problem resolve itself?* Putting problems in rank order leaves the less significant ones for last. Surprisingly, many of these less important problems resolve themselves or are solved by others before one can get to them. One less problem to solve leaves decision-making time and energy for other uses. *Is this my decision to make?* Many problems can be handled by other persons. They should be delegated to the people who are best prepared to deal with them; ideally, they should be delegated to the people whose work is most affected by them. Finally, *is this a solvable problem within the context of the organization?* The astute decision-maker recognizes the difference between problems that realistically can be solved and those that are simply not solvable, practically speaking.

Paul Nutt, a leading authority on decision-making in corporations, argues that half the decisions in organizations fail.[19] Why? In his opinion, the decision tactics that managers most often use are the ones that tend to fail the most. Managers take too many shortcuts. Too often, they merely copy the choices of others and try to sell these solutions to subordinates. While such copying seems practical and pragmatic, it fails to recognize unforeseen difficulties and delays. No two firms are alike and subtle adjustments are typically needed to copy another firm's solution. Subordinates may also end up believing that the manager is just imposing his or her clout—not working for the best interests of everyone. Something that is related to the overemphasis on immediate action is the tendency of managers to emphasize problems and solutions. Meanwhile, the tactics that are most related to success are not used enough. Managers need to focus on the outcomes they want, rather than the problems they see. Above all, managers need to use participation more. Let's take a closer look.

DECIDING WHO SHOULD PARTICIPATE

A mistake that is commonly made by many new managers and team leaders is presuming that they must solve every problem by making every decision themselves.[20] In practice, good organizational decisions are made by individuals who act alone, by individuals who consult with others, and by groups of people who work together.

Authority decisions are made by the manager or team leader, using information that he or she possesses and without involving others.

When individual decisions, also called **authority decisions**, are made, the manager or team leader uses information that he or she has, and the decision about what to do is made without involving others. This decision method often reflects the right to decide that goes with a person's position of formal authority in the organization. For instance, in deciding a rotation for lunch hours in a retail store, the manager may post a schedule. In **consultative decisions**, by contrast, inputs on the problem are wanted from other persons. Based on this information and how it is interpreted, the decision-maker makes a final choice. To continue the example, the manager may first tell subordinates that a lunch schedule is needed and ask them when they would like to schedule their lunch and why. Then, after having this information, the manager makes the decision. In other cases, true **group decisions** can be made by both consulting with others and allowing them to help make the final choice. To complete the example, the manager may hold a meeting to get everyone's agreement on a lunch schedule or a system for deciding how to make the schedule. More details on group decision-making were given in Chapter 9, which describes a variety of group decision-making techniques, including brainstorming, the nominal group technique, and the Delphi technique.

Consultative decisions are made by one individual after seeking input from or consulting with members of a group.

Group decisions are made by all members of the group.

As Figure 17.2. shows, Victor Vroom, Phillip Yetton, and Arthur Jago have developed a framework for helping managers choose which of these decision-making methods is the best one to use for different problem situations.[21] The central idea in their model is that the decision-making method that is used should always be appropriate to the problem being solved. The challenge is knowing when and how to use each of the possible methods, according to what the situation requires. They also further clarify the individual, consultative, and group decision options as follows:

Decision-making methods

- **AI** (*first variant on the authority decision*): The manager solves the problem or makes the decision alone, using information available at that time.

- **AII** (*second variant on the authority decision*): The manager obtains the necessary information from subordinate(s) or other group members and then decides on the solution to the problem. The manager may or may not tell subordinates what the problem is before obtaining the information from them. The subordinates provide the necessary information but do not generate or evaluate alternatives.

- **CI** (*first variant on the consultative decision*): The manager shares the problem with relevant subordinates or other group members individually, getting their ideas and suggestions without bringing them together as a group. The manager then makes a decision that may or may not reflect the subordinates' input.

- **CII** (*second variant on the consultative decision*): The manager shares the problem with subordinates or other group members, and brings them together to obtain their ideas and suggestions. The manager then makes a decision that may or may not reflect the subordinates' input.

- **G** (*the group or consensus decision*): The manager shares the problem with the subordinates as a complete group and helps the group reach a consensus on a final decision.

Figure 17.2 Selecting alternative decision-making methods: the Vroom and Jago decision process flowchart

Problem Attributes		Manager's Questions
QR	Quality requirement	How important is the technical quality of this decision?
CR	Commitment requirement	How important is subordinate commitment to the decision?
LI	Leader's information	Do you have sufficient information to make a high-quality decision?
ST	Problem structure	Is the problem well-structured?
CP	Commitment probability	If you were to make the decision by yourself, is it reasonably certain that your subordinate(s) would be committed to the decision?
GC	Goal congruence	Do subordinates share the organizational goals to be attained in solving this problem?
CO	Subordinate conflict	Is conflict among subordinates over preferred solutions likely?
SI	Subordinate information	Do subordinates have sufficient informatin to make a high-quality decision?

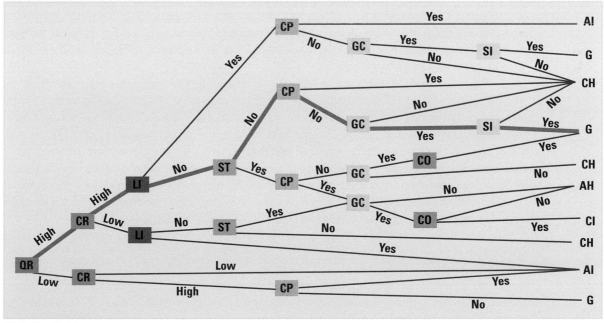

State the Problem

In the most recent version of this decision-making framework, Vroom and Jago use the flowchart shown in Figure 17.2 to help managers analyze problem situations and choose the most appropriate decision-making methods. Key issues are the quality requirements of a decision, the availability and location of the relevant information, the commitments needed to fully implement the decision, and the amount of time available. Although this model appears complex and cumbersome, its underlying logic offers a useful decision-making discipline. Try it by working through Figure 17.2 for an organizational problem that you are familiar with. The analysis forces you to recognize how time, quality requirements, information availability, and subordinate acceptance issues can affect decision outcomes. It also reminds you that all of the decision methods are important and useful. The key to effectively managing participation in decision-making is first knowing when to use each decision method and then knowing how to implement each method well.

KNOWING WHEN TO QUIT: ELIMINATING ESCALATING COMMITMENTS

An organization's natural desire to continue on a selected course of action reinforces some natural tendencies that decision-makers have.[22] Once the agonizing process of making a choice is apparently completed, executives make public commitments to implementing the choice, and once implementation begins, managers are often reluctant to change their minds and admit that a mistake has been made. Instead of backing off, the tendency is to press on to victory. This is called **escalating commitment**—continuing and renewing efforts on a previously chosen course of action, even though it is not working. Escalating commitment is reflected in the popular adage, "If at first you don't succeed, try, try, again."

> Escalating commitment is the tendency to continue a previously chosen course of action even when feedback suggests that it is failing.

Calgary-based oil and gas company Talisman Energy Inc.'s decision to invest in the African country Sudan is an example of bad decision-making. When Talisman bought a 25 percent interest in Sudan's oil fields in 1998, it was aware the country's problems. At the time, a 43-year civil war between the northern Arab government and southern tribes had claimed two million lives and displaced another four million people. The financial and political consequences of the company's involvement in that country were clear. Still, Talisman ignored its own due diligence and went ahead with the investment, then watched the value of its stock plummet. The company's only recourse was to sell out or withdraw. Talisman finally managed to sell its interests in Sudan in 2003.

In beginner-level finance courses, students learn about sunk costs. Money committed and spent is gone. The decision to continue is just that—a decision. It needs to be based on what investment is needed and the returns on that investment. This is one of the most difficult aspects of decision-making to get executives to accept, simply because so many of these executives rose to their positions by turning apparently losing courses of action into winners.[23] The tendency to escalate commitments is often stronger than the willingness to end them. Decision-makers may rationalize negative feedback as a temporary condition, protect their egos by not admitting that the original decision was a mistake, or characterize any negative results as a "learning experience" that can be overcome with added future effort.[24]

The self-discipline that an individual needs to have to be able to admit mistakes and change direction, however, is sometimes difficult to achieve. Escalating commitments are a form of decision entrapment that leads people to do things that the facts of a situation do not justify. We should be proactive in spotting "failures" and more open to reversing decisions or dropping plans that do not appear to be working.[25] But again, this is easier said than done. Good decision-makers know when to call it quits. They are willing to reverse previous decisions and to stop investing time and other resources in unsuccessful courses of action. As the late W. C. Fields is said to have muttered, "If at first you don't succeed, try, try, again. Then quit."

Technology, Culture, and Ethics in Decision-Making

In today's environments, the problems facing decision-makers in organizations seem to get ever more complex. For example, consider the following workplace trends:[26]

Key workplace trends

- Business units are becoming smaller in size: they are doing more outsourcing and employing fewer full-time workers.

- New, more flexible and adaptable organizational forms are replacing the traditional pyramid structures.

- Multifunctional understanding is increasingly important as organizations emphasize lateral coordination.

- Workers who have both technical knowledge and team skills are becoming more and more wanted.

- The nature of "work" is in flux as jobs change fast, require continuous learning, and are less bound by the "9-to-5" tradition of only doing exactly as instructed or directed.

Each of these trends is changing who is making the decisions and when, where, and how they are doing it. They are also contributing to the stresses and strains that come from the quest for higher and higher productivity which challenges the needs, talents, and opportunities of people at work. Some issues that make the decision-making process more complex include issues of information technology, culture, and ethics.

INFORMATION TECHNOLOGY AND DECISION-MAKING

As we have discussed throughout this book, today's organizations are becoming more and more sophisticated in how they use information technologies. Eventually, developments in the field of **artificial intelligence (AI)**—the study of how computers can be programmed to think like the human brain—will allow computers to replace many decision-makers.[27] Nobel laureate and decision scientist Herbert Simon is convinced that computers will someday be more intelligent than humans.

Already, the applications of AI to organizational decision-making are significant. We have access to decision-making support from expert systems that reason like human experts and follow "either-or" rules to make deductions. For example, if you call an advertised 800 number to apply for a home equity loan, you will not get a human but a computer program to take all the necessary information and provide confirmation of a loan. On the factory floor, decision support systems schedule machines and people to achieve maximum production efficiency.

Fuzzy logic that reasons beyond either-or choices and neural networks that reason inductively by simulating the brain's parallel processing capabilities is becoming an operational reality that goes much further than simple programmed decisions. Uses for such systems may be found everywhere, from hospitals where they check on medical diagnoses, to investment houses where they analyze potential investment portfolios, and to a wide and growing variety of other settings.[28]

Computer support for group decision-making, including developments with the Internet and with intranets, has broken the decision-making meeting out of traditional face-to-face interactions. With the software that is now available, problems can be defined and decisions can be made through virtual teamwork by people in geographically dispersed locations. We know that group decision software can be especially useful for generating ideas, such as in electronic brainstorming, and for improving the time efficiency of decisions. People working under electronically mediated conditions tend to stay focused on tasks and avoid the interpersonal conflicts and other

Artificial intelligence is the study of how computers can be programmed to think like the human brain.

problems that are common in face-to-face deliberations. On the negative side, decisions made by "electronic groups" risk being impersonal and, as a result, may have less commitment to them from the people responsible for their implementation and follow-through. There is also evidence that using computer technology for decision-making is better accepted by today's students than it is by persons who are already advanced in their organizational careers.[29] Erik Lockhart, associate director of the Queen's Executive Decision Centre at Queen's University, cautions that these systems are not foolproof: "If you don't understand group dynamics, you can get into trouble pretty quickly." The systems may "democratize" the decision-making process, he says, but "the technology is just a tool" and it remains "two-thirds talking."

What information technology will not do is deal with the issues raised by the "garbage can" model. The information technology promises a more orderly world where the process of choosing fits better with the traditional models. It extends the normal boundaries of rationality. For people, however, what is still on the information technology horizon are the most important decisions, the ones that come before the classical and standard approaches. These are pre-decision choices that are heavily influenced by cultural factors and ethics.

CULTURAL FACTORS AND DECISION-MAKING

Fons Trompenaars notes that culture is "the way in which a group of people solves problems."[30] It is only reasonable to expect that as cultures vary, so too will their choices about what is to be solved and how. For example, there are historical cultural preferences for solving problems. The approach favoured in this chapter emphasizes the North American view, which stresses decisiveness, speed, and individual selection of alternatives. This view focuses more on choice and less on implementation. Here in North America and other multicultural countries such as Argentina, Australia, and Singapore to name a few, we face the very differences within our borders and organizations. As discussed elsewhere in the book, this is a challenge but it also provides an opportunity to expand the methods and ideas to address and define problems and opportunities. Then again, the garbage can view suggests that implementation can proceed almost separately from the other aspects of decision-making.

GLOBALIZATION

CHC Helicopter Corporation is now the world leader in helicopter support service for offshore oil and gas operations, a status that was recently solidified when CHC acquired the Schreiner Aviation Group of the Netherlands. The company now operates a fleet of almost 400 helicopters and medium aircraft around the world and has a market that stretches from the Arctic to Antarctica, from Nigeria to Azerbaijan, and from Venezuela to Norway to Indonesia. In addition to having governments and the UN for customers, it also serves the top companies in the the oil industry, including Chevron, Shell, ExxonMobil, BP, and the Arabian Oil Company.

The secret to CHC's success is in part due to its company culture, which focuses on quality customer service. CHC is ISO 9001 certified, has a quality trained staff that believes in flexibility, develops strategic alliances, has a modern fleet of helicopters and other aircraft, and uses advanced management systems. To top it all off, CHC also distributes a quarterly employee newsletter, *Rotortales* to enhance employee teamwork across the globe. Thanks to this total systems approach, CHC has been able to establish long-term contracts around the world and to pull in revenue in the hundreds of millions of dollars—all this after starting with a single helicopter in 1978 in Newfoundland.

Other cultures place less emphasis on individual choice than on developing implementations that work. They start with what is workable and better rather than with the classical and behavioural comparison of current conditions with some ideal.[31] If a change can improve the current situation, even if it is not apparently directed toward a problem identified by senior management, subordinate managers may work together to implement it. And then senior management may be informed of the success of the change. To emphasize the importance of smooth implementation over grand decision-making, corporations may adopt systems that are similar to the Japanese *ringi* system where lower-level personnel indicate their written approval of proposals before changes are formally implemented. Written approval does not depend on whether or not the change should be done but on whether or not the group can actually implement it.[32]

In decision-making, culture has some impact on how problems are solved. It has more impact, however, on decisions about which concerns should get elevated to the status of problems that the firm needs to solve. For instance, the very fact that a procedure is old may make it more suspect in Canada and the United States than in France, with the result that old procedures are more likely to be thought of as problems in Canada and the United States.[33] This may be thought of as a kind of Western bureaucratic thinking.[34] The culture of the United States, sometimes described as being pluralistic, bluntly competitive, and impersonal, encourages this kind of cold, bureaucratic decision style. Here in Canada, on the other hand, while we too can be bureaucratic, we also tend to be more focused than our southern neighbours on the quality and equality of life for all, and this difference tends to affect what we see as problems that need to be solved. In other parts of the world, meanwhile, personal loyalties may determine decisions, and preserving harmony may be considered more important than achieving a bit more efficiency. In short, problems may be more person-centred and socially defined than bureaucratically proscribed.

While the aspects of gender differences that affect decision-making are beyond the scope of this book, we can still note in passing that the most noticeable differences between men and women involve perspectives on time and the tolerance for risk. As gender roles vary from culture to culture, however, it should be remembered that, while each person and team makes its own decisions, ultimately these decisions are tempered by the social and cultural backgrounds of the people making them.

ETHICAL ISSUES AND DECISION-MAKING

The subject of ethical behaviour in the workplace cannot be overemphasized, and it is worth reviewing once again the framework for ethical decision-making that was first introduced in Chapter 1. An *ethical dilemma* was defined as a situation in which a person must decide whether or not to do something that, although it would benefit the person or organization, may be considered unethical and perhaps illegal. Often, ethical dilemmas are associated with risk and uncertainty, and with non-routine problem situations. Just how you handle decisions under these circumstances—circumstances that you will inevitably face at some point during your career—may well be the ultimate test of your personal ethical framework.

An Effective Manager feature in Chapter 1 introduced a useful decision-making checklist for resolving ethical dilemmas. Before any decision is made, the checklist asks you to first answer some stiff questions about the decision you are considering.[35] To begin, it would have you ask: "Is my action legal? Is it right? Is it beneficial?" Second, it would have you ask: "How would I feel if my family found out about this? How would I feel if my decision were printed in the local newspaper?" Only after these questions are asked and satisfactorily answered does the model suggest that you take action. As a manager you also have the responsibility to integrate ethical decision-making into your part of the firm. Check The Effective Manager 17.2 for some help.

The Effective Manager | 17.2

SUGGESTIONS FOR INTEGRATING ETHICAL DECISION-MAKING

Infusing ethics into decision-making is difficult. Several scholars recommend the following:

- Develop a code of ethics and follow it.
- Establish procedures for reporting violations.
- Involve employees in identifying ethical issues.
- Monitor ethical performance.
- Reward ethical behaviour.
- Publicize efforts.

When it comes to the ethics of decision-making, the criteria that individuals use to define problems and the values that underlie these criteria must be considered.[36] Moral conduct is a factor in choosing problems, deciding who should be involved, estimating the impacts of alternatives, and selecting an alternative for implementation.

Moral conduct does not arise from after-the-fact embarrassment. As Fineman suggests, "If people are unable to anticipate shame or guilt before they act in particular ways, then moral codes are invalid.... Decisions may involve lying, deceit, fraud, evasion of negligence—disapproved of in many cultures. But ethical monitoring and control go beyond just the pragmatics of harm."[37] In other words, when you are the decision-maker, decision-making is not just a choice process that is automatically followed by implementation for the good of the organization. It involves your values and your morality whether or not you think it should. Thus, effective implemented choices need to not only solve a problem or take advantage of available choices but also match your values and help others. It is little wonder, then, that decision-making will likely be the biggest challenge of your organizational career.

CHAPTER 17 STUDY GUIDE

Summary

STUDY QUESTIONS

How are decisions made in organizations?

- Decision-making is a process of identifying problems and opportunities and choosing among alternative courses of action for dealing successfully with them.

- Organizational decisions are often made in risky and uncertain environments, where situations are ambiguous and information is limited.

- Routine and repetitive problems can be dealt with through programmed decisions; non-routine or novel problems require non-programmed decisions that are crafted to fit the current situation.

What are the useful decision-making models?

- According to classical decision theory, optimum decisions are made after carefully analyzing all possible alternatives and their known consequences.

- According to behavioural decision theory, most organizational decisions are made with limited information and by satisficing—that is, by choosing the first acceptable or satisfactory solution to a problem.

- According to the garbage can model, the main components of the choice process—problems, solutions, participants, choice situations—are all mixed up together in the "garbage can" of the organization.

How do intuition, judgement, and creativity affect decision-making?

- Intuition is the ability to quickly know and recognize the possibilities for action that will resolve a problem situation.

- Both systematic decision-making and intuitive decision-making are important in today's complex work environments.

- The use of judgemental heuristics—i.e., simplifying rules of thumb—is common in decision-making but can lead to biased results.

- Common heuristics include availability decisions based on recent events; representativeness decisions based on similar events; and anchoring and adjustment decisions based on historical precedents.

- Creativity in finding unique and novel solutions to problems can be improved through both individual and group problem—solving strategies.

How can the decision-making process be managed?

- Good managers know that not every problem requires an immediate decision; they also know how and when to delegate decision-making responsibilities.

- A common mistake is for a manager or team leader to make all decisions alone; instead, a full range of individual, consultative, and group decision-making methods should be used.

- The Vroom-Yetton-Jago model offers a way of matching problems with appropriate decision methods, based on quality requirements, information availability, and time constraints.

- Tendencies toward escalating commitment—continuing previously chosen courses of action even when they are not working—should be recognized in work settings.

How do technology, culture, and ethics influence decision-making?

- Technological developments are continuing to change the nature of organizational decision-making.

- Culture has a real impact: differences in culture determine who makes a decision and when, where, and how they make it.

- Ethics is involved in each stage of the decision-making process, and effective decision-making includes individual moral criteria and values.

KEY TERMS

Anchoring and adjustment heuristic (p. 348)

Artificial intelligence (p. 353)

Associative choices (p. 344)

Authority decisions (p. 350)

Availability heuristic (p. 348)

Behavioural decision theory (p. 344)

Certain environments (p. 342)

Classical decision theory (p. 344)

Confirmation trap (p. 348)

Consultative decisions (p. 350)

Creativity (p. 348)

Decision-making (p. 341)

Escalating commitment (p. 352)

Garbage can model (p. 346)

Group decisions (p. 350)

Heuristics (p. 348)

Hindsight trap (p. 348)

Intuition (p. 347)

Non-programmed decisions (p. 344)

Organized anarchy (p. 343)

Programmed decisions (p. 343)

Representativeness heuristic (p. 348)

Risk environments (p. 342)

Satisficing (p. 345)

Uncertain environments (p. 342)

SELF-TEST 17

MULTIPLE CHOICE

1. After a preferred course of action has been implemented, the next step in the decision-making process is to _____. (a) recycle the process (b) look for additional problems or opportunities (c) evaluate the results (d) document the reasons for the decision

2. In a(n) _____ environment, the decision-maker deals with probabilities regarding possible courses of action and their consequences. (a) certain (b) risk (c) organized anarchy (d) uncertain

3. In which kind of decision environment is associative choice most likely to occur? (a) organized anarchy (b) certainty (c) risk (d) satisficing

4. A manager who must deal with limited information and substantial risk is most likely to make decisions based on _____. (a) optimizing (b) classical decision theory (c) behavioural decision theory (d) escalation

5. A team leader who makes a decision not to launch a new product because the last new product launch failed is giving in to the _____ heuristic. (a) anchoring (b) availability (c) adjustment (d) representativeness

6. The five steps in the creativity process are preparation, _____, illumination, _____, and verification. (a) extension, evaluation (b) reduction, concentration (c) adaptation, extension (d) concentration, incubation

7. In Vroom's decision-making model, the choice among individual and group decision methods is based on criteria that include quality requirements, the availability of information, and _____. (a) the need for implementation commitments (b) the size of the organization (c) the number of people involved (d) the position power of the leader

8. The saying "If at first you don't succeed, try, try again" is most associated with a decision-making tendency called _____. (a) groupthink (b) the confirmation trap (c) escalating commitment (d) associative choice

9. One of the developments in artificial intelligence is _____ that attempt to have computers reason inductively in solving problems. (a) neural networks (b) expert systems (c) fuzzy logic (d) electronic brainstorms

10. Preferences for who makes decisions _____. (a) vary slightly across cultures (b) characterize individualistic cultures (c) are important only in high power distance (d) vary greatly across cultures

TRUE–FALSE

11. Most managerial decisions occur in certain environments.   T   F

12. Non-programmed decisions fit best with routine and repetitive problems.   T   F

13. Systematic decision-making is always preferred to intuitive decision-making.   T   F

14. Managers do not have to solve all the problems that come their way.   T   F

15. Escalating commitments is a way of improving the implementation of group decisions.   T   F

16. A good way to resolve a nagging problem is to implement some of the new information technology solutions.   T   F

17. The *ringi* system is a Japanese approach to gaining lower-level agreement and making sure that decisions can be implemented.   T   F

18. Group consensus is always preferred to the authority decision.   T   F

19. Impersonality in relationships is one possible disadvantage of electronic group decision-making.   T   F

20. In the final analysis, the turbulence in today's work environments makes decision-making impossible.   T   F

SHORT ANSWER

21. What are heuristics, and how can they affect individual decision-making?

22. What are the main differences among individual, consultative, and group decisions?

23. What is escalating commitment, and why is it important to be aware of it in decision-making?

24. What questions could a manager or team leader ask to help determine which problems should be dealt with and what priorities they should be given?

APPLICATIONS ESSAY

25. Your friends know you are taking OB courses and they constantly show you Dilbert cartoons in which managers are implementing decisions that are unrelated to problems. What insight can you share with them that will help them understand Dilbert better?

Conflict and Negotiation

Working around the Roadblocks

In the mid-1980s, Shasha Navazesh arrived in Toronto from Iran. Although Navazesh had a background in microbiology, he was drawn to the hospitality industry. Eventually he enrolled at George Brown College's culinary school to train as a pastry chef, where he began to reminisce of the bread that his mother and grandmother used to bake back in Iran. However, the bread that Navazesh remembered was different from the bread he found in Toronto.

Unfortunately, Navazesh could not find any courses teaching centuries-old methods of baking, so he began to experiment, eventually settling on a workable recipe. Navazesh also began to realize that there might be a market for such a product as organic foods were beginning to take hold in the marketplace. He decided to launch ShaSha Breads.

With little startup capital, Navazesh was able to rent the back of a bakery and its ovens from an owner on the verge of retirement. He then sunk the rest of his money into supplies. In the early days, Navazesh handled all the duties of his fledgling business: bread-making, packaging, sales, marketing, and deliveries. ISoon he had secured a few good accounts at health-food stores and specialty stores. But suddenly after a year of hope, the building housing the bakery was sold, leaving ShaSha Bread with customers and no bakery.

Despite the setback, Navazesh wanted to save his business. He became a "wandering baker", renting space after hours at local bakeries for $200 per night. Navazesh eventually saved enough money to rent space in a 2,000 square-foot former warehouse and eventually was able to buy the building.

Today, Navazesh has grown his business. Additionally, he has established the Artisan Bakers Quality Alliance (ABQA) to bring Ontario's artisan bakers together to share ideas, recipes, and techniques, to increase the availability of healthy bread in the market, and to educate consumers. He hopes to build an umbrella brand, similar to the Vintners Quality Alliance (VQA) for Ontario wines, and Navazesh is also the only baker in Canada to receive a National Research Council of Canada IRAP (Industrial Research Assistance Program) grant to do research on the bacteria culture or sourdough starter.

This chapter introduces you to conflict and negotiation as key processes of organizational behaviour that can have a major impact on the performance and satisfaction of people at work. As you read Chapter 18, keep in mind these key questions:

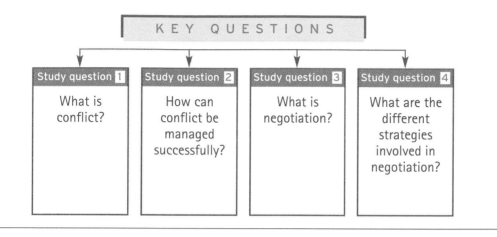

KEY QUESTIONS

Study question 1	Study question 2	Study question 3	Study question 4
What is conflict?	How can conflict be managed successfully?	What is negotiation?	What are the different strategies involved in negotiation?

The daily work of people in organizations is largely based on communication and interpersonal relationships. To implement courses of action in situations that are often complicated and stressful, managers must therefore have the interpersonal skills to work well with others.[1] The exchange of information in the workplace usually has a purpose and is intended to be persuasive.

At the same time, as we learned in Chapter 17, communication in interpersonal relationships is often the starting point for differences and disagreements that can create difficulties. Success in today's high-performance organizations increasingly requires a good understanding of the fundamentals of conflict and negotiation.

Conflict

Conflict occurs whenever there are disagreements in a social situation over substantive issues or whenever emotional antagonisms (e.g., dislike, mistrust, anger) create friction between individuals or groups—i.e., between the parties in conflict.[2] Managers and team leaders can spend a lot of time dealing with conflict, including conflicts in which the manager or leader is directly involved as one of the principal actors.[3] In other situations, the manager or leader may act as a mediator, or third party, whose job is to resolve conflicts between other people. In all cases, a manager or team leader must be comfortable with interpersonal conflict. This includes being able to recognize situations that have the potential for conflict and being able to deal with these situations in ways that will best satisfy the needs of both the organization and the people in conflict.[4]

Conflict occurs when parties disagree over substantive issues or when emotional antagonisms create friction between the parties.

TYPES OF CONFLICT

Substantive conflict involves fundamental disagreement over which ends or goals to pursue and how to achieve them.

Conflict as it is experienced in the daily workplace involves at least two basic forms. **Substantive conflict** is a fundamental disagreement over which ends or goals to pursue and how to achieve them.[5] A dispute with a boss about a plan of action, such as the marketing strategy for a new product, is an example of substantive conflict. When people work together day after day, it is only normal that there will eventually be different viewpoints on a variety of substantive workplace issues. At times, people will disagree over such things as group and organizational goals, the allocation of resources, the distribution of rewards, policies and procedures, and task assignments. Dealing with such conflicts successfully is an everyday challenge for most managers.

Emotional conflict involves interpersonal difficulties that arise over feelings of anger, mistrust, dislike, fear, resentment, and so on.

By contrast, **emotional conflict** involves interpersonal difficulties that arise over feelings of anger, mistrust, dislike, fear, resentment, and so on.[6] This conflict is commonly known as a "clash of personalities." Emotional conflicts can drain the energies of people and distract them from important work priorities. They can emerge from a wide variety of settings and are common among co-workers, as well as in superior–subordinate relationships. Emotional conflict between superiors and subordinates is perhaps the most upsetting organizational conflict for any person to experience. Unfortunately, competitive pressures in today's business environment and the resulting emphasis on downsizing and restructuring have created more situations in which the decisions of a "tough" boss can create emotional conflict.

FUNCTIONAL AND DYSFUNCTIONAL CONFLICTS

Conflict in organizations can be upsetting both to the individuals directly involved and to others who are affected by it. It can be quite uncomfortable, for example, to work in an environment in which two co-workers are continually hostile toward each other. In OB, however, as shown in Figure 18.1, it is recognized that there are two sides to conflict: the functional or constructive side, and the dysfunctional or destructive side.

Figure 18.1 The two faces of conflict: functional conflict and dysfunctional conflict

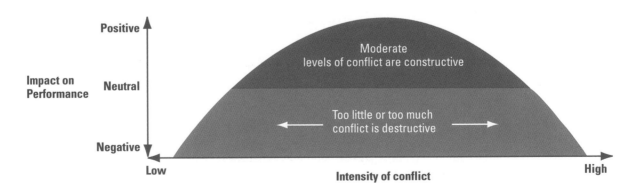

Functional conflict results in positive benefits to the individual, group, or organization.

Functional conflict, also called *constructive conflict or task conflict*, results in positive benefits to individuals, the group, or the organization. On the positive side, conflict can bring important problems to the surface so that they can be addressed. It can cause decisions to be considered carefully and perhaps reconsidered to ensure that the right path of action is being followed. It can increase the amount of information that can be used for decision-making. And it can offer opportunities for creativity that can improve individual, team, or organizational performance. Indeed, an effective manager is able to stimulate constructive conflict in situations where change and development are needed but, because people are satisfied with the status quo, there is no desire to make any changes..

Dysfunctional conflict, or *destructive conflict*, works to the individual's, group's, or organization's disadvantage. It is hurtful because it wastes energies, hurts group cohesion, promotes interpersonal hostilities, and generally creates a negative environment for workers. This occurs, for example, when two employees are unable to work together because of interpersonal differences (a destructive emotional conflict) or when the members of a committee fail to act because they cannot agree on group goals (a destructive substantive conflict). Destructive conflicts of these types can decrease work productivity and job satisfaction and contribute to absenteeism and job turnover. Managers must be alert to destructive conflicts and take action quickly to prevent or eliminate them, or at least minimize their disadvantages.

> Dysfunctional conflict works to the individual's, group's, or organization's disadvantage.

LEVELS OF CONFLICT

When someone has to deal personally with conflicts in the workplace, what matters is how well prepared he or she is to encounter and deal successfully with various types of conflict. People at work may encounter conflict at the intrapersonal level (conflict within the individual), the interpersonal level (individual-to-individual conflict), the intergroup level, or the interorganizational level.

Some conflicts that affect behaviour in organizations involve the individual by him- or herself. These **intrapersonal conflicts** often involve actual or perceived pressures that are caused by incompatible goals or expectations of the following types: *Approach–approach conflict* occurs when a person must choose between two positive and equally attractive alternatives. An example is having to choose between a valued promotion in the organization or a desirable new job with another firm. *Avoidance–avoidance conflict* occurs when a person must choose between two negative and equally unattractive alternatives. An example is being asked either to accept a job transfer to another town in an undesirable location or to have one's employment with an organization terminated. *Approach–avoidance* conflict occurs when a person must decide to do something that has both positive and negative consequences. An example is being offered a higher paying job whose responsibilities will require too much of one's personal time.

> Intrapersonal conflict occurs within the individual because of actual or perceived pressures caused by incompatible goals or expectations.

Interpersonal conflict occurs between two or more individuals who are against each other. It may be substantive or emotional, or both. Two individuals who are debating each other aggressively on the merits of hiring a job applicant is an example of a substantive interpersonal conflict. Two individuals who are continually in disagreement over each other's choice of work attire is an example of an emotional interpersonal conflict.

> Interpersonal conflict occurs between two or more individuals who are against each other.

Intergroup conflict that occurs among members of different teams or groups can also have a substantive and/or an emotional basis. Intergroup conflict is quite common in organizations, and it can make the coordination and integration of task activities very difficult.[7] The classic example is conflict among functional groups or departments in organizations, such as the marketing and manufacturing departments. The growing use of cross-functional teams and task forces is one way of trying to minimize such conflicts and promoting more creative and efficient operations.

> Intergroup conflict occurs among groups in an organization.

WORKPLACE DIVERSITY

David Whitsitt and his team at Petro-Canada's head office in Calgary had a tall task. They needed to develop an evaluation method to improve leadership competency and hence drive the company's competitive advantage. The belief that good leadership contributes to a working environment that produces strong business results was considered fundamental to making Petro-Canada an employer of choice. The system that was developed, the Leadership Feedback Process, is a version of the 360-degree feedback system that enables managers to clearly see how they are perceived by the people they supervise. An impressive 75 percent of participants say it is a good way to help leaders develop. At the same time, the company can combine the data from the companywide survey and identify the overall strengths and weaknesses of the company. But be careful. When Disney did its version of the 360-degree evaluation, the persons who selected friends to evaluate them were treated more honestly and tougher by their friends since they try to help you by being frank and constructive in their criticism.

Interorganizational conflict occurs between organizations.

Interorganizational conflict is most commonly thought of as the competition and rivalry that there is between firms that are operating in the same markets. A good example is the continuing battle between multinational businesses and their global rivals. RIM is fighting several court cases over whether or not it has infringed on patents of NTP of Chicago, with the result that the very future of its highly successful "BlackBerry" device is uncertain. But interorganizational conflict is a much broader issue than simply market competition. Consider, for example, disagreements between unions and the organizations that employ the union's members; between government agencies and the organizations that they regulate; between organizations and those who supply them with raw materials.

CULTURE AND CONFLICT

Society today shows many signs of strain in social relationships. We experience difficulties as a result of racial tensions, homophobia, gender gaps, and more. These problems can all be traced back to tensions between people who are different from each other in one way or another. They are also a reminder that culture and cultural differences must be thought of as potential sources of conflict.

Among the popular dimensions of culture discussed in Chapter 3, for example, substantial differences may be noted in time orientation. When persons from short-term cultures such as Canada and the U.S. try to work with persons from long-term cultures such as Japan and China, there is a high risk of conflicts developing over the urgency and timing of issues. This is also true when individualists work with collectivists and when persons from high power-distance cultures work with those from low power-distance cultures.[8] In each case, individuals who are not able to recognize and respect the impact of culture on behaviour may make it easier for dysfunctional situations to occur. On the other hand, when individuals are sensitive and respectful in cross-cultural work situations, it becomes easier to find ways to work together well and even benefit from the advantages that constructive conflict may offer.

WORKPLACE DIVERSITY

High-performance organizations like IBM have to capitalize on diversity. They must take full advantage of the talents and potential that there is in a multicultural workforce and workplace. As cultures vary around the world, the way business is done also varies. The best firms and their managers are culturally aware and they understand and respect diversity. J.T. Childs, Jr., vice president for Global Diversity at IBM, says: "Workforce diversity is the bridge between the workplace and the marketplace. And, it is anchored on ideals that guide how you treat citizens of all countries as potential customers." AT HSBC, which is named after its founding member, the Hongkong and Shanghai Banking Corporation, diversity is certainly valued. HSBC in Canada has national "Valuing Diversity" committees, comprising employees from various functions and levels within the organization, from both eastern and western Canada. The committees are involved in developing, implementing, and monitoring the company's "Valuing Diversity" initiatives. The goal is to create an environment that is supportive of individual needs and differences and a workplace where creativity, innovation, teamwork, and productivity can flourish. HSBC wants to sustain an environment where customers and employees are treated with respect and dignity, through executive leadership, outreach, policies and/or practices, and training initiatives.

Managing Conflict

Conflict can be handled in many ways, but the important goal is to achieve or make it possible for there to be true **conflict resolution**. This occurs when the reasons for a specific destructive conflict are eliminated. The process begins with a good understanding of the causes of the conflict and knowing what stage the conflict has reached.

Conflict resolution occurs when the reasons for a conflict are eliminated.

STAGES OF CONFLICT

Most conflicts develop in stages, as shown in Figure 18.2. Managers should be aware that unresolved prior conflicts encourage future conflicts of the same type or related ones. Rather than try to deny the existence of conflict or settle on a temporary resolution, it is always best to deal with important conflicts so that they are completely resolved.[9] *Conflict antecedents* are the conditions that are likely to develop into conflicts. When the antecedent conditions become the basis for substantive or emotional differences between people or groups, the stage of *perceived conflict* has been reached. Of course, only one of the conflicting parties may perceive the situation this way. It is important to distinguish between perceived and *felt conflict*. When conflict is felt, it is experienced as tension that motivates the person to take actions that will reduce the feelings of discomfort. For conflict to be resolved, all parties should both perceive it and feel the need to do something about it.

When conflict is openly expressed in behaviour, it is said to be manifest. A state of *manifest conflict* may be resolved by removing or correcting its antecedents. It can also be suppressed. With suppression, there is no change in the antecedent conditions; the manifest conflict behaviours are simply controlled. For example, one or both parties may choose to ignore the conflict when they interact with each other. *Suppression* is a superficial and often temporary form of conflict resolution. Indeed, we have already noted that unresolved and suppressed conflicts remain a problem. They may continue to fester and cause future conflicts over similar issues. As a temporary solution, however, suppression may be the best that a manager can achieve until the antecedent conditions can be changed.

Unresolved substantive conflicts can cause continued emotional discomfort and lead to dysfunctional emotional conflict between individuals. In contrast, truly resolved conflicts may create conditions that reduce the potential for future conflicts or make it easier to deal with them. Thus, any manager should be aware of the influence that *conflict aftermath* has on future occurrences of conflict.

Figure 18.2 The stages of conflict

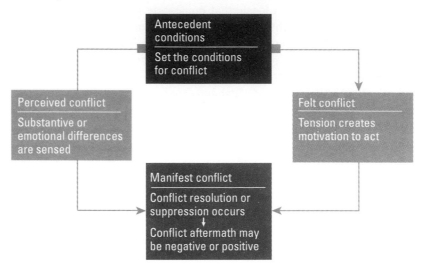

CAUSES OF CONFLICT

To deal successfully with conflict, a manager must first be familiar with several types of conflict situations. *Vertical conflict* occurs between hierarchical levels. It commonly involves supervisor–subordinate disagreements over resources, goals, deadlines, or performance results. *Horizontal conflict* occurs between persons or groups at the same hierarchical level. These disputes commonly involve goals that are incompatible, resources that are scarce, or purely interpersonal factors. A common variation of horizontal conflict is *line–staff conflict*. It often involves disagreements over who has authority and control over certain matters, such as personnel selection and termination practices.

OB Across Functions

Purchasing

Conflict Management in Supplier Relationships

Canadian engineering consulting firm ABCO Engineering and Operations Management Ltd. has developed unique supplier relationship management technology that helps ease the customer-supplier relationship. Its vSRM interface sends a company's purchase order requirements to suppliers and their responses back automatically. Using an Internet connection, customers and suppliers can be located anywhere in the world. The system can be set up in less than 24 hours and be integrated into ERP systems. It increases control over inventory and allows for timely and accurate information flow of purchase orders and release changes, essentially resolving conflicts and errors and improving supplier shipment performance.

www.abcoeng.com

Role conflicts are also common in work situations. This occurs when the communication of task expectations is inadequate or upsetting. As discussed for teamwork in Chapter 10, this often happens when what a person is expected to do is not clearly communicated, when excessive expectations result in job overloads, when insufficient expectations result in job underloads, or when expectations from different sources are incompatible.

Workflow interdependencies are the source of many conflicts. Disputes and open disagreements may erupt among people and units that have to co-operate to meet challenging goals.[10] When interdependence is high—that is, when a person or group must rely on contributions from one or more other people or groups to achieve its goals—conflicts often occur. You will notice this, for example, in a fast-food restaurant, when the people serving the food have to wait too long for it to be delivered from the cooks. Conflict also increases when individuals or groups do not have enough task direction or goals. *Domain ambiguities* are misunderstandings over such things as customer jurisdiction or how much responsibility a person or group has for the customer. Conflict is likely when individuals or groups are placed in ambiguous situations where it is difficult for them to understand just who is responsible for what.

Actual or perceived *resource scarcity* can lead to destructive competition. When resources are scarce, working relationships are likely to suffer. This is especially true in organizations that are experiencing downsizing or financial difficulties. As cutbacks occur, various individuals or groups try to position themselves to gain or retain as much as they can of the shrinking resource pool. They are also likely to try to resist resource redistribution, or to use countermeasures to prevent their resources from being redistributed to others.

Finally, *power or value asymmetries* in work relationships can create conflict. They exist when interdependent people or groups are substantially different from each other in terms of their status and influence, or in their values. Conflict due to asymmetry generally occurs, for example, when either a lower-power person needs the help of a higher-power person who does not respond, when people with dramatically different values are forced to work together on a task, or when a high-status person has to interact with and perhaps be dependent on someone with lower status.

INDIRECT CONFLICT-MANAGEMENT APPROACHES

Indirect conflict-management approaches try to solve conflict by avoiding direct dealings between personalities that could be in conflict. These approaches include reduced interdependence, appeals to common goals, hierarchical referral, and alterations in the use of mythology and scripts.

Reduced Interdependence   When workflow conflicts exist, managers can adjust the level of interdependency among the units or individuals.[11] One simple option is *decoupling*, or taking action to eliminate or reduce the required contact between parties in conflict. In some cases, the units' tasks can be adjusted to reduce the number of required points of coordination. The conflicting units can then be separated from each other, and each can be provided separate access to valued resources. Although decoupling may reduce conflict, it may also result in duplication and a poor allocation of valued resources.

Buffering is another approach that can be used when the inputs of one group are the outputs of another group. The classic buffering technique is to build an inventory, or buffer, between the two groups so that any output slowdown or excess is absorbed by the inventory and does not directly pressure the target group. Although it reduces conflict, this technique is increasingly unpopular because it increases inventory costs. A higher inventory goes against the elements of just-in-time delivery, which is now valued in operations management.

Conflict management can also be made easier by assigning people to serve as formal *linking pins* between groups that tend to be in conflict.[12] Persons in linking-pin roles, such as a project liaison, are expected to understand the operations, members, needs, and norms of their host group. They are supposed to use this knowledge to help their group work better with other groups when they have to accomplish mutual tasks. Though expensive, this technique is often used when different specialized groups, such as teams from engineering and sales, must closely coordinate their efforts on complex and long-term projects.

Appeals to Common Goals   An appeal to common goals can focus the attention of potentially conflicting parties on one mutually desirable conclusion. When the potential dispute is seen through a common framework that helps the parties recognize that they need each other in order to achieve common goals, petty disputes can be put in perspective. However, this can be difficult to achieve when past performance is poor and individuals or groups disagree over how to improve performance. In this negative situation, the manager needs to remember the tendency of individuals to use attribution—that is, they tend to blame poor performance on others or on external conditions. In this case, conflict resolution begins by making sure that the parties take personal responsibility for improving the situation.

HIGH-PERFORMANCE ORGANIZATIONS

Common goals drive the system when Wal-Mart steps up to meet, and beat, the competition. The world's largest retailer doesn't leave anything to chance, especially not the need for a compelling sense of common purpose and direction. Stop by the weekly Saturday meeting at the Bentonville, Arkansas, headquarters and listen to the cheer. "Who's number one?" chant the associates. "The customer. Always," they answer in unison. Keeping the focus, staying on goal, minding the values, sharing the vision—all are key to maintaining the common goals that bind together Wal-Mart's one million U.S. and 300,000 worldwide staff members in the quest for continuing growth. That was Sam's way and that remains the Wal-Mart way. The future danger concerns the more than 50 percent annual turnover of hourly staff and the difficulty in finding enough managers for the company's continuing expansion into food in the U.S., Sam's Clubs in Canada, and Wal-Mart stores in Europe and Mexico.[13]

Hierarchical Referral   *Hierarchical referral* uses the chain of command for conflict resolution. Here, problems are simply referred up the hierarchy for more senior managers to solve. Whereas hierarchical referral can be definitive in a particular case, it also has limitations. If conflict is severe and recurring, the continual use of hierarchical referral may not result in true conflict resolution. Senior managers who are far from the day-to-day affairs may not diagnose the real causes of a conflict, and the conflict resolution they propose may be superficial. Busy managers may tend to consider most conflicts as being the result of poor interpersonal relations and they may therefore act too quickly to replace a person who is seen as having a "personality" problem.[14]

Altering Scripts and Myths In some situations, conflict is superficially managed by *scripts*, or behavioural routines that become part of the organization's culture.[15] The scripts become rituals that allow the conflicting parties to express their frustrations and to recognize that they depend on each other through the larger corporation. An example is a monthly meeting of department heads that is held presumably for coordination and problem-solving but that actually becomes just a polite forum for superficial agreement.[16] Managers in such cases know their scripts and accept that it is hard to truly solve major conflicts. By sticking with the script, expressing only low-key disagreement and then quickly acting as if everything has been resolved, for instance, the managers publicly act as if problems are being addressed. Such scripts may be altered to allow and encourage a more active confrontation of issues and disagreements but in the short-term, the conflicts have been avoided.

DIRECT CONFLICT-MANAGEMENT APPROACHES

Figure 18.3 describes the five approaches to conflict management from the perspective of how much they emphasize co-operation and assertiveness in the relationship between the parties in conflict. Consultants and academics generally agree that true conflict resolution can occur only when the underlying substantive and emotional reasons for the conflict are identified and dealt with through a solution that allows all conflicting parties to "win."[17] (See The Effective Manager 18.1.) This issue of "Who wins?" is very important and can be looked at from the perspective of each party in the conflict.

Figure 18.3 Five ways to manage conflict

> **The Effective Manager** | **18.1**
>
> WHEN TO USE CONFLICT-MANAGEMENT STYLES
>
> - Collaboration and problem-solving is preferred for true conflict resolution when time and cost allow this approach.
> - Avoidance may be used when an issue is trivial or more important issues need attention, or when people need to cool down temporarily and regain perspective.
> - Authoritative command may be used when quick and decisive action is vital or when unpopular actions must be taken.
> - Accommodation may be used when issues are more important to others than to yourself or when you want to build "credits" you will be able to use in later issues.
> - Compromise may be used for temporary settlements of complex issues or to arrive at quick solutions when time is limited.

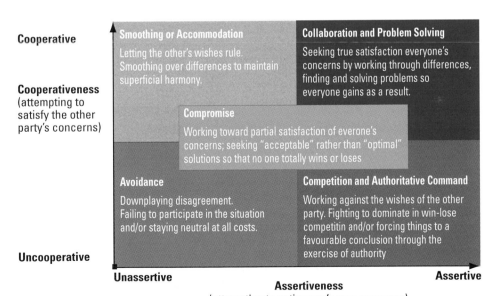

Avoidance involves pretending a conflict does not really exist.

Accommodation or **smoothing** involves treating differences as being small and finding areas of agreement.

Compromise occurs when each party gives up something of value to the other party.

Competition is trying to win by force, superior skill, or domination.

Authoritative command uses formal authority to end conflict.

Collaboration involves recognizing that something is wrong and needs attention through problem-solving.

Problem-solving uses information to resolve disputes.

Lose-Lose Conflict   *Lose-lose conflict* occurs when nobody really gets what he or she wants. The reasons for the conflict remain unchanged and a similar conflict is likely to occur in the future. Lose-lose conflicts often result when no one acts assertively and conflict management takes the forms described next. **Avoidance** is an extreme form of inattention; everyone simply pretends that the conflict does not really exist and hopes that it will go away. **Accommodation**, or **smoothing** as it is sometimes called, involves treating differences between the conflicting parties as being small and highlighting similarities and areas of agreement. This peaceful coexistence ignores the real essence of a specific conflict and often creates frustration and resentment. **Compromise** occurs when each party gives up something of value to the other party. As a result of no one getting what is really wanted, there are now antecedent conditions for future conflicts.

Win-Lose Conflict   In *win-lose conflict*, one party gets what it wants and the other party does not. This is a high-assertiveness and low-cooperation situation. It may result from outright **competition** in which one party wins through force, superior skill, or domination. It may also occur as a result of **authoritative command**, where a formal authority simply dictates a solution and specifies what is gained and what is lost by whom. Win-lose strategies do not address the root causes of the conflict and tend to suppress the desires of at least one of the conflicting parties. As a result, future conflicts over the same issues are likely to occur.

Win-Win Conflict   *Win-win conflict* is achieved by a blend of both high co-operation and high assertiveness.[18] **Collaboration** or **problem-solving** involves having all conflicting parties recognize that something is wrong and needs attention. It stresses gathering and evaluating information in solving disputes and making choices. Win-win conditions eliminate the reasons for continuing or reviving the conflict since nothing has been avoided or suppressed. All the relevant issues are raised and openly discussed. The ultimate test for a win-win solution is whether or not the conflicting parties see that the solution (1) achieves each other's goals, (2) is acceptable to both parties, and (3) establishes a process in which all the parties involved in the conflict feel a responsibility to be open and honest about facts and feelings. When success is achieved, true conflict resolution has occurred.

Although collaboration and problem-solving are generally favoured, one limitation is the time and energy it requires. It is also important to realize that both parties to the conflict need to be assertive and co-operative in order to develop a win-win joint solution. Finally, collaboration and problem-solving may not be feasible if the firm's dominant culture does not value co-operation.[19]

Negotiation

Talk about conflict! Picture yourself trying to make a decision in the following situation: You need to order a new state-of-the-art notebook computer for a staff member in your department. At the same time, another department plans to order a different brand. Your boss indicates that only one brand will be ordered. Of course, you believe the one chosen by your department is the best.

WHAT IS NEGOTIATION?

This is just a sample of the many situations that involve managers and others in negotiation—the process of making joint decisions when the parties involved have different preferences.[20]

Negotiation has special significance in work settings, where disagreements are likely to arise over such diverse matters as wage rates, task objectives, performance evaluations, job assignments, work schedules, work locations, and more.

NEGOTIATION GOALS AND OUTCOMES

In negotiation, two important goals must be considered: substance and relationship goals. *Substance goals* deal with outcomes that relate to the "content" issues that are under negotiation. The dollar amount of a wage agreement in a collective bargaining situation is one example. *Relationship goals* deal with outcomes that relate to how well the negotiating people and any constituencies they may represent are able to work with each other after the process is over. An example is the ability of union members and management representatives to work together effectively after a contract dispute has been settled.

Unfortunately, many negotiations result in damaged relationships because the negotiating parties become preoccupied with substance goals and self-interests. In contrast, *effective negotiation* occurs when substance issues are resolved and working relationships are maintained or even improved. It results in overlapping interests and joint decisions that are "for the better" of all parties. Three criteria for effective negotiation are described in The Effective Manager 18.2.

ETHICAL ASPECTS OF NEGOTIATION

To maintain good working relationships in negotiations, managers and the other parties in the negotiation should try to have high ethical standards. This goal is hard to achieve when there is an overemphasis on self-interests. The motivation to behave ethically in negotiations is tested by each party's desire to "get more" than the other from the negotiation or when it is believed that there are not enough resources to satisfy everyone.[21] After the negotiations have ended, the parties involved often try to rationalize or explain away less ethical behaviour as having been unavoidable, harmless, or justified. However, the questionable behaviours that are justified by after-the-fact rationalizations may be offset by long-run negative consequences, such as not being able to get what one wants the next time there are negotiations. At the very least, the unethical party may be the target of revenge tactics by the parties who feel they were at a disadvantage. Furthermore, once some people have behaved unethically in one situation, they may become entrapped by such behaviour and have a tendency to behave that way again in the future.[22]

ORGANIZATIONAL SETTINGS FOR NEGOTIATION

Managers and team leaders should be prepared to participate in at least four major action settings for negotiations. In *two-party negotiation*, the manager negotiates directly with one other person. In *group negotiation*, the manager is part of a team or group whose members are negotiating to arrive at a common decision. In *intergroup negotiation*, the manager is part of a group that is negotiating with another group to arrive at a decision about a problem or situation that is affecting both groups. And in *constituency negotiation*, the manager is negotiating with other persons, but each party—i.e., the manager and the other persons—is representing a broader constituency. A common example of constituency negotiation is when representatives of management and labour negotiate a collective bargaining agreement.

CULTURE AND NEGOTIATION

The existence of cultural differences in time orientation, individualism-collectivism, and power distance can have a substantial impact on negotiations. For example, when Canadian or U.S. businesses try to negotiate quickly with their Chinese counterparts, they often do so with the goal of getting definitive agreements that will govern a working relationship. Culture is not always on their side, however. A typical Chinese approach to negotiation might move much more slowly, require the development of good interpersonal relationships before reaching any agreement, show a reluctance to put everything in writing, and anticipate that any agreement that is reached can still be modified as future circumstances may require.[23] All this is quite the opposite of what negotiators expect when they are used to the more individualist and short-term Western culture.

| The Effective Manager | 18.2 |

CRITERIA OF AN EFFECTIVE NEGOTIATION

- *quality*—The results of the negotiation offer a "quality" agreement that is wise and satisfactory to all sides.
- *harmony*—The negotiation is "harmonious" and encourages rather than inhibits good interpersonal relations.
- *efficiency*—The negotiation is "efficient" and is no more time-consuming or costly than is absolutely necessary.

Negotiation Strategies

Managers and other workers frequently negotiate with each other over access to scarce organizational resources. These resources may be money, time, people, facilities, equipment, and so on. In all such cases, the general approach to the negotiation can have a major influence on its outcomes. In **distributive negotiation**, the focus is on "positions" that have been declared by conflicting parties. Each party is trying to claim certain portions of the available "pie"—that is, of the available resources. In **integrative negotiation**, sometimes called *principled negotiation*, the focus is on the merits of the issues. Everyone involved tries to enlarge the available pie rather than claim certain portions of it.[24] (See the Effective Manager 18.2.)

DISTRIBUTIVE NEGOTIATION

Distributive negotiation focuses on positions that have been declared by parties that are each trying to claim certain portions of the available pie.

Integrative negotiation focuses on the merits of the issues, and the parties involved try to enlarge the available pie rather than claim certain portions of it.

In distributive bargaining approaches, the participants would each ask the question, "Who is going to get this resource?" This question, and the context it gives for subsequent behaviour, will have a major impact on the negotiation process and outcomes. A case of distributive negotiation usually proceeds in one of two directions, and neither direction gives ideal results. *"Hard" distributive negotiation* happens when each party decides to refuse agreement until it gets its own way. This leads to competition, in which each party tries to dominate the other and tries to maximize its self-interests. The hard approach may lead to a win-lose outcome in which one party dominates and gains. Or it can lead to an impasse, with no agreement being reached.

"Soft" distributive negotiation, by contrast, happens when one party is willing to make concessions to the other to get things over with. In this case, one party tries to find ways to meet the other's desires. A soft approach leads to accommodation in which one party gives in to the other, or to compromise in which each party gives up something of value in order to reach agreement. In either case, some dissatisfaction is likely to eventually develop. Even when the soft approach results in compromise (e.g., splitting the difference between the initial positions equally), there may still be dissatisfaction because each party still has not gotten what it originally wanted.

Figure 18.4 An example of the bargaining zone in classic two-party negotiation

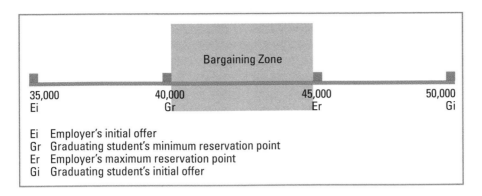

Ei Employer's initial offer
Gr Graduating student's minimum reservation point
Er Employer's maximum reservation point
Gi Graduating student's initial offer

Figure 18.4 introduces the case of the university graduate who is negotiating a job offer with a corporate recruiter.[25] The example shows the basic elements of classic two-party negotiation in distributive contexts. To begin, look at the situation from the graduate's perspective. She has told the recruiter that she would like a salary of $50,000; this is her initial offer. But she also has in mind a minimum reservation point of $40,000—the lowest salary that she will accept for this job. Thus, she communicates a salary request of $50,000 but is willing to accept one as low as $40,000. The situation is somewhat reversed from the recruiter's perspective. His initial offer to the graduate is $35,000, and his maximum reservation point is $45,000—this is the most he is prepared to pay.

The bargaining zone is defined as the range between one party's minimum reservation point and the other party's maximum reservation point. In Figure 18.4, the bargaining zone is $40,000 to $45,000. This is a positive bargaining zone since the reservation points of the two parties overlap. Whenever there is a positive bargaining zone, there is room for bargaining to occur. If the graduate's minimum reservation point had been greater than the recruiter's maximum reservation point (for example, $47,000), there would have been no room for bargaining. Classic two-party bargaining always involves the delicate tasks of first discovering the respective reservation points (one's own and the other party's) and then working toward an agreement that is somewhere within the resulting bargaining zone and is acceptable to each party.

> The bargaining zone in a negotiating situation is the zone between one party's minimum reservation point and the other party's maximum reservation point.

INTEGRATIVE NEGOTIATION

In the integrative approach to negotiation, participants would ask, "How can the resource best be used?" Notice that this question is very different from the one described for distributive negotiation. It is much less confrontational, and it permits a broader range of alternatives to be considered in the process. From the beginning, there is much more of a win-win orientation.

At one extreme, integrative negotiation may result from selective avoidance, in which both parties realize that there are more important things on which to focus their time and attention. The time, energy, and effort needed to negotiate may not be worth the rewards. Compromise can also play a role in the integrative approach, but it must have a lasting basis. This is most likely to occur when the compromise involves each party giving up something of perceived lesser personal value to gain something of greater value. For instance, in the classic two-party bargaining case over salary, both the graduate and the recruiter could expand the negotiation to include the starting date of the job. Since it will be a year before the candidate's first vacation, she may be willing to take a little less money if she can start a few weeks later. Finally, integrative negotiation may involve true collaboration. In this case, the negotiating parties do problem-solving to arrive at a mutual agreement that maximizes the benefits for each party.

HOW TO GAIN INTEGRATIVE AGREEMENTS

The integrative or principled approach is negotiation that is based on the merits of the situation. To reach truly integrative agreements, the participants must have supportive attitudes, constructive behaviours, and good information. These are the foundations for integrative agreements.[26]

Attitudinal Foundations There are three attitudinal foundations of integrative agreements. First, each party must approach the negotiation with a *willingness to trust* the other party. This is why ethics and maintaining relationships are so important in negotiations. Second, each party must show a *willingness to share information* with the other party. Without shared information, effective problem-solving is unlikely to occur. Third, each party must show a *willingness to ask concrete questions* of the other party. This further helps the sharing of information.

Behavioural Foundations During a negotiation, all behaviour is important for both its actual impact and the impressions it gives. Accordingly, the following behavioural foundations of integrative agreements must be carefully considered and included in any negotiator's repertoire of skills and capabilities:

Behavioural Foundations of Integrative Agreements

- the ability to separate the people from the problem so that emotional considerations do not affect the negotiation

- the ability to focus on interests rather than positions

- the ability to avoid making premature judgements

- the ability to keep the act of creating alternatives separate from the act of evaluating them

- the ability to judge possible agreements on an objective set of criteria or standards

Information Foundations The information foundations of integrative agreements are large. Each party has to be familiar with BATNA, which means the "best alternative to a negotiated agreement." That is, each party must know what he or she will do if an agreement cannot be reached. This requires both negotiating parties to identify and understand their personal interests in the situation. They must know what is really important to them in the situation, and they must come to understand how important the other party's interests are to that party. As difficult as it may seem, each party must achieve an understanding of what the other party values, even to the point of determining its BATNA.

COMMON NEGOTIATION PITFALLS

The negotiation process is certainly complex because of cultural and other considerations. It also often involves the many possible confusions of sometimes volatile interpersonal and group dynamics. Accordingly, negotiators need to guard against some common negotiation pitfalls or dangers.[27]

First, there is the tendency in negotiation to decide your position based on the assumption that, in order to gain your way, something must be subtracted from the other party's position. This *myth of the fixed pie* is a purely distributive approach to negotiation. The whole concept of integrative negotiation is based on the assumption that the pie can sometimes be expanded or used to the maximum advantage of all parties, not just one.

Second, because parties to negotiations often begin by stating their extreme demands, the possibility of *escalating commitment* is high. That is, once demands have been stated, people become committed to them and are reluctant to back down. Concerns for protecting one's ego and saving face may lead to an irrational escalation of conflict. Self-discipline is needed to spot this tendency in one's own behaviour, as well as in others.

Third, negotiators often develop *overconfidence* that their positions are the only correct ones. This can lead them to ignore the other party's needs. In some cases, negotiators completely fail to see the merits in the other party's position—merits that an outside observer would be sure to spot. Such overconfidence makes it harder to reach a positive common agreement.

Fourth, communication problems can cause difficulties during a negotiation. It has been said that "negotiation is the process of communicating back and forth for the purpose of reaching a joint decision."[28] This process can break down because of a *telling problem*—the parties do not really talk to each other, at least not in the sense of making themselves truly understood. It can also be damaged by a *hearing problem*—the parties are unable or unwilling to listen well enough to understand what the other party is saying. Indeed, positive negotiation is most likely when each party listens and frequently asks questions to clarify what the other party is saying. Each party occasionally needs to "stand in the other party's shoes" and to view the situation from that party's perspective.[29]

THIRD-PARTY ROLES IN NEGOTIATION

Negotiation may sometimes be accomplished through the intervention of third parties, such as when stalemates occur and it looks like matters cannot be resolved under current circumstances. In arbitration, such as the salary arbitration now common in professional sports, this third party acts as the "judge" and has the power to issue a decision that is binding on all parties—that is, all parties are obliged to respect the decision. This ruling takes place after the arbitrator listens to the arguments expressed by the parties in the dispute. In Ontario, for example, the Arbitration Act of 1991 establishes the rules and extent of the arbitration process but does not regulate or register the arbitrators. If the parties in arbitration want, the arbitrator can even base the rulings on religious beliefs and laws. However, the ruling is not binding if one party does not agree with it. In this case, the courts then become responsible for issuing a decision. Similar processes apply elsewhere in Canada.

In mediation, a neutral third party uses persuasion and rational argument to get the parties to reach a negotiated solution. This is a common approach in labour–management negotiations, where trained mediators that are acceptable to each side are called in to help resolve bargaining impasses. Unlike an arbitrator, the mediator is not able to dictate a solution.

In arbitration, a neutral third party acts as judge with the power to issue a decision that is binding on all parties.

In mediation, a neutral third party uses persuasion and rational argument to get the parties to reach a negotiated solution.

Summary

What is conflict?

- Conflict is any situation where there is disagreement over issues of substance or there are emotional antagonisms that create friction between individuals or groups.

- Conflict can be either substantive (based on work goals) or emotional (based on personal feelings).

- When it stays within limits that are acceptable, conflict can be a source of improved creativity and performance; it becomes destructive when it goes past these limits.

- Conflict situations in organizations occur in vertical and lateral working relations and in line–staff relations.

- Conflict usually develops through a series of stages, beginning with antecedent conditions and progressing into manifest conflict.

- Unresolved prior conflicts make it likely that there will be future conflicts of a similar nature.

How can conflict be managed successfully?

- Indirect forms of conflict management include appeals to common goals, hierarchical referral, organizational redesign, and the use of mythology and scripts.

- Direct conflict management proceeds with different combinations of assertiveness and co-operation from the parties in the conflict.

- Win-win conflict resolution is preferred; it is achieved through collaboration and problem-solving.

- Win-lose conflict resolution should be avoided; it is associated with competition and authoritative command.

What is negotiation?

- Negotiation occurs whenever two or more people with different preferences must make joint decisions.

- Managers may find themselves involved in various types of negotiation situations, including two-party, group, intergroup, and constituency negotiation.

- Effective negotiation occurs when issues of substance are resolved and human relationships are maintained or even improved in the process.

- Ethical conduct is important to successful negotiations.

What are the different strategies involved in negotiation?

- In distributive negotiation, each party focuses on establishing its position so that it can claim the portion that it wants of a "fixed pie."

- In integrative negotiation, sometimes called principled negotiation, the focus is on determining the merits of the issues and finding ways to satisfy each party's needs.

- The success of the strategies depends on avoiding common negotiating pitfalls and building good communication.

Accommodation or
smoothing (p. 370)

Arbitration (p. 375)

Authoritative command
(p. 370)

Avoidance (p. 370)

Bargaining zone (p. 372)

Collaboration (p. 370)

Competition (p. 370)

Compromise (p. 370)

Conflict (p. 361)

Conflict resolution (p. 364)

Distributive negotiation
(p. 372)

Dysfunctional conflict
(p. 363)

Emotional conflict (p. 362)

Functional conflict (p. 362)

Integrative negotiation
(p. 372)

Intergroup conflict (p. 363)

Interorganizational conflict
(p. 364)

Interpersonal conflict
(p. 363)

Intrapersonal conflict
(p. 363)

Mediation (p. 375)

Negotiation (p. 371)

Problem-solving (p. 370)

Substantive conflict (p. 362)

MULTIPLE CHOICE

1. A conflict that occurs as a fundamental disagreement over which ends or goals to pursue and how to accomplish them is known specifically as a(n) _____ conflict. (a) relationship (b) emotional (c) substantive (d) procedural

2. The indirect conflict-management approach that uses chain of command for conflict resolution is known as _____. (a) hierarchical referral (b) avoidance (c) organizational redesign (d) appeals to common goals

3. Which of the following is not a way in which conflict can be positive for a group or organization? (a) It can help identify otherwise neglected problems. (b) It can enhance creativity. (c) It can broaden the bargaining zone. (d) It can improve performance.

4. Lose-lose conflicts typically result from each of the following except_____. (a) competition (b) compromise (c) accommodation (d) avoidance

5. When would it be most effective for a manager to use accommodation? (a) when quick and decisive action is vital (b) when the manager wants to build "credit" for use in later issues (c) when people need to cool down and gain perspective (d) when the manager wants a temporary settlement of complex issues

6. According to the conflict management grid, the _____ conflict-management style is highly co-operative and assertive. (a) competition (b) compromise (c) accommodation (d) collaboration

7. The criteria for effective negotiation are _____. (a) harmony, efficiency, and quality (b) efficiency and effectiveness (c) ethics, practicality, and cost-effectiveness (d) quality, practicality, and productivity

8. _____ are two kinds of goals that should be considered in any negotiation. (a) Performance and evaluation (b) Task and substance (c) Substance and relationship (d) Task and performance

9. Which of the following statements is true? (a) Principled negotiation leads to accommodation. (b) Hard distributive negotiation leads to collaboration. (c) Soft distributive negotiation leads to accommodation or compromise. (d) Hard distributive negotiation leads to win-win conflicts.

10. The text mentions each of the following as a common negotiator pitfall except
_____. (a) falling prey to the myth of the "fixed pie" (b) rational escalation to conflict (c) overconfidence (d) listening to the other's needs (e) unethical behaviour

TRUE–FALSE

11. Intergroup conflict typically makes it easier to coordinate task activities.   T   F

12. Interpersonal conflicts can be substantive, emotional, or both.   T   F

13. Moderate levels of conflict are constructive.   T   F

14. When workflow interdependency is high, conflicts often occur.   T   F

15. The conflict-management grid classifies management styles along two dimensions: co-operativeness and assertiveness.   T   F

16. Two goals are at stake in any negotiation: distributive and integrative.   T   F

17. The most preferred approach to negotiation is distributive.   T   F

18. In integrative negotiations, everyone tries to enlarge the "pie."   T   F

19. BATNA requires that each party know what will be done if an agreement cannot be reached.   T   F

20. Two types of communication difficulties are common in negotiations: telling and hearing.   T   F

SHORT ANSWER

21. List and discuss three conflict situations faced by managers.

22. List and discuss the major indirect conflict-management approaches.

23. Under what conditions might a manager use avoidance or accommodation?

24. Compare and contrast distributive and integrative negotiation. Which is more desirable? Why?

APPLICATIONS ESSAY

25. Discuss the common pitfalls that you would expect to meet when you are negotiating your salary for your first job, and explain how you would try to best deal with them.

Change and Innovation

19

Renewed Airline Takes Flight

Air Canada has experienced a lot of turbulence in recent years. Canada's largest airline sought bankruptcy protection in 2003 and then re-emerged a year and a half later a restructured and streamlined air carrier. The success of its recovery from bankruptcy protection depended in large part on a creative and effective change management plan.

This plan included reducing operating costs, strengthening the balance sheet, reorganizing the corporate structure, and having a fleet renewal and marketing strategy. When announcing the completion of its restructuring process in September 2004, Air Canada said it reduced its debt and capitalized operating lease obligations from approximately $12 billion to less than $5 billion. It also raised $1.1 billion in new equity capital and had approximately $1.9 billion of cash on hand.

"We have fundamentally changed who we are," said Robert Milton, chairman, president and CEO of ACE Aviation Holdings Inc. "We have radically transformed this airline into a highly connected global network carrier offering the simplicity and ease of our low cost competitors."

Air Canada's various businesses segments, including Aeroplan, Air Canada Jazz, Destina.ca, Touram, Air Canada Technical Services, Air Canada Cargo, and Air Canada Groundhandling, now operate as separate legal entities, under parent holding company ACE Aviation Holdings Inc. The creation of ACE also necessitated the creation of new by-laws and a new board of directors.

Along with the corporate reorganization came an unveiling of a new look for the airline, including an updated design and colour scheme for its fleet, complete with a redesigned maple leaf on each airplane's tail; new uniforms for its 6,700 flight attendants and 2,900 airport customer service agents, who hadn't had a uniform change since 1995; a new in-flight entertainment system with personal television screens at each seat, featuring video and audio on demand; and lie-flat seats for international executive class passengers. These initiatives, which were to be introduced over the course of 2005, illustrate a renewed focus on providing customers with valued products and services.

The airline planned to introduce the changes "strategically and economically" to minimize costs. Painting the airplanes would take place over two years, according to the airline's regular maintenance program. In the meantime, a decal was placed on aircraft tails. The marketing campaign, which includes television and radio advertising featuring Celine Dion, was also produced within existing marketing budgets.

The airline's CEO credits the success of its transformation to its employees. "It's through their hard work, loyalty, and willingness to accept change that Air Canada has been transformed and positioned to succeed as a profitable, growing, competitive company in a rapidly changing industry," Mr. Milton said.

This chapter is about the important issues of change and innovation as they relate to developments in the modern workplace. As you read Chapter 19, keep in mind these key questions:

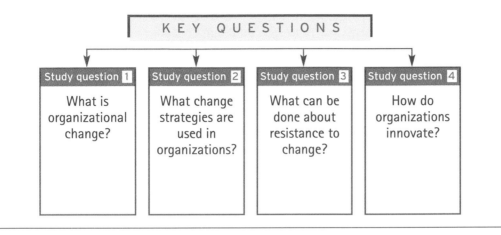

KEY QUESTIONS

Study question **1**	Study question **2**	Study question **3**	Study question **4**
What is organizational change?	What change strategies are used in organizations?	What can be done about resistance to change?	How do organizations innovate?

A recent *Harvard Business Review* article opens with this sentence: "The new economy has ushered in great business opportunities—and great turmoil. Not since the Industrial Revolution have the stakes of dealing with change been so high." The terms "turmoil" and "turbulence" are now often used to describe the current environment of business and management. The global economy is full of problems and opportunities, and is constantly bringing new surprises for even the most experienced business executives. At the heart of any successful response to the challenges of change are the people who make organizations work. This is what makes the insights of organizational behaviour so essential to leadership in change situations.

As the environment changes, organizations must change, too—not just in their quest for customers in highly competitive markets, but also in their quest to have the best in employee talents. Flexibility, competency, and commitment are the rules of the day. People in the new workplace must be comfortable in dealing with adaptation and continuous change. In addition to calls for greater productivity, a willingness to learn from the successes of others, total quality, and continuous improvement, everyone is also being called to achieve success while pursuing change and innovation. In the words of management consultant Tom Peters: "The turbulent marketplace demands that we make innovation a way of life for everyone. We must learn—individually and as organizations—to welcome change and innovation as vigorously as we have fought it in the past."[1]

Change in Organizations

"Change" is now the key word for many, if not most, organizations. Some of this change may be described as radical change, or frame-breaking change.[2] In OB, such change is generally called **transformational change**—change which results in a major overhaul of the organization or its component systems. Organizations that are experiencing transformational change make significant shifts in their basic, characteristic features, including their overall purpose

Transformational change radically alters the basic character of an organization.

and mission, their underlying values and beliefs, and their supporting strategies and structures.[3] In today's business environments, transformational changes often start with a critical event, such as a new CEO, a new ownership resulting from a merger or takeover, or a dramatic failure in operating results. When it occurs in the life cycle of an organization, such radical change is intense and it affects everything.

Another common form of organizational change is incremental change, or frame-bending change. This type of change is part of an organization's natural evolution. It happens often and is less traumatic. Typical changes of this type include the introduction of new products, new technologies, and new systems and processes. Although the nature of the organization remains mostly the same, incremental change builds on the existing ways of operating to improve these ways or extend them in new directions. The capability to improve continuously through incremental change is an important asset in today's demanding environments.

Change agents are people who take action to change the behaviour of people and systems.

The success of both radical and incremental change in organizations depends in part on **change agents** who lead and support the change processes. These are individuals and groups who take responsibility for changing the existing behaviour patterns of another person or social system. Although change agents sometimes are hired as consultants from outside the organization, any manager or leader in today's dynamic times is expected to be able to act as a change agent. Indeed, this responsibility is increasingly being defined as essential to the leadership role. Simply put, being an effective change agent means being a great "change leader."

ENTREPRENEURSHIP

He started by launching a student magazine, moved on to start a record company, and ended up being the brains and the drive behind the multibillion-dollar global conglomerate Virgin Group. We're talking about Richard Branson of course, named England's best business leader by his peers. Branson believes in starting companies rather than buying them. Says he: "We start from scratch each time as a way of making sure it's really ours." Change is part of the culture. "We split our ventures into smaller units when they get too big, so that each will become the swiftest at what it does best," says Branson. The Virgin brand is dedicated to service and value for its customers, and to an organizational culture focused on satisfaction, creativity, irreverence, and fun. Branson fits the image with an ever-present smile, open-necked shirt, and eye toward the future.[4]

PLANNED AND UNPLANNED CHANGE

Unplanned change occurs spontaneously and without a change agent's direction.

Not all change in organizations is the result of a change agent's direction. **Unplanned changes** occur spontaneously or randomly. They may be disruptive, such as a wildcat strike that ends in a plant closure, or beneficial, such as an interpersonal conflict that results in a new procedure being designed to smooth the flow of work between two departments. When the forces of unplanned change begin to appear, the appropriate goal is to act quickly to minimize any negative consequences and maximize any possible benefits. In many cases, unplanned changes can be used to good advantage.

Planned change is intentional and occurs with a change agent's direction.

In contrast, **planned change** is the result of specific efforts by a change agent. It is a direct response to someone's perception of a *performance gap*—a discrepancy between the actual situation and the situation that is wanted. Performance gaps may be seen as problems to be resolved or opportunities to be explored. Most planned changes may be regarded as attempts to deal with performance gaps in ways that benefit an organization and its members. For continuous improvement to occur, it is important to constantly look for performance gaps—both problems and opportunities—and to take action to resolve them.

ORGANIZATIONAL FORCES AND TARGETS FOR CHANGE

The forces for change that are driving all types and sizes of organizations are everywhere in today's dynamic work settings. They are found in the *organization–environment relationship*—for example, mergers, strategic alliances, and divestitures. These are all attempts by organizations to redefine its relationships with challenging social and political environments. They are found in the organizational life cycle—for example, changes in an organization's culture and structure. These are examples of how an organization must adapt as it evolves from birth through growth and toward maturity. They are found also in the *political nature of organizations*—for example, changes in internal control structures, including changes to benefits and reward systems. These are attempts by an organization to deal with changing political currents.

When an organization plans change that is based on any of these forces, it can aim these changes at a wide variety of components in the organization, most of which have already been discussed in this book. As shown in Figure 19.1, these targets include the organization's purpose, strategy, structure, and people, as well as its objectives, culture, tasks, and technology. When considering these targets, however, it must be recognized that each one is connected to many others in the workplace. Changes in one component are likely to require or involve changes in others. For example, a change in the basic tasks—what it is that people do—is almost always accompanied by a change in *technology*—the way in which these tasks are accomplished. Changes in tasks and technology usually also require alterations in structures, including changes in the patterns of authority and communication, as well as in the roles of workers. These technological and structural changes can, in turn, necessitate changes in the knowledge, skills, and behaviours of *people*—the members of the organization.[5] In all cases, of course, it is best to avoid the tendency to accept easy-to-implement, but questionable, "quick fixes" to problems.

Figure 19.1 Organizational targets for planned change

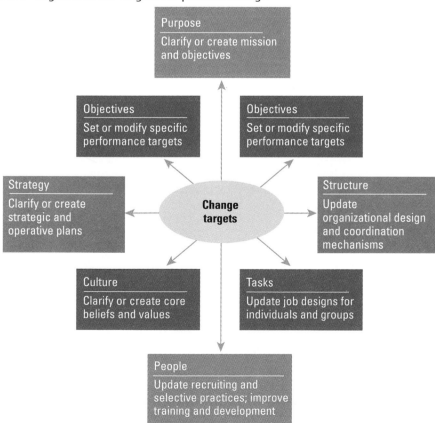

PHASES OF PLANNED CHANGE

Researchers suggest that the failure rate of organizational change attempts is as high as 70 per-cent.[6] The challenges of transformational change are especially large, as The Effective Manager 19.1 suggests.[7] A change initiative will have a better chance of succeeding, however, if one first understands the underlying processes of social change in organizations. Psychologist Kurt Lewin recommends that any change effort be viewed in three phases—unfreezing, changing, and refreezing—all of which must be well handled for a change to be successful.[8] He also sug-gests that we may become easily preoccupied with the changing phase and neglect the impor-tance of the unfreezing and refreezing phases.

Unfreezing is the stage where a situation is pre-pared for change.

Unfreezing In Lewin's model, **unfreezing** is the managerial responsibility of preparing a sit-uation for change. It involves disconfirming existing attitudes and behaviours to create a feel-ing that something new is needed. Unfreezing is easier to achieve if there are environmental pressures or if there is declining performance, recognition of a problem, or awareness that someone else has found a better way, among other things. Many changes are never tried or they fail simply because situations are not properly unfrozen to begin with.

Large systems seem particularly susceptible to what is sometimes called the boiled frog phenomenon.[9] This refers to the notion that a live frog will immedi-ately jump out when it is placed in a pan of hot water. When it is placed in cold water that is then heated very slowly, however, the frog will stay in the water until the water boils the frog to death. Organizations, too, can fall victim to similar cir-cumstances. When managers fail to monitor their environments, recognize the important trends, or sense the need to change, their organizations may slowly suf-fer and lose their competitive edge. Although the signals that change may be needed are available, they are not noticed or given any special attention—until it is too late. In contrast, the best organizations are led by people who are always on the alert and understand the importance of "unfreezing" in the change process. Compare Air Canada and WestJet. Based on what you know about these two air-lines, which one has been more successful at changing and adapting to the evolv-ing Canadian travelling public?

> ## The Effective Manager 19.1
>
> ### WHY TRANSFORMATIONAL EFFORTS FAIL
>
> - no sense of urgency
> - no powerful guiding coalition
> - no compelling vision
> - failure to communicate the vision
> - failure to empower others to act
> - failure to celebrate short-term wins
> - failure to build on accomplishments
> - failure to institutionalize results

Changing is the stage where specific actions are taken to create change.

Changing The **changing** stage involves taking action to modify a situation by changing things, such as the people, tasks, structure, or technology of the organization. Lewin believes that many change agents tend to fall into an activity trap. They skip over the unfreezing stage and start changing things too soon or too quickly. Although their intentions may be correct, the situation has not been properly prepared for change. This often leads to failure. Changing something is difficult enough in any situation; it is harder still without the proper foundations.

Refreezing is the stage where changes are rein-forced and stabilized.

Refreezing The final stage in the planned change process is **refreezing**. The goal here is to maintain the momentum of a change and eventually institutionalize it as part of the organiza-tion's normal routine. By doing this, refreezing secures the full benefits of long-lasting change. Refreezing involves positively reinforcing desired outcomes and providing extra support when there are difficulties. It involves evaluating progress and results, and assessing the costs and benefits of the change. And it allows for modifications to be made in the change to increase its success over time. When all of this is not done—in other words, when refreezing is neglect-ed—changes are often abandoned after a short time or they are only partly implemented.

Planned Change Strategies

Managers and other change agents use various strategies for mobilizing power, exerting influence over others, and getting people to support planned change efforts. As described in Figure 19.2, each of these strategies uses the various bases of social power discussed in Chapter 15. Note in particular that each power source has somewhat different implications for the planned change process.[10]

Figure 19.2 Power bases, change strategies, and predicted change outcomes

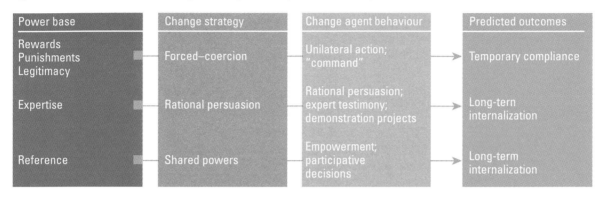

Power base	Change strategy	Change agent behaviour	Predicted outcomes
Rewards Punishments Legitimacy	Forced–coercion	Unilateral action; "command"	Temporary compliance
Expertise	Rational persuasion	Rational persuasion; expert testimony; demonstration projects	Long-tern internalization
Reference	Shared powers	Empowerment; participative decisions	Long-term internalization

FORCE-COERCION

A **force—coercion strategy** uses authority, rewards, and punishments as the main reasons to change. That is, the change agent acts unilaterally to "command" change through the formal authority of his or her position, to induce change through an offer of special rewards, or to force change through threats of punishment. People respond to this strategy mainly because they are afraid of being punished if they do not follow the change directive or because they hope to gain a reward if they do. The compliance to or acceptance of this change is usually temporary and continues only as long as the change agent and his or her legitimate authority are visible, or as long as the opportunities for rewards and punishments remain obvious.

A **force–coercion strategy** uses authority, rewards, and punishments to create change.

Your actions as a change agent using the force–coercion strategy might match the following profile:

> You believe that people who run things are basically motivated by self-interest and by what the situation offers them in potential personal gains or losses. Since you feel that people change only in response to such motives, you try to find out what they care about most (their vested interests) and then you put the pressure on. If you have formal authority, you use it. If not, you use whatever possible rewards and punishments you have access to and you do not hesitate to threaten others with these weapons. Once you find a weakness, you exploit it and are always wise to work "politically" by building supporting alliances wherever possible.[11]

RATIONAL PERSUASION

Change agents who use a **rational persuasion strategy** try to make change happen through the use of special knowledge, empirical support, or rational arguments. This strategy assumes

A **rational persuasion strategy** uses facts, special knowledge, and rational argument to create change.

that rational people will be guided by reason and self-interest in deciding whether or not to support a change. Expert power is used to convince others that the change will leave them better off than before. It is sometimes referred to as an *empirical-rational strategy* of planned change. When successful, this strategy results in a longer lasting, more naturalized change than does force–coercion.

As a change agent taking the rational persuasion approach to a change situation, you might behave as follows:

> You believe that people are basically rational and are guided by reason in their actions and decision-making. Once a specific course of action is shown to be in a person's self-interest, you assume that reason and rationality will cause the person to adopt it. Thus, you approach change with the objective of communicating—through information and facts—the essential "desirability" of change for the person whose behaviour you want to influence. If this logic is effectively communicated, you are sure the person will adopt the proposed change.[12]

SHARED POWER

A shared-power strategy uses participatory methods and emphasizes common values to create change.

A **shared-power strategy** actively and sincerely involves the people who will be affected by a change in planning and making key decisions about the change. Sometimes called a *normative–reeducative approach*, this strategy tries to use involvement and empowerment as a way to develop directions and support for change. It builds essential foundations, such as personal values, group norms, and shared goals, so that support for a proposed change happens naturally. Managers who use normative–reeducative approaches rely on the power of personal reference, and they also share power by allowing others to participate in planning and implementing the change. Given this high level of involvement, the strategy is likely to result in a longer lasting and internalized change.

As a change agent who shares power and adopts a normative–reeducative approach to change, you are likely to fit this profile:

> You believe that people have complex motivations. You feel that people behave as they do as a result of sociocultural norms and commitments to these norms. You also recognize that changes in these orientations involve changes in attitudes, values, skills, and significant relationships, not just changes in knowledge, information, or intellectual rationales for action and practice. Thus, when seeking to change others, you are sensitive to the supporting or inhibiting effects of group pressures and norms. In working with people, you try to find out their side of things and to identify their feelings and expectations.[13]

Resistance to Change

Resistance to change is an attitude or behaviour that shows unwillingness to make or support a change.

In organizations, **resistance to change** is any attitude or behaviour that indicates a person's unwillingness to make or support a desired change. Change agents often view any such resistance as something that must be "overcome" in order for change to be successful. This is not always true, however. It is helpful to view resistance to change as feedback that the change agent can use to help achieve change objectives.[14] Essentially, this constructive approach to resistance depends on recognizing that, when people resist change, they are defending something that is important to them and that appears threatened by the change attempt.

WHY PEOPLE RESIST CHANGE

People have many reasons to resist change. The Effective Manager 19.2 identifies fear of the unknown, insecurity, lack of a felt need to change, threat to vested interests, contrasting interpretations, and a lack of resources, among other possibilities. A work team's members, for example, may resist the introduction of advanced workstation computers because they have never used the operating system and are apprehensive. They may wonder whether the new computers will eventually be used as a reason for getting rid of some of them; or they may believe that they have been doing their jobs just fine and do not need the new computers to improve things. These and other viewpoints often create resistance to even the best and most well-intentioned planned changes.

Resistance to the Change Itself   Sometimes a change agent experiences resistance to the change itself. People may reject a change because they believe it is not worth their time, effort, or attention. To minimize resistance in such cases, the change agent should make sure that everyone who may be affected by a change knows specifically how it satisfies the following criteria:[15]

- *benefit*—The change should have a clear advantage for the people being asked to change; it should be perceived as "a better way."

- *compatibility*—The change should fit as well as possible with the existing values and experiences of the people being asked to change.

- *complexity*—The change should be only as complex as it needs to be; it must be as easy as possible for people to understand it and use it.

- *triability*—The change should be something that people can try on a step-by-step basis and make adjustments to as things progress.

Resistance to the Change Strategy   Change agents must also be prepared to deal with resistance to the change strategy. Someone who tries to get change through force–coercion, for example, may create resistance among individuals who resent management by "command" or the use of threatened punishment. People may resist a rational persuasion strategy if the data are suspect or the expertise of those supporting it is not clear. They may also resist a shared-power strategy that appears manipulative and insincere.

Resistance to the Change Agent   Resistance to the change agent is directed at the person who is implementing the change and often involves personality and other differences. Change agents who are isolated and aloof from other persons in the change situation, who appear self-serving, or who have a high emotional involvement in the changes are especially likely to have such problems. Research also indicates that change agents who differ from other persons in the change situation on such dimensions as age, education, and socio-economic factors may encounter greater resistance to change.[16]

HOW TO DEAL WITH RESISTANCE

An informed change agent has many options available to him or her for dealing positively with resistance to change, in any of its forms.[17] The first approach is education and communication. The objective is to educate people about a change before it is made and to help them under-

Criteria for Successful Changes

CGI Group

www.cgi.com

Montreal-based IT services firm CGI Group has acquired or merged with many companies since it was founded in 1976, often seamlessly and with little resistance. *Canadian Business* compares CGI to the Borg on Star Trek— only friendlier. The company has established a systematic approach to introducing employees, who are called "members," to the company's vision and the benefits. In fact, when merging with another company, CGI tries to maintain existing teams and often gives acquired managers more responsibility.

stand the logic of the change. Education and communication seem to work best when resistance is based on inaccurate or incomplete information. A second way is the use of participation and involvement. The goal of this approach is to allow others to help design and implement the changes. It asks people to contribute ideas and advice or to work on task forces or committees that may be leading the change. This approach is especially useful when the change agent does not have all the information that is needed to successfully handle a problem situation.

Facilitation and support involves providing assistance—both emotional and material—for people who are experiencing the hardships of change. A manager who is using this approach actively listens to problems and complaints, provides training in the new ways, and helps others to overcome performance pressures. Facilitation and support is highly recommended when people are frustrated by work constraints and difficulties that they are encountering in the change process. A negotiation-and-agreement approach offers incentives to people who are resisting or may resist the change. Tradeoffs are arranged to provide special benefits in exchange for assurances that the change will not be blocked. This approach is most useful when dealing with a person or group that will lose something of value as a result of the planned change.

Manipulation and co-optation makes use of hidden attempts to influence others, selectively providing information and consciously structuring events so that the desired change occurs. In some cases, leaders of the resistance may be "bought off" with special side deals to gain their support. Manipulation and co-optation are common when other tactics do not work or are too expensive. Finally, *explicit or implicit coercion* uses the force of authority to get people to accept change. Often, those who are resisting are threatened with a variety of undesirable consequences if they do not go along as planned. This may be done, for example, in crisis situations when speed is critical.

Figure 19.3 Methods for dealing with resistance to change

Method →	Use when →	Advantages →	Disadvantages
Education & communication	People lack information or have inaccurate information	Creates willingness to help with the change	Can be very time consuming
Participation & involvement	Other people have important information and/or power to resist	Adds information to change planning; builds commitment to the change	Can be very time consuming
Facilitation & support	Resistance traces to resource or adjustment problems	Satisfies directly specific resource or adjustment needs	Can be time consuming; can be expensive
Negotiation & agreement	A person or group will "lose" something because of the change	Helps avoid major resistance resistance	Can be expensive; can cause others to seek similar "deals"
Manipulation & cooptation	Other methods don't work or are too expensive	Can be quick and inexpensive	Can create future problems if people sense manipulation
Explicit & implicit coercion	Speed important and change agent has power	Quick; overpowers resistance	Risky if people get "mad"

Figure 19.3 summarizes additional insights into how and when each of these methods may be used to deal with resistance to change. Regardless of the chosen strategy, it is always

HIGH-PERFORMANCE ORGANIZATIONS

Since balancing its budget in 1997–98, the Government of Canada has put resources behind research and innovation. In February 2002, it launched a 10-year innovation strategy aimed at putting Canada among the world's most innovative countries. Canada's Innovation Strategy's goals include doubling current investments in research and development, making research and technological expertise available to firms of all sizes, raising the amount of venture capital financing, increasing the number of adults pursuing learning opportunities and enrolling in graduate studies at Canadian universities, and improving recruitment of foreign talent, including foreign students.

www.innovation.gc.ca

best to remember that the presence of resistance typically suggests that something can be done to achieve a better fit among the change, the situation, and the people affected. A good change agent deals with resistance to change by listening to feedback and acting accordingly.

Innovation is the process of creating new ideas and putting them into practice.

Product innovations introduce new goods or services to better satisfy customer needs.

Process innovations introduce into operations new and better ways of doing things.

Innovation in Organizations

The best organizations do not stagnate; they innovate.[18] And they are able to innovate on an ongoing basis—they value and expect "innovation," and it becomes a normal part of everyday operations. **Innovation** is the process of creating new ideas and putting them into practice.[19] It is how creative ideas find their way into everyday practices—and ideally these new practices improve customer service or organizational productivity. **Product innovations** result in the introduction of new or improved goods or services to better satisfy customer needs. **Process innovations** introduce new and better work methods and operations.

THE INNOVATION PROCESS

The basic steps in a typical process of organizational innovation are shown in Figure 19.4. They include:

1. *idea creation*—creating an idea through spontaneous creativity, ingenuity, and information processing

2. *initial experimentation*—establishing the idea's potential value and application

3. *feasibility determination*—identifying anticipated costs and benefits

4. *final application*—producing and marketing the new product or service, or implementing the new approach to operations

The innovation process is not complete until final application has been achieved. A new idea—even a great one—is not enough. In any organization, the idea must pass through all the stages of innovation and reach the point of final application before its value can be realized.

Harry Wasylyk and Larry Hansen

You may not know Harry and Larry's names, but you know their product. These two men, one from Winnipeg, the other from Lindsay, Ontario, developed the plastic garbage bag. Originally intended for industrial use, the concept of the garbage bag was eventually sold by the two men to Larry's employer, Union Carbide, and you now know their product as Glad garbage bags.

Figure 19.4 The innovation process: a case of new product development

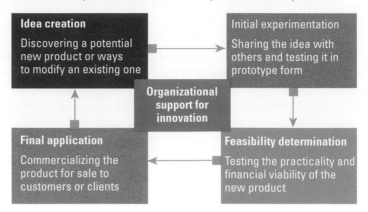

Idea creation
Discovering a potential new product or ways to modify an existing one

Initial experimentation
Sharing the idea with others and testing it in prototype form

Organizational support for innovation

Final application
Commercializing the product for sale to customers or clients

Feasibility determination
Testing the practicality and financial viability of the new product

FEATURES OF INNOVATIVE ORGANIZATIONS

The new workplace is placing great demands on organizations and their members to be continuously innovative. When we examine the characteristics of high-performance, innovative organizations, we observe certain common features. Highly innovative organizations have *strategies and cultures* that are built around a commitment to innovation. This includes tolerance for mistakes and respect for well-intentioned ideas that just do not work. Highly innovative organizations have *structures* that support innovation. They emphasize creativity through teamwork and cross-functional integration. They also use decentralization and empowerment to overcome the limitations of great size. In highly innovative organizations, *staffing* is done with a clear commitment to innovation. Special attention is given to the critical innovation roles of idea generators, information gatekeepers, product champions, and project leaders. Finally, innovative organizations benefit from *top-management support*. Senior managers provide good examples for others, eliminate obstacles to innovation, and try to get things done that make innovation easier. Former Johnson & Johnson CEO James Burke, for example, once said, "I try to give people the feeling that it's okay to fail," while Quad Graphics founder Harry V. Quadrucci practised what has been dubbed "management by walking away." The implication in both approaches is that employees know what needs to be done, and management's job is to trust and help them to do their best.[20]

ETHICS AND SOCIAL RESPONSIBILITY

The Canadian Centre for Ethics & Corporate Policy started out as an Anglican chaplaincy on Bay Street in Toronto's financial district. After focusing on the morals of downsizing in the '80s and '90s, this organization that has members from almost every major firm in Canada now focuses on broken partnerships, increasing understanding, the identification of best practices, and the development of ethically based leadership for organizations. Using awareness building, the sharing of learning and resources, and networking and referrals, the centre tries to "develop the opportunities to promote and maintain a high level of ethical orientation within organizations."[21]
www.ethicscentre.ca

Organizations that build positive work environments and make significant investments in their employees are best positioned to get the benefits of their full talents and work potential. As Stanford scholar and consultant Jeffrey Pfeffer says: "All that separates you from your competitors are the skills, knowledge, commitment, and abilities of the people who work for you. Organizations that treat people right will get high returns...."[22] That, in essence, is what the study of organizational behaviour is all about.

CHAPTER 19 STUDY GUIDE

Summary

What is organizational change?

- Planned change occurs because change agents, individuals, and groups make it happen to resolve performance problems or take advantage of performance opportunities.

- Transformational change radically alters the fundamental aspects of organizations, such as their purpose and mission, beliefs and values, and strategies and structures.

- Organizational targets for planned change include the organization's purpose, strategy, culture, structure, people, tasks, and technology.

- The planned change process requires attention to the three phases—unfreezing, changing, and refreezing.

What change strategies are used in organizations?

- Change strategies are the techniques that change agents use to get desired change in people and systems.

- Force–coercion change strategies use position power to force change through direct command or through rewards and punishments.

- Rational-persuasion change strategies use logical arguments and appeals to knowledge and facts to convince people to change.

- Shared-power change strategies involve other persons in planning and implementing change.

What can be done about resistance to change?

- Resistance to change should be expected and not feared; it is a source of feedback that can be used to improve a change effort.

- People usually resist change because they are defending something of value to them; they may focus their resistance on the change itself, the change strategy, or the change agent as a person.

- Strategies for dealing with resistance to change include education and communication, participation and involvement, facilitation and support, negotiation and agreement, manipulation and co-optation, and explicit or implicit coercion.

How do organizations innovate?

- Innovation is the process of creating new ideas and then implementing them in practical applications.
- Product innovations result in improved goods or services; process innovations result in improved work methods and operations.
- Steps in the innovation process normally include idea generation, initial experimentation, feasibility determination, and final application.
- Common features of highly innovative organizations include supportive strategies, cultures, structures, staffing, and senior leadership.

KEY TERMS

Change agents (p. 382)

Changing (p.384)

Force–coercion strategy (p. 385)

Innovation (p. 389)

Planned change (p. 382)

Process innovations (p. 389)

Product innovations (p. 389)

Rational-persuasion strategy (p. 385)

Refreezing (p. 384)

Resistance to change (p. 386)

Shared-power strategy (p. 386)

Transformational change (p. 381)

Unfreezing (p.384)

Unplanned change (p. 382)

SELF-TEST 19

MULTIPLE CHOICE

1. Performance gaps that create change situations include both problems to be resolved and _____. (a) costs to be avoided (b) people to be terminated (c) structures to be changed (d) opportunities to be explored

2. The presence or absence of a felt need for change is an issue in the _____ phase of planned change. (a) diagnostic (b) evaluative (c) unfreezing (d) changing

3. Which change strategy uses empirical data and expert power? (a) force–coercion (b) rational persuasion (c) shared power (d) authoritative command

4. What change strategy often creates only temporary compliance? (a) force–coercion (b) rational persuasion (c) shared power (d) normative re-education

5. A good change agent _____ resistance to change in order to best achieve change objectives. (a) eliminates (b) ignores (c) listens to (d) retreats from

6. According to the criterion of _____, a good change is clearly perceived as a better way of doing things. (a) benefit (b) triability (c) complexity (d) compatibility

7. Training in how to use a new computer technology is an example of managing resistance to change through _____. (a) participation and involvement (b) facilitation and support (c) negotiation and agreement (d) education and communication

8. The innovation process is not complete until _____ has occurred. (a) idea creation (b) invention (c) feasibility determination (d) final application

9. Innovative organizations are characterized by having _____. (a) strong hands-on management (b) a tolerance for mistakes (c) strongly reinforced structures (d) strong codes of communication

10. Refreezing ensures _____. (a) the organization returns to the original processes (b) stops the change processes from going any further (c) allows reviewing and improvements (d) allows management to once again gain control

TRUE–FALSE

11. The only significant change for today's organizations is radical or frame-breaking change.   T   F

12. Change agents, formally defined, are outside consultants hired to help managers change their organizations.   T   F

13. Changes in tasks, people, technology, and structures are often interrelated.   T   F

14. Positive reinforcement of desired behaviours is part of the refreezing phase of planned change.   T   F

15. The personality and style of the change agent may cause resistance to change.   T   F

16. The shared-power change strategy is the same as the rational-persuasion strategy.   T   F

17. A process innovation results in the creation of a new good or service.   T   F

18. Product champions and information gatekeepers play important innovation roles in organizations.   T   F

19. The perceptions of the change agents do not significantly affect their approach to the change situation.   T   F

20. Innovation is the creation of a new idea.   T   F

SHORT ANSWER

21. What should a manager do when forces for unplanned change appear?

22. What internal and external forces necessitate change in organizations?

23. What does the "boiled frog phenomenon" tell us about organizational change?

24. What are the major reasons for resistance to change and the most likely methods for dealing with them?

APPLICATIONS ESSAY

25 When George Maldanado became general manager of the local community recreation centre, he realized that many changes would be necessary to make the facility a true community resource. Having the benefit of a new grant, the centre had the funds for new equipment and expanded programming. All he needed to do now was to get the staff committed to new initiatives. Unfortunately, his first efforts to raise performance have been met with considerable resistance to change. A typical staff comment is, "Why do all these extras? Everything is fine as it is." How could George move the change process along by using the strategies for dealing with resistance to change that were discussed in the chapter?

Dynamics of Stress

Appendix

Stress is tension from extraordinary demands, constraints, or opportunities.

The processes of change and innovation often create new and increased pressures on the people involved in the change. **Stress** must be understood as tension that individuals experience when they are facing extraordinary demands, constraints, or opportunities.[1]

Source of Stress

Stressors are things that cause stress.

Any look toward your career future in today's dynamic times must include an awareness that stress is something you, as well as others, are sure to experience.[2] **Stressors** are the wide variety of things that cause stress for individuals. Some stressors can be traced directly to what people experience in the workplace, whereas others come from nonwork and personal factors.

WORK-RELATED STRESSORS

Without a doubt, work can be stressful and job demands can disrupt a person's work-life balance. A study of two-career couples, for example, found that some 43 percent of men and 34 percent of women felt that they worked more hours than they wanted to.[3] We know that work-related stress can come from many sources—from excessively high or low task demands, role conflicts or ambiguities, poor interpersonal relations, or career progress that is either too slow or too fast. A list of common stressors includes the following:

Possible Work-Related Stressors

- *task demands*—being asked to do too much or being asked to do too little
- *role ambiguities*—not knowing what one is expected to do or how work performance is evaluated
- *role conflicts*—feeling unable to satisfy multiple, possibly conflicting, performance expectations
- *ethical dilemmas*—being asked to do things that are against the law or against one's personal values
- *interpersonal problems*—experiencing bad relationships or working with others who do not get along
- *career developments*—moving too fast and feeling stretched; moving too slowly and feeling plateaued
- *physical setting*—being bothered by noise, pollution, a lack of privacy, or other unpleasant working conditions

NONWORK AND PERSONAL STRESSORS

A less obvious, though important, source of stress for people at work is the "spillover" effect from forces in their nonwork lives. Family events (e.g., the birth of a child), economic difficulties (e.g., the sudden loss of a big investment), and personal affairs (e.g., a separation or divorce) can all be extremely stressful. Since it is often difficult for people to completely separate their work and nonwork lives, stress of this nonwork sort can affect the way people feel and behave on the job, as well as away from it.

Another set of stressors includes personal factors, such as individual needs, capabilities, and personality. Stress can reach a destructive state more quickly, for example, when it is experienced by highly emotional people or by those who have low self-esteem. People who perceive a good fit between a job's requirements and their personal skills seem to have a higher tolerance for stress than people who feel less competent as a result of a person–job mismatch.[4] Basic aspects of personality are also important. The achievement orientation, impatience, and perfectionism of individuals with Type A personalities, for example, often create stress for them in work settings that others find relatively stress-free.[5]

BHP Billiton Diamonds
http://ekati.bhpbilliton.com
At the Ekati Diamond Mine, 300 kilometres from Yellowknife and 200 kilometres from the Arctic circle, the employees are encouraged to use the company's facilities. These include a running track, a gymnasium, racquetball courts, saunas, a games room, and television lounges. The health and well-being of the employees is a major focus for this company. BHP ranked sixth in Maclean's 2004 ranking of the top 10 physical workplaces.

STRESS AND PERFORMANCE

Stress is not always a negative influence on our lives. It has two faces—one positive and one negative.[6] **Constructive stress**, or *eustress*, acts in a positive way. Moderate levels of stress can increase work effort, stimulate creativity, and encourage greater diligence. You may know such stress as the tension that causes you to study hard before exams, or pay attention and complete assignments on time in a difficult class. **Destructive stress**, or *distress*, is dysfunctional for both the individual and the organization. Too much stress can overload and break down a person's physical and mental systems, resulting in absenteeism, turnover, errors, accidents, dissatisfaction, reduced performance, unethical behaviour, and even illness. Stanford scholar and consultant Jeffrey Pfeffer, for example, criticizes organizations for creating toxic workplaces when they have excessive practices.[7] A toxic company implicitly says to its employees: "We're going to put you in an environment where you have to work in a style and at a pace that is not sustainable. We want you to come in here and burn yourself out. Then you can leave."[8]

Constructive stress has a positive impact on both attitudes and performance.

Destructive stress has a negative impact on both attitudes and performance.

STRESS AND HEALTH

As is well known, stress can affect a person's health. It is a potential source of both anxiety and frustration, which can harm the body's physiological and psychological well-being over time.[9] Health problems that are associated with stress include heart attack, stroke, hypertension, migraine headache, ulcers, substance abuse, overeating, depression, and muscle aches. As noted in The Effective Manager A1, managers and team leaders should be alert to signs of excessive stress in themselves and their co-workers. Key symptoms to look for are changes from normal patterns, such as changes from regular attendance to absenteeism, from punctuality to tardiness, from diligent work to careless work, from a positive attitude to a negative attitude, from openness to change to resistance to change, or from co-operation to hostility.

The Effective Manager | A1

SIGNS OF EXCESSIVE STRESS
- change in eating habits
- change in alcohol consumption or smoking
- unhealthy feelings, such as aches and pains, an upset stomach
- restlessness, inability to concentrate, sleeping problems
- feelings of being tense, uptight, fidgety, nervous
- feelings of being disoriented, overwhelmed, depressed, irritable

Stress Management

Stress prevention involves minimizing the potential for stress to occur.

Stress prevention is the best first-line strategy in the battle against stress. It involves taking action to keep stress from reaching destructive levels in the first place. Personal and nonwork stressors must be recognized so that action can be taken to prevent them from having a negative impact. Persons with Type A personalities, for example, may exercise self-discipline; supervisors of Type A employees may try to model a lower-key, more relaxed approach to work. Family problems may be partially relieved by a change of work schedule; the anxiety caused by pressing family concerns may be reduced by simply knowing that your supervisor understands.

Stress management takes an active approach to deal with stress that is influencing behaviour.

Wellness involves maintaining physical and mental health to better deal with stress when it occurs.

Once stress has reached a destructive point, special techniques of **stress management** can be used. This process begins with the recognition of stress symptoms and continues with actions that help maintain a positive performance edge. The term **wellness** is increasingly used these days. Personal wellness means fulfilling one's physical and mental potential through a personal health promotion program.[10] This concept recognizes that people are responsible for improving and maintaining their wellness through a disciplined approach to physical and mental health. It requires attention to such factors as smoking, weight, diet, alcohol use, and physical fitness. Organizations can benefit from commitments to support personal wellness. A University of Michigan study indicates that firms have saved up to $600 per year per employee by helping them to cut the risk of significant health problems.[11] Joan Wade, the manager of Employee Benefits and Occupational Health and Safety and Wellness, Town of Richmond Hill, Ontario has noticed a drop in absenteeism since Richmond Hill introduced a wellness program. The saving of three-quarters of a day per employee per year translated into an annual savings of $68,000 or a $2 return for every dollar invested in employee health.[12]

organizationalbehaviour
SKILLSWORKBOOK

SUGGESTED APPLICATIONS OF WORKBOOK MATERIALS

I. Power Play Cases

Case	Suggested Chapter	Themes
1 A Question of Heart	6 Motivation and recruitment,	Motivation
2 Teamwork Canada	10 Teamwork and High-Performance Teams	Teamwork
3 At the Crossroads	13 Organizational Cultures	Culture
4 A True Leader	14 Leadership	Leadership
5 Who Gets to Play?	17 Decision-Making	Decision-Making

II. Cases for Critical Thinking

Case	Suggested Chapter	Cross-References and Integration

See companion website for on-line versions of many cases: www.wiley.com/canada/schermerhorn

Case	Suggested Chapter	Cross-References and Integration
1. Family Medical Group of Companies	1 Organizational Behaviour	organizational structure; design and culture; organizational change and innovation; decision making; leadership
2. Sun Microsystems Organization	2 The High-Performance Organization	human resource management; organizational cultures; innovation; information technology; leadership
3. New Rainbow Enterprises: The Grievous Gift	3 Gobalization	diversity and individual differences; perception and attribution; performance management; job design; communication; conflict decision-making
4. Never on a Sunday	4 Diversity and Individual Differences	ethics and diversity; organizational structure, design, and culture; decision-making; organizational change
5. Have it Working by Monday	5 Perception and Attribution	ethics and diversity; organizational structure, design, and culture; decision-making; organizational change
6. It Isn't Fair	6 Motivation and Reinforcement	perception and attribution; performance management and rewards; communication; ethics and decision-making
7 Canadian Products Limited	7 Human Resource Management Systems	organizational cultures; globalization; communication; decision-making
8. The Well-Paid Receptionist	8 Job Design	organizational design; motivation; performance management and rewards
9. The Forgotten Group Member	9 The Nature of Groups	teamwork; motivation; diversity and individual differences; perception and attribution; performance management and rewards communication; conflict; leadership
10. NASCAR's Racing Teams	10 Teamwork and High-Performance Teams	organizational cultures; leadership; motivation and reinforcement; communication
11. A Case of Doing Excellence	11 Strategy and the basic attributes of organizations	organizational structure, designs and cultures; performance management and rewards

Case	Suggested Chapter	Cross-References and Integration
12. Evergreen Technologies Ltd.	12 Strategic Competency and Organizational Design	organizational structure, designs and cultures; performance management and rewards
13. Motorola	13 Organizational Cultures	innovation; conflict and negotiation; leadership; change and stress
14. Sandra Lee, Principal of South Heights Public School	14 Leadership	organizational cultures; group dynamics and team work; motivation and reinforcement
15. Employment Equity at H.U.C.L.	15 Power and Politics	conflict; decision-making; organizatinal change; job design
16. The Poorly Informed Walrus	16 Information and Communication	diversity and individual differences; perception and attribution organizational; change and innovation
17. Outrage at Eastern	17 Decision-Making	organizational structure; culture; group dynamics and teamwork; diversity and individual differences
18. Countryside Environmental	18 Conflict and Negotiation	change, innovation, and stress; job designs; communication; power and politics
19. The New Vice-President	19 Change and Innovation	innovation; conflict and negotiation; leadership; change erformance management and rewards; diversity and individual differences; communication; power and influence and stress

III. Experiential Exercises

Exercise	Suggested Chapter	Cross-References and Integration
1. My Best Manager	1 Organizational Behaviour	leadership
2. Graffiti Needs Assessment	2 The High-Performance Organization	human resource management; communication
3. My Best Job	2 The High-Performance Organization	motivation; job design; organizational cultures
4. What Do You Value in Work?	2 The High-Performance Organization	diversity and individual differences; performance management and rewards; motivation; job design; decision-making
5. My Asset Base	2 The High-Performance Organization	perception and attribution; diversity and individual differences; groups and teamwork; decision-making
6. Expatriate Assignments	3 Globalization	perception and attribution; diversity and individual differences; decision-making
7. Cultural Cues	3 Globalization	perception and attribution; diversity and individual differences; decision-making; communication; conflict; groups and teamwork
8. Prejudice in Our Lives	4 Diversity and Individual Differences	perception and attribution; decision-making; conflict; groups and teamwork
9. How We View Differences	5 Perception and Attribution	culture; international; diversity and individual differences; decision-making; communication; conflict; groups and teamwork
10. Alligator River Story	5 Perception and Attribution	diversity and individual differences; decision-making; communication; conflict; groups and teamwork

Exercise	Suggested Chapter	Cross-References and Integration
11. *Teamwork and Motivation*	6 Motivation and Reinforcement	performance management and rewards; groups and teamwork
12. *The Downside of Punishment*	6 Motivation and Reinforcement	motivation; perception and attribution; performance management and rewards
13. *Annual Pay Raises*	7 Human Resource Management Systems	motivation; learning and reinforcement; perception and attribution; decision-making; groups and teamwork
14. *Tinkertoys*	8 Job Design	organizational structure; design and culture; groups and teamwork
15. *Job Design Preferences*	8 Job Design	motivation; job design; organizational design; change
16. *My Fantasy Job*	8 Job Design	motivation; individual differences; organizational design; change
17. *Motivation by Job Enrichment*	8 Job Design	motivation; job design; perception; diversity and individual differences; change
18. *Serving on the Boundary*	9 Nature of Groups	intergroup dynamics; group dynamics; roles; communication; conflict; stress
19. *Eggsperiential Exercise*	9 Nature of Groups	group dynamics and teamwork; diversity and individual differences; communication
20. *Scavenger Hunt—Team Building*	10 Teamwork and High-Performance Teams	groups; leadership; diversity and individual differences; communication; leadership
21. *Work Team Dynamics*	10 Teamwork and High-Performance Teams	groups; motivation; decision-making; conflict; communication
22. *Identifying Group Norms*	10 Teamwork and High-Performance Teams	groups; communication; perception and attribution
23. *Workgroup Culture*	10 Teamwork and High-Performance Teams	groups; communication; perception and attribution; job design; organizational culture
24. *The Hot Seat*	10 Teamwork and High-Performance Teams	groups; communication; conflict and negotiation; power and politics
25. *Organizations Alive!*	11 Teamwork and High-Performance Teams	decision-making; organization structures, designs, cultures
26. *Fast-Food Technology*	12 Strategy and the Basic Attributes of Organizations	organizational design; organizational culture; job design
27. *Alien Invasion*	13 Organizational Cultures	organizational structure and design; international; diversity and individual differences; perception and attribution
28. *Interview a Leader*	14 Leadership	performance management and rewards; group and teamwork; new workplace; organizational change and stress
29. *Leadership Skills Inventories*	14 Leadership	individual differences; perception and attribution; decision-making
30. *Leadership and Participation in decision-making*	14 Leadership	decision-making; communication; motivation; groups; teamwork

Exercise	Suggested Chapter	Cross-References and Integration
31. My Best Manager: Revisited	15 Power and Politics	diversity and individual differences; perception and attribution
32. Power Circles Exercise	15 Power and Politics	influence; power; leadership; change management
33. Active Listening	16 Information and Communication	group dynamics and teamwork; perception and attribution
34. Upward Appraisal	16 Information and Communication	perception and attribution; performance management and rewards
35. 360-degree Feedback	17 Decision-Making	communication; perception and attribution; performance management and rewards
36. Role Analysis Negotiation	17 Decision-Making	communication; group dynamics and teamwork; perception and attribution; communication; decision making
37. Lost at Sea	17 Decision-Making	communication; group dynamics and teamwork; conflict and negotiation
38. Entering the Unknown	17 Decision-Making	communication; group dynamics and teamwork; perception and attribution
39. Vacation Puzzle	18 Conflict and Negotiation	conflict and negotiation; communication; power; leadership
40. The Ugli Orange	18 Conflict and Negotiation	communication; decision-making
41. Conflict Dialogues	18 Conflict and Negotiation	conflict; communication; feedback; perception; stress
42. Force-Field Analysis	18 Conflict and Negotiation	decision-making; organization structures, designs, cultures

IV. Self-Assessment Inventories

Assessment	Suggested Chapter	Cross-References and Integration
1. Managerial Assumptions	1 Organizational Behaviour	leadership
2. A Twenty-First-Century Manager	1 Organizational Behaviour 2 The High-Performance Organization	leadership; decision-making; globalization
3. Turbulence Tolerance Test	1 Organizational Behaviour	perception; individual differences; organizational change and stress
4. Global Readiness Index	3 Globalization	diversity, culture, leading, perception, management skills, career readiness
5. Personal Values	4 Diversity and Individual Differences	perception; diversity and individual differences; leadership
6. Intolerance for Ambiguity	5 Perception and Attribution	perception; leadership
7. Two-Factor Profile	6 Motivation and Reinforcement	job design; perception; culture; human resource management

Assessment	Suggested Chapter	Cross-References and Integration
8. *Are You Cosmopolitan?*	7 Human Resource Management Systems 8 Job Designs	diversity and individual differences; organizational culture
9. *Group Effectiveness*	9 Nature of Groups	organizational designs and cultures; leadership
10. *Organizational Design Preference*	11 Strategy and the Basic Attributes of Organizations 12 Strtegic Competency and Organizational Design	job design; diversity and individual differences
11. *Which Culture Fits You?*	13 Organizational Cultures	perception; diversity and individual differences
12. *Least Preferred Coworker Scale*	14 Leadership	diversity and individual differences; perception; group dynamics and teamwork
13. *Leadership Style*	14 Leadership	diversity and individual differences; perception; group dynamics and teamwork
14. *"TT" Leadership Style*	14 Leadership 16 Information and Communication	diversity and individual differences; perception; group dynamics and teamwork
15. *Empowering Others*	15 Power and Politics 16 Information and Communication	leadership; perception and attribution
16. *Machiavellianism*	15 Power and Politics	leadership; perception and attribution
17. *Personal Power Profile*	15 Power and Politics	leadership; perception and attribution
18. *Your Intuitive Ability*	17 Decision-Making	diversity and individual differences
19. *Decision-Making Biases*	17 Decision-Making	teams and teamwork, communication, perception
20. *Conflict Management Styles*	18 Conflict and Negotiation	diversity and individual differences; communication
21. *Your Personality Type*	19 Change and Innovation	diversity and individual differences; job design Stress
22. *Time Management Profile*	19 Change and Innovation	diversity and individual differences Stress

Power Play Cases
BASED ON *GOLD RUSH 2002*

POWER PLAY CASE 1
A Question of Heart

- -

"I tell people that it's a one-goal difference between probably five teams; the competition is that good. But ultimately, we believe that we have more depth than other teams, we have more heart. Hopefully, that will make us successful."

> —*Wayne Gretzky, describing the situation he and the coaches were facing when building the men's Canadian hockey team for the 2002 Olympics. (Chapter 4: Coaches Meeting, Gold Rush 2002)*

If you made around $2 million per year[1] working at a physically gruelling job with limited time off during the summer, how motivated would you be to engage in more of the kind of work you do—on your own time and with no compensation?

This is the situation that faced Wayne Gretzky and the rest of the management group for Team Canada's entry into the 2002 Olympics. Despite its reputation as a hockey power, Canada had not won a gold medal in hockey in the Olympics since 1952.[2] Professional players from the NHL were able to compete for the first time at the 1998 games in Nagano, Japan. Canada was a pre-tournament favourite, but made it only as far as the quarter finals, losing to the Czech Republic in a

---

[1] The NHL average salary for 2002-2003 was $1.8 million, see www.NHL.com

[2] For a history of men's ice hockey at the Olympics, see http://www.canadianhockey.ca/e/teams/mens/olympics

The "normal" way of building a top amateur team would be to invite highly qualified players to a competitive camp, and then choose the best of the best for the team. For professional athletes, however, the prospect of coming to camp to "try out" with the possibility of being "cut" would be a turn-off. Gretzky was sensitive to this problem because he experienced first hand the reaction of a player who was "cut" from the 1998 team. (Chapter 2: First Meeting, *Gold Rush 2002*). Olympic rules also required Team Canada to name eight players on the team almost a year before the Olympics, in March 2001. The prestige of being named to the "first eight", or the disappointment of not being named, had to be managed as well.

The first eight players named by Gretzky and the coaching staff, based on their key statistics from the 2000-01 hockey season that immediately preceded their selection, were Mario Lemieux (as captain), Paul Kariya, Owen Nolan, Joe Sakic, Steve Yzerman, Scott Niedermayer, Chris Pronger, and Rob Blake.[3]

The relative rank of each player in the NHL was somewhat deceiving in that seven of the eight players named were the captains of their respective NHL teams (Rob Blake and Joe Sakic played for the same team—the Colorado Avalanche—where

shootout, then losing the bronze medal game to Finland to finish fourth overall. In fact, Gretzky had been a member of that 1998 team and felt the weight of Canada's disappointment with the result.

The challenge for Gretzky and the rest of the Team Canada management team was to bring together a group of players who could be motivated to give their best efforts, individually and as a team, towards the goal of obtaining an Olympic gold medal.

---

[3] The NHL statistics in the 2000-2001 hockey season for the first eight players chosen are listed below.

Player	Position	GP	G	A	P	Rank
Mario Lemieux (named captain)	Forward	43	35	41	76	27th
Paul Kariya	Forward	66	33	34	67	45
Owen Nolan	Forward	57	24	25	49	94th
Joe Sakic	Forward	82	54	64	118	2nd
Steve Yzerman	Forward	54	18	34	52	83th
Scott Niedermayer	Defence	57	6	29	35	24th
Chris Pronger	Defence	51	8	39	47	12th
Rob Blake	Defence	67	19	40	59	3rd

GP = Games Played in 2000–01 season (out of 82 games)
G = Goals scored
A = Assists
P = Total points
Rank = Rank vs. all NHL forwards or vs. all NHL defencemen, as appropriate.

Source: NHLPA website www.nhlpa.com

[4] Hockey Canada News Release http://www.canadianhockey.ca/news/2001/nr070.html

Sakic was the captain). Gretzky and his management team had selected these eight players for their "heart".

A total of 34 players were sent invitations to an Orientation camp for September 4–7, 2001 in Calgary, including four goaltenders (Patrick Roy, Eddie Belfour, Curtis Joseph, and Martin Brodeur).[4] Three more players were invited to attend during the camp, (including Jarome Iginla and Brendan Shanahan, who were later named to the 2002 Olympic team) for an ultimate total of 37 players. The Olympic team roster was limited to 23 players, which meant at least 14 of those attending the camp would not be named to the Olympic team.

Players and coaches at the camp were very enthusiastic, as shown in these quotes:

> "It's nice now that I'm here to give it all I got. You look around the room and you see players like Mario Lemieux, Lindros, the Niedermayers-guys like that-and it's just an honour to be here and be able to put that Team Canada jersey on."
>
> —*Richard Matvichuk, defenceman*

> "To be picked as one of the guys to attend the orientation camp is a great privilege. I'm just trying to get everything out of it that I can, take in the information and have some fun on the ice and to get to know everybody."
>
> —*Mike Peca, forward*

> "Our goal is to go to Salt Lake City and win the gold medal and, although the NHLPA didn't agree for us to go skate, I felt it was important to get the guys on the ice and everybody agreed."
>
> —*Mario Lemieux, Captain, Team Canada*

> "We were amazed at the kind of enthusiasm and the kind of energy that was brought forward by the players at the orientation camp and how they felt about being invited to come."
>
> —*Jacques Martin, Assistant Coach (Chapter 5: Orientation, Gold Rush 2002)*

Questions

1. Sports are often used as a metaphor in the business world. Consider how the players for Team Canada were recruited and their motivation for joining the Team Canada organization. What advice would you give to business organizations looking to recruit highly skilled professionals, based on the Team Canada 2002 experience?

2. Analyze the motivation of the players attending the orientation camp using at least one content theory and at least one process theory of motivation. Explain why you agree or disagree with the idea that Canadian players might have a stronger motivation to win the gold medal at the Olympics than players from other countries.

3. In November 2001, Patrick Roy held a news conference to announce that he would not be participating in the Olympics. At the time, Roy was seen as Canada's best goaltender and his lack of participation was seen as a blow to Canada's chances to win the Gold medal. Roy's reason for not participating in the Olympic Games was so that he could be better prepared for the NHL playoffs. Use expectancy theory to assess the strength of Roy's motivation to participate in the Olympics versus the NHL playoffs compared to that of Curtis Joseph (who played for the Toronto Maple Leafs) to explain why Patrick Roy made the decision he did. (Note: Roy's professional contract likely called for bonuses to be paid based on his performance in the playoffs, especially if his team, the Colorado Avalanche, won the championship. These contract provisions were standard among NHL goalies.)

4. What do you think Wayne Gretzky means when he says "we have more heart"? In your own words, describe what it means to have "heart". Using the NHLPA web site (www.nhlpa.com), research the playing history of two or more of the players Gretzky and the management team named as the first eight players on Team Canada. What evidence can you find in their playing history that these players have "heart"? ∎

POWER PLAY CASE 2
Teamwork Canada

The 4th place finish of the Canadian men's hockey at the 1998 Olympics in Nagano resulted in thorough changes to the men's hockey management team. Neither Mark Crawford nor any of the assistant coaches were retained in preparation for the 2002 Olympics. Similarly, the executive positions (Bob Clarke, General Manager with assistants Bob Gainey and Pierre Gauthier) were restructured and staffed with new people.[5]

However, the question was: would Wayne Gretzky as the new Executive Director (with Kevin Lowe as his assistant and Steve Tambellini as the Director of Player Personnel), and a new coaching staff headed by Pat Quinn, make a difference? The answer would be determined to a great extent on how the new managerial group worked together as a team.

A review of the biographies of the management team does not suggest that they were going to be successful, if experience in the role each was taking on was a predictor.[6]

When he was named Executive Director of Team Canada, Gretzky had no hockey management experience. Kevin Lowe had played with Gretzky when they were on the Stanley Cup-winning Oilers teams, and had some coaching experience in Edmonton. However, he had only been a General Manager there for about a year. Only Steve Tambellini was experienced in his role since he had been Vice-President of Player Development for the Vancouver Canucks and had filled several executive roles for the team.

The coaching staff presented a similar picture. Pat Quinn had no international coaching experience, serving as General Manager of two international men's teams. Neither Jacques Martin nor Ken Hitchcock had been on the coaching staff of an international men's hockey team. Wayne Fleming, however, did hold impressive international hockey coaching credentials, including coaching European teams prior to working with Canada's national teams.

The relationship between the coaches and players was a potential minefield. Curtis Joseph was one of the goalies mentioned early on as a Team Canada participant, and he was the goaltender for Quinn's team, the Toronto Maple Leafs. Would Quinn's opinions on Joseph be questioned on the basis that he was showing favouritism to one of his own? Gretzky was adamant that Mario Lemieux would be the captain of Team Canada. Would Lemieux's connection to Gretzky interfere with coaching decisions on playing strategy?

Deciding how to work together was the first step for the new team. Their success in doing so is measured by the following comment:

> You can have diversity of opinion but you have to respect the process and the people that are involved. One thing that I felt about the group that was put together by Bob Nicholson is that we have people that have brought an opinion, expect to be heard, and also can deal with the fact that maybe your opinion is not shared by everybody. And that, when we make a decision, we walk out with one mind.
> —Pat Quinn (Chapter 7: Final Selection, Gold Rush 2002)

Perhaps the most significant indication of the accomplishment of the 2002 Olympics hockey management team is that the executive and coaching staff remained intact for—and won—the next big hockey challenge, the World Cup of Hockey in September 2004.[7]

After another big international win for Canada, it's doubtful anyone would want to make changes to this team.

Questions

1. The chapter material outlines the steps required to create a high-performance team

---

[5] Biographies of the 1998 Olympic team participants can be accessed at http://www.canadianhockey.ca/e/teams/mens/olympics/1998/index.html

[6] Biographies of the 1998 Olympic team participants can be accessed at http://www.canadianhockey.ca/e/teams/mens/olympics/2002/rosters/can.html

(see "How to Create a High-Performance Team"). Describe the similarities between this list and the steps Wayne Gretzky took to build Team Canada's management team.

2. Although the members of the management team for Team Canada may have lacked in experience, they made up for it in other areas. Consider the attributes of high-performance teams. What evidence is there in Gold Rush 2002 that Team Canada's management team possessed these attributes?

3. Ken Hitchcock and Jacques Martin were both successful head coaches in the NHL at the time the 2002 team was formed, and Hitchcock was the only one to have coached a team to a Stanley Cup victory (twice, with the Dallas Stars). Wayne Fleming had the most international coaching experience, including previous Olympics (1992). Pat Quinn was named the head coach, without having any international coaching experience. This could have resulted in a divisive coaching staff with disagreements about the "best" way to coach Team Canada, but there appeared to be little controversy among the coaching staff. What factors were responsible for the coaching staff working together effectively as a team?

4. It would seem, from these clips of Gold Rush 2002 that experience performing in a particular role is not a necessary requirement when forming a high-performance team. If you were forming a team for a class project, would prior success in class projects be an important requirement for you if you could pick your team-mates? What would your criteria be and why?

5. What lessons can be learned from Team Canada for organizations seeking to build highly cohesive teams with positive high-performance? ■

---

7 Biographies of the 1998 Olympic team participants can be accessed at http://www.canadianhockey.ca/e/teams/mens/worldcup/2004/rosters/can.html

POWER PLAY CASE 3
At The Cross Roads

At the end of the round-robin portion of the men's Olympic hockey competition in Salt Lake City, Team Canada's record stood at one win (over Germany), one loss (to Sweden), and a tie (with Czechoslovakia). There had been rumours about player unhappiness with Pat Quinn's coaching style, and many critical comments about Team Canada's level of play. A repeat of the failure of the 1998 Olympic Games in Nagano looked like the likeliest outcome at this point.

The press conference following the game marked a turning point in Team Canada's fortunes when Wayne Gretzky passionately defended his team:

> We had a very emotional game tonight; I thought we played really well ... They [the Czech team] couldn't skate with us in the third period, they should have had 4 or 5 penalties ... If we did what they did tonight [spear and cross-check from behind a Canadian player], it would have been a big story. He blatantly tried to hurt him. I don't understand it. I think that guy should be suspended for the rest of the tournament. If it was a Canadian player that had did it, it would have been a big story. But a Czech player did it and it's okay ... I don't think we dislike those countries as much as they hate us. It's a fact. They don't like us, they want to see us fail, they love beating us ... we have got to get that same feeling towards them. Nobody wants us to win but our own players; our fans are loyal. People don't understand the pressure our guys are under ... Our country plays hard and we respect every team we play. We don't dislike them, but maybe sometimes when we start to dislike them we play better.
>
> —(Chapter 14: Czech Republic,
> Gold Rush 2002;
> Bonus: Gretzky's Press Conference,
> Gold Rush 2002)

Gretzky was reacting in part to the cultural assumptions about how Canadians play hockey compared to other countries. Followers of international hockey know the "reputations" that some countries have. Swedish teams are fast, good passers who are excellent offensively in the open ice but are not aggressive going after pucks in the corners. German teams play a strong defensive game but lack skilled offensive players. Russian teams play a strong "team" game with a disciplined system for moving the puck up the ice but lack passion and creativity. American teams feature all-star individual performers but have trouble playing as a team. Canadian teams play passionately, are creative offensively and tough defensively. But to some observers (especially European ones), the Canadian players are seen as "hooligans."

The challenge for Gretzky at this press conference was to focus on the positive culture of his team and reinforce it in the minds of the media as well as in the hearts of his own players. Gretzky and the management team had been working on exactly that from the start of building Team Canada and the Czech game represented a crossroads for this process. They had already faced an earlier challenge to the building of this culture with Patrick Roy's decision to not participate in the 2002 Olympics as a member of Team Canada. Roy would likely have been the first choice as the Team Canada goalie but his decision to not participate could have been a signal to other potential members of Team Canada that participating on the team was not important or that a gold medal win was not likely. The management team had to respond in a way that reinforced the winning culture that they were trying to build. Here are three responses:

> If he doesn't want to go, he doesn't want to go and we've got lots of guys who want to go, so we move on.
>
> —Pat Quinn, Head Coach

> Are we disappointed he's not going to be part of it? Absolutely. Does that mean we're not going to win? No.
>
> —Wayne Gretzky, Executive Director

We have three number ones [goaltenders] but all three have also said "I will do anything to be part of this team."

> —Steve Tambellini, Director of
> Player Personnel
> (Chapter 6: The Scouting Files,
> Gold Rush 2002)

Questions

1. Developing a high-performance organizational culture ought to be easy for a Canadian hockey team, but the history of Canadian hockey at the Olympics has not been successful. Describe the steps taken by Gretzky and the management team to build a common view of the team.

2. The chapter discusses how to create a collective identity and finding ways to work together. How did Team Canada approach each of the steps identified in the chapter?

3. The impact of cultural symbols is obviously important in this case. What symbols do you think were important for Team Canada and how were they used by the management team to build the identity of the 2002 Olympic team?

4. How important was the belief that the style of hockey Team Canada played was "different" from other countries, and different from previous Team Canada entries in international competition, to the creation of a strong high-performance culture? Why? Do businesses need to differentiate themselves the same way in order to create a strong culture? Why?

5. In a globally competitive business environment, do you believe it is necessary to "dislike" your competitors in order to have a strong high-performance culture? What similarities can you draw between Team Canada and a global business with a high-performance culture in the ways that culture is developed and maintained? ■

POWER PLAY CASE 4
A True Leader

The title sequence of Gold Rush 2002 replays the footage of the Canadian men's hockey team losing a shootout to the Czech Republic in a semi-final game of the 1998 Olympics in Nagano, Japan. A dejected Wayne Gretzky sits on the bench, the picture of utter disappointment with the loss and frustration that he was not one of the five players chosen to participate for Canada in the shootout. Gretzky had known that this would be his only chance to participate as a hockey player in the Olympics.

> "Wayne Gretzky had let it be known right from day one that he really wanted to be involved with the 2002 Olympics in Salt Lake City, anywhere from a stick boy to a water boy to [being] on the management team. It was very evident to myself that this is the person we wanted to lead Team Canada into Salt Lake City."
>
> —Bob Nicholson, President, Canadian Hockey Association
> (Chapter 2: First Meeting, Gold Rush 2002)

Gretzky considered it an honour to be asked to become Director of Team Canada, saying it was a simple decision for him to accept and he acknowledged the hard work ahead for his team. Everyone involved in hockey knew about Gretzky's passion for the sport, but what kind of a manger would he be? Could he be the leader of a hockey management team?

The key leadership positions on Team Canada included:

• Wayne Gretzky, as Executive Director, led the management team including coaches;

• Pat Quinn, as Head Coach (with Assistant Coaches Jacques Lemaire and Ken Hitchcock), led the team's preparation and managed the game on the ice; and

• Mario Lemieux, as Captain, led the players.

As Executive Director, Gretzky jumped to the role of leader with enthusiasm and before the first

game at the 2002 Olympics in Salt Lake City, said: "I learned from Glen Sather the best way to run an organization is hire the best people and we have a great staff. Pat [Quinn] and his coaching staff and Kevin [Lowe] and Steve Tambellini have been outstanding. If anything, we're over prepared…everything from who's picking up who from the airport to who's rooming with who to who's playing with who…we are ready." (Chapter 10: All-Star Game Meetings, Gold Rush 2002)

Pat Quinn addressed the coaches and training staff at the orientation camp, saying: "We'll be standing behind the bench in that gold medal game. That's what we're here for. If we go in prepared and planned, then we are going to come out of there with a pretty good feeling." (Chapter 5: Orientation, Gold Rush 2002)

Ken Hitchcock's perspective on his role with the team is "all about providing information to the players…I feel confident that if I watch another team play I can find a way to beat that team." (Chapter 4: Coaches Meeting, Gold Rush 2002)

The decision to hold an orientation camp was a difficult one because of opposition from the NHL union and the NHL Players Association (NHLPA). The management team was aware of this opposition but also knew that other countries would be holding camps or "exhibition games" of their own, regardless of the union's views. Invitations were sent out to the Canadian players to attend a voluntary orientation camp. According to Jacques Martin, "Basically, it was an opportunity for players to learn about how we want to play the game and also an opportunity for the coaches to get to know the players and experience first hand what kind of individuals we have."

Mario Lemieux was instrumental in getting the players onto the ice during the orientation camp, "Our goal is to go to Salt Lake City and win the gold medal and, although the NHLPA didn't agree for us to go skate, I felt it was important to get the guys on the ice and everybody agreed." The players invited to the orientation camp were a mix of talented players with varying levels of age and experience. Mario saw his role to "…make them [all] feel comfortable right off the bat—that's what I am able to do …"

Steve Tambellini commented, "That's what you want out of your captain: someone who commands respect of the group without demanding it himself. It's just a natural respect that they have. They want to listen to him and he has the ability to deliver on the ice. That's what Mario is capable of."

Despite the enthusiasm and positive energy, Team Canada ran into adversity at the Olympics. In the round-robin part of the tournament Team Canada lost to Sweden 5-2, barely beat Germany 3-2, and had to come from behind to tie the Czech team 3-3. After the game against the Czech Republic, Gretzky held an emotional press conference where he defended the team's play from the criticism the team was getting from the press (see chapter 13). Gretzky's statements at the press conference surprised many who had never before seen Gretzky so passionate off the ice.

His performance prompted the following observation

> "A true leader is a guy who takes twice his share of the blame and way less of the credit, and Wayne did a great job right there of deflecting the tension away from the players just to let them play the game."
> —Lanny MacDonald (Chapter 14: Czech Game, Gold Rush 2002)

Questions

1. Describe the traits that you think Wayne Gretzky, Pat Quinn, and Mario Lemieux each possess that exemplify leadership.

2. Common themes in behaviour-based leadership theories are that leaders exhibit a strong concern for "production" goals ("initiating structure") or for people ("consideration"). Find evidence from the case and/or the DVD clips of each type of leadership behaviour. Does one type of leadership behaviour predominate? Why? Do you think this is true for all organizations (why or why not)?

3. Team Canada can be viewed as an example of a high-performance work team. Do the formal leadership roles make any difference to highly talented hockey players? Consider the characteristics of a high-performance work team and apply them to the way Team Canada and its coaches operate.

4. One feature of increased globalization is the increase in competition for organizations to provide the best product or service for the global market. What advice would you give to a struggling organization based on Team Canada's 2002 experience? ■

POWER PLAY CASE 5
Who Gets to Play

If you were the person in charge of finding 23 players to represent Canada at the Olympics, how would you go about selecting the team?

This was just one of many decision-making challenges facing Wayne Gretzky and the managerial team preparing for the 2002 Olympics. Only two players from the 1998 Olympic team had retired—Wayne Gretzky and Ray Bourke—so forming the team for 2002 could have been as easy as naming Mario Lemieux (who was not available to play in 1998) and one other player.

But as Steve Tambellini observed, "Wayne was very strong in his opinion that we're going to take the very best players, regardless of age, whether they were 18 or 40 years old. We were going to take the best players. He really professed a belief that the very best players in the game could adapt to any situation." At the end of what Kevin Lowe described as "some interesting debate," the 23 players on Team Canada included just 13 players from the previous Olympic roster [8] and three of those 13 did not actually play in the 1998 Olympics. (Chapter 7: Final Selection, Gold Rush 2002)

At the coach's meeting in June, 2001, Head Coach Pat Quinn stated that he wanted to focus on "four lines and six defence", plus three goaltenders, which would mean 21 players in total. A discussion about the role of the two additional players concluded with Quinn stating that the last two players on the roster should know in advance they wouldn't play "unless the plane goes down." Quinn did not want to have any complaints from players about playing time at the Olympics as was the case with the 1998 team. As it turned out, the last player chosen at the meeting in December was Simon Gagne, who played in six games and scored a goal and added three assists during the Olympic Games![9]

Another decision that had to be made by the management team was whether or not they should try to bring potential team members together prior to the start of the 2001-02 NHL season. At the first meeting of the management group in February, 2001, this issue was debated. The European teams preparing for the Olympics had already determined to hold "internal competitions", which were contrary to the directives of the NHL Players Association. As a former player, Gretzky did not want to take any action that would be controversial with the players, but a consensus developed at the first meeting that Canadian players should be invited by Gretzky to come to a 'non-mandatory' camp in late summer. A reluctant Gretzky said, "Alright, that's the route we'll go—it's that simple."

But at the March 2001 announcement of the first eight players named to Team Canada, the subject came up again at the press conference, and it was clear that Gretzky was uncomfortable with the proposal to bring the players together, and had not yet taken any action to do so. Gretzky was eventually persuaded to issue the invitations and players enthusiastically arrived at the camp at the beginning of September 2001, despite the declarations of the NHL Players' Association.

All of the key decisions affecting the make-up of the team were made by consensus within the managerial group. After the first meeting Gretzky said, "We wanted to set the tone within our division of how this team is going to be run and, by that, I mean we're going to talk and debate about each and every player. Everyone's opinion is very important." This emphasis was echoed by Quinn in his comment, "When you have the sort of brain trust around that we have, then you use all of the information you have and get opinion." (Chapter 2: First Meeting, Gold Rush 2002)

Questions

1. Describe the type of decision facing Wayne Gretzky and the management team in picking the 23 players. Gretzky was adamant about not wanting to name eight players for the February 2002 Olympics in March, 2001. The reason he gave were to avoid hurt feelings of the players not named, but what other reasons might there be for deciding on all the players as late as possible? If you were Gretzky, when would you want to make the decision on the Team Canada roster and why?

2. Use the judgemental heuristics concepts presented in the chapter to explain how the players identified by the management team were chosen. Which do you believe is the dominant model for Gretzky's team and why? Describe any evidence you see in the video of the confirming trap in the selection of the final few players.

3. Gretzky was clear from the beginning that the managerial team would make decisions on player personnel together. Use the Vroom Jago model in the chapter to analyze his judgement about the best process to follow—do you agree that participative decision-making was the 'best' choice in this case? Under what circumstances should Gretzky have made the decisions on the player selection on his own? ■

cases for
CRITICAL THINKING

CASE 1
Family Medical Group of Companies

By Pauline Brockman and Andrew Templer

It's a bright April morning, and Bill Maron smiles towards the sun shining into his office. "Finally," he thinks to himself, "the missing piece to the puzzle that's going to have us move forward." But before Bill has long to dwell on this moment of satisfaction, the phone rings. It's his secretary Monica. "Nancy Meyers has arrived for your 9 a.m. meeting," Monica chants. After a brief moment, Bill turns his attention back to the issue at hand. "Thanks, Monica. Show her in."

Nancy is Bill's newest employee at the corporate head office of Family Medical. She was hired less than two weeks ago to be the director of human resources. Nancy has several years of human resources experience and particular expertise in human resource planning. Nancy has worked for major companies in the transportation industry throughout Canada and has gained a reputation for her energy and practical attitude. Bill needs Nancy to develop a comprehensive human resource plan for his two divisions (distribution and manufacturing). Continuing problems with morale, turnover, succession planning, and training have kept Bill from concentrating on his next endeavour: a new division that would provide home-nursing services.

Bill has just finished his daydreaming when Monica brings Nancy into the office. "Good morning, Nancy," Bill offers cheerfully with a firm handshake. "Have a seat," he says as he motions to the leather chairs in front of him. "I understand you are just the person to solve our HR problems."

Although Nancy was given selected information about the company and the challenges during her interviews, there is key information that Bill wants to share with her before she plunges into her new responsibilities. Nancy will also need to speak to the vice-presidents of each division. But, nevertheless, the appropriate place to start is at the beginning. Bill begins by giving Nancy a brief history of the company.

Family Medical Distribution

The original company, Family Medical Distribution, was created by the grandfather of Bill's wife, Helen. The company began operations in 1924 selling medical supplies, such as syringes and bandages, to local hospitals in the Kingston region. For 45 years, the company maintained its quiet but consistent presence in the local medical community. Over this time, the company built a solid reputation for quality products and reliable service, which the owner credited to his dedicated employees. Probably as a result of the company's small size, employees often felt like family members and stayed with the company until retirement.

Customer service was largely responsible for the company's early direction. The owner's philosophy was to satisfy the needs of the customer-regardless of what it might entail. Bill can't help but smile to himself when he recalls one of his favourite stories. Helen's grandfather, Mr. Halton, spent considerable time and energy to find and import a number of special religious articles from Europe as a favour to the nuns at St. Joseph's Hospital. It was these extraordinary business decisions that convinced Bill that Mr. Halton was as interested in building a socially useful organization as in making a reasonable income-evidenced by the modest bottom line each year on the income statements.

Bill shakes his head now when he thinks back to 1969 and how he came to purchase Family Medical Distribution. At the time, Bill was 30 years old and had a promising career as a Chartered Accountant with Ernst & Young. He worked long hours and enjoyed the challenges and perks of public accounting. Bill thought he'd be an accountant for life. Looking back now though, Bill is thankful for the bullish style of his father-in-law. When Mr. Halton became ill and passed away suddenly in 1968, it had been Helen's father who convinced

him to take the risk and purchase the business. Helen's father believed that Bill had the youthful energy and determination to take control of the foundering company.

Bill's Early Years

In the first few years, Bill had no choice but to learn about his company by rolling up his sleeves and getting involved. With only eight employees, Bill's role was far from glamorous (see Exhibit 1). Bill would often take customer orders, speak to vendors, and hunt for products in the warehouse-all within the same hour. Bill also spent countless hours on the road talking to customers and suppliers.

Bill's new surroundings had also been a bit of a letdown. The plush, modern facilities of Ernst & Young were out of reach for Family Medical. In fact, Family Medical Distribution consisted of a 1672 m2 warehouse and a single open-concept office for all staff to work in-including Bill. The office space was full of assorted old furniture that needed to be shunted around to allow staff enough room to manoeuvre from the coffee station back to the warehouse.

Despite the humble initial stages of ownership, Bill was driven to make his investment a success. Bill spent countless hours at Family Medical Distribution. He was determined to make the company grow beyond the boundaries of the Kingston region.

Thankfully, the efforts began to pay off. In the 15 years following 1969, Bill began to realize measured success. Family Medical Distribution had grown out of its original facilities when the company expanded into the rest of Ontario (especially Toronto) and later into the rest of the country through strategic acquisitions. By 1984, the company had become a true "national entity" with a distribution network that stretched from coast to coast. Branch offices in Vancouver, Winnipeg, Montreal, Fredericton, and

St. John's were now supplying hundreds of Canada's leading hospitals with quality medical products and systems (see Exhibit 2). Family Medical Distribution's reputation for service and quality had also grown nationally.

Need for Change

But Bill wasn't satisfied. By 1984, he craved a new entrepreneurial challenge. He had grown passionate about the medical business and the new technologies that were making significant improvements to medical treatments. Among the many changes, surgeries were becoming less invasive and hospital stays shorter. Bill's fervour for new technologies was not a secret. Family Medical Distribution had become a known supporter of leading-edge technology.

A few years earlier, Bill had received a frantic call from the emergency room supervisor at Toronto Hospital. Although it was quite late in the day, Bill, as usual, was in the office. A young accident victim was being transferred to Toronto Hospital and was in desperate need of a special non-invasive ventilator. Although considered new technology, the equipment was the young girl's best chance for a full recovery. Bill immediately ran back to the warehouse to gather the required equipment and accessories and headed to Toronto. Bill recalls the night vividly. It was 7:20 p.m. The sky was black with snow clouds, and Bill was determined to get to Toronto and make a difference.

He did. The girl survived. That special trip to Toronto had a lasting effect on Bill and strengthened his desire to make a difference in the medical community. As a distributor, Family Medical was limited in its ability to significantly advance technology. That trip to Toronto had given Bill the vision and desire to create a new division of Family Medical: a company responsible for developing and manufacturing innovative, new medical products.

Addition of Family Medical Manufacturing

Over the years, Bill had been approached by physicians many times to consider partnering in the manufacture and distribution of a particular invention. Bill was always careful to balance his interest and excitement against the potential risks. Such ventures typically require a substantial capital investment and particular expertise that was, at the time, not available in Family Medical Distribution.

Nearly two years after Bill's memorable trip to Toronto, an invention caught his attention-and the timing was right. Family Medical Distribution was operating smoothly and generating a reasonable income. Bill was presented with an idea that would help asthmatic patients, by more effectively delivering their medication through puffers. Like many great inventions, the principle behind the product actually appeared rather simple: a plastic holding chamber attached to the patient's puffer. The chamber would hold the medication until the patient was ready to inhale. Bill immediately funded the additional research necessary to perfect the prototypes and further analyze the market opportunities. After two years of laboratory research, the simple little product had become a complex, but nonetheless successful, innovation. In 1986, the AeroTube was launched and the new business division formalized under the name Family Medical Manufacturing.

Need for Help

By 1996, Bill was exhausted. The drastic funding cuts to the health-care community by both the federal and provincial governments in the 1990s had been squeezing the profits out of Family Medical Distribution. The company reacted to the industry chaos and drastic sales slump by reorganizing internal operations and refocusing the overall corporate direction. The company needed to make some radical changes in order to reverse the negative sales trends (see Exhibit 3).

Meanwhile, Family Medical Manufacturing continued to grow at an almost uncontrollable rate. The sales and marketing departments were aggressively promoting the AeroTube internationally. Within the past six years, the AeroTube had expanded its sales network to over 50 countries. New product-line extensions had been developed, but the resources were not available to begin producing and promoting the products. Although profits were significantly ahead of projections (see Exhibit 3), the growing pains within the company were becoming increasingly more obvious.

The demands of both companies were taking their toll on Bill. The pace was relentless, and despite working seven days a week, he could no longer keep up with the responsibilities of each company. After careful consideration, Bill decided he had no choice but to hire a vice-president for each company. Bill needed to relieve himself of many of the day-today tasks of each company to allow him time to manage the enterprise's overall direction.

New Vice-Presidents

Early in 1997, Sam Collins was promoted to vice-president of Family Medical Distribution. Sam had joined the company 15 years earlier and had successfully risen through the ranks. Sam was first hired as a sales representative for the province of New Brunswick and was a natural at building rapport with his customers. Sam had an easygoing personality and a sharp wit that customers loved. After eight years in the field, and some coaxing, Sam agreed to join head office in Kingston to become a marketing manager. Although leaving his roots in Maritime Canada was difficult, Sam made a successful transition into his new position. After this initial move, Sam continued to progress through the company, accepting opportunities as senior marketing manager, district sales manager, and director of marketing. Sam has always been considered a trusted and loyal employee. When Bill needed to create the vice-president's role in Family Medical Distribution, Sam was his obvious choice.

A few months later, Bill hired Mark Olsen to become the vice-president of Family Medical Manufacturing. Finding the right person for this position had been a bit more of a challenge. Bill needed to find someone with the experience and vision to continue expanding the markets for the AeroTube product line, yet who also possessed the technical ability to manage both the production and R&D departments. Mark's previous employer had been a related manufacturing company in the Kingston area. Mark had been quite successful as that company's director of the manufacturing and engineering operations. Although Mark is a relatively young vice-president at 45 years of age, his charm and approach to business have earned him respect. Mark studied engineering while at university, which has been helpful in overseeing the activities of the R&D division. Bill has been counting on Mark to grow the AeroTube line and expand the markets for new products.

"This is where I need your help, Nancy," offers Bill. "Family Medical Distribution is starting to make a financial turnaround but really needs some HR help to deal with the change process and the resulting fallout of staff. As well, Family Medical

Manufacturing really needs your help to develop an appropriate structure to cope with the growth. Both companies have made some strategic mistakes recently, which have resulted in the loss of some key staff to the competition. The environmental changes and our lack of organization have been very stressful for the staff. I think some staff have simply grown tired of waiting for top management to work out the problems. I really think addressing our human resource issues will help each of the companies gain control. I want to feel confident that both companies are on solid ground before we enter the home-nursing market."

Bill stopped for just a moment before proceeding. "Before I get ahead of myself, I really should give you some background on our human resources department."

Need for Human Resources Expertise

"In addition to hiring Sam and Mark in 1997, I also realized there was a need to formally establish a human resources department. The human resource issues in each of the companies had become increasingly more time-consuming and complex. It had become obvious that the need for human resources management had grown beyond an amateur's role and required a professional."

Bill stopped for a moment, and Nancy could see a cloud come over his eyes. Bill shook his head.

"Unfortunately, the HR department has been a bit of a disaster. The HR manager we hired has been on leave for the past 13 months. The human resources associate, Claire Jackson, has done a wonderful job and taken charge of the department, but the issues the department needs to address are just too much for her. In the past year, Claire has been spending almost all her time interviewing for vacant positions and handling the orientation and paperwork of the new employees. At any given time, she has a minimum of ten vacancies that she is working to fill. The growth in the manufacturing division has kept steady pressure on Claire to find quality staff, FAST. Although Claire has a clerk to help with the day-to-day paperwork, she really has not been able to deal with all the issues in the department. The training and development programs have really suffered. As well, we have not done any strategic planning or forecasting for either of the companies."

"You can now understand how delighted I was when you accepted the challenge and joined Family Medical. We certainly need your expertise in developing a human resource plan for the companies. We promoted Claire recently to the manager's position so that she would be ready to help you. I know you will find her a tremendous asset. The bottom line is, Nancy, the department is in desperate need of your leadership, and the company is in desperate need of your expertise. We need a solid human resource plan in order to move forward. I need the current problems addressed before I can create the home-nursing division.

"I'd like to give you a chance to prepare some preliminary information for the human resource plan before we meet again. I also know that you need to meet with Mark and Sam to gather their perspectives on things. Would it be okay to meet in two weeks to discuss the plan?"

Nancy's Initial Actions

Bill had been very clear; he wanted Nancy to develop a human resource plan to encompass both the manufacturing and distribution divisions. Nancy had to get moving-she just did not have the luxury of time to painstakingly review her every option. Bill wanted to meet with her in two weeks. She decided that the obvious place to begin was by finding out what her human resources manager and the two vice-presidents thought. Nancy asked Claire to write a brief memo to her outlining the pertinent issues in the human resources department (see Exhibit 4) and kept notes of the extensive interviews she had with Sam and Mark (see Exhibits 5 and 6).

With less than 10 days to go until her meeting with the president, Nancy closed her office door, turned off her phone, and began work on her strategy for the Family Medical Group of Companies.

Exhibit 1

Family Medical Distribution
December 31, 1967

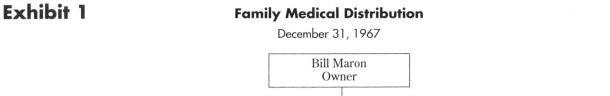

```
                          Bill Maron
                            Owner
```

| Jackie Zettle | Martin Soley | Ross McKinnon | Mary Mole |
| Accounting Clerk | Sales Representative | Sales Representative | Secretary |

| Bill Butter | Marg Rogers | Ron Brady/Jim Rush |
| Buyer | Customer Service | Warehouse |

Family Medical Group of Companies
April 30, 1999

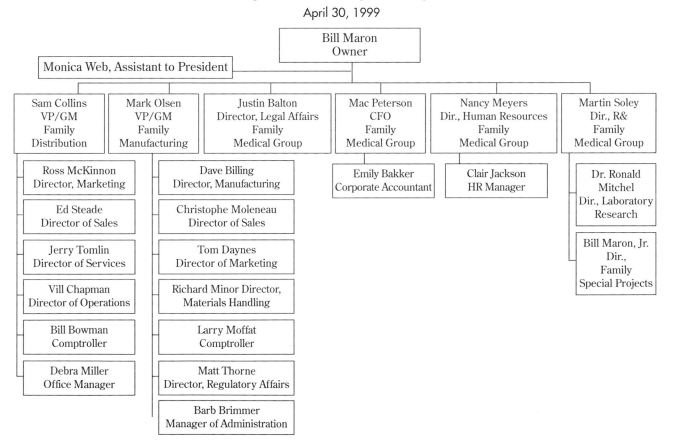

```
                                   Bill Maron
                                     Owner
```

Monica Web, Assistant to President

Sam Collins	Mark Olsen	Justin Balton	Mac Peterson	Nancy Meyers	Martin Soley
VP/GM	VP/GM	Director, Legal Affairs	CFO	Dir., Human Resources	Dir., R&
Family	Family	Family	Family	Family	Family
Distribution	Manufacturing	Medical Group	Medical Group	Medical Group	Medical Group

Ross McKinnon	Dave Billing		Emily Bakker	Clair Jackson	Dr. Ronald
Director, Marketing	Director, Manufacturing		Corporate Accountant	HR Manager	Mitchel
					Dir., Laboratory
Ed Steade	Christophe Moleneau				Research
Director of Sales	Director of Sales				

Jerry Tomlin	Tom Daynes		Bill Maron, Jr.
Director of Services	Director of Marketing		Dir.,
			Family
Vill Chapman	Richard Minor Director,		Special Projects
Director of Operations	Materials Handling		

| Bill Bowman | Larry Moffat |
| Comptroller | Comptroller |

| Debra Miller | Matt Thorne |
| Office Manager | Director, Regulatory Affairs |

| | Barb Brimmer |
| | Manager of Administration |

Exhibit 2

Time-line Family Medical Distribution

1924   Family Medical Distribution created by Herbert Halton, a former stock keeper for the Kingston General Hospital.

1968   Herbert Halton dies after a brief illness at the age of 70.

1969   Bill Maron purchases the company with a bank loan and the family house as collateral.

1971   Family Medical successfully expands the Ontario market with key customers in Toronto, Ottawa, London, and Windsor.

1975   Family Medical Distribution purchases a local distribution business in Montreal, Quebec. Under the purchase agreement, the 12 staff members in Montreal become the newest employees of Family Medical.

1977   Kirkland Medical is purchased in Vancouver, British Columbia. The business and staff become the western branch for Family Medical Distribution.

1978   A small operation in Winnipeg, Manitoba, is converted to Family Medical Distribution. Few customers are gained through the acquisition, but Family Medical Distribution is now able to comfortably supply all the western provinces.

1982   McArthur Medical Supplies is purchased. Both branches (Fredericton, New Brunswick, and St. John's, Newfoundland) are converted to Family Medical Distribution.

1986   Family Medical Manufacturing is created. Family Medical Group of Companies name is established to represent the corporate company.

Exhibit 3

Family Medical Group of Companies
Profit in (000s)

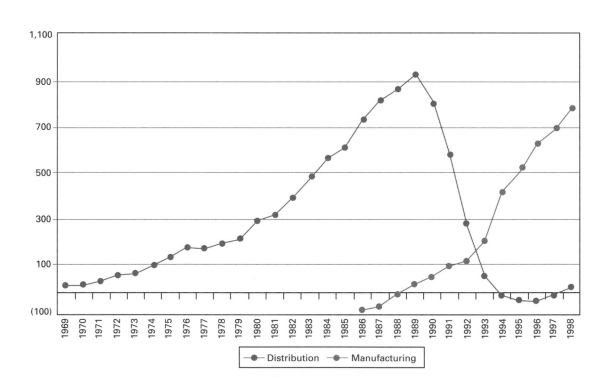

Exhibit 4

Notes to File: Sam Collins Interview

DATE: April 28, 1999

BCC: Bill Maron

RE: Interview with Sam Collins (Family Medical Distribution)

- Company has now grown to about 145 employees with most working in the sales, marketing, and operations departments. Many of the employees hired during Bill's early years continue to enjoy successful careers with the distribution business.

- Family Medical Distribution still has a solid reputation in the medical community but has been faltering in past five years due to government cutbacks in the medical industry. The restructuring has meant that hundreds of hospitals across the country have closed, while others have been forced to significantly reduce their number of beds.

- Sam feels the company has lacked a strategic focus and become "lazy" in the years leading up to the budget cuts.

- Sam is committed to returning Family Distribution to its former profitability. Sam feels personally responsible to deliver the bottom line to Bill.

- Family Medical Distribution has had to reposition itself as a specialty distributor of high-end medical products and systems in order to survive. The goal is to represent only key suppliers in Canada in the key areas of Critical Care, Anaesthesia, Respiratory Care, and Surgery.

- As a result of these industry stresses, there has been a significant change in the company's corporate culture. The new atmosphere is one of cost restraint and continuous change. The company has had to reduce its inventory and improve its processes to remain competitive in the increasingly smaller market.

- Sam has spent considerable effort evaluating the operations, sales, and marketing departments. He feels these areas will be the keys to turning the company around. He thinks the staff needs to work "smarter" and not "harder."

- Until recently, the company had operated for many years with relatively few changes. Many of the employees had a considerable amount of seniority, had risen through the ranks, and had hoped to retire from Family Medical. In the past two years, however, the external forces have created a need for change in the organizational mix and structure of the company. About five or six long-term employees have been terminated. Some of the vacancies have been filled from within the company, but the staff is still generally feeling nervous and uncertain. Sam has been pushing hard to focus the company and turn the company around.

- Sam is a bit hesitant about the role and value of an HR department. His past two years have been very disappointing with problems around hiring methods, confidentiality, knowledge/expertise, and lack of support for the new company Vision.

- Sam is willing to consider an HRP for Family Distribution but is more concerned with making the company profitable again.

Exhibit 5   Notes to File: Sam Collins Interview

Notes to File: Mark Olsen Interview

DATE: April 27, 1999

BCC: Bill Maron

RE: Interview with Mark Olsen (Family Medical Manufacturing)

- The pace has been hectic since Mark joined Family Medical Manufacturing two years ago. The company is very successful having continuously exceeded its growth and profit projections each year.

- The AeroTube is currently marketed in over 50 countries and secures about 47 percent of the market for valved holding chambers worldwide. The lab has also completed successful prototypes for two new products to be launched in the next year. One product will allow intubated patients in a hospital to receive their medications orally through puffers. The company is close to receiving approval from Canada's Health Protection Branch. The other product is a much larger version of the AeroTube and will soon be launched to veterinarians for use on animals with breathing problems.

- Bill still remains fairly involved in the day-to-day operations of Family Medical Manufacturing. This is the company that has brought him international recognition. Bill still approves all research projects that take place in our laboratory.

- The company has just moved into its "state-of-the-art" manufacturing facility in the past year. The building has been a showcase for other such companies in the region and boasts all the modern amenities including a programmable pass-card entry system, contemporary cafeteria with home-cooked meals, and a research & development lab worth over $3 million.

- The company now employs approximately 180 people (55 percent on the production line who work one of two shifts per day). The company also employs over 12 engineers and six laboratory technicians.

- Mark believes that staff is generally happy and that the company is positioned for yet another "better-than-expected" year.

Exhibit 6   Memo from Clair Jackson

INTEROFFICE MEMO

Date: April 23, 1999

To: Nancy Meyers

From: CLAIRE JACKSON

RE: Human Resource Issues

CONFIDENTIAL

The following list is a summary of the urgent/priority Human Resources issues that I have been working on in the past two months:

Family Medical Group (Corporate)
Our request for a part-time HR Assistant has been declined once again, and the purchase requisition for the HRIS has been put on hold until Mr. Maron gives further authorization.

Family Distribution
The staff at Family Distribution seems to be unsettled. Several staff members have left the company through terminations and voluntary resignations within the past two years. Most recently, Dorothy Haffrey was terminated after 16 years of service. Dorothy has had several formal complaints in her permanent record over the years for inappropriate behaviour and language. Despite several warnings her behaviour has not changed. Three weeks ago she swore at the Director of Marketing in the presence of a supplier. Although the staff does not generally condone Dorothy's behaviour, I believe they are genuinely concerned about their own futures. The staff at Family Distribution has also been applying aggressively for posted openings at Family Manufacturing.

Family Manufacturing
Four formal complaints have been submitted about the hiring practices at Family Manufacturing. These employees feel that they have been overlooked for key openings despite being able to fulfill the education and skills required for the positions. In all cases, the positions were filled by former employees of King Manufacturing (Mark Olsen's former employer). I completed the entire first round interviews and have reviewed the files carefully. The positions have all been filled with incumbents who can "hit the ground running." Mark felt Family Manufacturing did not have the time or luxury of training an internal employee.

Laura Davies, Senior Administrator, has tendered her resignation effective June 11th after not being successful in her application for the new Office Manager position. She has been a strong contributor to the overall administration of the company and has steadily been accepting increasing responsibility. During an informal meeting Laura shared the source of her unhappiness. Barb Brimner, the new Manager of Administration, inadvertently mentioned that Mark had promised her the position before the opening was posted. Laura has obviously perceived the hiring process to be unjust.

CASE 2
Sun Microsystems: "We're the dot in .com"

Developed by David S. Chappell, Ohio University; modified by Hal Babson

Columbus State Community College

What does it take to foster a computer revolution? Bill Gates's Microsoft model, based on distributed personal computers with software (largely Microsoft's) loaded on each individual machine, may be slowly giving way to a networked system long championed by McNealy's Sun Microsystems. In fact, McNealy has been one of the few computer industry leaders to take on Microsoft directly with a zeal and tenacity that is legendary. Steven M. Milunovich, an analyst with Merrill Lynch and Company, argues that "If you want to know where the computer industry is going, ask Sun."[1]

Note: The blue underscored words/phrases in this case indicate Internet links provided in the on-line version (http//www.wiley.com/canada/schermerhorn).

Sun Microsystems

Sun Microsystems was founded by Andreas Bechtolsheim, Bill Joy, Vinod Khosla, and Scott McNealy in 1982. The first Sun system, the Sun-1, was a high performance computer based on readily available, inexpensive components and the UNIX operating system largely developed by Joy while in graduate school at the University of California-Berkeley. From the very start, Sun resisted the so-called Microsoft Windows/Intel (Wintel) model and concentrated on high-end workstations, suitable for engineering, designers, Wall Street traders, and CAD/CAM applications.

Scott McNealy took over as president of Sun in 1984 and since then has waged a constant war with Bill Gates and Microsoft. At first, Sun's market niche of high-end workstations kept it from competing directly with personal computers. However, over time PCs acquired more and more computing power, putting them in more direct competition with workstations. As a consequence, Sun has branched out into other computer areas, with an emphasis on the Internet.

Sun built an entire line of computers based exclusively on its own designs, its own chips, dubbed Sparc, and its own software, a version of the UNIX operating system known as Solaris. As such, Sun stood alone as the "pure" alternative to the Wintel world.[2] This strategy was not without its detractors, who pointed out that Sun created problems for itself by requiring huge R&D expenses compared to those firms relying on Windows and Intel. Sun was spending 10.4% of its sales on R&D, compared to 4.5% at Compaq and 1.6% at Dell, who rely on Intel and Microsoft for much of their research.[3]

McNealy boasted that "There are three technology companies left in the computer world. Intel, Microsoft and Sun."[4] "They [Sun] are beginning to be viewed as much more credible as an end-to-end solution provider," said Joe Ferlazzo, an analyst at Technology Business Research. Sun offered an attractive alternative with the same operating system on everything from a $2,500 workstation with a single Sparc chip to a $1 million server with 64 parallel chips delivering as much computing power as an IBM mainframe. "That's what's needed in the ISP environment and in corporate computing" he added. In the opposite camp, Susan Whitney of IBM argued that "To believe that a single architecture will address all the business requirements is not a sound strategy."[5]

Undeterred, McNealy remained convinced of his mission, which is no less than to overthrow the personal computer. "The PC is just a blip. It's a big, bright blip," said McNealy. "Fifty years from now, people are going to look back and say: 'Did you really have a computer on your desk? How weird.'"[6] Analyst C. B. Lee of Sutro and Company and a former Sun manager argued that "McNealy shoots off his mouth too much. At some point, you've gotta be more mature."[7]

Offsetting McNealy's brashness was Ed Zander, chief operating officer for Sun, who exhibited a more conservative aura. "I think McNealy and Zander are kind of like yin and yang," said Milunovich from Merrill Lynch. "McNealy is the high priest of the religion. Ed is much more pragmatic. Having both is very good for Sun."[8]

One thing McNealy has been able to accomplish is the constant reinvention of Sun as times and external conditions change. Starting with workstations and their various components, he positioned the firm to offer top-of-the-line servers that power the Internet. With the development of Java and Jini, Sun evolved into a powerful software machine that served to drive the Internet and future "information appliances."

To do this, Sun recognized the need for talented people. Many observers rate Sun's employees among the most talented in Silicon Valley. To keep them in a competitive marketplace, Sun emphasized perks:

Family care: Adoptive parents received financial assistance. Lactation rooms helped new mothers return to work. In the San Francisco Bay Area, parents could take sick children to a special day-care center that cared for children with minor illnesses. Sun also offered a dependent-care spending account, a consultation and referral program, and an employee-assistance program providing short-term professional counseling.

Private workspace: When Sun designed its Menlo Park, California campus, the company asked employees for suggestions-and found that engineers prefer private offices over Dilbert-like cubicles. The engineers got the space they demanded for quiet development time.

Respecting employee time: Flexible hours and telecommuting helped accommodate busy schedules and keep employees from wasting time on California freeways. Train travelers could catch a special shuttle to Sun facilities, and the company reimbursed some commuting costs.[9]

Hard to Find Where the Sun Don't Shine

As early as 1987, Sun coined the phrase, "The network is the computer." [10] But it has only been with the full advent of the Internet coupled with Sun's Java programming language that all the pieces appeared to be falling into place to make this vision a reality. "Microsoft's vision was to put a mainframe on everybody's desktop," claims McNealy. "We want to provide dial tone for the Internet. We couldn't have more different visions."[11]

In 1995, Java was introduced as the first universal software designed from the ground up for Internet and corporate intranet developers to write applications that run on any computer, regardless of the processor or operating system.[12] In 1998 Sun introduced Jini, a technology that let computers and appliances connect to a network as simply as a telephone plugs into the wall.[13] Sun's objective was to make access to the Internet and computing as simple as picking up a phone and hearing a "<u>Webtone</u>."

Even Microsoft yielded to Java's appeal, licensing a version to develop its own line of software. Java's appeal was its ability to lower companies' IT costs because it runs unchanged on any device with a computer chip, enabling everything from wallet-sized cards to trucks to communicate over a network. However, Microsoft and Sun immediately got into a battle when Microsoft made a proprietary version of Java to run only on Windows programs. Sun sued. Sun claimed that network computing would herald a shift away from personal computers to more friendly appliances such as phones, digital assistants, and televisions. It hoped Java would provide the link to its powerful network servers with these network devices.[14] Microsoft preferred its <u>Windows CE</u> operating system to provide this link. In addition, it viewed Web appliances as "companions" rather than replacements to PCs.

The allure of a host of Internet devices was their ability to bring in more users. Their convenience and ease-of-use promoted a more ubiquitous presence for the Web and the information located there. Java goes after this "embedded" software market by powering the programs that run everything from phone switches to factory automation equipment.

Java-Powered Net "Appliances"

Network Computers
Stripped-down desktop computers run programs downloaded from the Internet.

TVs and Cable Set-Top Boxes
TCI was expected to distribute 20 million Java-equipped set-top boxes to encourage communication over cable.

Screenphones
Simple devices for straightforward services such as grocery ordering.

Cellular phones and pagers
Cellular phone manufacturers intended to use Java to offer new services through their cellular devices.

Smart Cards
Java smart cards programmed routine processes, such as airline ticket purchases, directly on the cards.

Cars
Navigation and diagnostic systems powered by Java programs.

Keys
Java-powered rings and pass cards.[15]

McNealy billed Java as the killer of Microsoft Windows. Sun claimed Java is ideally suited for the "network computer" (NC)-a lowcost machine that had no hard drive, relying instead on a network that would supply it with small Java programs. Plummeting personal computer prices stalled the takeoff of the NC, but McNealy and Sun remained committed to the idea. "Every day, 27,000 people (at Sun) get up and do one thing: network computing," claims Ed Zander. "That's a very, very powerful story."[16]

Sun-AOL-Netscape

On November 24, 1998, Sun signed an alliance agreement with America Online in association with AOL's $4.2 billion purchase of Netscape Communications. Access to Netscape's e-commerce software allowed Sun to hawk its servers and attract customers that wanted a more complete package.[17] In addition, Sun had access to one of the three largest portals on the Web. In exchange for providing $350 million in licensing, marketing, and advertising fees for the deal, AOL agreed to buy $500 million in Sun servers over the next three years.

Open system advocates were originally concerned about AOL's involvement in the deal. They felt that AOL might hinder the free distribution of Netscape's browser. However, Stephen Case, AOL founder, assured doubters that the partnership would continue to allow free access to Netscape's browser technology. He intended to depend on Sun Microsystems to develop systems to provide Internet access over next-generation devices.

As a partner with AOL and Netscape, Sun was in position to challenge IBM, Hewlett-Packard, and others in developing the systems that would let corporations rebuild their businesses in cyberspace. The challenge for Sun CEO Scott G. McNealy would be to behave like the top-tier industry leader that this deal could make him. And he would need to make sure that Sun not only talked like a good partner but behaved like one, too.[18]

A major factor in Sun's favour was a world in which companies would choose to outsource anything that's not a demonstrably clear competitive advantage. Things such as human resources, financials, e-mail, and Web hosting all would clearly follow in the steps of payroll and facility security-

that is, they would be outsourced. Sun had been saying that the network is the computer for at least a decade. Oracle had been talking the talk for about three years. SAP was founded on the principle of centralized control in the early 1970s. But no vendor had been able to convince any company that it should put its technological assets into someone else's hands. This started to change.[19]

The firm most strategically positioned to take advantage of this shift was Sun or possibly IBM Global Services. Scott McNealy stated several times that companies should never think about purchasing another server again. He means that companies should leave the costs of maintaining scalability and reliability of fundamental systems to someone that specializes in the technology.[20]

Even so, the Internet had to continue to evolve in order for Sun to realize its vision. John McFarlane, head of Solaris software, put it plainly: "We depend upon extreme reliability, availability and scalability as a market differentiator....I know from my seventeen years as a Nortel employee how much it hurts when there's a service failure of any kind, and how great it feels when the network would take a licking and keep on ticking. The same ethic applies at Sun. We run our own company systems on Sun, and our average downtime is about 22 minutes per-employee-per-year. Another way to put it is we experience about 99.96% uptime for every company user. We won a contract with the New York Stock Exchange because of our ability to deliver their required 99.99% uptime—and so far we're at 100%. If the Internet is truly to succeed as the next great communication medium for mainstream users, and the WebTone is to truly represent the same level of connectivity as the dial tone, then that level of reliability must be our model for all users. We call it the utility model of computing."[21]

With all these changes going on, how could a company cope? McNealy summed up his strategy by arguing, "If everybody thought that what we were doing was the right thing, everybody would do what we are doing. If you are controversial and you are wrong, you've got a big problem. You have to be very controversial and very right to make lots of money."[22]

In 2000, iPlanet E-Commerce Solutions, a Sun/Netscape Alliance, developed a business-to-business commerce platform which included buying, selling, billing, and much more. By 2001 the company was operating in 170 countries and had over $18 billion in revenues, and was surviving in 2002 as many so-called high-tech companies were struggling to continue their existence. By 2002, Sun had become the leading maker of UNIX-based servers to power computer networks and Web sites. Sun was making workstation computers and a wide range of tape-based storage systems. It was continuing to make its SPARC chips and Solaris operating system. The company had become a global giant with half of its sales outside of the United States.

Networked Systems vs. the PC

Scott McNealy championed the networked system in opposition to the Microsoft model of distributed personal computers loaded with software. As of 2002, McNealy's concept has failed to catch on. The reasons are fairly simple. The PC continues to be viewed as the best value. The networked system is not.

This perception has been fortified by the long-term trend of decreasing prices and increasing performance capabilities for the PC. "Network computers" and "Web appliances" have not been successful. According to Business Week: "Despite the backing of such heavyweights as Sun, Oracle, and IBM, network appliances (have) failed miserably. The reason is no mystery: They delivered a small fraction of the performance and flexibility of even a low-end PC at a large fraction of the cost."[23]

New Marketing Strategies

Sun's strategy of differentiating itself, that is, by branding its proprietary operating system, Solaris, keeping its product offerings simple, and heavily marketing itself as the "dot in dot-com" (e.g., its aggressive advertising campaign, "What can we dot-com for you?") paid off handsomely through the end of the first quarter of 2001. That campaign made Sun synonymous with the Internet and also made its servers the overwhelming choice of the dotcom and telecom companies, whose stock prices grew so rapidly prior to the start of the recession that began in 2000 but was not obvious until late in 2001. Hard times at many of these same companies have made Sun server systems available on the secondary market. New server sales to high-tech companies have therefore suffered.

Sales efforts then focused on health-care, retail, and government customers. These industries have substantial legacy computing environments, unlike the dot-com companies that accounted for such a large portion of Sun's sales previously. Sun therefore adjusted its strategy to make sure its offerings worked with other vendors' computing systems, built better relationships with systems integrators to better coordinate its equipment with existing environments, and recognized that any additional capacity has to be economically and efficiently deployed. In short, Sun thus sought to solve problems, instead of just adding computing capacity for its customers.[24]

As part of Sun's new strategy to be attractive to these new types of customers, Sun added the Linux operating system to help it compete in the low-end server market with IBM and Microsoft. Many analysts saw this as a defensive move that will ultimately dilute its message. According to Steven Shankland, "Sun has a lukewarm attitude about the Linux operating system, which competes with Sun's Solaris and is popular chiefly on Intel computer systems. But Sun is clear that it wants its Java software to run on all types of computers, and Linux machines work in concert to undermine the market power of Sun's foe Microsoft."[25]

Sun has lost its once-dominant share of the server market. According to TechUpdate.ZDnet: "Intel and IBM are now doing to Sun what Sun did to Digital Equipment in the mid-1980s. They are making an operating system with a tight hardware-software integration (such as DEC VAX in the 1980s, and Sun Solaris now) much less relevant, and ultimately turning the server market into a commodity (virtually entirely Intel chip-based) market. Ultimately, Linux will get fragmented and vendor-specific like Unix, but for now it has established a new commodity-like dynamic that favors high-volume, low-cost producers. With Intel's new generation of chips, almost any manufacturer can produce a high-performance box at a reasonable cost. Sun now has a two-front war to fight: Microsoft on one side, and the Intel/IBM/Linux camp on the other." [26]

Reinventing Sun: Web Services

Scott McNealy has "reinvented" Sun to reflect the change in external conditions. In the late 1980s and early 1990s, PCs acquired more computing power, putting them in more direct

competition with Sun's workstations. As a consequence, Sun branched out into other computer areas, with an emphasis on the Internet.

According to Peter Burrows: "Web services are shaping up to be the next big frontier in computing. Technology leaders foresee a day when all manner of jobs, from managing relationships with customers to coordinating with distributors, will be handled by services delivered over the Net rather than with traditional software programs, phones, and faxes. With its core dotcom and telecommunications markets in tatters, Sun's sales plunged 43% in the quarter that ended on Sept. 30 (2001). Faced with vicious price-cutting in the server business by Dell Computer Corp. and a resurgent IBM-Sun's No. 1 rival in corporate computing today-Sun has lost $268 million in the past two quarters. And some of its newer initiatives put it in direct competition with its allies, including software maker Oracle Corp. Meanwhile, Microsoft's Windows server operating system software is gaining market share...."[27]

Sun's high-end server technology is more popular with corporations than Microsoft's and it was optimistic that its unit sales would do well as the economy improved in late 2002, but the profit margin on its products was falling due to competition from IBM at the high end and from Windows- and Linux-based servers at the low end. Sun has the Java programming language but it does not control Java in the same way Microsoft controls Windows—it shares management of Java with 200 companies and cannot respond to customer complaints as easily as Microsoft.

To regain momentum, Sun is belatedly pushing into Web services by creating a platform for building services for corporations and independent software makers called Sun

ONE that will compete with Microsoft's .NET. One of the major problems confronting Sun at the present time is that during its period of rapid growth it overlooked Web services and must now try to catch up with Microsoft, which grabbed the lead in advancing an industry standard called XML for digitized data. XML is critical to Web services, since it lets data be passed among all kinds of computers and software programs.[28]

McNealy appears to have tried to develop an organization that achieves the satisfaction of customer needs with tasks done right the first time and with continuous improvement—the essence of total quality management. He has demonstrated vision that has brought out the best in people and has developed the intellectual capital needed to innovate, and provided a supportive organizational culture for such innovation. However, the problem is that he is up against a competitor who seeks to do the same things. The question then becomes: "Who can do it best?"

Review Questions

1. Discuss the authors' definition of high performance organizations. Is there anything you would add or delete?
2. Analyze Sun Microsystems based on the authors' five key characteristics of HPOs.
3. Does Sun represent a Greenfield or Redesign HPO?
4. McNealey has positioned Sun as a rival of Bill Gates's Microsoft. How could that have contributed to the effectiveness of Sun? ■

CASE 3
New Rainbow Enterprises: The Grievous Gift

By Joe S. Anderson, Northern Arizona University and Samuel Onyango Adhiambo, Andersen Consulting

Sean Harmon let out a long sigh as he stared out the window of his small office. He had just been talking to one of his employees from the main New Rainbow Enterprises retail store in town. As local director of operations for New Rainbow, Harmon was in charge of two stores which sold good quality "pre-owned" clothing and carried other apparel, appliances, and furniture on consignment. Having worked his way up in the organization for over 10 years in other parts of the state, Harmon was known for his long experience at New Rainbow; however, he had never been confronted with a situation quite like this one.

One of his employees, Matthew Odima Musoke, was quite obviously shaken and at the same time furious with his boss, store manager Jayne Richmond. Since hiring Musoke as a part-time employee over seven months earlier, Harmon has heard nothing but good reports about Musoke's performance from others in the New Rainbow organization. Until this afternoon, Harmon had believed that the main retail store was functioning better than it had in a while, certainly much better than the smaller second store on the east side of town. However, he was now forced to reconsider this belief in light of the heated conversation with Musoke. He had to find a way to resolve what had become an insurmountable clash between the very effective store manager and an (up to this point) exemplary employee. Sean Harmon sipped his coffee and wrote notes on a yellow legal pad while he reviewed the facts as he understood them.

The Employee

From the beginning, Matthew Odima Musoke had seemed an unusually good employee for New Rainbow. He was a graduate from East Africa, currently enrolled at the university in town, and pursuing his master's degree. He was in his early 30s, black, well-spoken and articulate in a pleasantly accented British English. He had been a high school teacher in his home country and had also done management consulting for a company there before moving to the United States. He had been in the United States for three years and had been working for New Rainbow Enterprises for slightly over seven months. He had definitely been in need of the part-time job when he was hired, but he was undoubtedly one of the best educated, brightest, and most motivated employees New Rainbow had ever hired.

Harmon thought back to the initial interview with Matthew Odima Musoke. The East African had been frank about never having worked for a woman: he was concerned about it. For that matter, he had never worked with any women. In the main New Rainbow store, all four of his co-workers would be women. He had wondered whether it would be more difficult getting along with a female boss than a male boss, since fewer women were in supervisory positions in Musoke's home country. However, the working relationship between Matthew Odima Musoke and his co-workers, especially manager Jayne Richmond, had turned out to be very good. Richmond repeatedly thanked Harmon for sending Musoke to her, and her initial evaluations of his work in her store were excellent. Harmon had found these performance reviews so outstanding that, following Richmond's recommendation, he had increased Musoke's initial $5.17 per hour pay to $5.70.

The Manager

Harmon respected Jayne Richmond in her role as manager of New Rainbow's main store. She had been with the company for nearly a year and during that time had promptly brought about significant improvements both in the appearance and operation of her store and in its sales volume. In addition, she had shown herself to be an efficient and usually friendly salesperson to the primarily low-income patrons of the store. Harmon believed Richmond to be an honest and forthright hard worker with a genuine interest in and strong commitment to running a quality operation in her store. Further, she seemed to be liked and respected by her four part-time employees. In addition to Matthew Odima Musoke and Jayne Richmond, there were two other white women and one African-American woman working in the store. It was a point of pride with both Richmond and Harmon, and with New Rainbow Enterprises, that their main store in town had a multi-ethnic work force.

Jayne Richmond was white and thirty-eight years old; she held a bachelor's degree in liberal arts from a large university. Beginning with a part-time job in a clothing store as she worked her way through college, she had accumulated nineteen years of experience in retail sales. She had

held management positions in two other stores before coming to New Rainbow. She was known for her friendly and fair approach to her employees when things were going well, but she could be a harsh and very demanding boss when there were problems in the store. For example, Harmon had noticed that Jayne took pride in her embossed coffee mug that proclaimed "I am the BOSS around here!" However, in spite of her tendency to be overly firm instead of friendly when things weren't going smoothly, Harmon had never heard anyone complain about Jayne Richmond for any reason. But that certainly wasn't the case this afternoon in his conversation with Matthew Odima Musoke.

The Incident

Harmon hadn't known why Musoke had wanted to meet with him, but he had welcomed the opportunity to speak with him. The manager of the smaller store on the east side of town would be leaving New Rainbow in three weeks, and Harmon hoped that he could convince Musoke to take the position of store manager at a modest increase in hourly pay and more hours each week. The issue of the promotion for Musoke was never discussed, though. Harmon had been taken by surprise by the East African's comments. He found he could remember them almost verbatim.

I thought I had a good working relationship with my co-workers and the customers, and I have been doing a good job. I had a pleasant relationship with the woman who is my boss, and I think we have been getting along pretty well, though I had wondered at the beginning how it would be to work for a woman. It turned out that wasn't anything of a problem, at all. I believed that Jayne Richmond and I had become good friends. I invited her to several functions at the university, and though she had other obligations

which couldn't allow her to attend, I felt that we were friends more than just co-workers in the store. I have been at New Rainbow for quite some time, and my performance evaluations have always been very high, so I believed that things were going well with my work, too. But yesterday Jayne Richmond called me in after hours to discuss something, which appeared to be something important from the way she presented it at first.

I met her in the little area in the back of the store that we use for an office, since there is really no separate office over there for the manager, so to speak. She took me in there and after some small talk she handed me a deodorant! I asked, "What is THIS?" I was quite surprised, as I could never imagine such a thing ever happening to me. She said that it was a deodorant; but I said, "Why are you giving this THING to me?"

She had nothing to say for a long time, and I asked her more than once. I asked, "Why are you giving me this thing? What are you trying to tell me by giving me this thing?" I could tell that she was having a hard time trying to talk about it, but I wanted to be completely clear about why she was trying to give me this THING, you understand. She finally said something, and I could tell that she was growing quite uncomfortable about this subject. She told me that she had been noticing an unusual and unpleasant smell around the store recently, and that some customers and some of the employees had remarked on the smell, as well. I asked what that had to do with me and she seemed even more uncomfortable. I continued to press her on the connection between me and that supposed smell and she finally opened up and told me that they had begun to notice the objectionable smell some time after I came to work here, so they decided that the smell must be coming from ME!

I must tell you that I have never been so insulted and infuriated in all my life! Where I come from, I would consider killing a person who had insulted me to such an extent. This is something extraordinarily serious in my country. But instead of retaliation, I know that I have to ignore this horrible insult to be able to continue to pursue my goals here in the USA. I cannot let my response to such an insult distract me from my higher purpose of earning my master's degree in this country. At the same time, I could not imagine being able to work with this woman any longer after she had made this terrible insult to me.

While Matthew Odima Musoke was relating this incident to Harmon, the director noticed that Musoke was visibly shaking with anger as he described the insult. Harmon was stunned! Before hearing about this incident, he had thought the two employees who got along together best were Musoke and Richmond. It appeared this was no longer the case, at all. Harmon asked Musoke whether there was more of the interaction to relate, and Musoke continued.

I told Jayne Richmond that I didn't believe that there was any particular smell coming from ME, and I also told her that I was earning my salary, and if I ever decided to buy one of those deodorant THINGS, I could do it from my own pay. I refused to accept the deodorant she was trying to give to me. I was so angry I had to leave rather abruptly. Then I called and asked to talk to

you, Mr. Harmon. I must tell you that I can no longer work with this woman who has insulted me in such an infuriating way.

The magnitude of the insult to the East African was totally unexpected to the director, and Harmon was temporarily at a loss for words. There was no question that Musoke was serious in not wanting to work with Richmond any longer, in spite of their previously good working relationship. Hannon further did not believe that he could make the situation better by trying to explain Richmond's actions, since the "gift" of the deodorant was perceived as such a hostile and insulting act by the East African.

The Decision

Sean Harmon reflected on the situation. He had told Matthew Odima Musoke that he would consider some solution to the problem. Musoke had stated that he would prefer to continue working for New Rainbow in some

capacity that required no further contact with Jayne Richmond, if that was possible. If no alternative to working with Jayne Richmond could be found, then Musoke saw no other alternative than to resign from New Rainbow Enterprises.

Harmon thought that transferring the East African to the east side store might be the solution to the problem. However, he wondered if the alleged body odour problem would be a stumbling block to Musoke's effective management of the smaller New Rainbow store. On two occasions Hannon had talked to Musoke in his office, and he had visited the main store several times; he had never noticed an odd smell in the store or an objectionable body odour from Matthew Musoke.

Harmon considered his possible courses of action. He needed to make a decision by morning: he'd promised to call Musoke first thing in the morning.

■

CASE 4
Never on a Sunday

Developed by Anne C. Cowden, California State University, Sacramento

McCoy's Building Supply Centers of San Marcos, Texas, have been in continuous successful operation for almost 70 years in an increasingly competitive retail business. McCoy's is one of the nation's largest family-owned and -managed building-supply companies, with sales topping $400 million. The company serves 10 million customers a year in a regional area currently covering New Mexico, Texas, Oklahoma, Arkansas, Mississippi, and Louisiana in 103 stores employing 1,600 employees. McCoy's strategy has been to occupy a niche in the market of small and medium-sized cities. McCoy's was originally a roofing business started by Frank McCoy in 1923; roofing remained the company's primary business until the 1960s, when it began to expand under the management of his son, Emmett McCoy.

McCoy's grounding principle is acquiring and selling the finest-quality products that can be found and providing quality service to customers. As an operations-oriented company, McCoy's has always managed without many layers of management. Managers are asked to concentrate on service-related issues in their stores: get the merchandise on the floor, price it, sell it, and help the customer carry it out. The majority of the administrative workload is handled through headquarters so that store employees can concentrate on customer service. The top management team (Emmett McCoy and his two sons, Brian and Mike, who serve as copresidents) has established 11 teams of managers drawn from the different regions McCoy's stores cover. The teams meet regularly to discuss new products, better ways for product delivery, and a host of items integral to maintaining customer satisfaction. Team leadership is rotated among the managers.

McCoy's has a workforce of 70 percent full-time and 30 percent part-time employees. McCoy's philosophy values loyal, adaptable, skilled employees as the most essential element of its overall success. To operationalize this philosophy, the company offers extensive on-the-job training. The path to management involves starting at the store level and learning all facets of operations before advancing into a management program. All management trainees are required to relocate to a number of stores. Most promotions come from within. Managers are rarely recruited from the outside. This may begin to change as the business implements more technology requiring greater reliance on college-educated personnel.

Permeating all that McCoy's does is a strong religious belief, including a strong commitment to community. In 1961 Emmett McCoy decided, in the wake of a devastating hurricane, to offer McCoy's goods to customers at everyday prices rather than charging what the market would bear. This decision helped establish McCoy's long-standing reputation of fair dealing, a source of pride for all employees, and allowed the company to begin its current expansion perspective. In 1989 McCoy's became a drug-free company. McCoy's takes part in the annual National Red Ribbon Campaign, "Choose to Be Drug Free." McCoy's also supports Habitat for Humanity in the United States and has provided support for low-income housing in Mexico.

Many McCoy family members are Evangelical Christians who believe in their faith through letting their "feet do it"—that is, showing their commitment to God through action, not just talk. Although their beliefs and values permeate the company's culture in countless ways, one very concrete way is reflected in the title of this case: Never on a Sunday. Even though Sundays are busy business days for retailers, all 103 McCoy's stores are closed on Sunday.

Review Questions

1. How do the beliefs of the McCoy family form the culture of this company?
2. Can a retailer guided by such strong beliefs compete and survive in the era of gigantic retailers such as Home Depot? If so, how?
3. Is such a strong commitment to social responsibility and ethical standards a help or a hindrance in managing a company?
4. How does a family-owned and -managed company differ from companies managed by outside professionals? ■

CASE 5

Have It Working By Monday Morning: A Case of Managing Change—Part I

by Bruce Fournier

Bob Johnson had taken his time finding a new opportunity. He had left Triton Manufacturing after repeated promises of an equity position and a free hand to run the business failed to materialize. He'd done his research. He'd looked at a lot of opportunities in several industries. "Aerospace", he'd concluded. "It's got all the right stuff…good margins, barriers to entry, room to maneuver. And it's got the glamour and challenge of high tech."

In his search, Bob had also come across a group of investors who shared his interest in aerospace. And it seemed like they would be great partners. They would only work with executives who had a significant amount of their own money at risk. They had asked him to keep in touch if he found anything he liked. They had even provided him with a couple of leads. And one of them was beginning to look pretty good.

Mavritek was one of those unlikely success stories. Georges Mavric, a refugee from Eastern Europe starts a machine shop in a garage. He does some tool work for other shops. He picks up some subcontract work. He gets invited to bid on some work. Then he's running a job shop. How did it happen? Well, first, it was the emphasis on quality. He was an old country craftsman, and those were the only kind of machinists he'd hire. But second, he and his guys, as he called them, could solve problems other shops wouldn't even look at. Sometimes it meant developing new techniques, but often as not, their solutions involved jury-rigging or modifying their equipment. Some of the pieces looked like real Rube Goldberg contraptions. But they got the job done. And the customers were usually delighted.

The negotiations were tough. Mavric had twice refused previous overtures from the investment group. He had been concerned that these "fancy businessmen" didn't have the commitment or expertise to deliver the kind of quality and innovation that had made the firm that bore his name first choice for third-tier aerospace manufacturing. But he'd gotten older since those earlier approaches and was anxious to enjoy some of the freedom he'd come to Canada to find. "And besides", he thought, "this Johnson seems pretty sharp. He promised not to change the name of the company and he said he would be the one who would actually run Mavritek." So the deal was consummated.

One of the things that had attracted Bob to Mavritek was its human capital. The equipment was old, but there was a large cadre of eccentric but excellent craftsmen. "They're crazy about quality," he told the investment group. "And with a little modernization, we can get productivity up pretty easily. There are a couple of niches we could easily slide into," Bob said.

But now it was time to get the rubber on the road. Bob knew that while quality was good, production was chaotic and costs were a lot higher than they needed to be. Technology was going to be an early short-term answer. But what technology, and how to implement it?

Bob approached a couple of the more experienced machinists. When he asked them what technology they thought Mavritek should acquire, Maurice's answer was fairly typical. "We don't need no new technology, Boss." Bob knew that wouldn't be an acceptable answer for the long term…and that it wouldn't satisfy the investment group. To be competitive in the longer term, productivity would have to be increased significantly. "So," Bob asked himself, "how do I get these old machinists to accept new technology?"

Discussion Questions

1. What can Bob Johnson do to get his workers interested in new technology?
2. Apply a Force Field Analysis to show what opportunities and barriers Johnson will face in implementing new technology.
3. How would you get new technology into Mavritek? Identify a strategy, then determine the specific steps necessary, and provide a Gantt chart showing the time sequence of your moves.

Part II

Bob was pretty sure by now. He had spent the last two days at the trade show, but had spent as much time talking to other attendees as he had to the vendors. A large CNC milling machine was what he needed to start the modernization of Mavritek. Financing wasn't going to be a problem. While the investment group had deep pockets, it preferred for its partners to operate their businesses independently. Cash flow was adequate to absorb the cost of the new machine provided that he could get it up to capacity quickly enough. He arranged for the machine to be delivered on a flatbed late on a Friday afternoon.

The truck's air horn was the signal Bob had been waiting for. As he descended the narrow stairway from the offices above the shop floor, Bob rehearsed his plan. This had to work. There probably wouldn't be any second chances. As he opened the door to the shop, the heat struck him like an advancing wall. And of course, there was the noise. With 40 machines cutting metal with metal, and with the whir and grind of turning and reciprocating machine heads, it was a noisy place. He had grown used to the smell of the cooling fluids used in the shop. In fact, he rather liked the oily smell.

As he strode purposely to the 12-foot metal door, he motioned to six of the more experienced machinists who had been working in that part of the shop. They fell into step behind him. He looked straight ahead and said nothing. As he reached the door, he gripped the chain and pulled it down hand over hand in deliberate, forceful strokes. As the door lurched up a foot and a half at a time, the back of a flatbed positioned a few feet from the threshold became visible to the workers gathered to Bob's left. On the back of the flatbed was a large, shiny,

green Cincinnati CNC milling machine.

Bob faced the men on his left, established eye contact, turned and pointed at the imposing machine on the flatbed, and said, "I want it working Monday morning. Over there," he said, pointing to a nearby space on the plant floor.

Bob turned, strode past the astonished workers, and returned up the stairs to his office. Gathering his briefcase and coat, he hurried to his car, parked to the right of the front door. "This had better work," he muttered to himself as he turned the key in the ignition.

Prediction Questions

1. Will the workers stay and work on such short notice?
2. If they stay, will they have the machine working by Monday morning?
3. How will they feel about how the task got assigned to them?
4. Use Situational Leadership to analyze Bob's actions.

Part III

When Bob arrived at the plant the Monday morning after the new CNC milling machine had been delivered, he went straight to the back of the plant where he hoped the team had been working all weekend. "What a relief," he sighed to himself as he was greeted by six obviously weary but smiling machinists. "We done it, Bob. It's working." It was Maurice. He was grinning like a Cheshire cat. The group couldn't have been more pleased with themselves.

Bob was pretty pleased, too. He had taken a large risk. The men were within their rights to have refused the weekend work. But Bob had watched them carefully in the few months that he'd been at Mavritek. These were the six that had done a lot of the machine modifications in the past. They were the ones that the less experienced men came to when they had a problem. They were the ones who were most proud of their craft. He'd picked the right ones for the job, alright. They hadn't let him down. He'd gambled and won.

Bob was profuse but sincere in his praise for these resourceful and willing partners of his…partners in change!

Bob told them what would be happening over the next month. Anyone who had met production requirements for the day was free to "play" with the new machine. There was a positive impact on productivity as workers, and not just the "original six", competed to complete their work early so they could get to explore the capabilities of the new big green toy. By the time the first month had passed, over two dozen machinists had spent time learning the capabilities of the new Cincinnati. There were times when several were at the machine at the same time.

After the first month, Bob announced the training policy: the CNC course on the Cincinnati would be available to anyone who wanted it, whether they were likely to be scheduled to work on the machine or not. By the time the machine was ready to go into production, four times as many operators had been trained as would be scheduled.

Discussion Questions

1. What were the crucial components of Bob's strategy that that assured the Monday morning success?
2. What factors is Bob manipulating with his play with the machine offer?
3. What impact will the training plan have?
4. What management/leadership concepts best explain Bob's strategy?

Part IV

When the Cincinnati was put into service about two months after its arrival, it was operating at less than 40 percent capacity. Gradually, workers who had had the opportunity to explore the new machine's capabilities, either through the course or by having had an informal exposure to the machine, began suggesting jobs that they had been doing on older technology machines that could be moved to the Cincinnati to take advantage of productivity or quality opportunities it offered. Within six months, the Cincinnati was operating at full capacity with jobs that provided margin benefits not achievable on Mavritek's conventional technology. Bob knew it was time for another piece of new equipment.

Bob went back down to the factory floor and selected a number of the people who had been involved with the Cincinnati and asked them to serve on a committee charged with identifying the next new machine which should be added to Mavritek's production arsenal. The committee's charge included identifying the type of machine needed for the kind of work that was expected over the next couple of years as well as identifying vendors and comparing performance and cost of the various options.

Bob chaired the committee, which carried out its mandate quickly and well. He was careful to give the team direction without giving them directions. He held back on his own opinions and expert knowledge, challenging the team members to do their own research and make their own decisions. The new machine, similar to the first, was loaded to full capacity within two months of its arrival.

Bob decided on a different strategy to acquire the next piece of new technology. He identified a team of experienced CNC operators and called them into the boardroom. A

new display case had been added on the north wall to show off the new precision parts Mavritek had been contracted to produce over the last year. As the men seated themselves around the table, Bob began. "We're at full capacity on the two new machines," he told them. "With the new orders we've been getting, we'll need more capacity soon. I really don't have time to track this down. Bring me a purchase order for whatever machine you think will position us to maintain this growth and I'll sign it." Before anyone could ask a question, Bob left the boardroom to take a phone call in his office.

The workers exchanged incredulous glances before the room erupted with questions. "There's no way old Mavric would have asked us to buy a new machine. Do you think Johnson really means it?" The discussion got more animated as it proceeded. There were questions about options. There were questions about the processes they should use to determine what machine to put on the purchase order. Before they left the room, they decided to investigate three machines. There was a Japanese model. It was the least expensive of the three, but had a good reputation. There was a German machine, but it was quite expensive. "Really," someone commented, "it's the Mercedes Benz of CNC milling machines." And finally, there was an American built Cincinnati machine that fell in between the Japanese and German machines, both price wise and in terms of features.

It was three weeks before the group brought a purchase order to Bob. They all crowded awkwardly just inside the door as Maurice handed the form to Bob. Taking just a cursory glance at it, Bob signed it and asked Maurice to take it to Wendell in purchasing. As Maurice was leaving Bob's office, Bob asked the remaining five operators, "Why did you bring me a purchase order for the Japanese machine?" "Because it was the best," they answered in unison. There was a nervous laugh at their all answering at the same time with the same answer. They began to speak again…. "When we talked to the vendors, we couldn't tell what was true and what was salesman's bull." "So we called some people we know who have the same machines." "We asked for information on downtime, cost of repairs, reliability and.…"

They were excited about the research they had done. And their answers to Bob's questions showed they had a strong commitment to the recommendation they had made. Bob thanked them for their excellent work and told them he was impressed with their thoroughness. Then he asked the question many people would like to have asked. "Did you think I wouldn't have signed the purchase order if it had been for the expensive machine?"

There was no hesitation. Maurice, who had come back from delivering the purchase order chimed in, "No. We were sure you would have signed it. But because of what we found out, it would have been a waste of money to buy the more expensive machines for the kind of work we do here. When we found out about the cost of repairs, downtime and all the other stuff, we really thought the Japanese machine would be a better value for Mavritek. We didn't pick it because it was cheap, we picked it because it was best."

As the workers filed out of his office, Bob couldn't help feeling just a little satisfaction. These were the same men who only a year ago had said, "We don't need no new technology, Boss."

Discussion Questions

1. Review the impact of Bob's actions on the Force Field Analysis you created after Part I. Which of his actions reduced the barriers?

Which increased the positive forces for change?
2. Use Vroom's motivation model to analyze the changes that have influenced the workers' environment (M=f(V×I×E).
3. How has Bob's approach influenced the job design aspects of the work? (i.e., Hackman and Oldham).
4. Use the Situational Leadership model to analyze each of the three major steps Bob used to get the new technologies implemented.
5. Create a Report Card for Bob based on Lewin's three-step approach to change (e.g., unfreeze, learn, refreeze).

Epilogue

Bob's purchase committee didn't stop doing their research when Bob signed the purchase order. From the time the new machine was installed, they began collecting performance data on it. It wasn't unusual for Bob to be stopped by one of the team during a plant walk around and be shown data that continued to demonstrate the wisdom of their recommendation. ∎

CASE 6
It Isn't Fair

Developed by Barry R. Armandi, SUNY–Old Westbury

Mary Jones was in her senior year at Central University and interviewing for jobs. Mary was in the top 1 percent of her class, active in numerous extracurricular activities, and highly respected by her professors. After the interviews, Mary was offered a number of positions with every company with which she interviewed. After much thought, she decided to take the offer from Universal Products, a multinational company. She felt that the salary was superb ($40,000), there were excellent benefits, and there was good potential for promotion.

Mary started work a few weeks after graduation and learned her job assignments and responsibilities thoroughly and quickly. Mary was asked on many occasions to work late because report deadlines were often moved forward. Without hesitation she said "Of course!" even though as an exempt employee she would receive no overtime.

Frequently, she would take work home with her and use her personal computer to do further analyses. At other times, she would come into the office on weekends to monitor the progress of her projects or just to catch up on the ever-growing mountain of correspondence.

On one occasion her manager asked her to take on a difficult assignment. It seemed that the company's Costa Rican manufacturing facility was having production problems. The quality of one of the products was highly questionable, and the reports on the matter were confusing. Mary was asked to be part of a team to investigate the quality and reporting problems. The team stayed in poor accommodations for the entire three weeks they were there. This was because of the plant's location near its resources, which happened to be in the heart of the jungle. Within the three-week period the team had located the source of the quality problem, corrected it, and altered the reporting documents and processes. The head of the team, a quality engineer, wrote a note to Mary's manager stating the following: "Just wanted to inform you of the superb job Mary Jones did down in Costa Rica. Her suggestions and insights into the reporting system were invaluable. Without her help we would have been down there for another three weeks, and I was getting tired of the mosquitoes. Thanks for sending her."

Universal Products, like most companies, has a yearly performance review system. Since Mary had been with the company for a little over one year, it was time for her review. Mary entered her manager's office nervous, since this was her first review ever and she didn't know what to expect. After closing the door and exchanging the usual pleasantries, her manager, Tom, got right to the point.

Tom: Well, Mary, as I told you last week this meeting would be for your annual review. As you are aware, your performance and compensation are tied together. Since the philosophy of the company is to reward those who perform, we take these reviews very sincerely. I have spent a great deal of time thinking about your performance over the past year, but before I begin I would like to know your impressions of the company, your assignments, and me as a manager.

Mary: Honestly, Tom, I have no complaints. The company and my job are everything I was led to believe. I enjoy working here. The staff are all very helpful. I like the team atmosphere, and my job is very challenging. I really feel appreciated and that I'm making a contribution. You have been very helpful and patient with me. You got me

involved right from the start and listened to my opinions. You taught me a lot and I'm very grateful. All in all I'm happy being here.

Tom: Great, Mary, I was hoping that's the way you felt because from my vantage point, most of the people you worked with feel the same. But before I give you the qualitative side of the review, allow me to go through the quantitative appraisal first. As you know, the rankings go from 1 (lowest) to 5 (highest). Let's go down each category and I'll explain my reasoning for each.

Tom starts with category one (Quantity of Work) and ends with category ten (Teamwork). In each of the categories, Tom has either given Mary a 5 or a 4. Indeed, only two categories have a 4 and Tom explains these are normal areas for improvement for most employees.

Tom: As you can see, Mary, I was very happy with your performance. You have received the highest rating I have ever given any of my subordinates. Your attitude, desire, and help are truly appreciated. The other people on the Costa Rican team gave you glowing reports, and speaking with the plant manager, she felt that you helped her understand the reporting system better than anyone else. Since your performance has been stellar, I'm delighted to give you a 10 percent increase effective immediately!

Mary: (mouth agape, and eyes wide) Tom, frankly I'm flabbergasted! I don't know what to say, but thank you very much. I hope I can continue to do as fine a job as I have this last year. Thanks once again.

After exchanging some parting remarks and some more thank-you's, Mary left Tom's office with a smile from ear to ear. She was floating on air! Not only did she feel the performance review process was uplifting, but her review was outstanding and so

was her raise. She knew from other employees that the company was only giving out a 5 percent average increase. She figured that if she got that, or perhaps 6 or 7, she would be happy. But to get 10 percent… wow!! Imagine…

Sue: Hi, Mary! Lost in thought? My, you look great. Looks like you got some great news. What's up?

Susan Stevens was a recent hire, working for Tom. She had graduated from Central University also, but a year after Mary. Sue had excelled while at Central, graduating in the top 1 percent of her class. She had laudatory letters of recommendation from her professors and was into many after-school clubs and activities.

Mary: Oh, hi, Sue! Sorry, but I was just thinking about Universal and the opportunities here.
Sue: Yes, it truly is…
Mary: Sue, I just came from my performance review and let me tell you, the process isn't that bad. As a matter of fact I found it quite rewarding, if you get my drift. I got a wonderful review, and can't wait till next year's. What a great company!
Sue: You can say that again! I couldn't believe them hiring me right out of college at such a good salary. Between you and me, Mary, they started me at $45,000. Imagine that? Wow, was I impressed. I just couldn't believe that they would… Where are you going, Mary? Mary? What's that you say, "It isn't fair"? What do you mean? Mary? Mary…

Review Questions

1. Indicate Mary's attitudes before and after meeting Sue. If there was a change, why?
2. What do you think Mary will do now? Later?
3. What motivation theory applies best to this scenario? Explain. ■

CASE 7
Canadian Products Limited

By Tupper Cawsey and Andrew Templer

Sharon Cliff, manager of human resource planning and development for Canadian Products Ltd., wondered what she should do in training and development for next year. Her training program for the previous two years at Canadian Products had been reasonably successful, but this year, she hoped to widen the training to all levels of management.

COMPANY BACKGROUND

Canadian Products is a multi-divisional corporation based in Montreal. Its five divisions design and manufacture a broad line of consumer and industrial products from electronics and home furnishings to industrial equipment (see Exhibit 1 for a partial organizational chart). In addition to the five divisions, Canadian Products has several wholly owned subsidiaries that provide it with raw materials and component parts.

Over the past 10 years Canadian Products had an annual compound growth of 8.6 percent. Last year, sales increased 12 percent to $520 million, and net income decreased 16 percent to $4.3 million. The decline in net income was attributed to increased global competition, increased raw material and supply costs, and unexpected startup costs of a new plant in Montreal. While sales of all product lines had increased, the president was aware that the market for their major product line was maturing and sales were projected to flatten in the coming years.

Top management continued to voice their concern for employees within the organization. Canadian Products had grown from only a few employees in 1930 to 1800 in 1963 and now over 3800. One year ago, the company had experienced the first strike in its history. Although a long and painful experience, the strike had resulted in improved employee-employer relations. As part of the improved relations, the president announced in the Annual Report that "the human resources division was broadly introducing training programs for all levels of management. Canadian Products recognizes the divisional needs created by rapid expansion, together with organizational changes made necessary to cope with such growth. Improved communications have resulted at all organizational levels. There has been a conscientious effort to renew one-to-one relationships with all employees. As a result, an improved rapport is evolving with salaried and hourly paid members and also with various union stewards representing employees at our various plant operations."

Concern for employees extended to managerial ranks as well. The company has had a long tradition of promoting from within. As a result, few managers of departmental level or higher ever left the company. Until recently, college degrees were not a prerequisite for success. While the company president had an MBA, many of the divisional general managers had risen from blue-collar ranks.

SHARON CLIFF'S BACKGROUND

Sharon Cliff was born in Arvida, Quebec, of anglophone parents. She was fluently bilingual and comfortable in both the French and English cultures as well. Before coming to Canadian Products three years ago, Sharon had worked for the federal government in training and development and had taught several years of high school. She decided to leave the civil service because "I needed a change. I had to do something more than was offered there."

Because of her lack of background in manufacturing, Sharon spent the first two months of her new job asking the various managers what they felt their training needs were. From this initial feedback, Sharon decided that her first training program at Canadian Products would involve the department managers in six days of workshops on a variety of topics. At the workshop, the first two days were spent on management concepts, while subsequent days dealt with such topics as interviewing and supervisor relations. Sharon felt that the program was successful but that it demonstrated the need for training below the department manager and manager levels. "If department managers needed as much training as they did, just imagine how much training the supervisors must need," she mused (see Exhibit 2 for a typical divisional organization). Because of this finding, last year's program revolved around supervisor training.

In addition to management training, Sharon ran several job instruction programs for sales personnel, secretarial staff, and the manufacturing operators. Sharon was also responsible for a five-member human resource planning training session.

THE TRAINING AND DEVELOPMENT PLANNING PROCESS

Sharon had found her initial visits with managers very useful as they helped form the basis for her training and development plan. She felt it was important that she determine not only the needs for training and development but also people's attitudes towards the plan. To do this she visited every division and department manager one-on-one and met with groups of department managers and managers. The six weeks of discussions were followed by an incubation period, during which the collected data were interpreted and a plan formulated. A rough draft of the program was then drawn up with an attempt to ensure "meaningful end results." Sharon stressed the need to assess and reassess training programs in order to obtain valid and valuable training. The rough draft of the program was then circulated to the managers and finally sent to top management for approval.

The final decision on the training plan was made by the Operations and Environment Committee of Canadian Products. Sharon felt that the presentation made to top management was only a formality. She didn't think she needed to sell it again at this late stage because they'd had so many chances to see and approve of the program.

A Typical Meeting on the Training and Development Plan

In order to provide an understanding of how training plans are developed, Sharon described a meeting with a divisional manager and his department manager: "A meeting with the general manager would precede the meeting with the whole group by about half an hour. I would sit down with the general manager and discuss my intentions and purposes. I hoped to satisfy the GM's need to initiate training-by-objectives rather than training-for-the-sake-of-training. My idea is to prepare the GM, analyze his thinking, and make him realize the impact he would have on the decision making of his subordinate group and himself. I hoped to make him feel

energized enough to ask questions at the group meeting-questions that would show he'd done some thinking. I wasn't trying to control the GM's thinking. I just discussed what the agenda would be-my objectives for holding that bigger meeting.

"I didn't want to put the general manager of Canadian Products in the position of controlling or dominating the group, because I saw him as my prime resource. There were so many training needs that I could see-I didn't wish to take the chair or assume the chief resource person's role. In particular, I didn't want to start telling Harry what Harry needed and Alice what Alice needed right in front of Joe who happened to be general manager.

"That was how the meeting was set up originally. Then I got into the larger meeting with the general manager and the group and introduced what was expected. I began with asking the general manager, 'Since you are the senior person in the organization-what do you need for yourself?' Asking the general manager seemed to get the ball rolling-if the boss were going to open up and speak, they all would. I did this because many people feel inhibited when taken out of their comfort zone and you put a fair amount of pressure on them. It's difficult to answer 'What do you need?' in front of the boss. Many would otherwise have a tough time saying 'I really don't know how to manage' or 'I really don't know how to do a performance review.'

"Frequently, managers can say what other people need, but can't describe what they need. I would then sit back and try to listen to the managers as they talked."

Training and Development Needs

The training and development plans for Canadian Products fell into several categories. The first category related to job or skills training. This

type of training was carried on within departments and sections of the organization and was handled primarily by line personnel, except for specific skills courses. These were under Sharon Cliff's department.

In addition, the top management was instituting a CQI (Continuous Quality Improvement) system that required further development. Last year, the formal programs concentrated on giving executives CQI concepts, while this year's training was to be concerned with implementation. Sharon still needed to decide the best manner of carrying out these plans.

Many managers also had needs specifically related to their functional areas, since many were new to their jobs. The company's growth meant that managers of major departments frequently had little experience and didn't know each other well. The organization, as a whole needed to develop a feeling of unity and cooperation.

In speaking about the general training needs of the organization, Sharon Cliff found that managers with even 10, 15, or 20 years also needed help. When I talked to senior managers on a one-to-one basis, they said they needed to communicate more effectively with the president and the Executive Committee. They needed to have better committee meetings that were chaired with more skill. Interestingly enough, every level of management identified the same needs for their bosses. Senior managers said, 'I've been here for 25 years and never had a formal performance review. Why is it critical to do one for my subordinates if my own boss doesn't feel it's important?'

"Only the newest managers had some kind of formal management training. Most managers had attended seminars or workshops over the years but had virtually nothing on management. Generally the first question I asked was, 'Which one of your job functions is responsible for most of your salary?' After a few twisted looks on their faces, their response was invariably 'management.' I asked them how many spent any time learning about management-whether by practice, learning in the classroom, or reading. I found that if a good article happened to come along about managing production supervisors they might read it but nothing more.

"In my meetings with managers, they mentioned a great number of concerns. Some of the managers talked of broader concepts, philosophies, and theories of management while others talked about practical issues in management such as interviewing techniques, appraisals, and performance reviews. They wanted to revise the whole review system and know how to put it into effective practice. In short, the managers needed more help in communication, interpersonal relationships, group decision making and on how to run more effective committees. There was so much to do in management development at every single level that you could almost set up a whole company to do nothing else.

"Canadian Products had a handful of beautiful managers who were being utilized as internal resources. Of those, eight were brand new, and two had been with the company almost since its formation."

SHARON CLIFF'S PERCEPTIONS

Sharon described herself as being looked on as the expert in the organization: "This had some advantages, in that I had credibility,' she commented. "But it also had some disadvantages in that everyone saw me as being 'different.' It became difficult to anticipate what people wanted and needed because they expected me to tell them. Of course, that was impossible. Consequently, I had to remain flexible with the program.

Frequently the managers' objectives and mine were different and had to be reconciled.

"One thing I feel is extremely important in our work is the need for follow-up and feedback on the job. There's no sense in launching a program unless it is accepted and carried out in a work environment. I insisted on carrying things through to the finish and, therefore, sometimes got into trouble. The trainers before me were very different. One was wholly practical and the other was totally conceptual. I think I'm a conceptualizer, but I like putting concepts into practice. I insist on a commitment by management to follow through.

"I think that I've been fairly successful with this approach so far. People are beginning to trust me within the organization. The other day I was asked to visit one of the subsidiaries, which had not previously invited anyone from the human resources division. This was the first opportunity that our division had to demonstrate our work!

"Sometimes I worry about the opinions the line managers have about me. Some of them doubt my usefulness and are reluctant to send managers on courses. However, the procedures I used in setting up the training and development plan seem to have helped. The paternalistic attitude of many senior managers is perhaps finally disappearing. Until recently, people who were promoted could never lose their job. I know of instances where serious errors have been made in promotions and nothing has been done.

"A couple of things that attracted me to Canadian Products were its philosophy that the employees are its most important asset and the company's concern with social responsibility. After a strike two years ago, a major initiative was undertaken to improve communications within the

organization and to solve some of the problems that had been created by rapid growth.

"Personally, I don't know how long I will stay with Canadian Products. I see myself as action-oriented, and I like getting things done. If things don't happen around here, I doubt that I'll stay. My goal is to be vice-president of human resources in some organization before I'm 40 [Sharon Cliff is now 35]. When I left government, I decided that one day I might regret leaving-but I have to try it. I still believe this."

RESOURCES AVAILABLE FOR THE TRAINING AND DEVELOPMENT PROGRAM

The primary resources required for the training and development program were the trainers, which could be drawn from a variety of sources. Internally, two people were available-Sharon Cliff and Bill Silver.

Sharon Cliff, as head of the human resource planning and development department, had five human resource planners and one human resource developer (Bill Silver) reporting directly to her. While some of Sharon's time could be used in training and development work, she had to devote considerable time to planning future programs and supervising the human resource planning section. Sharon felt that, at the very most, one-third of her time could be spent on actual training and development seminars.

Because the human resource planners were used for forecasting, career planning, and recruiting, only Bill Silver was available for training work. Bill had worked in education and administration before coming to Canadian Products. He had a BA in education with eight years of teaching and two years of administrative experience in a school. During that time,

Bill had considerable exposure as the football coach. Sharon Cliff was aware of Bill's perceptual and human relations abilities. She remarked that Bill was able to develop a trusting relationship with others very quickly.

In addition to the internal staff, Sharon considered bringing in outside consultants at varying costs. The company had already committed to several days of CQI training with George Odihome but was also considering Doug Bearett. His field of expertise was time management and his price was close to Odihome's. Sharon was also considering a local university professor from the business school. He didn't have the industry reputation, but was considerably less expensive. His educational background was certainly sufficient, but Sharon wondered if he would be as credible to Canadian Products managers as the other consultants. Another possibility was a group called Performance Management Inc. from Chicago. Sharon had recently received their folder in the mail, knew they were interested in team building, and thought they might be worth investigating.

If she wished, Sharon knew she could avoid the use of outside consultants entirely by relying on a series of films. Several good series on management concepts could be purchased for approximately $3,500 to $10,500 per series. These films would cover most modern management topics, but she wondered how quickly they would become dated.

Sharon Cliff considered all the available resources. Although her department operated on a set budget, departments would be charged for whatever services they used—$90 per person per day for workshops run by staff and varying rates for seminars run by external consultants. There was a definite need for demonstrating the value of training to the company, she reflected. ∎

Exhibit 1   Canadian Products Ltd., Divisional Organzation

(Partial Organizational Chart)

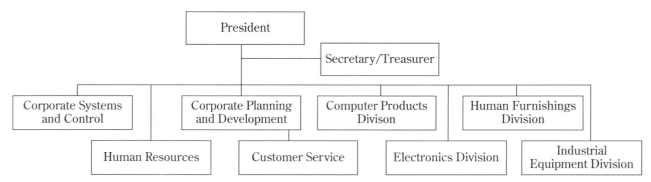

Exhibit 2   Canadian Products Ltd., Divisional Staff Organzation

(Partial Organizational Chart)

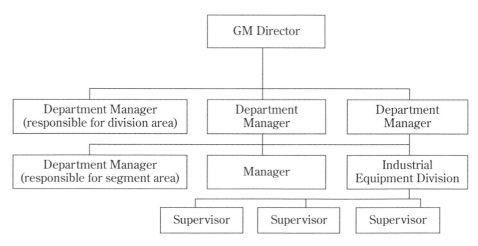

CASE 8

The Well-Paid Receptionist

By Roland B. Cousins, of LaGrange College. Management cooperated in the field research for this case, which was written solely for the purpose of stimulating student discussion. All individuals and incidents are real, but names and data have been disguised at the request of the organization.

Harvey Finley did a quick double take when he caught a glimpse of the figure representing Ms. Brannen's salary on the year-end printout. A hurried call to payroll confirmed it. Yes, his receptionist had been paid $127,614.21 for her services last year. As he sat in stunned silence, he had the sudden realization that, since his firm was doing so well this year, she would earn at least 10 to 15 percent more money during the current fiscal year. This was a shock, indeed.

With a second call to payroll, Harvey found out that Ms. Brannen's salary had been approximately $112,000 the year before last and $100,000 the year before that. She had been well paid for some time, he concluded.

Background

Harvey began his career as a service technician for a major manufacturer of copy machines. He received rather extensive technical training, but his duties were limited to performing routine, on-site maintenance and service for customers. After a year's experience as a service technician, he asked for and received a promotion to sales representative. In this capacity, he established many favorable contacts in the business community of Troupville and the surrounding towns. He began to think seriously about capitalizing on his success by opening his own business.

Then, seven years ago, he decided to take the plunge and start his own firm. He was tired of selling for someone else. When he mentioned his plan to his friends, they all expressed serious doubts; Troupville, a city of approximately 35,000 people located in the deep South, had just begun to recover from a severe recession. The painful memories of the layoffs, bankruptcies, and plummeting real estate values were too recent and vivid to be forgotten.

Undeterred by the sceptics, Harvey was optimistic that Troupville's slow recovery would soon become a boom. Even though his firm would certainly have to be started on a shoestring, Harvey thought his sales experience and technical competence would enable him to survive what was sure to be a difficult beginning. He was nervous but excited when he signed the lease on the first little building. A lifelong dream was either about to be realized or dashed forever. Troupville Business Systems was born.

While he had managed to borrow, rent, lease, or subcontract for almost everything that was absolutely necessary, he did need one employee immediately. Of course, he hoped the business would expand rapidly and that he would soon have a complete and competent staff. But until he could be sure that some revenue would be generated, he thought he could get by with one person who would be a combination receptionist/secretary and general assistant.

The typical salary for such a position in the area was about $14,000 per year; for Harvey, this was a major expense. Nevertheless, he placed what he thought was a well-worded ad in the "Help Wanted" section of the local newspaper. There were five applicants, four of whom just did not seem quite right for the position he envisioned. The fifth applicant, Ms. Cathy Brannen, was absolutely captivating.

Ms. Brannen was a twenty-seven-year-old divorcée with one small child. Her resume showed that she had graduated from a two-year office administration program at a state university. She had worked for only two employers following graduation, one for five years and the most recent for two years. Since returning to her hometown of Troupville two months ago, following her divorce, she had not been able to find suitable employment.

From the moment she sat down for the interview, Harvey and Ms. Brannen seemed to be on exactly the same wavelength. She was very articulate, obviously quite bright, and, most important, very enthusiastic about assisting with the start-up of the new venture. She seemed to be exactly the sort of person Harvey had envisioned when he first began to think seriously about taking the big plunge. He resisted the temptation to offer her the job on the spot, but ended the hour-long interview by telling her that he would check her references and contact her again very soon.

Telephone calls to her two former employers convinced Harvey that he had actually underestimated Ms. Brannen's suitability for the position. Each one said without equivocation that she was the best employee he had ever had in any position. Both former employers concluded the conversation by saying they would rehire her in a minute if she were still available. The only bit of disturbing information gleaned from these two calls was the fact that her annual salary had risen to $15,900 in her last job. Although Harvey thought that the cost of living was probably a bit higher in Houston, where she had last worked, he wasn't sure she would react favourably to the $14,000 offer he was planning to make. However, he was determined that, somehow, Cathy Brannen would be his first employee.

Ms. Brannen seemed quite pleased when Harvey telephoned her at home that same evening. She said she would be delighted to meet him at the office the next morning to discuss the position more fully.

Cathy Brannen was obviously very enthusiastic about the job as outlined in the meeting. She asked all of the right questions, responded quickly and articulately to every query posed to her, and seemed ready to accept the position even before the offer was extended. When Harvey finally got around to mentioning the salary, there was a slight change in Cathy's eager expression. She stiffened. Since Harvey realized that salary might be a problem, he decided to offer Cathy an incentive of sorts in addition to the $14,000 annual salary. He told her that he realized his salary offer was lower than the amount she had earned on her last job. And, he told her, he understood that a definite disadvantage of working for a new firm was the complete absence of financial security. Although he was extremely reluctant to guarantee a larger salary because of his own uncertainty regarding the future, he offered her a sales override in the amount of two percent of sales. He explained that she would largely determine the success or failure of the firm. She needed to represent the firm in the finest possible manner to potential customers who telephoned and to those who walked in the front

door. For this reason, the sales override seemed to be an appropriate addition to her straight salary. It would provide her with incentive to take an active interest in the firm.

Cathy accepted the offer immediately. Even though she was expecting a salary offer of $16,000, she hoped the sales override might make up the difference. "Who knows," she thought, "two percent of sales may amount to big money someday." It did not, however, seem very likely at the time. Troupville Business Systems began as a very small distributor of copy machines. The original business plan was just to sell copy machines and provide routine, on-site service. More extensive on-site service and repairs requiring that a machine be removed from a customer's premises were to be provided by a regional distributor located in a major city approximately 100 miles from Troupville.

Troupville Business Systems did well from the start. Several important changes were made in the services the firm offered during the first year. Harvey soon found that there was a greater demand for the leasing of copy machines, particularly the large expensive models which he originally planned to sell. He also soon discovered that his customers wanted to be able to contract directly with his firm for all of their service needs. Merely guaranteeing that he could get the machines serviced was not sufficient in the eyes of potential customers. In attempting to accommodate the market, he developed a complete service facility and began to offer leasing options on all models. These changes in the business all occurred during the first year. Growth during that year was steady but not spectacular. While sales continued to grow steadily the second year, it was early in the third year that Harvey made what turned out to be his best decision. He entered the computer business.

Harvey had purchased a personal computer soon after Troupville Business Systems was founded. The machine and its capabilities fascinated him, although he knew virtually nothing about computers. He was soon a member of a local users club, was subscribing to all the magazines, and was taking evening computer courses at the local university-in short, he became a computer buff. Harvey recognized the business potential of the rapidly growing personal computer market, but he did not believe that his original business was sufficiently stable to introduce a new product line just yet.

During his third year of operations, he decided the time was right to enter the computer business. He added to his product line a number of personal computers popular with small businesses in the area. This key decision caused a virtual explosion in the growth of his firm. Several key positions were added, including that of comptroller. By the fourth year of operations, computers produced by several other manufacturers had been added to Harvey's product line, and he had developed the capability of providing complete service for all products carried. His computer enterprise was not limited to business customers, because he quickly developed a significant walk-in retail trade. Rapid growth continued unabated.

During the first seven years of the company's existence, Cathy Brannen had proven truly indispensable. Her performance exceeded Harvey's highest expectations. Although her official position remained that of secretary/receptionist, she took it upon herself to learn about each new product or service. During the early years, Harvey often thought that she did a better job than he did whenever a potential customer called in his absence. Even after he acquired a qualified sales staff,

Harvey had no concerns when Cathy had to field questions from a potential customer because a regular salesperson was not available. The customer never realized that the professional young lady capably handling all inquiries was "only" the receptionist.

Cathy began performing fewer sales functions because of the increased number of professional salespersons, but her secretarial duties expanded tremendously. She was still Harvey's secretary, and she continued to answer virtually every telephone call coming into the business. Since her office was in an open area, she still was the first to greet many visitors. Cathy took a word processing course at a local business school shortly after joining the firm. As she began working with Harvey's first personal computer, she, too, developed into a computer aficionado and became the best computer operator in the firm.

The Current Situation

Harvey was shaken by the realization that Cathy Brannen had been paid over $127,000 last year. As he wondered what, if anything, should be done about her earnings, he began to reflect on the previous seven years.

Success had come almost overnight. It seemed as though Troupville Business Systems could do no wrong. The work force had grown at a rate of approximately 15 percent per year since the third year of opera-

tions. Seventeen people were now employed by the firm. While Harvey did acknowledge that some of this success was due to being in the right place at the right time, he also had reason to be proud of the choices he had made. Time had proven that all of his major decisions had been correct. He also could not overestimate Cathy's contribution to the success of the firm. Yes, certainly, one of the most important days in the life of the firm was the day when Cathy responded to his ad in the newspaper.

Success had brought with it ever-increasing demands on his time. He had never worked so hard, but the rewards were certainly forthcoming. First there was the new Jaguar, then the new home on Country Club Drive, the vacation home on the coast, the European trips. . . . Yes, success was wonderful.

During these years Cathy, too, had prospered. Harvey had not thought much about it, but he did remember making a joking comment the first day she drove her new Mercedes to work. He also remembered commenting on her mink coat at the company banquet last December. Cathy had been dazzling.

Now that Harvey realized what he was paying Cathy, he was greatly disturbed. She was making over twice as much money as anyone else in the firm with the exception of himself. The best salesman had earned an amount in the low sixties last year. His top managers were paid salaries

ranging from the high forties to the mid-fifties. The average salary in the area for executive secretaries was now probably between $22,000 and $25,000 per year. A good receptionist could be hired for under $20,000, and yet Cathy had been paid $127,614.21 last year. The sales override had certainly enabled Cathy to share in the firm's success. Yes, indeed.

As Harvey thought more and more about the situation, he kept returning to the same conclusion. He felt something had to be done about her compensation. It was just too far out of line with other salaries in the firm. Although Harvey was drawing over $200,000 per year in salary and had built an equity in the business of more than $1 million, these facts did not seem relevant as he pondered what to do. It seemed likely that a number of other employees did know about Cathy's compensation level. Harvey wondered why no one ever mentioned it. Even the comptroller never mentioned Cathy's compensation. This did seem quite odd to Harvey, as the comptroller, Frank Bain, knew that Harvey did not even attempt to keep up with the financial details. He relied on Frank to bring important matters to his attention.

With no idea of how to approach this problem, Harvey decided to begin by making a list of alternatives. He got out a piece of paper and, as he stared at the blank lines, overheard Cathy's cheerful exchange with a customer in the next room. ∎

CASE 9
The Forgotten Group Member

Developed by Franklin Ramsoomair, Wilfrid Laurier University

The Organizational Behaviour course for the semester appeared to promise the opportunity to learn, enjoy, and practice some of the theories and principles in the textbook and class discussions. Christine Spencer was a devoted, hard-working student who had been maintaining an A+ average to date. Although the skills and knowledge she had acquired through her courses were important, she was also very concerned about her grades. She felt that grades were paramount in giving her a competitive edge when looking for a job and, as a third-year student, she realized that she'd soon be doing just that.

Sunday afternoon. Two o'clock. Christine was working on an accounting assignment but didn't seem to be able to concentrate. Her courses were working out very well this semester, all but the OB. Much of the mark in that course was to be applied to the quality of groupwork, and so she felt somewhat out of control. She recollected the events of the past five weeks. Professor Sandra Thiel had divided the class into groups of five people and had given them a major group assignment worth 30 percent of the final grade. The task was to analyze a seven-page case and to come up with a written analysis. In addition, Sandra had asked the groups to present the case in class, with the idea in mind that the rest of the class members would be "members of the board of directors of the company" who would be listening to how the manager and her team dealt with the problem at hand.

Christine was elected "Team Coordinator" at the first group meeting. The other members of the group were Diane, Janet, Steve, and Mike. Diane was quiet and never volunteered suggestions, but when directly asked, she would come up with high-quality ideas. Mike was the clown. Christine remembered that she had suggested that the group should get together before every class to discuss the day's

case. Mike had balked, saying "No way!! This is an 8:30 class, and I barely make it on time anyway! Besides, I'll miss my Happy Harry show on television!" The group couldn't help but laugh at his indignation. Steve was the businesslike individual, always wanting to ensure that group meetings were guided by an agenda and noting the tangible results achieved or not achieved at the end of every meeting. Janet was the reliable one who would always have more for the group than was expected of her. Christine saw herself as meticulous and organized and as a person who tried to give her best in whatever she did.

It was now week 5 into the semester, and Christine was deep in thought about the OB assignment. She had called everyone to arrange a meeting for a time that would suit them all but seemed to be running into a roadblock. Mike couldn't make it, saying that he was working that night as a member of the campus security force. In fact, he seemed to miss most meetings and would send in brief notes to Christine, which she was supposed to discuss for him at the group meetings. She wondered how to deal with this. She also remembered the incident last week. Just before class started, Diane, Janet, Steve, and she were joking with one another before class. They were

laughing and enjoying themselves before Sandra came in. No one noticed that Mike had slipped in very quietly and had unobtrusively taken his seat.

She recalled the cafeteria incident. Two weeks ago, she had gone to the cafeteria to grab something to eat. She had rushed to her accounting class and had skipped breakfast. When she got her club sandwich and headed to the tables, she saw her OB group and joined them. The discussion was light and enjoyable as it always was when they met informally. Mike had come in. He'd approached their table. "You guys didn't say you were having a group meeting," he blurted. Christine was taken aback. "We just happened to run into each other. Why not join us?"

"Mike looked at them, with a noncommittal glance. "Yeah . . . right," he muttered, and walked away

Sandra Thiel had frequently told them that if there were problems in the group, the members should make an effort to deal with them first. If the problems could not be resolved, she had said that they should come to her. Mike seemed so distant, despite the apparent camaraderie of the first meeting.

An hour had passed, bringing the time to 3 p.m., and Christine found herself biting the tip of her pencil. The written case analysis was due next week. All the others had done their designated sections, but Mike had just handed in some rough handwritten notes. He had called Christine the week before, telling her that in addition to his course and his job, he was having problems with his girlfriend. Christine empathized with him. Yet, this was a group project! Besides, the final mark would be peer evaluated. This meant that whatever mark Sandra gave them could be lowered or raised, depending on the group's opinion about the value of the contribution of each member. She was definitely worried. She knew that Mike had creative ideas that could help to raise the overall mark. She was also concerned for him. As she listened to the music in the background, she wondered what she should do.

Review Questions

1. How could an understanding of the stages of group development assist Christine in leadership situations such as this one?
2. What should Christine understand about individual membership in groups in order to build group processes that are supportive of her workgroup's performance?
3. Is Christine an effective group leader in this case? Why or why not? ■

CASE 10
NASCAR's Racing Teams

Developed by David S. Chappell, Ohio University, modified by Hal Babson, Columbus State Community College

The most popular team sport, based on total spectator audience, is not basketball, baseball, football, or even soccer: it is stock car racing. The largest stock car racing group in the world is the National Association for Stock Car Auto Racing (NASCAR). The NASCAR Nextel Cup Series (previously identified as the Winston Cup Series), with 41 events at 24 U.S. tracks, kicks off in February at Daytona International Speedway and runs through November with the Ford 400 at Homestead-Miami Speedway in Miami.

Note: The blue underscored words/phrases in this case indicate Internet links provided in the on-line version (http/www.wiley.com/canada/schermerhorn).

NASCAR

NASCAR has become a marketing powerhouse. Not only are over 12 million fans attracted to race tracks, but another 250 million watch races on television. Drivers are involved in cable network shows as well as syndicated radio shows each week. NASCAR's official Web site, at www. nascar.com, ranks among the five most popular sites on the Internet, receiving 35 million hits each week. Companies such as the Coca-Cola Co. take advantage of NASCAR's popularity with merchandise, collectibles, apparel, accessories, toys, and other marketing tie-ins.

The race cars themselves have been described by some as "200 mile-per-hour billboards." As an organized sport, NASCAR is unique in that its drivers are treated like independent contractors rather than employees. As such, they must not only perform but also seek their own sponsors to finance their race teams. Traditional NASCAR sponsors include RJR Nabisco, Penzoil Quaker State, General Motors, M&M/Mars, Lowe's, and Proctor and Gamble. The popularity and success of NASCAR as a marketing tool continues to induce sponsors to enter the arena.

NASCAR enjoys a history of great drivers, including Richard Petty, Cale Yarborough, and Davey Pearson. A legend in the making is emerging in the league: Jeff Gordon. Jeff Gordon heads Hendrick Motorsport's # 24 Dupont Automotive Finishes team. In 2002, Jeff Gordon was not only recognized for his racing achievements but was designated as the 2002 Sports Ethics Fellow.

Jeff Gordon—Racing Sensation

Jeff Gordon, on the Nextel (Winston) Cup racing scene since 1993, has been a sensation ever since he started racing go-carts and quarter-midget cars at the age of 5. In 1979 and 1981, he was the quarter- midget national champion, and in 1990 he won the 1990 USAC midget championship. He has captured the imagination of race fans around the world, becoming the youngest driver ever to win three NASCAR Nextel Cup overall championships and has over 68 individual race wins in an nine-year span.

Gordon, 33, says his strong family upbringing in California and Indiana and his marriage to former Miss Winston beauty queen Brooke Sealy have made it easy. (However, in March 2002 Brooke filed for divorce from Jeff.) "There's no question Jeff has helped take our sport to the next level as far as image," said Ned Jarrett, a CBS analyst and two-time NASCAR champion during the 1960s. "He's helped raise the level of competition and also helped get the sport places it's never been before." The question becomes: What does Gordon have that others have trouble imitating?

As the driver of a successful race car, Gordon represents the most visible part of an incredibly complex team of individuals—all with a contribution to make on race day. "To build a winning team, you need three major ingredients—people, equipment, and money," stated Don Hawk, who was president of Dale Earnhardt, Inc. "You can't do it with only one, not even with two—you need all three. Look at Gordon. His team has crew chief Ray Evernham and the Rainbow Warriors pit crew—their multicolored uniforms match Gordon's multicolored car, the best in the garage area; they have the fastest and most reliable Chevrolet on the track; and they have great finances from DuPont. You couldn't do what they've done with just a great driver, just a great car, or an open pocketbook. You must have all three elements meshing. I liken a winning racing team to a Rubik's Cube: all the pieces must fit and be in the proper place."

The High-Performance Team

"Success is a ruthless competitor, for it flatters and nourishes our weaknesses and lulls us into complacency."

The quote above was found in the shop of Gordon's former crew chief, Ray Evernham, recognized by many in NASCAR as the premier crew chief in the business. While Gordon represented the star attraction, many believed that it was Evernham who pulled the whole act together. He was responsible for a group of over 120 technicians and mechanics with an annual budget estimated between $10 and $12 million! And he had strong opinions as to what it takes to consistently finish first: painstaking preparation, egoless teamwork, and thoroughly original strategizing—principles that apply to any high-performance organization.

You win as a team. Evernham believed that teams needed to experiment with new methods and processes. When he assembled his Rainbow Warriors pit crew, none of them had Nextel/Winston Cup experience and none worked on the car in any other capacity. With the use of a pit crew coach, the Rainbow Warriors provide Gordon with an approximately one-second advantage with each pit stop, which, at a speed of 200 miles per hour, equates to 300 feet of race track.

"When you coach and support a superstar like Jeff Gordon, you give him the best equipment possible, you give him the information he needs, and then you get out of the way. But racing is a team sport. Everyone who races pretty much has the same car and the same equipment. What sets us apart is our people. I like to talk about our "team IQ"—because none of us is as smart as all of us.

"I think a lot about people, management, and psychology: Specifically, how can I motivate my guys and make them gel as a team? I surround them with ideas about teamwork. I read every leadership book I can get my hands on. One thing that I took from my reading is the idea of a 'circle of strength.' When the Rainbow Warriors meet, we always put our chairs in a circle. That's a way of saying that we're stronger as a team than we are on our own."

Evernham backed up this belief in team by emphasizing team performance over individual performance. When the car won a race, everyone shared in the prize money. In addition, when Evernham earned money through personal-service activities such as speaking tours and autograph signings, he shared what he earned with the team. "I wouldn't be in a position to earn that income if it weren't for the team. Everyone should feel as if his signature is on the finished product."

The teamwork during a race could even include adversaries—as in other drivers. In an effort to make races competitive for fans, NASCAR uses several methods to make the cars approximately even in performance, thereby enhancing the competitive environment for the audience. To get ahead, racers depend on their friends in the form of cars that help aerodynamically "slingshot" them ahead of the pack. This may take the form of teammates (Jimmie Johnson and Brian Vickers for Hendrick Motorsports) or opponents.

Push for perfection but accept imperfection. High-performance teams are constantly improving, even in small ways. Evernham made use of every opportunity to learn something new. If the car was running well, Evernham would ask Gordon to find something wrong with it. "We always try to make the car perfect. But the car doesn't have to be perfect to win; it just has to be less imperfect than everyone else's car."

Don't strut your stuff. In the past, most crews concentrated on the car and relied on horsepower and driving talent to win the race. Evernham took a larger view that kept the egos in check: "There aren't many secrets in the Winston Cup, so you've got to protect as much information as you can. We want to have the fastest car on the track, but we don't want everyone else to know how fast we are. We don't show our hand until it's time to race or to qualify.

"We also try to mix things up on race day. We don't want to fall into patterns or to tip off the competition about our next pit stop. Since everyone can hear us on the scanners, we might use a code word to signal whether we're changing two tires or four. Sometimes, when the car is running well, Jeff might get on the radio and complain to me that the steering is tight, even though he's about to pass another driver. And that driver's crew chief will fall for it: 'Yeah, Gordon can't pass you right now, because he's tight.' The driver will leave a little opening and—boom—we're past him."

To win the race, drive by different rules. Evernham attacked each race as different from the last. He was constantly looking for even the smallest advantage that can give his race car and driver the edge. The team practices passing cars in unsuspected areas of the track, when their competition least expects it.

High-performance teams do not happen by chance; rather, they are the result of good recruiting and meticulous attention to learning every detail of the job. With multiple wins in every season since 1994 (despite a tremendous increase in the level of competition), the Gordon recipe for success has resulted in four Nextel Cup championships. Jeff Gordon wins approximately one of every four races he starts, a pace unmatched in modern times. However, on September 29, 1999, Ray Evernham resigned to form his own organization and was replaced with Brian Whitesell.

Whitesell took over as crew chief on an interim basis. With an engineering degree from Virginia Tech, Whitesell was one of the best-educated NASCAR crew chiefs. His brilliance was recognized by the legendary Dale Earnhardt when Jeff Gordon beat him in a race.

However, when Whitesell moved up to being team manager and the co-owner of the racing team along with Gordon, the search was on for a permanent replacement. The selection was Robbie Loomis. During the transition period and until Robbie Loomis became settled in the new position, Gordon went through six months without winning one race.

Robbie Loomis soon played a key role in a significant turnaround. In 2001 Jeff Gordon had a spectacular season: he was in the top 10 for the eighth season, and he ranked seventh in overall wins during his career. As of 2004 Gordon is within 16 victories of matching the record of Darrell Waltrip. Gordon is the only driver to attain over $75 million dollars in winnings.

What can be learned regarding the change in crew chief leadership and Jeff Gordon's continuing leadership? One test of leadership is how a group performs when the leader is not around. Another is how well a leader can turn a situation around. When Jeff Gordon lost his crew chief, Ray Evernham, there was a period of losses while the team was in transition. Nevertheless, the underlying strength of the team was obviously still there in spite of the losses. Jeff Gordon was

still there to inspire team members not to give up. The strength was fully utilized as the new team leader was able to grow, develop rapport and confidence with the team, and begin to function as a transformational leader.

Review Questions

1. Evaluate Jeff Gordon's race team on dimensions covered in the text's discussion of characteristics of high-performance teams.

2. Discuss Jeff Gordon's race team on dimensions covered in the text's discussion of methods to increase group cohesiveness.

3. Compare Gordon's race team on the methods of team building. Which one most applies to this situation?

4. What are the potential pros and cons when a successful team leader such as Evernham leaves and is replaced by someone else? ∎

CASE 11

A Case of Doing Excellence?

By Cheryl Harvey

September 5, 1995, was the day after Labour Day and the first time since spring that everyone was in the office. The vacations were over, kids were back in school, and it was a time for beginning again, a time to talk with the staff about what had to be done and how it was going to get done. There were some clear issues that had to be addressed. On July 21, the new Conservative provincial government had announced cutbacks in social services agency funding of 1.25% for the current year and 5% for next year. The government also planned to reduce payments to welfare recipients by 20% on October 1, a move which would place additional stress on many families and likely lead to more demand for the services this agency provided. Accreditation by the Ontario Association of Children's Aid Societies (OACAS) was scheduled for the first time in November. And then there was this research report.

Moe was puzzled and more than a little frustrated by the report. Was this or was this not an excellent organization? This agency had been chosen as an example of a place that seemed to fit the researcher's definition of excellence in human services organizations. But he wasn't sure what this report was saying. Was there something wrong here? Why?

Family and Children's Services of Guelph and Wellington County

Family and Children's Services of Guelph and Wellington County (F&CS) was a Children's Aid Society established in 1893 and, like the other 50 such agencies in Ontario, was

charged with the responsibility of enforcing the province's Child and Family Services Act. Section 15(3) sets out the functions of a Children's Aid Society as:

To investigate allegations or evidence that children who are under the age of sixteen years or are in the Society's care or under its supervision may be in need of protection;

To protect, where necessary, children who are under the age of sixteen years or are in the Society's care or under its supervision;

To provide guidance, counselling and other service to families for protecting children or for the prevention of circumstances requiring the protection of children.

F&CS was funded by both the provincial and the municipal governments in an 80-20 split mandated by the Act, and in 1994 operated with a budget of $4.9M. Two-thirds of that amount went to salaries, benefits, and training for a full-time equivalent staff of 61 social workers, child care workers and support staff. F&CS operated from three locations with its main office in Guelph, a city of 90,000, and smaller offices in Fergus and Arthur which served those communities, other small towns nearby, and rural areas in the county.

The agency's mission, "to advocate and provide for the protection of children, to support and strengthen families, and to promote the well-being of children in our communities," was carried out through the services it offered directly to children and their families as well as through its participation on various community committees and boards. It initiated and supported a wide range of community-based activities focused on preventing circumstances that might lead to children being at risk. For example, F&CS supported Onward Willow, Waverly, and Brant, all neighbourhood programs run largely by volunteers who provided child care, outreach to parents of newborns, employment readiness training (interview skills, resume writing), parent support groups, language classes for new Canadians, food distribution, and cooking clubs. The goal of all these activities was the development of these neighbourhoods as "villages" where the families that lived there supported each other. F&CS' emphasis on prevention set it apart from other Children's Aid Societies which focussed more narrowly on their child protection mandate.

In its direct services activities, F&CS emphasized that its role was not of a "baby snatcher" as Children's Aid Societies had traditionally been perceived. Rather, the agency viewed removing a child from home as a last resort and committed itself to using the least intrusive approach possible, preferring to sustain families to care for and support their own children. So, just as it aggressively pursued early prevention programs in the community, the agency focussed its direct client services on preventing the separation of children from their families. When separation was necessary, the emphasis was on either reuniting families quickly, or on planning a permanent placement for the child (for example, in an adoptive home).

F&CS was structured along service delivery lines, with three departments, Family Services, Children's Services, and Resources, devoted to direct services. Two administrative departments, Finance and Information Services, and Human Resources and Community Relations supported service delivery. Department managers reported to the Executive Director, Maurice (Moe) Brubacher, and these six persons formed the Management Team (see Exhibit 1).

Intake workers in the Family Services department responded to initial requests for service that might arise from a teacher, physician or other health care worker, a concerned neighbour or relative, or a parent. They investigated and assessed whether and how to intervene in situations of child abuse, high risk of abuse, severe parent-child conflict, abandonment, lack of supervision, and other circumstances that could leave parents unable to provide adequate care for their children. Many of these initial referrals were "brief services" of an hour or less, where, for example, a worker might respond to what turned out to be a request for information, might comfort a child who walked in upset and just needed to talk to someone for a while, or might give advice to a teacher who wanted to know how to discuss a disturbing incident with a child.

About half of these initial contacts resulted in cases opened (see Exhibit 2). These cases remained with the intake worker for up to 30 days while family counselling, crisis intervention, parent aides' support (provided by volunteers), or an abuse investigation took place. Most cases were closed during this period, but 20-30% were transferred to a Family Services worker whose work with the family could last for a couple of months or extend for several years. A family preservation worker from the Resources department, a parent aide volunteer, or an adoption worker from Children's Services might also be involved with the family, depending on its particular needs.

Where the risk to the child was so great, the parent-child conflict so intractable, the parents' ability to handle the child so poor, the child's difficulties so severe, that the situation could not be handled otherwise, the child was brought into care and F&CS became the child's legal guardian. The child was usually placed in a foster home or, less frequently, a group home or a children's mental health facility. A worker from the Children's Services department then worked with the child and the placement to reunite children to their family while the Family Services worker continued with the family towards that same goal.

The Resources department staff had a variety of responsibilities. They recruited, selected, trained, and supported foster parents; they coordinated the parent aide volunteer program, offered some group treatment programs, and worked in family preservation to offer intensive, short-term, in-home intervention with families where children would otherwise have been admitted to care.

Moe Brubacher

Moe Brubacher had been the Executive Director since 1989 and had worked at F&CS for 16 years. A manager in the Arthur office before becoming the E.D., Moe had thought a lot about what he wanted to accomplish in his new position:

"I felt very strongly committed to participatory decision making and to minimizing the hierarchy. The work I had done in North Wellington with the team that I worked with, I very much valued. The team, the people. In some ways it was the ideal thing, 'cause we had a small group of people. Seven or eight. Being out there on our own, we were very independent. I guess what I wanted to see here, was to be able to try and transpose some of those things that we valued so much there, to the larger organization."

"There were some things in terms of service that I was also concerned about. The numbers of children that were coming into care. I mean the difference between the number of children coming in to care in the north (Arthur) versus the south (Guelph) was very dramatic. I've always felt that the more competent and confident and committed that you are to working with families, the fewer children you bring into care. If you go in with an adversarial approach and an investigative approach, you're going to find problems and you're going to bring children into care and end up in court. But if you had done it with a different twist to start with, you wouldn't get there. So, that was another vision I had, was to try to push that one as far as we could. The third thing, beyond the service to the people that we serve directly, was the whole community – networking, and the need for somebody to take some leadership in that respect."

Moe worked with the board, the staff, others in the community, and with the Ministry to persuade them of his vision for F&CS and felt that his long days had been worthwhile. The last annual meeting held in April was a celebration of not just the activities of the previous year, but of the progress achieved over several years with the efforts of many individuals. The service statistics showed a steady decline in new admissions of children into care and an increase in the adoptions of children who were difficult to place. It seemed the agency's emphasis on the least intrusive intervention and on permanency planning was paying off.

Moe's attention to changing the leadership style in the organization also seemed to be working. For the first time ever, the staff association president had been invited to speak at this meeting and she was enthusiastic about how the agency was managed:

"… the fact that I am here speaks to several factors: it speaks to this agency's board which has demonstrated time and time again that it wants to hear from staff and include staff. It speaks to an agency director that is committed to involving staff in the decisions of the organization. It speaks to a management team that is flexible and open to staff involvement. And finally, it speaks to a staff membership that is willing to face the challenge of increased staff participation. Make no mistake –it is a challenge to us all because it asks all of us to step outside the traditional patterns of a typical bureaucracy."

Work in the community was also bearing fruit. F&CS would have social workers in two Guelph schools in the fall to aid its early intervention and prevention strategies. A pilot program to establish a shared intake system for all the children's services offered by F&CS, the Community Mental Health Clinic, and Community Alcohol and Drug Services had begun in Fergus in the summer. Integration promised to be a more efficient way for agencies to cooperate in providing services to clients in these days of dwindling resources and a better way to meet all of their needs. This "one-stop-access" would prevent the problems of potential clients not knowing where to go to get a particular service and perhaps finding themselves passed from agency to agency in search of the expertise they needed.

This initiative was a beginning step in moving to the integrated services model that F&CS and other members of the Wellington Children's Services Council advocated and was the result of several years' work.

Moe thought about all the changes that had taken place since 1989 and wondered about the future:

"There's the 80-20 rule. The first stuff is easy, and then the further you go to make the changes, the tougher it gets. So the first few years, tightening things up, reducing our children in care, that was a whole lot of fun, and that worked really well. But what do I do next? How do we go further?"
"There are frustrations with the Ministry, frustrations with the Association (OACAS) for putting so much of their energy into things like accreditation and quality assurance, and not balancing that very well with trying to pursue lots of innovative changes. I get frustrated internally that people don't want to change, people that are kind of locked into the traditional way, and have lots of reasons not to do things differently. Frustrations with the network of agencies for not being willing and able to trust one another more. And that happens on the front line, it happens among directors. We don't want to give things up. We're happy to do things differently as long as we get to keep everything we've got. We've made some progress, but the next step is tough."
" A year ago, I went through some really difficult personal times. There's the challenge to balance the internal stuff and the community stuff and the provincial stuff. And what's the appropriate balance without it being 60 hours a week? I've worked hard the last year to try to cut back time so I can do other things. All of it suffers to some extent. I look at some of the community stuff, and I realize that the last few Children's Council meetings, I haven't been there. I sort of feel guilty about that but, you can't be there and be in the bush at the same time. I can't be there and be here at the same time. I'm not sure what the answer is or what have I done or what haven't I done to set up expectations that people don't feel I'm meeting. And how to change the expectations. I think some of it is changing the expectations as much as it is changing my behaviour."

September 5, 1995

The research report addressed several different topics, and, smiling ruefully at himself, Moe scanned it again to escape from his bemused reflections. He wasn't sure exactly what he'd expected, but he knew it wasn't this. The researcher had attended the annual meeting, a board meeting, a manager/team leader meeting and a management team meeting. She had interviewed 23 persons from each level and from every department in the agency asking them about whether and how excellence was demonstrated on a variety of dimensions.

Moe focused briefly on the headings and some of the quotes the researcher had provided to illustrate her conclusions (see Appendix A), before turning to his keyboard to retrieve the agenda for tomorrow afternoon's management team meeting. He wanted to make sure he'd added the issues raised by the research report to the list of discussion items. Yes, there it was, right after the "accreditation readiness" update and before "implications of government cutbacks." Which of these issues were important to deal with? How? When? Moe opened his "priorities" file to sort through his thoughts and decide where to begin his week. It was going to be a very busy Fall. ∎

Exhibit 1 — Service Department

Family Services Department		Children's Services Department		Resources Depart.
North Wellington Team	*Centre Wellington Team*	*Adoption Team*	*Children's Services Team*	*Generic Social Workers*
Social Workers Heather Doering Rob Neill Nico van der Sluis Brian Wicke Intake Secretary Barbara Clark Team Leader Wanda Rae	Social Workers Lesley Goruk Cathy McGarthy *Deb Megens Intake Secretary Mary Ann Snoek Team Leader Anne Marie Simpson	Social Workers Rosemary Ceschan Jan Fecuck Ann Perk Rita Ryce Pregnancy Counselling Jynn Green Team Leader Sandra Berry	Social Workers Tom Caley Ron Harder Cindy Trodden Heather van- der Sluis Intake Secretary Carol Goll Team Leader Ann Colman	Mary Lou Fretz Al Koop Eva Marmurek Ann Nesbitt Leelie Pirie Cathy Smith Anita Vlaar – Foster Case & Support – Group Work – Prevention & Support – Child Abuse reatment Coordination After Hours Service Workers Family Preservation Workers Intake Secretary * Hazel Connell
Guelph Teams				
Social Workers Sylvia Danzie Andy Phillips Phil Potter Ron McHugh *Doreen Noreworth Team Leader Greg Sullivan I.R.O. Janice Morgan	Social Workers Celia Blair Jacqueline Guigue-Glaspell *Joyce Fyn Kirk Jenkins Gretchen Perry Team Leader Shelley Snyder			
Department Secretary	*Laurie Thyssen			
Manager – Alison Scott		**Manager – Pat Giles**		**Manager – Glory To**

Administrative Departments			
Finance & Information Services Department	**Human Resources & Community Relations Department**	Executive Director Moe Brubacher	Executive Assistant Colleen Reardon
Information Systems Co-ordinator Jocelyn Kelcher Data Entry Jan Vallas Accounting Jill Huson Purchase/File Clerk Carol Mast Receptionist Adalaine Masson	Co-ordinator of Volunteer & Community Relations Georgina Robertson Progrm Support Secretary Maria Hawker Administrative Assistant Joy Beaton	Board of Directors	Organizational Chart (July 1, 1995)
Manager – David Huson	**Manager – Jeanne Forsythe**		

Exhibit 2: Service Statistics

Family Services	1991	1992	1993	1994
Family service Referals	1288	1400	1570	1774
Cased Opened	774	696	823	845
Children Served	2491	2315	2719	2788
Child Abuse Cases	386	287	292	274
Foster Homes – Homes Open	83	79	75	74
Children's Services				
Children Admitted into Care	137	114	59	87
Children in Care (average)	103	114	59	87
Childre in Care (year end)	93	97	89	90
Children In Outside Paid Institutions	9	6	6	11
Total Days Care Provided	42,239	38,685	35,478	36,556
Adoption Services				
Adoption Placements	18	10	9	23
Children on Adoption Probation (year end)	19	23	18	19
Post Adoption Service – Families Served	27	30	27	28
Adoption disclosure Cases	170	144	133	147

Source: 1994 Annual Report

Appendix A

The Research Report (Extracts)

Clear Purpose

To really survive in this job, if you don't believe in it, it'll wear you down. This isn't just a job. This is more than that. And that can be really tough for the people that just want to work. (A manager/team leader)

Not everyone believes in the prevention stuff. (A staff member)

Serving Client Needs

If there's a need a client has, it's not a matter of, "Yes, we can," or, "No, we can't." It's, "What can we do?" and can we in any way suit the individual needs of that client. (A staff member)

I've heard for many, many years about the need for us to do some kind of a client satisfaction survey and we don't. We do staff satisfaction surveys over and over but we don't do them with the clients. (A staff member)

Commitments to Staff

The training that's provided to people I think is very good. I mean, whenever I've found something that I felt was really relevant, I was able to go. I've never gotten as much training as I have through here. I'm able to work with quite a bit of independence. Which I like. (A staff member)

Financially, we're doing pretty good. With respect to other agencies and I think with respect to other Children's Aids. And there's just lots of rewards from the nature of the job. (A staff member)

I've always said that if you can walk down the corridors of an organization and hear laughter, then you probably have a relatively healthy organization. And you can hear laughter in this building. (A manager/team leader)

I think we're really flexible in terms of our policies, our personnel policies. Personnel policies, like the family leave, the modified work week, educational needs.. I think we're really committed to staff in giving them the training when they first come in. (A manager/team leader)

There's a high level of trust. We're respected as professionals and trusted. And not being watched over—there's no sense of that. (A staff member)

We can accommodate your need to be human. And you just go and you come back to us when you can. 'Cause you're not gonna be any use to anybody when you're here anyway. And when you come back, you come back. Rejuvenated. You can go and you can concentrate on the family stuff, and you don't have to feel guilty about having to go. (A manager/team leader)

Commitments from Staff

The expectation back—that's not stated, but I know it—is that when I can work, I work harder. I think that's part of the payoff, is that what we expect from people is that commitment back. So that they too will be flexible about their time if we need them. That they too will be respectful of the kind of the freedom that's there, and not misuse that. And that they'll use the training. Most of the people here are really hardworking. (A manager/team leader)

It expects that we'll do our work very ethically, that we will represent the agency well. With the whole level of discomfort among certain people in the community around CAS, so, whatever we're doing out there, there's an element of PR in it. Even if we're out doing a home visit with someone, I mean, what we do gets repeated to their friends and gets repeated to their friends and gets repeated to their friends. (A staff member)

They expect us to use the training and education that we've had to be good social workers, to be fair, to listen, to give constructive input, to follow through on things –that's a really important thing. (A staff member)

I think the agency would expect good teamwork from people, support of each other. This isn't a good place to be a lone ranger. (A staff member)

Flexibility/ Adaptability

Sometimes there's been a perception that change has happened because Moe has an idea and we go with the idea. Then people just raise their eyebrows and say, well, where did this come from. An example of that right now is, there's a committee on around self-directed teams, and people's perception is that Moe has heard about this and it sounds good and so now, we're gonna do it. So that's the perception, that sometimes change takes place because it's an idea that Moe has. (A staff member)

Anyone can have an idea. As long as it's implemented properly and in stages and there's some consultation and a feedback loop and I think that's in place here. (A manager/team leader)

Sometimes I think we make change without really looking carefully at how its going to make our services to our clients better. So we may make it for other reasons than that. And that should be our real reason. (A staff member)

The best form of change in this organization is and has been that you see something working well and you build on it. And you reward it and you praise it and you highlight it. And then it continues to grow. And often that comes from the line in terms of someone really having a great idea. (A manager/team leader)

Internal Process

I think some of this partnership between staff and management is starting to become an expectation. You know, people are asking, we're asking to be more involved in the process and then, if we're all involved in it, then we'd all own it. 'Cause people can say, well you guys can make the decision, and we're saying sometimes, no, not necessarily. You're making this decision with us. And that's a shift. (A manager/team leader)

I think the day to day things are well run. I mean there is an order, a sense of order to what we do. (A staff member)

People in more direct contact with clients are encouraged to speak out about things, but then, there's a sense that what we say isn't really put to use. Sometimes, there's already an agenda. And it gets followed, no matter what people say. (A staff member)

We continue to struggle with conflict. It's not just office politics. It's people having really strong feelings about things, a real range of opinions. (A manager/team leader)

The workers are encouraged to talk to workers themselves rather than complain to their immediate superior. So that is constructive. People are honest and they do risk there. People who've been here the longest, three or four years, feel safe. (A manager/team leader)

Accreditation is driving us to write things down. There's so much focus on written policies and procedures. For everything. We're spending a lot of time documenting, making sure everything is in place for November. (A manager/team leader)

Sometimes I think we communicate really well and sometimes I think we really screwed it up, and sometimes I think that we get ahead of ourselves, like one part of us, like Moe for example, will be off on some sort

of goal in the community that doesn't really get translated back to us. So the community can receive one message and we're operating under another one. Or their expectations of us are very different because of what we say and what we're able to do, because we haven't learned what we can do completely to ...if we say we can do this, then we better be able to do it, and I think we ...that's where the striving comes in. I think we want to do it. We see the sense in doing it, but we haven't always got the mechanisms in place before we move or we move and we realize we've moved the wrong way. And I don't think we take the time with ourselves enough to make sure that we're stepping it out right. Sometimes we take a lot of time with it and we've missed the obvious. (A manager/team leader)

We don't know which decisions are Moe's, which belong to the management team, which are ours. We're supposed to have participatory decision making, but when and how, we don't always know. (A staff member)

I think we've underestimated some of that system stuff in trying to cut back in some of our admin services. I think we've cut back to the point where we've really hurt ourselves. (A manager/team leader)

Structure & System Fit

I've got people in all kinds of community, early intervention stuff. We're at the point where, does it make sense to stay structured the way we are, or are we going to change? (A manager/team leader)

There's too many managers and team leaders in case management conferences. If workers are supposed to be empowered, why are all the managers there? (A manager/team leader)

Striving

I think we're learning. I think that part of our striving is our learning. It feels like struggling along. I think we're pretty good at coming back to things. I don't think people let things go. (A manager/team leader)

There's always an attempt to improve on what's being done. For example, teamwork is already happening. What can we do to make teamwork work even better? This is going ok. What can we do to make sure that it's moving forward? There's never a complacency. (A staff member)

There's high expectations to do things better, not just to do things well, but to do them better. (A staff member)

Leadership

I think his beliefs, and his commitment, his energy, his sincerity, his work ethic, all of those things make him a real leader. He really believes in what he's doing and I think that comes through. And I think as much as people want to make fun of Moe and knock him, they will never be able to get him on that, because this guy is driven by what he thinks is the right thing for people. I think there's some really neat people in this organization who are really good leaders in leading different things. I think there's really good leadership in our staff association. When I look at some of the adoption team and how they have incorporated some of our permanency planning stuff with our front line? I mean they're real leaders in terms of the team work that they're doing and the kind of stuff that they're getting done. I think that's really good leadership. And I think there are some really good leaders, a whole bunch of different strengths, on our team. Some are really good at leading by not leading. Pat really lets

her team process things and sort of give~ them the information, and lets them do the job. She's got a sense of stability around her, where people feel they're always going to count on how she's going to be. I think that adds a whole element of security. I think that's a true leadership skill. (A manager/team leader)

I could probably learn to delegate more with them and they could take it on, but I need to let go. They keep telling me I need to let go of this, you need to let go of this. We can do this and we can do that. It's like I won't move unless I know how I can, so I have to be really clear before I can give it away. Once I give it away it's gone. But until I give it away, it can be really hard. (A manager/team leader)

I am singing Moe's praises because I do think he's a very good director. I think he's really helped to make a very positive name for this agency with other agencies. He's done a lot of work in developing new programs. He's worked really hard in that way. Community development's kind of his thing. I think that's a really excellent part of what goes on here. (A staff member)

Excellent?

I would hesitate to use the word excellent. I think that there are a lot of very positive things about the agency. And certainly it's been the place where I've gotten the most job satisfaction in all of the jobs that I've had. I think that there are a lot people who work very hard here. I think sometimes we ...I'm very glad this is confidential. (laughs) I think that there's too much effort put into making the appearance of things going well, and sometimes I think management has a hard time or is reluctant to take on some difficult issues. (A staff member)

Definitely. The ideology is that the clients are worthy. We're here for

a purpose. I find the people I work with are fun. I just was on vacation and I honestly miss this place when I'm not here. I really enjoyed my time off, but I called on Sunday to see how many messages I had, and not that I wanted to check my messages, but I was just excited about coming back on Monday. People are good. Management's good. I've always felt noticed. I've always felt appreciated. (A staff member)

Now. But if the funding changes much with this new government, that could have a big impact on services and on what we can do, should do, in the community. (A staff member)

Mostly. I think we have really good leadership. I think the director almost always makes the difference between being a good, or a very good, or an excellent organization. I don't think you can have an excellent organization without an excellent leader. Then, in that case, I think you can have pockets of excellence. I think there are some areas here that are more excellent than others, and there's times that are more excellent than others. (A manager/team leader)

What can prevent excellence? No one wants to do more. (A manager/ team leader)

Assignment Questions

1. What is organizational effectiveness? Organizational excellence? Is the researcher addressing the appropriate dimensions?
2. What issues can you identify from the report? Which of these should Moe deal with? How? When? ■

C A S E 1 2
Evergreen Technologies Ltd.

By Pauline Brockman and Andrew Templer

On a bright summer morning Alison Hayes, director—IT human resourcing for Evergreen Technologies Ltd. (ETL), opened the ToDo folder of her Palm Pilot and began adding in the words, "Evaluate work-from-home program." Mike Tulett, president of ETL, had just popped into Alison's office, supposedly just "in passing," but had immediately let it be known that he had important matters on his mind.

"We need to address this Alison," Mike said, waving a piece of paper in the air, "but I can't talk now because I've got a conference call with the Ministry of Transportation in a few minutes. We have to find some solutions to the work-from-home program, so can we meet at the end of the day to talk?"

Alison was barely able to nod before Mike strode off towards his office. She wondered what had brought on Mike's outburst. She guessed it was probably tied to her policy memo on managing telecommuting staff (see Exhibit 1). Though this was still a relatively new undertaking, she had not anticipated the depth of the reaction from employees and managers who could not take advantage of the work-from-home program.

The Company

In the last 10 years, Markham, Ontario, has grown to become Canada's new high-tech capital. In addition to being home to Evergreen Technologies Ltd. (ETL), Markham has also become the address for many of Canada's most notable high-tech companies, such as IBM, Sprint, ATI, Dell, and Onyx as well as hundreds of lesser-known start-ups.

ETL, founded in 1992 by an executive team with several years of both automotive and information technology experience, was formed to harness expertise and knowledge about the challenges of vehicle emissions in North America.

In the last few decades, smog has become a serious health and environmental concern in most major cities around the world. Greater levels of ground-level ozone have been created by mixing a growing amount of exhaust emissions from vehicles together with other environmental pollutants. This ground-level ozone, when mixed with sunlight, becomes the brown haze most people refer to as smog. As a result of the direct link between vehicles and the quality of the environment, emission-related projects have become a combined effort of the Ministry of the Environment (MOE) and Ministry of Transportation (MOT) in Canada and of the Department of Environmental Quality (DEQ) and the Department of Motor Vehicles (DMV) in the United States. Together, these organizations have begun to take a strong position to immediately decrease all forms of pollution in an attempt to reverse the negative effects on the earth's ozone layer.

ETL has responded to this market opportunity by developing and marketing the hardware and software necessary to implement and effectively administer vehicle inspection programs. Although the process and standards for vehicle emission inspections vary greatly from region to region and from country to country,

ETL's software, called Inspection Lane, has proved to be adaptable to the various types of emission inspection equipment available in North America. Although ETL is the only company of its kind in Canada, several impressive competitors in the United States have been vying for the lucrative state and provincial contracts. Despite this tough competition, however, ETL has been very successful in growing its business and reputation under the leadership of Mike Tulett, the company's president. Since its founding almost nine years ago, ETL has secured emissions-testing contracts in Texas, New Mexico, Colorado, Vermont, Virginia, Missouri, Georgia, and most recently, Ontario, Canada. This case is set halfway through Year 2 in the implementation of the Canadian contract. (See Exhibit 3.)

Ontario's "Drive Clean" Contract

In the late 1990s, Ontario responded to the need to reduce vehicle emissions with its own "Drive Clean" program. In terms of the program, as announced, all cars and light-duty trucks over three years of age in the Greater Toronto Area (GTA) would be required to begin scheduled vehicle-emission testing.

Owners of vehicles over three years of age would receive a notice approximately 90 days prior to their licence renewal stating that their car or light truck would require an emissions test. Owners would be required to take their automobile to a local, privately owned, licensed testing facility in their area (e.g., Canadian Tire) before the vehicle could obtain its annual licensing sticker. Vehicles would undergo the simple test, and within minutes the owners would receive a computer-generated report that stated whether the vehicle passed or failed the test, as well as an analysis of the pollutants coming from the tailpipe. An "emissions analyzer" in each facility would allow probes and other devices to capture output from the exhaust system and to check the gas cap for leaks. If the vehicle passed the test, the positive result would automatically be relayed to the Ministry of Transportation computer system so that the vehicle registration could be renewed by the deadline. If the vehicle failed the test, the owner would receive a report describing some of the potential causes of failure. Under the program, "failing" vehicles would need to be repaired and re-tested until a pass certificate was obtained.

ETL's Responsibility for The Test Project

As the successful bidder for the "Drive Clean" program, ETL is expected to take on a wide range of responsibilities for the emissions testing process. Its key task is the writing of software according to specifications provided by the MOE and MOT so that data captured on the analyzer can be safely transferred to the MOT's central database repository.

In addition to capturing the emissions data, ETL is required to look after other aspects of the testing process such as training emissions inspectors and performing station audits. The station audits are particularly necessary to ensure that stations follow the appropriate procedures and do not cheat the system or consumers by offering faulty readings and unnecessary repair claims. The data collected and systems developed by the technology group at ETL will be used to help identify suspect stations so that an undercover auditor can investigate and analyze the emissions testing system. Because thousands of stations exist within each province or

state, it would be impossible to perform an audit on each. The technology group will also be responsible for the billing aspect of the program to ensure that the government receives its share of the money paid for each emission test performed.

The Labour Market Facing ETL

While the Ontario Drive Clean project was good news financially for ETL, it has created significant work for the IT human resourcing department. A number of new staff had to be hired to run the project—all at a time when technology employees were in high demand. Not only do the number of technology jobs easily outnumber the number of qualified personnel, it is not at all unusual for developers to switch companies every couple of years. Like the rest of the industry, ETL has also been challenged by its ability to attract and retain highly qualified individuals, especially since very few have experience in emissions testing. Over the past five years only 3 of the 15 members of ETL's original Research and Development team have remained with the company. In addition, the database and Web development teams have undergone a complete transformation with nearly all staff now having transferred to other departments or having left the company entirely.

The Drive Clean project is proving particularly difficult to staff because none of the individuals coming to the company had prior emission-related experience and hence have required a significant learning curve to understand the business. As well, the delay in having the Ontario program implemented added to the staffing complexity. Now that the program has been approved there is sudden pressure for immediate implementation.

The Critical Nature of Staffing

One of the most significant challenges of a high-tech company is securing adequate levels of highly skilled staff. Whereas the information technology department is considered a support function in many traditional industries, at ETL the computer technicians, programmers, developers, and analysts are the driving force behind the company's success. Thus, high levels of turnover and unfilled positions are a source of considerable concern.

As director, IT human resourcing, Alison has been very frustrated by the company's difficulty in retaining its high-tech talent. In a few cases, the company's most mobile staff have been lured to the United States for salaries that range from US$15,000 to $55,000 more than those offered by ETL. Because ETL is in close proximity to several high-tech competitors, employees who are slightly unhappy or who continue to look for larger salaries are able to easily find other jobs. It is also a sad fact that some less scrupulous headhunter agencies make a lot of money out of work for the IT industry by placing and replacing employees between one client and another.

The IT industry also spans nearly all cultural and ethnic backgrounds. Due to significant shortages of qualified candidates in Canada, several of ETL's latest hires have come from Europe and the Middle East. Alison has found that overcoming language and cultural barriers has been both a difficult and slow process.

The Technology Group at ETL

The technology group at ETL has been responsible for developing and implementing the emissions-testing systems for the Drive Clean program. The group is divided into two major areas: development/support and infrastructure/quality control. (See the organization chart in Exhibit 2.)

Parallel with these major areas and similar to other high-tech organizations, the technology group has been divided into several subgroups or areas to handle business in a more efficient manner. The research and development team (R&D) is responsible for looking at the latest technologies, testing them, and piloting how they can be used in an upcoming project. The people in this team are often able to work from home because their job requires considerable investigation and thought, but not a lot of interaction with other team members. The work in this team typically requires employees to go off on their own with an idea and put in significant time and effort in order to return with the best solution. In this group, solitary work is often more productive.

The network and support team is responsible for the day-to-day operations of the business. This team consists of developers, database administrators, and network support personnel. Due to the nature of the work, this team is typically required to work on-site. Many of the programs have mandates to be operational "24-7" (24 hours per day, 7 days per week). Fines are usually incurred by this department for "system downtime" in excess of a predefined threshold (for example, 99.5 percent availability for the month). If the team is down for more than the threshold, ETL is fined by its customers for each hour of downtime.

The database team is responsible for the collection and storage of emission and program-related data. This information is the key to most of ETL's systems. This team is responsible for the database being available "24-7," ensuring system integrity, and doing new database development work. Although the team has a general framework of how the data should be stored, each jurisdiction usually has its own unique requirements that this department must implement and monitor.

The Web development team is responsible for organizing the volumes of data collected and making this information readily available for government organizations to access through the Internet. By providing its customers with simple access to the volumes of data, this team ensures clients are able to monitor the program to assure it's achieving the expected result. For instance, customers want data from a failed emissions test to match with data from a passed test after the repairs have been completed, so that a "reduction-in-pollution" can be calculated. This group can telecommute but must work closely with the database team.

As mentioned above, there has been considerable change in the technology group at ETL. The challenge has been to attract and retain highly qualified individuals. In five years, only 20 percent of the members of ETL's original research and development team remain with the company, and the database and Web development groups have undergone a complete transformation with nearly all staff having left for other departments or companies.

The Nature of the Work

Projects teams at ETL usually consist of multiple individuals from each of the different groups. Many times the various members of the technology group must work on more than one project at a time due to the length of projects and the coordination required between departments. Ensuring the right human resourcing and the right mix of time spent on projects can be, and has been, difficult for ETL to manage.

Development work can often involve a lot of thinking and require a great amount of concentration. Interruptions therefore are avoided whenever possible. A minor five-minute interruption would delay work by much more than five minutes as it is often difficult for the IT staff to get back to where they have left off. As a result, ETL encourages its staff to use e-mail first whenever possible. Before picking up the telephone to call a co-worker, staff members will often think "Do I really need the answer this minute or can I formulate this request in an e-mail?"

Members of the support group have a rotating support policy. Since systems must be operational "24-7" this might require evening work. ETL has developed a three-week rotation for each area of support. This means a staff member is "on support" for one week, "on backup" for one week, and has one week off. When a staff member must provide evening support that person is required to carry a pager and cell phone so that he or she may be contacted quickly and respond to any problems immediately. In order to compensate its staff for providing "24-7" service, ETL has given its support personnel a choice: either extra time off or extra monetary compensation.

Because ETL wants to avoid costly and inconvenient evening service calls, all staff are encouraged to create systems and procedures that require little support so staff can spend more time on development.

ETL's Work Atmosphere

The corporate culture at ETL, and other similar high-tech companies in the area, resembles little the manufacturing giants of the 1970s and 80s. ETL's office space is designed to be unceremoniously simple for maximum capacity and efficiency. As such, the space is carefully divided into a number of equal-sized cubicles, each carefully linked together with miles of cables, networked printers, and desktop computers. Since office space in the GTA is extremely limited and expensive, ETL has found it necessary to carefully consider the peaks and valleys in its human resource requirements. At present, ETL occupies nearly 100 percent of its available office space with no opportunity to expand without a physical move to a new facility.

For the most part, the atmosphere at ETL is serious. Inside the office, noise is generated by the clicking of keyboards and the hum from printers. High-tech work is also characterized by its constant need for high-level communication and teamwork, as most projects are quite sizable and include large numbers of developers and support personnel. Employees prefer e-mail and voicemail to written memos and lengthy group meetings. Like many other companies, ETL has a flex-hour policy, which accommodates the untraditional flow of IT work. With the approach of deadlines or the implementation of new programs, staff are often required to work long or odd work hours, which can create frequent or sudden surges in the workload.

The Plan to Meet the Needs of the Drive Clean Contract

In the 20 months leading up to the launch of the Drive Clean project, Mike and Alison had met several times to develop a strategy to deal with the human resource needs of the new contract. Even before the Drive Clean contract was formally ETL's, they had decided that they would need to hire an additional 30 IT specialists in addition to any staff who left to pursue other opportunities (see Exhibit 3, Project Timeline).

During this time Mike had become almost famous for his speech on the importance of the Ontario contract. "We need to manage this project carefully," Mike would start. "We can't afford to relax with the recent successes in the south. We knew the

competition would be anxious to take the business in our own backyard. I don't have to remind anybody that the margin on the Drive Clean project is tighter than usual. We have the resources and ability to make this project a success—BUT we need to manage the details. We can't afford to have our costs get away on this one. Staffing will be our single largest expenditure and we can't afford to mismanage this asset."

After several meetings, Mike and Alison finally agreed that of the 30 new hires, only 13 of the specialists would be offered full-time, permanent employment. Mike argued that once the project progressed to the implementation phase, certain expertise would no longer be needed.

The Work-From-Home Program

To help attract high-quality staff Alison had made a pitch to Mike to broaden the company's work-from-home program. Alison had argued that "those who would work from home can enjoy the flexibility of making their own hours while not having the expense or frustration of commuting to work each day. Thirty new hires is going to be a challenge in itself. The work-from-home program will certainly help us to attract the right employees in the job market. As well, the company will also benefit by not needing to physically expand the office area or invest in additional office furniture."

With less than ten months left until the official launch date, Mike and Alison had spent the last few weeks meeting with each of the department leaders to explain their strategy for the upcoming increase in personnel. The work-from-home program could be extended to many of the new hires as well as some of the existing staff. Each department head would be responsible for managing

the telecommuting situation in his or her department, including making the decisions about who would telecommute and who would work from the office.

Although department managers were not mandated to have a predetermined number of employees work from home, on several occasions Mike made sure to reinforce the benefits of such a program. "Without the program," Mike would explain, "the company will be forced to undergo an expensive move to a new facility. Adding on to the existing building is not possible, and a move would be extremely expensive. The fact that almost half the new hires will be on a one-year contract makes the decision not to move an easy one. To keep costs in line, we simply must find a way to manage the temporary growth in personnel through the work-from-home program."

Despite a great deal of planning and communication, however, several of the department managers had begun to express concern to Alison about the expected lack of accountability, teamwork, and communication that would result from a more intensive work-from-home program. In the past, the program had been used only periodically by a select group of staff members or for a few other temporary situations. After a few days of rather intense debate about the new program, Alison decided to develop an internal document outlining the managerial implications of the program in order to quell fears and to reinforce the basis of the program (see Exhibit 1).

The Immediate Challenge

Up to this point, Alison's department had been successful in securing eight new programmers and developers. Most had come from the GTA and were able to offer a variety of experience and knowledge for the early stages of the Drive Clean program. In several cases, the potential for an extensive work-from-home program was a strong factor in the new hires' decision to join ETL. However, with 22 more positions vacant and a dwindling number of applications, Alison was feeling a bit overwhelmed. "How on earth can I possibly manage everything!" she wondered to herself. "We need to secure several more staff in the upcoming weeks, but in the meantime we really need to make some decisions on the work-from-home program. How is this going to work? Who's going to be involved and how well are the remaining staff going to adjust?"

Alison's train of thought was interrupted as Mike walked into her office. She realized with a jolt that she had been thinking back over these issues for almost an hour and Mike's conference call was over already.

"The Ministry of Transportation are keen for us to get going and we need to get our work-from-home program in place," Mike started, as he eased himself into a chair across from Alison. "You know we have some issues to address with our internal staff before we can really get our human resources planning finalized. You may have addressed some of the managers' fears with your recent memo," Mike offered, "but you're probably aware of the rumblings as much as I am. Staff aren't happy and I'm concerned about the effects on our ability to implement the Drive Clean contract."

Mike stood up to leave. "Staff are concerned that they will be overlooked for the work-from-home program and are speculating that communication and interpersonal challenges with all the new hires will result in the failure of the Ontario project. Shall we meet in my office at

around 5 p.m. to decide what's to be done? I'd appreciate your proposals for making sure we have the human resources to complete the contract."

As Mike left her office, Alison realized that time was becoming increasingly tight to get the project off the ground. She knew she had to have some pretty convincing human resourcing proposals for her boss that afternoon and that she would have to address the issues surrounding the work-from-home program once and for all. She was beginning to wonder if the program would cause more harm than good to her human resources planning at ETL. Teleworking might be a great staffing solution in terms of cost savings and the bottom line, but not at the expense of destroying existing working relationships and processes. ∎

Exhibit 1

Memo

To: Department Managers

From: Alison Hayes

Date: March 23, 20XX

Re: The 'Work-from-Home' Project: A GUIDE for MANAGERS

It is important for you, as a manager, to remember that close supervision does not always mean good supervision; good supervision may be achieved without being close in proximity.

Here are some specifics that will help you achieve your goals:

Management skills. The same management skills used to manage employees working in the office apply to those telecommuting.

Work Assignments. Set up a means of communicating deadlines and project requirements. Discuss the expected quality and other criteria that might affect the successful completion of tasks. Communicate to employees what must be done, when it must be done, and who is to do it. The communication may take the form of a phone call, a weekly meeting, or memo. Use whatever means of communication is most comfortable for you. As a manager of off-site employees, the time you spend communicating with the remote workers will dictate the calibre of work they produce. Spend time communicating clearly and concisely the expectations you have of those employees.

Review Work Status. Set up intermediate periods to determine the progress of the tasks the employees are performing. The assessment may be at a designated point during the program, upon completion of certain tasks, or on a recurring basis, such as once a week on Monday.

Timetables. Work with these employees to develop reasonable and timely goals. The employees will clearly understand their workload and will be more focused in their work if they are following a timetable.

Coach and Develop Employees' Capabilities. There is limited time to spend with your remote employees to reinforce behaviour. Make the most of that time. Always reinforce positive behaviour. Bring unsatisfactory performance to the employee's attention immediately. Develop employee capabilities to correct deficiencies. Use the communications tools available to you to provide your employees with timely feedback. The feedback may be via voice mail, electronic mail, a phone call, or a face-to-face conversation.

Also remember that when managing telecommuting, the focus should not be on how the employee accomplishes the task, but whether the task is accomplished in a timely and complete manner. The bottom line is...you should already be familiar with these skills and be using them while supervising your employees located in the office.

If you need any assistance, please feel to contact me directly.

Exhibit 2   Evergreen Technologies Limited: Organization Chart

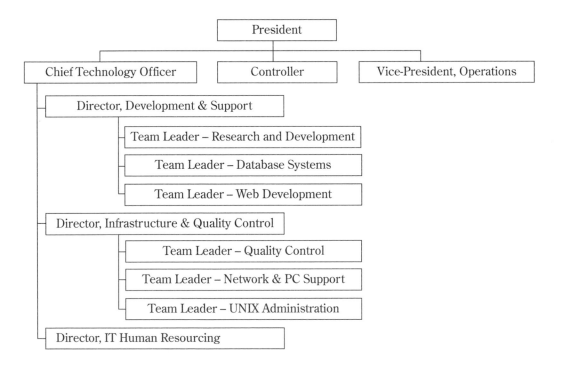

Exhibit 3   Evergreen Technologies Limited: Organization Chart

Project: Ontario-Drive Clean   Program Mgr: John Bergeron   Web: Hanish Bhatia   HR: Alison Hayes

Development: Carol Kilmer   Support: Mike Mauer   Database: Jamo Surmakki

STATUS UPDATE:

SCHEDULE

	Year 1		Year 2											Year 3					
	Nov.	Dec.	Jan.	Feb.	March	April	May	June	July	Aug.	Sept.	Oct.	Nov.	Dec.	Jan.	Feb.	March	April	Nov.	Jan.

Technical Plan Develop	●————————● 21st
HR requirement plan	● 3rd
Recruitment	●——————————————● 12th 23rd
Software - Phase I	●————● 21st 1st
Software - Phase II	●————————● 1st 10th
Test Facility Setup	●————————● 18th 15th
Software - Phase III	●————————● 10th 5th
Station Testing	●—● 15th 20th ●————● 5th 3rd
Web Access Testing	●————● 16th 17th
Mock Launch & Testing	● 30th
Program Launch	● 15th Proj. Complete

C A S E 1 3
Motorola: Seeking Direction

Up until the mid 1990s, Motorola Inc., world famous for its Six Sigma quality control program, was an early success story in the computer/electronics age and viewed on Wall Street as an American Icon. Motorola had moved from being a decentralized but integrated, narrowly focused electronics firm at $3 billion sales in 1980 to being a decentralized and disintegrated broad portfolio firm at $30 billion in sales in 2001.[1] Motorola had been one of the world's leading providers of wireless communications, semiconductors, electronic systems, components, and services. Its cellular phone, analog equipment, and pager products were identified among the very best in the mid 1990s. However, increased competition, the Asian economic crisis, and its short-sighted failure to quickly and fully embrace the digital revolution severely tarnished its operating results and image. In the April, 2004 issue of Business Week, Motorola ranked 308 of the top 500 companies of the S&P 500, with 3 F grades and 3 D grades out of 8 categories.[2] The question becomes: what can Motorola do to return to its former high-performance ways and what can new CEO Ed Zander do to change the recent record of failures, intracompany turf battles, and oversights?

Note: The blue underscored words/phrases in this case indicate Internet links provided in the on-line version (http://www.wiley.com/canada/schermerhorn).

The Making of Motorola

Motorola Inc. was founded by Paul V. Galvin in 1928. Motorola's long history of technological innovation began in the 1930s with the first car radio. In World War II, the Motorola Handie-Walkie Talkie went to war for the U.S. Army. Under the brand name "Motorola," suggesting "sound in motion" the company name was changed to Motorola, Inc. in 1947.[3] It was the goal of Motorola to provide products that would give people the time and freedom to explore new worlds and handle daily tasks in the most efficient manner.

Motorola has accomplished a number of firsts, including the first rectangular television picture tube, the first practical car radio, and pagers. In 1988, Motorola won the first Malcom Baldrige National Quality Award in recognition of quality in American business.

Beginning in 1987, Motorola began the design of IRIDIUM. The system was a satellite-based, wireless communications network. It consisted of 66 interconnected, low-orbiting satellites that delivered voice, data, fax, and paging through a hand-held phone. The development of IRIDIUM was intended to provide customers, including business professionals and travelers, with high-quality service at a reasonable rate.

As Motorola continued to expand its worldwide presence in the global marketplace through products and services, the need for talented personnel to uphold these established standards increased. In recognition of this, Motorola demonstrated a high commitment to seeking and developing a broad base of knowledgeable, highly trained employees, as evident through their innovative programs, provided by the establishment of Motorola University, and through the offering of expensive benefit plans to all Motorola associates.

Organizational Culture in Motorola

In the early 1990s, Motorola was recognized as a true high-performance organization with its innovations and socially responsible attitude. Its organizational culture was identified as a source of competitive advantage to the firm and one to be copied. Working in quality teams, members sought to provide the highest level of customer satisfaction, measuring defects in incidents per billion. These teams, however, were not always unified with other teams in the company. Motorola also earmarked more than $100 million a year for training, with everyone in the organization spending at least a week each year in the classroom at Motorola University, courtesy of the company.[4]

Motorola listed its fundamental objectives as total customer satisfaction: "To serve every customer better than our competitors do with products and services of excellent value and quality and thereby earn continued trust and support".[5]

Motorola wishes to accomplish this objective with respect for the individual, a statement it makes clear in its shared beliefs. Somewhere in the 1990s, this philosophy of satisfying customer needs became diluted by organizational egos.

Motorola's People

To treat each employee with dignity, as an individual; to maintain an open atmosphere where direct communication with employees affords the opportunity to contribute to the maximum of their potential and fosters unity of purpose with Motorola; to provide personal opportunities for training and development to ensure the most capable and most effective work force; to respect senior service; to compensate fairly by salary, benefits, and incentives; to promote on the basis of capability; and to practice the commonly accepted policies of equal opportunity and affirmative action.

Integrity and Ethics

To maintain the highest standards of honesty, integrity, and ethics in all aspects of our business—with customers, suppliers, employees, governments, and society at large—and to comply with the laws of each country and community in which we operate.[6]

From a proponent of leadership training to a leader in quality control processes, Motorola has created an internal climate that fostered high standards in a high-performance culture. The firm depended on Total Customer Satisfaction Teams (TCS) to ensure the firm's commitment to quality products and service. These teams were made up of almost 30 percent of Motorola's employees, and a goal of 10 times reduction of defects every two years puts pressure on the teams to constantly devise new ways to develop and deliver their products and services.[7]

However, organizational culture can sometimes be a two-edged sword. Strong and successful organizational cultures, like Motorola, may contribute to high performance for extended periods of time but may actually result in an inability to adjust when conditions change. It is important to foster a balance between stability and flexibility for change; an objective that is difficult to maintain in a global competition that has no respect for previous accomplishments or industrial icons. For the large firms, like Motorola, success in the short term causes problems with inflexibility toward paradigms of changing situations in the long term.

What Happened to Motorola on the Way to the 21st Century?

In early June 1998, then Motorola CEO Chris Galvin announced that the company would take a $1.95 billion charge and lay off 15,000 employees. Currently, Motorola is down to 88,000 employees from a peak of 147,000. Motorola's semiconductor business, which grew 23 percent in 1995, slowed to a 1 percent growth rate in 1998.[8] In recent years Motorola stock dropped dramatically, with a 52 week high on July 27, 2004 of $20.89, to a low of $9.03, and its share of the cellular phone market had plummeted as Motorola couldn't produce color-screen phones in volume.[9] Samsung came from nowhere to become the number two player by revenue after Nokia in the cell phone industry. Motorola's semiconductor unit had a lock on PDAs as recently as three years ago, but lost the lead to Intel. In 2003, the company eked out annual profits of $893 million on sales of $27 billion.[10] This profit would have been even less without the revenues from Motorola's chip business. Critics have come to a simple conclusion: Motorola does too many things—and not enough of them well. The company has earned the unenviable reputation of developing killer technology that got stuck in the labs.

Maggie Wilderotter, a former top executive with AT&T Wireless Services, provided insight into Motorola's problems. In the early 1990s, 85 percent of the cell phones sold to subscribers were made by Motorola. Their flip phones, the most advanced at the time, were in hot demand. AT&T decided that the future of cellular was digital, and over the next few years Wilderotter met repeatedly with the managers of Motorola at Motorola's Schaumberg, Illinois headquarters, urging them to develop a digital phone. Motorola kept stalling until the beginning of 1996, not long after AT&T had rolled out its digital network. Motorola unveiled its StarTAC phone: light, beautiful—and "analog". AT&T had no choice but to turn to cellular phone manufacturers Nokia and Ericsson for "digital" handsets. By the end of 1997, fewer than 40 percent of AT&T's wireless cell phones were made by Motorola.[11]

"It was bizarre," says Wilderotter. "We were very forthright with what we wanted. I don't know if they didn't listen or they thought it wasn't going to happen. It is absolutely amazing to me that they lost their way."[12] In 1998, Nokia replaced Motorola as the leading supplier of mobile handsets, a position Motorola had held since the mobile phone industry began.[13]

Much of Nokia's success was based on its digital technology. Motorola remained the world leader in the U.S. market where digital was slower to take off. When Motorola did provide a digital alternative in its popular Strata model, it retailed for $500, compared to Nokia's 6100 model selling at $200 with twice the battery life.[14]

Inspection of the company's IRIDIUM satellite system uncovered other weaknesses. While the system eliminated "dead cells" by providing complete global coverage, it came with a very expensive price tag. The phones have the look and weight of cell phones years ago along with a thick, ugly, black antenna.[15] Unfortunately, in order to function, the system needed a completely unobstructed view of the sky, with tall buildings and even thick foliage blocking transmissions.

Some of Motorola's troubles were external, including a drop in semiconductor sales due to the Asian economic crisis, increased competition in cellular products, and a decline in pager sales. Motorola tried to meet these challenges by attempting to restructure its operations in combination with cost-cutting measures. The situation illuminated the need for a culture that was both strong and responsive to such external factors. In the quickly changing high-technology field, companies were being forced to make rapid and costly choices among competing technologies. In facing the challenges of rapid technology, including the staying power of new products, Motorola appears laden with a history of 75 years' worth of stuffiness, obscure acronyms, and lack of a unified team approach.

Another concern for many investors and analysts was the presence and performance of Chris Galvin as chief executive officer (CEO) since 1997. Galvin abruptly left the company in September, 2003. He has since been replaced by new CEO Ed Zander, a loquacious individual of Sun Microsystems fame. Since arriving on the scene, Zander has been traveling worldwide, shaking hands, and getting an "earful" of adverse opinions of Motorola's lack of, or delays of, new electronic products by unhappy customers.[16]

Even before Zander's arrival, by 2002 Motorola made a plunge into digital technology, introducing a broad range of innovative products using digital technology. Zander has, however, begun to articulate a vision of Motorola in terms of its remaining four big end markets: the individual, the home, the auto, and the big organizations, which includes governments.[17] His focus will include collaboration across the company, targeting the mega-large business customers, potentially merging more units within the company, shedding employees, and developing new ways to combine wireless communications and the Net. Since Zander's arrival, Motorola has made impressive performances. On July 20, 2004 the company reported second-quarter sales up a healthy 41% compared to an anemic 2003. The star of these gains was the mobile-phone division, which has boosted revenues 67% to $3.9 billion dollars.[18] Two-way radios have received a big boost from increased spending by local and national government agencies on homeland-security concerns.

Motorola did decide to drop its boom-or-bust chip division. This leaves Motorola with essentially five businesses: cell phones, infrastructure equipment, two-way radio systems, the cable TV division, and one of Motorola's few recent success stories: electronic equipment for automobiles. Plans may be in the making for further mergers of units.

Review Questions

1. Discuss Motorola's relative success at the functions of organizational culture presented in the case.

2. How did Motorola lose its leading position in the electronics technology industry?

3. Discuss the various options managers might use in attempting to change the culture at Motorola.

4. How do you think employees at Motorola will react to the efforts of Ed Zander to bring the company back to a leader? ∎

C A S E   1 4

Sandra Lee, Principal of South Heights Public School

by Robert Ellis and Raymond Adamson

Part A

Sandra Lee hit bottom in February 1998. She was physically and emotionally drained by her experiences as the new Principal of an inner city school. Her previous teaching career had been marked by stunning success — in fact, she had gained a wide reputation as a leading educational innovator. All of this had meant nothing when she encountered the brick walls of South Heights Public School. After six months in which she attempted to infuse the school with a new vitality, she could see few changes that had made a difference in the lives of her students. Indeed, the only significant change was a campaign to get rid of her launched by a group of disaffected teachers. Should she resign and go back to the classroom she so loved or should she forge ahead?

The South Side

South Heights Public School of the Sherwood School Board is located in a small city in southern Ontario. The city is only a short commute from Toronto, and is widely known as an automobile manufacturing centre in Canada. Most of the inhabitants either work at the auto plants or at the other manufacturing and service enterprises that support them. There is also a significant commuting population that arrives and then leaves the city on a daily basis.

The school is located on the "South Side", in an area that was once a commercial centre. Over the years the focus of commerce has shifted to suburban shopping centres. The only recent commercial developments have been some fast food restaurants and a few service businesses, but they come and go and do little to create any sense of prosperity or revival for the area.

The residences around the school have also been largely neglected. Most of these were originally constructed as row housing for the immigrants who came to work at the auto plants after WWII. As the families of these workers prospered and moved on to other areas of the city and the province, their homes were converted to low rent and subsidized housing. Most of the current residents were attracted to the area for this reason: It is one of the cheapest places to live in Ontario. The South Side is known locally as the "welfare zone" since most of the residents are dependent on some form of government support.

There is chronic unemployment of about 70 percent in the South Heights school area. Many of the families are headed by a single parent, mostly women, and some of these families are third and fourth generation welfare recipients. The South Side is only a step from the North Side but it is a world away in terms of economic and social status. People on the North Side generally own their homes, have new cars, send their children to college, and most important, are employed. This level of stability and material well-being is almost non-existent on the South Side because the residents are largely transients, who appear unable to find or keep jobs for any sustained period of time.

This transience in their working lives is also reflected in the family structures. Many of the single mothers are young and became mothers in their mid to late teens. They were forced into major family responsibilities quite abruptly and were ill-prepared for their new parental role. They often had no network of family and few friends to advise them or support them. The men who filled the family position of "father" often stayed only a short time. The combination of these conditions of early motherhood,

absence of support networks, and replacement of the original spouse, created severe stresses. These were frequently expressed in violent confrontations among family members and often involved the children directly. Violence or threats of violence by parents and open defiance by children were commonplace methods of dealing with problems. This violent and defiant behaviour was frequently transferred to the school setting. Equally disturbing, many of the children came to school hungry, without haven eaten breakfast, and sometimes "with a bag of chips for lunch."

Another feature of the South Side culture was its association with drugs, violence and petty crime. Although the extent of this activity was less than what occurs in the worst areas of large cities, it further served to undermine the sense of security of children and parents.

South Heights Public School

Just as the South Side was neglected and run down, so was the school itself. Built in 1916 to serve children from kindergarten to grade 8, it was typical of the stolid and enduring institutional style of the times. With its brick walls and vaulting ceilings and windows, it was functional, but grey, drab and uninviting. Virtually nothing had been done over the years to renew the building, spruce it up or even keep it very clean. The school stood as a metaphor for the whole South Side. It was a challenge to the educational system, much as the area was to the municipality, but there seemed no collective will to change or redeem either one.

The school's location and reputation frightened off most experienced teachers. South Heights was often a first posting for new teachers and administrators, a place "where you would pay your dues." It hadn't always been so – indeed, the school had a rich and proud history. Past students

and teachers had fond memories of their days at South Heights and witnessed the continual neglect and decay of recent times with considerable regret.

One particular difficulty for the school was that a significant number of the parents had negative experiences when they were part of the school system. Many of them had been school dropouts and many others just turned off by formal schooling. In spite of this, most parents saw education as important for the lives of their children. The problem was that they did not know how to help their children be successful in school. Apart from this, given the conditions in which they lived, many parents were primarily concerned with survival. As a consequence, the parents did not get involved in the education process and did not particularly encourage school activities or interests for their children.

The school had such a poor reputation that it was continually rumoured to be closing. In fact, this was a focus of debate within the School Board: Should South Heights remain open or be closed? The School Board saw an aging school with a multitude of problems, and little else. As a result, very little was invested in the school to either improve or even maintain it. The result of all these forces was a school with little in the way of a future or hope.

An opportunity arose in 1997 to change this dismal picture. The Principal of South Heights was moving to another school and some senior officials of the Sherwood School Board saw this as a chance to intervene in this situation. The chair of the publicly-elected School Trustees commented, "South Heights had become a dumping ground for bad teachers. I was determined to veto the appointment of anyone who wasn't going to change this place." In the end the choice was a young Vice-Principal who had gained a strong reputation for innovative programs for children with disabilities, but who had relatively little administrative experience for the type of situation she would encounter at South Heights.

The New Principal: Sandra Lee

Sandra Lee became the Principal of South Heights Public School in 1997, coming upon the scene amid the conditions previously described. She was not happy about being placed at South Heights. Friends and peers advised her that South Heights would be a difficult situation to endure even for a short period of time. However, one did not turn down an administrative appointment. To do so would have effectively ended her career in administration. Since, in her own words, she was "very ambitious" about her career progress, she took the job. She came directly from a Vice-Principal position at a new model public school and the change to South Heights was far greater and more traumatic than she could ever have imagined.

Sandra's background in education was somewhat unusual in that her decision to become a teacher was taken later in life than most, after she had immigrated to Canada from Trinidad. She already had two children and she waited until her youngest was age two before she began her educational career. Sandra graduated from Teachers College as a special education teacher and embraced this as an anchor for her whole career. She had begun her practice teaching with mentally handicapped children and this early experience served to confirm her choice – this was what she wanted to do.

She spent the next 3 years working for the School Board on special education programs. Her specific focus at the time was children with developmental disabilities, which included children who were functioning at the lowest level within the educational system. Her goal was to discover ways that would really make a difference in their ability to learn and consequently in their quality of life. She also wanted to improve their status in the educational system and to attract many more competent educators into that part of the system. It was around this time that she developed what was to become an enduring foundation of her philosophy of education that, "there is always a way, you just have to find it." Her time at the School Board Office was followed by another three-year stint developing diagnostic and training classes for the learning disabled. Her proudest accomplishment was a writing program for children with learning disabilities. This was a singularly successful activity which provided her with a high profile at the Board as well as with other educators from all over the continent who came to observe the program. This program reflected her belief that, "... every child could bring out their ideas in writing."

From this foundation arose the idea of a Writing Guild, where children in the regular school program would write and present their own work during Education Week. She envisioned children in each town and city presenting their work to parents and members of the community, with panels of authors and illustrators to give the children guidance. To make this happen, she enlisted the support of a socially and politically skilful Principal to co-chair the Writing Guild. This support enabled the writing program to be successfully implemented in schools across the Board.

The final three-year period prior to her appointment as Vice-Principal involved a combination of expanding and developing her educational programs and positioning herself for promotion in the system. First, she enrolled in and completed a Masters of Education degree. She also took a leadership course through the School Board during this time, a course that emphasized the importance of both vision and a team approach to leadership. Participants in these courses and, more important, her mentors at the School Board, began to persuade her that she could have a wider impact on the school system as a Principal or executive administrator, than she could as a classroom teacher. Sandra finally succumbed to this advice and applied to be a Vice-Principal. She felt she was getting valuable support from senior Board administrators both for her programs and for her career moves. Whatever happened, Sandra was steadfast in her view that career moves would be taken only if they helped to promote programs she had developed for writing and for children with learning disabilities. Her application for Vice-Principal was successful and she was placed at Academy Hill Public School.

During her first year, Academy Hill was selected by the School Board as a pilot project for developing a cooperative learning program at the public school level. In this program children learned to work together in positive ways to build social and team skills. This provided a friendly environment for innovative programming. Quite conveniently, the Principal at Academy Hill was not very familiar with new program development, thus giving Sandra a fairly free rein. Once again her efforts were very successful and boosted her strong reputation for implementing new educational concepts. Indeed, she was gaining the attention and support of educators at the forefront of educational innovation and change.

Following her two-year stay at Academy Hill she took an internal Board transfer to Don Valley Public School. Her placement at Don Valley had been carefully planned to cultivate her administrative skills. Her new Principal worked with and managed people very well. She was advised by her mentors to observe and emulate those skills, with this note of caution: "… sometimes you go too fast. You think so far ahead and move so quickly, you leave people behind in the dust. We want you to learn that change takes time. You won't always have us around… ."

Welcome to South Heights Public School

Sandra's first visit to South Heights School was a horrifying experience. She arrived fresh from Don Valley, a new model suburban public school, and the contrast was shocking. The schools she had experience with were bright, happy places that welcomed students and teachers alike. To Sandra, South Heights looked dark and depressing. It exuded an institutional atmosphere from its square box-like shape to its brick exterior. There was some grass but no flowers to be seen anywhere. The school may have once been appealing but now it seemed to be part of a world that years of modern education has passed by completely.

While the outside was forbidding enough, the inside was even worse. The paint on some of the walls appeared to be original and on others it was peeling in patches. The dominant colours were green, yellow and burgundy and it created a drab and sombre effect. The classrooms were very spartan, containing little decoration beyond the desks and chalkboards. Classroom displays were neither colourful, nor eye appealing. Sandra found out later that decorations and other classroom embellishments were repeatedly stolen and any attempt to create a more appealing atmosphere had long been abandoned. The staff room was located in

a former coal bin in the basement. Isolated from the rest of the school, it was more squalid than the rest of the school, although it was decorated in the same style.

Sandra was not only shocked but also felt hurt and angry that a school would be allowed to deteriorate to such a state. Her first trip to South Heights was in early spring and she decided immediately that the first order of the day would be to clean and paint the place. The Board arranged for painting the school. Sandra enlisted family and friends and spent most of the summer sprucing up and decorating a new staff room. She also had murals painted in the school. The notion was to create "bright and happy" scenes and colours to relieve some of the interior gloom. Sandra admits that she did not have a clear strategy for improving conditions at the school beyond these initial steps. She essentially had no idea of what she should do next.

The first days of school had further surprises in store. Arriving early one morning, Sandra observed some parents waiting with their children in the schoolyard. She approached the parents, introduced herself and began with a few pleasantries. She could feel they were rather reticent and uncomfortable but she wanted to make contact and very shortly invited them inside for coffee. There was a brief hesitation and then one father blurted, "Lady, I don't want to have coffee with you. Just go to hell." Sandra had arrived at South Heights.

The confrontation with the parents foreshadowed what was going on throughout the school. In the halls, in the playground, in the classroom, students shouted incessantly at each other, and if shouting didn't resolve the issue, they slugged it out. Cathy, a first year teacher who arrived at the same time as Sandra, described what she encountered: "I grew up in a big family, a protected world. My initial reaction

in coming here was utter shock. When I was a kid, I wouldn't have looked at a teacher sideways. These children have grown up where they are not respected, they think it is normal, they don't know any different."

The staff knew the home life for most of the children reinforced this aggressive behaviour and the only responses the children seemed to understand were shouting even louder in return and using physical restraint to keep them in line. Some staff were shouting almost as much as the children! Sandra was appalled but the staff seemed hardly aware of their conduct. There were certainly many other school problems, no less discouraging, but these highly vocal confrontations seemed symbolic of a basic mistrust and resentment between the school and the families it was meant to serve.

Equally disturbing was how low standards had fallen in the school. Some staff were continually late for the start of their classes; others did not appear to have lesson plans prepared for their classes. The books in the school library appeared to be shelved on a random basis, and the library itself was closed as often as it was open. The school was not even kept clean; dust and dirt accumulated in the hallways and classrooms. Sandra felt she had to act quickly and she soon called a staff-planning meeting. The purpose was to devise a plan, at least for the year, to give the staff a sense of mission.

The planning meetings were conducted as a series so that the task was not perceived as too formidable. The format utilized the cooperative group techniques that Sandra had learned at Academy Hill and Don Valley. This cooperative technique involved assigning roles to each group member so that each person had to interact with others in order to fulfill their roles. This was intended to build team spirit as the plan was being developed.

The simple objective of the planning sessions was to identify what staff were doing that should be continued or expanded and what should be eliminated. A formal planning document evolved from these meetings identifying both positive and negative practices. Many of the items seemed to have Sandra's stamp on them but she insisted that the plan arose through consensus.

The central features of the school plan were grouped around the motto, "Together we light the way." This concept focused on teacher, student, and parent relationships that implied a partnership in the learning process. In keeping with this theme, other objectives were developed. These included an agreement that the learning process would be student-centred; focused on student needs, not teacher needs. It was also decided that teachers would make every effort to model appropriate behaviours for the students. This was obviously directed at eliminating aggressive verbal and physical confrontations among students, and between staff and students. However, it also included many other things, such as being on time, having lesson plans prepared for each class, standing at the door with a smile on your face and welcoming each student as they entered class, giving parents clear and detailed information on their child's progress on report cards, and generally taking personal responsibility for creating a good learning environment.

According to the plan, teachers were also expected to work together developing lesson plans so that both the content and consistency of instruction would improve. Teachers were responsible for the students' learning development, particularly their reading and writing skills. This presumably meant that teachers were accountable if a student's perform-

ance fell below some reasonable level of expectation.

Two months later, Sandra asked herself what had changed as a result of the school plan. In short, the answer was very little! The staff who had previously arrived late, and those who came to class unprepared, continued to do so. Those who engaged in verbal and physical confrontations with students continued this practice. She did take some comfort in the efforts of several new, enthusiastic teachers to implement the plan. She was also pleased that one of her initiatives to get parents more involved in the school was having some success. A group called "Parent Rap" was formed to bring parents and teachers together to discuss issues affecting the children. Unfortunately, just three parents were coming to the meetings on a regular basis.

Most senior teachers, however, were not cooperating with her attempts to change the school. Many of these teachers had not been to a professional development workshop in years, and were not simply sceptical toward her new approach to education, they were openly hostile and confrontational. Their opposition rested on the conviction that an authoritarian manner was the only thing that worked with these children. Further, their scepticism of new approaches had been strengthened by the failure of past efforts to make meaningful changes at South Heights.

Some of the confrontations with senior staff were quite unpleasant. For example, she refused to sign the report cards of one senior teacher because he wrote one or two words on each report card, rather than the detailed feedback they had agreed to provide to the parents. To the teacher this activity seemed pointless: "Would any of the parents bother reading this!" This teacher confronted her in the hallway and yelled at her in front of students and teachers. She told

him quietly, but firmly to go into her office. Once in her office he continued to yell and swept everything off her desk onto the floor. She received a visit the next day from an official of the teachers' union who said the problems she was having with this teacher could best be explained as, "... a new female Principal trying to intimidate the males in the system." This situation was similar to other hostile confrontations with the librarian and several of the senior teachers. She had only a vague knowledge of her rights as Principal to enforce standards, as standards had never been an issue in her previous experience.

Some of the senior staff had recently begun a campaign to have her dismissed, and tried to enlist other teachers and parents to their cause, in their words, "to save the children." A senior teacher who was sympathetic to Sandra's attempts to improve the school told her that the campaign was gaining momentum. She also confided to Sandra that she was not fully convinced of the ideas underlying the school plan.

Two events around this time brought her to an emotional low point in her life. Her father died suddenly, unexpectedly at the beginning of December. No one close to her had ever died and the pain she felt was "absolutely unendurable." She did not look forward to returning to South Heights after the Christmas break. A second event shortly thereafter brought her to the point of resignation. One day in early February she asked a female custodian to clean something up. The custodian screamed and yelled that she had "...ridiculous expectations ... the school was fine before you came here ... why don't you go back to where you came from!" Sandra was crushed. It was the "first time in my career I had experienced racism." Equally bad, she realized that "...even the custodian felt she could lace into me."

She drove home in tears. She knew "this is it: I can't take this any more." Should she resign now as Principal of South Heights? She could quickly return to developing programs for children with learning disabilities; indeed, the School Board would welcome her back. On the other hand, the children of South Heights desperately needed her help. The pain of her failure to make a meaningful change in their lives was acute. But if she stayed, what could she do to transform South Heights?

Discussion Questions

1. What are the problems here?
2. What are the important aspects of the situation confronting Sandra Lee upon her arrival at South Heights?
3. Why has the plan failed?
4. What theories and concepts help to explain the events in this case?
5. Should Sandra Lee resign and return to the classroom? What are the implications for her career if she chooses to return to the classroom? If she chooses to press on?
6. If she chooses to stay and attempt to transform South Heights, what should she do? What are the reasonable alternatives? What course of action should she pursue? How should she implement these actions?

Part B

After a weekend of soul-searching, Sandra Lee could see things more clearly. Her first six months as the new Principal of South Heights Public School had been pure hell. Sandra had been on the verge of resignation, but now she was determined to stay on as Principal and transform South Heights, a poor inner-city school. Her vision for the future of South Heights was taking shape: The school would become "the

heartbeat of the community." The central question concerning the future of South Heights, however, was not what the school should become, but rather how would it get there?

South Heights Public School

South Heights is located in an industrial city in Southern Ontario, a short distance from Toronto. The school is found on the "South Side" of the city, in an area that is both poor and neglected. Most of the families on the South Side are on welfare or other forms of government assistance. There is chronic unemployment of about 70% in the South Heights school area.

A single parent, who is typically the mother, was the head of many of the families. These women often became mothers at an early age and lacked parental skills. Shouting and threats of violence were commonly used techniques to discipline children. Instability was also a feature of the South Side culture, with family members changing and families moving in and out of the area. Involvement in the school on the part of parents and the broader community was virtually non-existent. South Heights Public School reflected the inherent neglect and lack of hope that characterized the South side area.

The future of the school was a subject of debate within the School Board: Should South Heights remain open or be closed? In 1997 the Principal of South Heights was moving to another school and senior officials at the Board saw an opportunity to change South Heights through fresh leadership. They selected a young Vice-Principal who had built a strong reputation for developing innovative education programs for children with learning disabilities, but who had little experience with children in the inner city.

Sandra Lee, the New Principal

Sandra Lee was appalled by what she encountered at South Heights in the summer of 1997. With its brick walls, vaulting ceiling and windows, South Heights appeared to be a cold, uninviting place. What was inside was even worse. The schools Sandra knew were bright, happy places that welcomed students and staff alike. South Heights was a shocking contrast: Classrooms and hallways were dirty, with paint peeling off the walls. The staff room at South Heights was in a former coal bin in the basement. It was filthy and decrepit, leaving anyone to wonder how staff could relax, let alone eat and mingle there. Sandra commented, "I would have died if I had eaten something there." What was most disturbing, however, was the level of violence within the school. Children settled their differences by shouting at each other, and when that didn't work, by fighting it out. Some staff members were also engaged in shouting and using physical force to control the children.

Sandra Lee set about to quickly change South Heights. She worked with staff to come up with a plan to change the school, encompassed by the motto, "Together We Light the Way". The plan involved teachers working together as a team to improve the quality of instruction, to create a warm and positive environment for the students and to provide parents with information about their child's progress. After several months, very little had changed at the school. In fact, Sandra was met with hostility from senior staff when she attempted to enforce elements of the plan. It was ironic that the only significant change she could see after 6 months was a campaign initiated by some disaffected senior staff members to have her dismissed.

Several events around this time brought Sandra to an emotional low point in her life. Her father died suddenly in December and the pain was "unendurable". In February 1998, Sandra approached the custodian at South Heights and asked her to clean up some leaves that had fallen off a plant onto the walkway. The custodian yelled and screamed that Sandra "…had ridiculous expectations… the school was fine before you came here" and told her to "…go back to where you came from." Sandra was crushed. This was the first racist comment she had experienced in her career. The effects of this confrontation and all the other events of the recent months led Sandra to the point of resignation. She drove home in tears and knew that "This is it: I can't take this anymore. Even the custodian felt she had the right to talk to a Principal that way, something had to change."

That weekend she weighed the option of resigning as Principal and returning to the classroom: "I'm a good teacher; 100 places would hire me at the drop of a hat. I refuse to let people treat me this way." Finally, the decision was made and she wrote a letter of resignation as Principal of South Heights Public School. "I've shed enough tears for this place." She told her husband to take the letter to the School Board Office on Monday morning. Her husband was alarmed, as he had never seen her quit anything in her life. He called a teacher friend who came over to the house to try to persuade her to stay at South Heights. Her friend's first line of argument didn't work: "You're going to wreck your career, you'll never get a chance to be a Principal again!" Sandra was not moved: "I don't care about a career where people treat me like this." The second line of argument had the desired effect: "So you're going to leave those kids that you said needed your help. You're not quitting those teachers, you're quitting those kids! Who's going to help

them if you leave? Who's going to make a difference for them?" For Sandra, "Once I saw it as giving up on them, I knew I had to stay. I had my focus again."

Sandra Lee Takes Charge

"Once I went back to South Heights on Monday morning, I was determined to take control and handle this situation. There was nothing worse that could happen to me. I had decided that I was the Principal of South Heights. I found the custodian in the staff room bragging to others about how she had told me off. I was furious that she was bold enough to do this. The first thing I did was call the custodian's supervisor and inform him that I didn't want the custodian back in the school. Under the Education Act, I am in charge of all personnel in the school and I asserted my rights as Principal to refuse anyone entry into the school."

"That afternoon I had a meeting with 5 people: the custodian, her supervisor, and 3 representatives from the union. I was not intimidated. Her supervisor didn't support what I was doing. One of the guys who represented her from the union was someone I had known at a previous school. I had treated him very well and he knew I was a good person. I told them I would not have someone speaking to the Principal like that. They knew she could be fired and they thought that is what I wanted. I personally didn't care what they did with her, but she wasn't coming back to the school. They asked if an apology and a transfer would be acceptable to me and I agreed to that."

"I had changed in the way I spoke, in the way I carried myself, in how much confidence I had. Before, I was in the 'nice girl' syndrome. I've never been authoritarian, never had to say, 'I expect this'. I may have presented myself as a weak person to the

staff. Now, I spoke to them as Principal of South Heights."

Sandra decided that she would not continue to tolerate some of the more objectionable behaviour she had encountered at South Heights. She began to document incidents involving a teacher who had yelled at her in front of staff and students and in a resultant meeting, angrily swept everything off her desk onto the floor. She also made her expectations regarding his behaviour very clear. When he "…slammed a kid against the wall, he was gone within two hours." Further, as Principal, Sandra had the power to re-assign staff to the classroom and did so in the case of the librarian who shelved books on a random basis and kept the library closed as often as it was open. Since he didn't want to be in the classroom, he soon put in for a transfer to another school. The teacher who led the mutiny held the position of academic resource person and Sandra also re-assigned her to the classroom. She replaced her with one of the new teachers who had been very supportive of the original change plan. The leader of the mutiny soon transferred as well.

Sandra's Philosophy for South Heights

Sandra reviewed the plan that she and the staff had developed last October. It was meant to get the staff working together as a team to transform South Heights into a warm and welcoming school with higher standards for both the staff and for the children. Teachers would also serve as role models to the children. In her words, "Most of all, I've got to show the kids that this is a place they want to be. We need to create a warm and welcoming atmosphere that is conducive to learning. No one will yell and scream at one another in this building. They have so much of this at home. This is not just a place of teaching and learning, but a place of healing and learning. We need to demonstrate that we love you, we care about you, and create a family here."

Hiring New Staff

She had encountered nothing but resistance from most senior staff in her attempts to implement this plan. Several members of the staff who opposed her would now be leaving and these were people that had given her the most trouble. This provided Sandra with the opportunity to hire teachers who would be more receptive to new ideas. Further, Sandra and several of the staff who had been supportive of change could work as a team in this recruitment process. Together they sought teachers for the coming year who "cared deeply" about the kids, were "enthusiastic" about changing a school like South Heights, and believed in "cooperation and teamwork". Near the end of each interview, candidates were asked, "Are you willing to make the commitment that will be required to make a difference for these kids?" In one case they interviewed a teacher who had previously received negative evaluations for "…criticizing and challenging every concept on which our educational system is based." Sandra and her team were deeply impressed. Her team joked about hiring "…rebels against the system like ourselves." Eventually, all but two of the senior teachers left and were replaced by teachers who were strongly supportive of innovative approaches to the long-term problems of South Heights.

Team Support and Development

A system was set up in Sandra's second year at South Heights for staff to help and support one another. One teacher explained, "I had a difficult time adjusting. I was overwhelmed by

the needs of the kids…standing in the middle of the classroom, hitting someone, throwing things, there's a load of family violence. It was awful, nothing I tried worked. I had taught for 30 years and felt I was failing. One day, a student was screaming at me in the hall, and Sandra and another teacher came and took him under their wing. One of the things I've appreciated, we are human beings, with a variety of needs…you have to be concerned about your own emotional well-being. If we didn't take care of ourselves, we can't take care of the kids." Another teacher added, "…dealing with these problems, helping them to be successful, you need the team and their support, otherwise you could go down the spiral very quickly." One teacher provided an example: "I was having problems last year. I was starting to spiral down and it was having an impact on the kids. I was burned out here and in my life. I went to the others and said I need your help, I'm thinking of leaving. I talked with Sandra and the others to get the feelings out. If I didn't have that I wouldn't have made it through the year."

To enable staff to see greater possibilities for change at South Heights, Sandra brought a Principal from an inner-city school in Western Canada to South Heights to conduct professional development workshops with staff. This person had high credibility with the staff because he had been successful in a situation similar to that found at South Heights.

Recognizing the Strengths and Potential in Others

Sandra was also "good at recognizing the strengths and leadership potential of other people." One teacher described how staff meetings evolved. "Staff meetings here are not like anywhere else. We had a workshop on collaboration that gave me some initial ideas. I came to the team

and said I want to try some changes. It will be difficult, so be patient. The focus of staff meetings is now shared decision-making and staff development. There has to be consensus, we almost never vote. We all have to take ownership. Everyone's opinion is valued—Sandra modelled that for us. Before you sat there and fell asleep. It started making sense for everyone to be a part of it; the secretary and custodian are part of it. When you see it, it demonstrates what we are as a group".

Several staff members provided examples. A teacher commented, "My last school was like living at the North Pole. Here they get to know your strengths. I got everyone using the Internet. I've grown more here than all my other schools combined." An Educational Assistant added, "I'm part of the team—it took me a year to get that through my head. At another school I was told, "Why are you going to staff meetings? You don't have to get involved."

The custodian described his role at South Heights, "There are great opportunities for me here. I started an environmental club and stressed to the kids how important it was to recycle. We asked parents to donate gardening tools and their time so that we could make this place look better. We now have a Community Planting Day where everyone, staff, students, parents, and members of the community, work together to plant the gardens around the school. I also like outdoor photography and fly-fishing. I used this to help one kid who was almost illiterate. I taught him how to tie flies. His reading has really improved since then. I never got a thank-you note before coming here, never had recognition in another school. I have a stack of thank-you notes two inches thick in my office. It would be hard to write a job description for what I do here."

Sandra explained how the team developed at South Heights. "During the first two years they definitely relied on me as leader, but now we are a community of leaders. With some level of mentoring, many of these teachers could become principals. At Academy Hill, I built a great team, but it disappeared when I left. At South Heights, I was very aware of building something that would be sustained."

Experiential Learning Programs

"We had made very little progress on the nature of the programs that these kids were exposed to. How could we find ways of making a difference to those kids?" A missing element in their lives was any connection to the workplace. For the most part, their parents did not work, and certainly not on any continuing basis. As a consequence, the children were not learning many of the skills that would make them employable and enable them to escape the cycle of poverty that had trapped their parents.

What Sandra envisioned was an Experiential Learning Program that could provide the skills needed to be a productive member of the workforce. A model that she found very helpful was the Employability Skills Profile developed by the Conference Board of Canada (see Appendix A). This would serve as a framework for what the children should be learning in the community and at school. Sandra was delighted when a number of local businesses offered their enthusiastic support for a program that allowed the students to gain valuable experience in the workplace.

Eliminating Violence

A number of other initiatives proved to be highly successful at South Heights. Sandra and her team managed to change the opening 'event' of the school year. A "rumble" with a rival school had always marked the beginning of school in September. This symbol of violence was replaced by the "Parade of Light" through the neighbourhood to celebrate the start of the school year. A "Respect Program" was launched to combat violence and racism in the school itself. Weekly respect lessons were taught in the classroom and a local service club provided incentives to reward students for practising respectful behaviours.

Community Involvement

Under the leadership of a junior teacher, "Parent Rap" began to draw more parents with each meeting. When it became clear to the parents that the meetings were intended to discuss what was important to them, attendance rose from just 3 parents to an average of 40. In turn, this had a positive impact on the children when they saw their parents becoming involved in the school. A breakfast program was funded by a local service club and helped to ensure that all students were at least meeting minimal nutritional requirements. Another service club donated the use of its gymnasium for recreational activities and for monthly assemblies. A "Triple S Program" rewarded students with gift certificates and movie passes for achievement in Scholastics, Sports/School activities, and Service

to the school/community. A "Reading Circle" brought parents, business people, politicians, and other members of the community to South Heights to read to the children in order to further their literacy skills.

According to Sandra, all of these programs were founded on personal relationships, on getting to know people who first become interested, and then committed to helping the children of South Heights. Further, each program was built in a step-by-step fashion: "…we would start with a little success." What underlies all of the programs developed at South Heights was the notion of partnerships, of all members of the community working together to ensure that these children are receiving the best education possible. The ultimate purpose of these initiatives was clear: "We always ask ourselves, is it good for the kids? That's the Litmus test for everything we do."

The school won a national award from the Conference Board of Canada for excellence in Business-Education Partnerships, among many other provincial and national awards they have received. On measures of scholastic achievement conducted by the Ministry of Education in the Province of Ontario, the school has made remarkable progress. Indeed, the children in this inner-city school are far exceeding the averages for the province across all subject areas tested. The expectations for the children of South Heights have progressed from being without hope, to believing that anything is possible for these children. ■

Appendix A

EMPLOYABILITY SKILLS PROFILE: The Critical Skills Required of the Canadian Workforce

Academic Skills	Personal Management Skills	Teamwork Skills
Those skills which provide the basic foundation to get, keep and progress on a job and to achieve the best results	The combination of skills, attitudes and behaviours required to get, keep and progress on a job and to achieve the best results	Those skills needed to work with others on a job and to achieve the best results

Canadian employers need a person who can:

Communicate

- Understand and speak the languages in which business is conducted
- Listen to understand and learn
- Read, comprehend and use written materials, including graphs, charts and displays
- Write effectively in the languages in which business is conducted

Think

- Think critically and act logically to evaluate situations, solve problems & make decisions
- Understand and solve problems involving mathematics and use the results
- Use technology, instruments, tools and information systems effectively
- Access & supply specialized knowledge from various fields (e.g., skilled trades, technology, physical sciences, arts and social sciences)

Learn

- Continue to learn for life

Canadian employers need a person who can demonstrate:

Positive Attitudes and Behaviours

- Self-esteem and confidence
- Honesty, integrity and personal ethics
- A positive attitude toward learning, growth and personal health
- Initiative, energy and persistence to get the job done

Responsibility

- The ability to set goals and priorities in work and personal life
- The ability to plan and manage time, money and other resources to achieve goals
- Accountability for actions taken

Adaptability

- A positive attitude towards change
- Recognition of and respect for people's diversity and individual differences
- The ability to identify and suggest new ideas to get the job done creatively

Canadian employers need a person who can:

Work with Others

- Understand and contribute to the organization's goals
- Understand and work within the culture of the group
- Plan and make decisions with others and support the outcomes
- Respect the thoughts and opinions of others in the group
- Exercise "give and take" to achieve group results
- Seek a team approach as appropriate
- Lead when appropriate, mobilizing the group for high performance

This document was developed by the Corporate Council on Education, a program of the National Business and Education Centre, The Conference Board of Canada.

CASE 15
Employment Equity at H.U.C.L.

By J. Janetos and T. Cawsey.

George Redpath had just returned to his office after attending an Executive overview entitled "Employment Equity: Challenge or Bureaucracy". As President of Huras- Utracki Canada Ltd. (H.U.C.L.) George was well aware of the parent company's (Huras-Utracki Ltd.—H.U.L.) involvement with U.S. Affirmative Action legislation (E.E.O.) since 1972. Redpath then called Steve Scott, Director of Personnel, and asked him to come to Redpath's office immediately. When Scott entered the President's office, Redpath said in his typical aggressive style—"Steve, the Federal Government is planning to pass Bill C-62 legislating Employment Equity within two months—I want your Employment Equity plan formulated for implementation in two months—June 1 not January 1 as originally planned."

Company Overview

Huras-Utracki Canada Ltd. (H.U.C.L.), is a Canadian sales and service subsidiary of the parent Huras-Utracki Ltd. (H.U.L.) based in California. H.U.L. has 62,000 employees worldwide and annual sales of four billion dollars in 1985. H.U.C.L., the Canadian subsidiary, has 800 employees located in 10 sales and service offices across Canada and annual sales of 160 million dollars the previous year.

Huras-Utracki Ltd. was founded in 1938 by Don Huras and Bob Utracki after they graduated from UCLA with electrical engineering degrees. The company has grown into a leading high technology company that manufactures over 10,000 products in the electronics field. These products can be subdivided into two broad categories: measurement (electronic instruments) and computation (computers).

H.U.L.'s success can be attributed to high quality products and a reputation for excellent research development and manufacturing processes. Both H.U.L. and H.U.C.L. have grown 20-25% on an annual basis during the previous six years, primarily driven by explosive growth in the computer market. Last year, however, was an extremely slow year for high technology companies. H.U.L. and H.U.C.L. experienced almost no growth.

Huras Utracki Canada Ltd. has existed in Canada for the past twenty-two years. The company has grown from 350 employees to 800 employees in the past seven years. The head office was originally in Quebec, however, in the early 1970's it was moved to Ontario due to rising separatist movement in the province of Quebec. In addition, the Canadian management team thought it was important to construct headquarters within the business hub of Canada.

Corporate Organization

H.U.C.L. has the challenge of selling and servicing H.U. products across Canada. The Canadian management team embarked on a decentralized management structure in the late 1970's. Currently, Canada is divided into three areas—Central, Western and Eastern with area head offices in Toronto, Edmonton and Montreal. Each area has a general management team as shown in Exhibit A. The decentralized structure was established for one purpose—TO BE CLOSE TO THE CUSTOMER. H.U.C.L. wanted to establish area management resources and computer systems in order to facilitate decision-making at the customer level. For example, the district management team in Calgary would use their senior management team in Edmonton for crucial sales and service decisions, instead of going to "those Easterners in the Toronto Head Office".

The Canadian Head Office for H.U.C.L. was based in Toronto in the same building as the Central Canadian area sales office and Toronto district sales office. The Corporate management team felt it was important to be close to the field operation and not to lose touch with customers or "front line" employees. The head office consisted of 80 employees or 10% of the H.U.C.L. employee population.

President George Redpath had just appointed two Vice-Presidents from the company ranks: Vice-President—Marketing, Frank James, a veteran H.U.C.L. senior sales manager and Vice-President—Finance and Administration, Jim Morris, the Corporate controller for twelve years (see Exhibit B for the Corporate Organization). In addition, Redpath had recently appointed Steve Scott as the new Director of Personnel reporting to the President. Steve had risen rapidly through the computer sales organization and was recently National Sales Manager for the Medical Electronics Products Group. Steve, however, did not have any personnel management experience and felt somewhat overwhelmed as he started his new position.

Company Philosophy ("The People Approach")

Huras-Utracki Ltd. has been a "family-oriented" company since its two-man inception in 1938. The success of the company can be attributed to maintaining the "family spirit" throughout all the international operations. This was accomplished by formulating manufacturing divisions with

1000 employees or less and by not allowing sales offices to exceed 200-400 employees. Decentralized decision-making was also inherent in all international sales/service and manufacturing operations. Employees were extremely motivated due to decentralized decision-making and subsequent job independence. Every employee was encouraged to be an entrepreneur with individualized Management By Objective Plans (MBO).

The "People Approach" is a company philosophy that dictates the norm for "people management" throughout all the international operations. The main principles of the "People Approach" are as follows: MBO, trust, individual dignity, teamwork, learn from mistakes, open door policy, training and development and profit sharing.

H.U.C.L. believed they had been successful over the years in implementing the "People Approach". This people philosophy resulted in low annual turnover (7-10% annually for the past seven years) and outstanding sales growth (20-25% annual growth over the past six years). The employee population also grew from 350 to 800 employees in the past six years. The past two years, however, combined slower sales growth and an increase in employee concerns. An employee attitude survey conducted the previous year indicated a strong loyalty to H.U.C.L. but "cracks" appeared in the following areas:
(1) management was too slow to act on poor performers
(2) few opportunities existed for employee growth and development
(3) there was too much emphasis on education/university degrees.

Employment Equity at H.U.C.L.

Steve Scott, the new Director of Personnel must now formulate an Employment Equity program for H.U.C.L. while:

(1) incorporating the "People Approach"
(2) introducing the program to a highly decentralized company and
(3) considering the employee concerns from the attitude survey (no career growth).

On this last point, Steve knew, from experience, that many H.U.C.L. women were not advancing up the traditional technical male sales/service corporate ladder. He wondered "how will the new legislation for Employment Equity reverse male domination in H.U.C.L. and Canadian industry? "In addition, how could he convince the top executive team (President and two V.P.'s) to support and implement a "top-down" acceptance of the Employment Equity Program?

In the past, the H.U.C.L. management team had been reluctant to formulate a specific Employment Equity Program. Now, federal legislation under Bill C-62 would force H.U.C.L. to construct an Employment Equity Action Plan with goals and a timetable as a necessary prerequisite for securing government contracts. (This method of enforcement is called contract compliance.) Twenty percent of H.U.C.L.'s business was selling products and services to the federal government.

Scott asked his systems specialist, Sally Harris to compile data from the company minicomputer to outline the percentage of females in various job categories. He thought this would be a good start in developing an Employment Equity Action Plan. The Federal legislation Bill C-62 would ask employers to track the percentage of minority employees (females, native Indians and handicapped) in the work force. Under contract compliance, companies would have to demonstrate plans to improve the numbers of minorities hired and promoted in order to remain on the Federal government supplier bid list. Exhibit C (data from 3 years previous) and Exhibit D (present data) demonstrate

male versus female in eight job groups from Sally Harris' computer analysis. In short, there was no marked improvement in the promotion of females to the management ranks. Scott was also able to compare the H.U.C. L. trend with the U.S. parent (H.U.L.) "Affirmative Action Review" (See Exhibit E).

An Employment Equity Committee was in existence at H.U.C.L. The committee headed by a technical software support manager. Her heart was in the right place but she did not have the time nor the background to lead a committee of other technical managers in a personnel related field (employment equity). In her last conversation with Scott, she stated "I want to resign from the committee".

Steve Scott's Challenge

Steve Scott has been very successful in his various sales management assignments. He would need all his "selling skills" in the new Director of Personnel position. The Employment Equity Action Plan was only one of many challenges. The Employee Attitude Survey indicated employees did not trust the Toronto Head Office personnel staff. Specifically employees and managers were concerned with the lack of confidentiality when discussing issues/problems with the personnel department. Scott's personnel staff was a mixture of young and inexperienced personnel professionals. In addition, Scott had four vacancies in his personnel department caused by transfers, promotion and one resignation.

Steve Scott finished another hectic day. His thoughts were on the Employee Equity Action Plan, poor personnel department credibility and four job vacancies to fill. Now ready to fight the rush hour traffic in his attempt to drive home, Scott contemplated aloud, "How can I obtain some meaningful progress on the employment equity front?" ■

Exhibit A

Decentralized Area Management Team
(Toronto, Montreal, Edmonton)

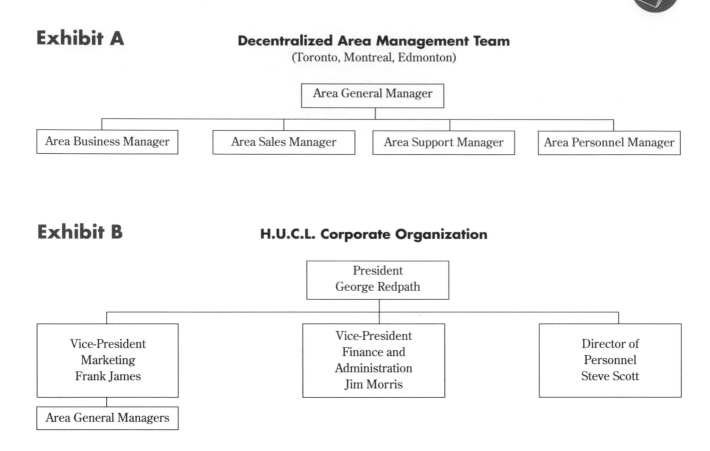

Exhibit B

H.U.C.L. Corporate Organization

Exhibit C

H.U.C.L. Employee Population
Three Years Previously

	Male	Female	Total	% Females
Sr. Management	11	0	11	0
Middle Management	3	0	3	0
Sales Management and Admin. Specialists	19	0	19	0
1st Line Supervisors	60	26	86	30.2
Sales Representatives	84	9	93	9.7
Sales Support Specialists	74	13	87	14.9
(Sales Trainees, Hardware/Software Specialists)				
Technical	117	4	121	3.3
Clerical/Admin. Support	35	136	171	79.5

Exhibit D

H.U.C.L. Employee Population
Present Data

	Male	Female	Total	% Females
Sr. Management	15	0	15	0
Middle Management	7	0	7	0
Sales Management	21	0	21	0
1st Line Supervisors and Admin. Specialists	59	42	101	41.6
Sales Representatives	113	9	122	7.4
Sales Support Specialists (Sales Trainees, Hardware/Software Specialists)	83	23	106	21.7
Technical	129	5	134	3.7
Clerical/Admin. Support	36	171	207	82.6

Exhibit E

U.S. Affirmative Action Review

	Total Number	Minority		Female	
		Total	Percent	Total	Percent
Managers and Supervisors					
Five Years Ago	3,887	376	9.7	799	20.5
Today	6,188	661	10.7	1583	25.6
Professionals					
Five Years Ago	7,239	787	10.9	1471	20.3
Today	12,379	1651	13.3	3610	29.2
Technicians					
Five Years Ago	3,039	383	12.6	471	15.5
Today	3,864	687	17.8	605	15.6
Skilled/Craft					
Five Years Ago	1,617	285	19.6	214	13.2
Today	1,923	409	21.3	345	17.9

CASE 16
The Poorly Informed Walrus

Developed by Barbara McCain, Oklahoma City University

"How's it going down there?" barked the big walrus from his perch on the highest rock near the shore. He waited for the good word. Down below, the smaller walruses conferred hastily among themselves. Things weren't going well at all, but none of them wanted to break the news to the Old Man. He was the biggest and wisest walrus in the herd, and he knew his business, but he had such a terrible temper that every walrus in the herd was terrified of his ferocious bark

"What will we tell him?" whispered Basil, the second-ranking walrus. He well remembers how the Old Man had raved and ranted at him the last time the herd had caught less than its quota of herring, and he had no desire to go through that experience again. Nevertheless, the walrus noticed for several weeks that the water level in the nearby Arctic bay had been falling constantly, and it had become necessary to travel much farther to catch the dwindling supply of herring. Someone should tell the Old Man; he would probably know what to do. But who? and how?

Finally Basil spoke up: "Things are going pretty well, Chief," he said. The thought of the receding water line made his heart grow heavy, but he went on: "As a matter of fact, the beach seems to be getting larger."

The Old Man grunted. "Fine, fine," he said. "That will give us a bit more elbow room." He closed his eyes and continued basking in the sun.

The next day brought more trouble. A new herd of walruses moved in down the beach and, with the supply of herring dwindling, this invasion could be dangerous. No one wanted to tell the Old Man, though only he could take the steps necessary to meet this new competition.

Reluctantly, Basil approached the big walrus, who was still sunning himself on the large rock. After some small talk, he said, "Oh, by the way, Chief, a new herd of walruses seems to have moved into our territory." The Old Man's eyes snapped open, and he filled his great lungs in preparation for a mighty bellow. But Basil added quickly, "Of course, we don't anticipate any trouble. They don't look like herring eaters to me. More likely interested in minnows. And as you know, we don't bother with minnows ourselves."

The Old Man let out the air with a long sigh. "Good, good," he said. "No point in our getting excited over nothing then, is there?"

Things didn't get any better in the weeks that followed. One day, peering down from the large rock, the Old Man noticed that part of the herd seemed to be missing. Summoning Basil, he grunted peevishly. "What's going on, Basil? Where is everyone?" Poor Basil didn't have the courage to tell the Old Man that many of the younger walruses were leaving every day to join the new herd. Clearing his throat nervously, he said, "Well Chief, we've been tightening up things a bit. You know, getting rid of some of the dead wood. After all, a herd is only as good as the walruses in it."

"Run a tight ship, I always say," the Old Man grunted. "Glad to hear that all is going so well."

Before long, everyone but Basil had left to join the new herd, and Basil realized that the time had come to tell the Old Man the facts. Terrified but determined, he flopped up to the large rock. "Chief," he said, "I have bad news. The rest of the herd has left you." The old walrus was so astonished that he couldn't even work up a good bellow. "Left me?" he cried. "All of them? But why? How could this happen?"

Basil didn't have the heart to tell him, so he merely shrugged helplessly. "I can't understand it," the old walrus said. "And just when everything was going so well."

Review Questions

1. What barriers to communication are evident in this fable?
2. What communication "lessons" does this fable offer to those who are serious about careers in the new workplace? ■

CASE 17
Outrage at Eastern

By Roland B. Cousins, LaGrange College and Linda E. Benitz, Powertel, Inc.

Charles Jackson, the plant manager at Eastern Plating for the last four years, felt mounting shock and revulsion as he read the lead article in the Evening Beacon. The article detailed allegations made against one of Eastern's employees, Marty Reid, by his 13-year-old stepdaughter and her mother, his wife. According to the story in the paper, Marty Reid had been molesting the young girl since she was eight years old. The stepdaughter had apparently run away from home two weeks before the article appeared and told her story to the police, who had found her walking down the highway five miles from her home. The step-daughter reported to police that she had suffered unspeakable abuse for almost five years. The girl's allegations were confirmed by her mother, who maintained she was too frightened of her husband to intervene and protect her daughter. The article further stated that Reid was charged with multiple felonies and jailed, but his parents and brother had pledged their property to bail him out of jail.

Jackson wondered if Reid would come to work as usual the next night. To be prepared for the possibility, he decided to review the employee handbook and determine what, if anything, he could or should do about Reid's continued employment. He also decided to review Reid's personnel record the next morning. Because Eastern Plating was located in a small community having only 10,000 residents, Jackson knew Reid would be the talk of the town and the plant tomorrow.

The Company

Eastern Plating was a small, privately owned, job-shop plating firm located in a rural area of the Deep South. The plant had moved from the northeast to its current location some years before. The move was rumored to be an effort to escape unions.

Eastern's current location was in a right-to-work state; since moving, there had never been a serious attempt to organize the workers. The company employed approximately 100 people, most of whom were white males in unskilled or semiskilled positions. The plant was located outside the town of Pineton, with a population of 10,000.

The per capita income in Pineton was low, even by regional standards, as a large percentage of the town's workforce held unskilled or semi-skilled positions in local manufacturing plants. There was some local agricultural activity, with the pulp-wood industry accounting for most of it. Although located in the "Bible Belt," Pineton had the reputation of being a rough, blue-collar town. In spite of the frequent Saturday night brawls at the local bars, the churches were full on Sunday morning.

The owners had one other similar plant, located several hundred miles from the Pineton plant. The corporate positions, what few there were, were located at the other plant, Central Plating and Finishing. Jackson reported to the president, who was the owner. Jackson had always been given a lot of autonomy in running the Eastern plant, and there was a minimum of bureaucracy, with few policies and procedures. The president rarely visited the plant, merely monitoring the plant operations by means of production reports.

Although there was a human resources department in the corporate offices, the director was more involved with corporate human resource strategy than with the day-to-day operations at either plant. A clerk at Eastern had responsibility for the human resource function. Although her time was filled primarily with payroll, insurance, and retirement matters, she had attended a two-day seminar covering other human resource functions including recruiting, selecting, training, disciplining, and employment law. She also kept all of the personnel records, including performance appraisals and disciplinary records.

It was generally known throughout the company that Jackson was expected to handle any and all problems arising in his plant by himself. There was no one to turn to at the other plant, unless he contacted the owner. Such a contact would be viewed by the owner as evidence of the plant manager's failure.

The company's disciplinary policies, found in the employee handbook, consisted of a few vague statements suggesting that employee misconduct would not be tolerated, and disciplinary measures would be applied progressively.

Marty Reid's Record

Upon arriving at work the following morning, Jackson immediately called the human resource assistant and requested Reid's folder. Because Jackson had only been at Eastern for four years and Reid was already working there when Jackson arrived, he did not know much about Reid's history with the firm. In reviewing the record, Jackson learned that Reid had been employed by Eastern for the last seven years, starting as a laborer when he was 30 years old. At the age of 37 and as the result of several promotions, Reid was currently a crane operator on the night shift.

Performance appraisals submitted by four different supervisors over the years had consistently rated his performance in the "good" range. There were two notations in the folder of oral warnings that had been given to Reid: one six years before for threatening a fellow employee and another four years before for the failure to call in when he was absent for one day. Overall, Reid's record was quite satisfactory—certainly better than the record of many workers at Eastern Plating.

In Reid's current job as crane operator, he spent most of his time alone in the crane's cab, manoeuvring the crane along the tracks that ran near the plant roof, approximately 40 feet above the plant floor and 30 feet above the tops of the open chemical vats, which ran down the centre of the plant floor. Although Jackson usually waved a greeting to Marty every morning when he made his walking tour of the plant, he had experienced very little personal contact with Reid during the four years since his appointment to plant manager at Eastern Plating.

The Employee Handbook

Jackson then took out his copy of the Eastern Plating Company's employee handbook to see what it said, if anything, about employees charged with crimes. The only statement that related to Marty's situation was the following sentence under the heading of Progressive Discipline: "An employee charged with a crime will be allowed to work as long as he/she is able to meet attendance and other work-related requirements."

A Visit From Reid

Charles Jackson put down the employee handbook and looked up as Reid walked through his office doorway.

Excuse me, Mr. Jackson, but I assume you read about me in the paper last night.

Yes, I did.

Well, Mr. Jackson, I want you to know there isn't a bit of truth to any of it.

My wife and her daughter just have it in for me. But the reason I wanted to see you this morning is just to tell you that I want to keep on working. I'm going to save up my vacation days, and I hope that will be enough to cover the days I'll have to miss for the trial. I hope that will not be a problem.

I don't foresee a problem, Marty.

Thanks, Mr. Jackson. I'll be back tonight for my shift.

More Visitors

For the remainder of the day, Jackson's thoughts kept coming back to Reid and the accusations made against him. Although he found it difficult to do, late in the day he tried to review some production charts. Suddenly, his concentration was broken by the sound of angry voices coming from the outer office.

His secretary buzzed him to tell him that several of the night shift employees wished to speak with him. "OK," Jackson responded as he laid the charts aside.

When his office door swung open, seven workers shuffled in, crowding his small office. Jackson was somewhat surprised because rarely did more than two workers want to see him at once. Jackson didn't have to wonder long why the men were there before the silence was broken by Mac, who was crowded closest to Jackson's desk.

Mr. Jackson, I'll get right to the point here. Me and the boys just wanted to let you know that we ain't going to work with Marty Reid any more. I'm sure you read the paper last night. Well, we've been hearing rumours for more than a week that something was going on, and Marty was being investigated for something. Most of us aren't saints, so we didn't think too much about it. But when we found out what he did, we all decided we wouldn't work with him. As a matter of fact, a couple of the boys said if he ever gets back up there on the crane, he'll probably fall to the floor or even into one of the acid vats. I know you're very concerned about plant safety and proud that we haven't had a really serious injury since the early 1980s, so I hope you will accept that this is a serious situation. We aren't working with a scumbag like that. Well, Mr. Jackson, that's all we wanted to say. Thanks for listening.

Although taken aback by Mac's statement, Jackson had the presence of mind to offer the following response:

Wait a minute, fellas. Reid has only been accused, and in our country a man is innocent until proven guilty. We have to wait for a jury to speak. ... Mr. Jackson, we don't need to hear from a jury. The word of that little girl and his old lady is good enough for us. We won't work with him. Period. And if you don't want an accident on the night shift, you'll just send him on his way. Thanks, Mr. Jackson.

The men filed out and closed the office door behind themselves. Jackson, somewhat shaken by the encounter, leaned back in his chair and wondered what he should do now. This was becoming serious, he thought. ■

CASE 18
Countryside Environmental Services

By Andrew Woodley and Tupper Cawsey

John straightened his tie as he walked down the hallway to the conference room. Vincent paced eagerly at his side. "You've told Andy and Gwen exactly what my role in this project is, haven't you?" Vincent muttered nervously to John. He was quite sure he knew the answer, but wanted to be sure he was going into this meeting in tune with John. Vincent had met with John on many occasions during the preceding month to negotiate his joining Countryside Environmental Services (CES). Once the contract had been negotiated, John had provided Vincent with a general orientation and overview of the company's operations. Now, Vincent was to meet the rest of the team.

"Oh don't worry, I'll make it clear in this meeting this morning" replied John. "As we've already discussed you're to be the guiding authority in this project, I'll be overseeing your progress however you will be responsible for the team's success or failure. We both know that you are more familiar than I of the procedures and politics involved in getting a landfill approved. We can benefit tremendously from your input. Yes, there's no doubting it, you'll be the key play Vincent." John hurried through this last sentence as they reached the meeting room and pushed open the door. He was pleased that Andy and Gwen were already seated and awaiting his arrival.

"We've been given the green light with the new name, so Countryside Environmental Services it is" John said with pride as he entered the small meeting room. This was an exciting moment in the history of Countryside Construction. It was the beginning of another venture for John and his company. Currently, Countryside employs eighty-five people and grosses more than $15 million. John attributed much of the company's success to his own management philosophy of diversity and perseverance.

John Hopkins established Countryside Construction some thirty years ago. The company started business as a small aggregate producer, excavating and selling sand and gravel from a local gravel pit. Today the company supplies aggregate to most of the region's sand blasting and construction businesses. Countryside also has a dominant presence in the local waste management industry. It ventured into waste management a decade ago after being awarded the City of Blensford's contract for the curb side pickup of household waste.

In response to this success, John created a new division of the company to handle waste management. It had been a successful venture for Countryside and John remained close to the action, personally managing the division. During the past five years the division acquired two additional contracts for the operation and management of two other County landfills.

Countryside Environmental Services (CES) had just been established as a spin off company from Countryside Construction to develop a new landfill on a parcel of land centred around one of the company's old gravel pits.

John had visualized owning his own landfill ever since Countryside first became involved in waste management. He believed that the owners of the landfills (in most cases the Government) pocketed all the profits. John was aware of the crippling environmental problems of the existing waste management system and knew that current landfill capacity was rapidly diminishing. He believed the economic potential for opening a new large scale landfill was promising.

Vincent Woodman had just been hired as the environmental consultant and manager of Countryside Environmental Services. Recently Vincent had vacated his seat on County Council, where he had been the County Warden and Reeve of the Town of Innsport for nine years. In this role, he had chaired the County Waste Management Committee and had represented the County on the Provincial Waste Management Steering Committee.

John was very pleased to have recruited Vincent. Vincent had developed an impressive reputation for effective input into waste management planning during his term in County politics. He eventually became frustrated with the lack of vision with which the County approached its worsening waste management problems. Vincent, like John could see that the increasing public outcry for environmentally safe landfills combined with a strong push towards the three R's (Reduce, Recycle and Reuse) was an opportunity for private enterprise. The best way to handle the Country's waste was for the County to enter into a joint venture with the private sector. The County simply did not have the necessary funds and pressure was mounting both from the public and provincial government officials for change. Vincent knew this better than anyone.

John pulled a few papers from his briefcase and shuffled them on the table. "Well I know you've met Andy and Gwen prior to today albeit for a brief moment. I've talked to Andy and Gwen about you joining CES and I am sure they are as enthusiastic as I am. However I should perhaps fill you in on my aspirations for this team and what I would like to see happen. As you know, Andy has been with us now for nearly three years in the capacity of Projects Engineer. Gwen is the Office Manager and joined us about six months prior to Andy." John was speaking quickly, his excitement evident. "Gwen is responsible for the day to day running of the office. She has been involved with the bookkeeping of some of our accounts. However I know that you are well acquainted with accounting Vincent. Andy will be in charge of all the technical/engineering work and Vincent, you will handle the political end of the plans as well as managing the project. I believe we have the basis for a solid and valuable group and I look forward to seeing progress. Vincent has briefed me on what we will need to concentrate on and he will be directing us through the environmental approval process. He has a wealth of knowledge and experience to share with us, so let's work together, be productive and have some fun at the same time." "Perhaps now is a good time, Vincent, for you to brief us on what you consider our plan of attack should be." John leaned back in his chair keen to listen to Vincent's remarks to this newly established team.

"Thank you John. I feel you have provided us with a very exciting opportunity here and I am honoured to be a part of this team. I believe we all have very valuable and relevant skills to utilize in this project and I can't stress enough the importance of working as a team. I truly believe we can make this vision of yours a reality."

"Just as I thought. A long winded politician." Gwen muttered for Andy's benefit. He heard her comment but decided to ignore it.

Vincent continued. "John, you have provided me with an overview of the situation here at Countryside. I would appreciate a day or so to settle in and become familiar with the environment. Then we could get together and go over some specific task assignments. For now you could all help me by answering a few questions. First of all have any business cards or letterhead been printed yet?" Vincent turned and faced Gwen.

"No, I haven't!" Gwen was quick to respond, determined that Vincent would not poke a hole in her armour. "I thought we should wait until we can come up with a company logo, perhaps a tree or a dove of something like that would be fitting. I'll organize that tomorrow."

"I think it is important to get that taken care of quickly. I have a meeting next week with the County Waste Management Committee and I would like to have some cards to hand out. Andy, it might be worthwhile for you to come along to the meeting." Vincent paused to consider his next remark.

Gwen interjected. "John, I think I should be a part of that County meeting as well. We know that County is cash strapped at the moment. I think I should give them some figures regarding the cost savings they could benefit from if they adopt our landfill proposal."

Vincent looked to John, a little startled by the authority in Gwen's

voice. John turned and looked out the window. Vincent continued. "I don't think that will be necessary for this meeting Gwen. They are not really interested in the costs right now, they just want a brief as to what approach we will be taking. It is encouraging to hear that you have already collected some cost data, perhaps you should pass it on to me. I'll combine it with the work I have already done. John had not informed me that any costings had been tabled yet. What figures have you put together?" Vincent enquired.

"Well I ummm…" Gwen stammered. "Well you know it's just preliminary figures. However I could get up and talk about costs just as well as any one else here and it sure would be a darn sight cheaper to have me there than you, Vincent."

Vincent again turned to John, hoping he would offer some comment to ease the situation. John continued to stare out the window. Vincent was concerned that he had not been forewarned of this conflict. He sat back carefully considering his next remarks, still hopeful that John would break the silence; "Gwen, I have been placed in charge of this project and I will not be requiring your presence at this meeting. I know the people on the Waste Management Committee well and I know what they are wanting to hear at this early stage. I respect your eager attitude, however must insist that I go alone or with Andy." Vincent paused, feeling satisfied that he had handled the situation well. He continued. "With John's approval I have drafted up a structural layout for the team, defining each individual's tasks and who they are responsible to. I shall bringing you all a copy in the next day or so. If you have any comments or suggestions regarding the content then please feel free to come and see me." Vince thought hard about this last comment, perhaps he would have to

revise Gwen's task description. "Well I feel that is all we need to cover today, so perhaps we could meet again in a couple of days. Does anyone have anything else which they feel needs to be discussed?" Vincent searched for somebody to take the conversation away from him.

Andy cleared his throat and addressed Vincent. "Perhaps we could sit down together after you have settled in and go over the current status of our landfill application in detail. We really have just touched the surface of what is required, but nonetheless there are several key site-specific facts that I can brief you on." Andy was a no nonsense, hard working individual who had been involved in a wide variety of projects in his time with the company. He looked forward to the work ahead of him. Vincent turned to face Andy, acknowledging the value of his suggestions with a smile.

John considered it was time to put an end to the meeting. "O.K. then. I think you have given us all a taste of what lies ahead. Perhaps next Tuesday we could meet again. Is that suitable?" John glanced around the room, noting everyone's agreement. "Let's wrap it up for now. Thank you all for your time. Gwen, could you stay behind for a minute? I want to go over a few things with you."

Vincent packed his suitcase and quickly left the room. "Wait up Andy," Vincent called to the young engineer as he closed the meeting room door and hurried down the hallway after him.

John gazed out the window, watching the passing traffic and waited till he could no longer hear Vincent and Andy as they continued down to the hallway, locked in serious conversation. "Well, what in the hell was that all about? Do you realize the position you're putting me in here?" John turned to face Gwen, and waited for her response. "Well?"

"I'm sorry, but I just can't understand why Vincent has to exclude me. Why does he have to get paid so much? It's a joke. How could you pay him so much more than me? I tell you now, I am not going to sit around here and have him tell me what to do. I'm the office manager, so I'm in charge of everyone in the office, that includes Vincent. O.K.!!" Gwen exclaimed. "Please understand me John, I want us all to be happy here but that isn't going to happen if we let this guy come in and start calling the shots."

"Listen Gwen, there is no doubting that you're an efficient and dependable worker. Everyone here recognizes and appreciates that, but I have to warn you, don't push it this time. Vincent seems to be a very nice and reasonable fellow and by all accounts he can add a great deal to this team. I don't believe your attack on him was necessary."

"Well John, you know I have been on edge with all that I am going through at home and perhaps I am overreacting somewhat, but I would like you to talk to Vincent and get him to include me in this waste management meeting at the County. I think it is very important that I attend. For what it's worth I could even take Andy's place, I know a little about the engineering of a landfill. I just think you need to have me there to keep an eye on things." Gwen was unrelenting.

John knew of the turmoil in Gwen's family life and felt a real sense of pain every time he thought about it. Gwen seemed to take every opportunity to fill John in on the current traumas with her husband. John had been divorced less than two years ago, he knew of the pain and the sense of rejection. He could not bring himself to look at Gwen, he just quietly said, "Just leave it with me, I'll have a word to Vincent about it, O.K.? Don't worry, we'll work something out."

Gwen smiled and got to her feet, feeling like she had salvaged some

grace from this morning's meeting. She liked John. She patted him on the shoulder and walked out the door.

John remained in the meeting room by himself for some time, contemplating the morning's events. He felt hopeful.

Vincent returned to his office after a lengthy conversation with Andy, who had filled him in on the internal workings of the company. Andy warned Vincent to tread lightly if he was going to confront John about Gwen's behaviour. He told him that it was a well-circulated rumour (and one that he did not believe) that John and Gwen were having an affair and that Gwen had been experiencing difficulties with her husband. Even though it was Vincent's first full day with the company, it was not a surprise when Andy mentioned that John was very supportive of Gwen and was allowing her tremendous flexibility at work. Gwen's behaviour of late apparently had many other people in the company on edge. Andy reported that two secretaries had just resigned and that he knew of three other staff members currently looking for new jobs. It was, according to Andy, no coincidence that this was occurring just as Gwen was becoming more difficult. John was not offering any assistance or advice to anyone apart from Gwen.

Vincent was interested to hear that John had asked for Andy's input in the selection of a secretary for Countryside Environmental. John, however, had made it clear at the time that he wanted Gwen to be transferred. Andy knew his objections would be in vain and so decided that he would have to learn to deal with the situation as best he could. Andy did however think highly of Gwen's work, but had pointed out that over the past six months her performance had suffered and her attitude to fellow employees had changed for the worse. He had lost a great deal of respect for her and now felt that work-

ing with her would be a very testing experience.

Vincent was surprised and appreciative of Andy's openness. He considered Andy to be believable and knew that John saw Andy as talented and credible. Vincent was all to familiar with situations like this and considered that the time to act was now, before the situation was allowed to get out of hand. He sat down at his desk and picked up the documents he had prepared for Gwen, defining her tasks and position. It was only now that he remembered that John had studied Gwen's job definition very closely and had made Vincent make several changes before approving it. Each alteration tended to make her job description vague and her position somewhat unclear. He decided that it was imperative to define exactly what she would and would not be required to do and who she would be accountable to. Vincent read through the documents again, making note of any changes he would like to make. In the light of the morning's events he knew he would have to discuss this further with John.

Vincent felt unsettled about the conflict that existed at Countryside and remembered all the petty squabbles, power struggles and internal politics he had to deal with in his term as County Warden. He was disgusted at the lack of maturity exhibited by some of his former colleagues and certainly did not want to be put in the same situation again. Vincent pushed his papers aside and reclined in his chair trying to relax. He considered the possibility that he was overreacting, but quickly dismissed this thought. He found himself wondering why he had chosen to accept John's offer to work for Countryside. Everything had seemed so promising and full of hope when he had met with John. One particular comment that John had made stuck in his mind. "If you have any troubles, then feel free to come and see me, my door is always open. I don't imagine however that you will encounter any major problems, the waste management division has been very successful in the past. I am excited to have you with us Vincent." Vincent had been very impressed with John; he had seemed very warm and sincere and had been a key factor in Vincent's final decision to accept the position. "…my door is always open." Vincent pondered over this comment for a minute before rising to his feet and heading down to John's office. He knocked lightly on the door and walked in. "Yes Vincent, what can I do for you?" John looked tired and worn out.

"I want to discuss with you Gwen's performance in the meeting this morning. I fail to see a need for the comments she made regarding her ability to outperform me at the County meeting. I'd appreciate it if you could provide me with some insight here." Vincent's statement was just what John had feared.

"Well you see Vincent, Gwen has always been an excellent performer here. She is just having a tough time with her personal life at the moment. I don't think there is any cause for alarm, she'll get over her problems soon and I know that she will bounce back to her former cheerful self. I ask you not to be overly critical of Gwen for now and that you give me a little time to work things out. We can't be too tough on her." John glanced up at Vincent, hoping he would understand.

"I would rather deal early with anything I see as potentially harmful to our progress, and this concerns me. If you consider that we should go easy, then I will respect your judgement. I just want you to know where I am coming from. Perhaps it would be advisable for one of us to sit down with her and go over just where she fits in here."

"No I don't think that is necessary. Don't let it get you down, it will clear itself up in time. Oh by the way,

I was pleased with the way you handled the meeting this morning." John turned back to his desk and began sorting through some papers. Vincent took the hint and decided to hold off discussing the issue further. He returned to his office to concentrate his efforts on becoming familiar with company protocol and making his office a more workable environment.

The next Monday morning, Vincent approached Andy and handed him a copy of his job description which included an itemization of both individual and group goals. Andy quickly glanced through the listed points but offered no immediate objections. Vincent suggested he take his time and thoroughly study the papers and come to him with any other comments.

Vincent looked around the cluttered office noting how claustrophobic it felt. Andy's desk was in one corner of the square room, desks belonging to secretaries were in two of the other corners and at the far end was Gwen's desk. Vincent was glad he had his own office. Since Gwen was away from her desk. Vincent pulled out her job description and scribbled on it:

> "INTER-OFFICE MEMO
> To: Gwen
> From: Vincent
> Subject: Job Description"

He placed the document on her desk and returned to his office.

About a minute after Gwen returned to her desk, Vincent heard her march boisterously past his office down the hall way in the direction of John's office. He suspected what the commotion was about and expected that he would soon be summoned into John's office. Much to his surprise he was not. Half an hour later John's office door was opened and Vincent heard John say "just leave it with me, I'll have a word with Vincent and straighten this out." Gwen glared at Vincent as she walked past him back

to her own desk. John left the office and Vincent did not see him again at all that day. Neither John nor Gwen approached him regarding the job description report.

One morning, a week later Vincent was the first to arrive at work. He noticed that a package had arrived overnight addressed to Countryside Environmental Services. It was from Hasty Print. He opened up the package and discovered that the company letterhead and business cards had arrived. He retrieved his own cards, and as he lifted them out of the box he uncovered Gwen's. He was shocked to see the title that appeared on them "MANAGER – FINANCE AND ACCOUNTS." His eyes nearly popped out of their sockets. He now understood why he had not heard the slightest mention of letterhead or business cards since their first meeting.

Vincent felt very frustrated and believed the team was going nowhere. Any efforts he made were being thwarted by Gwen. He considered that the time for letting things settle out had well passed and ass soon as John arrived in his office, he cornered him.

"Can I have a word with you John." John swivelled in his chair to see Vincent standing at his office door. Vincent's concern was noticeable both in his appearance and the serious tone of his voice.

"Sure, come on in." John replied.

Vincent closed the door behind him. "I am of the understanding that Gwen is the office manager. Is that correct?" Vincent paused and waited for John's response.

"Yes that is right." John said with some hesitation.

Vincent's voice increased in volume. "I have just this morning received our business cards. Are you aware of the title she has put down for herself?"

"Yes, she actually came to me last week to complain about the job description document you had given her. She was in quite a rage when she came storming in here. She figured she would be in charge of managing the finances of this project. You see she has just started going to night school for her Certified General Accountants certificate and I think she's pretty keen to practice what she is learning. I explained to her that you were responsible for deciding who did what and suggested that she sit down and discuss the matter with you. I figured that if she wanted to call herself the financial manager or anything else then so be it. You and I both know where she is at." John's face turned a pale shade of red. He could not bring himself to look up at Vincent. "Vincent I firmly believe that we should not intervene here. We need to give her some room and a bit more time to sort out her problems."

"Well John I'm no more for hitting someone when they're down than you are, but can you not see that she is the sole cause of the terrible atmosphere in this place. I'm not the only one that is affected here. I think we're in danger of losing some valuable players if you allow this kind of behaviour to continue. I have already been approached by a couple of the staff in this office who have voiced their objections. They believe she has changed dramatically over the past six months although certain individuals commented that she has always been somewhat bossy and power hungry. I gather my presence here has caused an escalation of the problem. I don't believe this is something we can just turn away from and hope that it will go away. It needs to be dealt with. When I first met with you I shared some concerns about the small size of this office and the necessity for a close knit team effort. I feel I can't perform effectively if this is allowed to continue." Vincent waited for John to respond to his comments, but was not surprised to receive nothing but

silence. John slowly got up from his chair and left the room. Vincent could see that he was very troubled. He desperately hoped that John could see the ramifications of his action.

A couple of days following Vincent's discussions with John, Gwen was away sick for two days. She returned to work one morning and began quizzing Andy as to what Vincent had been working on while she had been away. "Well I believe he was reading through the Environmental Assessment Act and making some notes. Perhaps you should ask him when he comes in." Andy was young and had become somewhat intimidated by her, a fact that she was well aware of.

"I thought you had already made some notes from the Act. You did didn't you?" Gwen continued, determined to create a scene.

Andy reluctantly replied "Well yes I did look at part of it, but that was some time ago."

Just as Andy finished these last comments, John walked into the office. Gwen was quick off the mark. "John, I think we need to do something about Vincent. Andy says Vincent has been duplicating work. That's a waste of time and with the money we pay him it's something we cannot afford."

"Well you're right, we don't need anyone to duplicate another person's work. I'll have to have a word to Vincent about that." John reached the coffee machine and filled his cup. He wanted to change the subject, but Gwen continued before he had a chance.

"And another thing," Gwen was winding up, "How is it that he can just come and go as he pleases, he is never in here before 8:30 a.m. Who gave him special rights?"

John ignored this last question and walked into his own office, hoping to escape the outburst. Andy had followed him and startled John when

he spoke. "John I feel I should clarify what Gwen was referring to in there about Vincent duplicating my work. I think that was a very unfair comment to make. She is taking what I said completely out of context. You see Vincent and I can read the same article, looking for different facts. That is exactly what happened here. I was looking for the engineering data, while Vincent was looking at the same papers with a political slant, extracting different material. I do not appreciate someone taking something I say out of context and blowing it up, especially in front of you. I ask you to consider this before you approach Vincent." Andy was rarely one to speak his mind, but felt a great sense of satisfaction with his remarks.

"Don't get your dander up Andy, I wasn't even going to mention it to Vincent. I was pretty sure that Vincent would not duplicate any work. Thanks for your comments though." John picked up his coffee and nervously smiled at Andy before taking a sip. Andy turned and left John's office, almost knocking over Gwen who was standing just around the corner, apparently listening in on what had been said.

Two months passed by. Vincent had been working for Countryside Environmental Services now for nearly three months. He was still feeling the frustrations of working with Gwen. Her behaviour continued to be erratic and her performance as a team member left a great deal to be desired. Vincent had approached John many times and on three specific occasions asked him to resolve the problems. Each time John had expressed his concern but asked Vincent to put up with the situation for a little longer. Vincent's personal secretary had resigned, stating that she required more time with her family. Vincent was well aware that the true reasons for her departure were not aired. In addition to this, Andy had confided with Vincent that he had been given a temporary offer of employment with a large mining company in the north of the province and would probably be accepting the offer when it is finalized. Vincent was very disturbed and troubled as to what he should do.

Questions to be Assigned

1. What are the key issues?
2. What is Gwen's, John's and Vincent's conflict management styles?
3. Discuss the differences between their styles making reference to specific examples from the case.
4. What conclusions can be drawn from (2)?
5. Structurally, is there anything wrong at CES?
6. Should Vincent continue to force the issue?
7. How can a win-win resolution be achieved? ■

CASE 19
The New Vice President

[Note: Please read only those parts identified by your instructor. Do not read ahead.]

Source: Adapted from Donald D. Bowen, et al., Experiences in Management and Organizational Behavior, 4th ed. (New York: Wiley), 1997.

Part A

When the new president at Mid-West U took over, it was only a short time before the incumbent vice president announced his resignation. Unfortunately, there was no one waiting in the wings, and a hiring freeze prevented a national search from commencing

Many faculty leaders and former administrators suggested that the president appoint Jennifer Treeholm, the Associate Vice President for Academic Affairs, as interim. She was an extremely popular person on campus and had 10 years of experience in the role of associate vice president. She knew everyone and everything about the campus. Jennifer, they assured him, was the natural choice. Besides, Jennifer deserved the job. Her devotion to the school was unparalleled, and her energy knew no bounds. The new president, acting on advice from many campus leaders, appointed Jennifer interim vice president for a

term of up to three years. He also agreed that she could be a candidate for the permanent position when the hiring freeze was lifted.

Jennifer and her friends were ecstatic. It was high time more women moved into important positions on campus. They went out for dinner to their every-Friday-night watering hole to celebrate and reflect on Jennifer's career.

Except for a brief stint outside of academe, Jennifer's entire career had been at Mid-West U. She started out teaching Introductory History, then, realizing she wanted to get on the tenure track, went back to school and

earned her Ph.D. at Metropolitan U while continuing to teach at Mid-West. Upon completion of her degree, she was appointed as an assistant professor and eventually earned the rank of associate based on her popularity and excellent teaching.

Not only was Jennifer well liked, but she devoted her entire life, it seemed, to Mid-West, helping to form the first union, getting grants, writing skits for the faculty club's annual follies, and going out of her way to befriend everyone who needed support.

Eventually, Jennifer was elected president of the Faculty Senate. After serving for two years, she was offered the position of associate vice president. During her 10 years as associate vice president, she handled most of the academic complaints, oversaw several committees, wrote almost all of the letters and reports for the vice president, and was even known to run personal errands for the president. People just knew they could count on Jennifer.

Review Questions

1. At this point, what are your predictions about Jennifer as the interim vice president?
2. What do you predict will be her management/leadership style?
3. What are her strengths? Her weaknesses? What is the basis for your assessment?

After you have discussed Part A, please read Part B.

Part B

Jennifer's appointment as interim vice president was met with great enthusiasm. Finally, the school was getting someone who was "one of their own," a person who understood the culture, knew the faculty, and could get things done.

It was not long before the campus realized that things were not moving and that Jennifer, despite her long-standing popularity, had difficulty making tough decisions. Her desire to please people and to try to take care of everyone made it difficult for her to choose opposing alternatives. (To make matters worse, she had trouble planning, organizing, and managing her time.)

What was really a problem was that she did not understand her role as the number-two person at the top of the organization. The president expected her to support him and his decisions without question. Over time the president also expected her to implement some of his decisions—to do his dirty work. This became particularly problematic when it involved firing people or saying "no" to old faculty cronies. Jennifer also found herself uncomfortable with the other members of the president's senior staff. Although she was not the only woman (the general counsel, a very bright, analytical woman was part of the group), Jennifer found the behavior and decision-making style to be different from what she was used to.

Most of the men took their lead from the president and discussed very little in the meetings. Instead, they would try to influence decisions privately. Often a decision arrived in a meeting as a "fait accompli." Jennifer felt excluded and wondered why, as vice president, she felt so powerless. In time, she and the president spent less and less time together talking and discussing how to move the campus along. Although her relations with the men on the senior staff were cordial, she talked mostly to her female friends.

Jennifer's friends, especially her close-knit group of longtime female colleagues, all assured her that it as because she was "interim." "Just stay out of trouble," they told her. Of course this just added to her hesitancy when it came to making tough choices.

As the president's own image on campus shifted after his "honeymoon year," Jennifer decided to listen to her friends rather than follow the president's lead. After all, her reputation on campus was at stake.

Review Questions

1. What is the major problem facing Jennifer?
2. What would you do if you were in her position?
3. Would a man have the same experience as Jennifer?
4. Are any of your predictions about her management style holding up?

Part C

When the hiring freeze was lifted and Jennifer's position was able to be filled, the president insisted on a national search. Jennifer and her friends felt this was silly, given that she was going into her third year in the job. Nonetheless, she entered the search process.

After a year-long search, the Search Committee met with the president. The external candidates were not acceptable to the campus. Jennifer, they recommended, should only be appointed on a permanent basis if she agreed to change her management style.

The president mulled over his dilemma, then decided to give Jennifer the benefit of the doubt and the opportunity. He appointed her permanent provost, while making the following private agreement with her.

1. She would organize her office and staff and begin delegating more work to others.
2. She would "play" her number two position, backing the president and echoing his position on the university's vision statement.
3. She would provide greater direction for the Deans who report to her.

Jennifer agreed to take the position. She was now the university's first female vice president and presided over a council of 11 deans, three of whom were her best female friends. Once again, they sought out their every-Friday-night watering hole for an evening of dinner and celebration.

Review Questions

1. If you were Jennifer, would you have accepted the job?
2. What would you do as the new, permanent, vice president?
3. Will Jennifer change her management style? If so, in what ways?
4. What are your predictions for the future?

Part D

Although people had predicted that things would be better once Jennifer was permanently in the job, things in fact became more problematic. People now expected Jennifer to be able to take decisive action. She did not feel she could.

Every time an issue came up, she would spend weeks, sometimes months, trying to get a sense of the campus. Nothing moved once it hit her office. After a while, people began referring to the vice president's office as "the black hole" where things just went in and disappeared.

Her immediate staff were concerned and frustrated. Not only did she not delegate effectively, but her desire to make things better led her to try to do more and more herself.

The vice president's job also carried social obligations and requests. Here again, she tried to please everyone and often ran from one evening obligation to another, trying to show her support and concern for every constituency on campus. She was exhausted, overwhelmed, and knowing the mandate under which she was appointed, anxious about the president's evaluation of her behavior.

The greatest deterioration occurred within her Dean's Council. Several of the male Deans, weary of waiting for direction from Jennifer regarding where she was taking some of the academic proposals of the president, had started making decisions without Jennifer's approval.

"Loose cannons," was how she described a couple of them. "They don't listen. They just march out there on their own."

One of the big problems with two of the deans was that they just didn't take "no" for an answer when it came from Jennifer. Privately, each conceded that her "no" sounded like a "maybe." She always left room open to renegotiate.

Whatever the problem, and there were several by now, Jennifer's ability to lead was being questioned. Although her popularity was as high as ever, more and more people on campus were expressing their frustrations with what sometimes appeared as mixed signals from her and the president and sometimes was seen as virtually no direction. People wanted priorities. Instead, crisis management reigned.

Review Questions

1. If you were president, what would you do?
2. If you were Jennifer, what would you do?

Conclusion

Jennifer had a few "retreats" with her senior staff. Each time, she committed herself to delegate more, prioritize, and work on time management issues, but within 10 days or so, everything was back to business as usual.

The president decided to hire a person with extensive corporate experience to fill the vacant position of Vice President of Finance and Administration. The new man was an experienced team player who had survived mergers, been fired and bounced back, and had spent years in the number-two position in several companies. Within a few months he had earned the respect of the campus as well as the president and was in fact emerging as the person who really ran the place. Meanwhile, the president concentrated on external affairs and fundraising.

Jennifer felt relieved. Her role felt clearer. She could devote herself to academic and faculty issues and she was out from under the pressure to play "hatchet man." As she neared the magic age for early retirement, she began to talk more and more about what she wanted to do next. ∎

Case Notes

Case 1

Copyright © 2000 Andrew Templer.

While it is not permitted to copy this case, copies or permission to reproduce are available from the Laurier Institute, Wilfrid Laurier University. Please contact the Laurier Institute at 519-884-0710 ext. 6997 or visit their website at www.wlu.ca/laurierinstitute and look under "Case Information". This material is not covered under authorization from CanCopy or any other reproduction rights organization.

Case 2

1. Hof, Robert; Hamm, Steve; and Sager, Ira. "Is the Center of the Computing Universe Shifting?," *Business Week*, January 19, 1999, pp. 64-72.

2. Helft, Miguel. "Sun Succeeds with Market Savvy, Pragmatism," *San Jose Mercury News*, December 6, 1998.

3. Hof, Hamm, and Sager, op. cit.

4. Ibid.

5. Ibid.

6. Ibid.

7. Ibid.

8. Helft, op. cit.

9. Merrick, Amy. "Companies Go the Extra Mile to Retain Employees," *R&D*, September 1998, p. S3.

10. Hof, Hamm, and Sager, op. cit.

11. Ibid.

12. "Sun Microsystems Homepage-History," http://www.sun.com/corporate over view/who/ html_history.html, April 20, 1999.

13. Hof, Hamm, and Sager, op. cit.

14. Helft, op. cit.

15. Hof, op. cit.

16. Helft, op. cit.

17. Hof, op. cit.

18. Sager, Ira; Yang, Catherine; Himelstein, Linda; and Gross, Neil. "Power-Play: AOL-Netscape-Sun," *Business Week*, December 7, 1998.

19. Taschek, John. "This Just In: The World Revolves Around Sun," *PC Week*, January 4, 1999, p. 48.

20. Ibid.

21. McFarlane, John. "Whose WebTone Is It, Anyway?," http://www.sun.com/corporate over view/news/ webtone.html, May 1998.

22. Helft, op. cit.

23. Wildstrom, Stephen H. "The PC: Imperfect and Indispensable," *Business Week*, September 3, 2001.

24. Graham-Hackett, Megan. "A New Dawn for Sun Microsystems?" *Business Week*, February 22, 2002.

25. Shankland, Steven. "Sun Boosts Java on Linux Gadgets," http://news.com/2100-1001-251821.html?legacy=cnet, January 31, 2001.

26. MetaGroup, "Making the Move to Linux," http://techupdate.zdnet/techupdate/stories/main/p,14179,2810801,0.html, September 7, 2001.

27. Burrows, Peter. "Sun's Defiant Face-Off," http://businessweek.com/magazine/content/01_47/b3758001.htm.

28. Ibid.

reasons http://businessweek.com/magazine/content/01_36/ b3747030.htm

solve http:www.businessweek.com/investor/content/feb2002/pi2002022_1909.htm

power http://news.com.com/2100-1001-251821.html?legacy =cnet

dominant http://techupdate.zdnet/techupdate/stories/main/ p,14179,2810801,0html

Peter Burrows http://businessweek.com/magazine/content/01_47/b3758001.htm

Case 3

Case 5

Case 7

Case 8

Case 10

1. Dodd, Annmarie. "The Fastest Sport on Earth-Fast-Moving and Fast-Growing, NASCAR Uses Its Loud, Folksy Appeal to Find New Racing Fans for the Future," *Daily News Record*, January 25, 1999.
2. Ibid.
3. Ibid.
4. Ibid.
5. Glick, Shav. "Dollar Signs: Sponsorships, Big Money Make NASCAR World Go 'Round," *Los Angeles Times*, February 14, 1999, p. D1.
6. Yost, Mark. "Companies Use NASCAR Races as Means to Rub Elbows, Boost Their Business," *Wall Street Journal*, February 22, 1999, p. B17B.
7. Dodd, op. cit.
8. "NASCAR Online: Jeff Gordon," http://www.nascar.com/winstoncup/drivers/GordJ01/index.html, February 19, 1999.
9. Cain, Holly. "Gordon Becomes Driving Force," *Seattle Times*, February 14, 1999, p. D1.
10. Glick, op. cit, p. D1.
11. Slater, Chuck. "Life in the Fast Lane," *Fast Company*, http://www.fastcompany.com/online/18/fastlane.html, October 1998.
12. Ibid.
13. Ibid.
14. Ibid.
15. Ibid.
16. Hinton, Ed. "Gordon's Gamble," *Sports Illustrated*, October 11, 1999.
17. Bechtel, Mark. "Like Old Times," *Sports Illustrated*, April 24, 2000.
18. Spencer, Lee. "Meet the Four-Time Champ-He's 30 Now," *Sporting News*, November 26, 2001. Robbie Loomis http://www.jeffgordon.com/team/bio_robbieloomis.html; record http://www.sportingnews.com/

Case 11

Case 12

Case 13

1. Canavan, Patrick. "Motorola: Agility for the Whole Organization," *Human Resource Planning*, September 1998, p. 13(1).
2. "Motorola Homepage-Timeline," http://www.mot.com/General/Timeline/timeln24.html, March 4, 1999.
3. "Managing People: Nicely Does It," *The Economist*, March 19, 1994, p. 84. "Motorola Homepage-Culture," http://www.mot.com/Employment/stand.htm, March 19, 1999.
4. "Organizational Culture Alignment," http://www.msdev.com/culture.htm, March 7, 1999.
5. Ibid.
6. Roth, Daniel. "From Poster Boy to Whipping Boy: Burying Motorola," *Fortune*, July 6, 1998, p. 28(2).
7. Ibid.
8. Cane, Alan. "Nokia Seizes Top Spot in Mobile Phones," *Financial Times* (London), February 8, 1999, p. 22.
9. Ibid.
10. Peltz, Michael. "Hard Cell," *Worth*, March 1999, pp. 45-47.
11. Mossberg, Walter. "Cures for PC Boredom: A Truly Global Phone and a Better Palm Pilot," *Wall Street Journal*, March 11, 1999, p. B1.
12. Peltz, op. cit.

Case 14

Case 15

Case 17

While it is not permitted to copy this case, copies or permission to reproduce are available from the Laurier Institute, Wilfrid Laurier University. Please contact the Laurier Institute at 519-884-0710 ext. 6997 or visit their website at www.wlu.ca/laurierinstitute and look under "Case Information". This material is not covered under authorization from CanCopy or any other reproduction rights organization.

Case 18

While it is not permitted to copy this case, copies or permission to reproduce are available from the Laurier Institute, Wilfrid Laurier University. Please contact the Laurier Institute at 519-884-0710 ext. 6997 or visit their website at www.wlu.ca/laurierinstitute and look under "Case Information". This material is not covered under authorization from CanCopy or any other reproduction rights organization.

experiential
EXERCISES

EXERCISE 1

My Best Manager

Procedure

1. Make a list of the attributes that describe the best manager you ever worked for. If you have trouble identifying an actual manager, make a list of attributes you would like the manager in your next job to have.

2. Form a group of four or five persons and share your lists.

3. Create one list that combines all the unique attributes of the "best" managers represented in your group. Make sure that you have all attributes listed, but list each only once. Place a check mark next to those that were reported by two or more members. Have one of your members prepared to present the list in general class discussion.

4. After all groups have finished Step 3, spokespersons should report to the whole class. The instructor will make a running list of the "best" manager attributes as viewed by the class.

5. Feel free to ask questions and discuss the results.

EXERCISE 2

Graffiti Needs Assessment: Involving Students in the First Class Session

Contributed by Barbara K. Goza, Visiting Associate Professor, University of California at Santa Cruz and Associate Professor, California State Polytechnic University, Pomona. From *Journal of Management Education*, 1993.

Procedure

1. Complete the following sentences with as many endings as possible.
   1. When I first came to this class, I thought . . .
   2. My greatest concern this term is . . .
   3. In 3 years I will be . . .
   4. The greatest challenge facing the world today is . . .
   5. Organizational behaviour specialists do . . .
   6. Human resources are . . .
   7. Organizational research is . . .
   8. The most useful question I've been asked is . . .
   9. The most important phenomenon in organizations is . . .
   10. I learn the most when . . .
2. Your instructor will guide you in a class discussion about your responses. Pay careful attention to similarities and differences among various students' answers.

EXERCISE 3

My Best Job

Procedure

1. Make a list of the top five things you expect from your first (or next) full-time job.
2. Exchange lists with a nearby partner. Assign probabilities (or odds) to each goal on your partner's list to indicate how likely you feel it is that the goal can be accomplished. (*Note:* Your instructor may ask that everyone use the same probabilities format.)
3. Discuss your evaluations with your partner. Try to delete superficial goals or modify them to become more substantial. Try to restate any unrealistic goals to make them more realistic. Help your partner do the same.
4. Form a group of four to six persons. Within the group, have everyone share what they now consider to be the most "realistic" goals on their lists. Elect a spokesperson to share a sample of these items with the entire class.
5. Discuss what group members have individually learned from the exercise. Await further class discussion led by your instructor.

EXERCISE 4

What Do You Value in Work?

Procedure

1. The following nine items are from a survey conducted by Nicholas J. Beutell and O. C. Brenner ("Sex Differences in Work Values," *Journal of Vocational Behavior*, Vol. 28, pp. 29–41, 1986). Rank order the nine items in terms of how important (9 = most important) they would be to you in a job.

How important is it to you to have a job that:
____ Is respected by other people?
____ Encourages continued development of knowledge and skills?
____ Provides job security?
____ Provides a feeling of accomplishment?
____ Provides the opportunity to earn a high income?

____ Is intellectually stimulating?
____ Rewards good performance with recognition?
____ Provides comfortable working conditions?
____ Permits advancement to high administrative responsibility?

2. Form into groups as designated by your instructor. Within each group, the *men in the group* will meet to develop a consensus ranking of the items as they think the *women* in the Beutell and Brenner survey ranked them. The reasons for the rankings should be shared and discussed so they are clear to everyone. The *women in the group* should not participate in this ranking task.

They should listen to the discussion and be prepared to comment later in class discussion. A spokesperson for the men in the group should share the group's rankings with the class.

3. (*Optional*) Form into groups as designated by your instructor, but with each group consisting entirely of men or women. Each group should meet and decide which of the work values members of the *opposite* sex ranked first in the Beutell and Brenner survey. Do this again for the work value ranked last. The reasons should be discussed, along with reasons that each of the other values probably was not ranked first . . . or last. A spokesperson for each group should share group results with the rest of the class.

Source: Adapted from Roy J. Lewicki, Donald D. Bowen, Douglas T. Hall, and Francine S. Hall, *Experiences in Management and Organizational Behavior,* 3rd ed. (New York: John Wiley & Sons, Inc., 1988), pp. 23–26. Used by permission.

EXERCISE 5

My Asset Base

A business has an asset base or set of resources that it uses to produce a good or service of value to others. For a business, these are the assets or resources it uses to achieve results, including capital, land, patented products or processes, buildings and equipment, raw materials, and the human resources or employees, among others.

Each of us has an asset base that supports our ability to accomplish the things we set out to do. We refer to our personal assets as *talents, strengths,* or *abilities.* We probably inherit our talents from our parents, but we acquire many of our abilities and strengths through learning. One thing is certain: we feel very proud of the talents and abilities we have.

Procedure

1. Printed here is a T chart that you are to fill out. On the right-hand side of the T, list four or five of your accomplishments—*things you have done of which you are most proud.* Your accomplishments should only include those things for which you can take credit, those *things for which you are primarily responsible.* If you are proud of the sorority to which you belong, you may be justifiably proud, but don't list it unless you can argue that the sorority's excellence is due primarily to your efforts.

However, if you feel that having been invited to join the sorority is a major accomplishment for you, then you may include it.

When you have completed the right-hand side of the chart, fill in the left-hand side by listing *talents, strengths,* and *abilities* that you have that have enabled you to accomplish the outcomes listed on the right-hand side.

2. Share your lists with other team members. As each member takes turn sharing his or her list, pay close attention to your own perceptions and feelings. Notice the effect this has on your attitudes toward the other team members.

3. Discuss these questions in your group:
   (a) How did your attitudes and feelings toward other members of the team change as you pursued the activity? What does this tell you about the process whereby we come to get to know and care about people?
   (b) How did you feel about the instructions the instructor provided? What did you expect to happen? Were your expectations accurate?

My Asset Base

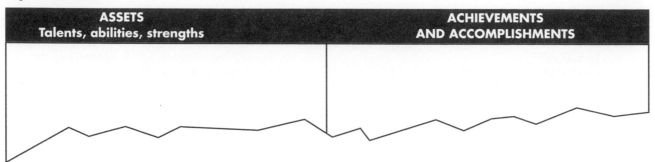

ASSETS Talents, abilities, strengths	ACHIEVEMENTS AND ACCOMPLISHMENTS

Source: Adapted from Donald D. Bowen et al., *Experiences in Management and Organizational Behavior,* 4th ed. (New York: John Wiley & Sons, Inc.), 1997.

EXERCISE 6

Expatriate Assignments

Contributed by Robert E. Ledman, Morehouse College

This exercise focuses on issues related to workers facing international assignments. It illustrates that those workers face a multitude of issues. It further demonstrates that managers who want employees to realize the maximum benefits of international assignments should be aware of, and prepared to deal with, those issues. Some of the topics that are easily addressed with this exercise include the need for culture and language training for the employees and their families and the impact that international assignments may have on an employee's family and how that may affect an employee's willingness to seek such assignments.

Procedure

1. Form into "families" of four or five. Since many students today have only one parent at home, it is helpful if some groups do not have students to fill both parental roles in the exercise. Each student is assigned to play a family member and given a description of that person. Descriptions of family members are given below.

2. Enter into a 20-minute discussion to explore how a proposed overseas assignment will affect the family members. Your goal is to try to reach a decision about whether the assignment should be taken. You must also decide whether the entire family or only the

Source: Robert E. Ledman, Gannon University. Presented in the Experiential Exercise Track of the 1996 ABSEL Conference and published in the *Proceedings* of that conference.

family member being offered the assignment will relocate. The assignment is for a minimum of two years, with possible annual extensions resulting in a total of four years, and your family, or the member offered the assignment, will be provided, at company expense, one trip back to the states each year for a maximum period of 15 days. The member offered the assignment will not receive any additional housing or cost-of-living supplements described in the role assignment if he or she chooses to go overseas alone and can expect his or her living expenses to exceed substantially the living allowance being provided by the company. In your discussion, address the following questions:

(a) What are the most important concerns your family has about relocating to a foreign country?

(b) What information should you seek about the proposed host country to be able to make a more informed decision?

(c) What can the member offered the assignment do to make the transition easier if he or she goes overseas alone? If the whole family relocates?

(d) What should the member offered the assignment do to ensure that this proposed assignment will not create unnecessary stress for him or her and the rest of the family?

(e) What lessons for managers of expatriate assignees are presented by the situation in this exercise?

Try to reach some "family" consensus. If a consensus is not possible, however, resolve any differences in the manner you think the family in the role descriptions would ultimately resolve any differences.

3. Share your answers with the rest of the class. Explain the rationale for your answers and answer questions from the remainder of the class.

4. (*Optional*) After each group has reported on a given question, the instructor may query the class about how their answers are consistent, or inconsistent, with common practice of managers as described in the available literature.

Descriptions of Family Members
Person Being Offered Overseas Assignment

This person is a middle- to upper-level executive who is on a fast track to senior management. He or she has been offered the opportunity to manage an overseas operation, with the assurance of a promotion to a vice presidency upon return to the states. The company will pay all relocation expenses, including selling costs for the family home and the costs associated with finding a new home upon return. The employer will also provide language training for the employee and cultural awareness training for the entire family. The employee will receive a living allowance equal to 20 percent of his or her salary. This should be adequate to provide the family a comparable standard of living to that which is possible on the employee's current salary.

Spouse of the Person Offered an Overseas Assignment (Optional)

This person is also a professional with highly transferable skills and experience for the domestic market. It is unknown how easily he or she may be able to find employment in the foreign country. This person's income, though less than his or her spouse's, is necessary if the couple is to continue paying for their child's college tuition and to prepare for the next child to enter college in two years. This person has spent 15 years developing a career, including completing a degree at night.

Oldest Child

This child is a second-semester junior in college and is on track to graduate in 16 months. Transferring at this time would probably mean adding at least one semester to complete the degree. He or she has been dating the same person for over a year; they have talked about getting married immediately after graduation, although they are not yet formally engaged.

Middle Child

This child is a junior in high school. He or she has already begun visiting college campuses in preparation for applying in the fall. This child is involved in a number of school activities; he or she is photographer for the yearbook and plays a varsity sport. This child has a learning disability for which services are being provided by the school system.

Youngest Child

This child is a middle school student, age 13. He or she is actively involved in Scouting and takes piano lessons. This child has a history of medical conditions that have required regular visits to the family physician and specialists. This child has several very close friends who have attended the same school for several years.

EXERCISE 7

Cultural Cues

Contributed by Susan Rawson Zacur and W. Alan Randolph, University of Baltimore

Introduction
In the business context, culture involves shared beliefs and expectations that govern the behaviour of people. In this exercise, *foreign culture* refers to a set of beliefs and expectations different from those of the participant's home culture (which has been invented by the participants).

Procedure
1. (10–15 minutes) Divide into two groups, each with colour-coded badges. For example, the blue group could receive blue Post-it notes and the yellow group could receive yellow Post-it notes. Print your first name in bold letters on the badge and wear it throughout the exercise.

Cultural Cues:	Your Culture:
Facial expression:	
Eye contact (note: you must have some eye contact in order to observe others):	
Handshake:	
Body language (note: must be evident while standing):	
Key words or phrases:	

Work with your group members to invent your own cultural cues. Think about the kinds of behaviours and words that will signify to all members that they belong together in one culture. For each category provided below, identify and record at least one important attribute for your culture.

Once you have identified desirable cultural aspects for your group, practise them. It is best to stand with your group and to engage one another in conversations involving two or three people at a time. Your aim in talking with one another is to learn as much as possible about each other—hobbies, interests, where you live, what your family is like, what courses you are taking, and so on, all the while practicing the behaviours and words identified above. It is not necessary for participants to answer questions of a personal nature truthfully. Invention is permissible because the conversation is only a means to the end of cultural observation. Your aim at this point is to become comfortable with the indicators of your particular culture. Practise until the indicators are second nature to you.

2. Now assume that you work for a business that has decided to explore the potential for doing business with companies in a different culture. You are to learn as much as possible about another culture. To do so, you will send from one to three representatives from your group on a "business trip" to the other culture. These representatives must, insofar as possible, behave in a manner that is consistent with your culture. At the same time, each representative must endeavour to learn as much as possible about the people in the other culture, while keeping eyes and ears open to cultural attributes that will be useful in future negotiations with foreign businesses. (*Note:* At no time will it be considered ethical behaviour for the representative to ask direct questions about the foreign culture's attributes. These must be gleaned from first-hand experience.)

While your representatives are away, you will receive one or more exchange visitors from the other culture, who will engage in conversation as they attempt to learn more about your organizational culture. You must strictly adhere to the cultural aspects of your own culture while you converse with the visitors.

3. (5–10 minutes) All travellers return to your home cultures. As a group, discuss and record what you have learned about the foreign culture based on the exchange of visitors. This information will serve as the basis for orienting the next representatives who will make a business trip.

4. (5–10 minutes) Select one to three different group members to make another trip to the other culture to check out the assumptions your group has made about the other culture. This "checking out" process will consist of actually practising the other culture's cues to see whether they work.

5. (5–10 minutes) Once the traveller(s) have returned and reported on findings, as a group, prepare to report to the class what you have learned about the other culture.

Source: Adapted by Susan Rawson Zacur and W. Alan Randolph from *Journal of Management Education,* Vol. 17, No. 4 (November 1993), pp. 510–516.

EXERCISE 8

Prejudice in Our Lives

Contributed by Susan Schor of Pace University and Annie McKee of The Wharton School, University of Pennsylvania with the assistance of Ariel Fishman of The Wharton School

Procedure

1. As a large class group, generate a list of groups that tend to be targets of prejudice and stereotypes in our culture—such groups can be based on gender, race, ethnicity, sexual orientation, region, religion, and so on. After generating a list, either as a class or in small groups, identify a few common positive and negative stereotypes associated with each group. Also consider relationships or patterns that exist between some of the lists. Discuss the implications for groups that have stereotypes that are valued in organizations versus groups whose stereotypes are viewed negatively in organizations.

2. As an individual, think about the lists you have now generated, and list those groups with which you identify. Write about an experience in which you were stereotyped as a member of a group. Ask yourself the following questions and write down your thoughts:

   (a) What group do I identify with?
   (b) What was the stereotype?
   (c) What happened? When and where did the incident occur? Who said what to whom?
   (d) What were my reactions? How did I feel? What did I think? What did I do?

   (e) What were the consequences? How did the incident affect myself and others?

3. Now, in small groups, discuss your experiences. Briefly describe the incident and focus on how the incident made you feel. Select one incident from the ones shared in your group to role-play for the class. Then, as a class, discuss your reactions to each role play. Identify the prejudice or stereotype portrayed, the feelings the situation evoked, and the consequences that might result from such a situation.

4. Think about the prejudices and stereotypes you hold about other people. Ask yourself, "What groups do I feel prejudice toward? What stereotypes do I hold about members of each of these groups?" How may such a prejudice have developed—did a family member or close friend or television influence you to stereotype a particular group in a certain way?

5. Now try to identify implications of prejudice in the workplace. How do prejudice and stereotypes affect workers, managers, relationships between people, and the organization as a whole? Consider how you might want to change erroneous beliefs as well as how you would encourage other people to change their own erroneous beliefs.

EXERCISE 9

How We View Differences

Contributed by Barbara Walker

Introduction

Clearly, the workplace of the future will be much more diverse than it is today: more women, more people of colour, more international representation, more diverse lifestyles and ability profiles, and the like. Managing a diverse workforce and working across a range of differences is quickly becoming a "core competency" for effective managers.

Furthermore, it is also becoming clear that diversity in a work team can significantly enhance the creativity and quality of the team's output. In today's turbulent business environment, utilizing employee diversity will give

the manager and the organization a competitive edge in tapping all of the available human resources more effectively. This exercise is an initial step in the examination of how we work with people whom we see as different from us. It is fairly simple, straightforward, and safe, but its implications are profound.

Procedure

1. Read the following:

Imagine that you are travelling in a rental car in a city you have never visited before. You have a one-hour drive on an uncrowded highway before you reach your destination. You decide that you would like to spend the time listening to some of your favourite kind of music on the car radio.

The rental car has four selection buttons available, each with a preset station that plays a different type of music. One plays *country music,* one plays *rock,* one plays *classical,* and one plays *jazz.* Which type of music would you choose to listen to for the next hour as you drive along? (Assume you want to relax and just stick with one station; you don't want to bother switching around between stations.)

2. Form into groups based on the type of music that you have chosen. All who have chosen country will meet in an area designated by the instructor. Those who chose rock will meet in another area, and so on. In your groups, answer the following question. Appoint one member to be the spokesperson to report your answers back to the total group.

Question
For each of the other groups, what words would you use to describe people who like to listen to that type of music?

3. Have each spokesperson report the responses of her or his group to the question in Step 2. Follow with class discussion of these additional questions:

(a) What do you think is the purpose or value of this exercise?
(b) What did you notice about the words used to describe the other groups? Were there any *surprises* in this exercise for you?
(c) Upon what sorts of data do you think these images were based?
(d) What term do we normally use to describe these generalized perceptions of another group?
(e) What could some of the consequences be?
(f) How do the perceptual processes here relate to other kinds of intergroup differences, such as race, gender, culture, ability, ethnicity, health, age, nationality, and so on?
(g) What does this exercise suggest about the ease with which intergroup stereotypes form?
(h) What might be ways an organization might facilitate the valuing and utilizing of differences between people?

Source: Exercise developed by Barbara Walker, a pioneer on work on valuing differences. Adapted for this volume by Douglas T. Hall. Used by permission of Barbara Walker.

EXERCISE 10

Alligator River Story

Source: From Sidney B. Simon, Howard Kirschenbaum, and Leland Howe, *Values Clarification, The Handbook,* rev. ed., copyright © 1991, Values Press, P.O. Box 450, Sunderland, MA. 01375. Send for a list of other strategy books from Value Press.

The Alligator River Story
There lived a woman named Abigail who was in love with a man named Gregory. Gregory lived on the shore of a river. Abigail lived on the opposite shore of the same river. The river that separated the two lovers was teeming with dangerous alligators. Abigail wanted to cross the river to be with Gregory. Unfortunately, the bridge had been washed out by a heavy flood the previous week. So she went to ask Sinbad, a riverboat captain, to take her across. He said he would be glad to if she would consent to go to bed with him prior to the voyage. She promptly refused and went to a friend named Ivan to explain her plight. Ivan did not want to get involved at all in the situation. Abigail felt her only alternative was to accept Sinbad's terms. Sinbad fulfilled his promise to Abigail and delivered her into the arms of Gregory. When Abigail told Gregory about her amorous escapade in order to cross the river, Gregory cast her aside with disdain. Heartsick and rejected, Abigail turned to Slug with her tail of woe. Slug, feeling compassion for Abigail, sought out Gregory and beat him brutally. Abigail was overjoyed at the sight of Gregory getting his due. As the sun set on the horizon, people heard Abigail laughing at Gregory.

Procedure
1. Read "The Alligator River Story."
2. After reading the story, rank the five characters in the story beginning with the one whom you consider the most offensive and end with the one whom you consider the least objectionable. That is, the character who seems to be the most reprehensible to you should be entered first in the list following the story, then the second most reprehensible, and so on, with the least reprehensible or objectionable being entered fifth. Of course,

you will have your own reasons as to why you rank them in the order that you do. Very briefly note these too.

3. Form groups as assigned by your instructor (at least four persons per group with gender mixed).
4. Each group should:
   (a) Elect a spokesperson for the group
   (b) Compare how the group members have ranked the characters
   (c) Examine the reasons used by each of the members for their rankings
   (d) Seek consensus on a final group ranking
5. Following your group discussions, you will be asked to share your outcomes and reasons for agreement or nonagreement. A general class discussion will then be held.

EXERCISE 11

Teamwork and Motivation

Contributed by Dr. Barbara McCain, Oklahoma City University

Procedure

1. Read this situation.

You are the *owner* of a small manufacturing corporation. Your company manufactures widgets—a commodity. Your widget is a clone of nationally known widgets. Your widget, "WooWoo," is less expensive and more readily available than the nationally known brand. Presently, the sales are high. However, there are many rejects, which increases your cost and delays the delivery. You have 50 employees in the following departments: sales, assembly, technology, and administration.

2. In groups, discuss methods to motivate all of the employees in the organization—rank order them in terms of preference.

3. Design an organization motivation plan that encourages high job satisfaction, low turnover, high productivity, and high-quality work.
4. Is there anything special you can do about the minimum-wage service worker? How do you motivate this individual? On what motivation theory do you base your decision?
5. Report to the class your motivation plan. Record your ideas on the board and allow all groups to build on the first plan. Discuss additions and corrections as the discussion proceeds.

Worksheet

Individual Worker	Team Member
Talks	
Me oriented	
Department focused	
Competitive	
Logical	
Written messages	
Image	
Secrecy	
Short-term sighted	
Immediate results	
Critical	
Tenure	

Directions: Fill in the right-hand column with descriptive terms. These terms should suggest a change in behaviour from individual work to teamwork.

The Downside of Punishment

Contributed by Dr. Barbara McCain, Oklahoma City University

Procedure

There are numerous problems associated with using punishment or discipline to change behaviour. Punishment creates negative effects in the workplace. To better understand this, work in your group to give an example of each of the following situations:

1. Punishment may not be applied to the person whose behaviour you want to change.

2. Punishment applied over time may suppress the occurrence of socially desirable behaviours.

3. Punishment creates a dislike of the person who is implementing the punishment.

4. Punishment results in undesirable emotions such as anxiety and agressiveness.

5. Punishment increases the desire to avoid punishment.

6. Punishing one behaviour does not guarantee that the desired behaviour will occur.

7. Punishment follow-up requires allocation of additional resources.

8. Punishment may create a communication barrier and inhibit the flow of information.

Source: Adapted from class notes: Dr. Larry Michaelson, Oklahoma University.

Annual Pay Raises

Contributed by Bonnie McNeely, Murray State University

Procedure

1. Read the job descriptions below and decide on a percentage pay increase for each of the eight employees.
2. Make salary increase recommendations for each of the eight managers that you supervise. There are no formal company restrictions on the size of raises you give, but the total for everyone should not exceed the $10,900 (a 4 percent increase in the salary pool) that has been bud-

geted for this purpose. You have a variety of information on which to base the decisions, including a "productivity index" (PI), which Industrial Engineering computes as a quantitative measure of operating efficiency for each manager's work unit. This index ranges from a high of 10 to a low of 1. Indicate the percentage increase _you_ would give each manager in the blank space next to each manager's name. Be prepared to explain why.

____ *A. Alvarez*   Alvarez is new this year and has a tough workgroup whose task is dirty and difficult. This is a hard position to fill, but you don't feel Alvarez is particularly good. The word around is that the other managers agree with you. PI = 3. Salary = $33,000.

____ *B. J. Cook*   Cook is single and a "swinger" who enjoys leisure time. Everyone laughs at the problems B.J. has getting the work out, and you feel it certainly is lacking. Cook has been in the job two years. PI = 3. Salary = $34,500.

____ *Z. Davis*   In the position three years, Davis is one of your best people, even though some of the other managers don't agree. With a spouse who is independently wealthy, Davis doesn't need money but likes to work. PI = 7. Salary = $36,600.

____ *M. Frame*   Frame has personal problems and is hurting financially. Others gossip about Frame's performance, but you are quite satisfied with this second-year employee. PI = 7. Salary = $34,700.

____ *C.M. Liu*   Liu is just finishing a fine first year in a tough job. Highly respected by the others, Liu has a job offer in another company at a 15 percent increase in salary. You are impressed, and the word is that the money is important. PI = 9. Salary = $34,000.

____ *B. Ratin*   Ratin is a first-year manager whom you and the others think is doing a good job. This is a bit surprising since Ratin turned out to be a "free spirit" who doesn't seem to care much about money or status. PI = 9. Salary = $33,800.

____ *H. Smith*   Smith is a first-year manager recently divorced and with two children to support as a single parent. The others like Smith a lot, but your evaluation is not very high. Smith could certainly use extra money. PI = 5. Salary = $33,000.

____ *G. White*   White is a big spender who always has the latest clothes and a new car. In the first year on what you would call an easy job, White doesn't seem to be doing very well. For some reason, though, the others talk about White as the "cream of the new crop." PI = 5. Salary = $33,000.

3. Convene in a group of four to seven persons and share your raise decision.

4. As a group, decide on a new set of raises and be prepared to report them to the rest of the class. Make sure that the group spokesperson can provide the rationale for each person's raise.

5. The instructor will call on each group to report its raise decisions. After discussion, an "expert's" decision will be given.

EXERCISE 14

Tinker Toys

Contributed by Bonnie McNeely, Murray State University

Materials Needed
Tinker Toy sets.

Procedure

1. Form groups as assigned by the instructor. The mission of each group or temporary organization is to build the tallest possible Tinker Toy tower. Each group should determine worker roles: at least four students will be builders, some will be consultants who offer suggestions, and the remaining students will be observers who remain silent and complete the observation sheet provided below.

2. Rules for the exercise:
   (a) Fifteen minutes allowed to plan the tower, but *only 60 seconds* to build.
   (b) No more than two Tinker Toy pieces can be put together during the planning.
   (c) All pieces must be put back in the box before the competition begins.
   (d) Completed tower must stand alone.

Observation Sheet

1. What planning activities were observed?

   Did the group members adhere to the rules?

2. What organizing activities were observed?

   Was the task divided into subtasks? Division of labour?

3. Was the group motivated to succeed? Why or why not?

4. Were any control techniques observed?

Was a timekeeper assigned?

Were backup plans discussed?

5. Did a clear leader emerge from the group?

What behaviours indicated that this person was the leader?

How did the leader establish credibility with the group?

6. Did any conflicts within the group appear?

Was there a power struggle for the leadership position?

Source: Adapted from Bonnie McNeely, "Using the Tinker Toy Exercise to Teach the Four Functions of Management, *Journal of Management Education,* Vol. 18, No. 4 (November 1994), 468–472.

EXERCISE 15

Job Design Preferences

Contributed by Lady Hanson, California State Polytechnic University, Pomona

Procedure

1. Use the left column to rank the following job characteristics in the order most important *to you* (1—highest to 10—lowest). Then use the right column to rank them in the order you think they are most important *to others*.

____ Variety of tasks ____
____ Performance feedback ____
____ Autonomy/freedom in work ____
____ Working on a team ____
____ Having responsibility ____
____ Making friends on the job ____
____ Doing all of a job, not part ____

____ Importance of job to others ____
____ Having resources to do well ____
____ Flexible work schedule ____

2. Form workgroups as assigned by your instructor. Share your rankings with other group members. Discuss where you have different individual preferences and where your impressions differ from the preferences of others. Are there any major patterns in your group—for either the "personal" or the "other" rankings? Develop group consensus rankings for each column. Designate a spokesperson to share the group rankings and results of any discussion with the rest of the class.

EXERCISE 16

My Fantasy Job

Contributed by Lady Hanson, California State Polytechnic University, Pomona

Procedure

1. Think about a possible job that represents what you consider to be your ideal or "fantasy" job. For discussion purposes, try to envision it as a job you would hold within a year of finishing your current studies. Write down a brief description of that job in the space below. Start the description with the following words—*My fantasy job would be* . . .

2. Review the description of the Hackman/Oldham model of Job Characteristics Theory offered in the textbook. Note in particular the descriptions of the core characteristics. Consider how each of them could be maximized in your fantasy job. Indicate in the spaces that follow how specific parts of your fantasy job will fit into or relate to each of the core characteristics.

(a) Skill variety:

(b) Task identity:

(c) Task significance:

(d) Autonomy:

(e) Job feedback:

3. Form into groups as assigned by your instructor. In the group have each person share his or her fantasy job and the descriptions of its core characteristics. Select one person from your group to tell the class as a whole about her or his fantasy job. Be prepared to participate in general discussion regarding the core characteristics and how they may or may not relate to job performance and job satisfaction. Consider also the likelihood that the fantasy jobs of class members are really attainable—in other words: Can "fantasy" become fact?

EXERCISE 17

Motivation by Job Enrichment

Procedure

1. Form groups of five to seven members. Each group is assigned one of the following categories:
   (a) Bank teller
   (b) Retail sales clerk
   (c) Manager, fast-food service (e.g., McDonald's)
   (d) Wait person
   (e) Receptionist
   (f) Restaurant manager
   (g) Clerical worker (or bookkeeper)
   (h) Janitor

2. As a group, develop a short description of job duties for the job your group has been assigned. The list should contain approximately four to six items.

3. Next, using job characteristics theory, enrich the job using the specific elements described in the theory. Develop a new list of job duties that incorporate any or all of the core job characteristics suggested by Richard Hackman and Greg Oldham, such as skill variety, task identity, and so on. Indicate for each of the new job duties which job characteristic(s) was/were used.

4. One member of each group should act as the spokesperson and will present the group's ideas to the class. Specifically describe one or two of the old job tasks. Describe the modified job tasks. Finally, relate the new job tasks the group has developed to specific job core characteristics such as skill variety, skill identity, and so on.

5. The group should also be prepared to discuss these and other follow-up questions:
   (a) How would a manager go about enlarging but not enriching this job?
   (b) Why was this job easy or hard?
   (c) What are the possible constraints on actually accomplishing this enrichment in the workplace?
   (d) What possible reasons are there that a worker would *not* like to have this newly enriched job?

EXERCISE 18 -------------------------------

Serving on the Boundary

Procedure

The objective of this exercise is to experience what it is like being on the boundary of your team or organization and to experience the boundary person's divided loyalties.

1. As a full class, decide on a stake you are willing to wager on this exercise. Perhaps it will be 5¢ or 10¢ per person or even more.
2. Form into teams. Select or elect one member from your team to be an expert. The expert will be the person most competent in the field of international geography.
3. The experts will then form into a team of their own.
4. The teams, including the expert team, are going to be given a straightforward question to work on. Whichever team comes closest to deriving the correct answer will win the pool from the stakes already collected. The question is any one of the following as assigned by the instructor: (a) What is the airline distance between Beijing and Moscow (in miles)? (b) What is the highest point in Texas (in feet)? (c) What was the number of American battle deaths in the Revolutionary War?
5. Each team should now work on the question, including the expert team. However, after all the teams come up with a verdict, the experts will be allowed to return to

their "home" team to inform the team of the expert team's deliberations.
6. The expert team members are now asked to reconvene as an expert team. They should determine their final answer to the question. Then, they are to face a decision. The instructor will announce that for a period of up to two minutes, any expert may either return to their home team (to sink or swim with the answer of the home team) or remain with the expert team. As long as two members remain in the expert team, it will be considered a group and may vie for the pool. Home teams, during the two-minute decision period, can do whatever they would like to do—within bounds of normal decorum—to try to persuade their expert member to return.
7. After the two minutes are up, teams will hand in their verdicts to the question, and the team with the closest answer (up or down) will be awarded the pool.
8. Class members should be prepared to discuss the following questions:
   (a) What did it feel like to be a boundary person (the expert)?
   (b) What could the teams have done to corral any of the boundary persons who chose not to return home?

EXERCISE 19 -------------------------------

Eggsperiential Exercise

Contributed by Dr. Barbara McCain, Oklahoma City University

Materials Needed

1 raw egg per group, 6 plastic straws per group, 1 yard of plastic tape, 1 large plastic jar

Procedure

1. Form into equal groups of five to seven people.
2. The task is to drop an egg from the chair onto the plastic without breaking the egg. Groups can evaluate the materials and plan their task for 10 minutes. During this period the materials may not be handled.
3. Groups have 10 minutes for construction.
4. One group member will drop the egg while standing on top of a chair in front of the class. One by one a representative from each group will drop their eggs.
5. Optional: Each group will name the egg.
6. Each group discusses their individual/group behaviours

during this activity. Optional: This analysis may be summarized in written form. The following questions may be utilized in the analysis:
   (a) What kind of group is it? Explain.
   (b) Was the group cohesive? Explain.
   (c) How did the cohesiveness relate to performance? Explain.
   (d) Was there evidence of groupthink? Explain.
   (e) Were group norms established? Explain.
   (f) Was there evidence of conflict? Explain.
   (g) Was there any evidence of social loafing? Explain.

EXERCISE 20

Scavenger Hunt — Team Building

Contributed by Michael R. Manning and Paula J. Schmidt, New Mexico State University

Introduction

Think about what it means to be a part of a team—a successful team. What makes one team more successful than another? What does each team member need to do in order for their team to be successful? What are the characteristics of an effective team?

Procedure

1. Form teams as assigned by your instructor. Locate the items on the list below while following these important rules:

   a. Your team *must stay together at all times*—that is, you cannot go in separate directions.

   b. Your team must return to the classroom in the time allotted by the instructor.

   The team with the most items on the list will be declared the most successful team.

2. Next, reflect on your team's experience. What did each team member do? What was your team's strategy? What made your team effective? Make a list of the most important things your team did to be succesful. Nominate a spokesperson to summarize your team's discussion for the class. What items were similar between teams? That is, what helped each team to be effective?

Items for Scavenger Hunt

Each item is to be identified and brought back to the classroom.

1. A book with the word "team" in the title.
2. A joke about teams that you share with the class.
3. A blade of grass from the university football field.
4. A souvenir from the state.
5. A picture of a team or group.
6. A newspaper article about a team.
7. A team song to be composed and performed for the class.
8. A leaf from an oak tree.
9. Stationery from the dean's office.
10. A cup of sand.
11. A pine cone.
12. A live reptile. (*Note:* Sometimes a team member has one for a pet or the students are ingenious enough to visit a local pet store.)
13. A definition of group "cohesion" that you share with the class.
14. A set of chopsticks.
15. Three cans of vegetables.
16. A branch of an elm tree.
17. Three unusual items.
18. A ball of cotton.
19. The ear from a prickly pear cactus.
20. A group name.

(*Note:* Items may be substituted as appropriate for your locale.)

Source: Adapted from Michael R. Manning and Paula J. Schmidt, *Journal of Management Education,* Building Effective Work Teams: A Quick Exercise Based on a Scavenger Hunt (Thousand Oaks, CA: Sage Publications, 1995), pp. 392–398. Used by permission. Reference for list of items for scavenger hunt from C. E. Larson and F. M. Lafas, *Team Work: What Must Go Right/What Can Go Wrong* (Newbury Park, CA: Sage Publications, 1989).

EXERCISE 21

Work Team Dynamics

Introduction

Think about your course work team, a work team you are involved in for another course, or any other team suggested by the instructor. Indicate how often each of the following statements accurately reflects your experience in the team. Use this scale:

1 = Always   2 = Frequently   3 = Sometimes   4 = Never

_____ 1. My ideas get a fair hearing.

_____ 2. I am encouraged for innovative ideas and risk taking.

_____ 3. Diverse opinions within the team are encouraged.

_____ 4. I have all the responsibility I want.

_____ 5. There is a lot of favoritism shown in the team.

_____ 6. Members trust one another to do their assigned work.

_____ 7. The team sets high standards of performance excellence.

_____ 8. People share and change jobs a lot in the team.

_____ 9. You can make mistakes and learn from them on this team.

_____ 10. This team has good operating rules.

Procedure

Form groups as assigned by your instructor. Ideally, this will be the team you have just rated. Have all team members share their ratings, and make one master rating for the team as a whole. Circle the items on which there are the biggest differences of opinion. Discuss those items and try to find out why they exist. In general, the better a team scores on this instrument, the higher its creative potential. If everyone has rated the same team, make a list of the five most important things members can do to improve its operations in the future. Nominate a spokesperson to summarize the team discussion for the class as a whole.

Source: Adapted from William Dyer, _Team Building,_ 2nd ed. (Reading, MA: Addison-Wesley, 1987), pp. 123–125.

EXERCISE 22 -

Identifying Group Norms

Procedure

1. Choose an organization you know quite a bit about.

2. Complete the questionnaire below, indicating your responses using one of the following:

> (a) Strongly agree or encourage it.
> (b) Agree with it or encourage it.
> (c) Consider it unimportant.
> (d) Disagree with or discourage it.
> (e) Strongly disagree with or discourage it.

_If_ an employee in this organization were to . . . _Most other employees would:_

1. Show genuine concern for the problems that face the organization and make suggestions about solving them . . . _____
2. Set very high personal standards of performance . . . _____
3. Try to make the workgroup operate more like a team when dealing with issues or problems . . . _____
4. Think of going to a supervisor with a problem . . . _____
5. Evaluate expenditures in terms of the benefits they will provide for the organization . . . _____

6. Express concern for the well-being of other members of the organization . . . _____
7. Keep a customer or client waiting while looking after matters of personal convenience . . . _____
8. Criticize a fellow employee who is trying to improve things in the work situation . . . _____
9. Actively look for ways to expand his or her knowledge to be able to do a better job . . . _____
10. Be perfectly honest in answering this questionnaire . . . _____

Scoring

A = +2, B = +1, C = 0, D = –1, E = –2   Score

1. Organizational/Personal Pride _____
2. Performance/Excellence _____
3. Teamwork/Communication _____
4. Leadership/Supervision _____
5. Profitability/Cost-Effectiveness _____
6. Colleague/Associate Relations _____
7. Customer/Client Relations _____
8. Innovativeness/Creativity _____
9. Training/Development _____
10. Candor/Openness _____

EXERCISE 23

Workgroup Culture

Contributed by Conrad N. Jackson, MPC, Inc.

Procedure

1. The bipolar scales on this instrument can be used to evaluate a group's process in a number of useful ways. Use it to measure where you see the group to be at present. To do this, *circle* the number that best represents *how you see the culture of the group.* You can also indicate how you think the group *should* function by using a different symbol, such as a square (□) or a caret (^), to indicate how you saw the group at some time in the past.
2. (a) If you are assessing your own group, have everyone fill in the instrument, summarize the scores, then discuss their bases (what members say and do that has led to these interpretations) and implications. This is often an extremely productive intervention to improve group or team functioning.
   (b) If you are assessing another group, use the scores as the basis for your feedback. Be sure to provide specific feedback on behaviour *you have observed* in

addition to the subjective interpretations of your ratings on the scales in this instrument.
   (c) The instrument can also be used to compare a group's self-assessment with the assessment provided by another group.

1. Trusting	1 : 2 : 3 : 4 : 5	Suspicious
2. Helping	1 : 2 : 3 : 4 : 5	Ignoring, blocking
3. Expressing feelings	1 : 2 : 3 : 4 : 5	Suppressing feelings
4. Risk taking	1 : 2 : 3 : 4 : 5	Cautious
5. Authenticity	1 : 2 : 3 : 4 : 5	Game playing
6. Confronting	1 : 2 : 3 : 4 : 5	Avoiding
7. Open	1 : 2 : 3 : 4 : 5	Hidden, diplomatic

Source: Adapted from Donald D. Bowen, et al., *Experiences in Management and Organizational Behavior,* 4th ed. (New York: John Wiley & Sons, Inc.), 1997.

EXERCISE 24

The Hot Seat

Contributed by Barry R. Armandi, SUNY–Old Westbury

Procedure

1. Form into groups as assigned by your instructor.
2. Read the following situation.

A number of years ago, Professor Stevens was asked to attend a departmental meeting at a university. He had been on leave from the department, but a junior faculty member discreetly requested that he attend to protect the rights of the junior faculty. The Chair, or head of the department, was a typical Machiavellian, whose only concerns were self-serving. Professor Stevens had had a number of previous disagreements with the Chair. The heart of the disagreements centred around the Chair's abrupt and domineering style and his poor relations with the junior faculty, many of whom felt mistreated and scared.

The department was a conglomeration of different professorial types. Included in the mix were behaviourists, generalists, computer scientists, and quantitative analysts. The department was

embedded in the school of business, which had three other departments. There was much confusion and concern among the faculty, since this was a new organizational design. Many of the faculty were at odds with each other over the direction the school was now taking.

At the meeting, a number of proposals were to be presented that would seriously affect the performance and future of certain junior faculty, particularly those who were behavioural scientists. The Chair, a computer scientist, disliked the behaviourists, who he felt were "always analyzing the motives of people." Professor Stevens, who was a tenured full professor and a behaviourist, had an objective to protect the interests of the junior faculty and to counter the efforts of the Chair.

Including Professor Stevens, there were nine faculty present. The accompanying diagram below shows the seating arrangement and the layout of the room. The ×s signify those faculty who were allies of the Chair. The +s are those opposed to the Chair and supportive of Professor Stevens, and the ?s were undecided and could be swayed either way. The circled numbers represent empty seats. Both **?**s were behaviourists, and the **+** next to them was a quantitative analyst. Near the door, the first **×** was a generalist, the two **+**s were behaviourists, and the second **×** was a quantitative analyst. The diagram shows the seating of everyone but Professor Stevens, who was the last one to enter the room. Standing at the door, Professor Stevens surveyed the room and within 10 seconds knew which seat was the most effective to achieve his objective.

3. Answer the following questions in your group.
   (a) Which seat did Professor Stevens select and why?
   (b) What is the likely pattern of communication and interaction in this group?
   (c) What can be done to get this group to work harmoniously?

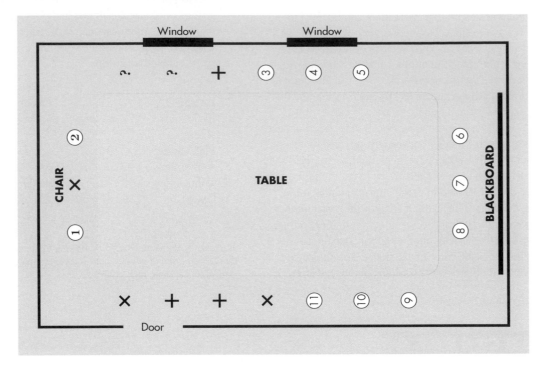

EXERCISE 25

Organizations Alive!

Contributed by Bonnie L. McNeely, Murray State University

Procedure

1. Find a copy of the following items from actual organizations. These items can be obtained from the company where you now work, a parent's workplace, or the university. Universities have mission statements, codes of conduct for students and faculty, organizational charts, job descriptions, performance appraisal forms, and control devices. Some student organizations also have these documents. All the items do not have to come from the same organization. *Bring these items to class.*

   (a) Mission statement
   (b) Code of ethics
   (c) Organizational chart
   (d) Job description
   (e) Performance appraisal form
   (f) Control device

2. Form groups in class as assigned by your instructor. Share your items with the group, as well as what you learned while collecting these items. For example, did you find that some firms have a mission, but it is not written down? Did you find that job descriptions existed, but they were not really used or had not been updated in years?

Source: Adapted from Bonnie L. McNeely, "Make Your Principles of Management Class Come Alive," *Journal of Management Education,* Vol. 18, No. 2, May 1994, 246–249.

EXERCISE 26 — — — — — — — — — — — — — — — — — — —

Fast-Food Technology

Contributed by D. T. Hall, Boston University, and F. S. Hall, University of New Hampshire

Introduction

A critical first step in improving or changing any organization is *diagnosing* or analyzing its present functioning. Many change and organization development efforts fall short of their objectives because this important step was not taken or was conducted superficially. To illustrate this, imagine how you would feel if you went to your doctor complaining of stomach pains and he recommended surgery without conducting any tests, without obtaining any further information, and without a careful physical examination. You would probably switch doctors! Yet managers often attempt major changes with correspondingly little diagnostic work in advance. (It could be said that they undertake vast projects with half-vast ideas.)

In this exercise, you will be asked to conduct a group diagnosis of two different organizations in the fast-food business. The exercise will provide an opportunity to integrate much of the knowledge you have gained in other exercises and in studying other topics. Your task will be to describe the organizations as carefully as you can in terms of several key organizational concepts. Although the organizations are probably very familiar to you, try to step back and look at them as though you were seeing them for the first time.

Procedure

1. In groups of four or six people, your assignment is described below.

One experience most people in this country have shared is that of dining in the hamburger establishment known as McDonald's. In fact, someone has claimed that twenty-fifth-century archeologists may dig into the ruins of our present civilization and conclude that twentieth-century religion was devoted to the worship of golden arches.

Your group, Fastalk Consultants, is known as the shrewdest, most insightful, and most overpaid management consulting firm in the country. You have been hired by the president of McDonald's to make recommendations for improving the motivation and performance of personnel in their franchise operations. Let us assume that the key job activities in franchise operations are food preparation, order-taking and dealing with customers, and routine cleanup operations.

Recently the president of McDonald's has come to suspect that his company's competitors—such as Burger King, Wendy's, Jack-in-the-Box, Dunkin' Donuts, various pizza establishments, and others—are making heavy inroads into McDonald's market. He has also hired a market research firm to investigate and compare the relative merits of the sandwiches, french fries, and drinks served in McDonald's and the competitor, and has asked the market research firm to assess the advertising campaigns of the two organizations. Hence, you will not need to be concerned with marketing issues, except as they may have an impact on employee behaviour. The president wants *you* to look into the *organization* of the franchises to determine the strengths and weaknesses of each. Select a competitor that gives McDonald's a good "run for its money" in your area.

The president has established an unusual contract with you. *He wants you to make your recommendations based upon your observations as a customer.* He does not want you to do a complete diagnosis with interviews, surveys, or behind-the-scenes observations. He wants your report in two parts. Remember, the president wants concrete, specific, and practical recommendations. Avoid vague generalizations such as "improve communications" or "increase trust." Say very clearly *how* management can improve organizational performance. Substantiate your recommendations by reference to one or more theories of motivation, leadership, small groups, or job design.

Part I

Given his organization's goals of profitability, sales volume, fast and courteous service, and cleanliness, the president of McDonald's wants an analysis that will *compare and contrast McDonald's and the competitor* in terms of the following concepts:

> Organizational goals
> Organizational structure
> Technology
> Environment
> Employee motivation
> Communication
> Leadership style
> Policies/procedures/rules/standards
> Job design
> Organizational climate

Part II

Given the corporate goals listed under Part I, what specific actions might McDonald's management and franchise owners take in the following areas to achieve these goals (profitability, sales volume, fast and courteous service, and cleanliness)?

> Job design and workflow

Organizational structure (at the individual restaurant level)
Employee incentives
Leadership
Employee selection

How do McDonald's and the competition differ in these aspects? Which company has the best approach?

2. Complete the assignment by going as a group to one McDonald's and one competitor's restaurant. If possible, have a meal in each place. To get a more valid comparison, visit a McDonald's and a competitor located in the same area. After observing each restaurant, meet with your group and prepare your 10-minute report to the executive committee.
3. In class, each group will present its report to the rest of the class, who will act as the executive committee. The group leader will appoint a timekeeper to be sure that each group sticks to its 10-minute time limit. Possible discussion questions include:
   (a) What similarities are there between the two organizations?
   (b) What differences are there between the organizations?
   (c) Do you have any "hunches" about the reasons for the particular organizational characteristics you found? For example, can you try to explain why one organization might have a particular type of structure? Incentive system? Climate?
   (d) Can you try to explain one set of characteristics in terms of some other characteristics you found? For example, do the goals account for structure? Does the environment explain the structure?

EXERCISE 27

Alien Invasion

Procedure

This is an exercise in organizational culture. You will be assigned to a team (if you are not already in one) and instructed to visit an organization by your instructor.

1. Visit the site assigned as a team working under conditions set forth in the "situation" below.
2. Take detailed notes on the cultural forms that you observe.
3. Prepare a presentation for the class that describes these forms and draw any inferences you can about the nature of the culture of the organization—its ideologies, values, and norms of behaviour.
4. Be sure to explain the basis of your inferences in terms of the cultural forms observed.

You will have 20 minutes to report your findings, so plan your presentation carefully. Use visual aids to help your audience understand what you have found.

Situation

You are Martians who have just arrived on Earth in the first spaceship from your planet. Your superiors have ordered you to learn as much about Earthlings and the way they behave as you can without doing anything to make them aware that you are Martians. It is vital for the future plans of your superiors that you do nothing to disturb the Earthlings. Unfortunately, Martians communicate by emitting electromagnetic waves and are incapable of speech, so you cannot talk to the natives. Even if you did, it is reported by the usually reliable Bureau of Interplanetary Intelligence that Earthlings may become cannibalistic if annoyed. However, the crash course in Earth languages taught by the bureau has enabled you to read the language.

Remember, these instructions limit your data collection to observation and request that you *not* talk to the "natives." There are two reasons for this instruction. First, your objective is to learn what the organization does when it is simply going about its normal business and not responding to a group of students asking questions. Second, you are likely to be surprised at how much you can learn by simply observing if you put your mind to it. Many skilled managers employ this ability in sensing what is going on as they walk through their plant or office area.

Since you cannot talk to people, some of the cultural forms (legends, sagas, etc.) will be difficult to spot unless you are able to pick up copies of the organization's promotional literature (brochures, company reports, advertisements) during your visit. Do not be discouraged, because the visible forms such as artifacts, setting, symbols, and (sometimes) rituals can convey a great deal about the culture. Just keep your eyes, ears, and antennae open!

EXERCISE 28

Interview a Leader

Contributed by Bonnie McNeely, Murray State University

Procedure

1. Make an appointment to interview a leader. It can be a leader working in a business or nonprofit organization, such as a government agency, school, and so on. Base the interview on the form provided here, but feel free to add your own questions.

2. Bring the results of your interview to class. Form into groups as assigned by your instructor. Share the responses from your interview with your group and compare answers. What issues were similar? Different? Were the stress levels of leaders working in nonprofit organizations as high as those working in for profit firms? Were you surprised at the number of hours per week worked by leaders?

3. Be prepared to summarize the interviews done by your group as a formal written report if asked to do so by the instructor.

Interview Questionnaire

Student's Name _____ Date _____

1. Position in the organization (title):
2. Number of years in current position:
   Number of years of managerial experience:
3. Number of people directly supervised:
4. Average number of hours worked a week:
5. How did you get into leadership?
6. What is the most rewarding part of being a leader?
7. What is the most difficult part of your job?
8. What would you say are the *keys to success* for leaders?

9. What advice do you have for an aspiring leader?
10. What type of ethical issues have you faced as a leader?
11. If you were to enroll in a leadership seminar, what topics or issues would you want to learn more about?
12. (Student's question)
    Gender: M____ F____ Years of formal education____
    Level of job stress: Very high____ High____
    Average____ Low____
    Profit organization____ Nonprofit organization____
    Additional information/Comments:

Source: Adapted from Bonnie McNeely, "Make Your Principles of Management Class Come Alive," *Journal of Management Education,* Vol. 18, No. 2, May 1994, 246–249.

EXERCISE 29

Leadership Skills Inventories

Procedure

1. Look over the skills listed below and ask your instructor to clarify those you do not understand.

2. Complete each category by checking either the "Strong" or "Needs Development" category in relation to your own level with each skill.

3. After completing each category, briefly describe a situation in which each of the listed skills has been utilized.

4. Meet in your groups to share and discuss inventories. Prepare a report summarizing major development needs in your group.

Instrument

	Strong	Needs Development	Situation		Strong	Needs Development	Situation
Communication	_____	_____	_____	Power and influence	_____	_____	_____
Conflict management	_____	_____	_____	Presentation and persuasion	_____	_____	_____
Delegation	_____	_____	_____	Problem solving and decision-making	_____	_____	_____
Ethical behaviour	_____	_____	_____	Stress management	_____	_____	_____
Listening	_____	_____	_____	Team building	_____	_____	_____
Motivation	_____	_____	_____	Time management	_____	_____	_____
Negotiation	_____	_____	_____				
Performance appraisal and feedback	_____	_____	_____				
Planning and goal setting	_____	_____	_____				

EXERCISE 30

Leadership and Participation in Decision Making

Procedure

1. For the 10 situations described below, decide which of the three styles you would use for that unique situation. Place the letter A, P, or L on the line before each situation's number.

> A—authority; make the decision alone without additional inputs.
>
> P—consultative; make the decision based on group inputs.
>
> L—group; allow the group to which you belong to make the decision.

Decision Situations

____ 1. You have developed a new work procedure that will increase productivity. Your boss likes the idea and wants you to try it within a few weeks. You view your employees as fairly capable and believe that they will be receptive to the change.

____ 2. The industry of your product has new competition. Your organization's revenues have been dropping. You have been told to lay off three of your ten employees in two weeks. You have been the supervisor for over one year. Normally, your employees are very capable.

____ 3. Your department has been facing a problem for several months. Many solutions have been tried and have failed. You finally thought of a solution, but you are not sure of the possible consequences of the change required or its acceptance by the highly capable employees.

____ 4. Flextime has become popular in your organization. Some departments let each employee start and end work whenever they choose. However, because of the cooperative effort of your employees, they must all work the same eight hours. You are not sure of the level of interest in changing the hours. Your employees are a very capable group and like to make decisions.

____ 5. The technology in your industry is changing faster than the members of your organization can keep up. Top management hired a consultant who has given the recommended decision. You have two weeks to make your decision. Your employees are capable, and they enjoy participating in the decision-making process.

____ 6. Your boss called you on the telephone to tell you that someone has requested an order for your department's product with a very short delivery date. She asked that you call her back with the decision about taking the order in 15 minutes. Looking over the work schedule, you realize that it will be very difficult to deliver the order on time. Your employees will have to push hard to make it. They are cooperative, capable, and enjoy being involved in decision-making.

_____ 7. A change has been handed down from top management. How you implement it is your decision. The change takes effect in one month. It will personally affect everyone in your department. The acceptance of the department members is critical to the success of the change. Your employees are usually not too interested in being involved in making decisions.

_____ 8. You believe that productivity in your department could be increased. You have thought of some ways that may work, but you're not sure of them. Your employees are very experienced; almost all of them have been in the department longer than you have.

_____ 9. Top management has decided to make a change that will affect all of your employees. You know that they will be upset because it will cause them hardship. One or two may even quit. The change goes into effect in 30 days. Your employees are very capable.

_____ 10. A customer has offered you a contract for your product with a quick delivery date. The offer is open for two days. Meeting the contract deadline would require employees to work nights and weekends for six weeks. You cannot require them to work overtime. Filling this profitable contract could help get you the raise you want and feel you deserve. However, if you take the contract and don't deliver on time, it will hurt your chances of getting a big raise. Your employees are very capable.

2. Form groups as assigned by your instructor. Share and compare your choices for each decision situation. Reconcile any differences and be prepared to defend your decision preferences in general class discussion. This exercise is designed to examine power and influence in the classroom setting. Specifically, it allows you to identify the combination of power bases used by your instructor in accomplishing his or her objectives for the course.

EXERCISE 31

My Best Manager: Revisited

Contributed by J. Marcus Maier, Chapman University

Procedure

1. Refer to the list of qualities—or profiles—the class generated earlier in the course for the "Best Manager."
2. Looking first at your Typical Managers profile, suppose you took this list to 100 average people on the street (or at the local mall) and asked them whether _____ (Trait X, quality Y) was "more typical of men or of women in our culture." What do you think *most* of them would say? That _____ (X, Y etc.) is more typical of *women*? or of *men*? Or of neither/both?[1] Do this for every trait on your list(s). (5 minutes)
3. Now do the same for the qualities we generated in our Best Manager profile. (5 min.)
4. A straw vote is taken, one quality at a time, to determine the class's overall gender identification of each trait, focusing on the Typical Managers profile (10–15 min.). Then this is repeated for the Best Manager profile (10–15 min.).[2]
5. Discussion. What do you see in the data this group has generated? How might you interpret these results? (15–20 min.)

Source: Based on Maier's 1993 article, "The Gender Prism," *Journal of Management Education,* 17(3), 285–314. 1994 Fritz Roethlisberger Award Recipient for Best Paper (Updated, 1996).

[1] This gets the participants to move outside of their *own* conceptions to their awareness of *societal* definitions of masculinity and femininity.

[2] This is done by a rapid show of hands, looking for a clear majority vote. An "f" (for "feminine") is placed next to those qualities that a clear majority indicate are more typical of women, an "m" (for "masculine") next to those qualities a clear majority indicate would be more typical of men. (This procedure parallels the median-split method used in determining Bem Sex Role Inventory classifications.) If no clear majority emerges (i.e., if the vote is close), the trait or quality is classified as "both" (f/m). The designations "masculine" or "feminine" are used (rather than "men" or "women") to underscore the *socially constructed* nature of each dimension.

EXERCISE 32

Power Circles

Contributed by Marian C. Schultz, University of West Florida

Procedure

1. Recall that the instructor's power includes the following major bases: (a) the authority that comes from the instructor's position (position power), (b) the knowledge, skill, and expertise of the instructor in the subject area (expert power), and (c) the regard in which you personally hold the instructor (referent power).

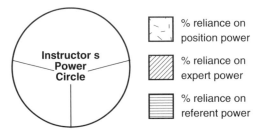

2. Indicate the configuration of power that is most evident in the way the instructor behaves in the course overall and according to the following "power circle." This circle can be filled in to represent the relative emphasis on the three power bases (e.g., 60 percent position, 30 percent expert, and 10 percent referent). Use the grid at the right to draw/fill in the circle to show the profile of instructor's power. The instructor will also complete a self-perceived power circle profile.

3. Consider also some possible special situations in which the instructor would have to use his or her power in the classroom context. Draw one power circle for each of the following situations, showing for each the power profile most likely to be used by the instructor to accomplish his or her goal.

- Instructor wants to change the format of the final examination.
- Instructor wants to add an additional group assignment to course requirements.
- Instructor wants to have students attend a special two-hour guest lecture on a Saturday morning.
- Instructor wants students to come to class better prepared for discussions of assigned material.

   The instructor will also complete a self-perceived power circle profile for each situation.

4. Share your power circles with those developed by members of your assigned group. Discuss the profiles and the reasons behind them in the group. Appoint one group member as spokesperson to share results in general class discussion. Discuss with the group the best way to communicate this feedback effectively to the instructor in the presence of all class members, and help prepare the spokesperson for the feedback session.

5. Have the instructor share his or her power profiles with the class. Ask the instructor to comment on any differences between the self-perceptions and the views of the class. Comment as a class on the potential significance to leaders and managers of differences in the way they perceive themselves and the ways they are perceived by others.

6. Discuss with the instructor and class how people may tend to favour one or more of the power bases (i.e., to develop a somewhat predictable power circle profile). Discuss as well how effective leaders and managers need to use power contingently, and modify their use of different power bases and power circle profiles to best fit the needs of specific influence situations.

EXERCISE 33

Active Listening

Contributed by Robert Ledman, Morehouse College

Procedure

1. Review active listening skills and behaviours as described in the textbook and in class.

2. Form into groups of three. Each group will have a listener, a talker, and an observer (if the number of students is not evenly divisible by three, two observers are used for one or two groups).

3. The "talkers" should talk about any subject they wish, but only *if* they are being actively listened to. Talkers should stop speaking as soon as they sense active listening has stopped.

4. The "listeners" should use a list of active listening skills and behaviours as their guide, and practise as many of them as possible to be sure the talker is kept talking. Listeners should contribute nothing more than "active listening" to the communication.

5. The "observer" should note the behaviours and skills used by the listener and the effects they seemed to have on the communication process.

6. These roles are rotated until each student has played every role.

7. The instructor will lead a discussion of what the observers saw and what happened with the talkers and listeners. The discussion focuses on what behaviours from the posted list have been present, which have been absent, and how the communication has been affected by the listener's actions.

Source: Adapted from the presentation entitled "An Experiential Exercise to Teach Active Listening," presented at the Organizational Behavior Teaching Conference, Macomb, IL, 1995.

EXERCISE 34

Upward Appraisal

Procedure

1. Form workgroups as assigned by your instructor.
2. The instructor will leave the room.
3. Convene in your assigned workgroups for a period of 10 minutes. Create a list of comments, problems, issues, and concerns you would like to have communicated to the instructor in regard to the course experience to date. *Remember,* your interest in the exercise is twofold:
   (a) to communicate your feelings to the instructor and
   (b) to learn more about the process of giving and receiving feedback.
4. Select one person from the group to act as spokesperson in communicating the group's feelings to the instructor.
5. The spokespersons should briefly convene to decide on what physical arrangement of chairs, tables, and so forth is most appropriate to conduct the feedback session. The

classroom should then be rearranged to fit the desired specifications.

6. While the spokespersons convene, persons in the remaining groups should discuss how they expect the forthcoming communications event to develop. Will it be a good experience for all parties concerned? Be prepared to critically observe the actual communication process.

7. The instructor should be invited to return, and the feedback session will begin. Observers should make notes so that they may make constructive comments at the conclusion of the exercise.

8. Once the feedback session is complete, the instructor will call on the observers for comments, ask the spokespersons for reactions, and open the session to discussion.

EXERCISE 35

360-Degree Feedback

Contributed by Timothy J. Serey, Northern Kentucky University

Introduction

The time of performance reviews is often a time of genuine anxiety for many organizational members. On the one hand, it is an important organizational ritual and a key part of the Human Resource function. Organizations usually codify the process and provide a mechanism to appraise performance.

On the other hand, it is rare for managers to feel comfortable with this process. Often, they feel discomfort over "playing God." One possible reason for this is that managers rarely receive formal training about how to provide feedback. From the manager's point of view, if done properly, giving feedback is at the very heart of his or her job as "coach" and "teacher." It is an investment in the professional development of another person, rather than the punitive element we so often associate with hearing from "the boss." From the subordinate's perspective, most people want to know where they stand, but this is usually tempered by a fear of "getting it in the neck." In many organizations, it is rare to receive straight, non-sugar-coated feedback about where you stand.

Procedure

1. Review the section of the book dealing with feedback before you come to class. It is also helpful if individuals make notes about their perceptions and feelings about the course *before* they come to class.
2. Groups of students should discuss their experiences, both positive and negative, in this class. Each group should determine the dimensions of evaluating the class itself *and* the instructor. For example, students might select criteria that include the practicality of the course, the way the material is structured and presented (e.g., lecture or exercises), and the instructor's style (e.g., enthusiasm, fairness).
3. Groups select a member to represent them in a subgroup that next provides feedback to the instructor before the entire class.
4. The student audience then provides the subgroup with feedback about their effectiveness in this exercise. That is, the larger class provides feedback to the subgroup about the extent to which students actually put the principles of effective feedback into practice (e.g., descriptive, not evaluative; specific, not general).

Source: Adapted from Timothy J. Serey, *Journal of Management Education,* Vol. 17, No. 2, May 1993. © 1993 by Sage Publications, Inc. Reprinted by permission of Sage Publications.

EXERCISE 36

Role Analysis Negotiation

Contributed by Paul Lyons, Frostburg State University

Introduction

A role is the set of various behaviours people expect from a person (or group) in a particular position. These role expectations occur in all types of organizations, such as one's place of work, school, family, clubs, and the like. Role ambiguity takes place when a person is confused about the expectations of the role. And sometimes, a role will have expectations that are contradictory—for example, being loyal to the company when the company is breaking the law.

The Role Analysis Technique, or RAT, is a method for improving the effectiveness of a team or group. RAT helps to clarify role expectations, and all organization members have responsibilities that translate to expectations. Determination of role requirements, by consensus—involving all concerned—will ultimately result in more effective and mutually satisfactory behaviour. Participation and collaboration in the definition and analysis of roles by group members should result in clarification regarding who is to do what as well as increase the level of commitment to the decisions made.

Procedure

Working alone, carefully read the course syllabus that your instructor has given you. Make a note of any questions you have about anything for which you need clarification or understanding. Pay particular attention to the performance requirements of the course. Make a list of any questions you have regarding what, specifically, is expected of you in order for you to be successful in the course. You will be sharing this information with others in small groups.

Source: Adapted from Timothy J. Serey, *Journal of Management Education,* Vol. 17, No. 2, May 1993. © 1993 by Sage Publications, Inc. Reprinted by permission of Sage Publications.

EXERCISE 37 -----------------------

Lost at Sea

Introduction

Consider this situation. You are adrift on a private yacht in the South Pacific when a fire of unknown origin destroys the yacht and most of its contents. You and a small group of survivors are now in a large raft with oars. Your location is unclear, but you estimate being about 1,000 miles south–southwest of the nearest land. One person has just found in her pockets five $1 bills and a packet of matches. Everyone else's pockets are empty. The following items are available to you on the raft.

Procedure

1. *Working alone,* rank in Column A the 15 items in order of their importance to your survival ("1" is most important and "15" is least important).
2. *Working in an assigned group,* arrive at a "team" ranking of the 15 items and record this ranking in Column B. Appoint one person as group spokesperson to report your group rankings to the class.
3. *Do not write in Column C* until further instructions are provided by your instructor.

Source: Adapted from "Lost at Sea: A Consensus-Seeking Task," in *The 1975 Handbook for Group Facilitators.* Used with permission of University Associates, Inc.

	A	B	C
Sextant	___	___	
Shaving mirror	___	___	
5 gallons of water	___	___	
Mosquito netting	___	___	
1 survival meal	___	___	
Maps of Pacific Ocean	___	___	
Floatable seat cushion	___	___	
2 gallons oil-gas mix	___	___	
Small transistor radio	___	___	
Shark repellent	___	___	
20 square feet black plastic	___	___	
1 quart of 20-proof rum	___	___	
15 feet of nylon rope	___	___	
24 chocolate bars	___	___	
Fishing kit	___	___	

EXERCISE 38 -----------------------

Entering the Unknown

Contributed by Michael R. Manning, New Mexico State University; Conrad N. Jackson, MPC, Inc., Huntsville, Alabama; and Paula S. Weber, New Mexico Highlands University

Procedure

1. Form into groups of four or five members. In each group spend a few minutes reflecting on members' typical entry behaviours in new situations and their behaviours when they are in comfortable settings.
2. According to the instructor's directions, students count off to form new groups of four or five members each.
3. The new groups spend the next 15–20 minutes getting to know each other. There is no right or wrong way to proceed, but all members should become more aware of their entry behaviours. They should act in ways that can help them realize a goal of achieving comfortable behav-

iours with their group.

4. Students review what has occurred in the new groups, giving specific attention to the following questions:
   (a) What topics did your group discuss (content)? Did these topics involve the "here and now" or were they focused on "there and then"?
   (b) What approach did you and your group members take to the task (process)? Did you try to initiate or follow? How? Did you ask questions? Listen? Respond to others? Did you bring up topics?
   (c) Were you more concerned with how you came across or with how others came across to you? Did

you play it safe? Were you open? Did you share things even though it seemed uncomfortable or risky? How was humour used in your group? Did it add or detract?

(d) How do you feel about the approach you took or the behaviours you exhibited? Was this hard or easy? Did others respond the way you had anticipated? Is there some behaviour you would like to do more of, do better, or do less of?

(e) Were your behaviours the ones you had intended (goals)?

5. Responses to these questions are next discussed by the class as a whole. (*Note:* Responses will tend to be mixed within a group, but between groups there should be more similarity.) This discussion helps individuals become aware of and understand their entry behaviours.

6. Optional individuals have identified their entry behaviours; each group can then spend 5–10 minutes discussing members' perceptions of each other:

(a) What behaviours did they like or find particularly useful? What did they dislike?

(b) What were your reactions to others? What ways did they intend to come across? Did you see others in the way they had intended to come across?

(Alternatively, if there is concern about the personal nature of this discussion, ask the groups to discuss what they liked/didn't like without referring to specific individuals.)

EXERCISE 39

Vacation Puzzle

Contributed by Barbara G. McCain and Mary Khalili, Oklahoma City University

Procedure

Can you solve this puzzle? Give it a try and then compare your answers with those of classmates. Remember your communicative skills!

Puzzle

Khalili, McCain, Middleton, Porter, and Quintaro teach at Oklahoma City University. Each gets two weeks of vacation a year. Last year, each took his or her first week in the first five months of the year and his or her second week in the last five months. If each professor took each of his or her weeks in a different month from the other professors, in which months did each professor take his or her first and second week?

Here are the facts:

(a) McCain took her first week before Khalili, who took *hers* before Porter; for their second week, the order was reversed.

(b) The professor who vacationed in March also vacationed in September.

(c) Quintaro did not take her first week in March or April.

(d) Neither Quintaro nor the professor who took his or her first week in January took his or her second week in August or December.

(e) Middleton took her second week before McCain but after Quintaro.

Month	Professor
January	
February	
March	
April	
May	
June	
July	
August	
September	
October	
November	
December	

Source: Adapted to classroom activity by Dr. Mary Khalili.

EXERCISE 40 -

The Ugli Orange

Introduction

In most work settings, people need other people to do their job, benefit the organization, and forward their career. Getting things done in organizations requires us to work together in cooperation, even though the ultimate objectives of those other people may be different from our own. Your task in the present exercise is learning how to achieve this cooperation more effectively.

Procedure

1. The class will be divided into pairs. One student in each pair will read and prepare the role of Dr. Roland, and one will play the role of Dr. Jones (role descriptions to be distributed by instructor). Students should read their respective role descriptions and prepare to meet with their counterpart (see Steps 2 and 3).
2. At this point the group leader will read a statement. The instructor will indicate that he or she is playing the role of Mr. Cardoza, who owns the commodity in question. The instructor will tell you
   (a) How long you have to meet with the other
   (b) What information the instructor will require at the end of your meeting

After the instructor has given you this information, you may meet with the other firm's representative and determine whether you have issues you can agree to.

3. Following the meetings (negotiations), the spokesperson for each pair will report any agreements reached to the entire class. The observer for any pair will report on negotiation dynamics and the process by which agreement was reached.
4. Questions to consider:
   (a) Did you reach a solution? If so, what was critical to reaching that agreement?
   (b) Did you and the other negotiator trust one another? Why or why not?
   (c) Was there full disclosure by both sides in each group? How much information was shared?
   (d) How creative and/or complex were the solutions? If solutions were very complex, why do you think this occurred?
   (e) What was the impact of having an "audience" on your behaviour? Did it make the problem harder or easier to solve?

Source: Adapted from Hall et al., *Experiences in Management and Organizational Behavior,* 3rd ed. (New York: John Wiley and Sons, Inc.), 1988. Originally developed by Robert J. House. Adapted by D. T. Hall and R. J. Lewicki, with suggested modifications by H. Kolodny and T. Ruble.

EXERCISE 41 -

Conflict Dialogues

Contributed by Edward G. Wertheim, Northeastern University

Procedure

1. Think of a conflict situation at work or at school and try to re-create a segment of the dialogue that gets to the heart of the conflict.
2. Write notes on the conflict dialogue using the following format

Introduction

- Background
- My goals and objectives
- My strategy
- Assumptions I am making

Dialogue (re-create part of the dialogue below and try to put what you were really thinking in parentheses).

Me:
Other:
Me:
Other, etc.

3. Share your situation with members of your group. Read the dialogue to them, perhaps asking someone to play the role of "other."
4. Discuss with the group:
   (a) The style of conflict resolution you used (confrontation, collaboration, avoidance, etc.)

(b) The triggers to the conflict, that is, what really set
        you off and why
    (c) Whether or not you were effective
    (d) Possible ways of handling this differently
5. Choose one dialogue from within the group to share
   with the class. Be prepared to discuss your analysis and
   also possible alternative approaches and resolutions for
   the situation described.

EXERCISE 42

Force-Field Analysis

Procedure

1. Choose a situation in which you have high personal
stakes (for example, how to get a better grade in course
X; how to get a promotion; how to obtain a position).
2. Using a version of the Sample Force-Field Analysis
Form on the next page, apply the technique to your situation.
   (a) Describe the situation as it now exists.
   (b) Describe the situation as you would like it to be.
   (c) Identify those "driving forces"—the factors that are
      presently helping to move things in the desired
      direction.
   (d) Identify those "restraining forces"—the factors that
      are presently holding things back from moving in
      the desired direction.

3. Try to be as specific as possible in terms of the above in
relation to your situation. You should attempt to be
exhaustive in your listing of these forces. List them all!
4. Now go back and classify the strength of each force as
weak, medium, or strong. Do this for both the driving
and the restraining forces.
5. At this point you should rank the forces regarding their
ability to influence or control the situation.
6. In small groups share your analyses. Discuss the usefulness and drawbacks to using this method for personal
situations and its application to organizations.
7. Be prepared to share the results of your group's discussion with the rest of the class.

Sample Force-Field Analysis Form

Current Situation:	Situation as You Would Like It to Be:
Driving Forces:	**Restraining Forces:**

self-assessment
INVENTORIES

Managerial Assumptions

Instructions

Read the following statements. Use the space to the left to write "Yes" if you agree with the statement, or "No" if you disagree with it. Force yourself to take a "yes" or "no" position for every statement.

1. Are good pay and a secure job enough to satisfy most workers?
2. Should a manager help and coach subordinates in their work?
3. Do most people like real responsibility in their jobs?
4. Are most people afraid to learn new things in their jobs?
5. Should managers let subordinates control the quality of their work?
6. Do most people dislike work?
7. Are most people creative?
8. Should a manager closely supervise and direct work of subordinates?
9. Do most people tend to resist change?
10. Do most people work only as hard as they have to?

11. Should workers be allowed to set their own job goals?
12. Are most people happiest off the job?
13. Do most workers really care about the organization they work for?
14. Should a manager help subordinates advance and grow in their jobs?

Scoring

Count the number of "yes" responses to items 1, 4, 6, 8, 9, 10, 12; write that number here as [X = ____]. Count the number of "yes" responses to items 2, 3, 5, 7, 11, 13, 14; write that score here [Y = ____].

Interpretation

This assessment sheds insight into your orientation toward Douglas McGregor's Theory X (your "X" score) and Theory Y (your "Y" score) assumptions. You should review the discussion of McGregor's thinking in Chapter 1 and consider further the ways in which you are likely to behave toward other people at work. Think, in particular, about the types of "self-fulfilling prophecies" you are likely to create.

_____

Source: Schermerhorn, John R. Jr., *Management,* 5th ed. (New York, John Wiley & Sons, Inc., 1996), p. 51. By permission.

ASSESSMENT 2

A Twenty-First-Century Manager

Instructions

Rate yourself on the following personal characteristics. Use this scale.

> S = Strong, I am very confident with this one.
>
> G = Good, but I still have room to grow.
>
> W = Weak, I really need work on this one.
>
> ? = Unsure, I just don't know.

1. *Resistance to stress:* The ability to get work done even under stressful conditions.
2. *Tolerance for uncertainty:* The ability to get work done even under ambiguous and uncertain conditions.
3. *Social objectivity:* The ability to act free of racial, ethnic, gender, and other prejudices or biases.
4. *Inner work standards:* The ability to personally set and work to high-performance standards.
5. *Stamina:* The ability to sustain long work hours.
6. *Adaptability:* The ability to be flexible and adapt to changes.
7. *Self-confidence:* The ability to be consistently decisive and display one's personal presence.
8. *Self-objectivity:* The ability to evaluate personal strengths and weaknesses and to understand one's motives and skills relative to a job.
9. *Introspection:* The ability to learn from experience, awareness, and self-study.
10. *Entrepreneurism:* The ability to address problems and take advantage of opportunities for constructive change.

Scoring

Give yourself 1 point for each S, and 1/2 point for each G. Do not give yourself points for W and ? responses. Total your points and enter the result here [PMF = ____].

Interpretation

This assessment offers a self-described *profile of your management foundations* (*PMF*). Are you a perfect 10, or is your PMF score something less than that? There shouldn't be too many 10s around. Ask someone who knows you to assess you on this instrument. You may be surprised at the differences between your PMF score as self-described and your PMF score as described by someone else. Most of us, realistically speaking, must work hard to grow and develop continually in these and related management foundations. This list is a good starting point as you consider where and how to further pursue the development of your managerial skills and competencies. The items on the list are recommended by the American Assembly of Collegiate Schools of Business (AACSB) as skills and personal characteristics that should be nurtured in college and university students of business administration. Their success—and yours—as twenty-first-century managers may well rest on (1) an initial awareness of the importance of these basic management foundations and (2) a willingness to strive continually to strengthen them throughout your work career.

_____

Source: See *Outcome Management Project,* Phase I and Phase II Reports (St. Louis: American Assembly of Collegiate Schools of Business, 1986 & 1987).

ASSESSMENT 3

Turbulence Tolerance Test

Instructions

The following statements were made by a 37-year-old manager in a large, successful corporation. How would you like to have a job with these characteristics? Using the following scale, write your response to the left of each statement.

> 4 = I would enjoy this very much; it's completely acceptable.
>
> 3 = This would be enjoyable and acceptable most of the time.
>
> 2 = I'd have no reaction to this feature one way or another, or it would be about equally enjoyable and unpleasant.
>
> 1 = This feature would be somewhat unpleasant for me.
>
> 0 = This feature would be very unpleasant for me.

_____ 1. I regularly spend 30 to 40 percent of my time in meetings.

_____ 2. Eighteen months ago my job did not exist, and I have been essentially inventing it as I go along.

_____ 3. The responsibilities I either assume or am assigned consistently exceed the authority I have for discharging them.

_____ 4. At any given moment in my job, I have on the average about a dozen phone calls to be returned.

_____ 5. There seems to be very little relation in my job between the quality of my performance and my actual pay and fringe benefits.

_____ 6. About 2 weeks a year of formal management training is needed in my job just to stay current.

_____ 7. Because we have very effective equal employment opportunity (EEO) in my company and because it is thoroughly multinational, my job consistently brings me into close working contact at a professional level with people of many races, ethnic groups and nationalities, and of both sexes.

_____ 8. There is no objective way to measure my effectiveness.

_____ 9. I report to three different bosses for different aspects of my job, and each has an equal say in my performance appraisal.

_____ 10. On average about a third of my time is spent dealing with unexpected emergencies that force all scheduled work to be postponed.

_____ 11. When I have to have a meeting of the people who report to me, it takes my secretary most of a day to find a time when we are all available, and even then, I have yet to have a meeting where everyone is present for the entire meeting.

_____ 12. The college degree I earned in preparation for this type of work is now obsolete, and I probably should go back for another degree.

_____ 13. My job requires that I absorb 100–200 pages of technical materials per week.

_____ 14. I am out of town overnight at least one night per week.

_____ 15. My department is so interdependent with several other departments in the company that all distinctions about which departments are responsible for which tasks are quite arbitrary.

_____ 16. In about a year I will probably get a promotion to a job in another division that has most of these same characteristics.

_____ 17. During the period of my employment here, either the entire company or the division I worked in has been reorganized every year or so.

_____ 18. While there are several possible promotions I can see ahead of me, I have no real career path in an objective sense.

_____ 19. While there are several possible promotions I can see ahead of me, I think I have no realistic chance of getting to the top levels of the company.

_____ 20. While I have many ideas about how to make things work better, I have no direct influence on either the business policies or the personnel policies that govern my division.

_____ 21. My company has recently put in an "assessment centre" where I and all other managers will be required to go through an extensive battery of psychological tests to assess our potential.

_____ 22. My company is a defendant in an antitrust suit, and if the case comes to trial, I will probably have to testify about some decisions that were made a few years ago.

_____ 23. Advanced computer and other electronic office technology is continually being introduced into my division, necessitating constant learning on my part.

_____ 24. The computer terminal and screen I have in my office can be monitored in my bosses' offices without my knowledge.

Scoring

Total your responses and divide the sum by 24; enter the score here [TTT = _____].

Interpretation

This instrument gives an impression of your tolerance for managing in turbulent times—something likely to characterize the world of work well into the [future]. In general, the higher your TTT score, the more comfortable you seem to be with turbulence and change—a positive sign. For comparison purposes, the average scores for some 500 MBA students and young managers was 1.5–1.6. The test's author suggests the TTT scores may be interpreted much like a grade point average in which 4.0 is a perfect A. On this basis, a 1.5 is below a C! How did you do?

Source: Peter B. Vail, _Managing as a Performance Art: New Ideas for a World of Chaotic Change_ (San Francisco: Jossey-Bass, 1989), pp. 8–9. Used by permission.

ASSESSMENT 4

Global Readiness Index

Instructions

Rate yourself on each of the following items to establish a baseline measurement of your readiness to participate in the global work environment.

Rating Scale:

1 = Very Poor   4 = Good
2 = Poor   5 = Very Good
3 = Acceptable

_____ 1. I understand my own culture in terms of its expectations, values, and influence on communication and relationships.

_____ 2. When someone presents me with a different point of view, I try to understand it rather than attack it.

_____ 3. I am comfortable dealing with situations where the available information is incomplete and the outcomes unpredictable.

_____ 4. I am open to new situations and am always looking for new information and learning opportunities.

_____ 5. I have a good understanding of the attitudes and perceptions toward my culture as they are held by people from other cultures.

_____ 6. I am always gathering information about other countries and cultures and trying to learn from them.

_____ 7. I am well informed regarding the major differences in government, political, and economic systems around the world.

_____ 8. I work hard to increase my understanding of people from other cultures.

_____ 9. I am able to adjust my communication style to work effectively with people from different cultures.

_____ 10. I can recognize when cultural differences are influencing working relationships and adjust my attitudes and behaviour accordingly.

Interpretation

To be successful in the twenty-first-century work environment, you must be comfortable with the global economy and the cultural diversity that it holds. This requires a _global mind-set_ that is receptive to and respectful of cultural differences, _global knowledge_ that includes the continuing quest to know and learn more about other nations and cultures, and _global work skills_ that allow you to work effectively across cultures.

Scoring

The goal is to score as close to a perfect "5" as possible on each of the three dimensions of global readiness. Develop your scores as follows.

Items (1 + 2 + 3 + 4)/4   = _____ Global Mind-Set Score

Items (5 + 6 + 7)/3   = _____ Global Knowledge Score

Items (8 + 9 + 10)/3   = _____ Global Work Skills Score

Source: Developed from "Is Your Company Really Global," _Business Week_ (December 1, 1997).

ASSESSMENT 5

Personal Values

Instructions

Below are 16 items. Rate how important each one is to you on a scale of 0 (not important) to 100 (very important). Write the numbers 0–100 on the line to the left of each item.

Not important				Somewhat important				Very important		
0	10	20	30	40	50	60	70	80	90	100

____ 1. An enjoyable, satisfying job.

____ 2. A high-paying job.

____ 3. A good marriage.

____ 4. Meeting new people; social events.

____ 5. Involvement in community activities.

____ 6. My religion.

____ 7. Exercising, playing sports.

____ 8. Intellectual development.

____ 9. A career with challenging opportunities.

____ 10. Nice cars, clothes, home, etc.

____ 11. Spending time with family.

____ 12. Having several close friends.

____ 13. Volunteer work for not-for-profit organizations, such as the cancer society.

____ 14. Meditation, quiet time to think, pray, etc.

____ 15. A healthy, balanced diet.

____ 16. Educational reading, TV, self-improvement programs, etc.

Scoring

Transfer the numbers for each of the 16 items to the appropriate column below, then add the two numbers in each column.

	Professional	Financial	Family	Social
	1. ____	2. ____	3. ____	4. ____
	9. ____	10. ____	11. ____	12. ____
Totals	____	____	____	____

	Community	Spiritual	Physical	Intellectual
	5. ____	6. ____	7. ____	8. ____
	13. ____	14. ____	15. ____	16. ____
Totals	____	____	____	____

Interpretation

The higher the total in any area, the higher the value you place on that particular area. The closer the numbers are in all eight areas, the more well-rounded you are. Think about the time and effort you put forth in your top three values. Is it sufficient to allow you to achieve the level of success you want in each area? If not, what can you do to change? Is there any area in which you feel you should have a higher value total? If yes, which, and what can you do to change?

Source: Robert N. Lussier, *Human Relations in Organizations,* 2nd ed. (Homewood, IL: Richard D. Irwin, 1993). By permission.

ASSESSMENT 6

Intolerance for Ambiguity

Instructions

To determine your level of tolerance (intolerance) for ambiguity, respond to the following items. PLEASE RATE EVERY ITEM; DO NOT LEAVE ANY ITEM BLANK. Rate each item on the following seven-point scale:

1	2	3	4	5	6	7
strongly disagree	moderately disagree	slightly disagree		slightly agree	moderately agree	strongly agree

Rating

_____ 1. An expert who doesn't come up with a definite answer probably doesn't know too much.

_____ 2. There is really no such thing as a problem that can't be solved.

_____ 3. I would like to live in a foreign country for a while.

_____ 4. People who fit their lives to a schedule probably miss the joy of living.

_____ 5. A good job is one where what is to be done and how it is to be done are always clear.

_____ 6. In the long run it is possible to get more done by tackling small, simple problems rather than large, complicated ones.

_____ 7. It is more fun to tackle a complicated problem than it is to solve a simple one.

_____ 8. Often the most interesting and stimulating people are those who don't mind being different and original.

_____ 9. What we are used to is always preferable to what is unfamiliar.

_____ 10. A person who leads an even, regular life in which few surprises or unexpected happenings arise really has a lot to be grateful for.

_____ 11. People who insist upon a yes or no answer just don't know how complicated things really are.

_____ 12. Many of our most important decisions are based on insufficient information.

_____ 13. I like parties where I know most of the people more than ones where most of the people are complete strangers.

_____ 14. The sooner we all acquire ideals, the better.

_____ 15. Teachers or supervisors who hand out vague assignments give a chance for one to show initiative and originality.

_____ 16. A good teacher is one who makes you wonder about your way of looking at things.

_____ Total

Scoring

The scale was developed by S. Budner. Budner reports test–retest correlations of .85 with a variety of samples (mostly students and health care workers). Data, however, are more than 30 years old, so mean shifts may have occurred. Maximum ranges are 16–112, and score ranges were from 25 to 79, with a grand mean of approximately 49.

The test was designed to measure several different components of possible reactions to perceived threat in situations which are new, complex, or insoluble. Half of the items have been reversed.

To obtain a score, first _reverse_ the scale score for the eight "reverse" items, 3, 4, 7, 8, 11, 12, 15, and 16 (i.e., a rating of 1 = 7, 2 = 6, 3 = 5, etc.), then add up the rating scores for all 16 items.

Interpretation

Empirically, low tolerance for ambiguity (high intolerance) has been positively correlated with:

• Conventionality of religious beliefs
• High attendance at religious services
• More intense religious beliefs
• More positive views of censorship
• Higher authoritarianism
• Lower Machiavellianism

The application of this concept to management in the 1990s is clear and relatively self-evident. The world of work and many organizations are full of ambiguity and change. Individuals with a _higher_ tolerance for ambiguity are far more likely to be able to function effectively in organizations and contexts in which there is a high turbulence, a high rate of change, and less certainty about expectations, performance standards, what needs to be done, and so on. In contrast, individuals with a lower tolerance for ambiguity are far more likely to be unable to adapt or adjust quickly in turbulence, uncertainty, and change. These individuals are likely to become rigid, angry, stressed, and frustrated when there is a high level of uncertainty and ambiguity in the environment. High levels of tolerance for ambiguity, therefore, are associated with an ability to "roll with the punches" as organizations, environmental conditions, and demands change rapidly.

Source: Based on Budner, S. (1962) Intolerance of ambiguity as a personality variable, _Journal of Personality,_ Vol. 30, No. 1, 29–50.

ASSESSMENT 7

Two-Factor Profile

Instructions

On each of the following dimensions, distribute a total of 10 points between the two options. For example:

Summer weather   (7) .... (3) Winter weather

1. Very responsible job   (___) .... (___) Job security

2. Recognition for work accomplishments   (___) .... (___) Good relations with co-workers

3. Advancement opportunities at work   (___) .... (___) A boss who knows his/her job well

4. Opportunities to grow and learn on the job   (___) .... (___) Good working conditions

5. A job that I can do well   (___) .... (___) Supportive rules, policies of employer

6. A prestigious or high-status job   (___) .... (___) A high base wage or salary

Scoring

Summarize your total scores for all items in the *left-hand column* and write it here: MF = _____ .

Summarize your total scores for all items in the *right-hand column* and write it here: HF = _____ .

Interpretation

The "MF" score indicates the relative importance that you place on motivating or satisfier factors in Herzberg's two-factor theory. This shows how important job content is to you.

The "HF" score indicates the relative importance that you place on hygiene or dissatisfier factors in Herzberg's two-factor theory. This shows how important job context is to you.

ASSESSMENT 8

Are You Cosmopolitan?

Instructions

Answer the questions below using a scale of 1 to 5: 1 representing "strongly disagree"; 2, "somewhat disagree"; 3, "neutral"; 4, "somewhat agree"; and 5, "strongly agree."

_____ 1. You believe it is the right of the professional to make his or her own decisions about what is to be done on the job.

_____ 2. You believe a professional should stay in an individual staff role regardless of the income sacrifice.

_____ 3. You have no interest in moving up to a top administrative post.

_____ 4. You believe that professionals are better evaluated by professional colleagues than by management.

_____ 5. Your friends tend to be members of your profession.

_____ 6. You would rather be known or get credit for your work outside rather than inside the company.

_____ 7. You would feel better making a contribution to society than to your organization.

_____ 8. Managers have no right to place time and cost schedules on professional contributors.

Scoring and Interpretation

A "cosmopolitan" identifies with the career profession, and a "local" identifies with the employing organization. Total your scores. A score of 30–40 suggests a cosmopolitan work orientation, 10–20 a "local" orientation, and 20–30 a mixed orientation.

_____

Source: Developed from Joseph A. Raelin, *The Clash of Cultures, Managers and Professionals* (Harvard Business School Press, 1986).

ASSESSMENT 9

Group Effectiveness

Instructions

For this assessment, select a specific group you work with or have worked with; it can be a college or work group. For each of the eight statements below, select how often each statement describes the group's behaviour. Place the number 1, 2, 3, or 4 on the line next to each of the 8 numbers.

Usually	Frequently	Occasionally	Seldom
1	2	3	4

_____ 1. The members are loyal to one another and to the group leader.

_____ 2. The members and leader have a high degree of confidence and trust in each other.

_____ 3. Group values and goals express relevant values and needs of members.

_____ 4. Activities of the group occur in a supportive atmosphere.

_____ 5. The group is eager to help members develop to their full potential.

_____ 6. The group knows the value of constructive conformity and knows when to use it and for what purpose.

_____ 7. The members communicate all information relevant to the group's activity fully and frankly.

_____ 8. The members feel secure in making decisions that seem appropriate to them.

Scoring

Add up the eight numbers and place an X on the continuum below that represents the score. Total _____

Effective group   8 . . . 16 . . . 24 . . . 32   Ineffective group

Interpretation

The lower the score, the more effective the group. What can you do to help the group become more effective? What can the group do to become more effective?

ASSESSMENT 10

Organizational Design Preference

Instructions

To the left of each item, write the number from the following scale that shows the extent to which the statement accurately describes your views.

> 5 = strongly agree
> 4 = agree somewhat
> 3 = undecided
> 2 = disagree somewhat
> 1 = strongly disagree

I prefer to work in an organization where:

1. Goals are defined by those in higher levels.
2. Work methods and procedures are specified.
3. Top management makes important decisions.
4. My loyalty counts as much as my ability to do the job.
5. Clear lines of authority and responsibility are established.
6. Top management is decisive and firm.
7. My career is pretty well planned out for me.
8. I can specialize.
9. My length of service is almost as important as my level of performance.
10. Management is able to provide the information I need to do my job well.
11. A chain of command is well established.
12. Rules and procedures are adhered to equally by everyone.
13. People accept authority of a leader's position.
14. People are loyal to their boss.
15. People do as they have been instructed.
16. People clear things with their boss before going over his or her head.

Scoring

Total your scores for all questions. Enter the score here [_____].

Interpretation

This assessment measures your preference for working in an organization designed along "organic" or "mechanistic" lines. The higher your score (above 64), the more comfortable you are with a mechanistic design; the lower your score (below 48), the more comfortable you are with an organic design. Scores between 48 and 64 can go either way. This organizational design preference represents an important issue in the new workplace. Indications are that today's organizations are taking on more and more organic characteristics. Presumably, those of us who work in them will need to be comfortable with such designs.

Source: John F. Veiga and John N. Yanouzas, *The Dynamics of Organization Theory: Gaining a Macro Perspective* (St. Paul, MN: West, 1979), pp. 158–160. Used by permission.

ASSESSMENT 11

Which Culture Fits You?

Instructions

Check one of the following organization "cultures" in which you feel most comfortable working.

1. A culture that values talent, entrepreneurial activity, and performance over commitment; one that offers large financial rewards and individual recognition.
2. A culture that stresses loyalty, working for the good of the group, and getting to know the right people; one that believes in "generalists" and step-by-step career progress.
3. A culture that offers little job security; one that operates with a survival mentality, stresses that every individual can make a difference, and focuses attention on "turn-around" opportunities.
4. A culture that values long-term relationships; one that emphasizes systematic career development, regular training, and advancement based on gaining of functional expertise.

Scoring

These labels identify the four different cultures: 1 = "the baseball team," 2 = "the club," 3 = "the fortress," and 4 = "the academy."

Interpretation

To some extent, your future career success may depend on working for an organization in which there is a good fit between you and the prevailing corporate culture. This assessment can help you learn how to recognize various cultures, evaluate how well they can serve your needs, and recognize how they may change with time. A risk taker, for example, may be out of place in a "club" but fit right in with a "baseball team." Someone who wants to seek opportunities wherever they may occur may be out of place in an "academy" but fit right in with a "fortress."

Source: Developed from Carol Hymowitz, "Which Corporate Culture Fits You?" *Wall Street Journal* (July 17, 1989), p. B1.

ASSESSMENT 12

Least Preferred Coworker Scale

Instructions

Think of all the different people with whom you have ever worked—in jobs, in social clubs, in student projects, or whatever. Next, think of the *one person* with whom you could work *least* well—that is, the person with whom you had the most difficulty getting a job done. This is the one person—a peer, boss, or subordinate—with whom you would least want to work. Describe this person by circling numbers at the appropriate points on each of the following pairs of bipolar adjectives. Work rapidly. There are no right or wrong answers.

Scoring

This is called the "least preferred coworker scale" (LPC). Compute your LPC score by totalling all the numbers you circled; enter that score here [LPC = ____].

Interpretation

The LPC scale is used by Fred Fiedler to identify a person's dominant leadership style. Fiedler believes that this style is a relatively fixed part of one's personality and is therefore difficult to change. This leads Fiedler to his contingency views, which suggest that the key to leadership success is finding (or creating) good "matches" between style and situation. If your score is 73 or above, Fiedler considers you a "relationship-motivated" leader; if your score is 64 and below, he considers you a "task-motivated" leader. If your score is between 65 and 72, Fiedler leaves it up to you to determine which leadership style is most like yours.

_____

Source: Fred E. Fiedler and Martin M. Chemers. *Improving Leadership Effectiveness: The Leader Match Concept,* 2nd ed. (New York: John Wiley & Sons, Inc., 1984). Used by permission.

Pleasant	8 7 6 5 4 3 2 1	Unpleasant
Friendly	8 7 6 5 4 3 2 1	Unfriendly
Rejecting	1 2 3 4 5 6 7 8	Accepting
Tense	1 2 3 4 5 6 7 8	Relaxed
Distant	1 2 3 4 5 6 7 8	Close
Cold	1 2 3 4 5 6 7 8	Warm
Supportive	8 7 6 5 4 3 2 1	Hostile
Boring	1 2 3 4 5 6 7 8	Interesting
Quarrelsome	1 2 3 4 5 6 7 8	Harmonious
Gloomy	1 2 3 4 5 6 7 8	Cheerful
Open	8 7 6 5 4 3 2 1	Guarded
Backbiting	1 2 3 4 5 6 7 8	Loyal
Untrustworthy	1 2 3 4 5 6 7 8	Trustworthy
Considerate	8 7 6 5 4 3 2 1	Inconsiderate
Nasty	1 2 3 4 5 6 7 8	Nice
Agreeable	8 7 6 5 4 3 2 1	Disagreeable
Insincere	1 2 3 4 5 6 7 8	Sincere
Kind	8 7 6 5 4 3 2 1	Unkind

ASSESSMENT 13

Leadership Style

Instructions

The following statements describe leadership acts. Indicate the way you would most likely act if you were leader of a work-group, by circling whether you would most likely behave in this way:

always (A); frequently (F); occasionally (O); seldom (S); or never (N)

A F O S N   1. Act as group spokesperson.

A F O S N   2. Encourage overtime work.

A F O S N   3. Allow members complete freedom in their work.

A F O S N   4. Encourage the use of uniform procedures.

A F O S N   5. Permit members to solve their own problems.

A F O S N   6. Stress being ahead of competing groups.

A F O S N   7. Speak as a representative of the group.

A F O S N   8. Push members for greater effort.

A F O S N   9. Try out ideas in the group.

A F O S N   10. Let the members work the way they think best.

A F O S N   11. Work hard for a personal promotion.

A F O S N   12. Tolerate postponement and uncertainty.

A F O S N   13. Speak for the group when visitors are present.

A F O S N   14. Keep the work moving at a rapid pace.

A F O S N   15. Turn members loose on a job.

A F O S N   16. Settle conflcts in the group.

A F O S N   17. Focus on work details.

A F O S N   18. Represent the group at outside meetings.

A F O S N   19. Avoid giving the members too much freedom.

A F O S N   20. Decide what should be done and how it should be done.

A F O S N   21. Push for increased production.

A F O S N   22. Give some members authority to act.

A F O S N   23. Expect things to turn out as predicted.

A F O S N 24. Allow the group to take initiative.
A F O S N 25. Assign group members to particular tasks.
A F O S N 26. Be willing to make changes.
A F O S N 27. Ask members to work harder.
A F O S N 28. Trust members to exercise good judgement.
A F O S N 29. Schedule the work to be done.
A F O S N 30. Refuse to explain my actions.
A F O S N 31. Persuade others that my ideas are best.
A F O S N 32. Permit the group to set its own pace.
A F O S N 33. Urge the group to beat its previous record.
A F O S N 34. Act without consulting the group.
A F O S N 35. Ask members to follow standard rules.

T ____   P ____

Scoring

1. Circle items 8, 12, 17, 18, 19, 30, 34 and 35.
2. Write the number 1 in front of a *circled item number* if you responded S (seldom) or N (never) to that item.
3. Write a number 1 in front of *item numbers not circled* if you responded A (always) or F (frequently).
4. Circle the number 1's which you have written in front of items 3, 5, 8, 10, 15, 18, 19, 22, 24, 26, 28, 30, 32, 34, and 35.
5. *Count the circled number 1's.* This is your score for leadership *concern for people.* Record the score in the blank following the letter P at the end of the questionnaire.
6. *Count the uncircled number 1's.* This is your score for leadership *concern for task.* Record this number in the blank following the letter T.

ASSESSMENT 14

"TT" Leadership Style

Instructions

For each of the following 10 pairs of statements, divide 5 points between the two according to your beliefs, perceptions of yourself, or according to which of the two statements characterizes you better. The 5 points may be divided between the a and b statements in any one of the following ways: 5 for a, 0 for b; 4 for a, 1 for b; 3 for a, 2 for b; 1 for a, 4 for b; 0 for a, 5 for b, but not equally (2 ½) between the two. Weigh your choices between the two according to the one that characterizes you or your beliefs better.

1. (a) As leader I have a primary mission of maintaining stability.
   (b) As leader I have a primary mission of change.
2. (a) As leader I must cause events.
   (b) As leader I must facilitate events.
3. (a) I am concerned that my followers are rewarded equitably for their work.
   (b) I am concerned about what my followers want in life.
4. (a) My preference is to think long range: what might be.
   (b) My preference is to think short range: what is realistic.

5. (a) As a leader I spend considerable energy in managing separate but related goals.
   (b) As a leader I spend considerable energy in arousing hopes, expectations, and aspirations among my followers.
6. (a) Although not in a formal classroom sense, I believe that a significant part of my leadership is that of teacher.
   (b) I believe that a significant part of my leadership is that of facilitator.
7. (a) As leader I must engage with followers at an equal level of morality.
   (b) As leader I must represent a higher morality.
8. (a) I enjoy stimulating followers to want to do more.
   (b) I enjoy rewarding followers for a job well done.
9. (a) Leadership should be practical.
   (b) Leadership should be inspirational.
10. (a) What power I have to influence others comes primarily from my ability to get people to identify with me and my ideas.
    (b) What power I have to influence others comes primarily from my status and position.

Scoring

Circle your points for items 1b, 2a, 3b, 4a, 5b, 6a, 7b, 8a, 9b, 10a and add up the total points you allocated to these items;

enter the score here [**T** = ____]. Next, add up the total points given to the uncircled items 1a, 2b, 3a, 4b, 5a, 6b, 7a, 8b, 9a, 10b; enter the score here [T = ____].

Interpretation

This instrument gives an impression of your tendencies toward "transformational" leadership (your **T** score) and "transactional" leadership (your T score). You may want to refer to the discussion of these concepts in Chapter 15. Today, a lot of attention is being given to the transforma-tional aspects of leadership—those personal qualities that inspire a sense of vision and desire for extraordinary accomplishment in followers. The most successful leaders of the future will most likely be strong in both "T"s.

_____
Source: Questionnaire by W. Warner Burke, Ph.D. Used by permission.

ASSESSMENT 15

Empowering Others

Instructions

Think of times when you have been in charge of a group—this could be a full-time or part-time work situation, a student workgroup, or whatever. Complete the following questionnaire by recording how you feel about each statement according to this scale.

> 1 = Strongly disagree
> 2 = Disagree
> 3 = Neutral
> 4 = Agree
> 5 = Strongly agree

When in charge of a group I find:

____ 1. Most of the time other people are too inexperienced to do things, so I prefer to do them myself.

____ 2. It often takes more time to explain things to others than just to do them myself.

____ 3. Mistakes made by others are costly, so I don't assign much work to them.

____ 4. Some things simply should not be delegated to others.

____ 5. I often get quicker action by doing a job myself.

____ 6. Many people are good only at very specific tasks, and thus can't be assigned additional responsibilities.

____ 7. Many people are too busy to take on additional work.

____ 8. Most people just aren't ready to handle additional responsibilities.

____ 9. In my position, I should be entitled to make my own decisions.

Scoring

Total your responses; enter the score here [____].

Interpretation

This instrument gives an impression of your *willingness to delegate.* Possible scores range from 9 to 45. The higher your score, the more willing you appear to be to delegate to others. Willingness to delegate is an important managerial characteristic. It is essential if you—as a manager—are to "empower" others and give them opportunities to assume responsibility and exercise self-control in their work. With the growing importance of empowerment in the new workplace, your willingness to delegate is well worth thinking about seriously.

_____
Source: Questionnaire adapted from L. Steinmetz and R. Todd, *First Line Management,* 4th ed. (Homewood, IL: BPI/Irwin, 1986), pp. 64–67. Used by permission.

ASSESSMENT 16

Machiavellianism

Instructions

For each of the following statements, circle the number that most closely resembles your attitude.

Statement	Disagree A Lot	Disagree A Little	Neutral	Agree A Little	Agree A Lot
1. The best way to handle people is to tell them what they want to hear.	1	2	3	4	5
2. When you ask someone to do something for you, it is best to give the real reason for wanting it rather than reasons that might carry more weight.	1	2	3	4	5
3. Anyone who completely trusts someone else is asking for trouble.	1	2	3	4	5
4. It is hard to get ahead without cutting corners here and there.	1	2	3	4	5
5. It is safest to assume that all people have a vicious streak, and it will come out when they are given a chance.	1	2	3	4	5
6. One should take action only when it is morally right.	1	2	3	4	5
7. Most people are basically good and kind.	1	2	3	4	5
8. There is no excuse for lying to someone else.	1	2	3	4	5
9. Most people forget more easily the death of their father than the loss of their property.	1	2	3	4	5
10. Generally speaking, people won't work hard unless forced to do so.	1	2	3	4	5

Scoring and Interpretation

This assessment is designed to compute your Machiavellianism (Mach) score. Mach is a personality characteristic that taps people's power orientation. The high-Mach personality is pragmatic, maintains emotional distance from others, and believes that ends can justify means. To obtain your Mach score, add up the numbers you checked for questions 1, 3, 4, 5, 9, and 10. For the other four questions, reverse the numbers you have checked, so that 5 becomes 1; 4 is 2; and 1 is 5. Then total both sets of numbers to find your score. A random sample of adults found the national average to be 25. Students in business and management typically score higher.

The results of research using the Mach test have found: (1) men are generally more Machiavellian than women; (2) older adults tend to have lower Mach scores than younger adults; (3) there is no significant difference between high Machs and low Machs on measures of intelligence or ability; (4) Machiavellianism is not significantly related to demographic characteristics such as educational level or marital status; and (5) high Machs tend to be in professions that emphasize the control and manipulation of people—for example, managers, lawyers, psychiatrists, and behavioral scientists.

Source: From R. Christie and F. L. Geis, *Studies in Machiavellianism* (New York: Academic Press, 1970). By permission.

ASSESSMENT 17 -

Personal Power Profile

Contributed by Marcus, Maier, Chapman University

Instructions

Below is a list of statements that may be used in describing behaviours that supervisors (leaders) in work organizations can direct toward their subordinates (followers). First, carefully read each descriptive statement, thinking in terms of *how you prefer to influence others*. Mark the number that most closely represents how you feel. Use the following numbers for your answers.

5 = Strongly agree
4 = Agree
3 = Neither agree nor disagree
2 = Disagree
1 = Strongly disagree

	Strongly Disagree	Disagree	Neither Agree nor Disagree	Agree	Strongly Agree
To influence others, I would prefer to:					
1. Increase their pay level	1	2	3	4	5
2. Make them feel valued	1	2	3	4	5
3. Give undesirable job assignments	1	2	3	4	5
4. Make them feel like I approve of them	1	2	3	4	5
5. Make them feel that they have commitments to meet	1	2	3	4	5
6. Make them feel personally accepted	1	2	3	4	5
7. Make them feel important	1	2	3	4	5
8. Give them good technical suggestions	1	2	3	4	5
9. Make the work difficult for them	1	2	3	4	5
10. Share my experience and/or training	1	2	3	4	5
11. Make things unpleasant here	1	2	3	4	5
12. Make being at work distasteful	1	2	3	4	5
13. Influence their getting a pay increase	1	2	3	4	5
14. Make them feel like they should satisfy their job requirements	1	2	3	4	5
15. Provide them with sound job-related advice	1	2	3	4	5
16. Provide them with special benefits	1	2	3	4	5
17. Influence their getting a promotion	1	2	3	4	5
18. Give them the feeling that they have responsibilities to fulfill	1	2	3	4	5
19. Provide them with needed technical knowledge	1	2	3	4	5
20. Make them recognize that they have tasks to accomplish	1	2	3	4	5

Scoring

Using the grid below, insert your scores from the 20 questions and proceed as follows: *Reward power*—sum your response to items 1, 13, 16, and 17 and divide by 4. *Coercive power*—sum your response to items 3, 9, 11, and 12 and divide by 4. *Legitimate power*—sum your response to questions 5, 14, 18, and 20 and divide by 4. *Referent power*—sum your response to questions 2, 4, 6, and 7 and divide by 4. *Expert power*—sum your response to questions 8, 10, 15, and 19 and divide by 4.

Interpretation

A high score (4 and greater) on any of the five dimensions of power implies that you prefer to influence others by employing that particular form of power. A low score (2 or less) implies that you prefer not to employ this particular form of power to influence others. This represents your power profile. Your overall power position is not reflected by the simple sum of the power derived from each of the five sources. Instead, some combinations of power are synergistic in nature—they are greater than the simple sum of their parts. For example, referent power tends to magnify the impact of other power sources because these other influence attempts are coming from a "respected" person. Reward power often increases the impact of referent power, because people generally tend to like those who give them things that they desire. Some power combinations tend to produce the opposite of synergistic effects, such that the total is less than the sum of the parts. Power dilution frequently accompanies the use of (or threatened use of) coercive power.

Reward	Coercive	Legitimate	Referent	Expert
1 ____	3 ____	5 ____	2 ____	8 ____
13 ____	9 ____	14 ____	4 ____	10 ____
16 ____	11 ____	18 ____	6 ____	15 ____
17 ____	12 ____	20 ____	7 ____	19 ____
Total ____	____	____	____	____
Divide by 4 ____	____	____	____	____

Source: Modified version of T. R. Hinken and C. A. Schriesheim, "Development and Application of New Scales to Measure the French and Raven (1959) Bases of Social Power." *Journal of Applied Psychology,* Vol. 74, 1989, 561–567.

ASSESSMENT 18

Your Intuitive Ability

Instructions

Complete this survey as quickly as you can. Be honest with yourself. For each question, select the response that most appeals to you.

1. When working on a project, do you prefer to:
   (a) Be told what the problem is but be left free to decide how to solve it?
   (b) Get very clear instructions about how to go about solving the problem before you start?
2. When working on a project, do you prefer to work with colleagues who are:
   (a) Realistic?
   (b) Imaginative?
3. Do you most admire people who are:
   (a) Creative?
   (b) Careful?
4. Do the friends you choose tend to be:

   (a) Serious and hard working?
   (b) Exciting and often emotional?
5. When you ask a colleague for advice on a problem you have, do you:
   (a) Seldom or never get upset if he or she questions your basic assumptions?
   (b) Often get upset if he or she questions your basic assumptions?
6. When you start your day, do you:
   (a) Seldom make or follow a specific plan?
   (b) Usually first make a plan to follow?
7. When working with numbers do you find that you:
   (a) Seldom or never make factual errors?
   (b) Often make factual errors?
8. Do you find that you:
   (a) Seldom daydream during the day and really don't enjoy doing so when you do it?

(b) Frequently daydream during the day and enjoy doing so?

9. When working on a problem, do you:
   (a) Prefer to follow the instructions or rules when they are given to you?
   (b) Often enjoy circumventing the instructions or rules when they are given to you?

10. When you are trying to put something together, do you prefer to have:
    (a) Step-by-step written instructions on how to assemble the item?
    (b) A picture of how the item is supposed to look once assembled?

11. Do you find that the person who irritates you *the most* is the one who appears to be:
    (a) Disorganized?
    (b) Organized?

12. When an expected crisis comes up that you have to deal with, do you:
    (a) Feel anxious about the situation?
    (b) Feel excited by the challenge of the situation?

Scoring

Total the number of "a" responses circled for questions 1, 3, 5, 6, 11; enter the score here [A = _____]. Total the number of "b" responses for questions 2, 4, 7, 8, 9, 10, 12; enter the score here [B = _____]. Add your "a" and "b" scores and enter the sum here [A + B = _____]. This is your *intuitive score*. The highest possible intuitive score is 12; the lowest is 0.

Interpretation

In his book *Intuition in Organizations* (Newbury Park, CA: Sage, 1989), pp. 10–11, Weston H. Agor states: "Traditional analytical techniques . . . are not as useful as they once were for guiding major decisions. . . . If you hope to be better prepared for tomorrow, then it only seems logical to pay some attention to the use and development of intuitive skills for decision making." Agor developed the prior survey to help people assess their tendencies to use intuition in decision making. Your score offers a general impression of your strength in this area. It may also suggest a need to further develop your skill and comfort with more intuitive decision approaches.

Source: AIM Survey (El Paso, TX: ENFP Enterprises, 1989). Copyright © 1989 by Weston H. Agor. Used by permission.

ASSESSMENT 19

Decision-Making Biases

Instructions

How good are you at avoiding potential decision-making biases? Test yourself by answering the following questions:

1. Which is riskier:
   (a) driving a car on a 400-mile trip?
   (b) flying on a 400-mile commercial airline flight?

2. Are there more words in the English language:
   (a) that begin with "r"?
   (b) that have "r" as the third letter?

3. Mark is finishing his MBA at a prestigious university. He is very interested in the arts and at one time considered a career as a musician. Is Mark more likely to take a job:
   (a) in the management of the arts?
   (b) with a management consulting firm?

4. You are about to hire a new central-region sales director for the fifth time this year. You predict that the next director should work out reasonably well since the last four were "lemons" and the odds favor hiring at least one good sales director in five tries. Is this thinking
   (a) correct?
   (b) incorrect?

5. A newly hired engineer for a computer firm in the Boston metropolitan area has 4 years' experience and good all-around qualifications. When asked to estimate the starting salary for this employee, a chemist with very little knowledge about the profession or industry guessed an annual salary of $35,000. What is your estimate?
   $_____ per year

Scoring

Your instructor will provide answers and explanations for the assessment questions.

Interpretation

Each of the preceding questions examines your tendency to use a different judgmental heuristic. In his book *Judgment in Managerial Decision Making,* 3rd ed. (New York: John Wiley & Sons, 1994), pp. 6–7, Max Bazerman calls these heuristics "simplifying strategies, or rules of thumb" used in making decisions. He states, "In general, heuristics are helpful, but their use can sometimes lead to severe errors....If we can make managers aware of the potential adverse impacts of using heuristics, they can then decide when and where to use them." This assessment offers an initial insight into your use of such heuristics. An informed decision maker understands the heuristics, is able to recognize when they appear, and eliminates any that may inappropriately bias decision-making.

Test yourself further. Before hearing from your instructor, go back and write next to each item the name of the judgmental heuristic (see Chapter 3 text discussion) that you think applies.

Then write down a situation that you have experienced and in which some decision-making bias may have occurred. Be prepared to share and discuss this incident with the class.

Source: Incidents from Max H. Bazerman, *Judgment in Managerial Decision Making,* 3rd ed. (New York: John Wiley & Sons, Inc., 1994), pp. 13–14. Used by permission.

ASSESSMENT 20

Conflict Management Styles

Instructions

Think of how you behave in conflict situations in which your wishes differ from those of one or more persons. In the space to the left of each statement below, write the number from the following scale that indicates how likely you are to respond that way in a conflict situation.

1 = very unlikely   2 = unlikely   3 = likely   4 = very likely

____ 1. I am usually firm in pursuing my goals.

____ 2. I try to win my position.

____ 3. I give up some points in exchange for others.

____ 4. I feel that differences are not always worth worrying about.

____ 5. I try to find a position that is intermediate between the other person's and mine.

____ 6. In approaching negotiations, I try to be considerate of the other person's wishes.

____ 7. I try to show the logic and benefits of my positions.

____ 8. I always lean toward a direct discussion of the problem.

____ 9. I try to find a fair combination of gains and losses for both of us.

____ 10. I attempt to work through our differences immediately.

____ 11. I try to avoid creating unpleasantness for myself.

____ 12. I try to soothe the other person's feelings and preserve our relationships.

____ 13. I attempt to get all concerns and issues immediately out in the open.

____ 14. I sometimes avoid taking positions that would create controversy.

____ 15. I try not to hurt others' feelings.

Scoring

Total your scores for items 1, 2, 7; enter that score here [*Competing* = ____]. Total your scores for items 8, 10, 13; enter that score here [*Collaborating* = ____]. Total your scores for items 3, 5, 9; enter that score here [*Compromising* = ____]. Total your scores for items 4, 11, 14; enter that score here. [*Avoiding* = ____]. Total your scores for items 6, 12, 15; enter that score here [*Accommodating* = ____].

Interpretation

Each of the scores above corresponds to one of the conflict management styles discussed in Chapter 15. Research indicates that each style has a role to play in management but that the best overall conflict management approach is collaboration; only it can lead to problem solving and true conflict resolution. You should consider any patterns that may be evident in your scores and think about how to best handle conflict situations in which you become involved.

Source: Adapted from Thomas-Kilmann, *Conflict Mode Instrument,* Copyright © 1974, Xicom, Inc., Tuxedo, NY 10987. Used by permission.

ASSESSMENT 21 — — — — — — — — — — — — — — —

Conflict Management Styles

Instructions

How true is each statement for you?

	Not True At All		Not True or Untrue		Very True
1. I hate giving up before I'm absolutely sure that I'm licked.	1	2	3	4	5
2. Sometimes I feel that I should not be working so hard, but something drives me on.	1	2	3	4	5
3. I thrive on challenging situations. The more challenges I have, the better.	1	2	3	4	5
4. In comparison to most people I know, I'm very involved in my work.	1	2	3	4	5
5. It seems as if I need 30 hours a day to finish all the things I'm faced with.	1	2	3	4	5
6. In general, I approach my work more seriously than most people I know.	1	2	3	4	5
7. I guess there are some people who can be nonchalant about their work, but I'm not one of them.	1	2	3	4	5
8. My achievements are considered to be significantly higher than those of most people I know.	1	2	3	4	5
9. I've often been asked to be an officer of some group or groups.	1	2	3	4	5

Scoring

Add all your scores to create a total score = _____.

Interpretation

Type A personalities (hurried and competitive) tend to score 36 and above. Type B personalities (relaxed) tend to score 22 and below. Scores of 23–35 indicate a balance or mix of Type A and Type B.

———————

Source: Adapted from Thomas-Kilmann, *Conflict Mode Instrument,* Copyright © 1974, Xicom, Inc., Tuxedo, NY 10987. Used by permission.

ASSESSMENT 22 — — — — — — — — — — — — — — —

Time Management Profile

Instructions

Complete the following questionnaire by indicating "Y" (yes) or "N" (no) for each item. Force yourself to respond "yes" or "no". Be frank and allow your responses to create an accurate picture of how you tend to respond to these kinds of situations.

_____ 1. When confronted with several items of similar urgency and importance, I tend to do the easiest one first.

_____ 2. I do the most important things during that part of the day when I know I perform best.

_____ 3. Most of the time I don't do things someone else can do; I delegate this type of work to others.

_____ 4. Even though meetings without a clear and useful purpose upset me, I put up with them.

_____ 5. I skim documents before reading them and don't complete any that offer a low return on my time investment.

_____ 6. I don't worry much if I don't accomplish at least one significant task each day.

_____ 7. I save the most trivial tasks for that time of day when my creative energy is lowest.

_____ 8. My workspace is neat and organized.

_____ 9. My office door is always "open"; I never work in complete privacy.

_____ 10. I schedule my time completely from start to finish every workday.

_____ 11. I don't like "to do" lists, preferring to respond to daily events as they occur.

_____ 12. I "block" a certain amount of time each day or week that is dedicated to high-priority activities.

Scoring

Count the number of "Y" responses to items 2, 3, 5, 7, 8, 12. [Enter that score here ____.] Count the number of "N" responses to items 1, 4, 6, 9, 10, 11. [Enter that score here ____.] Add together the two scores.

Interpretation

The higher the total score, the closer your behaviour matches recommended time management guidelines. Reread those items where your response did not match the desired one. Why don't they match? Do you have reasons why your behaviour in this instance should be different from the recommended time management guideline? Think about what you can do (and how easily it can be done) to adjust your behaviour to be more consistent with these guidelines. For further reading, see Alan Lakein, *How to Control Your Time and Your Life* (New York: David McKay), and William Oncken, *Managing Management Time* (Englewood Cliffs, NJ: Prentice Hall, 1984).

Source: John F. Veiga and John N. Yanouzas, *The Dynamics of Organization Theory: Gaining a Macro Perspective* (St. Paul, MN: West, 1979), pp. 158–160. Used by permission.

Glossary

Ability　A person's existing capacity to perform the various tasks needed for a given job.

Accommodation or smoothing　Involves playing down differences and finding areas of agreement.

Achievement oriented leadership　Emphasizes setting challenging goals, stressing excellence in performance, and showing confidence in people's ability to achieve high standards of performance.

Action research　The process of systematically collecting data on an organization, feeding it back for action planning, and evaluating results by collecting and reflecting on more data.

Active listening　Encouraging people to say what they really mean.

Adhocracy　An organizational structure that emphasizes shared, decentralized decision making; extreme horizontal specialization; few levels of management; the virtual absence of formal controls; and few rules, policies, and procedures.

Affective component　The component of an attitude that reflects the specific feelings regarding the personal impact of the antecedents.

Agency theory　Suggests that public corporations can function effectively even though its managers are self-interested.

Alternative dispute resolution　Involves a neutral third party who helps others resolve negotiation impasses and disputes.

Anchoring and adjustment heuristic　Bases a decision on incremental adjustments to an initial value determined by historical precedent or some reference point.

Aptitude　The capability of learning something.

Arbitration　When a neutral third party acts as judge with the power to issue a decision binding on all parties.

Artificial intelligence (AI)　Studies how computers can be programmed to think like the human brain.

Associative choices　Decisions which can be loosely linked to nagging continual problems but which were not specifically developed to solve the problem.

Attitude　Predisposition to respond in a positive or negative way to someone or something in one's environment.

Attribution theory　The attempt to understand the cause of an event, assess responsibility for outcomes of the event, and assess the personal qualities of the people involved.

Authoritarianism　The tendency to adhere rigidly to conventional values and to obey recognized authority.

Authoritative command　Uses formal authority to end conflict.

Authority decisions　Made by the manager or team leader without involving others using information he or she possesses.

Automation　Allows machines to do work previously accomplished by people.

Availability heuristic　Bases a decision on recent events relating to the situation at hand.

Avoidance　Involves pretending the conflict does not really exist.

Bargaining zone　The zone between one party's minimum reservation point and the other party's maximum reservation point in a negotiating situation.

Behavioural component　An intention to behave in a certain way based on a person's specific feelings or attitudes.

Behavioural decision theory　Views decision makers as acting only in terms of what they perceive about a given situation.

Behavioural perspective　Assumes that leadership is central to performance and other outcomes.

Behaviourally anchored rating scales (BARS)　A performance appraisal approach that describes observable job behaviours, each of which is evaluated to determine good versus bad performance.

Beliefs　Ideas about someone or something and the conclusions people draw about them.

Benefit cycle　A pattern of successful adjustment followed by further improvements.

Brainstorming　Generating ideas through "freewheeling" discussion and without criticism.

Bureaucracy　An ideal form of organization whose characteristics were defined by the German sociologist Max Weber.

Career planning   Creates long-term congruence between individual goals and organizational career opportunities.

Career planning and development   Working with managers and/or HR experts on career issues.

Career plateau   A position from which someone is unlikely to move to advance to a higher level of responsibility.

Career stages   Different points of work responsibility and achievement through which people pass during the course of their work lives.

Case study   An in-depth analysis of one or a small number of settings.

Causality   The assumption that change in the independent variable has caused change in the dependent variable.

Central tendency error   Occurs when managers lump everyone together around the average, or middle, category.

Centralization   The degree to which the authority to make decisions is restricted to higher levels of management.

Centralized communication networks   Networks that link group members through a central control point.

Certain environments   Provide full information on the expected results for decision-making alternatives.

Change agents   People who take action to change the behaviour of people and systems.

Changing   The stage in which specific actions are taken to create a change.

Channels   The pathways through which messages are communicated.

Charismatic leaders   Those leaders who, by force of their personal abilities, are capable of having a profound and extraordinary effect on followers.

Classical conditioning   A form of learning through association that involves the manipulation of stimuli to influence behaviour.

Classical decision theory   Views decision makers as acting only in terms of what they perceive about a given situation.

Coercive power   The extent to which a manager can use the "right of command" to control other people.

Cognitive components   The components of an attitude that are the beliefs, opinions, knowledge, or information a person possesses.

Cognitive dissonance   Describes a state of inconsistency between an individual's attitude and behaviour.

Cohesiveness   The degree to which members are attracted to a group and motivated to remain a part of it.

Collabouration   Involves recognition that something is wrong and needs attention through problem solving.

Collateral organization   Involves a representative set of members in periodic small-group, problem-solving sessions.

Communication   The process of sending and receiving symbols with attached meanings.

Communication channels   The pathways through which messages are communicated.

Competition   Seeks victory by force, superior skill, or domination.

Compressed work week   A work schedule that allows a full-time job to be completed in less than five full workdays.

Compromise   Occurs when each party involved in a conflict gives up something of value to the other.

Conceptual skill   The ability to analyze and solve complex problems.

Confirmation trap   The tendency to seek confirmation for what is already thought to be true, and to not search for disconfirming information.

Conflict   Occurs when parties disagree over substantive issues or when emotional antagonisms create friction between them.

Conflict resolution   Occurs when the reasons for a conflict are eliminated.

Confrontation meeting   An OD intervention designed to help determine how an organization might be improved and to start action toward such improvement.

Conglomerates   Firms that own several different unrelated businesses.

Consensus   A group decision that has the expressed support of most members.

Consideration   A highly considerate leader is sensitive to people's feelings and tries to make things pleasant for the followers.

Constructive stress   Stress that has a positive impact on attitudes and performance.

Consultative decisions   Decisions made by one individual after seeking input from or consulting with members of a group.

Content theories   Profiles different needs that may motivate individual behaviour.

Contingency approach   Seeks ways to meet the needs of different management situations.

Continuous improvement   The belief that anything and everything done in the workplace should be continually improved.

Continuous reinforcement   A reinforcement schedule that administers a reward each time a desired behaviour occurs.

Contrast effects   Occur when an individual's characteristics are contrasted with those of others recently encountered who rank higher or lower on the same characteristics.

Control   The set of mechanisms used to keep actions and outputs within predetermined limits.

Controlling   Monitoring performance and taking any needed corrective action.

Coordination   The set of mechanisms used in an organization to link the actions of its subunits into a consistent pattern.

Corporate governance   The oversight of management decisions by Boards of Directors.

Countercultures   Patterns of values and philosophies that outwardly reject those of the larger organization or social system.

Creativity   Generates unique and novel responses to problems and opportunities.

Critical incident diary   A method of performance appraisal that records incidents of unusual success or failure in a given performance aspect.

Cross-functional team   Brings together persons from different functions to work on a common task.

Cultural intelligence   The ability to identify, understand, and act effectively in cross-cultural situations.

Cultural relativism   The suggestion that ethical behaviour is determined by its cultural context.

Cultural symbol   Any object, act, or event that serves to transmit cultural meaning.

Culture   The learned and shared ways of thinking and acting among a group of people or society.

Decentralization   The degree to which the authority to make decisions is given to lower levels in an organization's hierarchy.

Decentralized communication networks   Networks that link all group members directly with one another.

Decision making   The process of choosing a course of action to deal with a problem.

Deficit cycle   A pattern of deteriorating performance that is followed by even further deterioration.

Delphi technique   Involves generating decision-making alternatives through a series of survey questionnaires.

Demographic characteristics   Background variables (e.g., age, gender) that help shape what a person becomes over time.

Destructive stress   Stress that has a negative impact on both attitudes and performance.

Developmental approaches   Systematic models of ways in which personality develops across time.

Directive leadership   Spells out the what and how of subordinates' tasks

Distributed leadership   The sharing of responsibility for meeting group task and maintenance needs.

Distributive justice   The degree to which all people are treated the same under a policy.

Distributive negotiation   Negotiation in which the focus is on positions staked out or declared by the parties involved who are each trying to claim certain portions of the available pie.

Diversity-consensus dilemma   The tendency for diversity in groups to create process difficulties even as it offers improved potential for problem solving.

Divisional departmentation   The grouping of individuals and resources by product, territories, services, clients, or legal entities.

Dogmatism   Leads a person to see the world as a threatening place and regard authority as absolute.

Domestic multiculturalism   Cultural diversity within a national population.

Dysfunctional conflict   Works to the group's or organization's disadvantage.

Effective communication   When the intended meaning equals the perceived meaning.

Effective groups   Groups that achieve high levels of task performance, member satisfaction, and team viability.

Effective manager   Leader of a team that consistently achieves high performance goals.

Efficient communication   Communication that is low cost in its use of resources.

Emotional adjustment traits   These traits measure how much an individual experiences emotional distress or displays unacceptable acts.

Emotional conflict   Conflict that involves interpersonal difficulties that arise over feelings of anger, mistrust, dislike, fear, resentment, and the like.

Emotional intelligence   The ability to manage oneself and one's relationships effectively.

Employee assistance programs   Provide help for employees that are experiencing stressful personal problems.

Employee involvement teams   Members of such teams meet regularly to examine work-related problems and opportunities.

Empowerment   The process that allows individuals and groups to make decisions affecting themselves and their work.

Environmental complexity   The magnitude of the problems and opportunities in the organization's environment as evidenced by the degree of richness, interdependence, and uncertainty.

Equity theory   Adams' theory, which posits that people will act to eliminate any felt inequity in the rewards received for their work in comparison with others.

ERG theory   Alderfer's theory, which identifies existence, relatedness, and growth needs.

Escalating commitment   The tendency to continue a previously chosen course of action even when feedback suggests that it is failing.

ESOPs   Like profit sharing, ESOPs are based on the total organization's performance, but measured in terms of stock price.

Ethical absolutism Assumption that a single moral standard applies to all cultures.

Ethical behaviour Behaviour that is morally accepted as "good" and "right."

Ethical dilemmas Situations that require a person to choose among actions that offer possible benefits while also violating ethical standards.

Ethics leadership Leadership with high moral standards.

Existence needs Desires for physiological and material well-being.

Expatriate A person who works and lives in a foreign country for an extended time.

Expectancy The probability that work effort will be followed by performance accomplishment.

Expectancy theory Vroom's theory that argues that work motivation is determined by individual beliefs regarding effort/performance relationships and work outcomes.

Expert power The ability to control another's behaviour because of the possession of knowledge, experience, or judgment that the other person does not have but needs.

External adaptation Reaching goals and dealing with outsiders. Issues concerned are the tasks to be accomplished, the methods used to achieve the goals, and methods of coping with success and failure.

Extinction The withdrawal of the reinforcing consequences for a given behaviour.

Extrinsic rewards Rewards given to the individual by some other person in the work setting.

Feedback The process of communicating how one feels about something another person has done or said.

Field survey A research design that relies on the use of some form of questionnaire for the primary purpose of describing and/or predicting some phenomenon.

FIRO-B theory Examines differences in how people relate to one another based on their needs to express and receive feelings of inclusion, control, and affection.

Flexible benefit plans Pay systems that allow workers to select benefits according to their individual needs.

Flexible manufacturing system Uses adaptive technology and integrated job designs to easily shift production among alternative products.

Flexible working hours Work schedules that give employees some daily choice in scheduling arrival and departure times from work.

Force-coercion strategy Uses authority, rewards, and punishments to create change.

Forced distribution A method of performance appraisal that uses a small number of performance categories, such as "very good," "good," "adequate," and "very poor" and forces a certain proportion of people into each.

Formal channels Communication pathways that follow the official chain of command.

Formal groups Officially designated groups for a specific organizational purpose.

Formalization The written documentation of work rules, policies, and procedures.

Functional conflict Results in positive benefits to the group.

Functional departmentation The grouping of individuals by skill, knowledge, and action yields.

Functional silos problem When persons working in different functions fail to communicate and interact with one another.

Fundamental attribution error The tendency to underestimate the influence of situational factors and to overestimate the influence of personal factors in evaluating someone else's behaviour.

Gain sharing A pay system that links pay and performance by giving the workers the opportunity to share in productivity gains through increased earnings.

Garbage can model Views the main components of the choice process-problems, solutions, participants, and choice situations-as all mixed up together in the garbage can of the organization.

Glass ceiling effect A hidden barrier limiting advancement of women and minorities in organizations.

Globalization Involves growing worldwide interdependence of resource suppliers, product markets, and business competition.

Global manager A manager who has the international awareness and cultural sensitivity needed to work well across national borders.

Global organizational learning The ability to gather from the world at large the knowledge required for long-term organizational adaptation.

Global outsourcing Domestic jobs are replaced with contract workers hired in other countries.

Goal setting The process of developing and setting motivational performance objectives.

Grafting The process of acquiring individuals, units, and/or firms to bring in useful knowledge to the organization.

Grapevine The network of friendships and acquaintances that transfers information.

Graphic rating scale A scale that lists a variety of dimensions thought to be related to high-performance outcomes in a given job and that one is expected to exhibit.

Group decisions Decisions that are made by all members of the group.

Group dynamics The forces operating in groups that affect the ways members work together.

Groups Involves two or more people working together regularly to achieve common goals.

Groupthink The tendency of cohesive group members to lose their critical evaluative capabilities.

Growth needs Desires for continued personal growth and development.

Halo effect Occurs when one attribute of a person or situation is used to develop an overall impression of the person or situation.

Halo error Results when one person rates another person on several different dimensions and gives a similar rating for each one.

Heuristics Simplifying strategies or "rules of thumb" used to make decisions.

Hierarchy of needs theory Maslow's theory that offers a pyramid of physiological, safety, social, esteem, and self-actualization needs.

High-context cultures Words convey only part of a message, while the rest of the message must be inferred from body language and additional contextual cues.

Higher-order needs Esteem and self-actualization in Maslow's hierarchy.

High-performance organization (HPO) An organization that is intentionally designed to bring out the best in people and produce sustainable organizational results.

Hindsight trap A tendency to overestimate the degree to which an event that has already taken place could have been predicted.

Horizontal specialization A division of labour through the formation of work units or groups within an organization.

House's path-goal theory of leadership Assumes that a leader's key function is to adjust his or her behaviours to complement situational contingencies.

Human capital The economic value of people with job-relevant abilities, knowledge, ideas, energies, and commitments.

Human resource strategic planning The process of hiring capable, motivated people to carry out the organization's mission and strategy.

Human resources The people who do the work that helps organizations fulfill their missions.

Human skill The ability to work well with other people.

Hygiene factors Factors in a job context, the work setting, that promote job dissatisfaction.

Inclusivity The degree to which the culture respects and values diversity and is open to anyone who can perform a job, regardless of their diversity attributes.

Individualism-collectivism The tendency of a culture's members to emphasize individual self-interests or group relationships.

Influence A behavioural response to the exercise of power.

Informal channels Do not follow the chain of command.

Informal groups Unofficial groups that emerge to serve special interests.

Information power Access to and/or control of information.

Information technology The combination of machines, artifacts, procedures, and systems used to gather, store, analyze, and disseminate information to translate it into knowledge.

Initiating structure This kind of leader is concerned with spelling out the task requirements and clarifying other aspects of the work agenda.

Innovation The process of creating new ideas and putting them in practice.

Instrumental values Values that reflect a per-son's beliefs about the means for achieving desired ends.

Instrumentality The probability that performance will lead to various work outcomes.

Integrative negotiation Negotiation in which the focus is on the merits of the issues, and the parties involved try to enlarge the available "pie" rather than stake claims to certain portions of it.

Intellectual capital The sum total of knowledge, expertise, and energy available from organizational members.

Interactional justice The degree to which people are treated with dignity and respect.

Interfirm alliances Announced cooperative agreements of joint ventures between two independent firms.

Intergroup conflict Occurs among groups in an organization.

Intergroup dynamics Relationships between groups cooperating and competing with one another.

Intergroup team building Helps groups improve their working relationships with one another and experience improved group effectiveness.

Intermittent reinforcement A reinforcement schedule that rewards behaviour only periodically.

Internal integration The creation of a collective identity and way of working and living together within an organization.

Interorganizational conflict Occurs between organizations.

Interpersonal conflict Occurs between two or more individuals in opposition to each other.

Intrapersonal conflict Occurs within the individual because of actual or perceived pressures from incompatible goals or expectations.

Intrinsic rewards Rewards received by the individual directly through task performance.

Intuition The ability to know or recognize quickly the possibilities of a situation.

Job analysis The procedure used to collect and classify information about tasks the organization needs to complete.

Job burnout Loss of interest in and satisfaction with a job due to stressful working conditions.

Job characteristics model Identifies five core job characteristics of special importance to job design—skill variety, task identity, task significance, autonomy, and feedback.

Job design The process of defining job tasks and the work arrangements to accomplish them.

Job enlargement Increases task variety by adding new tasks of similar difficulty to a job.

Job enrichment Increases job content by giving workers more responsibility for planning and evaluating duties.

Job migration The transferring of jobs from one country to another.

Job redesign Creates long-term congruence between individual goals and organizational career opportunities.

Job rotation Increases task variety by shifting workers among jobs involving tasks of similar difficulty.

Job satisfaction The degree to which individuals feel positively or negatively about their jobs.

Job sharing Allows one full-time job to be divided among two or more persons.

Job simplification Standardizes tasks and employs people in very routine jobs.

KISS principle Stands for "keep it short and simple."

Knowledge workers Employees whose major task is to produce new knowledge, typically through computer-oriented means.

Law of contingent reinforcement The view that, for a reward to have maximum reinforcing value, it must be delivered only if the desired behaviour is exhibited.

Law of effect The observation that behaviour which results in a pleasing outcome is likely to be repeated; behaviour that results in an unpleasant outcome is not likely to be repeated.

Law of immediate reinforcement The more immediate the delivery of a reward after the occurrence of a desirable behaviour, the greater the reinforcing effect on behaviour.

Leader match training Leaders are trained to diagnose the situation to match their high and low LPC scores with situational control.

Leadership A special case of interpersonal influence that gets an individual or group to do what the leader wants done.

Leadership prototype An image people have in their minds of what a model leader should look like.

Leading Creates enthusiasm to work hard to accomplish tasks successfully.

Learning An enduring change in behaviour that results from experience.

Least preferred coworker (LPC) scale A measure of a person's leadership style based on a description of the person with whom respondents have been able to work least well.

Legitimate power The extent to which a manager can use the "right of command" to control other people.

Leniency error The tendency to give relatively high ratings to virtually everyone.

Line units Work groups that conduct the major business of the organization.

Long-term/short-term orientation The degree to which a culture emphasizes long-term or short-term thinking.

Low-context cultures Cultures in which messages are expressed mainly by spoken and written words.

Low differentiation errors What occurs when raters restrict themselves to a small part of the rating scale.

Lower-order needs Physiological, safety, and social needs in Maslow's hierarchy.

Lump-sum increase A pay system in which people elect to receive their wage or salary increases in one or more "lump-sum" payments.

Maintenance activities Activities that support the emotional life of the group as an ongoing social system.

Management by objectives (MBO) A process of joint goal setting between a supervisor and a subordinate.

Management philosophy A philosophy that links key goal-related issues with key collaboration issues to come up with general ways by which the firm will manage its affairs.

Managerial mind-set An attitude or frame of mind about management.

Managerial script A series of well-known routines for problem identification and alternative generation and analysis common to managers within a ?rm.

Managers People who are formally responsible for supporting the work efforts of other people.

Masculinity-femininity The degree to which a society values assertiveness or relationships.

Matrix departmentation A combination of functional and divisional patterns wherein an individual is assigned to more than one type of unit.

MBWA Involves getting out of the office to directly communicate with others.

Mechanistic type (machine bureaucracy) Emphasizes vertical specialization and control with impersonal coordination and a heavy reliance on standardization, formalization, rules, policies, and procedures.

Mediation A neutral third party tries to engage the parties in a negotiated solution through persuasion and rational argument.

Merit pay A compensation system that bases an individual's salary or wage increase on a measure of the person's performance accomplishment during a specific time period.

Mimicry   The copying of the successful practices of others.

Mission statements   Written statements of organizational purpose.

Mixed messages   Misunderstandings that occur when a person's words say one thing while his or her nonverbal cues say something else.

Monochronic culture   Cultures in which people tend to do one thing at a time.

Motivating potential score   The extent to which the core characteristics of a job create motivating conditions.

Motivation   Forces within an individual that account for the level, direction, and persistence of effort expended at work.

Motivator factors   In job content, the tasks people actually do, are sources of job satisfaction.

Multiculturalism   Pluralism and respect for diversity in the workplace.

Multicultural workforces   Include workers from diverse ethnic backgrounds and nationalities.

Multinational corporation   A business with extensive international operations in more than one country.

Multiskilling   Team members are trained in skills to perform different jobs.

Mum effect   Occurs when people are reluctant to communicate bad news.

Need for achievement (nAch)   The desire to do better, solve problems, or master complex tasks.

Need for affiliation (nAff)   The desire for friendly and warm relations with others.

Need for power (nPower)   The desire to control others and influence their behaviour.

Negative reinforcement   The withdrawal of negative consequences, which tends to increase the likelihood of repeating the behaviour in similar settings; also known as avoidance.

Negotiation   The process of making joint decisions when the parties involved have different preferences.

New leadership   Emphasizes charismatic and transformational leadership approaches and various aspects of vision related to them, as well as self-directing work teams.

Noise   Anything that interferes with the effectiveness of communication.

Nominal group technique   Involves structured rules for generating and prioritizing ideas.

Nonprogrammed decisions   Decisions created to deal uniquely with a problem at hand.

Nonverbal communication   Communication that takes place through facial expressions, body movements, eye contact, and other physical gestures.

Norms   Rules or standards for the behaviour of group members.

Offshoring   Contracting out or outsourcing to workers in foreign countries.

Open systems   Systems that transform human and material resources into finished goods and services.

Operant conditioning   The process of controlling behaviour by manipulating, or "operating" on, its consequences.

Operations technology   The combination of resources, knowledge, and techniques that creates a product or service output for an organization.

Organic type   A professional bureaucracy that emphasizes horizontal specialization, extensive use of personal coordination, and loose rules, policies, and procedures.

Organization charts   Diagrams that depict the formal structures of organizations.

Organizational behaviour (OB)   The study of individuals and groups in organizations.

Organizational behaviour modification (OB Mod)   The systematic reinforcement of desirable work behaviour and the nonreinforcement or punishment of unwanted work behaviour.

Organizational communication   The process by which information is exchanged in the organizational setting.

Organizational (or corporate) culture   The system of shared actions, values, and beliefs that develops within an organization and guides the behaviour of its members.

Organizational design   The process of choosing and implementing a structural configuration for an organization.

Organizational development (OD)   The application of behavioural science knowledge in a long-range effort to improve an organization's ability to cope with change in its external environment and increase its problem-solving capabilities.

Organizational development interventions   Activities initiated to support planned change and improve work effectiveness.

Organizational effectiveness   Sustainable high performance in accomplishing mission and objectives.

Organizational governance   The pattern of authority, influence, and acceptable managerial behaviour established at the top of the organization.

Organizational learning   The process of acquiring knowledge and using information to adapt to successfully changing circumstances.

Organizational myth   A commonly held cause-effect relationship or assertion that cannot be empirically supported.

Organizational politics   The management of influence to obtain ends not sanctioned by the organization or to obtain sanctioned ends through nonsanctioned means and the art of creative compromise among competing interests.

Organizational strategy The process of positioning the organization in the competitive environment and implementing actions to compete successfully.

Organizational transformation The redesign of organizations to streamline, gain flexibility, and utilize new technologies for high performance.

Organizations Collections of people working together to achieve a common purpose.

Organized anarchy A form or division in a firm in a transition characterized by very rapid change and a lack of a legitimate hierarchy.

Organizing Dividing up tasks and arranging resources to accomplish them.

Output controls Controls that focus on desired targets and allow managers to use their own methods for reaching defined targets.

Output goals The goals that define the type of business an organization is in.

Outsourcing jobs Occurs when people outside a firm are contracted to perform scheduled job activities.

Paired comparison A comparative method of performance appraisal whereby each person is directly compared with every other person.

Participative leadership Focuses on consulting with subordinates and seeking and taking their suggestions into account before making decisions.

Perception The process through which people receive, organize, and interpret information from their environment.

Performance appraisal A process of systematically evaluating performance and providing feedback on which performance adjustments can be made.

Performance gap A discrepancy between the desired and actual state of affairs.

Permanent part-time work Permanent work of fewer hours than the standard week.

Personal bias error Occurs when a rater allows specific biases, such as racial, age, or gender, to enter into performance appraisal.

Personality Represents the overall profile or combination of characteristics that capture the unique nature of a person as that person reacts and interacts with others.

Personality dynamics The ways in which an individual integrates and organizes social traits, values and motives, personal conceptions, and emotional adjustment.

Planned change Intentional and occurs with a change agent's intentional direction.

Planning Sets objectives and identifies the actions needed to achieve them.

Polychronic culture A culture in which people tend to do more than one thing at a time.

Positive organizational behaviour The study and application of positively-oriented strengths and capacities.

Positive reinforcement The administration of positive consequences that tend to increase the likelihood of repeating the behaviour in similar settings.

Power The ability to get someone else to do something you want done or the ability to make things happen or get things done the way you want.

Power distance The willingness of a culture to accept status and power differences among its members.

Problem solving Uses information to resolve disputes.

Procedural justice The degree to which policies and procedures are properly followed.

Process consultation Helps a group improve on such things as norms, cohesiveness, decision-making methods, communication, conflict, and task and maintenance activities.

Process controls Controls that attempt to specify the manner in which tasks are to be accomplished.

Process innovations Innovations introducing into operations new and better ways of doing things.

Process power Control over methods of production and analysis.

Process reengineering The total rethinking and redesign of organizational process to improve performance and innovation; involves analyzing, streamlining, and reconfiguring actions and tasks to achieve work goals.

Process theories Theories that seek to understand the thought processes determining behaviour.

Product innovations Innovations that introduce new goods or services to better meet customer needs.

Profit-sharing plans Reward employees based on the entire organization's performance.

Programmed decisions Decisions that are determined by past experience as appropriate for a problem at hand.

Projection The assignment of personal attributes to other individuals.

Punishment The administration of negative consequences that tend to reduce the likelihood of repeating the behaviour in similar settings.

Quality circle Members of a quality circle meet regularly to find ways for continuous improvement of quality operations.

Quality of work life (QWL) The overall quality of human experiences in the workplace.

Ranking A comparative technique of performance appraisal that involves rank ordering of each individual from best to worst on each performance dimension.

Rational persuasion The ability to control another's behaviour because, through the individual's efforts, the person accepts the desirability of an offered goal and a reasonable way of achieving it.

Rational persuasion strategy Uses facts, special knowledge, and rational argument to create change.

Realistic job previews Previews which provide applicants with an objective description of a job and organization.

Recency error A biased rating that develops by allowing the individual's most recent behaviour to speak for his or her overall performance on a particular dimension.

Recruitment The process of attracting the best qualified individuals to apply for a job.

Referent power The ability to control another's behaviour because of the individual's desire to identify with the power source.

Refreezing The stage in which changes are reinforced and stabilized.

Reinforcement The administration of a consequence as a result of behaviour.

Reinforcement theories They emphasize the means through which operant conditioning takes place.

Relatedness needs Desires for satisfying interpersonal relationships.

Reliability The consistency and stability of a score from a measurement scale.

Representative power The formal right conferred by the firm to speak for and to a potentially important group.

Representativeness heuristic Bases a decision on similarities between the situation at hand and stereotypes of similar occurrences.

Resistance to change An attitude or behaviour that shows unwillingness to make or support a change.

Restricted communication networks Link subgroups that disagree with one another's positions.

Reward power The extent to which a manager can use extrinsic and intrinsic rewards to control other people.

Risk environments Business environments that provide probabilities regarding expected results for decision-making alternatives.

Rites Standardized and recurring activities used at special times to influence the behaviours and understanding of organizational members.

Rituals System of rites.

Role A set of expectations for a team member or person in a job.

Role ambiguity Occurs when someone is uncertain about what is expected of him or her.

Role conflict Occurs when someone is unable to respond to role expectations that conflict with one another.

Role negotiation A process through which individuals clarify expectations about what each should be giving and receiving as group members.

Role overload Occurs when too much work is expected of the individual.

Role underload Occurs when too little work is expected of the individual.

Romance of leadership People attribute romantic, almost magical qualities to leadership.

Sagas Embellished heroic accounts of the story of the founding of an organization.

Satisficing Decision making that chooses the first alternative that appears to give an acceptable or satisfactory resolution of the problem.

Scanning Looking outside the firm and bringing back useful solutions to problems.

Schemas Cognitive frameworks that represent organized knowledge about a given concept or stimulus developed through experience.

Scientific method A key part of the OB research foundations, which involves four steps: the research question or problem, hypothesis generation or formulation, the research design, and data gathering, analysis, and interpretation.

Selection The series of steps from initial applicant screening to hiring.

Selective perception The tendency to single out for attention those aspects of a situation or person that reinforce or emerge and are consistent with existing beliefs, values, and needs.

Self-concept The view individuals have of themselves as physical, social, and spiritual or moral beings.

Self-directing work teams Teams that are empowered to make decisions about planning, doing, and evaluating their work.

Self-fulfilling prophecy The tendency to create or find in another situation or individual that which one has expected to find.

Self-managing teams Same as self-directing work teams.

Self-monitoring Reflects a person's ability to adjust his or her behaviour to external, situational (environmental) factors.

Self-serving bias The tendency to deny personal responsibility for performance problems but to accept personal responsibility for performance success.

Shamrock organizations Firms that operate with a core group of permanent workers supplemented by outside contractors and part-time workers.

Shaping   The creation of a new behaviour by the positive reinforcement of successive approximations to the desired behaviour.

Shared-power strategy   Uses participative methods and emphasizes common values to create change.

Simple design   An organization configuration involving one or two ways of specializing individuals and units.

Situational control   The extent to which leaders can determine what their groups are going to do and what the outcomes of their actions and decisions are going to be.

Skill-based pay   A system that rewards people for acquiring and developing job-relevant skills in number and variety relevant to the organization's need.

Social capital   The performance potential represented in the relationships maintained among people at work.

Social facilitation   The tendency for one's behaviour to be influenced by the presence of others in a group.

Social information processing theory   An approach that believes that individual needs and task perceptions result from socially constructed realities.

Social loafing   Occurs when people work less hard in groups than they would individually.

Social responsibility   The obligation of organizations to behave in ethical and moral ways.

Social traits   Surface-level traits that reflect the way a person appears to others when interacting in various social settings.

Socialization   Orienting new employees to the firm and its work units.

Societal goals   Goals that reflect the intended contributions of an organization to the broader society.

Sociotechnical systems   Organizational systems that integrate people and technology into high-performance work settings.

Sources and types of values   Parents, friends, teachers, and external reference groups can all influence individual values.

Span of control   The number of individuals reporting to a supervisor.

Staff units   Groups that assist the line units by performing specialized services for the organization.

Stakeholders   People and groups with an interest or "stake" in the performance of the organization.

Standardization   The degree to which the range of actions in a job or series of jobs is limited.

Status congruence   The consistency between a person's status within and outside of a group.

Stereotyping   When one thinks of an individual as belonging to a group or category and the characteristics commonly associated with the group or category are assigned to the individual.

Stimulus   Something that incites action.

Strategy   The process of positioning the organization in the competitive environment and implementing actions to compete successfully.

Stress   Tension from extraordinary demands, constraints, or opportunities.

Stress management   An active approach to deal with stress that is influencing behaviour.

Stress prevention   Minimizing the potential for stress to occur.

Stressors   Things that cause stress.

Strictness error   The tendency to give everyone a low rating.

Structural redesign   Involves realigning the structure of the organization or major subsystem in order to improve performance.

Subcultures   Unique patterns of values and philosophies within a group that are not consistent with the dominant culture of the larger organization or social system.

Substantive conflict   Fundamental disagreement over ends or goals to be pursued and the means for their accomplishment.

Substitutes for leadership   Make a leader's influence either unnecessary or redundant in that they replace a leader's influence.

Supportive leadership   Focuses on subordinate needs, well-being, and promotion of a friendly work climate.

Survey   feedback Begins with the collection of data via questionnaires from organization members or a representative sample of them.

Sweatshops   Employ people that must work under adverse labour conditions

Synergy   The creation of a whole that is greater than the sum of its parts.

Systems goals   Goals concerned with conditions within the organization that are expected to increase its survival potential.

Task activities   Actions that directly contribute to the performance of important group tasks.

Task performance   The quantity and quality of work produced.

Team building   A collaborative way to gather and analyze data to improve teamwork.

Teams   People working actively together to achieve a common purpose for which they are all accountable.

Teamwork   Occurs when group members work together in ways that utilize their skills well to accomplish a purpose.

Technical skill   An ability to perform specialized tasks.

Telecommuting Working at home or in a remote location that uses computer and telecommunication linkages with the office.

Temporary part-time work Temporary work of fewer hours than the standard week.

Terminal values A person's preferences concerning the "ends" to be achieved.

Theory A set of systematically interrelated concepts, definitions, and hypotheses that are advanced to explain and predict phenomena.

360-degree evaluation (also called 360-degree feedback) A comprehensive approach that uses evaluations of bosses, peers, and subordinates but also self-ratings, customer ratings, and others outside the work unit.

Total quality management (TQM) A total commitment to high-quality results, continuous improvement, and meeting customer needs.

Training Provides the opportunity to acquire and improve job-related skills.

Trait perspectives Assume that traits play a central role in differentiating between leaders and nonleaders or in predicting leader or organizational outcomes.

Transactional leadership Involves leader-follower exchanges necessary for achieving routine performance agreed upon between leaders and followers.

Transformational leadership Occurs when leaders broaden and elevate followers' interests and followers look beyond their own interests for the good of others.

Transformational change radically shifts the fundamental character of an organization.

Two-factor theory Herzberg's theory that identifies job context as the source of job dissatisfaction and job content as the source of job satisfaction.

Type A orientation A personality orientation characterized by impatience, desire for achievement, and perfectionism.

Type B orientation A personality orientation characterized by an easygoing and less competitive nature than Type A.

Uncertain environments Business environments that provide no information to predict expected results for decision-making alternatives.

Uncertainty avoidance The cultural tendency to be uncomfortable with uncertainty and risk in everyday life.

Unfreezing The stage of the change process at which a situation is prepared for change.

Unplanned change Change that occurs spontaneously and without a change agent's direction.

Valence The value to the individual of various work outcomes.

Validity The degree of confidence one can have in the results of a research study.

Value congruence Occurs when individuals express positive feelings upon encountering others who exhibit values similar to their own.

Value creation The extent to which an organization satisfies the needs of strategic constituencies.

Values Broad preferences concerning appropriate courses of action or outcomes.

Vertical specialization A hierarchical division of labour that distributes formal authority.

Virtual groups Groups that work together via computer networks.

Virtual organization An ever-shifting constellation of ?rms, with a lead corporation, that pool skills, resources and experiences to thrive jointly.

Virtual team A work team that convenes and operates with its members linked together electronically via networked computers.

Wellness Maintaining physical and mental health to better deal with stress when it occurs.

Whistleblower Someone within the organization who exposes the wrongdoings of others in order to preserve high ethical standards.

Workforce diversity Differences based on gender, race and ethnicity, age, and able-bodied-ness.

Work-life balance Deals with the demands from one's work and personal affairs.

Zone of indifference The range of authoritative requests to which a subordinate is willing to respond without subjecting the directives to critical evaluation or judgment.

End Notes

CHAPTER 1

[1] See Jeffrey Pfeffer, *The Human Equation: Building Profits by Putting People First* (Boston: Harvard Business School Press, 1998) and Charles O'Reilly III and Jeffrey Pfeffer, *Hidden Value: How Great Companies Achieve Extraordinary Results with Ordinary People* (Boston: Harvard Business School Press, 2000.

[2] John Huey, "Managing in the Midst of Chaos," *Fortune* (April 5, 1993), pp. 38–48. See also Tom Peters, *Thriving on Chaos* (New York: Knopf, 1991); Jay R. Galbraith, Edward E. Lawler III, and Associates, *Organizing for the Future: The New Logic for Managing Organizations* (San Francisco: Jossey-Bass, 1993); William H. Davidow and Michael S. Malone, *The Virtual Corporation: Structuring and Revitalizing the Corporation of the 21st Century* (New York: Harper Business, 1993); Charles Handy, *The Age of Unreason* (Boston: Harvard Business School Press, 1990) and *The Age of Paradox* (Boston: Harvard Business School Press, 1994). Peter Drucker. *Managing in a Time of Great Change* (New York: Truman Talley, 1995) and *Management Challenges for the 21st Century* (New York: Harper, 1999).

[3] See Daniel H. Pink, "Free Agent Nation," *Fast Company* (December 1997), pp. 131ff; and Tom Peters, "The Brand Called You," *Fast Company* (August/September 1997).

[4] Robert B. Reich, "The Company of the Future," *Fast Company* (November 1998), p. 124ff.

[5] Based on Jay A. Conger, *Winning 'em Over: A New Model for Managing in the Age of Persuasion* (New York: Simon & Schuster, 1998), pp. 180–181; Stewart D. Friedman, Perry Christensen, and Jessica DeGroot, "Work and Life: The End of the Zero-Sum Game, *Harvard Business Review* (November/December 1998): 119–129; and C. Argyris, "Empowerment: The Emperor's New Clothes," *Harvard Business Review:* (May/June 1998): 98–105.

[6] The foundation report on diversity in the American workplace is *Workforce 2000: Work and Workers in the 21st Century* (Indianapolis: Hudson Institute, 1987). For comprehensive discussions, see Martin M. Chemers, Stuart Oskamp, and Mark A. Costanzo, *Diversity in Organizations: New Perspectives for a Changing Workplace* (Beverly Hills, CA: Sage, 1995); and Robert T. Golembiewski, *Managing Diversity in Organizations* (Tuscaloosa, AL: University of Alabama Press, 1995).

[7] See R. Roosevelt Thomas, Jr. with Marjorie I. Woodruff, *Building a House for Diversity* (New York: AMACOM, 1999); R. Roosevelt Thomas, "From Affirmative Action to Affirming Diversity," *Harvard Business Review* (March/April 1990): 107–117; and *Beyond Race and Gender: Unleashing the Power of Your Total Workforce by Managing Diversity* (New York: AMACOM, 1992).

[8] For discussions of the glass ceiling effect see Ann M. Morrison, Randall P. White, and Ellen Van Velso, *Breaking the Glass Ceiling* (Reading, MA: Addison-Wesley, 1987); Anne E. Weiss, *The Glass Ceiling: A Look at Women in the Workforce* (New York: Twenty First Century, 1999); Debra E. Myerson and Joyce K. Fletcher, "A Modest Manifesto for Shattering the Glass Ceiling," *Harvard Business Review* (January/February 2000).

[9] For more information see Statistics Canada, www.statcan.ca.

[10] David A. Thomas and Suzy Wetlaufer, "A Question of Color: A Debate on Race in the U.S. Workplace," *Harvard Business Review* (September/October 1997): 118–132. *Business Week* (August 6, 2001), p. 22; "Change at the Top," *Wall Street Journal* (March 9, 1999), p. B12; *The 2000 Catalyst Census of Women Corporate Officers and Top Earners* (New York: Catalyst 2000). For a look at corporate best practices, see Catalyst, *Advancing Women in Business: The Catalyst Guide* (San Francisco: Jossey-Bass, 1998).

[11] James G. March, *The Pursuit of Organizational Intelligence* (Malden, MA: Blackwell, 1999).

[12] See Peter Senge, *The Fifth Discipline* (New York: Harper, 1990); D. A. Garvin, "Building a Learning Organization," *Harvard Business Review* (November/December 1991): 78–91; Chris Argyris, *On Organizational Learning,* 2nd ed. (Malden, MA: Blackwell, 1999).

[13] Information from www.eg.com/global/gcr.nsf.

[14] See Jay W. Lorsch ed., *Handbook of Organizational Behavior* (Englewood Cliffs, NJ: Prentice Hall, 1987), for a general overview.

[15] Geert Hofstede, "Cultural Constraints in Management Theories," *Academy of Management Executive,* 7 (1993): 81–94.

[16] For more on mission statements see Patricia Jones and Larry Kahaner, *Say It and Live It: The 50 Corporate Mission Statements That Hit the Mark* (New York: Currency/Doubleday, 1995) and John Graham and Wendy Havlick, *Mission Statements: A Guide to the Corporate and Nonprofit Sectors* (New York: Garland Publishers, 1995).

[17] James C. Collins and Jerry I. Porras, "Building Your Company's Vision," *Harvard Business Review* (September/October 1996): 65–77.

[18] Hydro Quebec , http://www.hydroquebec.com.

[19] Reich, op. cit. (1998).

[20] See Michael E. Porter. *Competitive Strategy: Techniques for Analyzing Industries and Competitors* (New York: Free Press, 1980) and *Competitive Advantage: Creating and Sustaining Superior Performance* (New York: Free Press, 1986).

[21] Gary Hamel and C. K. Prahalad, "Strategic Intent," *Harvard Business Review* (May/June 1989): 63–76; and Richard A. D'Aveni, *Hyper Competition: Managing the Dynamics of Strategic Maneuvering* (New York: Free Press, 1994).

[22] Murray Demolition, http://www.murraydemolition.com.

[23] See Dave Ulrich, "Intellectual Capital = Competence ? Commitment," *Harvard Business Review* (Winter 1998): 15–26.

[24] "What Makes a Company Great?" *Fortune* (October 26, 1998), p. 218.

[25] See Brian Dumaine, "The New Non-Manager Managers," *Fortune* (February 22, 1993), pp. 80–84; and Walter Kiechel III, "How We Will Work in the Year 2000," *Fortune* (May 17, 1993), p. 38.

[26] The review is from Henry Mintzberg, *The Nature of Managerial Work* (New York: Harper & Row, 1973). For related and further developments, see Morgan W. McCall, Jr., Ann M. Morrison, and Robert L. Hannan, *Studies of Managerial Work: Results and Methods, Technical Report No. 9* (Greensboro, NC: Center for Creative Leadership, 1978); John P. Kotter, *The General Managers* (New York: Free Press, 1982); Fred Luthans, Stuart Rosenkrantz, and Harry Hennessey, "What Do Successful Managers Really Do?" *Journal

of *Applied Behavioral Science* 21, No. 2 (1985): 255–270; Robert E. Kaplan, *The Warp and Woof of the General Manager's Job, Technical Report No. 27* (Greensboro, NC: Center for Creative Leadership, 1986); and Fred Luthans, Richard M. Hodgetts, and Stuart A. Rosenkrantz, *Real Managers* (New York: HarperCollins, 1988)

27 John R. Schermerhorn, Jr., *Management,* 7th ed. (New York: Wiley, 2000).

28 Mintzberg, op. cit. (1973). See also Henry Mintzberg, *Mintzberg on Management* (New York: Free Press, 1989) and "Rounding Out the Manager's Job," *Sloan Management Review* (Fall 1994): 11–26.

29 Kotter, op. cit., (1982); John P. Kotter, "What Effective General Managers Really Do," *Harvard Business Review,* 60 (November/December 1982): 161. See Kaplan, op. cit., 1984.

30 Herminia Ibarra, "Managerial Networks," Teaching Note: #9–495–039, Harvard Business School Publishing, Boston, MA.

31 Robert L. Katz, "Skills of an Effective Administrator, *Harvard Business Review,* 52 (September/October 1974): 94. See also Richard E. Boyatzis, *The Competent Manager: A Model for Effective Performance* (New York: Wiley, 1982).

32 Daniel Goleman, *Emotional Intelligence* (New York: Bantam, 1995) and *Working with Emotional Intelligence* (New York: Bantam, 1998). See also his articles "What Makes a Leader," *Harvard Business Review* (November/December 1998): 93–102, and "Leadership that Makes a Difference," *Harvard Business Review* (March/April 2000): 79–90, quote from p. 80.

33 Conger, op. cit., 1998.

34 A good overview is available in Linda K. Trevino and Katherine J. Nelson, *Managing Business Ethics,* 2nd ed. (New York: Wiley, 1999).

35 See Blair Sheppard, Roy J. Lewicki, and John Minton, *Organizational Justice: The Search for Fairness in the Workplace* (New York: Lexington Books, 1992); and Jerald Greenberg, *The Quest for Justice on the Job: Essays and Experiments* (Thousand Oaks, CA: Sage Publications, 1995); Robert Folger and Russell Cropanzano, *Organizational Justice and Human Resource Management* (Thousand Oaks, CA: Sage, 1998); Mary A. Konovsky, "Understanding Procedural Justice and its Impact on Business Organizations," *Journal of Management,* 26 (2000): 489–511.

36 Interactional justice is described by Robert J. Bies, "The Predicament of Injustice: The Management of Moral Outrage," in L. L. Cummings & B. M. Staw (eds.), *Research in Organizational Behavior,* Vol. 9 (Greenwich, CT: JAI Press, 1987), pp. 289–319. The example is from Carol T. Kulik and Robert L. Holbrook, "Demographics in Service Encounters: Effects of Racial and Gender Congruence on Perceived Fairness,*" Social Justice Research* (in press).

37 See Steven N. Brenner and Earl A. Mollander, "Is the Ethics of Business Changing?" *Harvard Business Review,* 55 (January/February 1977): 50–57; Saul W. Gellerman, "Why 'Good Managers Make Bad Ethical Choices,'" *Harvard Business Review,* 64 (July/August 1986): 85–90; Barbara Ley Toffler, *Tough Choices: Managers Talk Ethics* (New York: John Wiley, 1986); Justin G. Longnecker, Joseph A. McKinney, and Carlos W. Moore, "The Generation Gap in Business Ethics," *Business Horizons,* 32 (September/October 1989): 9–14; John B. Cullen, Vart Victor, and Carroll Stephens, "An Ethical Weather Report: Assessing the Organization's Ethical Climate," *Organizational Dynamics* (Winter 1990): 50–62; Dawn Blalock, "Study Shows Many Execs Are Quick to Write Off Ethics," *Wall Street Journal* (March 26, 1996), p. C1.

38 Based on Gellerman, op. cit., 1986.

39 A classic book is Archie B. Carroll, *Business and Society: Managing Corporate Social Performance* (Boston: Little Brown, 1981).

40 For research on whistleblowers, see Paula M. Miceli and Janet P. Near, *Blowing the Whistle* (New York: Lexington, 1992).

41 Douglas McGregor, *The Human Side of Enterprise* (New York: McGraw-Hill, 1960).

42 David A. Nadler and Edward E. Lawler III, "Quality of Work Life: Perspectives and Directions," *Organizational Dynamics* 11 (1983): 22–36; the discussion of QWL, in Thomas G. Cummings and Edgar F. Huse, *Organizational Development and Change* (St. Paul, MN: West, 1990); and Stewart D. Friedman, Perry Christensen, and Jessica DeGroot, "Work and Life: The End of the Zero-Sum Game," *Harvard Business Review* (November– December 1998): 119–129.

43 Pfeffer, *The Human Equation: Building Profits by Putting People First,* op. cit., p. 292.

Source Notes

Vignette: Husky Injection Molding Systems, http://www.husky.ca, accessed May 17, 2004; "Husky woos workers with unique perks," *The Globe and Mail*, August 20, 2001; Hewitt Associates LLC Website "Best employers in Canada share five key traits," December 2003, *Hewitt News and Information*, http://www.hewitt .com, accessed May 17, 2004.

Aaron Bernstein, "Low-Skilled Jobs" *Business Week* (February 26, 2001 p. 91). Florida A & M University. Diana Kunde, "Black University, Corporations Find Close Ties Benefit Everyone," *The Columbus Dispatch* (October 5, 1998), p. 4; www.famu.edu.

Microsoft Great Plains information from Robert B. Reich, "The Company of the Future," *Fast Company* (November 1998), p. 124ff.

CHAPTER 2

1 This discussion comes from Course Notes for Management 5371, *Managing Organizational Behavior and Organizational Design,* prepared by Barry A. Macy, Texas Tech University, Fall 2001.

2 Personal Communication with Barry A. Macy, March 5, 1999.

3 "What Makes a Company Great?" *Fortune* (October 26, 1998), p. 218.

4 See Thomas A. Stewart, "Planning a Career Without Managers," *Fortune* (March 20, 1995), pp. 72–80.

5 Workplace Visions (September/October 1998), p. 2.

6 Lester Thurow, *Head to Head: The Coming Economic Battle among Japan, Europe, and America* (New York: Morrow, 1992) and Barry A. Macy, *Successful Strategic Change* (San Francisco: Barrett-Koehler, in preparation).

7 Organization for Economic Cooperation and Development (OECD), http://www.oecd.org.

8 Nina Munk, "The New Organization Man," *Fortune* (March 16, 1998), pp. 63–64.

9 Thurow.

10 See, for example, Jay R. Galbraith, Edward E. Lawler III, and Associates, *Organizing for the Future: The New Logic for Managing Organizations* (San Francisco: Jossey-Bass, 1993); and Peter Drucker, *Managing in a Time of Great Change* (New York: Truman Talley, 1995).

11 Michael Hammer and James Champy, *Reengineering the Corporation* (New York: Harper Collins, 1993).

12 See Gary Hammel and Jeff Sampler, "The e-Corporation," *Fortune* (December 7, 1998), pp. 79–90; and David Kirkpatrick, "The E-Ware War," *Fortune* (December 7, 1998), pp. 115–117.

13 William H. Davidow and Michael S. Malone, *The Virtual Corporation: Structuring and Revitalizing the Corporation of the 21st Century* (New York: Harper Business, 1993). Also, Andrew Kupfer, "Alone Together: Will Being Wired Set Us Free?" *Fortune* (March 20, 1995), pp. 94–104.

14 See Daniel H. Pink, "Free Agent Nation," *Fast Company* (December, 1997), pp. 131ff; and Tom Peters, "The Brand Called You," *Fast Company* (August/September 1997).

15 Charles Handy, *The Age of Unreason* (Boston: Harvard Business School Press, 1990). See also his later book, *The Age of Paradox* (Boston: Harvard Business School Press, 1994).

16 Jeffrey Pfeffer, *The Human Equation: Building Profits by Putting People First* (Boston: Harvard Business School Press, 1998).

17 See Dave Ulrich, "Intellectual Capital = Competence ? Commitment," *Harvard Business Review* (Winter 1998), pp.15–26.

18 Bradley L. Kirksman, Kevin B. Lowe, and Dianne P. Young, "The Challenge in High Performance Work Organizations," *Journal of Leadership Studies,* Vol. 5, No. 2 (Spring 1998): 3–15.

19 Kirksman, Lowe, and Young, p. 5.

20 See Kirksman, Lowe, and Young, ibid., for a discussion of this point, and Kirksman, Lowe, and Young, *High Performance Work Organizations* (Greensboro, NC: Center for Creative Leadership, 1999), for a more detailed treatment of high performance organizations.

21 Kirksman, Lowe, and Young (1998); Course Notes for Barry Macy, Management 5371, Texas Tech University (Fall 2001).

22 Kirksman, Lowe, and Young (1998), pp. 5, 6.

23 Ibid., p. 5.

24 C. B. Gibson and B. L. Kirksman, "Our Past, Present and Future in Teams: The Role of the Human Resources Professional in Managing Team Performance," in A. L. Kraut and A. K. Korman (eds.), *Changing Concepts and Practices for Human Resources Management: Contributions from Industrial Organizational Psychology* (San Francisco: Jossey-Bass, in press).

25 P. S. Goodman, R. Devadas, and T. L. Hughson, "Groups and Productivity: Analyzing the Effectiveness of Self Managing Work Teams," in J. P. Campbell and R. J. Campbell (eds.), *Productivity in Organizations: New Perspectives from Industrial and Organizational Psychology* (San Francisco: Jossey-Bass, 1988), pp. 295–237.

26 Robert E. Markland, Shawnee K. Vickery, and Robert A. Davis, *Operations Management,* 2nd ed. (Cincinnati, OH: Southwestern Publishing, 1998), p. 646.

27 Lee J. Kraijewski and Larry R. Ritzman, *Operations Management,* 5th ed. (Reading, MA: Addison-Wesley, 1989), pp. 158–159.

28 Ibid.

29 See Eryn Brown, "VF Corp. Changes Its Underware," *Fortune* (December 7, 1998), pp. 115–118; Edward Cone, "Inching Along," *Baseline* (October 2001), pp. 57–59.

30 See D. A. Garvin, "Building a Learning Organization," *Harvard Business Review* (July–August 1993): 78–91; and Danny Miller, "A Preliminary Typology of Organizational Learning: Synthesizing the Literature," *Journal of Management,* Vol. 22, No. 3 (1996), pp. 485–505.

31 Kirksman, Lowe, and Young (1998), pp. 6–7.

32 Macy, *Successful Strategic Change.*

33 Macy, Course Notes (Fall 2001).

34 See Macy, *Successful Strategic Change.*

35 Kirksman, Lowe, and Young (1998), pp. 7–12.

36 Ibid.

37 Ibid., p. 9.

38 Macy, Management 5371, Course Notes (Fall 2001).

39 Ibid.

40 Kirksman, Lowe, and Young (1998), pp. 10–12.

41 O'Toole, p. 15.

42 See B. A. Macy and J. Izumi, "Organizational Change, Design, and Work Innovation: A Meta-Analysis of 131 North American Field Studies— 1961–1991," in W. A. Pasmore and R. W. Woodman (eds.), *Research in Organizational Change and Development,* Vol. 7 (Greenwich, CT: JAI Press, 1993), pp. 235–311.

43 Kirkman, Lowe, and Young (1998), pp. 11–12.

44 O'Toole.

45 Macy, *Successful Strategic Change.*

46 The discussion in this section is based on Howard D. Putnam, *The Winds of Turbulence* (New York: Harper Business, 1991); Christy E. Dockrey, *Southwest Airlines: A Texas Airline in an Era of Deregulation* (unpublished Master's thesis, Texas Tech University, 1996); Kevin Frieberg and Jackie Frieberg, *Nuts* (Austin, TX: Bard Press, 1996); Joan M. Feldman, "IT, Culture and Southwest," *Air Transport World,* Vol. 37, No. 5 (May 2000), pp. 45–49; Perry Flint, "Back on Schedule," *Air Transport World,* Vol. 37, No. 11 (November 2000), pp. 47–51.

47 WestJet, http://www.westjet.ca.

Source Notes

Vignette: summarized from Justin Fox, "Nokia's Secret Code," *Fortune* (May 1, 2000), pp. 161–174; see also www.nokia.com.

Pyramid from Thomas A. Stewart, "Planning a Career without Managers," *Fortune* (March 20, 1995), pp. 72–80.

Generation X values/preferences adapted from Barry A. Macy, *Successful Strategic Change* (San Francisco: Barett-Koehler, in preparation). On, Stock to Grow On," *Fortune* (January 8, 2001), p. 151; High performance organization components adapted from Bradley L. Kirksman, Kevin B. Lowe, and Dianne P. Young, "The Challenge of Leadership in High Performance Work Organizations," *Journal of Leadership Studies,* Vol. 5, No. 2 (1998), p. 8.

Saturn Corporation information from Jack O'Toole, *Forming the Future: Lessons from the Saturn Corporation* (Cambridge, MA: Blackledge, 1996), Chs. 1–5; Effective manager information developed from E. E. Lawler III, "Total Quality Management and Employee Involvement: Are They Compatible?" *Academy of Management Executive,* Vol. 8, No. 1 (1994), pp. 68–76.

CHAPTER 3

1 *The Invisible Continent* (New York: Harper Business, 2000).

2 Kenichi Ohmae, *The Invisible Continent* (New York: Harper Business, 2000); *The Borderless World* (New York: Harper Business, 1989). Peter F. Drucker, "The Global Economy and the Nation-State," *Foreign Affairs* (September/October 1997).

3 See Michael Porter's three-volume series *The Competitive Advantage of Nations, Competitive Advantage,* and *Competitive Strategy* (New York: The Free Press, 1998).

4 Kenichi Ohmae, *The Evolving Global Economy* (Cambridge, MA: Harvard Business School Press, 1995); Kenichi Ohmae, "Putting Global Logic First," *Harvard Business Review* (January/February 1995), pp. 119–125; and, Jeffrey E. Garten, "Can the World Survive the Triumph of Capitalism?" *Harvard Business Review* (January/February, 1997), pp. 67–79.

5 William B. Johnson, "Global Workforce 2000: The New World Labor Market," *Harvard Business Review* (March/April 1991), pp. 115–127.

6 See Porter, op. cit.; Kenichi Ohmae *The End of the Nation State: The Rise of Regional Economies* (New York: The Free Press, 1995); and William Greider, *One World, Ready or Not: The Manic Logic of Global Capitalism* (New York: The Free Press, 1998).

7 For more information see Industry Canada's website, http://strategis.ic.gc.ca.

8 Michael E. Porter, "Clusters and the New Economics of Competition," *Harvard Business Review* (November–December 1998).

9 Mzamo P. Mangaliso, "Building Competitive Advantage from Unbunfu: Management Lessons from South Africa," *Academy of Management Executive,* Vol. 15 (2001), pp. 23–33.

10 James A. Austin and John G. McLean, "Pathways to Business Success in Sub-Saharan Africa," *Journal of African Finance and Economic Development,* Vol. 2 (1996), pp. 57–76; Information from "International Business: Consider Africa," *Harvard Business Review,* Vol. 76 (January/February 1998), pp. 16–18.

11 Robert T. Moran and John R. Risenberger, *Making Globalization Work: Solutions for Implementation* (New York: McGraw-Hill, 1993); "Don't Be an Ugly-American Manager," *Fortune* (October 16, 1995), p. 225; and, "A Way to Measure Global Success," *Fortune* (March 15, 1999), pp. 196–197.

12 "Working Overseas—Rule No. 1: Don't Miss the Locals," *Business Week* (May 15, 1995), p. 8.

13 "Don't Be an Ugly-American Manager," op. cit., p. 225; Vanessa Houlder, "Foreign Culture Shocks," *Financial Times* (March 22, 1996), p.12.

14 Geert Hofstede, *Culture's Consequences: International Differences in Work-Related Values* (Beverly Hills, CA.: Sage Publications, 1980); and, Fons Trompenaars, *Riding the Waves of Culture: Understanding Cultural Diversity*

in Business (London: Nicholas Brealey Publishing, 1993). For an excellent discussion of culture, see also Chapter 3, "Culture: The Neglected Concept," in Peter B. Smith and Michael Harris Bond, *Social Psychology Across Cultures,* 2nd ed. (Boston: Allyn & Bacon, 1998).

[15] Geert Hofstede, *Culture and Organizations: Software of the Mind* (London: McGraw-Hill, 1991).

[16] A good overview of the world's cultures is provided in Richard D. Lewis, *When Cultures Collide: Managing Successfully Across Cultures* (London: Nicholas Brealey Publishing, 1996).

[17] Benjamin L. Whorf, *Language, Thought and Reality* (Cambridge, MA: MIT Press, 1956).

[18] Edward T. Hall, *Beyond Culture* (New York: Doubleday, 1976).

[19] A classic work and the source of our examples is Edward T. Hall, *The Silent Language* (New York: Anchor Books, 1959).

[20] Allen C. Bluedorn, Carol Felker Kaufman, and Paul M. Lane, "How Many Things Do You Like to Do at Once?" *Academy of Management Executive,* Vol. 6 (November 1992), pp. 17–26.

[21] Edward T. Hall's book *The Hidden Dimension* (New York: Anchor Books, 1969; Magnolia, MI: Peter Smith, 1990) is a classic reference and the source of our examples. See also Edward T. Hall, *Hidden Differences* (New York: Doubleday, 1990).

[22] The classic work is Max Weber, *The Protestant Ethic and the Spirit of Capitalism* (New York: Scribner, 1930). For a description of religious influences in Asian cultures, see S. Gordon Redding, *The Spirit of Chinese Capitalism* (New York: Walter de Gruyter, 1990).

[23] Hofstede, op. cit. (1980). Geert Hofstede and Michael H. Bond, "The Confucius Connection: From Culture Roots to Economic Growth," *Organizational Dynamics,* Vol. 16 (1988), pp. 4–21.

[24] Hofstede, op. cit. (1980).

[25] Chinese Culture Connection, "Chinese Values and the Search for Culture-Free Dimensions of Culture," *Journal of Cross-Cultural Psychology,* Vol. 18 (1987), pp. 143–164.

[26] Hofstede and Bond, op. cit., 1988: and Geert Hofstede, "Cultural Constraints in Management Theories," *Academy of Management Executive,* Vol. 7 (February 1993), pp. 81–94. For a further discussion of Asian and Confucian values, see also Jim Rohwer, *Asia Rising: Why America Will Prosper as Asia's Economies Boom* (New York: Simon & Schuster, 1995), and Chapter 3 on "China" in Lewis, op. cit. (1996).

[27] For an example, see John R. Schermerhorn, Jr., and Michael H. Bond, "Cross-Cultural Leadership Dynamics in Collectivism + High Power Distance Settings," *Leadership and Organization Development Journal,* Vol. 18 (1997), pp. 187–193.

[28] Nancy J. Adler, *International Dimensions of Organizational Behavior,* 2nd ed. (Boston: PWS-Kent, 1991).

[29] Trompenaars, op. cit. (1993).

[30] Alvin Toffler, *The Third Wave* (New York: William Morrow, 1980).

[31] Information from "Sweatshop Wars," *The Economist* (February 27, 1999), pp. 62–63.

[32] See Hofstede, op. cit. (1980, 1993); Adler, op. cit. (1991).

[33] Adler, op. cit. (1991).

[34] For more information see Statistics Canada, www.statcan.ca.

[35] For more information see United Nations website, www.un.org.

[36] See J. Stewart Black and Hal B. Gregersen, "The Right Way to Manage Expats," *Harvard Business Review* (March/April 1999).

[37] See Rosalie Tung, "Expatriate Assignments: Enhancing Success and Minimizing Failure," *Academy of Management Executive* (May 1987), pp. 117–126; and Adler, op. cit. (1991).

[38] Nancy J. Adler, "Reentry: Managing Cross-Cultural Transitions," *Group and Organization Studies,* Vol. 6, No. 3 (1981), pp. 341–356; and Adler, op. cit. (1991).

[39] For a discussion of international business ethics, see Thomas Donaldson and Thomas W. Dunfee, *Ties That Bind* (Boston: Harvard Business School Press, 1999); Thomas Donaldson, "Values in Tension: Ethics Away from Home," *Harvard Business Review* (September/October 1996), pp. 48–62; and, Debora L. Spar, "The Spotlight and the Bottom Line," *Foreign Affairs* (March/April 1998).

[40] "Cracking Down on Overseas Bribes," *Business Week* (March 1, 1999), p. 41

[41] "Business Ethics: Sweatshops," *The Economist* (February 27, 1999), pp. 62–63.

[42] Information from Council for Economic Priorities Accreditation Agency Web site: www.cepaa.org.

[43] Donaldson, op. cit. (1996).

[44] Ibid.; Thomas Donaldson and Thomas W. Dunfee, "Towards a Unified Conception of Business Ethics: Integrative Social Contracts Theory," *Academy of Management Review,* Vol. 19 (1994), pp. 252–285; and Donaldson and Dunfee, op. cit. (1999). For a related discussion see John R. Schermerhorn, Jr., "Alternative Terms of Business Engagement in Ethically Challenging Environment," *Business Ethics Quarterly* (1999), forthcoming.

[45] Geert Hofstede, "Motivation, Leadership and Organization: Do American Theories Apply Abroad?" *Organizational Dynamics,* Vol. 9 (1980), pp. 43+; Hofstede, op cit. (1993).

[46] Two classic works are William Ouchi, *Theory Z: How American Businesses Can Meet the Japanese Challenge* (Reading, MA: Addison-Wesley, 1981); Richard Tanner and Anthony Athos, *The Art of Japanese Management* (New York: Simon & Schuster, 1981).

[47] See J. Bernard Keys, Luther Tray Denton, and Thomas R. Miller, "The Japanese Management Theory Jungle—Revisited," *Journal of Management,* Vol. 20 (1994), pp. 373–402; and "Japanese and Korean Management Systems," Ch. 13 in Min Chen, *Asian Management Systems* (New York: Routledge, 1995).

Source Notes

Vignette: http://www.inco.com

Information from "A Global Sightseeing Tour," *Business Week* (February 1, 1999), pp. ENT3.

"Just a Wee Bit of Life in Silicon Glen," *World Business* (March/April 1996), p. 13.

Council on Economic Priorities Accreditation Agency Web site, www.cepaa.org.
   Developed from Geert Hofstede, *Culture's Consequences* (Beverly Hills, CA: Sage Publications, 1980).

Developed from Fons Trompenaars, *Riding the Waves of Culture* (London: Nicholas Brealey Publishing, 1993).

Developed from Nancy J. Adler, *International Dimensions of Organizational Behavior,* 2nd ed. (Boston: Kent, 1991).

John R. Schermerhorn, Jr., *Management,* 6 ed. (New York, Wiley, 1999), p. 118. Used by permission.

CHAPTER 4

[1] J. Laabs, "Interest in Diversity Training Continues to Grow," *Personnel Journal* (October 1993), p. 18.

[2] L. R. Gomez-Mejia, D. B. Balkin, and R. L. Cardy, *Managing Human Resources* (Englewood Cliffs, NJ: Prentice-Hall, 1995), p. 154.

[3] John P. Fernandez, *Managing a Diverse Workforce* (Lexington, MA: D. C. Heath, 1991); D. Jamieson and Julia O'Mara, *Managing Workplace 2000* (San Francisco: Jossey-Bass, 1991).

[4] T. G. Exner, "In and Out of Work," *American Demographics* (June 1992), p. 63, and A. N. Fullerton, "Another Look at the Labor Force," *Monthly Labor Review* (November 1993), p. 34; M. K. Foster and B. J. Orser, "A Marketing Perspective on Women in Management," *Canadian Journal of Administrative Sciences,* Vol. 11, No. 4 (1994), pp. 339–345: L. Gardenswartz and A. Rowe, "Diversity Q & A," *Mosaics* (March/April, 1998), p. 3.

5 Canadian Charter of Rights and Freedoms and Employment Equity Act available at http://laws.justice.gc.ca.

6 Krefting and Kryzstofiak, p. 10.

7 See E. Macoby and C. N. Jacklin. *The Psychology of Sex Differences* (Stanford, CA: Stanford University press, 1974); G. N. Powell, *Women and Men in Management* (Beverly Hills, CA: Sage Publications, 1988): T. W. Mangione. "Turnover—Some Psychological and Demographic Correlates," in R. P. Quinn and T. W. Mangione (eds.), *The 1969–70 Survey of Working Conditions* (Ann Arbor: University of Michigan Survey Research Center, 1973); R. Marsh and H. Mannan, "Organizational Commitment and Turnover: A Predictive Study," *Administrative Science Quarterly* (March 1977), pp. 57–75; R. J. Flanagan, G. Strauss, and L. Ulman, "Worker Discontent and Work Discontent and Work Place Behavior," *Industrial Relations* (May 1974), pp. 101–23; K. R. Garrison and P. M. Muchinsky, "Attitudinal and Biographical Predictions of Incidental Absenteeism," *Journal of Vocational Behavior* (April 1977), pp. 221–230; G. Johns, "Attitudinal and Nonattitudinal Predictions of Two Forms of Absence from Work," *Organizational Behavior and Human Performance* (December 1978), pp. 431–44; R. T. Keller, "Predicting Absenteeism from Prior Absenteeism, Attitudinal Factors, and Nonattitudinal Factors," *Journal of Applied Psychology* (August 1983), pp. 536–540.

8 Statistics Canada, http://www.statcan.ca/Daily/English/020619/d020619b.htm; http://www.statcan.gc.ca/english/freepub/89F0133XIE/89F0133XIE2003000.pdf

9 American association of Ritired Persons, *The Aging Work Force* (Washington, D.C.: AARP, 1995), p. 3.

10 Canadian Human Rights Commission, www.chrc-ccdp.ca/media_room/news_ releases-en.asp?id=195

11 Paul Mayrand, "Older Workers: A Problem or the Solution?" *AARP Textbook Authors' Conference Presentation* (October 1992), p. 29; G. M. McEvoy and W. F. Cascio, "Cumulative Evidence of the Relationship Between Employee Age and Job Performance," *Journal of Applied Psychology* (February 1989), pp. 11–17.

12 For more information see Statistics Canada, www.statcan.ca.

13 See Fernandez, p. 236; *Mosaics,* Vol. 4, No. 2 (March/April, 1998, p. 4.

14 Fernandez; *Mosaics* (March/April, 1998).

15 See Taylor H. Co and Stacy Blake, "Managing Cultural Diversity: Implications for Organizational Competitiveness," *Academy of Management Executive,* Vol. 5, No. 3 (1991), p. 45.

16 For more information see Statistics Canada, www.statcan.ca.

17 Ibid.

18 Larry L. Cummings and Donald P. Schwab, *Performance in Organizations: Determinants and Appraisal* (Glenview, IL: Scott, Foresman, 1973), p. 8.

19 See J. Hogan, "Structure of Physical Performance in Occupational Tasks," *Journal of Applied Psychology,* Vol. 76 (1991), pp. 495–507.

20 Patricia Best, "Sleeping pretty," *Report on Business Magazine*, March 2004.

21 See N. Brody, *Personality: In Search of Individuality* (San Diego, CA: Academic Press, 1988), pp. 68–101; C. Holden. "The Genetics of Personality," *Science* (August 7, 1987), pp. 598–601.

22 See Geert Hofstede, *Culture's Consequences: International Differences in Work-Related Values,* abridged ed. (Beverly Hills: Sage Publications, 1984).

23 Chris Argyris, *Personality and Organization* (New York: Harper & Row, 1957); Daniel J. Levinson, *The Seasons of a Man's Life* (New York: Alfred A. Knopf, 1978); Gail Sheehy, *New Passages* (New York: Ballantine Books, 1995).

24 M. R. Barrick and M. K. Mount, "The Big Five Personality Dimensions and Job Performance: A Meta Analysis," *Personnel Psychology,* Vol 44 (1991), pp. 1–26, and "Autonomy as a Moderator of the Relationships Between the Big Five Personality Dimensions and Job Performance," *Journal of Applied Psychology* (February 1993), pp. 111–118.

25 See Jim C. Nunnally, *Psychometric Theory,* 2nd ed. (New York: McGraw Hill, 1978), Ch. 14.

26 See David A. Whetten and Kim S. Cameron. *Developing Management Skills,* 3rd ed. (New York: Harper Collins, 1995), p. 72.

27 Raymond G. Hunt, Frank J. Krzystofiak, James R. Meindl, and Abdalla M. Yousry, "Cognitive Style and Decision Making," *Organizational Behavior and Human Decision Processes,* Vol. 44, No. 3 (1989), pp. 436–453. For additional work on problem-solving styles, see Ferdinand A. Gul. "The Joint and Moderating Role of Personality and Cognitive Style on Decision Making," *Accounting Review* (April 1984), pp. 264–277; Brian H. Kleiner, "The Interrelationship of Jungian Modes of Mental Functioning with Organizational Factors: Implications for Management Development," *Human Relations* (November 1983), pp. 997–1012; James L. McKenney and Peter G. W. Keen, "How Managers' Minds Work," *Harvard Business Review* (May/June 1974), pp. 79–90.

28 Some examples of firms using the Myers-Briggs Indicators are J. M. Kunimerow and L. W. McAllister, "Team Building with the Myers-Briggs Type Indicator: Case Studies," *Journal of Psychological Type,* Vol. 15 (1988), pp. 26–32; G. H. Rice, Jr. and D. P. Lindecamp, "Personality Types and Business Success of Small Retailers," *Journal of Occupational Psychology,* Vol. 62 (1989), pp. 177–182; and B. Roach, *Strategy Styles and Management Types: A Resource Book for Organizational Management Consultants* (Stanford, CA: Balestrand Press, 1989).

29 For more information see Statistics Canada, www.statcan.ca.

30 J. B. Rotter, "Generalized Expectancies for Internal versus External Control of Reinforcement," *Psychological Monographs,* Vol. 80 (1966), pp. 1–28.

31 Don Hellriegel, John W. Slocum, Jr., and Richard W. Woodman, *Organizational Behavior,* 5th ed. (St. Paul, MN: West, 1989), p. 46.

32 See John A. Wagner III and John R. Hollenbeck, *Management of Organizational Behavior* (Englewood Cliffs, NJ: Prentice-Hall, 1992), Ch. 4.

33 Niccolo Machiavelli, *The Prince,* trans. George Bull (Middlesex, UK: Penguin, 1961).

34 Richard Christie and Florence L. Geis, *Studies in Machiavellianism* (New York: Academic Press, 1970.

35 See M. Snyder, *Public Appearances/Private Realities: The Psychology of Self-Monitoring* (New York: W. H. Freeman, 1987).

36 Snyder.

37 Adapted from R. W. Bonner, "A Short Scale: A Potential Measure of Pattern A Behavior," *Journal of Chronic Diseases,* Vol. 22 (1969). Used by permission.

38 See Meyer Friedman and Ray Roseman, *Type A Behavior and Your Heart* (New York: Alfred A. Knopf, 1974). For another view, see Walter Kiechel III, "Attack of the Obsessive Managers," *Fortune* (February 16, 1987), pp. 127–128.

39 Viktor Gecas, "The Self-Concept," in Ralph H. Turner and James F. Short, Jr. (eds.), Vol. 8, *Annual Review of Sociology* (Palo Alto, CA: Annual Review, 1982), p. 3. Also see Arthur P. Brief and Ramon J. Aldag, "The Self in Work Organizations: A Conceptual Review," *Academy of Management Review* (January 1981), pp. 75–88; and Jerry J. Sullivan, "Self Theories and Employee Motivation," *Journal of Management* (June 1989), pp. 345–363.

40 Compare Philip Cushman, "Why the Self Is Empty," *American Psychologist* (May 1990), pp. 599–611.

41 Based in part on a definition in Gecas, p. 3.

42 Suggested by J. Brockner, *Self-Esteem at Work* (Lexington, MA: Lexington Books, 1988) p. 144; and Wagner and Hollenbeck, pp. 100–101.

43 See P. E. Jacob, J. J. Flink, and H. L. Schuchman, "Values and Their Function in Decisionmaking," *American Behavioral Scientist,* Vol. 5, Suppl. 9 (1962), pp. 6–38.

44 See M. Rokeach and S. J. Ball Rokeach, "Stability and Change in American Value Priorities, 1968–1981," *American Psychologist* (May 1989), pp. 775–784.

45 Milton Rokeach, *The Nature of Human Values* (New York: Free Press, 1973).

46 See W. C. Frederick and J. Weber, "The Values of Corporate Managers and

Their Critics: An Empirical Description and Normative Implications," in W. C. Frederick and L. E. Preston (eds.), *Business Ethics Research Issues and Empirical Studies* (Greenwich, CT: JAI Press, 1990), pp. 123–144.

[47] Gordon Allport, Philip E. Vernon, and Gardner Lindzey, *Study of Values* (Boston: Houghton Mifflin, 1931).

[48] Adapted from R. Tagiuri, "Purchasing Executive: General Manager or Specialist?" *Journal of Purchasing* (August 1967), pp. 16–21. Bruce M. Maglino, Elizabeth C. Ravlin, and Cheryl L. Adkins, "Value Congruence and Satisfaction with a Leader: An Examination of the Role of Interaction," unpublished manuscript (Columbia, SC: University of South Carolina, 1990), pp. 8–9.

[49] Maglino, Ravlin, and Adkins.

[50] Daniel Yankelovich, *New Rules! Searching for Self-Fulfillment in a World Turned Upside Down* (New York: Random House, 1981); Daniel Yankelovich, Hans Zetterberg, Burkhard Strumpel, and Michael Shanks, *Work and Human Values: An International Report on Jobs in the 1980s and 1990s* (Aspen, CO: Aspen Institute for Humanistic Studies, 1983); William Fox, *American Values in Decline: What We Can Do* (Gainesville, FL: 1st Books Library, 2001).

[51] See Jamieson and O'Mara, pp. 28–29.

[52] Compare Martin Fishbein and Icek Ajzen, *Belief, Attitude, Intention and Behavior: An Introduction to Theory and Research* (Reading, MA: Addison-Wesley, 1973).

[53] See A. W. Wicker, "Attitude versus Action: The Relationship of Verbal and Overt Behavioral Responses to Attitude Objects," *Journal of Social Issues* (Autumn 1969), pp. 41–78. Notes N-7

[54] Leon Festinger, *A Theory of Cognitive Dissonance* (Palo Alto, CA: Stanford University Press, 1957).

[55] H. W. Lane and J. J. DiStefano (eds.), *International Management Behavior* (Scarborough, Ontario: Nelson Canada, 1988), pp. 4–5; Z. Abdoolcarim, "How Women Are Winning at Work," *Asian Business* (November 1993), pp. 24–29.

[56] For more information see Royal Bank of Canada, www.rbc.com.

Source Notes

Vignette: Tess Kalinowski, "Celebrating cultures in classes," *Toronto Star*, October 12, 2003, A4; Tess Kalinowski, "Not quite ready for Grade 1 skills," *Toronto Star*, November 22, 2003, A23; Human Resources Development Canada (HRDC) Website, "Understanding the Early Years: Dixie Bloor Mississauga children off to good start in life," November 21, 2003, available online at www.hrdc-drhc.gc.ca/common/news/dept/031121.shtml, accessed December 14, 2003; HRDC Website, "Early Childhood Development in the Dixie Bloor Community of Mississauga, Ontario," September 2003, available online at www.hrdc-drhc.gc.ca/sp-ps/arb-dgra/publications/research/2003docs/SP-583-09-03/e/SP-583-09-03_E_toc.shtml, accessed December 14, 2003; CTV.ca Website, "Number of foreign-born Canadians at 70-year high," available online at www.ctv.ca/servlet/ArticleNews/story/CTVNews/1043156830054_49//, accessed December 14, 2003; and Statistics Canada, "2001 Census," available online at www12.statcan.ca/english/census01/home/index.cfm, accessed December 14, 2003.

Effective Manager information from Gary N. Powell, "One More Time: Do Male and Female Managers Differ?" *Academy of Management Executive*, Vol. 4, No. 3 (1995), p. 74.

Summarized from Adam Gorlick, "Challenged, Yet Empowered," *Dallas Morning News* (November 19, 2000), p. 14A.

Summarized from Vikes Bajag, "Tech Professionals Often Find Challenging Work Abroad," *Dallas Morning News* (July 2, 2000), p. 16L.

Continuum excerpted from Chris Argyris, *Personality and Organization* (New York: Harper & Row, 1957).

Problem-Solving Summary based on R. P. McIntyre and M. M. Capen, "A

Cognitive Style Perspective on Ethical Questions," *Journal of Business Ethics*, Vol. 12 (1993), p. 631; D. Hellriegel, J. Slocum, and Richard Woodman, *Organizational Behavior*, 7th ed. (Minneapolis: West Publishing, 1995), Ch. 4. Summarized from Crayton Harrison, "Banks Finding Diversity Pays Off Several Ways," *Dallas Morning News* (August 13, 2000), p. 23L.

Based on M. Rokeach. *The Nature of Human Values* (New York: Free Press, 1973).Information summarized from Theresa Love: Success Story," *Dallas Morning News* (September 3, 2000), p. 18L.

Effective Manager information from Michelle N. Martinez, "Health Care Firm Seeks to Measure Diversity," *HR News* (October 1997), p. 6.

CHAPTER 5

[1] H. R. Schiffmann, *Sensation and Perception: An Integrated Approach*, 3rd ed. (New York: Wiley, 1990).

[2] Example from John A. Wagner III and John R. Hollenbeck, *Organizational Behavior* 3rd ed. (Upper Saddle River, NJ: Prentice-Hall, 1998), p. 59.

[3] See M. W. Levine and J. M. Shefner, *Fundamentals of Sensation and Perception*, Georgia T. Chao and Steve W. J. Kozlowski, "Employee Perceptions on the Implementation of Robotic Manufacturing Technology," *Journal of Applied Psychology*, Vol. 71 (1986), pp. 70–76; Steven F. Cronshaw and Robert G. Lord, "Effects of Categorization, Attribution, and Encoding Processes in Leadership Perceptions," *Journal of Applied Psychology*, Vol. 72 (1987), pp. 97–106.

[4] See Robert Lord, "An Information Processing Approach to Social Perceptions, Leadership, and Behavioral Measurement in Organizations," in B. M. Staw and L. L. Cummings (eds.), *Research in Organizational Behavior*, Vol. 7 (Greenwich, CT: JAI Press, 1985), pp. 87–128; T. K. Srull and R. S. Wyer, *Advances in Social Cognition* (Hillsdale, NJ: Erlbaum, 1988); U. Neisser, *Cognitive and Reality* (San Francisco: W. H. Freeman, 1976), p. 112.

[5] See J. G. Hunt, *Leadership: A New Synthesis* (Newbury Park, CA: Sage Publications, 1991), Ch. 7; R. G. Lord and R. J. Foti, "Schema Theories, Information Processing, and Organizational Behavior," in H. P. Simms, Jr., and D. A. Gioia (eds.), *The Thinking Organization* (San Francisco: Jossey-Bass, 1986), pp. 20–48; S. T. Fiske and S. E. Taylor, *Social Cognition* (Reading, MA: Addison-Wesley, 1984).

[6] See J. S. Phillips, "The Accuracy of Leadership Ratings: A Categorization Perspective," *Organizational Behavior and Human Performance*, Vol. 33 (1984), pp. 125–138; J. G. Hunt, B. R. Baliga, an M. F. Peterson, "Strategic Apex Leader Scripts and an Organizational Life Cycle Approach to Leadership and Excellence," *Journal of Management Development*, Vol. 7 (1988), pp. 61–83.

[7] D. Bilimoria and S. K. Piderit, "Board Committee Membership Effects of Sex-Biased Bias," *Academy of Management Journal*, Vol. 37 (1994), pp. 1453–1477.

[8] Dewitt C. Dearborn and Herbert A. Simon, "Selective Perception: A Note on the Departmental Identification of Executives," *Sociometry*, Vol. 21 (1958), pp. 140–144.

[9] J. P. Walsh, "Selectivity and Selective Perception: An Investigation of Managers' Belief Structures and Information Processing," *Academy of Management Journal*, Vol. 24 (1988), pp. 453–470.

[10] J. Sterling Livingston, "Pygmalion in Management," *Harvard Business Review* (July/August 1969).

[11] D. Eden and A. B. Shani, "Pygmalian Goes to Boot Camp," *Journal of Applied Psychology*, Vol. 67 (1982), pp. 194–199.

[12] See B. R. Schlenker, *Impression Management: The Self-Concept, Social Identity, and Interpersonal Relations* (Monterey, CA: Brooks/Cole, 1980); W. L. Gardner and M. J. Martinko, "Impression Management in Organizations," *Journal of Management* (June 1988), p. 332; R. B. Cioldini, "Indirect Tactics of Image Management: Beyond Banking," in R. A. Giacolini and P. Rosenfeld (eds.), *Impression Management in the Organization* (Hillsdale, NJ:

Erlbaum, 1989), pp. 45–71.

[13] See H. H. Kelley, "Attribution in Social Interaction," in E. Jones, et al. (eds.), *Attribution: Perceiving the Causes of Behavior* (Morristown, NJ: General Learning Press, 1972).

[14] See Terence R. Mitchell, S. G. Green, and R. E. Wood, "An Attribution Model of Leadership and the Poor Performing Subordinate," in Barry Staw and Larry L. Cummings (eds.), *Research in Organizational Behavior* (New York: JAI Press, 1981), pp. 197–234; John H. Harvey and Gifford Weary, "Current Issues in Attribution Theory and Research," *Annual Review of Psychology,* Vol. 35 (1984), pp. 427–459.

[15] R. M. Steers, S. J. Bischoff, and L. H. Higgins, "Cross Cultural Management Research," *Journal of Management Inquiry* (Dec. 1992), pp. 325–326; J. G. Miller, "Culture and the Development of Everyday Causal Explanation," *Journal of Personality and Social Psychology,* Vol. 46 (1984), p. 961–978.

[16] A. Maass and C. Volpato, "Gender Differences in Self-Serving Attributions About Sexual Experiences," *Journal of Applied Psychology,* Vol. 19 (1989), pp. 517–542.

[17] See J. M. Crant and T. S. Bateman, "Assignment of Credit and Blame for Performance Outcomes," *Academy of Management Journal* (February 1993), pp. 7–27;

[18] E. C. Pence, W. E. Pendelton, G. H. Dobbins, and J. A. Sgro, "Effects of Causal Explanations and Sex Variables on Recommendations for Corrective Actions Following Employee Failure," *Organizational Behavior and Human Performance* (April 1982), pp. 227–240.

[19] See F. Fosterling, "Attributional Retraining: A Review," *Psychological Bulletin* (Nov. 1985), pp. 496–512.

Source Notes

Vignette: SmartLabrador Project Website, available online at http://project.smartlabrador.ca/home.php, accessed December 14, 2003; ColabNet Website, available online at www.colabnet.nf.ca, accessed December 14, 2003; Industry Canada, "Smart Communities," available online at http://smartcommunities.ic.gc.ca/index_e.asp, accessed December 14, 2003.

Data reported in Edward E. Lawler III, Allan M. Mohrman, Jr., and Susan M. Resnick, "Performance Appraisal Revisited," *Organizational Dynamics,* Vol. 13 (Summer 1984), pp. 20–35.

p. 18L. Information from Roger J. Volkema, "Ethicality in Negotiations: An Analysis of Perceptual Similarities and Differences between Brazil and the United States," *J. Business Research,* Vol. 45 (May 1999), pp. 59–68. Information from James Pecht, "Accountants Leaving Nerd Image Behind," *Dallas Morning News* (October 15, 2000), p. 20L.

Information from Carla D'Nan Bass, "Title Confusion Can Slow Job Searches Experts Say," *Dallas Morning News* (October 17, 1999), p. 16L.

Information from "Technology to Put 'Black Box' in Cars on Horizon," *Lubbock Avalanche Journal* (June 25, 2000), p. 3E.

Information from Christine W. Letts, William P. Ryan, and Allen Grossman, *High Performance Non-Profit Organizations* (New York: Wiley, 1999), pp. 93–96.

Information from John R. Schermerhorn, Jr., "Team Development for High Performance Management," *Training and Development Journal,* Vol. 40 (November 1986), pp. 38–41.

Information from B. R. Schlinker, *Impression Management: The Self Concept, Social Identity, and Interpersonal Relations* (Monterey, CA: Brooks Cole, 1980).

CHAPTER 6

[1] See John P. Campbell, Marvin D. Dunnette, Edward E. Lawler III, and Karl E. Weick, Jr., *Managerial Behavior Performance and Effectiveness* (New York: McGraw-Hill, 1970), Ch. 15.

[2] For a review article that identifies a still-relevant need for more integration among motivation theories, see Terrence R. Mitchell, "Motivation—New Directions for Theory, Research and Practice," *Academy of Management Review* 7 (January 1982): 80–88.

[3] Geert Hofstede, "Cultural Constraints in Management Theories," *Academy of Management Executive* 7 (February 1993): 81–94.

[4] Geert Hofstede, *Culture's Consequences: International Differences in Work-Related Values,* abridged ed. (Beverly Hills, CA: Sage Publications, 1984).

[5] For good overviews of reinforcement-based views, see W. E. Scott Jr., and P. M. Podsakoff, *Behavioral Principles in the Practice of Management* (New York: Wiley, 1985); Fred Luthans and Robert Kreitner, *Organizational Behavior Modification and Beyond* (Glenview, IL: Scott, Foresman, 1985).

[6] For some of B. F. Skinner's work; see his *Walden Two* (New York: Macmillan, 1948), *Science and Human Behavior* (New York: Macmillan, 1953), and *Contingencies of Reinforcement* (New York: Appleton-Century-Crofts, 1969).

[7] E. L. Thorndike, *Animal Intelligence* (New York: Macmillan, 1911), p. 244.

[8] Adapted from Luthans and Kreitner, op. cit. (1985).

[9] This discussion is based on ibid.

[10] Both laws are stated in Keith L. Miller, *Principles of Everyday Behavior Analysis* (Monterey, CA: Brooks/Cole, 1975), p. 122.

[11] See John Putzier and Frank T. Novak, "Attendance Management and Control," *Personnel Administrator* (August 1989): 59–60.

[12] This example is based on a study by Barbara Price and Richard Osborn, "Shaping the Training of Skilled Workers," working paper (Detroit: Department of Management, Wayne State University, 1999).

[13] Metso Automation SCADA Solutions Ltd., www.metsoautomation.com.

[14] Robert Kreitner and Angelo Kiniki, *Organization Behavior,* 2nd ed. (Homewood, IL: Irwin, 1992).

[15] These have been used for years; see K. M. Evans, "On-the Job Lotteries: A Low-Cost Incentive That Sparks Higher Productivity," *Compensation and Benefits Review* 20, No. 4 (1988): 63–74; A. Halcrow, "Incentive! How Three Companies Cut Costs,"*Personal Journal* (February 1986), p. 12.

[16] A. R. Korukonda and James G. Hunt, "Pat on the Back Versus Kick in the Pants: An Application of Cognitive Inference to the Study of Leader Reward and Punishment Behavior," *Group and Organization Studies* 14 (1989): 299–234.

[17] Edwin A. Locke, "The Myths of Behavior Mod in Organizations," *Academy of Management Review* 2 (October 1977): 543–553. For a counterpoint, see Jerry L. Gray, "The Myths of the Myths about Behavior Mod in Organizations: A Reply to Locke's Criticisms of Behavior Modification," *Academy of Management Review* 4 (January 1979): 121–129.

[18] Robert Kreitner, "Controversy in OBM: History, Misconceptions, and Ethics," in Lee Frederiksen, ed., *Handbook of Organizational Behavior Management* (New York: Wiley, 1982), pp. 71–91.

[19] W. E. Scott, Jr., and P. M. Podsakoff, *Behavioral Principles in the Practice of Management* (New York: Wiley, 1985); also see W. Clay Hamner, "Reinforcement Theory and Contingency Management in Organizational Settings," in Richard M. Steers and Lyman W. Porters (eds.), *Motivation and Work Behavior,* 4th ed. (New York: McGraw-Hill, 1987), pp. 139–165; Luthans and Kreitner, op. cit. (1985); Charles C. Manz and Henry P. Sims, Jr., *Superleadership* (New York: Berkeley, 1990).

[20] Abraham Maslow, *Eupsychian Management* (Homewood, IL: Irwin, 1965), and *Motivation and Personality,* 2nd ed. (New York: Harper & Row, 1970).

[21] Lyman W. Porter, "Job Attitudes in Management: II. Perceived Importance of Needs as a Function of Job Level," *Journal of Applied Psychology* 47 (April 1963): 141–148.

[22] Douglas T. Hall and Khalil E. Nougaim, "An Examination of Maslow's Need Hierarchy in an Organizational Setting," *Organizational Behavior and Human Performance* 3 (1968): 12–35; Porter, op. cit. (1963); John M.

Ivancevich, "Perceived Need Satisfactions of Domestic Versus Overseas Managers," 54 (August 1969): 274–278.

23 Mahmoud A. Wahba and Lawrence G. Bridwell, "Maslow Reconsidered: A Review of Research on the Need Hierarchy Theory," *Academy of Management Proceedings* (1974): 514–520; Edward E. Lawler III and J. Lloyd Shuttle, "A Causal Correlation Test of the Need Hierarchy Concept," *Organizational Behavior and Human Performance* 7 (1973): 265–287.

24 Nancy J. Adler, *International Dimensions of Organizational Behavior,* 2nd ed. (Boston: PWS-Kent, 1991), p. 153.; Richard M. Hodgetts and Fred Luthans, *International Management* (New York: McGraw-Hill, 1991), Ch. 11.

25 Clayton P. Alderfer, "An Empirical Test of a New Theory of Human Needs," *Organizational Behavior and Human Performance* 4 (1969): 142–175; Clayton P. Alderfer, *Existence, Relatedness, and Growth* (New York: Free Press, 1972); Benjamin Schneider and Clayton P. Alderfer. "Three Studies of Need Satisfaction in Organization," *Administrative Science Quarterly* 18 (1973): 489–505.

26 Lane Tracy, "A Dynamic Living Systems Model of Work Motivation," *Systems Research* 1 (1984): 191–203; John Rauschenberger, Neal Schmidt, and John E. Hunter, "A Test of the Need Hierarchy Concept by a Markov Model of Change in Need Strength," *Administrative Science Quarterly* 25 (1980): 654–670.

27 Sources pertinent to this discussion are David C. McClelland, *The Achieving Society* (New York: Van Nostrand, 1961); David C. McClelland, "Business, Drive and National Achievement," *Harvard Business Review* 40 (July/August 1962): 99–112; David C. McClelland, "That Urge to Achieve," *Think* (November/December 1966): 19–32; G. H. Litwin and R. A. Stringer, *Motivation and Organizational Climate* (Boston: Division of Research, Harvard Business School, 1966), pp. 18–25.

28 George Harris, "To Know Why Men Do What They Do: A Conversation with David C. McClelland," *Psychology Today* 4 (January 1971): 35–39.

29 David C. McClelland and David H. Burnham, "Power Is the Great Motivator," *Harvard Business Review* 54 (March/April 1976): 100–110; David C. McClelland and Richard E. Boyatzis, "Leadership Motive Pattern and Long-Term Success in Management," *Journal of Applied Psychology* 67 (1982): 737–743.

30 P. Miron and D. C. McClelland, "The Impact of Achievement Motivation Training in Small Businesses," *California Management Review* (Summer 1979): 13–28.

31 The complete two-factor theory is well explained by Herzberg and his associates in Frederick Herzberg, Bernard Mausner, and Barbara Bloch Synderman, *The Motivation to Work,* 2nd ed. (New York: Wiley, 1967); and Frederick Herzberg, "One More Time: How Do You Motivate Employees?" *Harvard Business Review* 46 (January/February 1968): 53–62.

32 From Herzberg, op. cit. (1968), pp. 53–62.

33 See Robert J. House and Lawrence A. Wigdor, "Herzberg's Dual-Factor Theory of Job Satisfaction and Motivation: A Review of the Evidence and a Criticism," *Personnel Psychology* 20 (Winter 1967): 369–389; and Steven Kerr, Anne Harlan, and Ralph Stogdill, "Preference for Motivator and Hygiene Factors in a Hypothetical Interview Situation," *Personnel Psychology* 27 (Winter 1974): 109–124; Nathan King, "A Clarification and Evaluation of the Two-Factor Theory of Job Satisfaction," *Psychological Bulletin* (July 1970): 18–31; Marvin Dunnette, John Campbell, and Milton Hakel, "Factors Contributing to Job Satisfaction and Job Dissatisfaction in Six Occupational Groups," *Organizational Behavior and Human Performance* (May 1967): 143–174; R. J. House and L. Wigdor, "Herzberg's Dual Factor Theory of Job Satisfaction and Motivation: A Review of the Evidence and a Criticism," *Personnel Psychology* (Summer 1967): 369–389.

34 Adler, op. cit. (1991), Ch 6; Nancy J. Adler and J. T. Graham, "Cross Cultural Interaction: The International Comparison Fallacy," *Journal of International Business Studies* (Fall 1989): 515–537; Frederick Herzberg, "Workers Needs: The Same around the World," *Industry Week* (September 27, 1987), pp. 29–32.

35 See, for example, J. Stacy Adams, "Toward an Understanding of Inequality," *Journal of Abnormal and Social Psychology* 67 (1963): 422–436; and J. Stacy Adams, "Inequity in Social Exchange," in L. Berkowitz (ed.), *Advances in Experimental Social Psychology,* Vol. 2 (New York: Academic Press, 1965), pp. 267–300.

36 Adams, op. cit. (1965).

37 These issues are discussed in C. Kagitcibasi and J. W. Berry, "Cross-Cultural Psychology: Current Research and Trends," *Annual Review of Psychology* 40 (1989): 493–531.

38 Victor H. Vroom, *Work and Motivation* (New York: Wiley, 1964).

39 See Vroom (1964).

40 See Terence R. Mitchell, "Expectancy Models of Job Satisfaction, Occupational Preference and Effort: A Theoretical, Methodological, and Empirical Appraisal," *Psychological Bulletin* 81 (1974): 1053–1077; Mahmoud A. Wahba and Robert J. House, "Expectancy Theory in Work and Motivation: Some Logical and Methodological Issues," *Human Relations* 27 (January 1974): 121–147; Terry Connolly, "Some Conceptual and Methodological Issues in Expectancy Models of Work Performance Motivation," *Academy of Management Review* 1 (October 1976): 37–47; Terrence Mitchell, "Expectancy-Value Models in Organizational Psychology," in N. Feather (ed.), *Expectancy, Incentive and Action* (New York: Erlbaum & Associates, 1980).

41 See Lyman W. Porter and Edward E. Lawler III, *Managerial Attitudes and Performance* (Homewood, IL: Irwin, 1968).

42 See Adler (1991).

43 See William E. Wymer and Jeanne M. Carsten, "Alternative Ways to Gather Opinions," *HR Magazine* 37, 4 (April 1992): 71–78.

44 The Job Descriptive Index (JDI) is available from Dr. Patricia C. Smith, Department of Psychology, Bowling Green State University; the Minnesota Satisfaction Questionnaire (MSQ) is available from the Industrial Relations Center and Vocational Psychology Research Center, University of Minnesota.

45 Barry M. Staw, "The Consequences of Turnover," *Journal of Occupational Behavior* 1 (1980): 253–273; John P. Wanous, *Organizational Entry* (Reading, MA: Addison-Wesley, 1980).

46 Charles N. Greene, "The Satisfaction-Performance Controversy," *Business Horizons* 15 (1972): 31; Michelle T. Iaffaldano and Paul M. Muchinsky, "Job Satisfaction and Job Performance: A Meta-Analysis," *Psychological Bulletin* 97 (1985): 251–273; Greene, op. cit. (1972), pp. 31–41; Dennis Organ, "A Reappraisal and Reinterpretation of the Satisfaction-Causes-Performance Hypothesis," *Academy of Management Review* 2 (1977): 46–53; Peter Lorenzi, "A Comment on Organ's Reappraisal of the Satisfaction-Causes-Performance Hypothesis," *Academy of Management Review* 3 (1978): 380–382.

47 Porter and Lawler (1968).

48 This integrated model is consistent with the comprehensive approach suggested by Martin G. Evans, "Organizational Behavior: The Central Role of Motivation," in J. G. Hunt and J. D. Blair (eds.), *1986 Yearly Review of Management of the Journal of Management* 12 (1986): 203–222.

Source Notes

Vignette: Zenon Environmental Inc. Website, available online at www.zenonenv.com, accessed May 19, 2004; Mark McNeil, "Oakville's Zenon tops list of Canada's good companies," *Hamilton Spectator*, 2002, available online at www.corporateknights.ca/resources/media/spectator1.asp, accessed May 19, 2004.

Information from David Whitford, "A Human Place to Work," *Fortune* (January 8, 2001), pp. 108–120.

Information from Carla D'Nan Bass, "It's Pay Plan, not Perks, That Sales Workers Want," *Dallas Morning News* (July 9, 2000), p. 11L.

Information from Worldcom 1997 Annual Report, pp. 36, 56. Information from "Best Companies: Helping Themselves," *Fortune* (January 8, 2001), p. 158.

Information from Crayton Harrison, "Banks Offering Incentives to Boost Customer Service," *Dallas Morning News* (January 7, 2001), p. 19L.

Information from "It's a Good Thing Overseas Too: Martha Goes Global," *Lubbock Avalanche Journal* (March 4, 2001), p. 5D. Information from Carla D'Nan Bass, "Incentive Programs Never

Take a Holiday," *Dallas Morning News* (July 30, 2000), p. 14L. Information from "Best Companies: Brainy Builders," *Fortune* (January 8, 2001), p. 154.

CHAPTER 7

[1] For a good discussion of human resource management strategy and its linkage to overall management strategy, see A. J. Templer and R. J. Cattaneo, "A Model of Human Resources Management Effectiveness," *Canadian Journal of Administrative Sciences,* Vol. 12, No. 1, (1995) pp. 77–88.

[2] See J. R. Schermerhorn, Jr., *Management,* 5th ed. (New York: Wiley, 1996), Ch. 12; G. M. Bounds, G. H. Dobbins, and O. S. Fowler, *Management: A Total Quality Perspective* (Cincinnati: South-Western, 1995), Ch. 9; L. R. Gomez-Mejia, D. B. Balkin, and R. L. Cardy, *Managing Human Resources* (Englewood Cliffs, NJ: Prentice-Hall, 1995), chs 2, 6.

[3] Bounds, Dobbins, and Fowler, pp. 313–318.

[4] Bounds, Dobbins, and Fowler, p. 315.

[5] Bounds, Dobbins, and Fowler, p. 317; Gomez-Mejia, Balkin, and Cardy, pp. 97–98.

[6] Summarized from Bounds, Dobbins, and Fowler, pp. 319–321; Gómez-Mejia, Balkin, and Cardy, Ch. 6; Schermerhorn, pp. 290–293.

[7] See "Blueprints for Service Quality: The Federal Express Approach," *AMA Management Briefing* (New York: AMA Publications, 1991).

[8] Based on A. Uris, *Eighty-eight Mistakes Interviewers Make and How to Avoid Them* (New York: AMA Publications, 1988).

[9] Public Service Commission of Canada, http://www.psc-cfp.gc.ca.

[10] B. B. Gaugler, D. B. Rosenthal, G. C. Thornton, and C. Bentson, "Meta-Analysis of Assessment Center Validity," *Journal of Applied Psychology,* Vol. 72 (1987), pp. 493–511; G. M. McEvoy and R. W. Beatty, "Assessment Centers and Subordinate Appraisals of Managers: A Seven-Year Study of Predictive Validity," *Personnel Psychology,* Vol. 42 (1989), pp. 37–52. See also Nortel Networks, (www.nortel.ca), Sun Life Financial (www.sunlife.ca).

[11] P. M. Muchinsky, "The Use of Reference Reports in Personnel Selection: A Review and Evaluation," *Journal of Occupational Psychology,* Vol. 52 (1979), pp. 287–297; "Background checks on the Rise," *Dallas Morning News* (November 11, 2001), pg. L.

[12] This training discussion based on Bounds, Dobbins, and Fowler, pp. 326–329; Schermerhorn, pp. 294–295; S. R. Robbins, *Organizational Behavior,* 7th ed. (Englewood Cliffs, NJ: Prentice-Hall, 1996), pp. 641–644.

[13] Canadian Plastics Sector Council,www.cpsc-ccsp.ca/Employee%20Retention/Baytech_Plastics.htm.

[14] Much of the initial discussion in this section is based on Daniel C. Feldman, "Careers in Organizations: Recent Trends and Future Directions," *Journal of Management,* Vol. 15 (June 1989), pp. 135–156; Irving Janis and Dan Wheeler, "Thinking Clearly about Career Choices." *Psychology Today* (May 1978), p. 67; Walter Kiechel III, "How We Will Work in the Year 2000," *Fortune* (May 17, 1993), pp. 38–52.

[15] Charles Handy, *The Age of Unreason* (Boston: Harvard Business School Press, 1991).

[16] This discussion combines earlier and later career development literature based on Janis and Wheeler, p. 67; Daniel J. Levinson, *The Seasons of a Man's Life* (New York: Knopf, 1978): Douglas T. Hall, *Careers in Organizations* (Santa Monica, CA: Goodyear, 1975); Lloyd Baird and Kathy Krim, "Career Dynamics: Managing the Superior-Subordinate Relationship," *Organizational Dynamics* (Spring 1983), p. 47; Paul H. Thompson, Robin Zenger Baker, and Norman Smallwood, "Improving Professional

Development by Applying the Four-Stage Career Model," *Organizational Dynamics* (Autumn 1986), pp. 49–62; Thomas P. Ference, James A. F. Stoner, and E. Kirby Warren, "Managing the Career Plateau." *Academy of Management Review,* Vol. 2 (October 1977), pp. 602–612; Gail Sheehy, *New Passages: Mapping Your Life across Time* (New York: Ballantine Books, 1995).

[17] "Strategic Issues in Performance Appraisal, Theory and Practice," *Personnel,* Vol. 60 (Nov./Dec. 1983), p. 24; GómezMejia, Balkin, and Cardy, Ch. 8; "Performance Appraisal: Current Practices and Techniques," *Personnel* (May/June 1984), p. 57.

[18] See G. P. Latham and K. N. Wexley, *Increasing Productivity Through Performance Appraisal* (Reading, MA: Addison-Wesley, 1981), p. 80.

[19] See R. J. Newman, "Job Reviews Go Full Circle," *U.S. News and World Report* (November 1, 1993), pp. 42–43; J. A. Lopez, "A Better Way?" *Wall Street Journal* (April 13, 1994), p. R6; M. S. Hirsch, "360 Degrees of Evaluation," *Working Woman* (August 1994), pp. 20–21; B. O'Reilly, "360 Degree Feedback Can Change Your Life," *Fortune* (October 17, 1994), pp. 93–100; see *Leadership Quarterly;* Vol. 9, No. 4 (1998), special issue on "360 Degree Feedback in Leadership Research," pp. 423–474; Stephen; P. Robbins, *Organizational Behavior,* 8th ed. (Upper Saddle River, NJ: Prentice Hall, 1998), p. 568.

[20] Robert C. Hill and Sara M. Freedman, "Managing the Quality Process: Lessons from the Baldrige Award Winner," *Academy of Management Executive,* Vol. 6 (February 1992), p. 84.

[21] For more details, see Latham and Wexley, op. cit. (1981); Stephen J. Carroll and Craig E. Schneier, *Performance Appraisal and Review Systems* (Glenview, IL: Scott, Foresman, 1982).

[22] See George T. Milkovich and John W. Boudreau, *Personnel/Human Resource Management: A Diagnostic Approach,* 5th ed. (Plano, TX: Business Publications, 1988).

[23] For a detailed discussion, see S. J. Carroll and H. L. Tosi, Jr., *Management of Objectives: Application and Research* (New York: Macmillan, 1976); A. P. Raia, *Managing by Objectives* (Glenview, IL: Scott, Foresman, 1974).

[24] For discussion of many of these errors, see David L. Devries, Ann M. Morrison, Sandra L. Shullman, and Michael P. Gerlach, *Performance Appraisal on the Line* (Greensboro, NC: Center for Creative Leadership, 1986), Ch. 3.

[25] E. G. Olson, "The Workplace Is High on the High Court's Docket," *Business Week* (October 10, 1988), pp. 88–89.

[26] Based on J. J. Bernardin and C. S. Walter, "The Effects of Rater Training and Diary Keeping on Psychometric Error in Ratings," *Journal of Applied Psychology,* Vol. 61 (1977), pp. 64–69; see also R. G. Burnask and T. D. Hollman, "An Empirical Comparison of the Relative Effects of Sorter Response Bias on Three Rating Scale Formats," *Journal of Applied Psychology,* Vol. 59 (1974), pp. 307–312.

[27] W. F. Cascio and H. J. Bernardin, "Implications of Performance Appraisal Litigation for Personnel Decisions," *Personnel Psychology,* Vol. 34 (1981), pp. 221–222.

[28] See David Shar, "Comp Star Adds Efficiency and Flexibility to Performance Reviews," *HR Magazine* (October 1997), pp. 37–42.

[29] For complete reviews of theory, research, and practice, see Edward E. Lawler III, *Pay and Organizational Effectiveness* (New York: McGraw-Hill, 1971); Edward E. Lawler III, *Pay and Organization Development* (Reading MA: Addison-Wesley, 1981); Edward E. Lawler III, "The Design of Effective Reward Systems," in Jay W. Lorsch (ed.), *Handbook of Organizational Behavior* (Englewood Cliffs, NJ: Prentice-Hall, 1987), pp. 255–271.

[30] As an example, see D. B. Balkin and L. R. Gómez-Mejia (eds.), *New Perspectives on Compensation* (Englewood Cliffs, NJ: Prentice-Hall, 1987).

[31] Jone L. Pearce, "Why Merit Pay Doesn't Work: Implications from Organization Theory," in David B. Balkin and Luis R. Gómez-Mejía, pp. 169–178; Jerry M. Newman, "Selecting Incentive Plans To Complement Organizational Strategy," in Balkin and Gómez-Mejía, pp. 214–224; Edward E. Lawler III, "Pay for Performance: Making It Work," *Compensation and*

Benefits Review. Vol. 21 (1989), pp. 55–60.

[32] See Daniel C. Boyle, "Employee Motivation that Works," *HR Magazine* (October 1992), pp. 83–89. Kathleen A. McNally, "Compensation as a Strategic Tool," *HR Magazine* (July 1992), pp. 59–66.

[33] S. Caudron, "Master the Compensation Maze," *Personnel Journal* (June 1993), pp. 640–648.

[34] N. Gupta, G. E. Ledford, G. D. Jenkins, and D. H. Doty, "Survey Based Prescriptions for Skill-Based Pay," *American Compensation Association Journal.* Vol. 1, No. 1 (1992), pp. 48–59; L. W. Ledford, "The Effectiveness of Skill-Based Pay," *Perspectives in Total Compensation,* Vol. 1, No. 1 (1991), pp. 1–4.

[35] See Brian Graham-Moore, "Review of the Literature," in Brian Graham-Moore and Timothy L. Ross (eds.), *Gainsharing* (Washington, DC: The Bureau of National Affairs, 1990), p. 20.

[36] S. E. Markham, K. D. Scott, and B. L. Little, "National Gainsharing Study: The Importance of Industry Differences," *Compensation and Benefits Review* (Jan./Feb. 1992), pp. 34–45.

[37] Gómez-Mejía, Balkin, and Cardy, pp. 410–411.

[38] Gómez-Mejía, Balkin, and Cardy, pp. 409–410.

[39] C. O'Dell and J. McAdams, "The Revolution in Employee Benefits," *Compensation and Benefits Review* (May/June 1987); pp. 68–73.

Source Notes

Vignette: Taleo Website, available online at www.taleo.com, accessed May 18, 2004; Taleo U.K., Case Study—Nation Bank of Canada, available online at www.recruitsoft.co.uk/en/knowledge/media/pdf/CaseStudy_NBC.pdf, accessed May 18, 2004.

Ryan J. Danielson "Cross-Training at Peace River Pulp: A Case Study," Industrial Relations Centre, Queen's University, Kingston, ON, 2000. http://www.industrialrelationscentre.com/infobank/current_issues_series/cross-training_at_peace_river_pulp.pdf.

Information from Cora Daniels, "To Hire a Lumber Expert, Click Here," *Fortune* (April 3, 2000), pp. 267–270.

Information from Charles L. Ehrenfeld, "Their Lifeblood," *Lubbock Avalanche Journal* (November 18, 2001), pp. 14–15

Cross-Functional information from *Lubbock Avalanche Journal* (December 31, 1998), p. 86.

Information from Catalina Camia, "Political Help Wanted," *Dallas Morning News* (July 9, 2000), p. 8A.

Effective Manager information from A. Uris, *Eighty-eight Mistakes Interviewers Make and How to Avoid Them* (New York: AMA Publications, 1988).

Information from Vikas Bajaj, "Job Rotations Churn Out a Versatile Work Force," *Dallas Morning News* (June 11, 2000), p. 24L.

Information from Crayton Harrison, "Staffing Program Can Create Tech Teams—In 48 Hours," *Dallas Morning News* (April 15, 2001), p. 13L.

Information from Carla D'Nan Bass, "Health-Care Pros Have Many Training Options," *Dallas Morning News* (July 23, 2000), p. 35L.Performance Review Form adapted from Andrew D. Szilagi, Jr., and Marc J. Wallace, Jr. *Organizational Behavior and Performance,* 3rd ed. (Glenview, IL: Scott, Foresman, 1983), pp. 393–394.

Adapted from J. P. Campbell, M. D. Dunnette, R. D. Arvey, and L.V. Hellervik, "The Development Evaluation of Behaviorally Based Rating Scales," *Applied Psychology,* Vol. 57 (1973), p. 18. Copyright 1973 by the American Psychological Association. Reprinted by permission of publisher and authors.

Effective Management information from J. Zignon, "Making Performance Appraisal Work for Teams," *Training* (June 1994), pp. 58–63.

CHAPTER 8

[1] Frederick W. Taylor, *The Principles of Scientific Management* (New York: W.W. Norton, 1967).

[2] Information from "Building the S80: More Than a Sum of Its Parts," *Volvo S80* (1998); company Web site: www.volvo.com.

[3] Frederick Herzberg, "One More Time: How Do You Motivate Employees?" *Harvard Business Review* 46 (January/February 1968), pp. 53–62.

[4] Paul J. Champagne and Curt Tausky, "When Job Enrichment Doesn't Pay," *Personnel,* Vol. 3 (January/February 1978), pp. 30–40.

[5] For a complete description, see J. Richard Hackman and Greg R. Oldham, *Work Redesign* (Reading, MA: Addison-Wesley, 1980).

[6] See J. Richard Hackman and Greg Oldham, "Development of the Job Diagnostic Survey," *Journal of Applied Psychology,* Vol. 60 (1975), pp. 159–170.

[7] Hackman and Oldham, op. cit. For forerunner research, see Charles L. Hulin and Milton R. Blood, "Job Enlargement Individual Differences, and Worker Responses," *Psychological Bulletin,* Vol. 69 (1968), pp. 41–55; Milton R. Blood and Charles L. Hulin, "Alienation, Environmental Characteristics and Worker Responses," *Journal of Applied Psychology,* Vol. 51 (1967), pp. 284–290.

[8] Gerald Salancik and Jeffrey Pfeffer, "An Examination of Need-Satisfaction Models of Job Attitudes," *Administrative Science Quarterly,* Vol. 22 (1977), pp. 427–456; Gerald Salancik and Jeffrey Pfeffer, "A Social Information Processing Approach to Job Attitude and Task Design," *Administrative Science Quarterly,* Vol. 23 (1978), pp. 224–253.

[9] George W. England and Itzhak Harpaz, "How Working Is Defined: National Contexts and Demographic and Organizational Role Influences," *Journal of Organizational Behavior* (July 1990), pp. 253–266.

[10] William A. Pasmore, "Overcoming the Roadblocks to Work-Restructuring Efforts," *Organizational Dynamics,* Vol. 10 (1982), pp. 54–67; Hackman and Oldham, op. cit. (1975).

[11] See William A. Pasmore, *Designing Effective Organizations: A Sociotechnical Systems Perspective* (New York: Wiley, 1988).

[12] *The Economist* (October 17, 1998), p. 116.

[13] See Malcolm S. Salter and Wayne A. Edesis, "Wolfsburg at the Center," *Harvard Business Review* (July/August 1991).

[14] Peter Senker, *Towards the Automatic Factory: The Need for Training* (New York: Springer-Verlag, 1986).

[15] See Ramchandran Jaikumar, "Postindustrial Manufacturing," *Harvard Business Review,* Vol. 44 (1986), pp. 69–76.

[16] See Thomas M. Koulopoulos, *The Workflow Imperative: Building Real World Business Solutions* (New York: Van Nostrand Reinhold, 1995).

[17] Information from "The Business Imperative for Workflow & Business Process Reengineering," *Fortune* (November 27, 1995), special advertising supplement.

[18] Open-Text Corporation, www.opentext.com/solutions/platform/business-process-management.

[19] Edwin A. Locke, Karyll N. Shaw, Lise M. Saari, and Gary P. Latham, "Goal Setting and Task Performance: 1969–1980," *Psychological Bulletin,* Vol. 90 (July/November 1981), pp. 125–152; Edwin A. Locke and Gary P. Latham, "Work Motivation and Satisfaction: Light at the End of the Tunnel," *Psychological Science,* Vol. 1, No. 4 (July 1990), pp. 240–246; and Edwin A. Locke and Gary P. Latham, *A Theory of Goal Setting and Task Performance* (Englewood Cliffs, NJ: Prentice-Hall, 1990).

[20] Gary P. Latham and Edwin A. Locke, "Goal Setting—A Motivational Technique That Works," *Organizational Dynamics,* Vol. 8 (Autumn 1979), pp. 68–80; Gary P. Latham and Timothy P. Steele, "The Motivational Effects of Participation versus Goal-Setting on Performance," *Academy of Management Journal,* Vol. 26 (1983), pp. 406–417; Miriam Erez and Frederick H. Kanfer, "The Role of Goal Acceptance in Goal Setting and Task Performance," *Academy of Management Review,* Vol. 8 (1983), pp. 454–463; and R. E. Wood and E. A. Locke, "Goal Setting and Strategy Effects on Complex Tasks," in B. Staw and L. L. Cummings (eds.), *Research in Organizational Behavior* (Greenwich, CT: JAI Press, 1990).

[21] See E. A. Locke and G. P. Latham, "Work Motivation and Satisfaction," *Psychological Science,* Vol. 1, No. 4 (July 1990), p. 241.

[22] Ibid.

23 Information available at www.zeroknowledge.com/en/company/careers.php; http://www.profitguide.com/enewsletters/profiteer/article.jsp?content=77.

24 For a good review of MBO, see Anthony P. Raia, *Managing by Objectives* (Glenview, IL: Scott, Foresman, 1974);

25 Ibid.; also, Steven Kerr summarizes the criticisms well in "Overcoming the Dysfunctions of MBO," *Management by Objectives,* Vol. 5, No. 1 (1976).

26 For overviews, see Allan R. Cohen and Herman Gadon, *Alternative Work Schedules: Integrating Individual and Organizational Needs* (Reading, MA: Addison-Wesley, 1978); and Jon L. Pearce, John W. Newstrom, Randall B. Dunham, and Alison E. Barber, *Alternative Work Schedules* (Boston: Allyn & Bacon, 1989). See also Sharon Parker and Toby Wall, *Job and Work Design* (Thousand Oaks, CA: Sage, 1998).

27 B. J. Wixom Jr., "Recognizing People in a World of Change," *HR Magazine* (June 1995), pp. 7–8; and "The Value of Flexibility," *Inc.* (April 1996), p. 114.

28 Steven Chase, "Web pharmacies fear web tightening," *The Globe and Mail,* Nov. 12, 2004.

29 C. Latack and L. W. Foster, "Implementation of Compressed Work Schedules: Participation and Job Redesign as Critical Factors for Employee Acceptance," *Personnel Psychology,* Vol. 38 (1985), pp. 75–92.

30 "Aetna Life & Casualty Company," *Wall Street Journal* (June 4, 1990), p. R35; (June 18, 1990), p. B1.

31 *Business Week* (December 7, 1998), p. 8.

32 Getsy M. Selirio, "Job Sharing Gains Favor as Corporations Embrace Alternative Work Schedule," *Lubbock Avalanche-Journal* (December 13, 1992), p. 2E.

33 Ann Walmsley, "Making it Work," *Today's Parent,* April 1999; www.todays parent.com/lifeasparent/workfinance/ article.jsp?content=440& page=1]

34 "Making Stay-at-Homes Feel Welcome," *Business Week* (October 12, 1998), pp. 153–155.

35 T. Davenport and K. Pearlson, "Two Cheers for the Virtual Office," *Sloan Management Review* (Summer 1998), pp. 51–64.

36 "Making Stay-at-Homes Feel Welcome," op. cit.

37 HRSDC, *Work-Life Balance in Canada, A Report to Ministers Responsible for Labour in Canada,* Chapter IV, 2002; www.hrsdc.gc.ca/asp/ gateway.asp?hr=/en/lp/spila/wlb/rtm/07chapter_4.shtml&hs=wnc

38 Daniel C. Feldman and Helen I. Doerpinghaus, "Missing Persons No Longer: Managing Part-Time Workers in the '90s," *Organizational Dynamics* (Summer 1992), pp. 59–72.

Source Notes

Vignette: RBC Financial Group Website, <http://www.rbc.com>, accessed August 11, 2004

"When Is a Temp Not a Temp?" *Business Week* (December 7, 1998), pp. 90–91.

Figure 8.2 adapted from J. Richard Hackman and Greg R. Oldham, "Development of the Job Diagnostic Survey," *Journal of Applied Psychology,* Vol. 60 (1975), p. 161. Used by permission.

Based on Edwin A. Locke and Gary P. Latham: "Work Motivation and Satisfaction: Light at the End of the Tunnel," *Psychological Science,* Vol. 1, No. 4 (July 1990), p. 244.

CHAPTER 9

1 For a good discussion of groups and teams in the workplace, see Jon R. Katzenbach and Douglas K. Smith, "The Discipline of Teams," *Harvard Business Review* (March/April, 1993), pp. 111–120.

2 Harold J. Leavitt and Jean Lipman-Blumen, "Hot Groups," *Harvard Business Review* (July/August 1995), pp. 109–116.

3 See, for example, Edward E. Lawler, III, *High-Involvement Management* (San Francisco: Jossey-Bass, 1986).

4 For more information see CGI Group, www.cgi.com.

5 Marvin E. Shaw, *Group Dynamics: The Psychology of Small Group Behavior,* 2nd ed. (New York: McGraw-Hill, 1976).

6 Bib Latane, Kipling Williams, and Stephen Harkins, "Many Hands Make Light the Work: The Causes and Consequences of Social Loafing," *Journal of Personality and Social Psychology,* Vol. 37 (1978), pp. 822–832; E. Weldon and G. M. Gargano, "Cognitive Effort in Additive Task Groups: The Effects of Shared Responsibility on the Quality of Multi-attribute judgments," *Organizational Behavior and Human Decision Processes,* Vol. 36 (1985), pp. 348–361; John M. George, "Extrinsic and Intrinsic Origins of Perceived Social Loafing in Organizations," *Academy of Management Journal* (March 1992), pp. 191–202; and W. Jack Duncan, "Why Some People Loaf in Groups While Others Loaf Alone," *Academy of Management Executive,* Vol. 8 (1994), pp. 79–80.

7 D. A. Kravitz and B. Martin, "Ringelmann Rediscovered," *Journal of Personality and Social Psychology,* Vol. 50 (1986), pp. 936–941.

8 A classic article is by Richard B. Zajonc, "Social Facilitation," *Science,* Vol. 149 (1965), pp. 269–274.

9 Laurel Hyatt, "Interview with… Greg Anderson, vice president, human resources, Janssen-Ortho Inc.," *Workplace Today,* September 2003.

10 Rensis Likert, *New Patterns of Management* (New York: McGraw-Hill, 1961).

11 For a good discussion of task forces, see James Ware, "Managing a Task Force," Note 478-002, Harvard Business School, 1977.

12 For more information see Hoffmann-La Roche Limited, www.rochecanada.com.

13 See, for example, Leland P. Bradford, *Group Development,* 2nd ed. (San Francisco: Jossey-Bass, 1997).

14 J. Steven Heinen and Eugene Jacobson, "A Model of Task Group Development in Complex Organization and a Strategy of Implementation," *Academy of Management Review,* Vol. 1 (October 1976), pp. 98–111; Bruce W. Tuckman, "Developmental Sequence in Small Groups," *Psychological Bulletin,* Vol. 63 (1965), pp. 384–399; and Bruce W. Tuckman and Mary Ann C. Jensen, "Stages of Small Group Development Revisited," *Group & Organization Studies,* Vol. 2 (1977), pp. 419–427.

15 See J. Richard Hackman, "The Design of Work Teams," in Jay W. Lorsch (ed.), *Handbook of Organizational Behavior* (Englewood Cliffs, NJ: Prentice Hall, 1987), pp. 343–357.

16 David M. Herold, "The Effectiveness of Work Groups," in Steven Kerr, ed., *Organizational Behavior* (New York: Wiley, 1979), p. 95; see also the discussion of group tasks in Stewart, Manz, and Sims, op. cit. (1999), pp. 142–143.

17 Ilgen, et al., op. cit. (1997); and Warren Watson, "Cultural Diversity's Impact on Interaction Process and Performance," *Academy of Management Journal,* Vol. 16 (1993).

18 L. Argote and J. E. McGrath, "Group Processes in Organizations: Continuity and Change" in C. L. Cooper and I. T. Robertson (eds.), *International Review of Industrial and Organizational Psychology* (New York: Wiley, 1993), pp. 333–389.

19 See Daniel R. Ilgen, Jeffrey A. LePine and John R. Hollenbeck, "Effective Decision Making in Multinational Teams," in P. Christopher Earley and Miram Erez (eds.), *New Perspectives on International Industrial/Organizational Psychology* (San Francisco: New Lexington Press, 1997), pp. 377–409.

20 William C. Schultz, *FIRO: A Three-Dimensional Theory of Interpersonal Behavior* (New York: Rinehart, 1958).

21 William C. Schutz, "The Interpersonal Underworld," *Harvard Business Review;* Vol. 36 (July/August, 1958), p. 130.

22 Katzenbach and Smith, op. cit. (1993).

23 E. J. Thomas and C. F. Fink, "Effects of Group Size," in Larry L. Cummings and William E. Scott (eds.), *Readings in Organizational and Human Performance* (Homewood, IL: Irwin, 1969), pp. 394–408.

24 Shaw, op. cit. (1976).

25 George C. Homans, *The Human Group* (New York: Harcourt Brace, 1950).

26 For more information see Mount Sinai Hospital's website at www.mtsinai.on.ca

27 For a discussion of intergroup dynamics, see Schein, op. cit. (1988), pp. 106–115.

28 "Producer Power," *The Economist* (March 4, 1995), p. 70.

29 The discussion is developed from Schein, op. cit. (1988), pp. 69–75.

30 Ibid., p. 73.

31 Developed from guidelines presented in the classic article by Jay Hall, "Decisions, Decisions, Decisions," *Psychology Today* (November 1971), pp. 55–56.

32 Norman R.F. Maier, "Assets and Liabilities in Group Problem Solving," *Psychological Review,* Vol. 74 (1967), pp. 239–249.

33 Ibid.

34 Irving L. Janis, "Groupthink," *Psychology Today* (November 1971), pp. 33–36; Irving L. Janis, *Groupthink,* 2nd ed. (Boston: Houghton Mifflin, 1982). See also J. Longley and D. G. Pruitt, "Groupthink: A Critique of Janis' Theory," in L. Wheeler (ed.), *Review of Personality and Social Psychology* (Beverly Hills, CA: Sage Publications, 1980): Carrie R. Leana, "A Partial Test of Janis's Groupthink Model: The Effects of Group Cohesiveness and Leader Behavior on Decision Processes," *Journal of Management,* Vol. 11, No. 1 (1985), pp. 5–18. See also Jerry Harvey, "Managing Agreement in Organizations: The Abilene Paradox," *Organizational Dynamics* (Summer 1974), pp. 63–80.

35 Psychologists for Social Responsibility (Washington, D.C.), www.psysr.org/groupthink%20overview.htm; Center for Media & Democracy Disinfopedia, www.disinfopedia.org/wiki.phtml?title=Groupthink.

36 Janis, op. cit. (1982).

37 Gayle W. Hill, "Group versus Individual Performance: Are N1 1 Heads Better Than One?" *Psychological Bulletin,* Vol. 91 (1982), pp. 517–539.

38 These techniques are well described in George P. Huber, *Managerial Decision Making* (Glenview, IL: Scott, Foresman, 1980); and Andre L. Delbecq, Andrew L. Van de Ven, and David H. Gustafson, *Group Techniques for Program Planning: A Guide to Nominal Groups and Delphi Techniques* (Glenview, IL: Scott, Foresman, 1975); and William M. Fox, "Anonymity and Other Keys to Successful Problem-Solving Meetings," *National Productivity Review;* Vol. 8 (Spring 1989), pp. 145–156.

39 Delbecq et al., op. cit. (1975); Fox, op. cit. (1989).

40 R. Brent Gallupe and William H. Cooper, "Brainstorming Electronically," *Sloan Management Review* (Fall 1993), pp. 27–36.

Source Notes

Vignette: Information from David Kirkpatrick, "The Second Coming of Apple," *Fortune* (November 9, 1998), pp. 86–92. See also Brent Schlender, "The Three Faces of Steve," *Fortune* (November 9, 1998), pp. 96–104; www.apple.com.

University of Alberta, http://www.hrs.ualberta.ca/index.aspx?Page=12.

EDS: Information from Eric Matson, "The Seven Sins of Deadly Meetings," *Fast Company Handbook of the Business Revolution* (New York: Fast Company, 1997), p. 31.

Developed from Edgar H. Schein. *Process Consultation,* Vol. 1. Copyright © 1988 (Addison-Wesley Publishing Company), Chapter 6.

CHAPTER 10

1 Jon R. Katzenbach and Douglas K. Smith, "The Discipline of Teams," *Harvard Business Review* (March/April 1993a), pp. 111–120; and Jon R. Katzenbach and Douglas K. Smith, *The Wisdom of Teams: Creating the High-Performance Organization* (Boston: Harvard Business School Press, 1993b).

2 Jay A. Conger, *Winning 'em Over: A New Model for Managing in the Age of Persuasion* (New York: Simon & Schuster, 1998).

3 Ryan J. Danielson "Cross-Training at Peace River Pulp: A Case Study," Industrial Relations Centre, Queen's University, Kingston, ON, 2000; www.industrialrelationscentre.com/infobank/current_issues_series/cross-training_at_peace_river_pulp.pdf.

4 Katzenbach and Smith, op. cit. (1993a and 1993b).

5 See also Jon R. Katzenbach, "The Myth of the Top Management Team," *Harvard Business Review,* Vol. 75 (November/December 1997), pp. 83–91.

6 Information from Robert B. Reich, "The Company of the Future," *Fast Company* (November 1998), p. 124+.

7 Telus Corporation, www.telus.com.

8 Katzenbach and Smith, op. cit. (1993a and 1993b).

9 For a good overview, see Greg L. Stewart, Charles C. Manz, and Henry P. Sims, *Team Work and Group Dynamics* (New York: Wiley, 1999).

10 Katzenbach and Smith, op. cit. (1993a), p. 112.

11 Developed from ibid. (1993a), pp. 118–119.

12 See Stewart et al., op. cit. (1999), pp. 43–44.

13 See Daniel R. Ilgen, Jeffrey A. LePine and John R. Hollenbeck, "Effective Decision Making in Multinational Teams," in P. Christopher Earley and Miriam Erez (eds.), *New Perspectives on International Industrial/Organizational Psychology* (San Francisco: New Lexington Press, 1997), pp. 377–409.

14 Ilgen, et al., op. cit. (1997); and Warren Watson, "Cultural Diversity's Impact on Interaction Process and Performance," *Academy of Management Journal,* Vol. 16 (1993).

15 For an interesting discussion of sporting team see Ellen Fagenson-Eland, "The National Football League's Bill Parcells on Winning, Leading, and Turning Around Teams," *Academy of Management Executive,* Vol. 15 (August 2001), pp. 48–57; and, Nancy Katz, "Sports Teams as a Model for Workplace Teams: Lessons and Liabilities," *Academy of Management Executive,* Vol. 15 (August, 2002), pp. 56–69.

16 For a good discussion of team building, see William D. Dyer, *Team Building,* 3rd ed. (Reading, MA: Addison-Wesley, 1995).

17 Developed from a discussion by Edgar H. Schein, *Process Consultation* (Reading MA: Addison-Wesley, 1969), pp. 32–37; Edgar H. Schein, *Process Consultation: Volume I* (1988), pp. 40–49.

18 The classic work is Robert F. Bales, "Task Roles and Social Roles in Problem-Solving Groups," in Eleanor E. Maccoby, Theodore M. Newcomb, and E. L. Hartley (eds.), *Readings in Social Psychology* (New York: Holt, Rinehart & Winston, 1958).

19 For a good description of task and maintenance functions, see John J. Gabarro and Anne Harlan, "Note on Process Observation," Note 9-477-029 (Harvard Business School, 1976).

20 See Daniel C. Feldman, "The Development and Enforcement of Group Norms," *Academy of Management Review,* Vol. 9 (1984), pp. 47–53.

21 See Robert F. Allen and Saul Pilnick, "Confronting the Shadow Organization: How to Select and Defeat Negative Norms," *Organizational Dynamics* (Spring 1973), pp. 13–17; Alvin Zander, *Making Groups Effective* (San Francisco: Jossey-Bass, 1982), Ch. 4; Daniel C. Feldman, op. cit. (1984).

22 For a summary of research on group cohesiveness, see Marvin E. Shaw, *Group Dynamics* (New York: McGraw-Hill, 1971), pp. 110–112, 192.

23 Information from Stratford Shermin, "Secrets of HP's 'Muddled' Team," *Fortune* (March 18, 1996), pp. 116–120.

24 See Kenichi Ohmae, "Quality Control Circles: They Work and Don't Work," *Wall Street Journal* (March 29, 1982), p. 16; Robert P. Steel, Anthony J. Mento, Benjamin L. Dilla, Nestor K. Ovalle, and Russell F. Lloyd, "Factors Influencing the Success and Failure of Two Quality Circles Programs," *Journal of Management,* Vol. 11, No. 1 (1985), pp. 99–119; Edward E. Lawler III, and Susan A. Mohrman, "Quality Circles: After the Honeymoon," *Organizational Dynamics,* Vol. 15, No. 4 (1987), pp. 42–54.

25 See Jay R. Galbraith, *Designing Organizations* (San Francisco: Jossey-Bass, 1998).

26 Jerry Yoram Wind and Jeremy Main, *Driving Change: How the Best Companies Are Preparing for the 21st Century* (New York: The Free Press, 1998), p. 135.

27 Jessica Lipnack and Jeffrey Stamps, *Virtual Teams: Reaching Across Space, Time, and Organizations with Technology* (New York: Wiley, 1997). See also Bombardier's website at www.bombardier.com/index.jsp?id=3_0&lang=en&file=/en/3_0/3_3/3_3.html.

28 For a review of some alternatives, see Jeff Angus and Sean Gallagher, "Virtual Team Builders—Internet-Based Teamware Makes It Possible to Build Effective Teams from Widely Dispersed Participants," *Information Week* (May 4, 1998).

29 Christine Perey, "Conferencing and Collaboration: Real-World Solutions for Business Communications," *Business Week* special advertising section (1999).

30 R. Brent Gallupe and William H. Cooper, "Brainstorming Electronically," *Sloan Management Review* (Fall 1993), pp. 27–36.

31 William M. Bulkeley, "Computerizing Dull Meetings Is Touted as an Antidote to the Mouth That Bored," *Wall Street Journal* (January 28, 1992), pp. B1, B2.

32 See Gallupe and Cooper, op. cit. (1993).

33 For early research on related team concepts, see Richard E. Walton, "How to Counter Alienation in the Plant," *Harvard Business Review* (November/December 1972), pp. 70–81; Richard E. Walton, "Work Innovations at Topeka: After Six Years," *Journal of Applied Behavior Science,* Vol. 13 (1977), pp. 422–431; Richard E. Walton, "The Topeka Work System: Optimistic Visions, Pessimistic Hypotheses, and Reality," in Zager and Rosow (eds.), *The Innovative Organization,* Ch. 11.

34 Information from Vanaja Dhanan and Cecille Austria, "Where Workers Manage Themselves," *World Executive's Digest* (October 1992), pp. 14–16.

35 Additional discussion of TI in Malaysia is found in Stewart et al. (1999), pp. 18–26; see also Texas Instruments at www.ti.com.

Source Notes

Charles Schwab & Co.: Information from Eric Matson, "The Seven Sins of Deadly Meetings," *Fast Company Handbook of the Business Revolution* (New York: Fast Company, 1997), p. 31.

John R. Schermerhorn, Jr., *Management,* 5th ed. (New York: Wiley, 1996), p. 274. Used by permission.

National Broadband Task Force, www.broadband.gc.ca/pub/media/nsc/report/nsc_report_en.pdf.

Winning Management Teams, CEO Perspectives, Government of Ontario, 2002 available at www.ontariocanada.com/ontcan/en/PDF_HTML/Priority-2/w-e-winning-teams.htm.

Sertapak Group, website at www.sertapak.com/about/ourteam/manufacturing.html.

Air Liquide website at www.ca.airliquide.com/en/corporate/careers_air/what_makes_all_special/our_people.asp.

Clemmer Group website at www.clemmer.net/speaking/dcco_mgrt.shtml.

Canadian Outback website at www.canadianoutback.com/teambuilding_adventures.php

Second City website at www.secondcity.com/corporate/services/index.asp.

Alberta Pacific Forest Industries Inc. website at www.alpac.ca/About_Al-Pac/Training.htm.

CHAPTER 11

1 The view of strategy provided here is a combination of perspectives drawn from several sources including Alfred D. Chandler, *The Visible Hand: The Managerial Revolution in America* (Cambridge, MA: Belnap, 1977); Michael E. Porter, *Competitive Strategy* (New York: Free Press, 1980); L. R. Jauch and R. N. Osborn, "Toward an Integrated Theory of Strategy," *Academy of Management Review* 6 (1981): 491–498; B. Wernefelt, "A Resource-based View of the Firm," *Strategic Management Journal* 5 (1984): 171–180; J. B. Barney, "Firm Resources and Sustained Competitive Advantage," *J. Management* 17 (1991): 99–120; Michael A. Hitt, R. Duane Ireland, and Robert E. Hoskisson, *Strategic Management: Competition and Globalization* (Cincinnati, OH: Southwestern, 2001).

2 H. Talcott Parsons, *Structure and Processes in Modern Societies* (New York: Free Press, 1960).

3 See Terri Lammers, "The Effective and Indispensable Mission Statement," *Inc.* (August 1992): 1, 7, 23, for instance, and I. C. MacMillan an A. Meshulack, "Replacement versus Expansion: Dilemma for Mature U.S. Businesses," *Academy of Management Journal* 26 (1983): 708–726.

4 See Stewart R. Clegg and Cynthia Hardy, "Organizations, Organization and Organizing," in Clegg, Hardy, and Nord (eds.), *Handbook of Organizational Studies* (1996), pp. 1–28 and William H. Starbuck and Paul C. Nystrom, "Designing and Understanding Organizations," in P. C. Nystrom and W. H. Starbuck (eds.), *Handbook of Organizational Design: Adapting Organizations to Their Environments* (New York: Oxford University Press, 1981).

5 See Jeffery Pfeffer, "Barriers to the Advance of Organization Science," *Academy of Management Review* 18, No. 4 (1994): 599–620; Richard M. Cyert and James G. March, *A Behavioral Theory of the Firm* (Englewood Cliffs, NJ: Prentice-Hall, 1963). A good discussion of organizational goals is also found in Charles Perrow, *Organizational Analysis: A Sociological View* (Belmont, CA: Wadsworth, 1970) and in Richard H. Hall, "Organizational Behavior: A Sociological Perspective," in Jay W. Lorsch (ed.), *Handbook of Organizational Behavior* (Englewood Cliffs, NJ: Prentice-Hall, 1987), pp. 84–95.

6 See Osborn, Hunt, and Jauch (1985).

7 Janice Beyer, Danta P. Ashmos, and R. N. Osborn, "Contrasts in Enacting TQM: Mechanistic vs. Organic Ideology and Implementation," *Journal of Quality Management* 1 (1997): 13–29, and for an early treatment, see Paul R. Lawrence and Jay W. Lorsch, *Organization and Environment* (Homewood, IL: Irwin, 1969).

8 Chandler, op. cit. (1977).

9 For reviews, see Osborn, Hunt, and Jauch (1985); Clegg, Hardy, and Nord (1996).

10 See Prashant C. Palvia, Shailendra C. Palvia, and Edward M. Roche, *Global Information Technology and Systems Management: Key Issues and Trends* (Nashua, NH: Ivy League Publishing, 1996).

11 For instance, see J.E.M. McGee, M. J. Dowling, and W. L. Megginson, "Cooperative Strategy and New Venture Performance: The Role of Business Strategy and Management Experience," *Strategic Management Journal* 16 (1995): 565–580 and James B. Quinn, *Intelligent Enterprise: A Knowledge and Service BasedParadigm for Industry* (New York: Free Press, 1992).

12 See P. Candace Deans, *Global Information Systems and Technology: Focus on the Organization and Its Functional Areas* (Harrisburg, PA: Ideal Group Publishing, 1994) and Osborn, Hunt, and Jauch (1985).

13 Haim Levy and Deborah Gunthorpe, *Introduction to Investments,* 2nd ed. (Cincinatti, OH: South-Western, 1999).

14 William G. Ouchi and M. A. McGuire, "Organization Control: Two Functions," *Administrative Science Quarterly* 20 (1977): 559–569.

15 This discussion is adapted from W. Edwards Deming, "Improvement of Quality and Productivity Through Action by Management," *Productivity Review* (Winter 1982): 12, 22; and W. Edwards Deming, *Quality, Productivity and Competitive Position* (Cambridge, MA: MIT Center for Advanced Engineering, 1982).

16 For related reviews, see W. Richard Scott, *Organizations: Rational, Natural, and Open Systems,* 2nd ed. (Englewood Cliffs, NJ: Prentice-Hall. 1987): Osborn, Hunt, and Jauch (1985); Clegg, Hardy, and Nord (1996).

17 See Osborn, Hunt, and Jauch (1985), pp. 273–303 for a discussion of centralization/decentralization.

18 Ibid.

19 For reviews of structural tendencies and their influence on outcomes, also see Scott (1987); Clegg, Hardy, and Nord (1996).

20 Ibid.

21 For a good discussion of the early use of matrix structures, see Stanley Davis, Paul Lawrence, Harvey Kolodny, and Michael Beer, *Matrix* (Reading, MA: Addison-Wesley, 1977).

22 See P. R. Lawrence and J. W. Lorsch, *Organization and Environment:*

Managing Differentiation and Integration (Homewood, IL: Richard D. Irwin, 1967).

23 See Osborn, Hunt, and Jauch (1985).

24 Max Weber, *The Theory of Social and Economic Organization,* translated by A. M. Henderson and H. T. Parsons (New York: Free Press, 1947).

25 These relationships were initially outlined by Tom Burns and G. M. Stalken, *The Management of Innovation* (London: Tavistock, 1961).

26 See Henry Mintzberg, *Structure in Fives: Designing Effective Organization*s (Englewood Cliffs, NJ: Prentice-Hall, 1983).

27 Ibid.

28 Ibid.

29 See Osborn, Hunt, and Jauch (1984) for an extended discussion.

30 See Peter Clark and Ken Starkey, *Organization Transitions and Innovation—Design* (London: Pinter Publications, 1988).

Source Notes

The bulk of this chapter was originally based on Richard N. Osborn, James G. Hunt, and Lawrence R. Jauch, *Organization Theory: Integrated Text and Cases* (Melbourne, FL: Krieger, 1985). For a more recent but consistent view, see Lex Donaldson, "The Normal Science of Structural Contingency Theory," in Stewart R. Clegg, Cynthia Hardy, and Walter R. Nord (eds.), *Handbook of Organizational Studies* (London: Sage Publications, 1996), pp. 57–76.

Marcus B. Osborn, "Organizational Structure at First Community Financial," working paper, Department of Public Administration, Arizona State University, Tempe, AZ, 1999.

Canadian National –CN website at www.cn.ca/companyinfo/history/en_About OurStory.shtml, under "North America's Railroad, 1999.

Stockwatch website at http://new.stockwatch.com/swnet/utilit/utilit_ products.aspx.

Quality Solutions Inc. website at www.qualitysolutions.ca/tqm.htm.

Alcan website at www.alcan.com/web/publishing.nsf/Content/ About+Alcan+-+Company+Structure.

Natural Resources Canada website at www2.nrcan.gc.ca/dmo/aeb/English/ ReportDetail.asp?x=232&type=rpt#top.

Bell Canada Enterprises website at http://www.bce.ca.

CHAPTER 12

1 The view of strategy as a process of co-evolution was drawn from several sources, including Alfred D. Chandler, *The Visible Hand: The Managerial Revolution in America* (Cambridge, MA: Belnap, 1977); Michael E. Porter, *Competitive Strategy* (New York: Free Press, 1980); L. R. Jauch and R. N. Osborn, "Toward an Integrated Theory of Strategy," *Academy of Management Review* 6 (1981): 491–498; B. Wernefelt, "A Resource-based View of the Firm," *Strategic Management Journal* 5 (1984): 171–180; J. B. Barney, "Firm Resources and Sustained Competitive Advantage," *J. Management* 17 (1991): 99–120; Ross Marion, *The Edge of Organization: Chaos and Complexity Theories of Formal Social Systems* (London, Sage, 1999); Arie Lewin, Chris Long, and Timothy Caroll, "The Coevolution of New Organizational Forms," *Organization Science* 10 (1999): 535–550; Michael A. Hitt, R. Duane Ireland, and Robert E. Hoskisson, *Strategic Management: Competition and Globalization* (Cincinnati, OH: Southwestern, 2001).

2 R. N. Osborn, J. G. Hunt, and L. Jauch, *Organization Theory Integrated Text and Cases* (Melbourne, FL: Krieger, 1984), pp. 123–215.

3 See Henry Mintzberg, *Structure in Fives: Designing Effective Organizations* (Englewood Cliffs, NJ: Prentice-Hall, 1983).

4 For a comprehensive review, see W. Richard Scott, *Organizations: Rational, Natural, and Open Systems,* 2nd ed. (Englewood Cliffs, NJ: Prentice-Hall, 1987).

5 See Peter M. Blau and Richard A. Schoenner, *The Structure of Organizations* (New York: Basic Books, 1971); Joan Woodward, *Industrial Organization: Theory and Practice* (London: Oxford University Press, 1965).

6 Ibid.

7 Gerardine DeSanctis, "Information Technology," in Nigel Nicholson (ed.),

Blackwell Encyclopedic Dictionary of Organizational Behavior (Cambridge, MA: Blackwell Publishers, Ltd., 1995), pp. 232–233.

8 James D. Thompson, *Organization in Action* (New York: McGraw-Hill, 1967).

9 Woodward (1965).

10 For reviews, see Osborn, Hunt, and Jauch (1984); and Louis Fry, "Technology-Structure Research: Three Critical Issues," *Academy of Management Journal* 25 (1982): pp. 532–552.

11 Mintzberg (1983).

12 Charles Perrow, *Complex Organizations: A Critical Essay,* 3rd ed. (New York: Random House, 1986).

13 Mintzberg (1983).

14 Prashant C. Palvia, Shailendra C. Palvia, and Edward M. Roche, *Global Information Technology and Systems Management: Key Issues and Trends* (Nashua, NH: Ivy League Publishing, 1996).

15 DeSanctis (1995).

16 P. Candace Deans, *Global Information Systems and Technology: Focus on the Organization and Its Functional Areas* (Harrisburg, PA: Ideal Group Publishing, 1994).

17 Osborn, Hunt, and Jauch (1984).

18 David A. Nadler and Michael L. Tushman, *Competing by Design: The Power of Organizational Architecture* (New York: Oxford University Press, 1997).

19 David Lei, Michael Hitt, and Richard A. Bettis, "Dynamic Capabilities and Strategic Management," *Journal of Management* 22 (1996): pp. 547–567.

20 Melissa A. Schilling, "Technological Lockout: An Integrative Model of the Economic and Strategic Factors Driving Technological Success and Failure," *Academy of Management Review* 23, No. 2 (1998): 267–284.

21 Jack Veiga and Kathleen Dechant, "Wired World Woes: www.help," *Academy of Management Executive* 11, No. 3 (1997): 73–79.

22 Jaana Woiceshyn, "The Role of Management in the Adoption of Technology: A Longitudinal Investigation," *Technology Studies* 4, No. 1 (1997): 62–99.

23 Janice Beyer, Danta P. Ashmos, and R. N. Osborn, "Contrasts in Enacting TQM: Mechanistic vs Organic Ideology and Implementation," *Journal of Quality Management* 1 (1997): 13–29.

24 Veiga and Dechant (1997).

25 Michael A. Hitt, R. Duane Ireland, and Robert E. Hoskisson, *Strategic Management: Competitiveness and Globalization* (Cincinnati, OH: South-Western College Publishing, 2001).

26 This section is based on R. N. Osborn and J. G. Hunt, "The Environment and Organization Effectiveness," *Administrative Science Quarterly* 19 (1974): 231–246; and Osborn, Hunt, and Jauch (1984).

27 See R. N. Osborn and C. C. Baughn, "New Patterns in the Formation of U.S. Japanese Cooperative Ventures," *Columbia Journal of World Business* 22 (1988): 57–65.

28 R. N. Osborn, *The Evolution of Strategic Alliances in High Technology,* working paper (Detroit: Department of Management, Wayne State University, 2001); and Shawn Tully, "The Modular Corporation," *Fortune* (February 8, 1993).

29 . Huber, "Organizational Learning: The Contributing Process and the Literature," *Organization Science* 2, No. 1 (1991): 88–115.

30 J. W. Myer and B. Rowan, "Institutionalized Organizations: Formal Structure as Myth and Ceremony," *American Journal of Sociology* 83 (1977): 340–363.

31 Bandura, *Social Learning Theory* (Englewood Cliffs, NJ: Prentice-Hall, 1977).

32 See, for example, A. M. Morrison, R. P. White, and E. Van Velsor, *Breaking the Glass Ceiling* (Reading, MA: Addison-Wesley, 1987); J. D. Zalesny and J. K. Ford, "Extending the Social Information Processing Perspective: New Links to Attitudes, Behaviors and Perceptions," *Organizational Behavior and Human Decision Processes* 47 (1990): 205–246; M. E. Gist, C. Schwoerer, and B. Rosen, "Effects of Alternative Training Methods of Self-Efficacy and Performance in Computer Software

Training," *Journal of Applied Psychology* 74 (1989): 884–91; D. D. Sutton and R. W. Woodman, "Pygmalion Goes to Work: The Effects of Supervisor Expectations in a Retail Setting," *Journal of Applied Psychology* 74 (1989): 943–950; M. E. Gist, "The Influence of Training Method on Self-Efficacy and Idea Generation among Managers," *Personnel Psychology* 42 (1989): 787–805.

[33]See M. E. Gist, "Self Efficacy: Implications in Organizational Behavior and Human Resource Management," *Academy of Management Review* 12 (1987): 472–485; A. Bandura, "Self Efficacy Mechanisms in Human Agency," *American Psychologist* 37 (1987): 122–147.

[34]J. March, *Decisions and Organizations* (Oxford: Basil Blackwell, 1988).

[35]R. N. Osborn, and D. H. Jackson, Leaders, "Riverboat Gamblers on Purposeful Unintended Consequences in the Management of Complex Technologies," *Academy of Management Journal* 31 (1988): 924–947.

[36]See A. L. Stinchcombe, *Economic Sociology* (New York, Academic Press, 1983).

[37]Ibid.

[38]Osborn and Jackson (1988).

[39]bid.

[40]O. P. Walsch and G. R. Ungson, "Organization Memory," *Academy of Management Review* 16, No. 1 (1991): 57–91.

[41]A. A. Marcus, *Business and Society: Ethics Government and the World of Economy* (Homewood, IL: Richard D. Irwin, 1993).

[42]Ibid.

Source Notes

Bomardier information from: news release, Dec. 9, 2003; http://www.bombardier.com/index.jsp?id=3_0&lang=en&file=/en/3_0/pressrelease.jsp%3Fgroup%3D3_0%26lan%3Den%26action%3Dview%26mode%26Dlist%26year%3Dnull%26id%3D2228%26sCateg%3D3_0; Bomardier press releases: Wichita, Kansas, March 12, 2004; Orlando, Florida, October 06, 2003, Pretoria, September 20, 2002; http://www.bombardier.com/index.jsp?id=3_0&lang=en&file=/en/3_0/pressreleaselist.jsp%3Fgroup%3D3_0%26lan%3Den%26action%3Dview%26mode%3Dlist%26year%3D1997

GlaxoSmithKline website at www.gsk.ca.

Workopolis.com

Andy Holloway, "Ready, set —wait," Canadian Business, March 19, 2001, www.canadianbusiness.com/article.jsp?content=21371.

InterActive Corp. website at www.iac.com/index/overview/overview_factsheet.html.

Statistics Canada website at www.statcan.ca/Daily/English/040225/d040225c.htm; http://www.statcan.ca/Daily/English/990223/d990223.htm#ART2; Mark Uhrbach and Bryan van Tol, "Broadband Internet: Removing the Speed Limit for Canadian Firms," Science, Innovation and Electronic Information Division, www.statcan.ca/english/research/11-621-MIE/11-621-MIE2004016.htm#4.

Nortel Networks information from "Low morale crushing Nortel's innovation," CBC Ottawa news, Oct 7 2002, http://ottawa.cbc.ca/regional/servlet/View?filename=nortelinnov021007, http://www.nortelnetworks.com/employment/faq.html, "Nortel CEO: Downsizing plans within two weeks," Cnews, Tech News, Sept. 9, 2004 http://cnews.canoe.ca/CNEWS/TechNews/TechInvestor/2004/09/09/622293-cp.html.

Canadian Advanced Technology Alliance website at www1.cata.ca/cata/catainfo/index.cfm.

"De Beers pleads guilty in price fixing case," The Associated Press, July 13, 2004, MSNBC News, www.msnbc.msn.com/id/5431319.

City of Markham website at www.markham.ca/markham/channels/edo/InterEcoAll.htm.

Treasury Board of Canada website at http://www.tbs-sct.gc.ca/pubs_pol/dcg-pubs/tb_h4/holdings-fonds05_e.asp.

CHAPTER 13

[1] Edgar Schein, "Organizational Culture," *American Psychologist,* Vol. 45 (1990), pp. 109–119; and E. Schein, *Organizational Culture and Leadership* (San Francisco: Jossey-Bass, 1985).

[2] Schein (1990).

[3] This example was reported in an interview with Edgar Schein, "Corporate Culture Is the Real Key to Creativity," *Business Month* (May 1989), pp. 73–74.

[4] For early work, see T. Deal and A. Kennedy, *Corporate Culture* (Reading, MA: Addison-Wesley, 1982); and T. Peters and R. Waterman, *In Search of Excellence* (New York: Harper & Row, 1982), while more recent studies are summarized in Joanne Martin and Peter Frost, "The Organizational Culture War Games: The Struggle for Intellectual Dominance," in Stewart R. Clegg, Cynthia Hardy, and Walter R. Nord (eds.), *Handbook of Organization Studies* (London: Sage Publications, 1996), pp. 599–621.

[5] Schein (1985).

[6] For an extended discussion, see J. M. Beyer and H. M. Trice, "How an Organization's Rites Reveal Its Culture," *Organizational Dynamics* (Spring 1987), pp. 27–41.

[7] A. Cooke and D. M. Rousseau, "Behavioral Norms and Expectations: A Quantitative Approach to the Assessment of Organizational Culture," *Group and Organizational Studies* 13 (1988), pp. 245–273.

[8] Martin and C. Siehl, "Organization Culture and Counterculture," *Organizational Dynamics* 12 (1983), pp. 52–64.

[9] Ibid.

[10] See R. N. Osborn, "The Aftermath of the Daimler and Detroit," Working Paper, Department of Management, Wayne State University 2001.

[11] See Pfeffer (1998). Taylor Cox, Jr., "The Multicultural Organization," *Academy of Management Executive,* Vol. 2, No. 2 (May 1991), pp. 34–47.

[12] For more information on Cisco Systems see website at www.cisco.com.

[13] Carl Quintanilla, "DU-UDE: CEOs, Feeling Out of Touch with Junior Employees, Try to Get 'Withit,'" *Wall Street Journal,* (November 10, 1998), p. 1.

[14] Schein (1985), pp. 52–57.

[15] Peters and Waterman (1982).

[16] Schein (1990).

[17] H. Gertz, *The Interpretation of Culture* (New York: Basic Books, 1973).

[18] Beyer and Trice (1987). HP's new advertisement at www.shopping.hp.com/cgibin/hpdirect/shopping/scripts/generic_store/ generic_subcategory_view.jsp?landing=handhelds&category=handhelds&subcat1=classic_performance&catLevel=2&BV_SessionID=@@@@0754168907.1101419508@@@@&BV_EngineID=ccdhadddegkikemcfngcfkmdflldfjk.0.

[19] *Business Week* (November 23, 1992), p. 117.

[20] H. M. Trice and J. M. Beyer, "Studying Organizational Cultures Through Rites and Ceremonials," *Academy of Management Review,* Vol. 3 (1984), pp. 633–669.

[21] J. Martin, M. S. Feldman, M. J. Hatch, and S. B. Sitkin, "The Uniqueness Paradox in Organizational Stories," *Administrative Science Quarterly,* Vol. 28 (1983), pp. 438–453.

[22] Deal and Kennedy (1982).

[23] Osborn and Baughn (1994).

[24] R. N. Osborn and D. Jackson, "Leaders, River Boat Gamblers or Purposeful Unintended Consequences," *Academy of Management Journal,* Vol. 31 (1988), pp. 924–947.

[25] G. Hofstede and M. H. Bond, "The Confucius Connection: From Cultural Roots to Economic Growth," *Organizational Dynamics,* Vol. 16 (1991): 4–21.

[26] This section is based on R. N. Osborn and C. C. Baughn, *An Assessment of the State of the Field of Organizational Design* (Alexandria, VA: U.S. Army Research Institute, 1994).

[27] Martin and Frost (1996).

[28] Warner Burke, *Organization Development* (Reading, MA: Addison-Wesley, 1987); Wendell L. French and Cecil H. Bell, Jr., *Organization*

Development, 4th ed. (Englewood Cliffs, NJ: Prentice-Hall, 1990); Edgar F. Huse and Thomas G. Cummings, *Organization Development and Change,* 4th ed. (St. Paul, MN: West, 1989).

[29] Warren Bennis, "Using Our Knowledge of Organizational Behavior," in Lorsch, pp. 29–49.

[30] Excellent overviews are found in Cummings and Huse (1989), pp. 32–36, 45; and French and Bell (1990).

[31] Richard Beckhard, "The Confrontation Meeting," *Harvard Business Review,* Vol. 45 (March/April 1967), pp. 149–155.

[32] See Dale Zand, "Collateral Organization: A New Change Strategy," *Journal of Applied Behavioral Science* 10 (1974): 63–89; Barry A. Stein and Rosabeth Moss Kanter, "Building the Parallel Organization," *Journal of Applied Behavioral Science,* Vol. 16 (1980), pp. 371–386.

[33] J. Richard Hackman and Greg R. Oldham, *Work Redesign* (Reading, MA: Addison-Wesley, 1980).

Source Notes

Vignette: Vancouver City Savings Credit Union Website, available online at www.vancity.com, accessed May 12, 2004; Go Green Website, "Vancouver city savings credit union, a worthy investment," available online at www.gogreen.com/choices/yourbiz/case5.html, accessed May 12, 2004; Katherine MacKlem, "Top 100 employers", *Maclean's Magazine,* October 20, 2003, available online at www.macleans.ca/webspecials/article.jsp?content=20031020_67488_67488, accessed May 12, 2004; "Fade to black, depression in the workplace," Warren Shepell Consultants Corporation, Newroom, July/August 2002, available online at www.warrenshepell.com/newsroom/news-aug2002.asp, accessed May 12, 2004.

For a recent discussion of the resurgence of interest in individuals within organizations, see Jeffery Pfeffer, *The Human Equation: Building Profits by Putting People First* (Boston: Harvard Business School Press, 1998). Greg Keenan, Eric Reguly, and Andrew Willis, "Union could derail Stelco financing," *The Globe and Mail,* Nov. 18, 2004.

http://www.theglobeandmail.com/servlet/ArticleNews/TPStory/LAC/20041 18/RSTELCO18/TPBusiness/?query=GM+changes

Figure 13.1, by permission of the Regents. Copyright 1969 by the Regents of the University of California. Reprinted from *California Management Review* 12, No. 2 (1996),

CHAPTER 14

[1] See J. P. Kotter, *A Force for Change: How Leadership Differs from Management* (New York: Free Press, 1990).

[2] See Bernard M. Bass, *Bass and Stogdill's Handbook of Leadership,* 3rd ed. (New York: Free Press, 1990).

[3] See Alan Bryman, *Charisma and Leadership in Organizations* (London: Sage Publications, 1992), Ch. 5.

[4] Ralph M. Stogdill, *Handbook of Leadership* (New York: Free Press, 1974).

[5] Based on information from Robert J. House and Ram Aditya, "The Social Scientific Study of Leadership: Quo Vadis?" *Journal of Management,* Vol. 23 (1997), pp. 409–474; Shelley A. Kirkpatrick and Edwin A. Locke, "Leadership: Do Traits Matter?" *The Executive,* Vol. 5, No. 2 (1991), pp. 48–60; Gary Yukl, *Leadership in Organizations,* 3rd ed. (Upper Saddle River, NJ: Prentice-Hall, 1998), Ch. 10.

[6] Rensis Likert, *New Patterns of Management* (New York: McGraw-Hill, 1961).

[7] Bass, op. cit. Ch. 24.

[8] G. B. Graen and M. Uhl-Bien, "Relationship-Based Approach to Leadership: Development of Leader-Member Exchange (LMX) Theory of Leadership Over 25 Years: Applying a Multi-Level Multi-Domain Perspective," *Leadership Quarterly,* Vol. 6 (Summer 1995), pp. 219–247.

[9] R. J. House and R. Aditya, "The Social Scientific Study of Leadership: Quo Vadis?" *Journal of Management,* Vol. 23 (1997), pp. 409–474.

[10] Kirkpatrick and Locke; Yukl, Ch. 10; J. G. Hunt and G. E. Dodge, "Management in Organizations," *Handbook of Psychology* (Washington, DC: American Psychological Association, 2000).

[11] This section is based on Fred E. Fiedler and Martin M. Chemers, *Leadership* (Glenview, IL: Scott-Foresman, 1974).

[12] This discussion of cognitive resource theory is based on Fred E. Fiedler and Joseph E. Garcia, *New Approaches in Effective Leadership* (New York: Wiley, 1987).

[13] See L. H. Peters, D. D. Harke, and J. T. Pohlmann, "Fiedler's Contingency Theory of Leadership: An Application of the Meta-analysis Procedures of Schmidt and Hunter," *Psychological Bulletin,* Vol. 97 (1985), pp. 274–285.

[14] Yukl, op. cit.

[15] F. E. Fiedler, M. M. Chemers, and L. Mahar. *Improving Leadership Effectiveness: The Leader Match Concept,* 2nd ed. (New York: Wiley, 1984).

[16] For documentation see Fred E. Fiedler and Linda Mahar, The Effectiveness of Contingency Model Training: A Review of the Validation of Leader Match," *Personnel Psychology* (Spring 1979), pp. 45–62; Fred E. Garcia, Cecil H. Bell, Martin M. Chemers, and Dennis Patrick, "Increasing Mine Productivity and Safety through Management Training and Organization Development: A Comparative Study," *Basic and Applied Social Psychology* (March 1984), pp. 1–18; Arthur G. Jago and James W. Ragan, "The Trouble with Leader Match Is that It Doesn't Match Fiedler's Contingency Model," *Journal of Applied Psychology* (November 1986), pp. 555–559.

[17] See Yukl, op. cit.; R. Ayman, M. M. Chemers, and F. E. Fiedler, "The Contingency Model of Leadership Effectiveness: Its Levels of Analysis," *Leadership Quarterly,* Vol. 6 (Summer 1995), pp. 147–168.

[18] This section is based on Robert J. House and Terence R. Mitchell, "Path-Goal Theory of Leadership," *Journal of Contemporary Business* (Autumn 1977), pp. 81–97.

[19] House and Mitchell, op. cit.

[20] C. A. Schriesheim and L. L. Neider, "Path-Goal Theory: The Long and Winding Road," *Leadership Quarterly,* Vol. 7 (1996), pp. 317–321; M. G. Evans, "Commentary on R. J. House's Path-Goal Theory of Leader Effectiveness," *Leadership Quarterly,* Vol. 7 (1996), pp. 305–309.

[21] R. J. House, "Path-Goal Theory of Leadership: Lessons, Legacy, and a Reformulated Theory," *Leadership Quarterly,* Vol. 7 (1996), pp. 323–352.

[22] See the discussion of this approach in Paul Hersey and Kenneth H. Blanchard, *Management of Organizational Behavior* (Englewood Cliffs, NJ: Prentice Hall, 1988) and Paul Hersey, Kenneth Blanchard, and Dewey E. Johnson, *Management of Organizational Behavior,* 8th ed. (Upper Saddle River, NJ: Prentice Hall, 2001).

[23] R. P. Vecchio and C. Fernandez, "Situational Leadership Theory Revisited," in M. Schnake (ed.), *1995 Southern Management Association Proceedings* (Valdosta, GA: Georgia Southern University 1995), pp. 137–139; Claude L. Graeff, "Evolution of Situational Leadership Theory: A Critical Review," *Leadership Quarterly,* Vol. 8 (1997), pp. 153–170.

[24] The discussion in this section is based on Steven Kerr and John Jermier, "Substitutes for Leadership: Their Meaning and Measurement," *Organizational Behavior and Human Performance,* Vol. 22 (1978), pp. 375–403; Jon P. Howell, David E. Bowen, Peter W. Dorfman, Steven Kerr, and Phillip M. Podsakoff, "Substitutes for Leadership: Effective Alternatives to Ineffective Leadership," *Organizational Dynamics* (Summer 1990), pp. 21–38.

[25] Phillip M. Podsakoff, Peter W. Dorfman, Jon P. Howell, and William D. Todor, "Leader Reward and Punishment Behaviors: A Preliminary Test of a Culture-Free Style of Leadership Effectiveness," *Advances in Comparative Management,* Vol 2 (1989), pp. 95–138; T. K. Peng, "Substitutes for Leadership in an International Setting," unpublished manuscript, College of Business Administration, Texas Tech University (1990); P. M. Podsakoff and S. B. MacKenzie, "Kerr and Jermier's Substitutes for Leadership Model: Background, Empirical Assessment, and Suggestions for Future Research," *Leadership Quarterly* (1996).

[26] See T. R. Mitchell, S. G. Green, and R. E. Wood, "An Attributional Model of Leadership and the Poor Performing Subordinate: Development and

Validation," in L. L. Cummings and B. M. Staw (eds.), *Research in Organizational Behavior,* Vol. 3 (Greenwich, CT: JAI Press, 1981), pp. 197–234.

[27] James G. Hunt, Kimberly B. Boal, and Ritch L. Sorenson, "Top Management Leadership: Inside the Black Box," *Leadership Quarterly,* Vol 1 (1990), pp. 41–65.

[28] C. R. Gerstner and D. B. Day, "Cross-cultural Comparison of Leadership Prototypes," *Leadership Quarterly,* Vol. 5 (1994), pp. 122–134.

[29] Hunt, Boal, and Sorenson, op. cit.

[30] See J. Pfeffer, "Management as Symbolic Action: The Creation and Maintenance of Organizational Paradigms," in L. L. Cummings and B. M. Staw (eds.), *Research in Organizational Behavior,* Vol. 3 (Greenwich, CT: JAI Press, 1981), pp. 1–52.

[31] James R. Meindl, "On Leadership: An Alternative to the Conventional Wisdom," in B. M. Staw and L. L. Cummings (eds.), *Research in Organizational Behavior,* Vol. 12 (Greenwich, CT: JAI Press, 1990), pp. 159–203.

[32] Compare with Bryman; also see James G. Hunt and Jay A. Conger (eds.), Special issue, Part 1, *The Leadership Quarterly,* Vol. 10, No. 2 (1999), entire issue.

[33] See R. J. House, "A 1976 Theory of Charismatic Leadership," in J. G. Hunt and L. L. Larson (eds.), *Leadership: The Cutting Edge* (Carbondale, IL: Southern Illinois University Press, 1977), pp. 189–207.

[34] R. J. House, W. D. Spangler, and J. Woycke, "Personality and Charisma in the U.S. Presidency," *Administrative Science Quarterly,* Vol. 36 (1991), pp. 364–396.

[35] R. Pillai and E. A. Williams, "Does Leadership Matter in the Political Arena? Voter Perceptions of Candidates Transformational and Charismatic, Leadership and the 1996 U.S. Presidential Vote," *Leadership Quarterly.* Vol. 9 (1998), pp. 397–416.

[36] See Jane M. Howell and Bruce J. Avolio, "The Ethics of Charismatic Leadership: Submission or Liberation," *Academy of Management Executive,* Vol. 6 (May 1992), pp. 43–54.

[37] Jay Conger and Rabindra N. Kanungo, *Charismatic Leadership in Organizations* (San Francisco: Jossey-Bass, 1998).

[38] Conger and Kanungo, op. cit.

[39] B. Shamir, "Social Distance and Charisma: Theoretical Notes and an Exploratory Study," *Leadership Quarterly,* Vol. 6 (Spring 1995), pp. 19–48.

[40] See B. M. Bass, *Leadership and Performance Beyond Expectations* (New York: Free Press, 1985); A. Bryman, *Charisma and Leadership in Organizations* (London: Sage Publications, 1992), pp. 98–99.

[41] B. M. Bass, *A New Paradigm of Leadership* (Alexandria, VA: U.S. Army Research Institute for the Behavioral and Social Sciences, 1996).

[42] Bryman, op. cit., Ch. 6; B. M. Bass and B. J. Avolio, "Transformational Leadership: A Response to Critics," in M. M. Chemers and R. Ayman (eds.), *Leadership Theory and Practice: Perspectives and Directions* (San Diego, CA: Academic Press, 1993), pp. 49–80; Kevin B. Lowe, K. Galen Kroeck, and Nagaraj Sivasubramanium, "Effectiveness Correlates of Transformational and Transactional Leadership: A Meta-Analytic Review of the MLQ Literature," *Leadership Quarterly,* Vol. 7 (1996), pp. 385–426.

[43] See Bradley L. Kirman, Kevin B. Lowe, and Dianne P. Young, "The Challenge in High Performance Organizations," *The Journal of Leadership Studies,* Vol. 5, No. 2 (1998), pp. 3–15.

[44] Charles C. Mantz and Henry P. Sims, Jr., "Leading Teams to Lead Themselves: The External Leadership of Self-Managed Work Teams," *Administrative Science Quarterly,* Vol. 32 (1987), pp. 106–128; Susan G. Cohen, Lei Chang, and Gerald E. Ledford, Jr., "A Hierarchical Construct of Self-Management Leadership and Its Relation to Quality of Work Life and Perceived Work GroupEffectiveness," *Personnel Psychology,* Vol. 50 (1997), pp. 275–308.

[45] Manz and Sims, op. cit.

[46] Cohen, Chang, and Ledford, op. cit.

[47] Bass, *New Paradigm;* Bass and Avolio, op. cit.

[48] See Jay A. Conger and Rabindra N. Kanungo, "Training Charismatic Leadership: A Risky and Critical Task," in Jay A. Conger, Rabindra N. Kanungo, and Associates (eds.), *Charismatic Leadership: The Elusive Factor in Organizational Effectiveness* (San Francisco: Jossey-Bass, 1988), Ch. 11.

[49] See J. R. Kouzes and B. F. Posner, *The Leadership Challenge: How to Get Extraordinary Things Done in Organizations* (San Francisco: Jossey-Bass, 1991).

[50] Marshall Sashkin, "The Visionary Leader," in Conger and Kanungo, *Charismatic Leadership: The Elusive Factor in Organizational Effectiveness,* Ch. 5.

Source Notes

Summarized from Cheryl Hall, "The Right Stuff," *Dallas Morning News* (October 22, 2000), pp. 1H–2H. Trait-based information from Robert J. House and Ram Aditye, "The Social Scientific Study of Leadership: Quo Vadis?" *Journal of Management,* Vol. 23 (1987), pp. 405–474; Shelby A. Kirkpatrick and Edwin A. Locke, "Leadership: Do Traits Matter?" *The Executive,* Vol. 5, No. 2 (1991), pp. 48–60; Gary Yukl, *Leadership in Organizations* (Upper Saddle River, NJ: Prentice Hall, 1998), Ch. 10.

Summarized from Sharyn Obsatz, "Blind Since Age 23, Exec Works to Help Disabled," *Dallas Morning News* (July 16, 2000), p. 3F.

Summarized from Cheryl Hall, "Building Her Own Vision," *Dallas Morning News* (May 28, 2000), pp. 1H–2H.

Fiedler model based on F. E. Fiedler and M. M. Chemers, *Leadership and Effective Management* (Glenview, IL: Scott, Foresman, 1974). Path–goal adapted from Richard N. Osborn, James G. Hunt, and Lawrence R. Jauch, *Organizational Theory: An Integrated Approach* (New York: Wiley, 1980), p. 464.

From Paul Hersey and Kenneth H. Blanchard, *Management of Organizational Behavior* (Englewood Cliffs, NJ: Prentice Hall, 1988), p. 171. Used by permission.

Based on Steven Kerr and John Jermier, "Substitutes for Leadership: Their Meaning and Measurement," *Organizational Behavior and Human Performance,* Vol. 22 (1978), p. 387; Fred Luthans, *Organizational Behavior,* 6th ed. (New York: McGraw-Hill, 1992), Ch. 10.

Summarized from Jeremy Cowen, "Sharp Focus," *Lubbock Avalanche-Journal* (November 15, 2001), pp. 6, 22. Summarized from Chris Van Wagenen, "Software Helps to Track Tunes," *Lubbock Avalanche Journal* (April 9, 2000), p. 1E.

Close and Distant based on Boas Shamir, "Social Distance and Charisma: Theoretical Notes and an Exploratory Study," *Leadership Quarterly,* Vol. 6 (1995), pp. 19–48.

Summarized from "Success Story," *Dallas Morning News* (September 10, 2000), p. 22L.

Effective Manager based on B. M. Bass, *Leadership and Performance Beyond Expectations* (New York: Free Press, 1985).

Leader behaviour information from Charles C. Manz and Henry P. Sims, "Leading Workers to Lead Themselves: The External Leadership of Self Managed Work Teams," *Administrative Science Quarterly,* Vol. 32 (1987), pp. 106–128; and Susan G. Cohen, Lei Chang, and Gerald E. Ledford, Jr. "A Hierarchical Construct of Self-Management Leadership and Its Relationship to Quality of Work Life and Perceived Work Group Effectiveness," *Personnel Psychology,* Vol. 50 (1997), pp. 275–308.

Self-Directing Work Teams information from Delphi Packard Electric Systems, Brookhaven Facility, *Summary Managers Network Information Packet* (Lubbock, TX: Center for Productivity and Quality of Work Life, Texas Tech University, May 1995).

OB Across Functions information from Burk Uzzle, "John Deere Runs on Chaos," *Fast Company* (November 1998), p. 173.

Effective Manager information from Jay A. Conger and Rabindra N. Kanungo, "Training Charismatic Leadership: A Risky and Critical Task," In J. A. Conger, R. N. Kanungo and Associates (eds.), *Charismatic*

Leadership: The Elusive Factor in Organizational Effectiveness (San Francisco: Jossey-Bass, 1988), Ch 11.

CHAPTER 15

[1] We would like to thank Janice M. Feldbauer, Michael Cakrt, Judy Nixon, and Romuald Stone for their comments on the organization of this chapter and the emphasis on a managerial view of power.

[2] Rosabeth Moss Kanter, "Power Failure in Management Circuit," *Harvard Business Review* (July/August 1979): 65–75.

[3] John R. P. French and Bertram Raven, "The Bases of Social Power," in Dorwin Cartwright (ed.), *Group Dynamics Research and Theory* (Evanston, IL, Row, Peterson, 1962), pp. 607–623.

[4] We have added process, information, and representative.

[5] John P. Kotter, "Power, Success, and Organizational Effectiveness," *Organizational Dynamics* 6 (Winter 1978): 27; David A. Whetten and Kim S. Cameron, *Developing Managerial Skills* (Glenview, IL: Scott, Foresman, 1984), pp. 250–259.

[6] David Kipinis, Stuart M. Schmidt, Chris Swaffin-Smith, and Ian Wilkinson, Patterns of Managerial Influence: Shotgun Managers, Tacticians, and Bystanders," *Organizational Dynamics* 12 (Winter 1984): 60, 61.

[7] Ibid., pp. 58–67; David Kipinis, Stuart M. Schmidt, and Ian Wilkinson, "Intraorganizational Influence Tactics: Explorations in Getting One's Way," *Journal of Applied Psychology* 65 (1980): 440–452.

[8] Warren K. Schilit and Edwin A. Locke, "A Study of Upward Influence in Organizations," *Administrative Science Quarterly,* 27 (1982): 304–316.

[9] Ibid.

[10] Stanley Milgram, "Behavioral Study of Obedience," in Dennis W. Organ (ed.), *The Applied Psychology of Work Behavior* (Dallas: Business Publications, 1978), pp. 384–398. Also see Stanley Milgram, "Behavioral Study of Obedience," Journal of Abnormal *and Social Psychology* 67 (1963): 371–378; Stanley Milgram, "Group Pressure and Action Against a Person," *Journal of Abnormal and Social Psychology* 69 (1964): 137–143; Some Conditions of Obedience and Disobedience to Authority," *Human Relations* 1 (1965): 57–76; Stanley Milgram, *Obedience to Authority* (New York: Harper & Row, 1974).

[11] Chester Barnard, *The Functions of the Executive* (Cambridge, MA: Harvard University Press, 1938).

[12] Ibid.

[13] See Steven N. Brenner and Earl A. Mollander, "Is the Ethics of Business Changing?" *Harvard Business Review* 55 (February 1977): 57–71; Barry Z. Posner and Warren H. Schmidt, "Values and the American Manager: An Update," *California Management Review* 26 (Spring 1984): 202–216.

[14] Although the work on organizational politics is not extensive, useful reviews include a chapter in Robert H. Miles, *Macro Organizational Behavior* (Santa Monica, CA: Goodyear, 1980); Bronston T. Mayes and Robert W. Allen, "Toward a Definition of Organizational Politics," *Academy of Management Review* 2 (1977): 672–677; Gerald F. Cavanagh, Dennis J. Moberg, and Manuel Velasquez, "The Ethics of Organizational Politics," *Academy of Management Review* 6 (July 1981): 363–374; Dan Farrell and James C. Petersen, "Patterns of Political Behavior in Organizations," *Academy of Management Review* 7 (July 1982): 403–412; D. L. Madison, R. W. Allen, L. W. Porter, and B. T. Mayes, "Organizational Politics: An Exploration of Managers' Perceptions," *Human Relations* 33 (1980): 92–107.

[15] Mayes and Allen, "Toward a Definition of Organizational Politics," p. 675.

[16] Jeffrey Pfeffer, *Power in Organizations* (Marshfield, MA: Pitman, 1981), p. 7.

[17] Michael Sconcolfi, Anita Raghavan, and Mitchell Pacelle, "All Bets Are Off: How the Salesmanship and Brainpower Failed at Long Term Capital," *Wall Street Journal* (November 16, 1998), pp. 1, 18–19.

[18] B. E. Ashforth and R. T. Lee, "Defensive Behavior in Organizations: A Preliminary Mobel," *Human Relations* (July 1990): 621–648; personal communication with Blake Ashforth, December 1998.

[19] See Pfeffer (1981); M. M. Harmon and R. T. Mayer, *Organization Theory for Public Administration* (Boston: Little, Brown, 1984); W. Richard Scott, *Organizations: Rational, Natural and Open Systems* (Englewood Cliffs, NJ: Prentice-Hall, 1987).

[20] Developed from James L. Hall and Joel L. Leldecker, "A Review of Vertical and Lateral Relations: A New Perspective for Managers," in Patrick Connor (ed.), *Dimensions in Modern Management,* 3rd ed. (Boston: Houghton Mifflin, 1982), pp. 138–146, which was based in part on Leonard Sayles, *Managerial Behavior* (New York: McGraw-Hill, 1964).

[21] See Jeffrey Pfeffer, *Organizations and Organization Theory* (Boston: Pitman, 1983); Jeffrey Pfeffer and Gerald R. Salancik, *The External Control of Organizations* (Englewood Cliffs, NJ: Prentice-Hall, 1978).

[22] R. N. Osborn, "A Comparison of CEO Pay in Western Europe, Japan and the U.S.," working paper (Detroit: Department of Management, Wayne State University, 1998).

[23] Source: Pamela L. Perrewe, Gerald R. Ferris, Dwight D. Frink, and William P. Anthony, "Political Skill: An Antidote for Workplace Stressors," *Academy of Management Executive* 14:3 (2001): 115–120.

[24] Amy J. Hillman and Michael A. Hitt, Corporate Political Strategy Formulation: A Model of Approach Participation and Strategy Decisions," *Academy of Management Review* 24:3 (1999): 825–842.

[25] Douglas A. Schuler, "Corporate Political Strategy and Foreign Competition: The Case of the Steel Industry," *Academy of Management Journal* 29:3 (1996): 720–732.

[26] Op. cit. Hillman and Hitt, 1999.

[27] See the early work of James D. Thompson, *Organizations in Action* (New York: McGraw-Hill, 1967) and more recent studies by R. N. Osborn and D. H. Jackson, "Leaders, Riverboat Gamblers, or Purposeful Unintended Consequences in Management of Complex Technologies," *Academy of Management Journal* 31 (1988): 924–974; M. Hector, "When Actors Comply: Monitoring Costs and the Production of Social Order," *Acta Sociologica* 27 (1984): 161–183; T. Mitchell and W. G. Scott, "Leadership Failures, the Distrusting Public and Prospects for the Administrative State," *Public Administration Review* 47 (1987): 445–452.

[28] J. J. Jones, *The Downsizing of American Potential* (New York: Raymond Press, 1996).

[29] This discussion is based on Cavanagh, Moberg, and Velasquez (1981); and Manuel Velasquez, Dennis J. Moberg, and Gerald Cavanagh, "Organizational Statesmanship and Dirty Politics: Ethical Guidelines for the Organizational Politician," *Organizational Dynamics* 11 (1983): 65–79, both of which offer a fine treatment of the ethics of power and politics.

Source Notes

Vignette: See "Microsoft and the Browser Wars," *Seattle Times* (November 18, 1998), pp. C1–3: "ASAP Interview with Bill Gates," *Forbes ASAP* (1992), p. 84; "Identity Crises," *Forbes Magazine* (May 25, 1992), p. 82; "Microsoft Aims Its Arsenal at Networking," *Business Week* (October 12, 1992), pp. 88–89; "The PTC and Microsoft," *Business Week* (December 28, 1992), p. 30; "The PC Wars Are Sweeping into Software," *Business Week* (July 13, 1992), p. 132; Top 10 reasons to get Windows XP Home Edition, www.microsoft.com/windowsxp; Eric Wildstrom, "Microsoft: How it Became Stronger than Ever," businessweek.com/magazine/content/01-23/63735001.htm.

Linda Corman, "As Good as It Gets: The 1998 Compensation Survey," *CFO* (November 1998), pp. 41–54.

www.Dell.com/uslen/gen/corporate; www.dell.com/.

CHAPTER 16

[1] Bill Gates, "Bill Gates' New Rules," *Time* (March 22, 1999), pp. 72–84. This is an excerpt from Bill Gates, *The Speed of Thought: Using a Digital Nervous System* (New York: Warner Books, 1999). See Henry Mintzberg, *The Nature of Managerial Work* (New York: Harper & Row, 1973); Morgan W. McCall, Jr., Ann M. Morrison, and Robert L. Hannan, *Studies of Managerial Work: Results and Methods, Technical Report No. 9* (Greensboro, NC: Center for Creative Leadership, 1978); and John P. Kotter, *The General Managers*

(New York: Free Press, 1982).

2 Surveys reported on line at the American Management Association Web site (www.amanet.org): "The Passionate Organization" (September 26–29, 2000) and "Managerial Skills and Competence" (March/April, 2000).

3 Baseline survey reported in Lucent Technologies, *1998 Annual Report.*

4 See Angelo S. DeNisi, and Arraham N. Kluger, "Feedback Effectiveness: Can 360-degree Appraisals Be Improved?" *Academy of Management Executive* 14 (2000): 129–139.

5 See Axelrod (1996).

6 See Richard L. Birdwhistell, *Kinestics and Context* (Philadelphia: University of Pennsylvania Press, 1970).

7 Edward T. Hall, *The Hidden Dimension* (Garden City, NY: Doubleday, 1966).

8 See D. E. Campbell, "Interior Office Design and Visitor Response," *Journal of Applied Psychology* 64 (1979): 648–653; P. C. Morrow and J. C. McElroy, "Interior Office Design and Visitor Response: A Constructive Replication," *Journal of Applied Psychology* 66 (1981): 646–650.

9 M. P. Rowe and M. Baker, "Are You Hearing Enough Employee Concerns?" *Harvard Business Review* 62 (May/June 1984): 127–135.

10 This discussion is based on Carl R. Rogers and Richard E. Farson, "Active Listening" (Chicago: Relations Center of the University of Chicago).

11 Modified from an example in ibid.

12 Richard V. Farace, Peter R. Monge, and Hamish M. Russell, *Communicating and Organizing* (Reading, MA: Addison-Wesley, 1977), pp. 97–98.

13 The statements are from *Business Week* (July 6, 1981), p. 107.

14 See A. Mehrabian, *Silent Messages* (Belmont, CA: Wadsworth, 1981).

15 See C. Barnum and N. Woliansky, "Taking Cues from Body Language," *Management Review* 78 (1989): 59; S. Bochner (ed.), *Cultures in Contact: Studies in Cross-Cultural Interaction* (London: Pergamon, 1982); A. Furnham and S. Bocher, *Culture Shock: Psychological Reactions to Unfamiliar Environments* (London: Methuen, 1986); "How Not to Do International Business," *Business Week* (April 12, 1999); Yori Kagegama, "Tokyo Auto Show Highlights," Associated Press (October 24, 2001).

16 See Gary P. Ferraro, "The Need for Linguistic Proficiency in Global Business," *Business Horizons* 39 (May/June, 1966): 39–46.

17 This research is reviewed by John C. Athanassiades, "The Distortion of Upward Communication in Hierarchical Organizations," *Academy of Management Journal* 16 (June 1973): 207–226.

18 F. Lee, "Being Polite and Keeping MUM: How Bad News is Communicated in Organizational Hierarchies," *Journal of Applied Social Psychology* 23 (1993): 1124–1149.

19 Thomas J. Peters and Robert H. Waterman, Jr., *In Search of Excellence* (New York: Harper & Row, 1983).

20 Portions of this section are adapted from John R. Schermerhorn, Jr., *Management,* 5th ed. (New York: Wiley, 1996), pp. 375–378. Used by permission.

21 Networking is considered an essential managerial activity by Kotter (1982).

22 Peters and Waterman (1983).

23 For more information see Intuit Canada at www.intuit.com/canada.

24 *Business Week* (May 16, 1994), p. 8.

25 The concept of interacting, coacting, and counteracting groups is presented in Fred E. Fiedler, *A Theory of Leadership Productivity* (New York: McGraw-Hill, 1967).

26 Research on communication networks is found in Alex Bavelas, "Communication Patterns in Task-Oriented Groups," *Journal of the Acoustical Society of America* 22 (1950): 725–730. See also "Research on Communication Networks," as summarized in Marvin E. Shaw, *Group Dynamics: The Psychology of Small Group Behavior* (New York: McGraw-Hill, 1976), pp. 137–153.

27 See "e.Biz: What Every CEO Should Know about Electronic Business," *Business Week,* Special Report (March 22, 1999).

28 Information from Alison Overholt, "Intel's Got (Too Much)

29 Deborah Tannen, *Talking 9 to 5* (New York: Avon, 1995).

30 Deborah Tannen, *You Just Don't Understand: Women and Men in Conversation* (New York: Ballantine Books, 1991).

31 Deborah Tannen, "The Power of Talk: Who Gets Heard and Why," *Harvard Business Review* (September/October, 1995): 138–148.

32 Reported by *Working Woman* (November 1995), p. 14.

33 Ibid.

34 For an editorial opinion, see Jayne Tear, "They Just Don't Understand Gender Dynamics," *Wall Street Journal* (November 20, 1995), p. A14.

35 For more information see The Office of the Privacy Commissioner at http://www.privcom.gc.ca/fs-fi/02_05_d_17_e.asp.

Source Notes

Vignette: Industry Canada website, "Success Story: Canadian Tire," May 31, 2004, available online at http://strategis.ic.gc.ca/epic/internet/incts-scf.nsf/en/s100144e.html, accessed June 4, 2004; Andy Holloway, Andrew Wahl, Zena Olijnyk, Laura Bogomolny, "The Best Managers in Canada, Most Innovative Executive, Janice Wismer," *Canadian Business Magazine*, April 26, 2004, available online at http://www.canadianbusiness.com/features/article.jsp?content=200404026_59684_59684&page=4 accessed June 4, 2004; Manitoba Association for Distributed Learning and Training Website, "Canadian Tire: A case study for Quality E-Learning in Business" 2004 conference May 7, 2004, available online at http://www.madlat.ca/presentations/Making%20Virtual%20Learning%20 Effective, accessed June 4, 2004. Eryn Brown, "VF Corp. Changes its Underware," *Fortune* (December 7, 1998), pp. 115–118; and "Stitching Together an E-Corporation," *Fortune* (December 7, 1998), p. 117; corporate Web site: www.vfc.com.

John R. Schermerhorn, Jr., *Management,* 5th ed. (New York: Wiley, 1996), p. 377. Used by permission.

CHAPTER 17

1 For concise overviews, see Susan J. Miller, David J. Hickson, and David C. Wilson, "Decision-Making in Organizations," in Stewart R. Clegg, Cynthia Hardy, and Walter R. Nord (eds.), *Handbook of Organizational Studies* (London: Sage Publications, 1996), pp. 293–312; George P. Huber, *Managerial Decision Making* (Glenview, IL: Scott, Foresman, 1980).

2 This section is based on Michael D. Choen, James G. March, and Johan P. Olsen, "The Garbage Can Model of Organizational Choice," *Administrative Science Quarterly* 17 (1972): 1–25 and James G. March and Herbert A. Simon, *Organizations* (New York: Wiley, 1958), pp. 137–142.

3 See KPMG, www.kpmg.ca/en/services/advisory/err/governanceRiskMgmt.html.

4 This traditional distinction is often attributed to Herbert Simon, *Administrative Behavior* (New York: Free Press, 1945), but an available source is Herbert Simon, *The New Science of Management Decision* (New York: Harper & Row, 1960).

5 Ibid.

6 Also see Mary Zey (ed.), *Decision Making: Alternatives to Rational Choice Models* (Thousand Oaks, CA: Sage Publications, 1992).

7 Simon, *Administrative Behavior.*

8 For discussions, see Cohen, March, and Olsen (1972); Miller, Hickson, and Wilson (1996); and Michael Masuch and Perry LaPontin, "Beyond Garbage Cans: An AI Model of Organizational Choice," *Administrative Science Quarterly* 34 (1989): 38–67.

9 Weston H. Agor, *Intuition in Organizations* (Newbury Park, CA: Sage Publications, 1989).

10 Henry Mintzberg, "Planning on the Left Side and Managing on the Right," *Harvard Business Review* 54 (July/August 1976): 51–63.

11 See Weston H. Agor, "How Top Executives Use Their Intuition to Make Important Decisions," *Business Horizons* 29 (January/February 1986): 49–53; and Agor (1989).

12 The classic work in this area is found in a series of articles by D.

Kahneman and A. Tversky, "Subjective Probability: A Judgment of Representativeness," *Cognitive Psychology* 3 (1972): 430–454; "On the Psychology of Prediction," *Psychological Review* 80 (1973): 237–251; "Prospect Theory: An Analysis of Decision under Risk," *Econometrica* 47 (1979): 263–291; "Psychology of Preferences," *Scientific American* (1982): 161–173; "Choices, Values, Frames," *American Psychologist* 39 (1984): 341–350.

13 Definitions and subsequent discussion based on Max H. Bazerman, *Judgment in Managerial Decision Making,* 3rd ed. (New York: Wiley, 1994).

14 Cameron M. Ford and Dennis A. Gioia, *Creative Action in Organizations* (Thousand Oaks, CA: Sage Publications, 1995).

15 G. Wallas, *The Art of Thought* (New York: Harcourt, 1926). Cited in Bazerman (1994).

16 E. Glassman, "Creative Problem Solving," *Supervisory Management* (January 1989): 21–26; and B. Kabanoff and J. R. Rossiter, "Recent Developments in Applied Creativity," *International Review of Industrial and Organizational Psychology* 9 (1994): 283–324.

17 Information from Kenneth Labich, "Nike vs. Reebok," *Fortune* (September 18, 1995), pp. 90–106.

18 James A. F. Stoner, *Management,* 2nd ed. (Englewood Cliffs, NJ: Prentice-Hall, 1982), pp. 167–168.

19 Paul C. Nutt, "Surprising but True: Half the Discussions in Organizations Fail," *Academy of Management Executive* 13:4 (1999): 75–90.

20 Ibid.

21 Victor H. Vroom and Philip W. Yetton, *Leadership and Decision Making* (Pittsburgh: University of Pittsburgh Press, 1973); Victor H. Vroom and Arthur G. Jago, *The New Leadership* (Englewood Cliffs, NJ: Prentice-Hall, 1988).

22 Barry M. Staw, "The Escalation of Commitment to a Course of Action," *Academy of Management Review* 6 (1981): 577–587; Barry M. Staw and Jerry Ross, "Knowing When to Pull the Plug," *Harvard Business Review* 65 (March/April 1987): 68–74. See also Glen Whyte, "Escalating Commitment to a Course of Action: A Reinterpretation," *Academy of Management Review* 11 (1986): 311–321.

23 Joel Brockner, "The Escalation of Commitment to a Failing Course of Action: Toward Theoretical Progress," *Academy of Management Review* 17 (1992): 39–61; J. Ross and B. M. Staw, "Organizational Escalation and Exit: Lessons from the Shoreham Nuclear Power Plant," *Academy of Management Journal* 36 (1993): 701–732.

24 Bazerman (1994), pp. 79–83.

25 See Brockner (1992); Ross and Staw (1993); and J. Z. Rubin, "Negotiation: An Introduction to Some Issues and Themes," *American Behavioral Scientist* 27 (1983): 135–147.

26 See "Computers That Think Are Almost Here," *Business Week* (July 17, 1995): 68–73.

27 A. R. Dinnis and J. S. Valacich, "Computer Brainstorms: Two Heads Are Better Than One," *Journal of Applied Psychology* (February 1994): 77–86.

28 For an expanded discussion of such ethical frameworks for decision making, see Linda A. Travino and Katherine A. Nelson, *Managing Business Ethics* (New York: Wiley, 1995).

29 B. Kabanoff and J. R. Rossiter, "Recent Developments in Applied Creativity," *International Review of Industrial and Organizational Psychology* 9 (1994): 283–324.

30 Fons Trompenaars, *Riding the Waves of Culture: Understanding Cultural Diversity in Business* (London: Nicholas Brealey Publishing, 1993), p. 6.

31 See ibid., pp. 58–59.

32 For a good discussion of decision making in Japanese organizations, see Min Chen, *Asian Management Systems* (New York: Routledge, 1995).

33 Nancy J. Adler, *International Dimensions of Organizational Behavior,* 2nd ed. (Boston: PWS-Kent, 1991).

34 See Miller, Hickson, and Wilson (1996).

35 We would like to thank Kristi M. Lewis for emphasizing the importance of identifying criteria and weighing criteria and urging us to include this section on ethics.

36 Stephen Fineman, "Emotion and Organizing," in Clegg, Hardy, and Nord, *Handbook of Organizational Studies,* pp. 542–580.

37 For an expanded discussion of ethical frameworks for decision making, see Linda A. Travino and Katherine A. Nelson, *Managing Business Ethics* (New York: Wiley, 1995); Saul W. Gellerman, "Why 'Good' Managers Make Bad Ethical Choices," *Harvard Business Review* 64 (July/August 1986): 85–90 and Barbara Ley Toffler, *Tough Choices: Managers Talk Ethics* (New York: Wiley, 1986).

Source Notes

http://www.analog.com/processors/resources/beginnersGuide/introduction.html#whatis; http://www.mosaid.com/corporate/news-events/releases-2000/000720.php

Andrew Nikiforuk, "Company loves misery," *Canadian Business,* March 20, 2000.

http://www.canadianbusiness.com/article.jsp?content=10595; http://www2.ccnmatthews.com/3gCNRP/pdf/20030312132n.pdf

www.REI.com.

www.jackinthebox.com

www.Pella.com

www.Nolledrilling.com

Nokia Annual Report, 1997, p. 22. Analog.com/publications/DSP; Otis Port and Paul C. Judge,

"Chips That Mimic the Human Senses," *Business Week* (November 30, 1998), pp. 158–159.

S.S. Harrington, "What Corporate America is Teaching About Ethics," *Academy of Management & Education 11* (1991): 21–30; Don Hellriegel, John Slocum and Richard Woodman *Organizational Behavior* (Minneapolis: West Publishing, 1999).

Reprinted from Victor H. Vroom and Arthur G. Jago, *The New Leadership* (Englewood Cliffs, NJ: Prentice-Hall, 1988), p. 184. Used by permission of the authors.

CHAPTER 18

1 See, for example, Henry Mintzberg, *The Nature of Managerial Work* (New York: Harper & Row, 1973); and John R.P. Kotter, *The General Managers* (New York: Free Press, 1982).

2 One of the classic discussions is by Richard E. Walton, *Interpersonal Peacemaking: Confrontations and Third-Party Consultation* (Reading, MA: Addison-Wesley, 1969).

3 Kenneth W. Thomas and Warren H. Schmidt, "A Survey of Managerial Interests with Respect to Conflict," *Academy of Management Journal* 19 (1976): 315–318.

4 For a good overview see Richard E. Walton, *Managing Conflict: Interpersonal Dialogue and Third Party Roles,* 2nd ed. (Reading, MA: Addison-Wesley, 1987) and Dean Tjosvold, *The Conflict-Positive Organization: Stimulate Diversity and Create Unity* (Reading, MA: Addison-Wesley, 1991).

5 Walton (1969).

6 Ibid.

7 Richard E. Walton and John M. Dutton, "The Management of Interdepartmental Conflict: A Model and Review," *Administrative Science Quarterly* 14 (1969): 73–84.

8 Geert Hofstede, *Culture's Consequences: International Differences in Work-Related Values* (Beverly Hills: CA: Sage Publications, 1980), and Geert Hofstede, "Cultural Constraints in Management Theories," *Academy of Management Executive* 7 (1993): 81–94.

9 These stages are consistent with the conflict models described by Alan C. Filley, *Interpersonal Conflict Resolution* (Glenview, IL: Scott, Foresman, 1975); and Louis R. Pondy, "Organizational Conflict: Concepts and Models," *Administrative Science Quarterly* 12 (September 1967): 269–320.

10 Information from "Capitalizing on Diversity: Navigating the Seas of the Multicultural Workforce and Workplace," *Business Week,* Special Advertising Section (December 4, 1998).

11 Walton and Dutton (1969).

12 Rensis Likert and Jane B. Likert, *New Ways of Managing Conflict* (New York: McGraw-Hill, 1976).

13 Information from "Saturday Morning Fever," *Economist* (December 8, 2001): 56.

14 See Jay Galbraith, *Designing Complex Organizations* (Reading, MA: Addison-Wesley, 1973); David Nadler and Michael Tushman, *Strategic Organizational Design* (Glenview, IL: Scott, Foresman, 1988).

15 E. M. Eisenberg and M. G. Witten, "Reconsidering Openness in Organizational Communication," *Academy of Management Review* 12 (1987): 418–426.

16 R. G. Lord and M. C. Kernan, "Scripts as Determinants of Purposeful Behavior in Organizations," *Academy of Management Review* 12 (1987): 265–277.

17 See Filley (1975); and L. David Brown, *Managing Conflict at Organizational Interfaces* (Reading, MA: Addison-Wesley, 1983).

18 Ibid., pp. 27, 29.

19 For discussions, see Robert R. Blake and Jane Strygley Mouton, "The Fifth Achievement," *Journal of Applied Behavioral Science* 6 (1970): 413–427; Kenneth Thomas, "Conflict and Conflict Management," in M. D. Dunnett (ed.), *Handbook of Industrial and Organizational Behavior* (Chicago: Rand McNally, 1976), pp. 889–935; and Kenneth W. Thomas, "Toward Multi-Dimensional Values in Teaching: The Examples of Conflict Behaviors," *Academy of Management Review* 2 (1977): 484–490.

20 For an excellent overview, see Roger Fisher and William Ury, *Getting to Yes: Negotiating Agreement Without Giving In* (New York: Penguin, 1983). See also James A. Wall, Jr., Negotiation: Theory and Practice (Glenview, IL: Scott, Foresman, 1985).

21 Roy J. Lewicki and Joseph A. Litterer, *Negotiation* (Homewood, IL: Irwin, 1985), pp. 315–319.

22 Ibid., pp. 328–329.

23 For a good discussion, see Michael H. Bond, *Behind the Chinese Face* (London: Oxford University Press, 1991); and Richard D. Lewis, *When Cultures Collide*, Ch. 23 (London: Nicholas Brealey Publishing, 1996).

24 Following discussion is based on Fisher and Ury (1983); and Lewicki and Litterer (1985).

25 This example is developed from Max H. Bazerman, *Judgment in Managerial Decision Making*, 2nd ed. (New York: Wiley, 1991), pp. 106–108.

26 For a detailed discussion, see Fisher and Ury (1983), and Lewicki and Litterer (1985).

27 Developed from Bazerman (1991), pp. 127–141.

28 Fisher and Ury (1983), p. 33.

29 Lewicki and Litterer (1985), pp. 177–181.

Source Notes

Vignette: ShaSha Bread Website, www.shashabread.com, accessed August 8, 2004; Donna Jean Mckinnon, "There's good bread making good bread," *Toronto Star*, no date; John Morstad, "Raising bread to a higher level," *The Globe and Mail*, November 27, 1999; Rebecca Maxwell, "Working toward the collective good," *Bakers Journal*, April 2002; Carol Neshevich, "For love of bread," *Foodservice & Hospitality Magazine*, March 2001.

John R. Schermerhorn, Jr., *Management*, 6th ed. (New York: Wiley, 199), p. 341. Used by permission. HRM News: Information from Carol Kleiman, "Performance Review Comes 'Full Circle,'" *Columbus Dispatch* (January 31, 1999), p. 291.

Deloitte Touche: Information from Sue Shellenbarger, "Three Myths that Make Managers Push Staff to the Edge of Burnout," *Wall Street Journal* (March 17, 1999), pl. B1.

EEOC: Information from "Suspect Age Bias? Try Proving It," *Fortune* (February 1, 1999), p. 58.

CHAPTER 19

1 Tom Peters, *Thriving on Chaos* (New York: Random House, 1987); Tom Peters, "Managing in a World Gone Bonkers," *World Executive Digest* (February 1993), pp. 26–29; and Tom Peters, *The Circle of Innovation* (New York: Alfred A. Knopf, 1997).

2 See David Nadler and Michael Tushman, *Strategic Organizational Design* (Glenview, IL: Scott, Foresman, 1988); and Noel M. Tichy, "Revolutionize Your Company," *Fortune* (December 13, 1993), pp. 114–118.

3 Jerry I. Porras and Robert C. Silvers, "Organization Development and Transformation," *Annual Review of Psychology,* Vol. 42 (1991), pp. 51–78.

4 Information from "Entrepreneurs Speak at HBS," *Harvard Business School Bulletin* (February 1999), p. 6; corporate Web site: www.virgin.com.

5 The classic description of organizations on these terms is by Harold J. Leavitt, "Applied Organizational Change in Industry: Structural, Technological and Humanistic Approaches," in James G. March (ed.), *Handbook of Organizations* (Chicago: Rand McNally, 1965). This application is developed from Robert A. Cooke, "Managing Change in Organizations," in Gerald Zaltman (ed.), *Management Principles for Nonprofit Organizations* (New York: American Management Association, 1979). See also David A. Nadler, "The Effective Management of Organizational Change,? in Jay W. Lorsch (ed.), *Handbook of Organizational Behavior* (Englewood Cliffs, NJ: Prentice-Hall, 1987), pp. 358–369.

6 Beer and Mitra (2000), op cit., p. 133.

7 John P. Kotter, "Why Transformation Efforts Fail," *Harvard Business Review* (March/April, 1995), pp. 59–67.

8 Kurt Lewin, "Group Decision and Social Change," in G. E. Swanson, T. M. Newcomb, and E. L. Hartley (eds.), *Readings in Social Psychology* (New York: Holt, Rinehart & Winston, 1952), pp. 459–473.

9 Tichy and Devanna (1986), p. 44.

10 The change strategies are described in Robert Chin and Kenneth D. Benne, "General Strategies for Effecting Changes in Human Systems," in Warren G. Bennis, Kenneth D. Benne, Robert Chin, and Kenneth E. Corey (eds.), *The Planning of Change,* 3rd ed. (New York: Holt, Rinehart & Winston, 1969), pp. 22–45.

11 Example developed from an exercise reported in J. William Pfeiffer and John E. Jones, *A Handbook of Structural Experiences for Human Relations Training,* Vol. II (La Jolla, CA: University Associates, 1973).

12 Ibid.

13 Ibid.

14 Donald Klein, "Some Notes on the Dynamics of Resistance to Change: The Defender Role," in Bennis et al. (eds.), *The Planning of Change* (1969), pp. 117–124.

15 See Everett M. Rogers, *Communication of Innovations,* 3rd ed. (New York: Free Press, 1993).

16 Ibid.

17 John P. Kotter and Leonard A. Schlesinger, "Choosing Strategies for Change," *Harvard Business Review,* Vol. 57 (March/April 1979), pp. 109–112.

18 A classic work in this area is Peter F. Drucker, *Innovation and Entrepreneurship* (New York: Harper, 1985).

19 Edward B. Roberts, "Managing Invention and Innovation," *Research Technology Management* (January/February 1988), pp. 1–19. For an extensive case study, see John Clark, *Managing Innovation and Change (Thousand Oaks, CA: Sage Publications*, 1995). For a comprehensive update on innovation in industry, see "Innovation in Industry," *The Economist* (February 20, 1999), pp. 5–18.

20 Quotes from Kenneth Labich, "The Innovators," *Fortune* (June 6, 1988), pp. 49–64.

21 For more information see the Canadian Centre for Ethics and Corporate Policy website at www. ethicscentre.ca

22 Pfeffer (1998).

Source Notes

Richard Pascale, "Change How You Define Leadership and You Change How You Run a Company," *Fast Company, The Professor Series* (Boston: Fast Company, 1998).

Red Roof Inns: Information from Mike Pramik, "Wellness Programs Give Businesses Healthy Bottom Line," *The Columbus Dispatch* (January 18, 1999), pp. 10–11.

Lonnie Johnson: Information from Patricia J. Mays, "Gun Showers Wealth on Inventor," *The Columbus Dispatch* (January 24, 1999), p. 6B

Photo Credits

Chapter 1
2 Courtesy of Husky Injection Molding Systems Ltd.; 5 Courtesy of The Directors College; 7 Courtesy of Ernst & Young; 9 Courtesy of Murray Demolition Corp.; 16 Courtesy of TD Bank Financial Group; 16 Courtesy of Endpoint Research.

Chapter 2
22 Courtesy of Nokia Corporation; 27 PhotoDisc, Inc.; 28 Courtesy of 1-800-GOT-JUNK?; 29 PhotoDisc, Inc.; 30 Courtesy of WestJet.

Chapter 3
38 Courtesy of INCO Limited; 40 Canadian Press/Ben Margot; 43 Corbis Digital Stock; 47 Canadian Press/Fred Chartrand; 49 Courtesy of AIESEC; 50 PhotoDisc, Inc.

Chapter 4
56 Courtesy of Markham Gateway Public School; 59 PhotoDisc, Inc.; 63 Corbis Digital Stock; 73 Courtesy of BC Hydro Aboriginal Relations; 66 Courtesy of Royal Bank of Canada.

Chapter 5
80 Courtesy of SmartLabrador Initiative; 87 PhotoDisc, Inc.; 89 PhotoDisc, Inc.; 90 PhotoDisc, Inc.

Chapter 6
96 Courtesy of ZENON Environmental Inc.; 99 Courtesy of Fairmont Hotels & Resorts; 108 PhotoDisc, Inc.; 112 Courtesy of Research In Motion.

Chapter 7
120 Courtesy of National Bank of Canada; 122 Corbis Digital Stock; 123 PhotoDisc, Inc.; 125 Courtesy of Baytech Plastics; 126 Courtesy of On-Line Support; 127 PhotoDisc, Inc.

Chapter 8
144 Courtesy of Royal Bank of Canada; 146 Courtesy of Volvo Cars; 149 Courtesy of University of Alberta; 152 PhotoDisc, Inc.; 153 Courtesy of Domtar/Photographer Pierre Crevier; 154 PhotoDisc, Inc.; 155 Associated Press/Bebeto Matthews; 157 PhotoDisc, Inc.

Chapter 9
164 Courtesy of Apple Computer, Inc.; 166 Courtesy of CGI Group; 167 PhotoDisc, Inc.; 168 Courtesy of Hoffmann-La Roche Limited; 172 Courtesy of EDS; 174 Canadian Press/Steve White.

Chapter 10
182 Canadian Press/Mike Sturk; 184 Canadian Press/Kevin Frayer; 186 Courtesy of Air Liquide; 187 Courtesy of Cyberplex Inc.; 188 Canadian Press/Steve White; 195 Courtesy of Peoplesoft; 196 Courtesy of Texas Instruments.

Chapter 11
202 Courtesy of Tatham Group; 204 Courtesy of St. John Ambulance; 211 PhotoDisc, Inc.; 214 Canadian Press/Paul Chiasson; 215 PhotoDisc, Inc.; 218 Courtesy of SNC-Lavalin.

Chapter 12
228 Courtesy of WestJet; 232 Courtesy of Marnie Walker; 233 Corbis Digital Stock; 235 Courtesy of Research In Motion; 238 PhotoDisc, Inc.; 240 Courtesy of Monster Worldwide;242 Courtesy of the Town of Markham; 247 Courtesy of ProCarta, Inc.

Chapter 13
252 Courtesy of Vancouver City Savings Credit Union; 254 PhotoDisc, Inc.; 256 Courtesy of Ethics Quality Inc.; 257 Canadian Press/Joe Cavaretta; 259 Courtesy of ACE Bakery; 263 Canadian Press/Scott Audette; 264 Courtesy

of WestJet.

Chapter 14
274 Canadian Press/Jeff McIntosh; 287 Corbis Digital Stock; 289 Courtesy of Treasury Board of Canada Secretariat; 291 Courtesy of Deere & Company.

Chapter 15
298 Canadian Press/Joe Cavaretta; 301 PhotoDisc, Inc.; 306 Corbis Digital Stock; 316 Canadian Press/Paul Chiasson; 317 Canadian Press/Gilles LaFrance.

Chapter 16
322 Canadian Press/Frank Gunn; 325 Corbis Digital Stock; 331 Courtesy of Intuit Canada; 335 Courtesy of VF Corporation.

Chapter 17
340 PhotoDisc, Inc. 342 Courtesy of MOSAID Technologies; 343 Canadian Press/Don Denton; 345 Courtesy of Nokia Corporation; 347 Canadian Press/Steve White; 354 Courtesy of CHC Helicopter Corp.

Chapter 18
360 PhotoDisc, Inc.; 364 Courtesy of PetroCanada; 365 Associated Press/Fabian Bimmer; 366 PhotoDisc, Inc.; 368 Canadian Press/Fred Lum; 371 Courtesy of Deloitte.

Chapter 19
380 Courtesy of Air Canada; 382 Canadian Press/Aaron Harris; 387 Courtesy of CGI Group; 389 PhotoDisc, Inc.; 389 Courtesy of Leanne Rancourt; 390 Courtesy of the Ethics Centre.

Appendix
Canadian Press/Bob Weber.

Power Play Case 1
Canadian Press/Tom Hanson; Case 1 Canadian Press/Paul Chiasson.

Organization Index

Organization Index

Name Index

Subject Index